King and Emperor

King and Emperor

A New Life of Charlemagne

JANET L. NELSON

UNIVERSITY OF CALIFORNIA PRESS

University of California Press, one of the most distinguished university presses in the United States, enriches lives around the world by advancing scholarship in the humanities, social sciences, and natural sciences. Its activities are supported by the UC Press Foundation and by philanthropic contributions from individuals and institutions. For more information, visit www.ucpress.edu.

University of California Press
Oakland, California

Published in the United Kingdom by Allen Lane

Library of Congress Cataloging-in-Publication Data

Names: Nelson, Janet L. (Janet Laughland), 1942- author.
Title: King and emperor : a new life of Charlemagne / Janet L. Nelson.
Description: Oakland, California : University of California Press, [2019] |
Includes bibliographical references and index. |
Identifiers: LCCN 2019006653 (print) | LCCN 2019010384 (ebook) | ISBN
9780520973947 (ebook) | ISBN 9780520314207 (cloth : alk. paper)
Subjects: LCSH: Charlemagne, Emperor, 742-814. |
France—Kings and rulers—Biography. | France—History—To 987. |
Europe—History—392-814.
Classification: LCC DC73 (ebook) | LCC DC73 .N454 2019 (print) | DDC
944/.0142092 [B] —dc23
LC record available at https://lccn.loc.gov/2019006653

Manufactured in the United States of America

28 27 26 25 24 23 22 21 20
10 9 8 7 6 5 4 3

To Christine and Fritz, *sine quibus non*

Contents

List of Illustrations

Fuller descriptions of and comments on the images can be found on pp. 495–500.

List of Maps

Elements from Map 10 are courtesy of Lacey Wallace, University of Lincoln. Map 11 is courtesy of T. Kraus, J. Müller et al., Abbildung 25, p. 120. Map 12 courtesy of Lukas Werther, University of Jena. Map 13 after P. D. King, 1987. Map 14 after Classen, 1971. Map 15 courtesy of Mike McCormick, Harvard University.

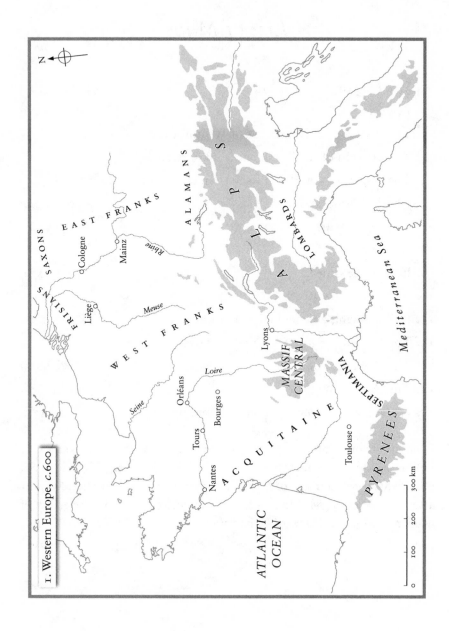

1. Western Europe, c.600

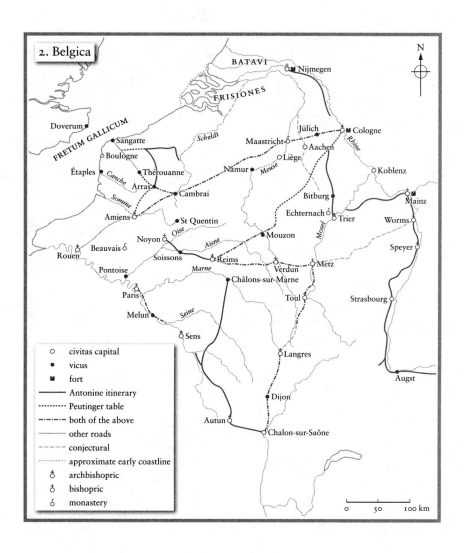

2. Belgica

N

BATAVI
FRISIONES

Doverum

FRETUM GALLICUM

Sangatte
Boulogne
Étaples
Thérouanne
Arras
Cambrai

Scheldt

Maastricht
Namur
Liège

Jülich
Aachen

Cologne

Rhine

Koblenz

Bitburg
Echternach
Trier

Mosel

Mainz
Worms

Amiens
St Quentin

Oise

Noyon
Beauvais
Rouen
Soissons
Pontoise

Aisne
Reims

Mouzon

Marne

Verdun
Metz

Speyer

Paris
Melun

Seine

Châlons-sur-Marne

Toul

Strasbourg

Sens

Langres

Canche
Somme

Meuse

Augst

Dijon

Autun
Chalon-sur-Saône

	civitas capital
●	vicus
⌘	fort
——	Antonine itinerary
········	Peutinger table
–·–·–	both of the above
——	other roads
– – –	conjectural
·······	approximate early coastline
⚲	archbishopric
⚲	bishopric
♀	monastery

0   50   100 km

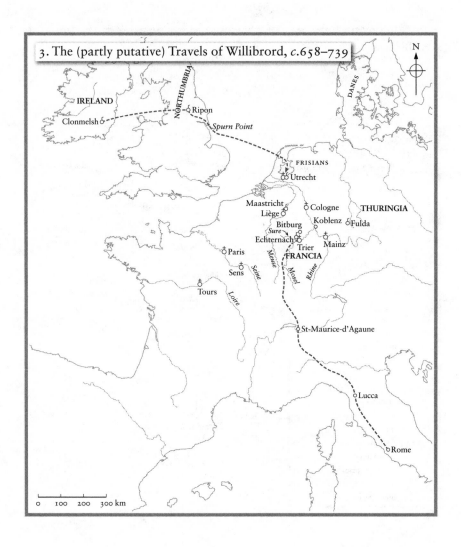

3. The (partly putative) Travels of Willibrord, c.658–739

N

IRELAND

NORTHUMBRIA

DANES

Clonmelsh ⚭

Ripon

Spurn Point

FRISIANS

Utrecht

Maastricht
Liège

Cologne

THURINGIA

Koblenz

Fulda

Bitburg

Sure

Echternach

Mainz

Trier

FRANCIA

Paris

Sens

Seine

Meuse

Mosel

Rhine

Tours

Loire

St-Maurice-d'Agaune

Lucca

Rome

0   100   200   300 km

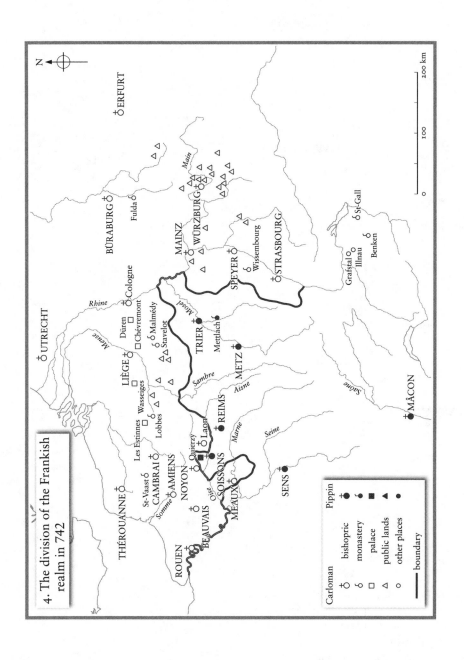

4. The division of the Frankish realm in 742

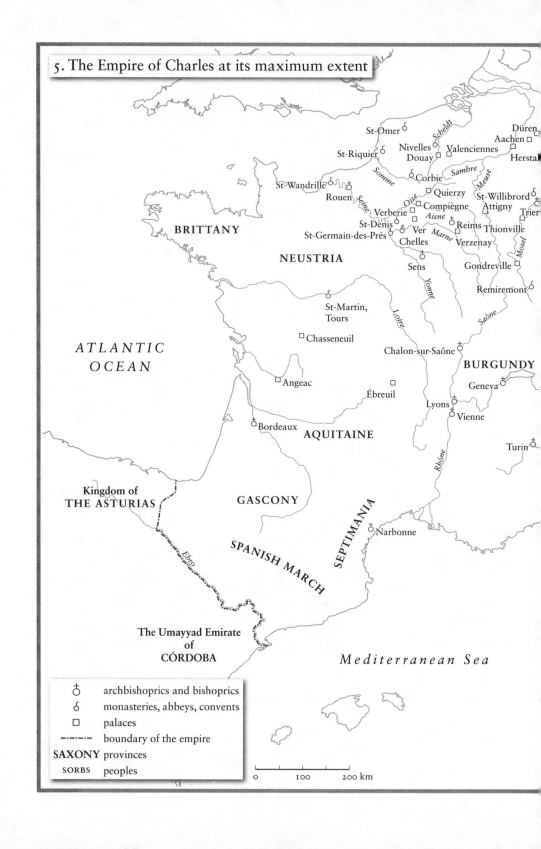

5. The Empire of Charles at its maximum extent

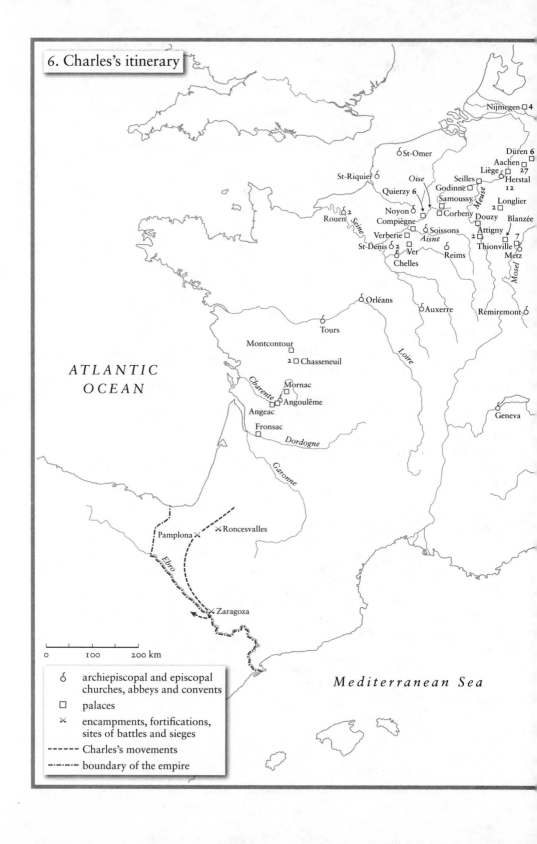

6. Charles's itinerary

Nijmegen □ 4

Düren 6 □
Aachen □
Liège ᛦ □ 27
Herstal 12

St-Omer ᛦ
Seilles □
Longlier □

St-Riquier ᛦ
Oise
Godinne □
Blanzée

Quierzy 6 □
Samoussy □
Douzy □

Noyon ᛦ □ Corbeny □
Attigny

Rouen ᛦ 2
Seine
Compiègne ᛦ
Soissons ᛦ
2 □ Thionville
7 □

Verberie □
Aisne
Metz

St-Denis ᛦ 2 □
Ver
Reims ᛦ
Mosel

Chelles ᛦ

Orléans ᛦ
Auxerre ᛦ
Rémiremont ᛦ

Tours ᛦ

Montcontour □
Loire

2 □ Chasseneuil

ATLANTIC
OCEAN

Mornac □
Charente
Angoulême
□
Geneva ᛦ

Angeac

Fronsac □
Dordogne

Garonne

Pamplona ✗ ✗ Roncesvalles

Ebro

✗ Zaragoza

Mediterranean Sea

0   100   200 km

ᛦ   archiepiscopal and episcopal
    churches, abbeys and convents

□   palaces

✗   encampments, fortifications,
    sites of battles and sieges

----- Charles's movements

-·-·- boundary of the empire

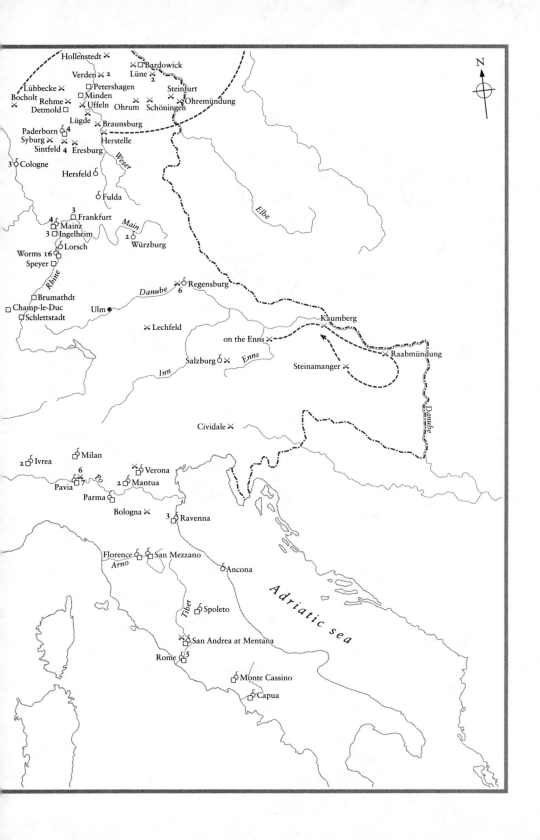

N

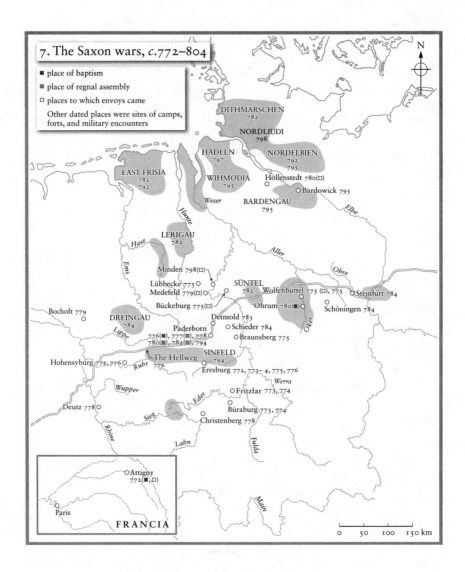

7. The Saxon wars, c.772–804

- ■ place of baptism
- ▣ place of regnal assembly
- □ places to which envoys came

Other dated places were sites of camps, forts, and military encounters

N

DITHMARSCHEN
782

NORDLIUDI
798

HADELN
797

NORDELBIEN
792
795

EAST FRISIA
782
792

WIHMODIA
795

Hollenstedt 780(□)

Bardowick 795

Weser

BARDENGAU
795

Elbe

Hunte

Aller

LERIGAU
782

Hase

Obre

Ems

Minden 798(□)

Lübbecke 775 ○
Medefeld 779(□) ○

SÜNTEL
782

Wolfenbüttel 775 (□), 775

Steinfurt 784

Bückeburg 775(□)

Ohrum 780(■)

Schöningen 784

Bocholt 779

DREINGAU
784

Detmold 783

○ Schieder 784

Lippe

Paderborn
776(▣), 777(▣), 778
780(▣), 782(▣), 794

○ Braunsberg 775

Oker

Hohensyburg 778, 776 ○

Ruhr

The Hellweg
776

SINFELD
794

Eresburg 772, 773–4, 775, 776

Wupper

Eder

Werra

○ Fritzlar 773, 774

Deutz 778 ○

Büraburg 773, 774

Sieg

Christenberg 778

Rhine

Lahn

Fulda

○ Attigny
772(■,□)

Paris

Main

FRANCIA

0   50   100   150 km

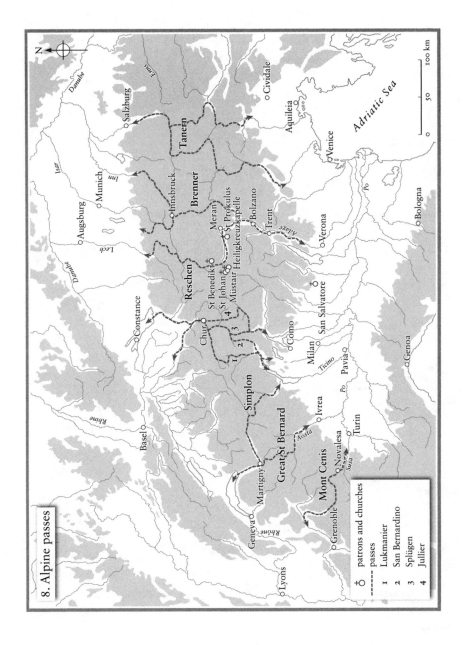

8. Alpine passes

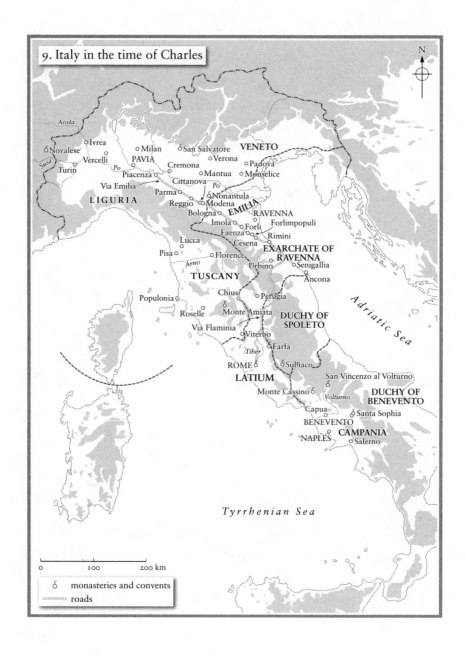

9. Italy in the time of Charles

N

Aosta

Novalese   Ivrea   Milan   San Salvatore   VENETO
Vercelli   PAVIA   Verona   Padova
Susa   Turin   Po   Cremona   Monselice
              Piacenza   Mantua
    Via Emilia   Cittanova   Po
    Parma   Nonantula
LIGURIA   Reggio   Modena
              Bologna   EMILIA   RAVENNA
              Imola   Forlì   Forlimpopuli
              Faenza   Rimini
    Lucca   Cesena
    Pisa   Florence   EXARCHATE OF
                    RAVENNA
    Arno   Urbino   Senigallia
    TUSCANY   Ancona

    Populonia   Chiusi   Perugia   Adriatic Sea
    Roselle   Monte Amiata   DUCHY OF
                    SPOLETO
    Via Flaminia   Viterbo
    Tiber   Farfa
    ROME   Subiaco
    LATIUM   San Vincenzo al Volturno
    Monte Cassino   Volturno   DUCHY OF
                    BENEVENTO
    Capua   Santa Sophia
    BENEVENTO   CAMPANIA
    NAPLES   Salerno

Tyrrhenian Sea

0   100   200 km

6   monasteries and convents
        roads

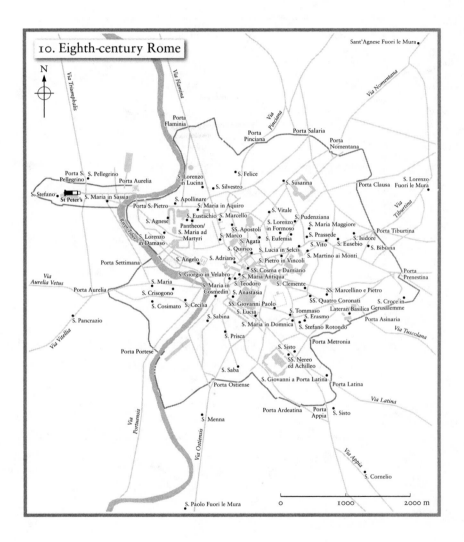

10. Eighth-century Rome

N

Sant'Agnese Fuori le Mura

Via Triumphalis
Via Flaminia
Via Nomentana

Porta
Flaminia

Via Pinciana

Porta
Pinciana
Porta Salaria
Porta
Nomentana

Porta S.   S. Pellegrino
Pellegrino   •   •
Porta Aurelia
S. Lorenzo
in Lucina   •   • S. Felice
• S. Susanna
Porta Clausa
S. Lorenzo
Fuori le Mura

S. Stefano •
St Peter's
S. Maria in Sassia
• S. Silvestro

Porta S. Pietro
• S. Apollinare
S. Maria in Aquiro •
• S. Vitale
Via Tiburtina

S. Eustachio S. Marcello •
• S. Pudenziana
S. Lorenzo   S. Maria Maggiore
in Formoso •   •
Porta Tiburtina

S. Agnese •
Pantheon/
S. Maria ad
Martyri
SS. Apostoli •
S. Marco
• S. Eufemia
• S. Prassede
• S. Isidore

S. Lorenzo
in Damaso
S. Agata •
• S. Vito
S. Eusebio •
• S. Bibiana

S. Quirico •
S. Lucia in Selcis
S. Martino ai Monti •

Porta Settimana
• S. Adriano
S. Pietro in Vincoli •

S. Angelo •
SS. Cosma e Damiano
Porta
Prenestina

Via
Aurelia Vetus
S. Maria •
S. Giorgio in Velabro •
S. Maria Antiqua
S. Teodoro •
S. Clemente •

Porta Aurelia
S. Crisogono •
S. Maria in
Cosmedin
S. Anastasia •
SS. Marcellino e Pietro •
S. Croce in
Gerusalemme

S. Cosimato • S. Cecilia •
SS. Giovanni Paolo
SS. Quattro Coronati •
Lateran Basilica

S. Pancrazio •
S. Lucia •
S. Tommaso •
Porta Asinaria

Via Vitellia
S. Sabina •
S. Erasmo •
Via Tuscolana

S. Maria in Domnica •
S. Stefano Rotondo •

S. Prisca •

Porta Portese
S. Sisto •
Porta Metronia

SS. Nereo
ed Achilleo

S. Saba •

S. Giovanni a Porta Latina •
Porta Latina

Porta Ostiense
Via Latina

Porta Ardeatina
Porta
Appia
• S. Sisto

S. Menna •

River Tiber

Via Portuensis
Via Ostiensis
Via Appia

• S. Cornelio

0   1000   2000 m

S. Paolo Fuori le Mura •

11. Plan of the phase of archaeological finds
(and still standing buildings) at the time of Charles,
as of February 2013

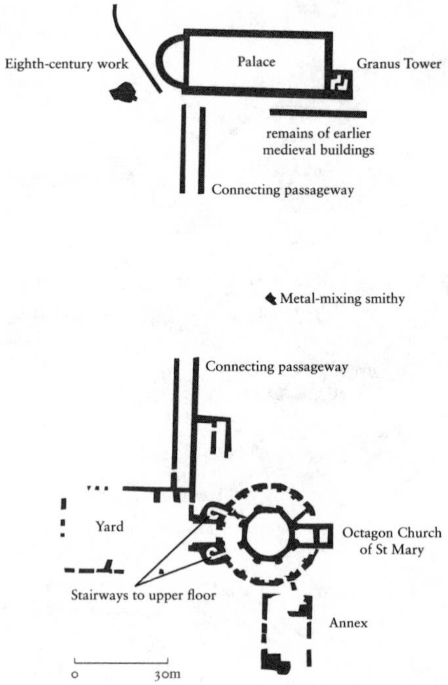

Eighth-century work

Palace

Granus Tower

remains of earlier
medieval buildings

Connecting passageway

Metal-mixing smithy

Connecting passageway

Yard

Octagon Church
of St Mary

Stairways to upper floor

Annex

0   30m

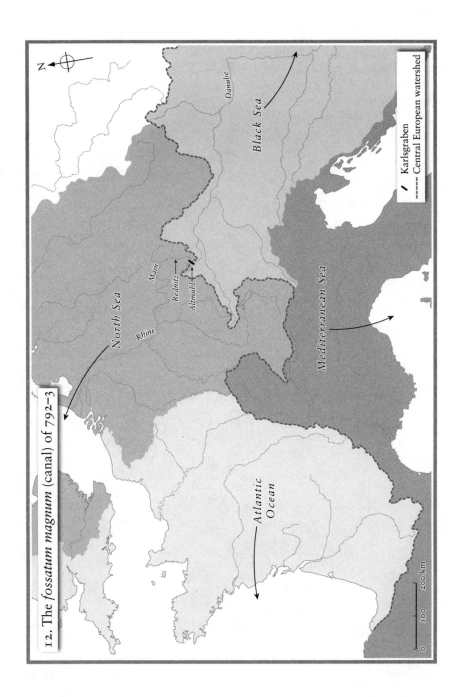

12. The *fossatum magnum* (canal) of 792–3

13. The *Divisio* of 806

Nimwegen 4

Gent
Aachen 27
Boulogne
S. Omer
Herstal 12
Lüttich
Valenciennes 2
Seilles
Orville
S. Riquier
Godinne
Laon
Quierzy 6
Samoussy Longlier 2
Rouen 2
Noyon
Corbeny
Douzy
Compiègne
Attigny 2
Verberie
Soissons
Diedenhofen 7
S. Denis 2
Ver
Reims
Blanzée
Chelles
Verzenay
Metz
Gondreville
Gondreville
Champ-le-duc
Remiremont

Orléans
Auxerre
Tours

ATLANTIC
OCEAN
Montcontour
Chasseneuil

Mornac
Angeac
Angoulême

Genf
Gr. S. Bernard

Fronsac
Dordogne

M. Cenis

Garonne

K A R

L U D W I G

Seine

Loire

Ebro

Roncesvalles
Pamplona

Zaragoza

Mediterannean Sea

0   100   200 km

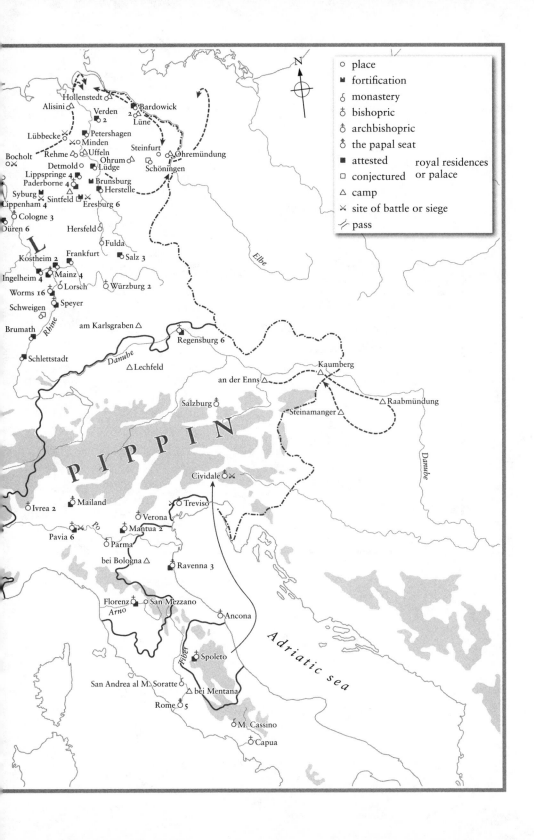

N

place
fortification
monastery
bishopric
archbishopric
the papal seat
attested
conjectured
camp
site of battle or siege
pass

royal residences
or palace

Hollenstedt
Alisini
Verden
Bardowick
Lüne
Petershagen
Lübbecke
Rehme
Minden
Steinfurt
Ohremündung
Bocholt
Uffeln
Ohrum
Detmold
Lüdge
Schöningen
Lippspringe 4
Brunsburg
Paderborne 4
Herstelle
Syburg
Eresburg 6
Cippenham 4
Sintfeld
Cologne 3
Düren 6
Hersfeld
Fulda
Frankfurt
Salz 3
Kostheim 2
Ingelheim 4
Mainz 4
Worms 16
Lorsch
Würzburg 2
Schweigen
Speyer
Brumath
am Karlsgraben
Schlettstadt
Regensburg 6
Lechfeld
an der Enns
Kaumberg
Salzburg
Steinamanger
Raabmündung

Elbe

Rhine

Danube

Danube

PIPPIN

Cividale
Mailand
Treviso
Ivrea 2
Verona
Mantua 2
Pavia 6
Parma
bei Bologna
Ravenna 3
Florenz
San Mezzano
Arno
Ancona
Spoleto
San Andrea al M. Soratte
bei Mentana
Rome 5
M. Cassino
Capua

Adriatic sea

Po

Tiber

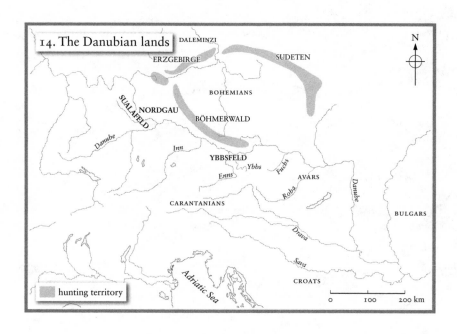

14. The Danubian lands

DALEMINZI

ERZGEBIRGE

SUDETEN

N

BOHEMIANS

SUALAFELD

NORDGAU

BÖHMERWALD

Danube

Inn

YBBSFELD

Ybbs

Fuchs

Enns

Roba

AVARS

Danube

CARANTANIANS

BULGARS

Drava

Sava

Adriatic Sea

CROATS

hunting territory

0   100   200 km

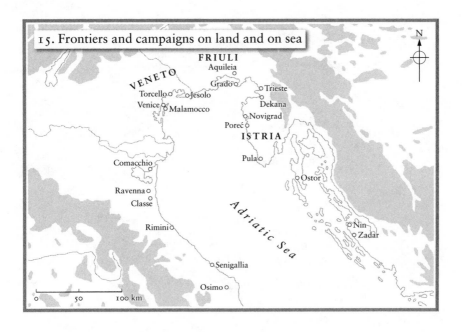

15. Frontiers and campaigns on land and on sea

FRIULI
Aquileia
VENETO
Grado
Torcello — Jesolo
Venice — Malamocco
Trieste
Dekana
Novigrad
Poreč
ISTRIA
Pula
Comacchio
Ravenna
Classe
Ostor
Rimini
Nin
Zadar
Senigallia
Osimo
Adriatic Sea

N

0   50   100 km

List of Genealogies

Genealogy A: Arnulfings, Pippinds, Carolingians

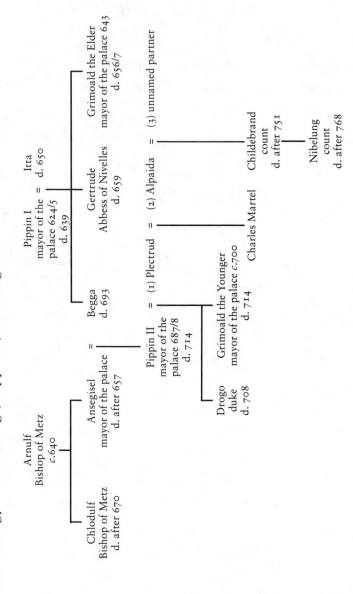

Arnulf
Bishop of Metz
c.640

Chlodulf
Bishop of Metz
d. after 670

Ansegisel
mayor of the palace
d. after 657

=

Begga
d. 693

Pippin I
mayor of the
palace 624/5
d. 639

=

Itta
d. 650

Gertrude
Abbess of Nivelles
d. 659

Grimoald the Elder
mayor of the palace 643
d. 656/7

Pippin II
mayor of the
palace 687/8
d. 714

=

(1) Plectrud

=

(2) Alpaida

=

(3) unnamed partner

Drogo
duke
d. 708

Grimoald the Younger
mayor of the palace c.700
d. 714

Charles Martel

Childebrand
count
d. after 751

Nibelung
count
d. after 768

Genealogy B: The descendants of Pippin and Alpaida

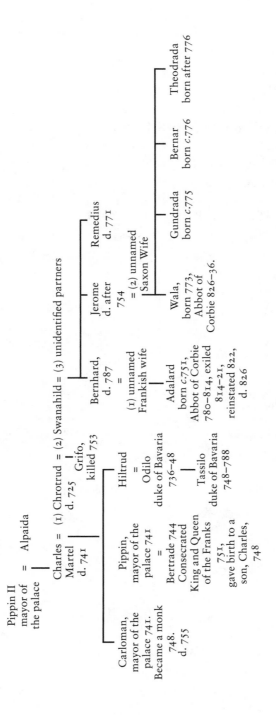

Genealogy C: The family of Charles

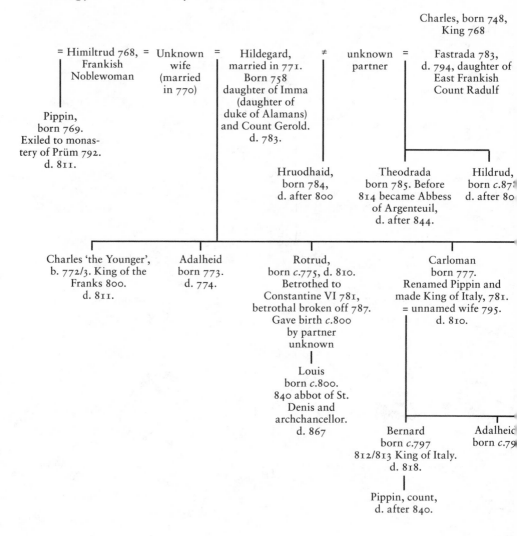

Charles, born 748,
King 768

= Himiltrud 768, = Unknown = Hildegard, ≠ unknown = Fastrada 783,
Frankish wife married in 771. partner d. 794, daughter of
Noblewoman (married Born 758 East Frankish
in 770) daughter of Imma Count Radulf
(daughter of
Pippin, duke of Alamans)
born 769. and Count Gerold.
Exiled to monas- d. 783.
tery of Prüm 792.
d. 811.

Hruodhaid, Theodrada Hildrud,
born 784, born 785. Before born c.87?
d. after 800 814 became Abbess d. after 80
of Argenteuil,
d. after 844.

Charles 'the Younger', Adalheid Rotrud, Carloman
b. 772/3. King of the born 773. born c.775, d. 810. born 777.
Franks 800. d. 774. Betrothed to Renamed Pippin and
d. 811. Constantine VI 781, made King of Italy, 781.
betrothal broken off 787. = unnamed wife 795.
Gave birth c.800 d. 810.
by partner
unknown

Louis
born c.800.
840 abbot of St.
Denis and
archchancellor. Bernard Adalheid
d. 867 born c.797 born c.79?
812/813 King of Italy.
d. 818.

Pippin, count,
d. after 840.

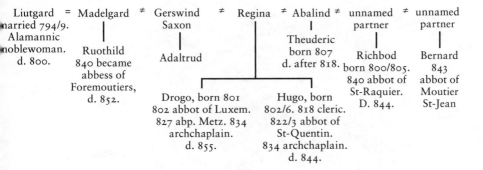

Liutgard = Madelgard ≠ Gerswind ≠ Regina ≠ Abalind ≠ unnamed ≠ unnamed
married 794/9.   Saxon   partner   partner
Alamannic   Theuderic
noblewoman.   Ruothild   born 807   Richbod   Bernard
d. 800.   840 became   Adaltrud   d. after 818. born 800/805.   843
         abbess of   840 abbot of   abbot of
       Foremoutiers,   St-Raquier.   Moutier
          d. 852.   Drogo, born 801   Hugo, born   D. 844.   St-Jean
                  802 abbot of Luxem.   802/6. 818 cleric.
                  827 abp. Metz. 834   822/3 abbot of
                  archchaplain.   St-Quentin.
                  d. 855.   834 archchaplain.
                          d. 844.

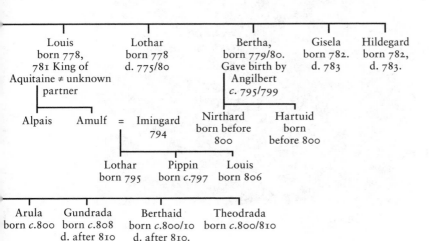

Louis   Lothar   Bertha,   Gisela   Hildegard
born 778,   born 778   born 779/80.   born 782.   born 782,
781 King of   d. 775/80   Gave birth by   d. 783   d. 783.
Aquitaine ≠ unknown   Angilbert
    partner   c. 795/799

Alpais   Amulf   =   Imingard   Nirthard   Hartuid
                     794   born before   born
                        800   before 800

       Lothar   Pippin   Louis
     born 795   born c.797   born 806

Arula   Gundrada   Berthaid   Theodrada
born c.800 born c.808   born c.800/10 born c.800/810
       d. after 810   d. after 810.

Bronze equestrian statuette of Charles.

I

Introduction

1. AN EXTRAORDINARY MAN

This book's subject is a man who was by any standards extraordinary: a many-sided character whose sixty-five years of life and doings were driven by unremitting physical energy and intellectual curiosity. He was a man of many parts, a warlord who conquered an empire, a man of peace and a judge who promised 'for each their law and justice', a man who presided over church councils as a prince and defender of the Latin Church, a person who preached and practised both *caritas* (charity) and *amor* (love) and knew the value of giving to the less powerful and the less wealthy, a person whose interests ranged from viewing the night-sky and sending men to supervise the repair of Christian sites in the Holy Land to keeping in touch with kings and potentates from Ireland and northern Spain to Constantinople and Baghdad, a man of flesh-and-blood, a family-man who had at least nine sexual partners, fathered at least nineteen children, and was grandfather to at least eleven more. Charles was someone whose personality still shines through the texts and artefacts and memories he left and the stories (some edifying, some bawdy) that were told about him decades, then centuries, after his time.

Writing a book about Charles, who lived between 748 and 814, in the midst of a period popularly known as the Dark Ages, takes some nerve. All historical biographers, whoever their subjects, have the gift of hindsight denied to their subjects, and face the occupational hazards of teleology – reading back hypothetical causes from later phenomena – and anachronism – an approach inappropriate for the historical time to which the subject belonged. In Charles's case, the biographer has a mine of evidence about the relevant time and context: evidence that can be presented to modern readers for their own inspection. I have sometimes approached Charles from unfamiliar angles which can be unexpectedly illuminating. I have not assumed that Charles was a 'Great Man' (truth to tell, I was taught at my mother's knee to bridle at those words); nor have I thought of him as 'The Father of Europe', or 'The Lighthouse of Europe' (though those were names that a contemporary poet conferred on him). I am even less keen on pinning a national label on 'German' *Karl der Große*, Charles the Great, or borrowing 'French' *Charles-le-magne*, which means the same thing, and which English-speaking peoples have assimilated in modern times. In this book, unless I am quoting someone else, I call my subject Charles, or use one or another of the languages spoken by his contemporaries: Latin *Carolus*, Old High German *Karlus* or Romance *Karlo*. From Christmas Day 800, Charles entitled himself in documents: 'Charles, most serene augustus, crowned by God, great peacemaking emperor, governing the Roman Empire, and similarly, by the grace of God, King of the Franks and of the Lombards'. Two phrases here are not platitudes but statements of heaven-sent legitimacy; for Charles, 'crowned by God', and 'by the grace of God' meant what they said. *Un*said in his title, but equally important in underpinning Charles's legitimacy, was his idea of the mutual trust between king and his faithful men. A German historian put this in a nutshell: *consensus fidelium* (the consensus of the faithful men) was the 'complementary concept' to the Christian ideal of kingship.[1]

From the 1090s onwards, when Frankish armies marched to the Holy Land in the footsteps they believed were Charles's, many people across the centuries have thought his life worth remembering – or re-imagining. 'Great Men', long known as such and put on school curricula, sometimes remain popular, even now, as national symbols and symptoms of identity. Since the twelfth century, *Charlemagne* has remained a widely known historical figure because of his fortuitous connections with French Crusades, with pilgrimage to Santiago de Compostela, with heroic French poetry, and – as *Karl der Große* – with political prophecy and German imperial propaganda. In modern times, he has been memorialized by modern rulers and ideologues including Kaiser Wilhelm II and Adolf Hitler. After the Second World War, Charles was reconstructed as the icon of Europe; and it's since then that his biography-industry has thrived, especially in Germany but also in France and Italy, Catalonia and Croatia. Charles is more solidly grounded in contemporary evidence than most other persons whose status, power, patronage and posthumous celebrity have ensured their name-recognition by modern citizens of Europe. Behind the myth is a life, a narrative of lived experience. The approaches taken in this book will include an acceptance that Charles colluded in the construction of his own story, thus making his biography in part an illusion.[2] At the same time, sufficient evidence survives to enable Charles's psychology and subjectivity to be perceived and retrieved, up to a point. In what follows, more will be made than ordinarily of Charles's relationships with his kin, and with women. Distance remains, but feelings of strangeness and connection are not incompatible. A paradoxical sense of being distant yet close is what the late Karl Leyser (a medievalist who specialized on the tenth century) evoked, with another layer of paradox: 'the world of the tenth century is, or ought to be, strange to us'.[3] A number of recent biographers of Charles have taken Leyser's message to heart. Strangeness is often precisely what draws people nowadays to remote periods of the past.

II. CHARLES AND HIS BIOGRAPHERS

There are many books in several European languages that offer excellent narratives or thematic accounts of Charles's reign.[4] Some authors have shied away from claiming to write biography, or, instead, claimed, perhaps in a subtitle, to have written a biography yet not actually delivered on that claim.[5] The usual explanation given, tacit or explicit, is lack of the sort of material available for individual lifespans in more modern times, or even ancient times. Cicero, for instance, left large numbers of letters, public and personal; St Augustine of Hippo's *Confessions* were a spiritual autobiography of his early life, but he also left many letters and sermons that included elements of life-writing.[6] Charles, by contrast, left very few letters or other personal reminiscences giving direct access to his thoughts, experiences or intentions. The material is difficult, sometimes treacherous: I have often been conscious of skating on very thin ice.

Difficult is not impossible. Evidence for the personal can come in unexpected genres: royal charters, for instance, employed symbols, metaphor and rhetoric as codes which can be cracked, as can the actual code known as Tironian notes, or Carolingian shorthand.[7] In Charles's case, many reported actions are credited to him by contemporary or near-contemporary writers, who make it possible to infer something of his motives and thoughts and, from those, connect him *indirectly* with readers. Sometimes evidence for men and women close to or affected by him is available too, the more welcome for being infrequent. When the biographer happens on such evidence, the possibilities for drawing plausible inferences multiply. They become cues: the biographer interrupts the narrative flow to include pieces, often substantial, of contemporaries' writings, and to work these hard. Though this often means making readers too work hard, the rewards soon become apparent.

My approach in this book resembles in some ways that of an old-fashioned biographer. It is sequential, in a way that reduces, even it can't avoid them, the risks of teleology. Some modern biographies of Charles have been structured thematically, treating themes one by one, across time – say, the thirty years of Charles's Saxon Wars, or of church reforms that spanned his reign. Others have from the outset denied the possibility of writing Charles's life on the grounds that his personality is unknowable. My starting assumption is that more of Charles's personality can be known than first meets the eye. This book therefore goes chronologically, following Charles's life as he lived it, and as we all live our lives – in hope but also in ignorance of what would or could follow a given perception, decision or act. Books about early medieval history (and this is often the case with more modern histories too) are thickly larded with must-haves, perhapses and probablies: attempts at calibrating what can never be more than best-guesses. In the writings of historians, avowals of ignorance appear often, but writing chronologically helps reduce the need for them. My chosen tactic – it can hardly be dignified as a method – is as far as possible to omit those qualifying words and phrases. Otherwise, I have tried to follow historians' ground rules: first, go for the sources, treat them critically but also sympathetically; and then do the same with the historiography, which is vast and largely in German. Fortunately, excellent German books on Charles are increasingly often being translated not too long after they first appear. Celebratory commemorations in 2000 of Charles's imperial coronation in 800, and in 2014 of his death in 814, brought floods of new publications, and in several cases translations soon after. When modern-language teaching in UK secondary schools is steadily declining, the appearance from North American, British and Dutch presses of more translations of Continental works on pre-modern European history is all the more welcome. A British-born biographer, or self-professed 'biographer', of Charles can't help being internationalist.

The first biography of Charles was written in Latin by a contemporary, Einhard, born at or near Mainz c.770 and so a generation younger than his subject. Einhard had his own approach to writing a life. He was familiar with the genre of saints' Lives (*vitae*), and happily borrowed from it. It so happened that he had the benefit of another kind of model as well. Einhard was sent at seven or so, the usual age when an infant became a boy, to be educated at the monastery of Fulda. Multi-talented, he did not become a monk, but re-entered lay life when Abbot Baugulf sent him to join the court of Charles sometime in the mid-790s, and he subsequently married. Einhard did not lose touch with Fulda, where the library had a manuscript of the *Lives of the Caesars* written by the Roman historian Suetonius, a rare work in Charles's realm. Einhard may have read Suetonius's work while at Fulda or, more likely, later when he had a copy of his own at his estate at Mulinheim in Hesse. Some fifteen years after Charles's death, Einhard wrote his *Life of Charles – Vita Karoli* – skilfully and selectively borrowing from Suetonius, and also from Cicero.[8] He had strong personal motives: a deep sense of obligation to Charles and his family, who had 'nurtured' him at court, and a wish to save Charles's deeds from the oblivion of posterity. Einhard had been among Charles's leading counsellors, and he remained an influential figure at the court of Charles's son Louis, where for a while he may have been the tutor of Louis' eldest son Lothar. Like Charles himself, Einhard became more deeply concerned with religion as he grew older, and – like Charles – ever keener to aid the salvation of his contemporaries by mobilizing heavenly powers through prayer and good works (Charles's preferred method) or saints' relics (Einhard's preference).

Though Einhard had withdrawn somewhat from public life when competition between interests and policy-options at Louis' court grew fiercer (flaring into a full-scale political crisis in 828), he decided, early in 829, and with a view to recovering some of his old influence, to write the *Life*, hoping that from it, not only Louis, but senior counsellors and a junior generation too would find messages and a model for public life in the present.[9] The *Life* was short and memorable. Einhard, who was anything but naïve, sent a copy to someone he knew well: 'Here is the book for you!' he wrote in his prologue, using the familiar second-person singular form of address in Latin, *tu*. 'You' was Gerward, the court librarian, who passed it on to Louis with a little dedicatory verse commending Einhard as its author. It soon came to be regarded as a model ruler-biography, a mirror for princes and for their advisers. The *Life* presented lively personal details of Charles that have proved irresistible to readers ever after. The spread of manuscript copies (much slower than of books in a print culture, of course) was rapid for the ninth century, suggesting eager readers and listeners, who almost certainly included Louis' youngest son Charles, born in 823 and named after his grandfather. Many translations, or reworkings of Charles's story, sometimes into vernacular languages as well as Latin, show the *Life*'s appeal to readers and hearers in succeeding centuries: the latest count is 'over 123 manuscripts'.[10]

Modern historians have tended to give the *Life* a cool reception. They have severely criticized its errors and its deliberate silences, and flatly rejected some of Einhard's statements. They have seen as a major drawback his use of Suetonius' way of structuring his *Lives* thematically, with public life, consisting mainly of wars, followed by private life. They have lamented, though they have not really tried to account for, Einhard's omission of such important matters as administrative measures and aristocratic involvement in government, topics for which evidence has to be sought elsewhere. I shall not forego using Einhard's *Life*, however, nor even the monk Notker of St-Gall's gossipy and anecdotal *Deeds of Charles*, written in the early 880s, which drew much on Einhard's work. All biographies are authorial constructs, and those of Einhard and Notker (not to mention the present author's) are no exceptions. Nevertheless, both transmit, beneath liberal sprinklings of ninth-century spice, nutritious grains of historicity in stories and memories. Einhard especially conveys a strong sense of Charles as a man and a vivid personality. 'I was present', he asserts in his prologue, 'and I know these things by the witness of my own eyes, as they say.' Autopsy, literally, 'seeing for yourself', does not necessarily yield truth in any straightforward way – and indeed Einhard was quoting 'the witness of my own eyes' from a third-century bishop's letter mentioning St Paul's ascent into Heaven. But I think some psychological truths are inescapably there in the *Life of Charles*.

Charles's physical traits are described in c. 22. Confidence in their accuracy is dented a little by the number of phrases lifted from Suetonius' *Lives*, and the fact that Einhard's personal acquaintance with Charles began in the emperor's later years (as suggested by the reference to his 'fine white hair'):

> His body was large and strong. He was tall but not unduly so – his height was seven times the length of his own foot. The top of his head was round, his eyes were large and lively, his nose was a little larger than average, he had fine white hair and a cheerful and attractive face. So standing or sitting, his presence was greatly increased in authority and dignity. His neck was short and thick, his stomach protruded a bit, but the symmetry of the other parts hid these flaws. His pace was firm and the whole bearing of his body powerful. His voice was indeed clear but, given his size, not as strong as might have been expected. His health was good until four years before he died . . . He exercised regularly by riding and hunting which came naturally to him . . . He was so good at swimming that no-one was considered better than him.'[11]

Though this book's subtitle labels the man Charlemagne, and, of course, name-recognition appeals to readerships (and publishers), in the body of the book itself I had already decided not to refer to him by that moniker. 'Charlemagne' is certainly distinctive, but it is anachronistic (none of Charles's contemporaries used it) and cumbersome, and it asserts what needs to be (yet seldom is) defined or demonstrated – greatness, which is just what I wanted to insist was no foregone conclusion. Instead I call my subject, simply, Charles. I differentiate his grandfather Charles by using his nickname Martel, 'The Hammer', and his son by calling him 'Charles the Younger' or 'Young Charles'. I have entitled my book in plain English, 'A New Life'. As for how to write it, I have borrowed royal advice from another source, Lewis Carroll's *Alice's Adventures in Wonderland*: ' "Begin at the beginning," the King said, very gravely, "and go on till you come to the end: then stop".' It is good advice for the writer of a life-story, for an end will certainly come ... But even 'going on' is not always plain sailing, because of the patchiness of the evidence for Charles's life.

In the evidence that remains, especially for the latter half of the reign, a character-trait of this man that shines out is his sociability. The names, and sometimes quite a lot more than names, of his close family, and of some of his counsellors and friends, are known, though even the best efforts to find out much about these relationships leave glaring blanks. Clerics and monks and nuns are disproportionately represented in the record, partly because of their professional grip on literacy (this was far from being a monopoly, however, and the span of Charles's life covered a great extension of *lay* literacy), but also because of the much higher chances of the survival of church archives than lay archives. About laypeople, it is always harder to find evidence of lives over time. For instance, a name that coincidentally resonated over the centuries was that of Roland, one of Charles's *palatini*, 'men of the palace' (or as later French authors called them, the king's *paladins*). A thread of references can be spun to show 'Roland' as a count in Charles's entourage at the palace of Herstal in 772; as an official in charge of a mint issuing Charles's Type-One (768–91) pennies; and as Count of the Breton March killed in the ambush of Charles's rearguard at Roncesvaux on 15 August 778.[12]

Later in this book, I largely resist the temptation to cite material which is late (written some seventy years after Charles's death) and locally gleaned from oral traditions preserved in and around the monastery of St-Gall. Notker of St-Gall (*c*.840–912, also known as 'Notker the Stammerer') used Einhard's *Vita Karoli* and wrote between 885 and 887 in the genre of *Gesta* – 'Deeds' – for a royal patron, Charles's great-grandson Charles III (emperor 881–7 – his nickname 'the Fat' dates from the twelfth century). Two of Notker's many stories are worth quoting in the context of Charles's personality and sense of humour (jokes are always significant clues).[13] The first is this:

> The habits of men change, and when the Franks, who were fighting with the Gauls, saw them proudly wearing little striped cloaks and were delighted by this novelty, they abandoned their ancient customs and began to copy those of the Gauls. At first the strictest of emperors did not forbid this, because this style of clothing seemed to him most suitable for waging war. But when he found that the Frisians were abusing his permission

and selling these little short cloaks for the same price as the old large ones, he gave orders that no-one should buy from them at the customary price any cloaks except the big ones which were very broad and very long; and he added, 'What's the use of those little napkins? When I'm in bed, I can't cover myself up in them, when I'm out riding I can't protect myself against wind and rain, and when I have to go off to answer a call of nature, I suffer from freezing-cold legs!'

The second is this:

[In the midst of wars and man-management] the great-hearted emperor in no way omitted to send envoys bearing letters and gifts to all kind of rulers of very distant places; and from these, in return, were sent the honours of all these provinces. When, from the midst of the Saxon war, he sent envoys to the king at Constantinople, the king asked them whether the kingdom of his son Charles was at peace or was it suffering incursions from neighbouring peoples? The chief envoy replied that all was at peace except that a certain people called the Saxons were disturbing the frontiers with very frequent raids. 'O dear!', said that man who was sluggish in idleness and useless for any warlike action, 'why does my son struggle against enemies who are so few, have no reputation and completely lack manly courage? You can have that people, together with everything that belongs to them!' When the envoy returned and reported this to the most warlike Charles, he laughed and said: 'That king would have done you a lot more of a good turn if he'd given you a pair of linen pants for your long journey back.'

III. OTHER SOURCES, OTHER GENRES

By early medieval standards, there is rather a lot of textual evidence for Charles as a historical actor. The most important reason for this sudden plenitude is that charters become unprecedentedly plentiful during his reign: some 7,000 survive, in originals or later copies, made at the request of property-donors both ecclesiastical and lay.[14] These documents, usually recording gifts to churches, reveal huge amounts of information about the social and economic history of Charles's reign at local and regional levels. The 164 surviving charters of Charles himself are especially valuable for the light they, and in particular their timing and place of issue, throw on political relationships and Charles's own political calculations. Charles's reign also saw the issuing of unprecedentedly numerous, full and detailed administrative documents called capitularies, together with their ecclesiastical equivalents, decrees of church councils and orders issued by bishops, acting more or less at Charles's behest.[15] These cover every kind of governmental action, from the summoning of armies and the running of local judicial assemblies to the issuing and control of coinage and the making of lists of everything from the services owed by peasants on royal estates to hostages and relics of saints. In Italy after the Frankish conquest of 774, a separate kingdom of Lombardy continued to exist with, after 781, a king of its own: Charles's son Pippin, who had his own chancery and issued his own capitularies.[16] In Aquitaine, also a separate kingdom under Charles's son Louis, no capitularies were issued, apparently, and extremely few royal charters survive; instead, the supervisory role of tutors appointed by Charles, and a stream of commands from Charles himself, continued throughout Charles's reign.

Viewed through a wider lens, there was more literacy about in Charles's reign than in any previous early medieval one. This is a major dimension of what modern historians call the Carolingian Renaissance.[17] People – women as well as men – were writing in more diverse genres and forms, from long and fancy letter-poems by *literati* to short messages of the 'send more socks' variety.[18] Letters, especially those written by Charles's most-favoured scholar, the Anglo-Saxon Alcuin of York (c.735–804), many to the king, or about the king, give some of the fullest evidence for Charles the man. Alcuin, like his fellow-countryman Cathwulf, the Spaniard Theodulf, the Italians Paul and Peter, and the Irishmen Clement and Dungal, had been lured to Charles's court, and wrote revealingly in various genres about life and work there. Other letters written to Charles from outside his realm, and especially the letters written to him by successive popes between the 760s and 791 (when the relevant collection, the *Codex Carolinus*, ends), provide invaluable evidence of not just diplomacy and high politics but a whole world of religious beliefs and practices in which the exchange of gifts, including prayers and favours, was prominently involved.[19]

As well as the charters, poems, letters, capitularies and lists, a wealth of annals and chronicles were produced, some by clerics at or near Charles's court, others written up by church communities in the regions,

concerned about local issues of their own yet with court contacts.[20] The
court was 'not a set of buildings but a collection of people'.[21] The court
was movable: demands of war and political cohesion on the one hand,
the management of food supplies on the other, required the ruler's itinerancy between palaces with their associated royal lands and hunting
forests. From the 790s the court became increasingly based at Aachen.
The court, or court-connected, annals' horizons reflected this shift.
Annals produced in regional locations like Salzburg or Regensburg in
Bavaria, or Wissembourg in the Mosel area reflected it too, yet never
lost sight of local concerns. Annals often recorded, however partially
and indirectly, Charles's interests, aims and hopes, and connected them
with outcomes, as when well-planned military campaigns outside Francia brought plunder back home. Later in the reign, the pattern may
have shifted from plunder to tribute, that is, more regular transfers of
revenue to the Aachen court, a trend assisted by Charles's strengthened
grip on coinage management. The annal-writers, whether court-based
or local, also signalled how the best-laid schemes could be foiled by
unforeseeable disasters, as when 90 per cent of Charles's horses died in
an equine pestilence, or when famine struck Francia, or when tried and
trusted men were slain in battles or ambushes, or succumbed to malaria
on summer campaigns in Italy.[22] Even in a world where war, inherently
high-risk, was endemic, and men were expected, and trained, to be warriors, Charles grieved over such losses. Yet when news came out of the
blue that the Danish king had been slain 'by one of his own retinue, a
vassal' (*a quodam suo satellite, a suo vassallo*), Charles seized what he
rightly saw as a golden opportunity to redirect events on the northern
frontier and to have the vassal's deed recorded. When Charles's own
son plotted to kill his father and his younger half-brothers, he was
foiled by a cleric who alerted Charles at the last minute: the measure of
the king's relief was recorded by the court annalist, who noted the
lavish scale of the gifts Charles bestowed on those who had refused
to join the plotters. The production of annals at York continued a
Northumbrian tradition that was augmented by news Alcuin sent home
from Francia during the 790s, while Frankish annal-writers, at the court
and elsewhere, benefitted from information flowing across the Channel
from several Anglo-Saxon kingdoms. Annals attest to the flow of communications and news across Charles's realm and beyond.

Two other sources that shed light on particular aspects of Charles's reign, each of them for different reasons, contribute perspectives of unique value. The first, written in Constantinople in the years c.810–15, was the *Chronicle* (*Chronographia*) of Theophanes, an aristocrat brought up at the imperial court with extensive connections. His interest in the west was variable, but on some topics his evidence is important – for instance on the Empress Eirene's initiative in proposing her son's betrothal to Charles's daughter Rotrud, on military encounters in the eastern Mediterranean, and on Charles's imperial coronation.[23] The second source was a *Chronicle* written in the eighth century in Latin by Creontius (Crantz), the chancellor – or chief counsellor – of Duke Tassilo of Bavaria; the early-modern scholar Aventinus (1477–1534) translated it into German. This work adds a distinctively Bavarian voice to those of other contributors to the contemporary historiography, providing details of Tassilo's wars with the Carantanians (Carinthians).[24]

At Rome, scribes in papal employ maintained the production, some-what episodically, of the *Lives of the Popes*. These writers did not regularly record even what was going on in their own backyards, and their eyes only spasmodically turned to Francia; however, when they did, their testimony is uniquely valuable, not just because, like letters, they reflect strictly contemporary reactions, but because their views were *not* Frankish, and they were *not* looking out from Charles's court.[25] Rome's eighth-century information-network, as revealed in the papal letters, stretched especially densely from Benevento, Naples, Amalfi and other cities south of Rome, and from the Adriatic ports via the Mediterranean, to Constantinople in the east; and north of Rome through central Italy to the Lombard heartlands and the Alps.

In Aquitaine, that is, Gaul south of the Loire and west of the Rhône, an important text reflecting a regional view was the substantial part of the *Life* of Charles's son Louis that was written up on the basis of infor-mation from one of Louis' Aquitanian closest advisers during his tenure of the sub-kingdom between 781 and 814. This, together with an Aqui-tanian chronicle, the letters of Aquitanian churchmen and also of Aquitanian laypersons in need of protection, gives historians access to a vast region which the Frankish and court-focused annals hardly ever reached. These various bits of evidence make very clear Charles's strong if spasmodic interest in Aquitanian affairs and a growing investment in the Spanish March, involving contacts with Christian kings in the Asturias. To fill out this map of Charles's geographical horizons: there survives a list, compiled in 808 by trusted agents sent at his behest and working on the spot, of Christian communities in the Holy Land. Charles sought and duly received statistical information about personnel and locations, in order to send them material help. This document shows better than anything else the extent of Charles's ambition and the actual reach of his regime. It also shows a good deal of what motivated him in the latter years of his reign. Finally, in the church Charles built at Aachen, there is not a text but a body: the physical remains of Charles himself, bones that have been inspected thrice in modern times. They confirm what Einhard's text says about the man's height – 6'3" – and they tend to support recent textual findings of his age at death, on which more below.

This brief and selective summary of the main types of evidence is put here at the beginning for positive reasons: first, to indicate how and why it is possible to write an account of Charles's reign; second, to suggest that it's possible sometimes to impute to Charles calculations, motives, plans and decisions, as well as emotions; and third, to claim that Charles's physical being is in part knowable, and that he enjoyed good health for almost the whole of what for those times, and for a layman, was an unusually long life. This third point was important for Charles, and for those he ruled (a modern parallel would be Queen Victoria): it did not guarantee, but it did I think contribute immensely towards, a sense of continuity and stability, a sense that he was fortunate, divinely blessed, a sense of trust evoked and sustained between the king and his people, his faithful ones (*fideles*). Charles's own constancy, praised by Einhard, might be said to have been reflected in *their* constancy.

Sufficient as the evidence is to encourage modern readers to gain some acquaintance with Charles, beginning to feel at home with him is a moment to feel wary. Karl Leyser's words about strangeness, remember, are words of warning. The values and priorities of Charles and his contemporaries are not ours – though neither are they wholly different. Love of children or siblings, and rivalries between them, the value of trust and the horror of mistrust, a sense of wry or ribald humour that could turn to insult: all these we can share, up to a point. Yet we gain deeper understandings only by keeping our distance, and by being stringently and precisely critical. Poems, for instance, had classical echoes that dulled but didn't silence the sound of axes' grinding. Annals were not just records but constructs, designed and timed to strengthen particular loyalties, persuade audiences at court or in specific localities to accept a particular version of events, or to signal changing priorities. The timing of the compilation of annals at court was determined by the need to produce a justificatory dossier for Charles's engineering of the condemnation of Duke Tassilo of Bavaria and his family at Ingelheim in June/July 788. In October, Charles and his arch-chaplain, Bishop Angilram of Metz, were at Regensburg. There Charles issued a charter donating the Bavarian ducal monastery of Chiemsee to the Carolingian ancestral church of Metz, 'recalling to our control the duchy of Bavaria, alienated from us in a faithless manner (*infideliter*) by the malign men Odilo [Tassilo's father] and our kinsman Tassilo'.

Charles summoned a small team of churchmen, including Alcuin, to stay at Aachen over the winter of 788–9 and to produce the *Admonitio generalis*, a capitulary issued in letter-form by 'Ego Carolus', and an unprecedentedly full set of instructions, old and new, on law and morals. Its call to general heart-searching presupposed plans for wide distribution, and the number of its manuscripts produced in the latter years of Charles's reign show that the plans were implemented. The selection of papal letters, the *Codex Carolinus*, collected in 791 when Charles was residing at Regensburg, was originally accompanied by a parallel selection – now lost – of letters from the emperors in Constantinople. Every one of these texts was a characteristic product, not just political but ideological, of Charles's world: each had its timing and purpose. Charles and his agents were learning to become planners on a more than merely regnal scale.

IV. THE BROAD CONTEXT OF FRANKISH HISTORY BEFORE CHARLES

A biography needs to be set in a broader context, not just of changes in the few generations immediately preceding the life of the subject, but of longer-term continuities. At this point, therefore, and drawing heavily on other scholars' work (while keeping references to a minimum), I want to present a brief and rather general sketch of the transformation of the Roman world from the fourth century to the end of the early eighth.

The migration of peoples (*ethnē* in Greek, in Latin *gentes* and hence, in adjectival form, 'ethnic' or 'gentile'; often translated into English as 'tribes') who called themselves Goths and had previously lived as agriculturalists in the lands north of the Black Sea, where archaeological evidence reveals their distinctive pottery, forms of burial and settlement, started in the later fourth century. It was then that Hunnic nomads, driven by drought on the Eurasian steppes and population pressure, began to move westwards, pushing the Goths away from their old lands and forcing them 'across the imperial frontier en masse', where they imposed terms on the East Roman emperor. They spoke various versions of Germanic languages, had shared cultural traits, and their elites cherished 'gentile' origin-myths and variant forms of customary laws that defined and legitimized their identity. 'The Goths' split between western and eastern branches – Ostrogoths, who settled in Italy and Visigoths, who settled in Spain – but they were in fact composed of many different ethnic groups. The Vandals comprised a similar mixture and, after traversing Gaul and Spain, settled in North Africa. In the course of the fourth and fifth centuries, Saxons settled in north Germany; Franks, whose name allegedly meant 'Fierce Ones' or 'Free Ones', settled in the Rhineland, with Thuringians to the east of them; Alamans, meaning 'All Men', settled to the east of the upper Rhine (hence *Allemagne*). Burgundians settled in southern Gaul. By c.500, these movements and settlements of peoples had produced a patchwork-quilt effect, which with a degree of improvisation modern scholars can map.[26]

The history of the Franks is comparatively well-documented from the sixth century onwards. Though the Franks had a sense of common descent, distinct Frankish kingdoms emerged from the transformation of the western Roman Empire in the fifth and sixth centuries through processes of dynastic succession and division. Early medieval scholars who wrote about the Franks regarded them as distinctively warlike. Whether or not that was true, in the course of three or four generations they conquered the Roman provinces west of the Rhine, together known as 'the Gauls', or simply 'Gaul'. The Franks were distinctive in a second sense too: unlike other rulers and peoples who had accepted, and clung to, a heretical form of Christianity known as Arianism, the earliest Frankish warlord to be called king, Clovis (481–511), chose to convert to Catholic Christianity, as adopted by the Emperor

Constantine in the early fourth century and maintained by Roman emperors from the 360s on. The Franks' Catholicism eased their co-existence and merging with the continuing indigenous Catholic population of late Roman Gaul; and when the Roman Empire faded out of existence in the West, the Frankish kingdom, now long Catholic, survived, and thrived.[27] Indeed, the Franks were distinguished by their orthodoxy, and by their kings' determination to destroy heresy.

A third way of Frankish distinctiveness was central to their kingship. Whereas other kingdoms operated a more or less elective succession-system, 'In the kingdom of the Franks, kings come forth from the family', as Pope Gregory I (590–604) put it in a homily on the Gospels. Called after a mythical ancestor, Merovech, the Merovingian dynasty was fundamental to the Franks' identity and continuity. Like other family inheritances, the kingdom was divided between heirs, and two Merovingian kingdoms eventually crystallized: an eastern one, Austrasia, and a western or 'new' one, Neustria. Accidents of births and (often violent) deaths resulted in a reunited kingdom under Chlothar II (613–29).

In 623, Chlothar appointed as mayor of the Austrasian palace for his young son Dagobert a magnate named Pippin, whom later historians labelled 'of Herstal', a family property north of Liège on the river Meuse, to differentiate him from later namesakes. The mayoralty was functionally similar to the post of *princeps palatii*, 'chief man of the palace', or *secundus a rege*, 'second man after the king' in the Persian Empire, as described in the biblical Book of Esther (an important reference-point for medieval scholars). In the course of the seventh century, mayors increasingly helped run Merovingian kingdoms by managing the palace, that is, the court and the centre of administration, and, like kingship, the post came to be regarded as hereditary.

Royal power dwindled from *c.*670 because of decisions, or accidents, that punctuated the dynasty's history: divisions of the kingdom, assassinations of kings and a series of child-successions. The mayors of the palace, in principle right-hand-men, became in practice powers-behind-the-throne. In the palace, where feasting and drinking and boasting could put peace at risk, the mayor preserved it. The mayor was also a military leader in his own right, able to extend *his* protection (*mundeburdium*) over 'a bishop or abbot along with his men, retainers and friends (*homines, gasindi, amici*), and those under his patronage (*mitio*)'.

This text is a form-document, a model anonymized for general use, as notaries and lawyers still use form-documents today.[28] Historians have long undervalued them *because* they anonymize ('A' grants 'B' property 'C' on date 'D'), rather than referring to actual people and places and giving actual dates. Notaries in the early Middle Ages found formulae valuable because they quickly met the needs of clients wanting, for instance, to make a will, or assign a dowry. Efficient charter-production depended on the use of formulae. Their sheer usefulness is now being properly appreciated as evidence of social realities; and historians are becoming clever at dating and localizing them. The form-document on *mundeburdium* just-mentioned refers to people living under ecclesiastical patronage, who included peasants on church lands. Other formulae refer to similar arrangements involving lay magnates and their peasants. Through such chain-relationships, royal power was delegated to the mayor by the king and exercised in law-courts as legal advocacy for clients, and their dependants. Justice, as well as protection and patronage, was becoming an 'ordinary name of power', also designated 'Carolingian justice'.[29]

In the latter part of the seventh century, when Frankish kings' effective power had shrunk and mayors controlled the palace, Pippin II, whom later chroniclers cast as Pippin of Herstal's grandson, became mayor. Pippin II was not born to mayoralty, though: he was a mayor laboriously self-made, first, by his marriage to Plectrud, heiress to rich lands between the rivers Meuse and Mosel and another cluster not far from Herstal, and second, by his victory in war between eastern and western Frankish aristocratic factions in 687. Well after these events, a two-layered genealogical fudge confected by eighth-century scholars made Pippin II's mother, Begga, Pippin of Herstal's daughter, and inserted as Begga's husband Ansegisel, son of Bishop Arnulf of Metz. The palace was the mayor's place of power as well as, if diminishingly, the king's. A standard form of address for a bishop offering the mayor a Christmas gift expressed the nature and focus of the political relationships in which the mayor's legitimacy was rooted: 'To the famous lord and ornament of the magnates of the royal palace and son in Christ of the universal catholic church.' The mayoralty's tendency to become dynastic combined with the weakening of kingship left a space for 'the ornament of the magnates of the royal palace' to fill.

To make war successfully, whether against regional rivals or, at the king's or mayor's command, against enemies beyond the Franks' frontiers, lay aristocrats needed to attract warriors to their followings. Late seventh- and early eighth-century narrative sources are full of men identified as *gasindi* (companions), *vassi* (boys), *fideles* (faithful men), *amici* (friends) and *satellites* (armed retainers), who constituted the warbands of warlords. The transformation of the Roman world was about them as well. It was a story of interconnected levels of dependence and routes to social mobility. Early medieval narratives, from annals to saints' lives, show that war played an important part in the acquisition and distribution of wealth. The methods by which lay and ecclesiastical lords acquired more wealth from their peasants' labours on the land become easier to see in the eighth century, thanks to larger numbers of documents made by churchmen, whether charters recording church property, surveys of peasant dues, or – again – legal formularies usable by lay persons, from kings to the relatively humble, to record a variety of social arrangements in which high and low, at least in some regions, could negotiate terms.

Among the Franks, the people to whom Charles belonged, kings had been the greatest of warlords in the sixth and earlier seventh centuries. By *c*.700, however, kings had not only ceded war-leadership, along with much governmental power, to mayors of the palace, but they had lost their grip on peoples beyond their frontiers who had once been subject to their overlordship but had now become effectively independent. The Bavarians are a good example. They lived in the lands covering what are now southern Bavaria and western Austria (see Map 1). Their laws had been 'given' them by a Merovingian king. By the early eighth century their warleaders (*duces* – dukes) had converted to Christianity and were running Bavaria under their own steam. Their ruling family, the Agilolfings, with branches sprawling into Alamannia and Lombardy, held the dukedom by hereditary right, and their elite was divided into five aristocratic families (*genealogiae*), whose names were recorded at the opening of the version of the Law of the Bavarians codified *c*.740.

A family as a universal form of social life sounds very familiar, but an early medieval *familia* or *genealogia* is, in fact, a good example of what makes early medieval people seem strange to us. Before *c*.700 there is simply too little evidence to construct family trees for any but royalty and a small handful of aristocratic families, and even these are full of gaps, especially where women are concerned. Still, for these few families, there is for the first time in the timespan covered by this book sufficient material to offer some plausible reconstructions, especially where prosopographers (scholars interested in names and family-connexions) have been busy. It is easily assumed that a family was a group with clear boundaries, that men and women knew who belonged and who didn't, and that they had a strong sense of family identity and solidarity. These are the very features that make families sound familiar. But closer acquaintance often makes them seem much less familiar. Aristocratic families, or clans, like the Bavarian Huosi, were riven with rivalries. Relationships between brothers, and between uncles and nephews, were especially liable to produce conflict, most of all in royal families, since kingship itself, looked at as a global phenomenon, was a uniquely scarce resource.[30] Fraternal disputes over the family inheritance were common. In such conditions, 'family identity' and 'the bonds of kinship' became problematic. Identities and bonds were real enough, and generated visible solidarities. Yet, under pressure, family branches, far from hanging together often hung separately.

Similar considerations apply to marriage. The conjugal bond was basic to social relations, yet among the Franks the twin practices of serial monogamy and polygamy persisted into this period, producing fault-lines often considered more typical of the harem than of a Christian household. A form of rivalry that attracted particular attention from chroniclers was that between the families of successive wives, or of wives at the same time, with the relationships funded by different forms of property-exchange. Modern historians of medieval marriage have tried to find ways round such conundrums by inventing the institution of *Friedelehe*, a form of private marriage not involving the alliance between families of like status that was the key feature of legal marriage, and the category of *Friedelfrau*, love-bride, or secondary wife. These inventions have been rejected only in recent historiography, not before time, and a larger variety of partnerships seen to have existed, complicating conflicts in some cases, allowing for more comfortable flexibility in others. Different near-contemporary accounts of these relationships reveal conflicting interpretations cooked up to justify different parties' positions after the event.

Intergenerational tensions can exist in any family, but, given the marital practices just described, they arose especially often in elite or royal ones. This is clause 9 in the Law of the Bavarians (whose rulers were dukes rather than kings):

> *De filiis ducum, si protervi fuerint.* Concerning the sons of dukes, if they are rebellious.
>
> If a duke's son is so proud and foolish that he wants to dishonour his father by [listening to] the advice of bad men, or to seize his kingdom from him by force . . . he must know that this is to act against the law [for which the penalty is to lose his inheritance, and also be exiled should the king or the father, i.e. the duke, so wish].

The ellipsis indicates where I have left out a vital set of conditions that qualify this statement:

> . . . so long as his father is still capable of fighting a case in a legal dispute, and going on campaign, and judging the people, and leaping on to his horse in a manly fashion, and brandishing his weapons, and is not deaf or blind, and is able in all respects to carry out the king's orders . . .

This passage is the 'essential requirements' section of a Bavarian duke's job spec. So long as the duke ticked these boxes, he held his job according to law.

Kings and *duces* alike were important for aristocrats, and also for people of lesser rank (including peasants), because they provided leadership in war and justice, i.e. procedures for settling disputes, in peace. Mayors of the palace needed followers just as kings did, and by *c.*700 the Frankish mayors were becoming more successful than their kings in attracting and keeping followers. This did not solve the endemic problems of conflict between the Neustrians and Austrasians, and the Austrasian mayoral dynasty itself was riven by conflict. It did mean, however, that a warlord with courage, flair and luck could achieve a sudden reversal of fortune, essentially through speed of reaction. In 718, the Austrasian mayor Charles Martel led his forces to victory over the Neustrians at Soissons and chased his defeated enemies across the Loire at Orléans; then he moved north-east and across the Rhine and as far as the river Weser deep in Saxony, and finally back to his homelands in the area of Liège – some 1,400km on old Roman roads and, east of the Rhine, old warpaths.[31] Martel's performance in that year proved that nothing succeeded like success.

V. MORE ABOUT DISTANCE

In a large realm, the problems of distance remained, both in war and in peace. In the heyday of the Roman Empire, imperial messengers could ride around 70 miles in a day, covering the 280km – 175 miles – from Rome to Ravenna in about two and a half days.[32] The scale and speed of such a communication-network bears comparison in some ways (not in the volume of correspondence, certainly, but in the speed news could travel) to the courier-link with its 106 relay-stations that connected Madrid to the Spanish Netherlands in the reigns of Charles V and Philip II in the sixteenth century. Crucial information took weeks or even months to arrive. In an exceptional case, a courier achieved the phenomenal average speed of 150km (some 93 miles) a day travelling from Brussels to Madrid. Fernand Braudel, writing on the global empire of Philip II of Spain in the sixteenth century, quoted from Philip's last advice to his son in which he blamed the problems of his reign on 'the distance that separates one state and another'. Braudel himself gave deep consideration to distance as 'public enemy number 1'. Taking a different tack, Geoffrey Parker quoted a British diplomat's complaint in 1917 of 'the rapidity of communication by telegraph and telephone', which 'leave no time for reflection or consultation and demand an immediate and often hasty decision'.[33] Like the diplomat, Parker thought you could have too much of a good thing. Eighth-century statistics on communication are guesstimates. Still, they are enough to suggest that Charles, in evaluating his sources and resources, and their limits, in war and also in peace, had to factor in the geography of distance. In eighth-century communications, as in modern times, it was a question of balancing the need for information and the need to decide on a response.

In warfare, the problems of distance were not so different in the nineteenth century before the railways from those encountered by Charles's father and Charles himself in the eighth, when mounted armies, though not larger than a few thousand men, could move fast, covering perhaps 30km per day. As for communications, a messenger at the ready, using known routes with staging-posts for a change of horses, could cover 100km per day. A ruler had to be ready to respond to unexpected news: his answer would depend not only on the time available but on other priorities *at the time*. Given a speedy messenger, news of the attempted assassination of Pope Leo III in Rome on 25 April 799 probably reached Charles at Aachen, 1,500km away, early in the second week of May. Charles immediately sent the news to Alcuin, who was now based at Tours. Alcuin hoped and expected Charles to react swiftly by leading an army into Italy to rescue and reinstall the pope. But at this moment, it turned out, the pope was not Charles's priority. First, there was a Saxon campaign to win; second, and connected, there were tensions to resolve within his own family, that is, between Charles and his sons. Leo found other rescuers, and fled to Charles in Saxony, arriving in late August.

Events and rumours evoked a flurry of correspondence meanwhile. Messengers worked overtime. Archbishop Arn of Salzburg, at Paderborn in Saxony with Charles, sent a letter to Alcuin at Tours containing highly sensitive allegations about the pope's private life. Alcuin read it with only his student Candidus present, and then, anxious that it might fall into anyone else's hands, told him to put it into the fire 'so that no scandal might arise through the carelessness of the man who looks after my correspondence'. In June and July 799, the number of letters sent by Alcuin to Charles and others was especially high: roughly one letter per fortnight has survived. Eventually, by November, Arn, with Charles's arch-chaplain Hildebald, archbishop of Cologne, and a retinue big enough to double as an army, had escorted the pope the 1,500km back to Rome. For comparison, from 787–9, there survive seven letters sent from Pope Hadrian to Charles, which contain the shadow-forms of the letters from Charles which had prompted the papal responses.

VI. MAPS

Though many books on Charles have had a map or two, few writers have seriously reckoned with the potential of maps to make sense of political and economic geography and of the specific changes that occurred in the eighth century. An important aim of *this* book has been to make the most of what maps can provide. Maps at the cutting edge of GPS technology are available online, where references are also given. But incorporating maps into the book itself allows the reader to move from text to visualization of political and economic data in familiar formats, and back again. First and fundamentally, maps present readers with such physical features in landscapes as the locations of rivers and mountains. It can easily be grasped how these both divide and connect zones of economic and political power, and at the same time suggest probabilities of contests within regions and the marking of boundaries between realms. The English language had no adjective to denote areas ruled, *regna* in Latin (meaning kingdoms and also what modern historians label sub-kingdoms, for instance Aquitaine, or Neustria), until Susan Reynolds resurrected the handy word 'regnal', which will be used in this book.[34]

The economic, political and military significance of rivers and river-valley regions needs more emphasis than it has often received; and this applies to the late Roman/early Frankish period as much as to the eighth century.[35] In every period, rivers determine much of the topography of power. Roman fortresses on the west bank of the Rhine, for instance, became urban and ecclesiastical centres under the Franks. Trade passed along rivers and, as Roman emperors had done, Frankish kings established toll-points to tap traders' profits. That the Rhine was an artery as well as a formidable barrier was something the Romans recognized – as did Charles, centuries later, when he rebuilt the Roman bridge (using the old piles) over the river at Mainz. Similarly, the huge mountain-spines of the Alps, the Pyrenees and the Apennines are key to Charles's construction and practice of empire; for instance in the tactics, political as well as military, that Charles employed in planning for his Italian campaign in 773–4, or his expedition into Spain in 778, or in the conquest of Bavaria in 791–3. The best-laid plans could not always forestall disaster, however, as Charles's men learned to their cost at the pass of Roncesvaux where, as Einhard wrote, putting it mildly, 'the terrain was against them'.

Until the 790s, Charles's practice of government was in the main itinerant.[36] Rivers featured strongly in itineraries and the locations of palaces. Two of the seventh-century Merovingians' favoured palaces were in old Roman cities that were also on rivers: Metz at the confluence of the Mosel and the Seille; and Paris on the Seine. A significant change in the seventh century saw Merovingian kings residing more often in palaces at rural estate-centres (*villae*), such as Quierzy. The Arnulfing mayors of the palace occasionally continued this practice;

and the first Carolingian king, Pippin, in the first decade of his reign stayed at Verberie and Compiègne. It was at Quierzy that Pippin welcomed, in 743, an important religious and political figure, Virgil the Irishman, later to become archbishop of Salzburg. In mid-winter 753–4, Pope Stephen II had come from Rome and been invited by Pippin to stay at St-Denis. Then

> Pippin took his leave with the venerable pontiff's advice, favour and prayers, and made his way to the place called Quierzy with all the dignitaries of his royal power and imbued them with the great father's holy advice. There, having agreed to a plan made with the pope, they decided how it would be carried out.

Pope Stephen's celebration of Easter (24 April) at Quierzy was an event that inextricably combined and celebrated the political and religious in the new kingship. The river Oise downstream from Quierzy was useful for travel and for transport. The royal family, the court and the resident service personnel would all have found this palace and its environs delightful rather than formidable. Pippin is documented as staying there four times, and he overwintered there thrice. Some residences mattered much more than others. Early Carolingian itinerancy can be overstated. The date of Charles's birth is well-documented as 2 April 748. It may well be that he was born at Quierzy and that, during his growing years, that palace was a familiar environment. In those years and for several decades to come, an Aachen 'capital' would remain unimaginable.

When more information becomes available in Charles's reign, it becomes clear that palaces where king and household overwintered had to be ready to host stays of many hundreds of people for up to five or six months. The people who organized these stays, *senescalci* and *mansionarii* (who must surely have been aided by women as well as men), were among the regime's key personnel. So too were the *iudices* or estate-managers, who ran the extensive royal estates and provisioning and transport systems in the surrounding territory. These necessary resources included often very large tracts of forest or *foresta*, meaning land outside (*foris*) the areas of common use or the estates of aristocrats and churches, and also parks (*brogili*): land reserved for the use of the king and his men to hunt in for the purposes of food-supply, exercise and military training, with a significant element of competitiveness. Places where kings were to be found were also places where kings wanted to be seen, and seen at work amidst their counsellors, officials and servants. People seeking justice, or bringing complaints, came to palaces for judgments. Only from the mid-790s on did the Aachen palace become *the* court.

Mapping churches across later Merovingian and early Carolingian times is easier to do because increasing quantities of evidence are available, partly because more of that evidence is archaeological. Cities (*civitates*) which had once been nodes of Roman imperial government now became places where bishops lived in former Roman governmental buildings where their cathedrals were located. Episcopal churches and rural churches, and extra-mural cemeteries, in what had been Roman cities have been excavated at Cologne, Lyons, Metz, Paris and Tours, to name only a few. There were urban and suburban monasteries, often founded by bishops, sometimes on lands that were a king's to give away; and there were, especially from the seventh century, rural monasteries maintained by the patronage of rulers, aristocrats and lesser landowners. Additionally, there were monasteries located in such demanding early medieval landscapes as the Jura: versions of the deserts in which monasticism had originally taken root.

The landed properties of rulers and aristocrats, and also churches, could be increased through warfare and through gift, often in the form of dower and dowry. Far from being somehow opposed, family concerns and religious concerns were connected, just as were the interests of patrons and families on the one hand, and of managers and members of ecclesiastical communities on the other. Lay and ecclesiastical landlords belonged to the same families and acquired land by concerted action. Sons of aristocrats, trained for war, enlisted in the warbands of lay and ecclesiastical elites. To put it another way, an abbot or abbess was at once a spiritual leader and, if not actually a family member, hand-in-glove with the family-patrons. By 700, while this was the set-up in many parts of the west, it was most clearly so in Francia, where denser charter-evidence becomes available earliest, and where kings of the Merovingian dynasty generously provided lands for monasteries and allowed 'free election' of abbots by monks, but neither imposed services on them, nor exactly owned them.

VII. TRADING-PLACES

Trading-places and markets appear from the later seventh century in a variety of sources, especially in Gaul north of the Loire and in Frisia, as increasing wealth in the countryside created demand for more exchange and more media of exchange, encouraging overseas trade in the North Sea area. It was not just because monasteries were good at producing and preserving texts that trade and markets were recorded in monastic chronicles and saints' *Lives*: monasteries, uncoincidentally sited on or very near rivers or deltas, were deeply involved in these exchanges.[37] The later Merovingians lost control of the coin supply, and as gold became harder to get hold of, and silver easier and of much lower value, they began to issue silver coins, or pennies. Enterprising local powers and power-brokers began to issue their own pennies from mints often located in or near old Roman cities where bishops and counts were based.[38] A map of trading-places and mints begins to look rather messy because ecclesiastical institutions need to be mapped in the same places. Where historians track these in church records that include royal grants to churches to manage and take tolls, archaeologists find material evidence of craft production, and stray coin-finds which numismatists can interpret in terms of local and regnal politics. The map would become very messy, in fact, because numbers of find-spots and hoards change so strikingly over the eighth century, and specifically in the reign of Charles. This is why more than one map is needed.

Economic change in the eighth century is documented by new types of material evidence. Archaeologists have excavated trading-places and productive sites, finding objects and coins suggestive of markets. They have also excavated palaces and churches and revealed imposing buildings and glorious wall-paintings.[39] Working in collaboration with natural scientists, especially molecular biologists, some archaeologists are reconstructing vital statistics hitherto inaccessible. The cessation of the endemic disease that plagued Europe and the Mediterranean world from the sixth century to the early eighth can be demonstrated. Unchecked by endemic disease, population tended to rise.[40] Thus, in the four centuries after AD300, falling populations had reduced the labour-supply, enabling peasants to strike better bargains with landlords. However, once labour became more plentiful, aristocrats were able to extract more from their peasants in the way of services or rents. The sheer patchiness of the evidence is in part accidental, but it also reflects what has been called 'the leopard-spot geographical pattern', where regions containing more or less independent peasant communities were interspersed with dependent ones under lordly exploitation.[41] Any generalized model of peasants' lot improving while that of landlords necessarily went the other way, or vice versa – in other words, a zero-sum game – is too crude to be meaningful, and in any case bears no relation to the economy presently under discussion. Different conditions existed patchily yet simultaneously within regions and localities. Archaeological evidence lends increasing support to this reading.

Recent investigations of the retreat of Swiss glaciers due to relative warm and dry conditions indicate that the 'Medieval Warm Period' began somewhat earlier than hitherto thought, in the mid-eighth century.[42] Coincidentally, between 764 and 823 there was a break in extreme climatic events produced by volcanic emissions. No severe winters from that cause occurred during those decades. There were three serious famines (778–9, 792–3 and 805–6) and two devastating animal epidemics (in 791 and 810). Otherwise, however, it seems that Charles's reign, free of exogenous dire impacts on the economy, was a relatively lucky period for the European population.

VIII. VITAL STATISTICS

Some of the sorts of problems confronted by historians of the early Middle Ages will by now be very clear. They arise not so much from absence or even shortage of evidence, nor from its patchiness which intensifies the difficulty of assessing change over time, nor even from the frustration of encountering silence on the very things you realize you subconsciously expected to hear. They arise from cultural distance, and the experience of finding the early Middle Ages strange, which is, for readers as well as writers of books about the period, the beginning of wisdom. The most obvious of vital statistics – precise dates of birth and death and their locations – are what a modern state routinely collects about its citizens nowadays, and what census-data makes generally accessible. In the case of even the best-documented earlier medieval persons, that data, those statistics, are nearly always impossible to find.

Take birth: there were two sets of Frankish laws, one with twelve as the age of adulthood, the other fifteen. A high-born youth's coming of age was publicly marked by a ritual arming. But there is no evidence for how the moment was determined. Senior family members would see visible signs of puberty – a growth spurt; a sprouting beard; a voice breaking – from which they could count back to the date of birth somewhat approximately, assuming they wanted to know it. Even for the sons of kings, until the middle of the ninth century, day and month birthdates are, with one exception, not recorded.

The exception is Charles himself. The question of *when* exactly Charles was born in terms of day and month has been solved by historians applying both judgement and luck. In a manuscript datable to the second quarter of the ninth century from Lorsch, a monastery particularly close to the Carolingian family, and concerned with the commemoration of its members, a scribe noted, '*IIII. Non. Apr. Nativitas domni et gloriosissimi Karoli imperatoris*', using here the ancient Roman dating-form, in modern terms '2 April', with the information: 'The birth of the lord and most glorious emperor Charles.' The first scholar to call attention to this note in the Lorsch manuscript was Jean Mabillon (1632–1707), in a 1704 supplement to his *De Re Diplomatica* ('On the Study of Documents'), published in 1681 with the aim of setting out rules for critically assessing the genuineness or otherwise of early medieval charters. The great medieval historian Marc Bloch (1886–1944) said of 1681: 'that year, the year of the publication of *De Re Diplomatica*, was truly a great one in the history of the human mind.'

So far, so good: the Lorsch scribe gave day and month. What about the year? A German historian, Karl Ferdinand Werner (1924–2008), Director of the German Historical Institute in Paris, pointed out that at Lorsch in the mid-ninth century, the monks' concern, part of a longstanding system which included saints' days, was liturgical commemoration *every* year on a particular day and month. In a paper given in Paris in 1972, published in German in 1973 and in French in 1975, Werner pointed out that the argument for accepting the date of 742 as the year of Charles's birth came from one source: Einhard's *Life of Charles*. Einhard professed to know next to nothing about Charles's early life (he may have professed that in order to avoid having to present Charles as a junior family member). He knew (because he was almost certainly there) Charles's deathdate: 28 January 814. He also knew from Suetonius that the Emperor Augustus had died aged seventy-two. In the absence of other evidence, and keen to score a symbolic point, he asserted that Charles too had died 'in the seventy-second year of his age'. So great was Einhard's authority with most later historians right down to the twentieth century, that 742 as the year of Charles's birth became set in historiographical stone. Werner not only showed the feebleness of the accepted orthodoxy, he also pointed to strong evidence against it in a little group of additions (the earliest at the year 747, the latest at 770) to a set of annals written up more or less contemporaneously by someone close to a Carolingian court. At 747 the scribe had written: *'Et ipso anno fuit natus Karolus rex'* ('and in that year, King Charles was born'). Where other historians had called this a mistake and reiterated Einhard's assertion that Charles died in his 'seventy-second year', Werner recognized Einhard's statement as baseless, and the annalist's statement as reliable because of this author's privileged position in space and time.

In 1995, a German historian of a younger generation, Matthias Becher, offered a small qualification to Werner's argument. Becher observed that the author of these annals, like many other annalists of this period, dated the start of each year from Easter, a movable feast, and that in 747 Easter fell on 24 April. But many writers then (as in our own system now, though far from globally) used 1 January as the start-date of a new year, and on that reckoning, 2 April belonged in 748. The Lorsch writer had used the annalists' reckoning. Thus a not very well-founded birthdate of 2 April 742 has yielded to a well-founded one: 2 April 748. Thanks to Werner and Becher between them, then, Charles's lifespan has been reduced from seventy-two years to not quite sixty-six.

The further implications of the new fact, or, to borrow the term now widely used by scholars in digital humanities, 'factoid' (meaning 'what historians have agreed is a fact'), will be discussed in various contexts later in the book. This exemplary case of scholarly revisionism shows the difficulty of knowing for certain the most basic of vital statistics, even of one of the best-documented people of the early Middle Ages. In itself, however, it does not necessarily show anything much about how Charles and his contemporaries thought and felt about remembering birthdays, or, for that matter, deathdays. Scholars used to accept, for instance, that the births and deaths of children were regarded as unimportant by parents in so-called 'traditional' cultures because infant mortality was so common that emotional investment in children was discouraged.[43] Even in source-poor times, this absence of evidence is not evidence of absence. In itself, the very fact of the recording of Charles's own birth, or the birth or death of a child or sibling, indicated something significant to Charles and/or to other family members. The records of these life-events, however infrequent their survival, signalled things that mattered to Charles and the people of his world: the importance of dynasty, the role of royal women in politics, relationships between father and daughters as well as between father and sons, and between siblings. Similar observations apply to another type of bond that affected Charles politically and personally, that is, the mutual obligations and affection between him as lord and the men who served him faithfully, in war and in government. That the deaths of his men mattered much to Charles can be inferred from recorded evidence of his reactions to the losses of Roland and his men at Roncesvaux in 778, and to a Frankish defeat in Saxony in 782.

Charles's life is documented thinly by comparison with some later medieval lives and very many modern ones, and also very unevenly. Evidential dead-ends are met often. Nevertheless, and in part compensating for those, are the variety, and the occasional density, of the contemporary evidence. Variety of genre makes for serious problems of comparison. How, for instance, can the weight of a series of letters be assessed against that of a series of instructions to royal officials or a set of annals, or – to move beyond texts – a partially excavated palace (Aachen) assessed against a still-standing church (Charles's great one at Aachen, or Theodulf's small one at Germigny near St-Benoît-sur-Loire)? What is the evidential value of a poem? The verse-epitaph survives at the church of St-Arnulf, Metz of Charles's daughter Hildegard, named after her mother Queen Hildegard who died within days of giving birth to her; baby Hildegard herself died only a few weeks later. According to the poet, the epitaphs of both queen (her deathdate recorded in annals as 30 April 783) and daughter were written at Charles's command. The baby's epitaph was no doubt, as literary scholars have said, a practised courtier's production of conventional sentiments in stylish imitation of classical models to suit the needs of his royal patron. On other criteria, the poem might be read and assessed differently, in terms of the psychological responses of parents, siblings, nurses and nannies:

Hildegard, bitter death took you away untimely
As the cold north wind snatches away the buds of the
    cypresses in spring,
you did not live for even a year.
You never had a first birthday.
Little girl, little maiden, you left behind grief that
    was not little.
You pierce as with a spear the royal heart of your father,
And bearing your mother's name, you renew the sorrow
    of her death
After you scarcely lived 40 days.[44]

IX. EIGHTH-CENTURY TRANSFORMATIONS

By the early eighth century the Roman world had been transformed from one great empire into, working from east to west, a Muslim caliphate in western Asia, the Near East and North Africa; a territorially diminished eastern Roman Christian empire, Byzantium; and a multiplicity of kingdoms and peoples in what had been the western Roman empire. Muslim conquests, concentrated in the 630s–60s, had made division a fact of life. Yet east–west communications persisted in the late seventh and early eighth centuries. There were diplomatic contacts and symbolic skirmishes between Damascus and Constantinople and Rome. In 691–2, the Ecumenical Council in the Trullan palace in Constantinople was attended by 211 bishops from the east Roman sees and legates from Jerusalem, Alexandria, Antioch and Rome. The Byzantine Emperor Justinian II sent master mosaicists to help adorn Jerusalem's Dome of the Rock, now being converted into a mosque (he did the same again for the Great Mosque in Damascus in 708–11). On 5 October 710, at the emperor's invitation, Pope Constantine I (707–15), a native of Syria, set out with a huge retinue for Constantinople, returning to Rome almost exactly a year later (having been detained by illness – normally the two-way journey by sea took about two months). The biographer of Pope Gregory II (715–31) recorded the siege of Constantinople by a Muslim fleet of 'unspeakable Saracens', in 717–18, and its defence by the Emperor Leo III. The Visigothic kingdom of Spain was conquered by a mainly Berber Muslim army of 'the unspeakable race of the Hagarenes' from Ceuta in North Africa in 711. The biographer further noted the letter sent to the pope by 'Eudo duke of the Franks' in 721, recalling that Gregory had

> the previous year sent him three sponges from those provided for use on his own table . . . At the time war [with the Saracens] was beginning [in 721], Eudo prince of Aquitaine had given them to his people to consume in small amounts, and of those who had shared in them not one had been injured or killed. [Eudo also stated] that 375,000 [Saracens] were killed on one day [and] that only 1500 Franks had died in the war.[45]

Whatever else can be made of this information, it shows contacts between the papacy and Franks and/or Aquitanians, who were certainly not considered unspeakable at the pope's court. Papal biographers also mention exchanges between Gregory II and King Liutprand of the Lombards, and between Gregory III and 'His Excellency Charles [Martel] who then ruled the kingdom of the Franks'.

By the mid-eighth century, changes in the wider world and the transformations of the seventh century had brought into being distinct heirs and inheritances: three Empires of Faith, each internally diverse, each driven and unified by religious fervour.[46] Rome's legacy to the caliphate was a tax-taking regime with huge paid armies, an incoming Arab minority, identified by its language and obedience to Islam, ruling over populations consisting through the eighth century of large Christian and Jewish majorities in the vast Near-Eastern territories of Egypt and Syria. The East Roman Empire, though hugely diminished in size and under enormous pressure, fought back, firmly retaining its great capital Constantinople, its state apparatus and tax system, Christian Roman law, multiple written languages, hegemonic Greek culture and identity, strong naval presence in the eastern Mediterranean and Adriatic seas, and political control, still, of much of Italy under the overall authority of the exarch based in Ravenna. An Arab fleet kept Constantinople under siege in 717–18: a trial which the 'queen-city', protected by its patron the Virgin Mary, Queen of Heaven, withstood, and to which Emperor Leo III (717–41) responded by jacking up fiscal demands in Italy, and – in an extraordinary ideological experiment – favouring a policy of iconoclasm (the destruction of icons) capable of motivating his own armies to confront iconoclastic Islam. While the exarch pleaded in vain for the emperor's help, Constantinople's control of its provinces in Italy was shaken but not broken.

In the west, Muslim warriors largely drawn from the local Berber population in North Africa, with leaders egged on by the Umayyad caliph in Damascus, crossed the Straits of Gibraltar and conquered Iberia between 711 and 714. Soon Muslim troops were raiding into the former Roman province of Narbonnensis (known to Charles and his contemporaries as Septimania), which had been an integral part of the Hispanic kingdom ruled until 711 by Visigothic kings. There were also Muslim raids east beyond the Rhône into Provence and north into Aquitaine. After the 670s, leaders in both these large regions had appeared increasingly seldom at any Merovingian palace, and though they still acknowledged Merovingian kings and retained ties with Frankish aristocrats, they became in effect independent princes. As such, they were willing when it suited them to ally with Muslims, but when Muslim raids became too severe, they opposed them, and sought help further afield.[47] A third Empire of Faith was being constructed, with Latin-using Christian rulers and princes, their supporters, popes and assorted ecclesiastics as active collaborators in this re-formation, in which the Franks were increasingly prominent. The next chapter – the proper beginning of this book – will focus on the decades following c.700, the parts played by Charles's grandparents and parents, and other kin, and by lay and ecclesiastical supporters of the mayoral dynasty; and then trace the formative changes in the Franks' political and social world as it had come to be when Charles was born into it on 2 April 748.

The tomb of Abbot Willibrord at Echternach.

2

Family Stories Charles Might Have Known

I. FREDEGAR'S STORY

In the early Middle Ages, high-status families might transmit their stories through the written word.[1] More likely was transmission through oral traditions and social memory rooted in places and spaces. Charles's story began with his great-great-grandfather Arnulf, in the seventh century. The story-teller was Fredegar, author of a *Chronicle* in four books. Fredegar continued the history-writing tradition of Gregory of Tours (d.594) but from a distinctly secular and more easterly viewpoint, indicating the authorship of a layman interested in Burgundy and Austrasia. Arnulf, bishop of Metz and Pippin 'I' (so-called by modern historians to differentiate him from later namesakes), mayor of the palace of Austrasia, appear in the *Chronicle* acting together in the same faction (*factio*), and dying at about the same time, *c.*640. Fredegar completed his work in the early 660s. Though he had given Pippin 'I' an enthusiastic write-up, he drew a veil over the assassination of Pippin's son Grimoald, which occurred *c.*660. Coincidentally or not, the family of Pippin disappeared from the historical record for a decade or so just about when Fredegar stopped writing.[2]

II. GISELA'S STORY

Well over 160 years after Bishop Arnulf's death, a writer in 804 or 805, at a time in Charles's reign when the question of the succession was reaching a moment of decision, stopped writing a set of annals known to modern historians as the *Annales Mettenses Priores* (*AMP*), the

Earlier Annals of Metz (though they had little to do with Metz except as a Carolingian burial-place, and their earlier part does not look like a set of annals).[3] The *AMP* author, uniquely, referred to the *Pippinii*, meaning the offspring of Pippin 'II'; and the story unfolded here is that of the Carolingians. Some modern historians have been tempted, rightly I think, to infer an author or patron who was a member of the dynasty, with a strong interest in the great convent of Chelles, near Paris, mentioned in the *AMP* at a key moment, 804. That the work breaks off in 805 could suggest a link with the author's death. Residing at the convent of Chelles between sometime in the late eighth century and her death, 'a few years before her brother', was Gisela, the sister of Charles – though in a charter she issued on 13 June 799 she identified herself not as a sister but as 'the most noble daughter of the late King Pippin and Queen Bertrada'.[4] The author/patron began with a paean of praise to Pippin 'II', whose mother, Begga, was the daughter of Pippin 'I', and whose father was Ansegisel, identified by others writing in the eighth century – but not by *this* author, who was perhaps deliberately discreet on the bishop's fatherhood – as the son of Arnulf. The mentions of Chelles, and the insistent theme of the Pippinids' dynastic history, send strong signals about the *AMP*'s sources and purposes. The text begins with a uniquely full and fulsome account of Pippin 'II', and the author shows a recurring interest in female historical characters (good and bad), among them Anstrud, the Neustrian heiress to whom Pippin 'II' arranged the marriage of his son Drogo shortly after the battle of Tertry, which turned out to be the key to Pippin's growing influence in Neustria. These traits strengthen the case for regarding Gisela as the person who commissioned the *AMP* and even having a quasi-authorial role in it. There will be more to say later in this book about the circumstances of the *AMP*'s production. For the moment, the *AMP*'s unique information about Pippin 'II' in that early section seems to depend on near-contemporary material. Breaking a self-imposed historians' 'rule' to assume that, other things being equal, the nearer a text is in date to events recorded the likelier it is to be best-informed, I make the *AMP* an exception to that rule, and place its details on Pippin 'II' as 'the second story', and Gisela as conscientious keeper of family memory. On further sections of the *AMP*, however, and given that this is a unique and at the same time extremely tendentious source, I take a more sceptical view and try to justify so doing.[5]

III. THE STORY AS TOLD BY THE AUTHOR OF GERTRUDE'S *LIFE*

Late in the seventh century, in a saint's life and an account of a set of miracles, the Pippinid genealogy was first given shape and 'defined by women'.[6] The first of these women was Itta, Charles's great-great-great-grandmother, whose daughter Gertrude (born *c*.621) had, according to the author of her *Life*, chosen the life of a nun. The *Life* written up in *c*.670, within twenty years of Gertrude's death, stresses Itta's position as *materfamilias*, at whose knee sat her daughter. Gertrude became abbess of a convent founded on Itta's primary estate, Nivelles.[7] Gertrude's *Life* also mentions Fosses, another of Itta's estates, and the book of Gertrude's miracles (written up *c*.700) mentions a third, Andennes, to which Itta's other daughter, Begga, retired in her widowhood (and in due course gained a reputation for sanctity herself). These texts show that Itta was a rich heiress, and that in marrying Pippin 'I' she had brought Nivelles, Fosses and Andennes into their joint possession. A genealogy produced at Metz very early in the ninth century shows Begga, the younger daughter of Itta and Pippin, marrying Arnulf's son and producing Pippin 'II'. Thus Begga was 'a *sine qua non* of the Pippinid family'.[8] Her elder sister Gertrude, 'given to God', had become abbess of Nivelles founded by the widowed Itta when her inherited lands were hers to grant.[9] Itta and Begga had 'defined' the genealogy, but Gertrude was every bit as important a character in the family history: her contribution was not through motherhood but through early and well-established sanctity, as set out in her *Life* and her miracles. It was not surprising that Nivelles became a dynastic cult-site especially cherished by the women of the family. More surprising, but worth pondering, was the rhetorical question of the author of Gertrude's *Life*, 'Who living in Europe does not know the loftiness of the names and the localities of her lineage?'

IV. THE STORY AS TOLD AT NOTRE DAME, SOISSONS

Another historical narrative, the *Liber Historiae Francorum* (*LHF*), written up *c*.727 but in fact ending in 721, focused not on a family but on a people and a region – the Franks and Neustria; indeed to this author the Franks *were* the Neustrians.[10] In the earlier sections of the story, the *LHF*-author drew on an abbreviated version of the *Histories* of Gregory of Tours, showing a particular interest in the Frankish queens who had been prominent therein, and also in Soissons and the Oise-valley region. From these evident interests, some modern historians have reasonably enough inferred that the author was a nun writing in the great convent of Notre Dame, Soissons.[11] She showed little sign of interest in Austrasia or the Pippin family up to *c.*675, but from then on, she recorded the main points of the career of Charles's great-grandfather Pippin 'II' (640/650–714), though not in chronological order: first she highlighted Pippin's victory over the Neustrians at Tertry (687), followed by his return to Austrasia, but only then did she note, as it were in flashback, that Pippin, evidently some time before, had married 'the very noble Plectrud' and had two sons by her, the elder of whom, Drogo, had been made duke of Champagne. The *LHF*-author, a few lines later, notes that Pippin had another wife (unnamed) by whom he had a son called Charles (later nicknamed Martel) who was 'well-educated, with exceptional qualities and military ability'.[12]

V. BEDE'S STORY

Pippin 'II' was not just a figure of interest for Frankish authors with Pippinid links. He caught the attention of a younger contemporary across the Channel who was, among other things, a historian. This was Bede (672/3–735), who completed his *Ecclesiastical History of the English People* in 731. Bede had been offered as a child to the monastic life at Wearmouth-Jarrow. Though he never left his native Northumbria, his world of contacts, like that of the inmates of Nivelles, reached far and wide. In the last of the five books of his *Ecclesiastical History*, he recorded the activities of Pippin 'warleader of the Franks' (*dux Francorum*) in supporting the preaching of Anglo-Saxon missionaries to partly Christianized or pagan people on the Continent. In the early 690s, Pippin had extended his rule into southern Frisia, where he helped the Northumbrian cleric Willibrord (657/8–739) establish a base, and then sent him to Rome, to get papal authority to preach. Willibrord was also 'hoping to receive relics of the blessed apostles and martyrs of

Christ, so that, when he had . . . founded churches . . . he might have relics to put into them, dedicating each church to the saint whose relics they were'.[13] When Pippin heard that two of Willibrord's Anglo-Saxon fellow-preachers had been killed by still-pagan Old Saxons, he 'had their bodies brought to him and buried them with much splendour in the church at Cologne', thereby treating them as martyrs.[14] Then, 'at the urging of his wife Plectrud', Pippin gave Suidbert, another of Willibrord's companions, land at Kaiserwerth on the east bank of the Rhine, some 40km downstream from Cologne, so that he could build a monastery.[15] Pippin, in 695, sent Willibrord on a second visit to Rome, to be consecrated by the pope as 'archbishop of the Frisians at Pippin's request'.[16] Soon after Willibrord's return, 'the wealthy and noble widow Irmina', Plectrud's mother, granted him lands on which to build a monastery at Echternach, a little to the west of Trier on the river Sûre, an affluent of the Mosel. This is the one piece of evidence that comes from a contemporary document, rather than from Bede, but it fits neatly with the rest of what Bede knew.[17] In 708 Willibrord made his archiepiscopal seat at Utrecht 'in his [Pippin's] famous fortress'.[18] Bede's narrative connected these people and places. His interest in Willibrord and his companions arose from his strong sense that their efforts were a return-gift for the conversion of the Anglo-Saxons by papal and Frankish efforts, the subject of his *Ecclesiastical History*.[19] In a world of pious warlords and noble ladies, Bede's religious impulse generated political support. The actions of preachers and powerful laypeople complemented each other: these men and women cherished the same goals with equal sincerity. Locating relics in strongholds like Utrecht and Cologne fortified religious and political authority in a local landscape, and at the same time intensified and perpetuated contacts with Rome.

VI. THE STORIES OF CHILDEBRAND AND NIBELUNG, OR, THE 'CONTINUATORS OF FREDEGAR'

Sometime after the *LHF*-author stopped work, in 727, a new author compiled a radically revised version of Fredegar's *Chronicle*, and added to it a version of the *LHF* (known as 'B') from chapter 42 down to its final chapter 53. The Continuator made some significant additions about the Pippinids to the *LHF*'s account of events between 711 and 719, left awkward gaps and confusions in the 720s, but from the 730s offered an original and – this goes without saying – highly tendentious narrative down to 751, with a second continuation from there to 768. At chapter 33, which deals with the events of 751, the author reports the election and consecration of Pippin 'III' 'together with Queen Bertrada'. At chapter 34, one manuscript has this:

> Up to here, the illustrious man Count Childebrand, uncle of the just-mentioned King Pippin, very conscientiously saw to the writing of this *History* or *Deeds of the Franks*. From this point the record goes on under the supervision of the illustrious man Nibelung, son of Childebrand, who was also a count.

Modern historians know this father-and-son pair as the Continuators of Fredegar.[20]

For the 730s, the First Continuator's story, gap-ridden and woolly though it is, becomes a key source of information. For the period 741 to 768, both Childebrand and Nibelung are exceptionally important because they wrote quite independently of other eighth-century annalists, whether those who wrote more or less contemporaneously (but with frustrating brevity) or, the best-known of works in this genre, the *Annales regni Francorum* (*ArF*), which were not written contemporaneously but in 789/790 (though using older material). In the rest of this chapter, and in the next, I will make the most of the Continuators of Fredegar. The years when Charles Martel's sons ruled as mayors of the palace from 741 to 747, then when Pippin 'III' ruled as sole mayor and, finally and especially, when the Second Continuator took over, Pippin's reign as king (751–68), were formative years for the Carolingian regime and for the Charles who is the subject of this book. The Second Continuator ends with Pippin 'III's death, the division of the kingdom, and the consecrations of Pippin's sons Charles and Carloman.

Both Childebrand and Nibelung wrote to glorify the dynasty and the Franks: 'substantial and partisan', and with a 'triumphal gloss', fairly sums up a two-edged narrative that sometimes parts company from 'the realities of what is described'.[21] Childebrand and Nibelung were not authors in the modern sense, but patrons, commissioners, or supervisors of *gesta*, and – in Childebrand's case – a self-identified actor in them. Their lands lay in Burgundy, and they spent some of their time looking after their interests there. At other times they seem to operate at the court or palace, in the mayoral or later royal entourage. These men were *of* the ruling family, yet they were not entirely *in* it. Childebrand's mother seems to have been a concubine, not a wife, of Martel. Childebrand and Nibelung did not bear Pippinid names, after all, and it is not clear how much difference this made in practice: Pippin 'II's grandsons were named Arnulf, Hugh, Pippin and Gotfrid (sons of Drogo), and Theodoald (son of Grimoald). Canon-law rules of course existed in Frankish books, but to project what passed for norms in the 750s back to *c.*700 is anachronistic. In practice, contingencies of birth and death still determined claims to succession in the kingdom of the Franks. One of Mayor Pippin 'II's two sons was a heartbeat away from sudden death when, in 714, he entered a church to pray for his father's recovery from illness and himself fell victim to an assassin's blade.[22] History encourages counterfactual thoughts: in 747, what if Martel's two sons had succumbed to illness, or if the two sons of Pippin 'III' (neither of whom as yet had a son) had died in, say, 768? Was it unthinkable that, in the one case, Childebrand in 747, or in the other, Nibelung in 768, could have put in a bid for the Frankish realm? An uncertainty principle was built with a vengeance into dynastic succession.

VII. A COMPOSITE STORY

The rest of this chapter combines elements of the above stories into an 'all-in' tale that then extends into the latter part of the life of Pippin 'II', and the lives of his children. Why include so much backstory when this book's subject is Charles, elder son of Pippin 'III'? The answer is that this one exceptionally well-documented family provides Charles with a context. Readers who have encountered and felt (the more often the better) the strangeness of a world in which the protagonists were warlords and -ladies, holy men and impresarios of ritual performances, and have acquainted themselves with the landscapes in which these people purposefully engaged in actions and interactions and pursued social and political goals, are better placed to reconstruct or re-imagine Charles's life.

On Ascension Day, 13 May 706, Pippin and Plectrud, daughter of the wealthy widow Irmina, asserted their rights over, and gave more land to, Willibrord's church at Echternach. Pippin, in marrying Plectrud, had made what was hers become his too, the more easily since she had sisters but no brother. The couple's gift on this auspicious day highlights the intersection of family wealth and the endowment of holy places, following rhythms of acquisition and redistribution that played across generations in families, and across the periods of office of church-custodians. Short-term flux occurred within long-term stability.[23] Pippin and Plectrud had had two charters drawn up. In one, they called Echternach 'our monastery', declared that it was 'built on our property', and gave it an extra endowment which Plectrud had acquired from her deceased uncle, Irmina's brother, 'so that the community could prosper there for all time, on this condition that this same monastery henceforth remains in the domination and defence of us and our heirs'.[24] In the second charter the donors confirmed the grant of the monastery to Willibrord and laid down that after his death the brethren should elect for themselves the next abbot 'on condition that he would be faithful to us and our heirs and live according to his holy order, and that they should remain under our protection and defence'. If any relative should contest this in the future, they would 'incur the wrath of Almighty God and should make amends according to the value of the property at that time, as well as paying the [royal] treasury a fine of 10 lb. of gold and 20 lb. of silver'.[25] For Pippin and Plectrud, rights to 'dominate and defend', and being assured of the personal fidelity of the abbot, were the surest available forms of control.[26] Willibrord, intending to found churches in Frisia, fulfilled his hope of bringing many relics back from Rome to install in altars.[27] Relic-veneration, though never prescribed by any ecclesiastical decree (and that can come as a surprise), had long since been embedded in religious practice. It was at once the product and the sign of spontaneous lay–ecclesiastical collaboration.[28] Approach the strangeness of this early-medieval world sympathetically, and you hold in tension the notions of value suggested by relics from Rome and the monetary penalty imposed on those who took back lands their kin had given to monasteries.

Monastic rules stipulated the election of abbots by their communities, but kin and patrons, and abbots themselves, played large parts in abbatial appointments. Willibrord's successors as abbots of Echternach were his close relatives, Aldbert, and then Beornrad.[29] With much at stake, tensions around abbatial succession could flare into disputes between kin. Similar tensions and disputes over kings' successions had punctuated Frankish history for some two hundred years, usually involving violent conflict between rival Merovingians. The emergence of the mayoralty of the palace produced a form of dual leadership (comparable to that of caliph and vizier in the Muslim world of the Abbasid period – c.750–1258) with governmental functions and wealth passing slowly but surely from king to mayor in an obscure process that began with two royal assassinations in the 670s and extended across the ensuing five decades.[30] In the *LHF*, the deaths and reign-years of kings went on being recorded until the text stopped in 727, while from the early 670s onwards the mayor Pippin 'II' was entitled *princeps* ('chief man').[31] It was a sign of Bede's awareness of political realities in Francia that after Chlothar III (d.673) he mentioned Frankish mayors but never kings. Not only were Merovingians now evidently becoming figures who were more totemic than powerful, they were becoming hard to find. In 715, when Dagobert III died without an obvious heir, 'the Franks put on the throne a cleric named Daniel, after waiting for his hair to grow, and named him Chilperic'; five years later 'the Franks put as king over them Theuderic, son of Dagobert III, brought up (*nutritus*) in the convent of Chelles'.[32] Thus kings could still be found in the age of Martel with a lease on legitimacy. But – thanks to Martel – it turned out that the lease had not long to run.

Pippin 'II' fathered, from two wives, a number of potential heirs in an increasingly hereditary-looking regime. Pippin and Plectrud produced two sons. The elder, Drogo (born probably in the 670s), duke of Champagne, had four sons, while the younger, Grimoald (born perhaps in the 680s), was mayor of the palace of Austrasia, and had one son, Theodoald, by a concubine.[33] Pippin and Alpaida had one son, born in 688, called Charles, 'Carlo in his own language' (and first nick-named 'Martel' in the ninth century; I use the nickname consistently to differentiate him from his later namesakes), who in turn had a son named Carloman, born 708/709, and a second son, Pippin 'III', born in 714 or 715.[34] Some scholars have thought fit to call Pippin 'II' a polygamist. I doubt if he or his contemporaries would ever have thought of the situation in such terms. The *LHF* c. 48 describes Plectrud as *uxor nobilissima et sapientissima* ('wife most noble and most wise'), while the Continuator c. 5 calls her *uxor nobilis et prudentissima* ('wife noble and most prudent'). The *LHF* says Martel was born 'from another wife' (*uxor*) but doesn't name her, whereas the Continuator c. 6 calls Alpaida by her name and identifies her as *uxor nobilis et eligans* ('wife noble and attractive').[35] Some modern historians have found it impossible to believe that polygamy was practised by people whom texts of *c.*700 represented as Christianized long ago. Instead those historians constructed the half-way house of a *Friedelehe*, an informal and thus reversible union somewhere between marriage and concubinage, and a convenient option for elite Frankish men. Alpaida was cited as a good example of a *Friedelfrau*. Historians of canon law seem to have been much more bothered than were the elite Franks themselves about their sexual customs. Recently, *Friedelehe* has been convincingly exposed as a figment of some modern wishful thinking.[36] Flexible attitudes to concubinage and the claims of concubines' offspring seem to have coexisted with a recognized distinction between the inheritance rights of offspring of wives and a man's right to leave his property to concubines' sons and to nephews.

In the decades around 700, real power made mayoralty what kingship had so long been, 'a scarce resource', succession to which was inevitably contested.[37] In 708, Pippin's son Drogo died, and his son Arnulf succeeded to his dukedom in Champagne. Not long after, the mayor of the Frankish palace, Pippin's younger son and presumptive heir Grimoald, married the daughter of the Frisian duke, which, given years of conflict between Franks and Frisians, looks like a conciliatory move that strengthened Grimoald.[38] Early in 714 Pippin was already a sick man. On 2 March, he was too ill to attest the foundation-charter of the convent of Susteren granting control to Willibrord, and so had to get Plectrud to confirm the grant on his behalf.[39] He pointedly added that Willibrord's successor should be similarly loyal to 'our son Grimoald and his sons and our son Drogo and his sons, our grandsons'.[40] Pippin was in effect denying the claims of Martel and his son Carloman (born *c.*708).[41] But Grimoald, on his way to visit his sick father, stopped to pray at Liège in the church dedicated to St Lambert (a bishop of Maastricht murdered in 703 and now venerated by, among others, Pippin and Plectrud); and 'there in the church, Grimoald was assassinated'.[42] Though no source pins the blame on Martel, he would have had to be exceptionally altruistic not to see the murder as offering some advantage to him and his own son. The dying Pippin's reaction was to muster enough strength to have Grimoald's little son (*parvulus*), Theudoald, installed as mayor of the Neustrians.[43] Whether the Susteren charter of 2 March or Pippin's death on 16 December 714 was the prompt, Martel set about fathering another son himself.

Pippin's influence over Neustria had always been limited.[44] When the Frisian duke, Radbod, struck an opportunistic alliance with the Neustrians and unleashed Frisian attacks in the area around Utrecht, Willibrord fled south to Echternach.[45] The rival branches of the Pippinid family and their claims to Pippin's legacy became embroiled in old hostilities between Neustrians and Austrasians. Competition was rooted in property, and the competitors were often women. Plectrud and Alpaida was not so much 'natural' as 'structural' rivals.[46] Each had inherited lands not so far distant from each other, and these can be mapped in the Echternach charters: Plectrud's in the lower Meuse valley and to the east thereof, at Cologne; Alpaida's further up the Meuse in the area north of Liège, and with southerly outliers in the area of Echternach (see Map 2).[47] The charter-evidence suggests that the wealth of Plectrud's family far outdid that of Alpaida, but this can become a circular argument; Plectrud's family compared with Alpaida's is much better documented.[48] It is hard to identify any of Alpaida's siblings, whereas a genealogy can show Plectrud and her four sisters as the offspring of Irmina and Hubert.[49] It was Plectrud, Theodoald's grandmother, who maintained his mayoralty after her husband's death, and 'did everything by her own counsel and rulership' (*suo consilio atque regimine cuncta agebat*). 'Everything' included imprisoning her stepson Martel at Cologne, her stronghold, seemingly as soon as possible after Pippin's death.[50] Whatever the prison regime there, it is not likely to have included marital visits. Martel's second son was presumably conceived sometime in 714. No wonder that Martel in 715 sank from source-historical view. History may be written by the winners, but they or their descendants often need patience to await the winning.

In a battle near Compiègne on 26 September 715, Neustrians led by their mayor Ragamfred confronted Austrasians supporting Plectrud's mayor Theodoald. The Neustrians triumphed. Little Theodoald, whom the Austrasians had brought to the battlefield for luck, was whisked away from the scene in the nick of time, while Plectrud withdrew to Cologne, and the Austrasians 'chose' the Neustrian mayor as their mayor too.[51] During Plectrud's absence, Martel managed 'with difficulty' to escape from imprisonment, but he had not yet established his leadership of the Austrasians strongly enough to respond when the Neustrians, allied with Radbod's Frisians, attacked again early in 716.

Meanwhile Martel's wife, Rotrud, had given birth to a son.[52] Nothing more is known about Rotrud, except the note of her death in 725 in an early set of annals, and a belated implicit acknowledgement that she had also been the mother, in 708 or 709, of Martel's first-born, Carloman.[53] The baby was called Pippin, after his grandfather: it was a name that conveyed an important message of family belonging.[54] In the decades around 700 a group of names seems to have crystallized as identifying members of a family that modern historians call 'the Pippinids', after the name of the earliest-documented ancestor, Pippin 'I', but perhaps already labelled early in the eighth century as *Pippinii*, 'the Pippins'.[55] Furthermore, because there was already a 'Pippin', Drogo's son, in Plectrud's branch of the family, the name of the new baby in the same generation but in Alpaida's alternative branch was a striking assertion of parity on the part of Martel and Rotrud vis-à-vis Plectrud.

Baptismal celebrations seem to have been postponed. Early in 716, still with insufficient men, Martel went into battle against the Neustrians and Frisians, and for the first and last time in his career, lost.[56] The Neustrian victors made for Cologne where 'they forced Plectrud to yield up much treasure' – the treasure of the Austrasian mayoralty. In April, as the Neustrians withdrew westwards towards the Meuse, Martel ambushed them near Amblève and seized that treasure. It was one of those reversals of fortune that dramatically changed the options available to the protagonists. Plectrud's position was seriously weakened and Martel's hugely strengthened. Just a month after this, on 31 May, the saint's day of Lambert, his remains were translated to Liège by Plectrud's kinsman Bishop Hubert of Maastricht, with the approval of Martel.[57] This announcement of Martel's newly won power also looks like an attempt to reconcile the two branches of the family.

The baptizing of Martel's little son was very probably part of this rapprochement. Baptism had connotations beyond naming, at once much larger, for baptism integrated the child into the Christian community, and much more closely personal, for it established a bond of spiritual kinship between godparents and godchild, and a spiritual paternity between the officiant and the baby. This bond between baptizer and baptized, documented earlier in Frankish history, was to be publicized and raised to high symbolic status in the second half of the eighth century by successive popes.[58] Only very exceptionally is an officiating cleric mentioned by name: the case of Martel's and Rotrud's baby boy is one such exception. The cleric who baptized him was Willibrord (it is a mere supposition, but a pleasing one, that Echternach was the site of the baptism). The story of the baptism, to which no date is attached, appears in a text of the late eighth century, but the fact that that text was the *Life of Willibrord* written by the Northumbrian Alcuin, a kinsman of Willibrord, lends it credibility. In naming the child Pippin, Martel did more than offer an olive-branch: he staked his own claim to succeed to the mayoralty. Willibrord died in 739, and since the charter-record of the *Pippinii* is almost a blank in the 720s and 730s, there is no knowing how often Pippin himself saw Willibrord. Yet the child when he became a man remembered Echternach in a donation.[59]

Baptism created another special relationship: that between Martel and Willibrord as co-fathers. Willibrord's connections with the *Pippinii* up to this point had been with Plectrud and the branch of the family she embodied. They extended now to include Martel and his branch. It has been argued that Willibrord 'defected' from Plectrud, adroitly exchanging her patronage for Martel's when it was politic to do so.[60] A more plausible alternative reading is that Willibrord, as a charismatic peacemaker and a faithful custodian of Echternach, was keen to heal the rift between the branches of the *Pippinii* and that the *Pippinii* themselves sought an entente.[61] In 716/717, Duke Arnulf, one of Plectrud's grandsons, gave Echternach his share of the family inheritance at Bollendorf, a few kilometres along the river Sûre.

On 21 March 717, Martel had won a decisive battle against the Neustrians at Vinchy near Cambrai, and carried off rich booty into Austrasia; then at Cologne, after facing down Plectrud for once and for all, he seized his father's treasure, and – here the author suggests cause and effect – 'set up a king for himself by the name of Chlothar [IV – of Austrasia]'.[62] Just a month after Vinchy, the duke (*dux*) of the Thuringians, Heden II (who had perhaps fought alongside Martel at Vinchy), made gifts of property to Echternach at Arnstadt and Hammelburg near Würzburg: generosity suggesting friendship with Martel.[63] Early in 718 Martel beat the Neustrians again, this time with their ally, Duke Eudo of Aquitaine, at Soissons, a site, like Vinchy, on the old Austrasian-Neustrian frontier. Martel chased the defeated Neustrians – with Eudo and King Chilperic and his treasure – to Paris and then south to Orléans and across into Aquitaine. Martel shrewdly sent envoys to Eudo with the offer of a friendship treaty, to which Eudo responded by sending Martel both Chilperic *and* his treasure. Martel was lucky as well as shrewd: he had gained control of Chilperic's treasure, and when Chlothar IV died later in 718, the Austrasian treasure too remained in Martel's hands. Martel's access de facto to both the Neustrian and Austrasian treasuries gave him the power to attract troops, and to maintain them, their horses and their equipment in the field over a period of months rather than weeks.

What followed was something that both contemporary writers and modern historians have considered impressive in itself and significant for the future: Martel attacked Saxon territory 'and laid it waste with a mighty blow as far as the Weser'. Paul Fouracre's maps show that Martel had moved some 200km east of the Rhine and in a region unprovided with Roman roads.[64] Writers of annals in the 720s and 730s, with hindsight, were able to record the campaigns of Martel starting from 'firstly, against Saxons' in 718, and continuing with more wars on Saxons in 720, 722, 729 and 738.[65] In other years, in between these offensives, attacks were launched into Bavaria (twice), Swabia, Gascony (twice) and Frisia (twice), against the Saracens (twice), into Provence, and again into Gascony, against the sons of Eudo. Distant encounters were not always hostile: they sometimes involved negotiations, and marriage-alliances, which in the case of the Agilolfings straddled Bavaria and Alemannia; and with the Lombards, Martel always seems to have kept good relations.[66] The frequency of these references to aggression far beyond the eastern and north-eastern frontiers of the Franks is something strikingly new, however, and nowhere more so than in the Saxon campaign of 718. This was a sequel to Martel's pursuit of his enemies from Soissons across Neustria and as far as Paris on the Seine and Orléans on the Loire: add to that the distance required to move the army back north-east, crossing the Oise and the Meuse to reach, say, Cologne, and from there to the Weser and back, and an estimate of 'at least 1,300km' covered by Martel and his men over the year seems entirely plausible.[67]

On 23 February 718, the only precise date available for Martel's itinerary in that critical year, Martel had made Echternach a gift of his share in the Bollendorf estate. For Willibrord, ever keen to recharge the great project of evangelizing the Frisians, and finding secular power to maximize the effectiveness of mission, this was not a moment to transfer his loyalty to Plectrud, or play off one kinsman against another, but rather to encourage the *Pippinii* to make their divided property more energy-efficient by reuniting it.[68] At this point, Martel had everything to gain by enthusiastic collaboration. His charter for Echternach was perhaps issued from Vigy on the Mosel, 15km north-east of Metz.[69] If Martel's war-journey to Soissons took him another 250km from the Metz area early in 718, his 'energy and military skill' look yet more impressive. Finally, though, into any calculation must be factored the boost to morale experienced by Martel. He had given the churches of St Peter and St Paul at Echternach 'for the good of my soul' before the battle of Soissons, and – what Martel and his followers surely saw as a material pay-off – acquired earthly treasures after it.[70]

As his father had done, Martel supported Willibrord in Utrecht by confirming and extending Pippin's grants.[71] He also took into his 'protection and defence' another Anglo-Saxon holy man and missionary, Boniface (*c*.680–754), whom Pope Gregory II had ordained a bishop in 722, in Rome. On his way north again, Boniface visited the court of the Lombard king Liudprand (712–44) at Pavia, and, once back in Francia, he handed Martel a papal letter of recommendation, in which Gregory explained Boniface's task as 'preaching to the peoples of the *gens* of Germany and those variously dwelling on the east bank of the Rhine'.[72] As a man of the English people himself, Boniface wrote to 'all the Catholics of the descent-group and people of the English' (*stirps et prosapia Anglorum*) to urge their prayers for the pagan Saxons.[73] Like Willibrord, Boniface knew all about the need for support from the powers that were; indeed he had 'an almost opportunistic sense for what was possible'.[74] Thanks to Duke Heden, Thuringia already offered fertile ground. In the seventh century, Thuringian leaders had co-operated with Merovingian overlords, and by now, much of Franconia and Thuringia had already been targeted by Christian missionaries. Where the Thuringians were concerned, Boniface was content to seek 'what was possible' by deepening Christianization in ways that did not hit headlines. Bede never mentioned Boniface. But on 1 December 722 Gregory wrote to five named Thuringian Christian magnates to praise their faith and urge them to co-operate with Boniface.[75]

Towards the end of his life, Martel was planning to establish a bishopric at Heden's old residence, Würzburg, on the river Main, with the approval of the pope and with Burchard, one of Boniface's followers, as the new see's first bishop; and among Martel's last thoughts on the succession (see p. 56 below) was the assignment of Thuringia to his elder son Carloman.[76] Würzburg was now a Frankish stronghold, especially as Heden's long-lived daughter Immina was the abbess of St Mary's convent there. She apparently now became abbess at the new Karlburg too.[77] What might seem locations remote from each other were now connected by bonds of patronage and protection that benefitted from the relative ease of riverine communications between, say, Würzburg on the Main, Trier on the Mosel, and nearby Echternach on the Sûre. Among the Saxons, the mission field was much stonier, and Boniface was realistic when he asked his compatriots for prayers rather than resources in men and materiel. His efforts in central Germany were made easier by Martel's successful campaign against the Saxons in 738 which made more secure, at least in the short run, the routes to and within Thuringia. Martel's protection of Boniface lasted until his own death in 741.

VIII. THE BIGGER PICTURE

Edward Gibbon famously wrote in chapter 52 of his masterwork, *The Decline and Fall of the Roman Empire*, that had Martel not defeated the Muslim conquerors of Spain in 732 at the battle of Poitiers, 'the Arabian fleet might have sailed without a naval combat into the mouth of the Thames. Perhaps the interpretation of the Koran would now be taught in the schools of Oxford, and her pulpits might demonstrate to a circumcised people the sanctity and truth of the revelation of Mahomet.'[78] Muslim armies in Spain, since 711, did pose problems for the inhabitants of Gaul, especially the front-line region of Aquitaine, just across the Pyrenees. But resistance, led by Duke Eudo, was fierce, and mostly successful. The author of a lively chronicle, in Latin, by a Christian cleric living under Muslim rule was preoccupied with politics and war, and said nothing about the religion of the conquerors. The author's usual term for them was *Sarraceni*, which in Roman times had meant inhabitants of the Arabian Peninsula, and he called the conquered territory a *regnum*, its ruler a governor. Elite Spanish Christians in this period adopted a realistic attitude to their Saracen rulers: they negotiated terms with the governor in Córdoba who ran a regime based far less on tax or tribute than on the support of local landowners, whatever their religion.[79] The plundering-raid led by the governor Abd ar-Rahman far into the north of Aquitaine in 733 (the chronicle-author alleged that he planned to take a crack at plundering St-Martin's, Tours) was a one-off raid: after its failure, it was never tried again.[80] Gibbon's 'perhaps' was and is a non-starter. Septimania and Provence offered the Saracens closer and richer targets until the 790s. After the Frankish capture of Barcelona in 801, a more-or-less stable frontier-zone was established in the Spanish March.[81]

A ninth-century allegation that Martel plundered churches to fund his wars grew over centuries into a larger assertion about the origins of feudalism. That myth-totem has been as comprehensively felled by recent historians as was the oak at the Saxon shrine of Geismar felled by St Boniface, according to the author of his *Vita*, Willibald, writing in the 760s for the devotees of the recently martyred saint.[82] Likewise, the claim that early eighth-century bishops were in need of reform and/or especially acquisitive and hence keen to build up regional power to threaten that of Martel himself, has now been seriously undermined.[83] Theories of ecclesiastical change centred on the age of Martel have not withstood searching examination of earlier periods, which has revealed large continuities between the later seventh century and the eighth. Martel's patronage of churches was as effective, and selective, as his father's had been, and as carefully managed. To strengthen his position in Neustria, he made St-Wandrille, the monastery-cum-trading-place at the mouth of the Seine, a conspicuous beneficiary of his protection. In return the abbot granted out lands (*precaria*) to his own men, often kinsmen, to hold as temporary landlords, and also to an agreed quota of the mayor's men who owed fighting-service in the mayor's army.[84] This was hardly a system: rather, sets of ever-changing networks and transactions were organized by churchmen and laypeople (more is known about elites, but lesser folk were certainly involved too) for their mutual benefit. Striking evidence is to be found already in the Form-ulary (a collection of form-documents) compiled by the monk Marculf, *c.*700, and in the subsequent use of the relevant formulae in charters.[85] Martel himself 'moved briskly in on St-Denis'.[86] Meanwhile a powerful abbot or lay magnate could found a monastery like Prüm, Murbach or

Hornbach, or made a monastery their heir by testament, as at Flavigny or Novalesa, their charters spelling out the spiritual benefits of what were at the same time 'investments in wealth and power' for themselves and their descendants.[87]

Revisionist views of old verities lead back to families, and ahead to the ways in which these 'investments' began to affect the generation of Martel's offspring. What sort of childhood and youth was experienced by young *Pippinii* detailed at Genealogy B (p. xxxiii), and when did succession problems surface?

Of Drogo's four sons, Hugh, the priest, accumulated a raft of ecclesiastical posts, including the see of Rouen, through which he supported his uncle's regime in Neustria until his death in 730. Arnulf may or may not have been one of the two sons of Drogo who were kept in confinement in 723 'and one of them died'.[88] Nothing more is known of Pippin and Gotfrid. As for Theodoald, their cousin, last heard of being spirited away from the battlefield near Compiègne in 715, he may or may not be identified with the 'Thiedold' in a charter in favour of Willibrord issued by Martel in 723.[89] Theodoald's luck certainly ran out when Martel died in 741: *Carolus mortuus et Theodold interfectus est* ('Charles [Martel] died and Theodold was killed').[90] 'Dynastic shedding' with 'the problem of power both critical and unresolved' was to remain characteristic of the Carolingians: structurally necessary, tragic for those shed.[91]

In Martel's branch of the family, Carloman, identified as Martel's *filius*, attested at Herstal on 1 January 724 yet another gift by Martel to Willibrord's fortress-church at Utrecht.[92] A reasonable inference is that Carloman was now of age, at fifteen (b.708), whereas his brother Pippin, still a minor, did not attest.[93] A further possible inference is that Carloman now had a household of his own, but there is no direct evidence on this, nor of where and how he was brought up; that he was nurtured at Echternach is a hypothesis of modern vintage.[94] The birthdate of Hiltrud, the only daughter of the family, is unknown, though she was of an age to elope in 741 (see below). The record of the death of the children's mother, Rotrud, in 725 gives no mention of where she was buried, or where she died, possibly in giving birth to Hiltrud – whose elopement would then have followed soon after menarche.

For Pippin, Martel's younger son, there is more evidence. Two documents from the 750s, issued by Pippin after he had become king, show that he spent time when young at the monastery of St-Denis, near Paris.

In the earlier one, granting confiscated lands to the monastery, Pippin mentioned that he had been 'nurtured' there (*ubi enotriti fuimus*).[95] This has generally been taken to mean that Pippin had been educated at St-Denis, with a further possible implication that his parents meant to offer him as an oblate. In fact St-Denis, like other monasteries in this period, no longer housed monks but *clerici* (canons) who were closely connected with the secular world. Charters show that St-Denis sustained a number of small religious houses in its ambit, some of them female; and a set of legal formulae from the monastery includes, as item I, a bishop's answer to an abbess's question of what should be done with a nun who committed adultery. Formularies were practical texts, intended for repeated use, and the bishop's answer, deploying an array of canonical prescriptions, was firm but sympathetic: replace vigorous sex with rigorously exhausting prayer. To put such behaviours in a wider context: evidence from England and from Italy, as well as from seventh- and eighth-century Frankish hagiography, indicate the porousness of female enclosure when widows, children and god-children resided in convents without being under vows. Excavations of eighth- and early-ninth-century material unearthed at Flixborough, Lincolnshire, illustrate the difficulty of distinguishing 'monastic' from 'secular' settlement when there is no textual evidence. This could of course be a case of both/and. The charter-evidence partly compensates for the lack of comparable eighth-century archaeological data from St-Denis.[96]

The second document is a royal judgment in a dispute over tolls that pitted St-Denis against the lay officer responsible for toll-collection, Count Gerald of Paris.[97] The monastery's agents testified that 'the lord king Pippin himself affirmed that he had always seen from his early childhood that those tolls were possessed and collected on the part of St-Denis' (*Ipse dominus rex Pippinus adfirmabat quod semper a sua infantia ipsos teloneos partebus sancti Dionisii habere et colligere vidisset*). Additionally, two women are recorded in a collection of the saint's miracles written up at St-Denis c.830 (late evidence, but with signs of being based on institutional memory and archives rather than imagination) as taking a special interest in St-Denis. One was Swanahild, Pippin's stepmother, Martel's second wife, and the other the wife of Count Gerald, Rotrud (perhaps a close relative of Pippin's mother).[98] Bertrada, the wife of Pippin himself, is said very explicitly to have been

involved in the economic activities, in textile production and in trading, at the annual fair of St-Denis.[99] On this evidence, not only Pippin
in his childhood, but, later, his wife as well, in her widowhood after
768, resided (not necessarily continuously) in the nurturing environment of St-Denis, just as the Merovingian Theuderic IV (720–37) was
nurtured (*enutritus*) at Chelles.[100] Pippin's whereabouts in the 720s,
before and after his mother's death in 725, are simply undocumented.
But by *c*.727/730, he had reached the age of twelve and Frankish
manhood.[101]

Over the next two generations, Pippin's own sons and his legitimate
grandsons in due course were all treated as young adults, capable of
fighting and taking part in assemblies, and, most important, being
given political and military responsibilities, often publicly announced
in a memorable ritual such as investiture with weapons. No such rite of
passage, or assigning of adult responsibilities, is documented for either
of Martel's sons. One explanation is that Martel deliberately, and successfully, withheld responsibility from his sons in order to keep power
in his own hands, especially power to control the succession.[102] If so,
this was an exception, for delegation of power to a regional level –
historians often use the term 'sub-kingdom', though there was no
contemporary equivalent – was a tactic commonly chosen by early
medieval kings. The relative stability of the king's position was a key
factor. Martel was not a king; instead he co-existed with one, until
737.[103] The Merovingian dynasty retained its distinctively long-haired
kings, its naming-practices, and its aura: at Meaux in the mid-ninth
century, women danced as they sang 'a public song in the style of
country folk', about Chlothar II's campaigns against the Saxons two
hundred years before.[104] By 717, Martel had won the power to choose
his king, and he had two sons to succeed him. His triumph was recent,
though, and the dramatic strengthening of Austrasia at Neustria's
expense still lay in the future.[105]

The prospects of Martel's sons Carloman and Pippin altered when,
very soon after Rotrud's death in 725, Martel remarried.[106] After campaigning against the Alamans and Swabians, and also 'subduing' the
borderlands of the Bavarians, Martel had brought home with him Swanahild, niece of the Bavarian Duke Hugbert. She soon gave birth to a
son, Grifo, in (probably) 726.[107] There is no mention of the reactions of
either Carloman or Pippin, both by then past the age of *infantia*; nor of

either of them fighting at the battle of Poitiers (733) whence their father derived such fame. According to the early ninth-century *AMP*, perhaps drawing on social memory, Martel took both these sons with him to Aquitaine in 735 to receive the loyalty-oath of Duke Hunald.[108]

Grifo's existence raised questions about shares in any future division of the realm of the Franks. On her mother's side, Swanahild was a niece of Odilo, who had become duke of Bavaria in 736, and on good terms with both Martel and King Liutprand of the Lombards; she was also a niece on her father's side of Guntrud, who had married the young King Liutprand (712–44) in 715.[109] Martel himself was intent on reviving close bonds with both Bavarians and Lombards. Political relations between Bavarians, Lombards and Franks were at the same time famil-ial relations, between Agilolfings, Lombard royals and Pippinids. High-born women were not just 'good to think with' as security for deals between families: often they were also extremely active protag-onists in their own right.[110]

In the rest of this chapter information from Childebrand's 'house-chronicle' is interwoven with other material down to 748, when Charles, the main subject of this book, was born.[111] Childebrand – aka the Con-tinuator of Fredegar – focused on Martel's wars and campaigns: against Frisians (in 734); against resisters in Burgundy, where the writer had lands, and so a special stake (in 733 and 735), and Martel's first target was Lyons; against Saxons, labelled *rebellantes* and *paganissimi* (in 738); in Aquitaine (735); and in Provence (736) where *dux* Maurontus and other Neustrian and Burgundian Franks allied with 'Ishmahelites' or Saracens (labelled *gens valida*) against Martel, were defeated, and had their lands confiscated.[112] A striking feature of the 730s was the repeated targeting of Burgundy, first by Martel (733, 735), then by Childebrand (736) who mentioned himself by name as Martel's right-hand man (*vir industrius*) in a campaign around Avignon, and in the third person as Martel's '[half-]brother' in wars in the Narbonnais and the far south-west, and again in Provence.[113] These campaigns recorded plunder and devastation that in scale and detail support the idea that this was an eye-witness account.

Childebrand's story then became more diffuse. The order of events as he listed them might not have tallied with their order in time; but a focus on concerns about the succession became increasingly evident. Letters and gifts arrived from Pope Gregory III (the date(s) have to be inferred from one of the letters) and there were reciprocal gifts from Martel, carried by Abbot Grimo of Corbie, whose name sounds Pippinid, and the recluse Sigobert of St-Denis, whose name sounds Merovingian, but could equally well be Anglo-Saxon.[114] In 740, 'after consulting his great men, Martel made a division of his *regna* [the plural spoke volumes about how contemporaries thought about land and power] between Carloman the first-born raised up over Austrasia and Swabia, and Pippin, the younger one, to be sent to Burgundy, Neustria, and Provence.' Then 'the same year, Duke Pippin raised an army, and with his uncle Duke Childebrand and a great number of leading men and many phalanxes of warriors they headed for Burgundy and occupied the borderlands (*fines regionum*)'.[115] A complementary action on Carloman's part seems plausible, and the fact that Carloman had a son, Drogo, makes it all the more likely, though no source mentions it.[116]

Neither Childebrand nor any other Frankish source mentioned Pippin's being sent by his father to Italy. The unique record is that of Paul the Deacon, in the final scrappy pages of his *History of the Lombards* (written up in *c*.790), with no date given, but apparently in the context of events in 738: 'Charles *princeps Francorum* sent his son Pippin to Liutprand [king of the Lombards], so that he [Liutprand] could receive his [Pippin's] hair. Liutprand, cutting off Pippin's hair became a "father" (*pater*) to him, and sent him back to his actual father (*genitor*) loaded with royal gifts.'[117] This tale has recently been set in an Italian and Mediterranean context that forbids any interpretation of the hair-cutting as a designation of Pippin to kingship, but usefully highlights Martel's determination to stand by his alliance with Liutprand in co-operating against Saracen attacks, which quickly materialized.[118]

Childebrand was silent on the death of King Theuderic IV (in 737), and the ensuing interregnum. Charters went on being issued in Alsace and Burgundy, but dated by the number of years since Theuderic's death. This was a form of 'lawyers' time' which conveyed a sense of legitimacy through historical memory.[119] But such formulae could neither disguise the fact that Martel was now a mayor without a king nor conceal the existence of Theuderic's son. Martel had gone far towards constructing a new dynastic legitimacy. Rotrud and Swanahild had been recognized successively as lawful wives. His three sons by another woman who never received such recognition (modern historians label her a concubine, though she was of high birth) were given names denoting ineligibility for succession: Jerome and Remigius were put in ecclesiastical posts, while Bernard, the eldest, remained in lay life, married and produced a family.[120] When Martel divided his *regna* between Carloman and Pippin in 740, he was already a sick man.[121]

From Bavaria in 740, Duke Odilo of Bavaria arrived at Martel's court. If the succession-plan had by then been not just sketched but implemented, it could follow that, rather than having been driven out by enemies (as some have thought), Odilo was keen to pursue with Martel the church-strategy for Bavaria that Boniface had arranged with Gregory III on his third visit to Rome in 737–8: one of Martel's last acts was to give consent to the creation of new bishoprics, including Würzburg.[122] Odilo had other plans too, which fitted well with his keenness to collaborate with Martel. A lightning romance between Odilo and Hiltrud seems unlikely. Instead, the most probable scenario is that a marriage-alliance with Martel's daughter was already on the agenda when Odilo arrived in Francia. What certainly ensued was that he made Hiltrud pregnant and she gave birth to a son, Tassilo, in mid-741, while Martel was still living.[123] Childebrand told no lies, but simply said nothing. His next piece of information for 740 followed his report of the division of lands between Carloman and Pippin, and, in the present tense, of his own involvement in Pippin's Burgundian campaign.

The Continuator's next sentence strikes the reader forcibly as the most surprising in his work: 'Meanwhile, something that is pain and grief to say, ruin is being stirred up, there have appeared new signs in the sun and in the moon and in the stars, and also the most sacred order of Easter has been thrown into confusion.'[124] Borrowing, with minor adaptations and a change of tense, from Luke 21:25, '*erunt signa in sole et luna et stellis* (there shall be signs in the sun, and in the moon, and in the stars)', the Continuator's apocalyptic cry echoes Christ's words on the eve of his betrayal and death. The 'disturbance of the order of Easter' seems to be a metonym for confusion.[125]

Childebrand immediately reports signs of reordering and settlement: *Carlus nimpe princeps Parisius basilicam sancti Dionisii martyris multa munera ditavit* ('Of course Charles the ruler endowed the church of the martyr-saint Denis with many gifts.')[126] Boldly counteracting grim portents, Martel persisted in two striking appropriations of symbolic capital: he stayed at the old Merovingian palace of Quierzy in the Oise valley, and gave large gifts, including the old Merovingian estate at Clichy near Paris, to St-Denis, a prime Merovingian cult-site which, though infrequently used as a royal mausoleum, was the burial-place of Dagobert and Clovis II.[127] This was where Martel's second son Pippin had received part of his upbringing. It was where Swanahild, Martel's wife, had been engaging in an appropriation of her own, in league with the count of Paris, of the tolls that rightfully belonged to the abbey (see above). Martel had chosen to be buried at St-Denis. He died at Quierzy on 22 October 741, and his body was taken to St-Denis from there, maybe via the Oise and the Seine.[128] Swanahild and Grifo probably took leading roles in these arrangements. Pippin already had close contacts with the abbey, and St-Denis lay in his territory.[129] But it seems unlikely that either he or Carloman saw this as a moment of familial rapprochement.

The grim portents were not imaginary. A near-contemporary source's statement, in a juxtaposition suggesting connection, that 'Martel died and Theodoald was killed' was one sign that intra-familial rivalries remained intense.[130] A still-clearer and contemporary sign was a letter of Boniface requesting 'Grifo son of Carlus . . . if God shall give power to you [*tibi*], . . . to help all the servants of God in Thuringia and protect the Christians from the hostility of the heathens'. The syntax of this letter changes to the second person plural at this point, and continues:

> And know that we are offering prayers to God for you (*Et cognoscite, quod memoria vestra nobiscum est coram Deo*) according to the way your father when he was alive and [your] mother commended you to me a long time ago now (*et sicut et pater vester vivus et mater iam olim mihi commendarunt*) . . . And meanwhile remember dearest sons what the Psalmist said: 'All flesh is as grass . . . ' (*Interea memento, filii carissimi, quia iuxta vocem psalmigrafi, 'Homo sicut foenum dies eius . . .'* Ps 103:15).[131]

At the time of writing, in far-off Thuringia, Boniface had some idea that Grifo, now of age, was possibly in with a chance of sharing Martel's inheritance; but, foreseeing the likelihood that Carloman and Pippin would emerge as the winners, he sent similar letters to them as well.

The *AMP* author (and more briefly, but maybe drawing on the same source(s) as the *AMP*, the *Annales regni Francorum*) assigns Swanahild an important role unmentioned in the contemporary sources, alleging that this 'monstrous woman' (*improba mulier*) persuaded her dying husband to assign a share in his inheritance to her son consisting of 'parts of Neustria, Austrasia and Burgundy', thereby arousing the indignation of the Franks, and that 'by a malign plan' she got Grifo to occupy Laon and declare war on his [half-] brothers.[132] This story has been generally accepted by historians, but the absence of any contemporary support makes it hard to swallow. The contemporary Continuator of Fredegar mentions Swanahild at this point only in the context of her 'nefarious plan' to ensure Hiltrud's escape to join Odilo and to marry him 'against the will and advice of her brothers [Carloman and Pippin]'.[133] Once Carloman and Pippin had joined forces, any moment of opportunity for Grifo had gone.[134] His capture, in 741 at Laon by the count, Charibert, in charge of that stronghold, who promptly handed him over to Carloman, is reported only in those later sources, but there may be some connection here with Pippin's choice, three years later, of the count's daughter as his bride.[135] Childebrand never mentions Grifo – but Childebrand's son, the second Continuator, does, some years later (?753) in the context of Grifo's flight to Aquitaine, then Burgundy, in a desperate attempt to reach Lombardy, and finally his death in battle (he still had an army) in the Alps.[136] Grifo's story, and his ability to retain support, has evidently been distorted and in part suppressed.

To revisit the weeks after Martel's death: though it is not clear when Odilo went back to Bavaria, it is clear that Hiltrud and her baby son joined him there late in 741 or early 742. According to the Continuator, 'meanwhile the Gascons had rebelled' against the Franks on their own account, and Carloman and Pippin co-ordinated a winter campaign deep into Aquitaine, subdued the *Romani*, that is, the local population, reached Bourges and burned its suburbs, drove Duke Hunald into flight, ravaged the region, destroyed the fortress of Loches some 50km south-east of Tours, and, before returning north with their captives, halted at Vieux-Poitiers, some 30km north-east of modern Poitiers, and there implemented their father's division plan in 742.[137] The armies of the two brothers acted as an assembly of faithful men whose approval legitimated the division of Martel's *regna*.[138]

From 741, warfare east of the Rhine is the major theme for Childebrand, but another source now echoed him: the *ArF* author. Capitalizing on their Vieux-Poitiers agreement, Carloman and Pippin attacked the

Alamans in autumn 742 and received their submission; in 743, Odilo and his Bavarians rebelled against his 'kinsmen' – his brothers-in-law – who campaigned eastwards as far as the Lech, and heavily defeated Odilo.[139] These wars tested the nerve of Carloman and Pippin. Militarily successful, yet conscious of a deficit of legitimacy, in 743 they set up another Merovingian king, Childeric III – an event unmentioned in any narrative source but visible in the regnal years of charters. This king had a son, too, and their very existence apparently helped stabilize Carloman's and Pippin's joint regime.

A complementary story can be reconstructed from the records of church councils during these years. Both Carloman and Pippin were keen patrons of Boniface's efforts to improve the moral standards of churchmen and restore the institutional rhythms of councils. The first such council is dated 21 April 742: 'I Carloman, *dux* and *princeps* of the Franks, with the counsel of the servants of God and of my chief men have summoned Boniface and six bishops in my realm (*regnum*) and their clergy.'[140] The seven-point agenda was a fundamentally conservative one, reiterating the rules of clerical life, especially for bishops, and requiring clergy to teach the people to shun pagan practices. To a second council in March 743, at Estinnes in the Hennegau in Austrasia, Carloman summoned not just bishops but 'counts and prefects', powerful laymen. The main topic was military preparedness. It was decided that a proportion of church lands be kept at Carloman's disposal to fund grants to his fighting-men of *precaria* of church lands, at an annual rent to the relevant church of 12 pence per holding.[141] There was a brief reference to canon law prohibitions of 'adulteries and incestuous marriages'. Six months later, at a council summoned by Pope Zacharias in Rome, a much fuller set of decrees was issued against clerical liaisons and the prohibited degrees of relationship for would-be married lay couples. On 2 March 744, '*Ego Pippinus*, I Pippin, *dux* and *princeps* of the Franks', summoned a Neustrian council where heretics were condemned, clergy and laity forbidden to fornicate, and both husbands and wives forbidden to take a second spouse while the first was still living.[142]

Marital matters were now on the public agenda, and, one way or another, Pippin's thoughts now turned in the direction of marriage. His older brother Carloman was now in his mid-thirties with several children, the oldest of them, Drogo, almost of age. Joint campaigns had been successfully waged in the east as well as in Aquitaine, but it was the regions under Carloman's rule that posed greater threats of ongoing resistance. In 744, Pippin, aged twenty-six, chose a wife, or rather, he and the bride, Bertrada, and her father, the count of Laon, negotiated a mutually satisfactory marriage deal. The couple were cousins, and some of their inherited properties adjoined each other.[143] But their relationship was not so close as to run across any incest prohibition; nor, it has been pointed out, would the aristocracy 'be willing to welcome a law that forced their own lord to give up his own marriage-plans', given that they were 'probably already so likely to react in a "highly political" manner in those days' [!].[144] Again, the marriage might threaten the hitherto apparently close entente between the brothers, and at the very least would affect the interests of Carloman and his offspring, especially Drogo, the oldest. Still, the situation remained manageable, even welcome.

Two years later, however, things looked different. Carloman was now thirty-eight, and had just won a victory over the Alamans at Cannstatt so crushing as to involve the demise of 'a substantial part of the Alamannic nobility'. 'Cannstatt did for Alamannic land-holding what Hastings did for Anglo-Saxon land-holding.'[145] Immense confusion ensued, although Alamannic responses are not recorded. The highly political contemporary Frankish view of Childebrand was that the Alamans had broken their faith and were therefore 'rebels' who deserved to be slaughtered; no less robust was Childebrand's assertion that Carloman, having conceived a deep desire for the monastic life, had committed his son Drogo into the hands of his brother and left for Rome, so that 'by this succession, Pippin was strengthened in his kingdom'.[146] Another probably contemporary text, the *Annales Petaviani*, is alone in connecting Carloman's decision to leave Francia for Rome with 'contrition' for his brutal treatment of the Alamans: 'he felt contrite (*compunctus*) and because of this abandoned his kingdom'.[147]

Modern interpretations have varied. On one view, Pippin, who had had good relations with his brother up to this point and wished him well, acknowledged that Drogo was now of age and was genuinely willing for him to succeed to his father's mayoralty, and in sending Carloman off with gifts for the pope was signalling his commitment to a protective alliance with Rome. On this view, these complicated rearrangements made it understandable that the brothers agreed there would be 'no campaign that year', though this information in later annals appears in 745 instead of 747.[148] On another view, Carloman's enthusiasm for religious reforms had always exceeded Pippin's, and fraternal relations were already worsening once Pippin's marriage in 744 signalled his increasingly self-interested intentions.[149] Amid muddled and conflicting bits and pieces of evidence, the family stories show structures of politics and patterns of violence that point to intra-family conflict rather than co-operation. Pippin, while devout, was at the same time devoutly convinced of his own claims to rule, and at the expense of his brother and his nephew. Carloman, now nearing forty and, as it turned out, with only a few more years to live, may have felt ready to abandon the world – but only having settled the matter of Drogo's succession at the August 747 assembly. Drogo probably lacked sufficient support to sustain his mayoralty, and Pippin was already set on leaving him to twist in the wind. This must have been a moment of general uncertainty. The unidentifiable person in Boniface's following who wrote, in late 747 or the beginning of 748, to someone called Andhun to ask 'whether our bishop [i.e. Boniface] should attend the synod of the duke of the western provinces or go to [?that of] Carloman's son' was in a quandary.[150] It seems no coincidence that Childebrand has so little to say about the events of 749 and 750, except that these were two years in which no wars happened, while the author of the *ArF* offers a clearly retrospective view from *c*.790 confined to the wheeling and dealing between Pippin and Rome, passing over 751 and 752 in silence.

Looking back over the family stories that might have become known to Charles and the generation before his, I think it's time to consider one further genre: chronicles and annals. These narratives entered the early medieval scholarly repertoire in Ireland and Anglo-Saxon England in the late seventh and early eighth centuries.[151] In Francia, scribes in some well-supplied monastic establishments picked up this practice, though it was often limited to the recording of the deaths of holy men and notes on exceptional weather. What was to become a prime source of such narrative productions in Francia during Charles's long life was the *Annales regni Francorum*, the 'Annals of the realm of the Franks' (*ArF*).[152] These annals begin in 741 with an end: the end of Martel's life – 'Charles mayor of the palace died' (*Karlus maior domus diem obiit*). The entry for 742 records the concerted campaign of Carloman and Pippin against the Aquitanians and the division of the realm of the Franks between the brothers. The entries for 743 and 744 baldly mention the military actions of Carloman and Pippin against Bavarians and Saxons. The 745 entry records Carloman's decision – which was itself a remarkable story – to retire from the world: an event with the notable consequence, because of essential preparations on the parts both of Carloman as traveller and of Pippin as reconfigurer of the family- and home-front, that 'there was no campaign that year'.

Perhaps the *ArF* were kept up a little patchily at first – there are two blank years in 751 and 752. But however patchy, the annalistic material seems to have been collected more or less regularly, and finally, in 788, when Charles had it compiled at his court into a dossier to be used in the prosecution of the Bavarian Duke Tassilo and his wife Liutperga, with the objective of removing the couple and their offspring from power and so clearing the way for Charles's takeover of Bavaria. This was a dossier that depended on a carefully constructed historic narrative.[153] Once the dossier had been made, dissemination was the next logical step for Charles – and the evidence of relatively numerous copies bears out that that had been part of the plan.[154] Beyond the recording of aims and outcomes by annalists generally reckoned to have had court connections, Charles grew to foresee the means to creating and maintaining 'a harmonious and Christian whole of a disparate realm'.[155]

Meanwhile, in 747, Charles was no more than a twinkle in Pippin's eye. In any case, a focus on Pippin alone is too narrow here. I want to end this chapter by widening the focus to include Bertrada, and adding some details about dates. Reconsidering dates can have the effect of changing the whole picture.[156] Here the first key item of evidence is the marriage date of Pippin and Bertrada, '744'. The date is uniquely credible because it comes from the records of the monastery of Prüm, founded by Bertrada's grandmother (Bertrada 'the elder') and her son Charibert in 721, and re-founded by Pippin and Bertrada in 762. The ninth-century author of the *Annals of Prüm* anachronistically gave the pair the titles king and queen but would not have misdated their marriage: 'the marriage of king Pippin and queen Bertrada' (*conjunctio Pippini regis et Bertrade regine*).[157] The second key item is the letter of an Anglo-Saxon scholar, Cathwulf *peregrinus* (the 'pilgrim' or 'foreigner'), to Bertrada and Pippin's son, King Charles, in or about 775, which listed, as the first of a series of 'special blessings' bestowed on

Charles by God, the conception of the king himself, 'by the dignity of the king [Pippin] and queen [Bertrada] and in addition by the prayers and especially those who were praying to God, most of all the mother, as it then pleased God [to grant]'.[158] The couple's prayers – 'especially the mother's' – had been answered after something over three years of childlessness. Since fecundity was precisely what was expected of a high-born wife, it was unsurprising that Bertrada, in particular, was anxious to deliver, just as the biblical Hannah (1 Samuel 2:1–10) had delivered when God had marvellously answered her prayers and she conceived a son, Samuel. A little further on in Cathwulf's letter, he quoted this passage in writing to the king. One way of explaining these exceptional features of Cathwulf's letter is to consider the possibility that Bertrada, a woman divinely tried and divinely chosen, now, at the time of Cathwulf's writing, a widow 'consecrated to God', and growing old as a figure held in great honour with her son, was herself the source of the story about Charles's being conceived by God's response to her prayers. If, by a further small stretch of imagination (and thanks to the insights of two very generous colleagues) the scene is imagined at St-Denis, it can now be argued that that was where Cathwulf was living, and where Bertrada herself semi-permanently resided too, in the abbaye de St-Denis-aux-Dames. It is in this setting that the story of Bertrada's prayers, and their outcome, rings true.[159]

To return to the outcome of Bertrada's prayers is to return to 747, the year in which she discovered she was pregnant. Bertrada and her women did not have to wait for Hincmar of Reims to tell them (as he did the Frankish elite in 860 in the famous divorce case of King Lothar II and Queen Theutberga) that though bishops lacked personal experience of such matters, their investigations could expose 'the virgin secrets of girls and women'.[160] Bertrada and her ladies-in-waiting had that knowledge, and so could work out that Bertrada in August was two months pregnant. Working back from what is now known to have been Charles's birthdate, 2 April 748, modern investigators can infer that the date of conception must have been around the beginning of June 747. Bertrada of course did not know that the baby would be a son, but because God had granted to her what he had granted to Hannah, and for similar reasons, she devoutly believed so. And because, at the big assembly at Düren in mid-August, Carloman had publicly announced, 'afire with inextinguishable devotion', his decision to retire to Rome, bearing rich gifts to the pope from his brother Pippin, and believing his son Drogo was safely 'committed into Pippin's hands', he hastened on his way gladly, Bertrada equally gladly waved him good-bye. Thus was it that, as contemporary annals reported, 'Carloman migrated to Rome, and in that same year, King Charles was born.'[161] Pippin, whatever he had promised, or meant, where Drogo was concerned, was now a father with a son of his own. That son was given the name of his grandfather, Charles. For both parents he was a much-wanted baby – and that, as any child psychologist knows, gives an infant the best possible start in life.

The River Oise at Quierzy.

3

The Child in the Picture

I. BIRTH AND LANGUAGE

The rest of this book will be – as it says on the cover – a Life. This needs to be reaffirmed because it is not self-evident. True, Johannes Fried, a leading scholar in the Charlemagne-field, has linked his assertion that in Charles's case 'a biography in the modern sense is impossible' to the fact that (with one possible exception) 'not a single record of Charles's words, or those of any of his five bed-partners, or of any of his children, has survived'.[1] Fried has affirmed, rightly, that the *Vita* of Charles written by Einhard in 829, though its influence has persisted (and evolved), could not be called 'a biography in the modern sense'.[2] Precious few records have survived of Charles's words, but those few are precious indeed. Any 'source' is a more-or-less imaginative construct, to be checked and tested against others for what weight it can bear. Reliability is always relative. I aim to make the most of as many details of Charles's personal life as turn out to be available, and to weave them into what, from his early years on, was also a public life. The subject of *this* chapter is a child-life, and as such is even more patchily documented than the ensuing life-stages. Still, scraps of information and memorable vignettes do survive, to be set more or less convincingly in the frame of a family history.

An obvious opening question about any individual is where they were born. In Charles's case, the short answer is: birthplace unknown. Much later myths on this subject can be ignored. Real clues lie not only in a number of places known from the evidence of charters, whose formal traits include a statement about place of issue, indicating where, as well as when, one or both of Charles's parents were residing, but in narrative sources that also record the parents' stays, when, during the months of winter, the couple's regular practice was to stay in a well-organized estate-centre (*villa*) or palace. That stay on 11 February 748 of Pippin (and I assume Bertrada too) at the palace of Ver, identifiable as probably Vaires-sur-Marne, 6km west of Lagny-sur-Marne, is suggestive, given Charles's birthdate of 2 April.[3] In light of the guess, and some supporting evidence, offered in Chapter 1, I will risk a higher stake on Quierzy as Charles's birthplace.

What was Charles's *patrius sermo*, his paternal language (as Einhard put it)?[4] The narrative sources mentioned in Chapter 2 give some prominence to Quierzy, while the charters attest stays at Compiègne (an old Merovingian palace) and Verberie.[5] Frequent residence in the Oise valley could imply that the main language spoken at the court of Pippin and Bertrada was a form of 'rustic Roman', that is, a language evolving into Romance.[6] But they and many of their courtiers and servants may have been bilingual in various forms of Romance and Old High German, and a similar situation probably prevailed in the valleys of the Meuse, Mosel and the Middle Rhine. Einhard said Charles spoke, in addition to his *patrius sermo* (native language), Latin and a bit of Greek,[7] and *patrius sermo* has been taken to mean some form of Old High German.[8] However, language usage was varied and rapidly evolving throughout Charles's life and reign.[9] From the mid-790s on, Einhard would have encountered a court full of largely German speakers at Aachen, but since Charles's earlier life had been mostly spent, campaigning apart, in areas where various forms of 'rustic Roman' were spoken, and mutually intelligible, in practice he would have been bilingual from childhood in languages that were early forms of French and German. In those languages, Bertrada, her women, and the baby's wet-nurse or nanny, were his likeliest teachers of songs and stories.

II. 751, BEFORE 22 OCTOBER

In an original charter confirming all the lands of St-Denis in what had formerly been Carloman's kingdom, Pippin, as mayor of the palace, requested the monastery's perpetual prayers 'for us and for our sons and for the stability of the kingdom of the Franks'.[10] The plural 'sons' indicates both that Charles's younger brother, Carloman, was born shortly before his parents had become king and queen, and that Pippin and Bertrada and their two sons were now very close to being regarded by his entourage and by the community at St-Denis as a royal family.[11]

III. 751, NOVEMBER

For Charles himself, the first memorable event in his early years may well have been the consecration of his parents as king and queen, sometime in November 751 when the boy was a little over three and a half.[12] On this event, a huge edifice of speculative and often confessionally driven writing has been built on meagre and problematic evidence. Older generations of historians, with liberal use of hindsight, either, as Protestants, decried a papal triumph or, as Roman Catholics, welcomed it. Either way, they identified a revolution. More recent historians have broken out of the teleological trap, in some cases downgrading the event's authenticity to the extent of doubting whether it occurred at all.[13] I accept the account of Childebrand, the first Continuator of Fredegar, because it was written closer to the event than that of any other writer: 'The pre-eminent Pippin, by the election of all the Franks to the seat of the kingdom, by the consecration of the bishops and by the princes' subjecting themselves, together with Queen Bertrada was raised into the kingdom, as the order of antiquity requires.'[14]

That the three years following Charles's birth are exceptionally poorly documented could reflect Pippin's exceptional difficulties in getting the consensus and acceptance of bishops and lay aristocrats and other regional powers within and around Francia to recognize his rule as legitimate. As promised to Carloman, his elder brother, Pippin had negotiated a deal with his nephew Drogo. He had also won compliance from his half-brother Grifo. He had kept lines of communication open to Italy, trying to maintain the longstanding alliance with the Lombards. Already in 747, Pope Zacharias had written to the bishops, abbots and *principes* welcoming their willingness, as reported by Pippin, to be *unanimes* and *cooperatores*, and succinctly setting out the meaning of this co-operation as *nobis orantibus et illis bellantibus*, 'with us [i.e. pope and clergy] praying and them [i.e. *principes* and secular men and warriors] fighting'.[15] By the summer of 751, Pippin was ready to seek an understanding with Zacharias which would be tantamount to getting papal collusion for a coup against the Merovingian king, with the Frankish elite's approval. He sent envoys to Rome.[16]

Pippin was in a good position to invoke historic continuity as a basis of legitimacy, for by now, the Franks had long been Christianized and acculturated to Christian kingship.[17] There was, as Childebrand wrote, an old custom (*antiquitus ordo*), or set of procedures, for king-making, which included scenarios of election and recognition.[18] But old custom was just one side of Pippin's case for change. The other involved innovation. Deposing a Merovingian king and his son, after two and a half centuries of dynastic continuity, needed powerful justifying. By 751, in a trend accelerating in the late seventh and early eighth centuries – and particularly during the 740s – lay proprietorial rights over monasteries had become embedded in the cultural landscape of local and regional power.[19] Pippin himself was a conspicuous beneficiary. Tonsuring and incarceration in a monastery had become acceptable ways of silencing now-*un*acceptable people.[20] According to annals written several decades after the event, King Childeric III and his son were deposed and tonsured at St-Médard, Soissons; the father incarcerated at St-Bertin, the son at St-Wandrille/Jumièges.[21] The 'where' of Pippin's inauguration was the abbey of St-Médard, Soissons, where a stone's throw away in the old *civitas* there was a royal residence. The 'how' and 'with whom' were more innovative still: Pippin received 'the consecration of bishops' (*consecratio episcoporum*), and as part of the same occasion, the king's wife, Bertrada, was also consecrated. The combination of these procedures was anything but improvised: it had been very carefully thought through in such a way as to be at once familiarly old, and familiarly new. The familiarly old was hallowed by Scripture, both in the Old Testament, where priests and kings were described as anointed, and also the New, where the Apostle Peter had assembled the Christian faithful into a *genus electum, regale sacerdotium, gens sancta, populus acquisitionis . . . qui aliquando non populus, nunc autem populus Dei*, 'a chosen race, a royal priesthood, a holy nation, a people acquired . . . formerly not a *populus* but now a *populus Dei*' ('people of God', I Peter 2:9–10). The familiarly new feature was rooted in readings of biblical figures and events as 'types' or models, translated from ancient Israel's past to the Frankish present. Already materialized in the anointings performed in baptism and post-baptismal confirmation (typologized as spiritual rebirths and strengthenings) and the anointings of priests' hands at ordination, the consecration of the king was performed by bishops.[22] An *un*familiarly new feature, finally, which had no biblical warrant, was the consecration of the queen.[23] This feature, I think, was the shared brainchild of Pippin and Bishop Chrodegang of Metz: the right man in place at the right time.[24]

Rituals, rather than 'working magic *on*' the minds of the actors and agents themselves, worked *in* them – in this case, to reproduce a shared Frankish-Christian identity, carefully contextualizing decisions and actions in a time and culture.[25] For those participating in and witnessing the words and actions of November 751, what they experienced depended on an understanding of a cluster of *related* rituals, all involving anointment with oil. The meaning of these in now-familiar contexts had been explained and demonstrated by bishops to their flocks, more generally by clergy to laity, and also, crucially, by seniors to juniors.[26] Though clear evidence is centuries later, it can stand in nevertheless for the medieval everyday. A father took his son to local courts so as to familiarize the lad with assembly business and train him for participation as an adult.[27] In a similar way, parents took their small children to see their siblings baptized in church.[28] The inaugurations of Pippin and Bertrada happened, not just 'at Soissons', a place long-celebrated in Merovingian history as a royal residence, but in the abbey of St-Médard, the burial-place of one of the most famed of Merovingian kings, Chlothar I.

The choice of St-Médard for the deposition and tonsuring of Childeric III and his son marked the closure of Merovingian history. Choosing the same site for the double inaugurations of Pippin and Bertrada at once obliterated the old dynasty and announced the advent of the new.[29] In the earlier half of Charles's reign there would be parallels in two cases, that of the Lombard dynasty in 774 and the Bavarian Agilolfing dynasty in 788, where rulers and their wives or sons were deposed and humiliated and incarcerated while the Frankish king and queen superseded those they had ousted, by force and forceful forgetting.[30] In both Lombardy and Bavaria, the representatives of the old dynasties were soon afterwards removed far away from their inherited landscapes, literally re-placed, in confinement, while the incoming dynasty organized its own provisional inauguration in a site near that of the old one, and mobilized their own junior generations to impose an artificial continuity. Michel Foucault saw dynasty engendered and sustained by 'bio-power': human resources embodied in the living and the dead, changing shape through time, self-consciously, but also selectively, cultivating memories of its own past, and generating forms of governmentality, identity and religiosity specific to what has been called 'a family-state'.[31] In the formative moment that created Charles's empire and would hold it together was a set of practices in which dynasty was central.[32] From these dynastic exclusions and appropriations, and the parts played by the installing of members of younger generations, would come further interesting outcomes. For now, the point to underline is the use of ritual to mark, and impose, both change and continuity. In this context, even the very young could have important parts to play. In 1953, Charles's distant descendant Prince Charles, son of Queen Elizabeth II, watched, aged four and a half, from an upper gallery his mother's consecration as queen in Westminster Abbey, burial-place of kings, while his grandmother pointed out what was going on. I will venture a surmise that Charles son of Pippin and Bertrada was present at his parents' consecrations in 751, making perhaps his first public appearance in a venerable abbey that was the burial-place of Frankish kings. Charles's parents trusted him to play out his part well, contributing to the entrenchment of their success: a coup that had changed Charles's life and prospects for good.

IV. 753/4 – A SMALL BOY WITH A BIG ROLE

The year 751 marked another coup in another kingdom: the success of the Lombard king Aistulf (749–56) in gaining control of Ravenna and its territory, Constantinople's outpost in the West. When, on 26 March 752, Stephen II took the papal throne, he worried far less about Greeks than about Lombards who now encroached on what had been the Byzantine exarchate, where local elites and their leading officials (*duces*) were carving out estates for themselves.[33] Meanwhile Aistulf demanded a tribute from the Roman duchy itself, putting further pressure on papal coffers. It did not take Stephen long to become involved in negotiations with the Franks for the protection of Rome and its territory. Pippin sent an emissary, Abbot Droctegang of Jumièges to Rome, where he arrived in the spring of 753. (That Theoderic, the son of the deposed Childeric III, had been tonsured as a cleric at Jumièges in 752 could suggest that Pippin's choice of Droctegang as emissary was connected with his role as custodian of the last Merovingian – perhaps as a reward for it; and the use of abbots as emissaries was certainly a Carolingian innovation.) Droctegang journeyed back to Francia along with a Roman cleric (he was to return to Rome with Pippin's reply), bringing further pleas from Pope Stephen, and two letters: one to Pippin, urging further efforts, the other – which may well have come as a flattering surprise – 'to those glorious men, our sons, all the *duces* of the people of the Franks (*omnibus ducibus gentis Francorum*) . . . you who love St Peter and are committed to his interests.' Pippin's response was all the pope could have wished for. The king sent to Rome two very powerful men whom he specially trusted, Chrodegang of Metz and a leading Frankish aristocrat, Duke Autchar, 'to bring the pope back' with them to Francia.[34] Stephen set out from Rome with a large following on 14 October, and, stopping at Pavia only for fruitless talks with Aistulf, they crossed the Great St Bernard pass to St-Maurice d'Agaune, where two further royal servants awaited them, Abbot Fulrad of St-Denis and Duke Rothard, for the final lap of their journey.[35]

Meanwhile, the second Continuator of Fredegar, Childebrand's son Nibelung, who had taken over the continuator's task in 751, recounted how Pippin, after a summer campaign against Saxons, took much plunder and came homewards by way of Bonn on the Rhine, where he heard news of Grifo's death. When Pippin reached Thionville on the Mosel, he learned that Stephen, with his large following and many gifts, had already crossed the Alps and was hurrying north to meet him.

> Hearing this with joy and gladness and with the greatest care for his [the pope's] reception, Pippin gave orders that his son Charles should go south to meet him, and escort him to the royal estate at Ponthion into Pippin's presence. And there Stephen the Roman pope came into the king's presence, and there he distributed largesse with many gifts both for the king and for the Franks, and seeking help against the people of the Lombards and their king Aistulf . . . Then King Pippin told Pope Stephen to stay for the winter at the city of Paris in the monastery of the martyr St Denis, and [he] took a great deal of trouble over this and gave it much careful attention. Pippin also sent envoys to Aistulf asking him, out of respect

for the most holy Apostles SS Peter and Paul, not to campaign in an enemy's fashion in the territory of Rome, and requesting him to stop making frivolous, impious and illegal demands, in a way the *Romani* had never before done.[36]

Compare the account in the *Vita Stephani II* in the *Liber Pontificalis*:

(c. 25) When the king heard that the blessed pope had arrived, he came very quickly to meet him, along with his wife, sons and dignitaries. On this account, he sent his son, Charles by name, nearly 100 miles with some of his chief men, to meet the angelic pope. He himself was at his palace at the place called Ponthion, some 3 miles distant. He dismounted from his horse and prostrated himself on the ground in great humility, along with his wife, his sons, and his chief men, and welcomed the holy pope; and he walked along for some distance beside his saddle-horse, like a groom . . .

(c. 26) . . . Then they all . . . set out for the palace . . . on the 6th day of January, on the Solemnity of Christ's Epiphany . . . There they sat together inside the oratory, and there and then the blessed pope besought the Christian king in tears to arrange for peace-treaties on behalf of St Peter and the *Res Publica* of the Romans. And at that moment Pippin satisfied the blessed pope with an oath that he would make every effort to obey his orders and advice, and in accordance with the pope's wishes, that he would restore the exarchate of Ravenna and the rights and places of the *Res Publica* by every means possible.

(c. 27) But as the winter season was pressing, he asked the holy pope to make his way with all his companions to Paris, to spend the winter at the venerable monastery of St Denis. This he did, and he and the Christian Pippin went to that venerable monastery; it was the Lord's will that some days later, the lord pope anointed the Christian king Pippin, with his two sons, by Christ's grace kings of the Franks.[37]

It is easy to spot that the *Vita* author and Nibelung offered different emphases. The *Vita* author was interested in setting Charles, whom he named, firmly in the context of his family, his father, mother and younger brother – i.e. Carloman, born in 751, whom the author did not name – and added that all four prostrated themselves before the pope. Nibelung had nothing on the family's acting together in this way.

According to the *Vita* author, Stephen anointed Pippin and his two sons, 'by Christ's grace kings of the Franks', and the reality of these events is buttressed by later allusions in a charter of Pippin's and in Stephen's letter to Pippin and his sons.[38] Nibelung had no stake in mentioning these; his father had highlighted episcopal consecration as a key feature of Pippin's inauguration in 751. This explains Nibelung's silence: there were two different stories: one papal, one Frankish.

In these two different sources, though, there is a common element of particular interest because it consists of the *same* information about the five-year-old Charles: both Nibelung and the author of Stephen II's *Vita* describe the role played by Charles in being sent out to escort the pope to Ponthion. The *Vita* author gives more detail: he gives the distance Charles with his retinue travelled out from Thionville to meet Stephen as 'nearly 100 miles', but this is really a secondary matter. There may be some intertextuality going on between this *Vita* and another in the *Liber Pontificalis*, the *Vita* of Pope Constantine I (708–15), which also includes the son of a ruler (Tiberius, co-ruler with his father the Byzantine emperor Justinian II) being sent out to welcome the pope.[39] But this does not diminish the significance and credibility of Charles's escort-duty. That papal and Frankish sources essentially concur in highlighting Charles's high-profile role suggests that the story of Charles being given the task of riding out to meet the pope was a true one. Charles's parents, staging events for an audience consisting of their leading clergy and magnates, put the spotlight on this child. To single him out for a special role vis-à-vis the pope signalled an exceptional future for him.

One further dimension of the relationships created by Pope Stephen with Pippin and his family was that of spiritual compaternity. The analogy was with the bond of spiritual paternity between the officiating priest at a baptism with the child baptized, and of spiritual co-fatherhood between godparents and parents.[40] By consecrating Pippin's and Bertrada's sons, the pope became their spiritual father and spiritual co-parent of their parents who thereafter rejoiced in the titles of *compater* and *commater*. This was to remain a relationship *ex officio*, as it were, formally re-created by succeeding popes (Paul I, brother of Stephen II, and Stephen III and Hadrian).[41] It was a good (though short-lived) example of a papal creative experiment in elaborating bonds with Frankish rulers.[42] After Pope Hadrian, the practice was abandoned: presumably a sign of responsiveness to changed circumstances and Charles's preference.

Pope Stephen was not the only great personage to arrive in Francia from Italy that winter. Pippin's brother Carloman, 'now a monk', made a similar journey north at about the same time. According to the *ArF*, Carloman, under pressure from the Lombard king Aistulf, had come from his monastery to derail the pope's plans and dissuade Pippin from invading Italy. Perhaps Carloman saw his sons again in Francia. But Pippin's mind was made up; and when he, apparently together with Bertrada, and the pope left Francia for Italy in early summer 754, Carloman, already a sick man, travelled with them. By then, according to the well-informed author of the *Annales Petaviani*, Carloman's sons had been tonsured. Perhaps for the first time, Charles and his brother had been left at home in one of the Oise valley palaces while their mother set off with her husband on an Italian *iter* (a word meaning both 'journey' and 'campaign'), which for her was cut short by the decision (hers? Pippin's?) to 'remain with' her brother-in-law at Vienne, where Carloman died on 17 August, and whence his body was taken to Monte Cassino for burial.[43] Whether, or in what sense, Carloman's 'remaining' was custodial, and whether Bertrada was taking care of him as Shakespeare's Lady Macbeth took care of King Duncan, is disputed by historians. Readers should judge for themselves, taking into account that from this time, there is no further reference in any source to Carloman's sons, Pippin's nephews.

V. 755: HOW CHARLES LOST HIS FIRST MILK TOOTH

If successive ritual inaugurations confirmed the new regime, a constant flow of supernatural power was believed necessary to sustain it. In the thought-world of Frankish Christianity, intercessory prayer, especially that of monks, was considered the efficient mobilizer of saintly intervention. In 751 St Médard, in 754 St Denis and, with the pope as intermediary, St Peter, could be regarded as active agents in the regime's maintenance. Another mighty saint was Germanus (or Germain), bishop of Paris (d.576), whose monastery, St-Germain-des-Prés, on the left bank of the Seine at Paris, was granted freedom from tolls by Pippin at a date between 751 and 768.[44] In 755, according to an author writing in the early ninth century (or writing later in that century using early ninth-century material), there was a *translatio*, that is, a solemn removal to a new and finer tomb, of St Germain's remains in an impressively well-attended ritual in which the royal family participated. The story was long ago dismissed as without historical basis, and more recently has been consigned to the 'late legend' category.[45] I am not alone, however, in thinking that a case can be made for its having been told in the early ninth century, during the lifetime of Charles, and by Charles himself.[46] The author of the text lays no claim to have been present at St Germain's *translatio*, but says he has heard the story from Charles himself 'who was present as a seven-year-old at his father's act of piety and recalled what he saw with admirable fluency'.[47] The story as Charles told it began with a problem that could have proved fatal to any *translatio*: Pippin and a large retinue of bishops, clergy, monks and great men were quite unable to move the saint's sarcophagus. A possibly interpolated passage in the story then describes what happened when Pippin made a special offer of an important estate to St Germain: miraculously, the sarcophagus became movable. The story then details a further hitch:

'Because the carrying-poles had been made very long to allow as many people as possible to share the pious labour, it had become impossible to lower the sarcophagus into the hole prepared for it. When everyone urged that the poles be shortened Pippin objected: "The sarcophagus might be damaged. Some safer plan must be found".' No sooner had he spoken than the sarcophagus moved of its own accord: 'While everyone was stupefied and put their hands to their mouths in alarm, it slipped quickly off the poles and dropped into the hole . . . When they had all looked into the hole, they saw that the sarcophagus, which they'd feared shattered, was safe and sound. Clearly this was the work of angels. And while everyone marvelled, I while playing about as boys will [remember this is still Charles speaking], slipped down by accident into the hole. And there I soon lost my first tooth.'

Despite some scholars' scepticism, others have found the story plausible. My own contribution has been the ancillary one of drawing attention to the exceptional, even unique, nature of what I had expected to find was a popular medieval folktale-motif, and, further, proposing a history of the story's transmission via Charles to Irmino, abbot of

St-Germain in Charles's latter years and among the witnesses to Charles's testament, made in 811, and recorded, witnesses and all, by Einhard in the *Vita Karoli*.[48] I dwell on this story because I read it as both psychologically and historically true. Isidore of Seville, the seventh-century encyclopedist who endorsed the scheme of the seven ages of man, called the second stage of a male child's life *pueritia*, boyhood, which he also considered 'years of discretion'. He further defined its beginning as 'when the teeth are changed'. It was the age when a high-born boy might well be offered as an oblate to a monastery, or sent to live in the household of a great noble. Charles in later life recalled the day of St Germain's *translatio* as the time when his boyhood began, the very public moment when he began to understand discipline. His story was at the same time a kind of confession: a small miracle connecting with a large one. Charles's tale revealed, and can still reveal, a well-trained memory and a gift for narrating, and an alert, responsive and engaging personality. The man recollecting his child-self confidently connected with the saint. The natural loss of the tooth signalled a supernatural gain. Modern readers of the story gain unique access to Charles, boy and man.[49]

VI. 757 AND 759: TWO MORE SIBLINGS FOR CHARLES

According to the author of the *Vita* of Pope Paul (consecrated 29 May 757), it was Stephen II who, on his visit to Francia, had promised Pippin that he would build a church, close to St Peter's, in honour of Petronilla, believed to have been Peter's daughter, and that he would transfer her body from outside the city into its spiritual heart.[50] The author explained that to fulfil the promise of his predecessor and elder brother, Paul 'immediately' after Stephen's death (26 April), 'began operations at the cemetery ... two miles from Rome where St Petronilla had once been buried [and] removed the venerable and holy body along with the marble sarcophagus in which it lay ... and brought it to St Peter's [on the Vatican] and placed the holy body in the mausoleum next to St Andrew's.'[51] Permanent prayers were to be offered there for the Franks and their ruler in the sanctuary of 'their helper (*auxiliatrix*) Petronilla'.[52] At an unknown date in 757, Bertrada gave birth to Gisela,

Charles's sister.[53] In 758, Pippin sent Abbot Wulfard of St-Martin, Tours, to Rome, bearing Gisela's baptismal shawl to Pope Paul who (he informed Pippin) placed it in the oratory at St Peter's, which was dedicated to the Franks' *auxiliatrix*. Addressing Pippin as 'spiritual co-father' and calling the baby, whose name he apparently didn't yet know, *dulcissima et amantissima spiritalis filia*, 'sweetest and most beloved spiritual daughter', Paul said he had received the shawl as receiving the baby girl 'as if she had actually been there' (*tamquam praesentialiter*).[54] The sending of the shawl was 'a virtual ritual'.[55] It recreated and reinforced the bond of compaternity between spiritual father (the pope, *ex officio*) and Pippin and Bertrada, the actual co-parents of, now, a daughter as well as two sons.[56] Paul choreographed the ritual. Pippin, now committed to protect the papacy, had his own dynastic reasons for wanting the compaternal relationship to continue. A number of Paul's subsequent letters included by name Gisela as well as her two elder brothers, and their parents, in the pope's prayers for the royal family.[57] Hearing such papal letters read out before the court was a strong reminder to the royal children of their place in the family and in the dynasty.[58] Later chapters of this book will show the importance of Charles's relationship with his younger sister and of her role in maintaining contacts with the succeeding generation.[59]

Under the year 759, the compiler of the *ArF* (writing *c*.790) recorded the birth of a third son to Bertrada, and, not long after, recorded the child's short life, and his death: 'Pippin gave the child his own name, Pippin; but he lived only two years and died in the third.' The mention of this baby Pippin's birth and death is exceptional for three reasons: deaths of infant children are reported extremely seldom; the naming of this third boy-child after his father seemed to privilege him and perhaps to promise him a share in the paternal inheritance; and this Pippin's existence was remembered nearly thirty years after his death. For a modern historian to note the child's existence, and to wonder why the annalist included it, is also exceptional: Johannes Fried's suggestion that Charles himself, who was, after all, the patron/commissioner of these annals, made a point of registering baby Pippin's life and death is apropos. It made psychological sense. Perhaps the thirteen-year-old big brother had felt the child's loss keenly. Not only did he wish it to be remembered decades later: he was in a position to have it recorded in the annals he commissioned.[60]

VII. TWO MORE LITTLE SISTERS

Bertrada bore her husband two other children, both girls, named Rothaid and Adelhaid. Neither lived long, it seems. Both were buried in Metz, now in the mid-eighth century being constructed as a focus of Arnulfing dynastic memory: 'it was there that the kings descending from St Arnulf placed the bodies of those dear to them'.[61] Yet, these lost babes were commemorated, two decades later, in epitaphs written by Paul the Deacon at Charles's behest during the brief period (c.782–5) when this accomplished poet was attached to Charles's court. Paul's own brother had been taken as a hostage to Francia after a failed Lombard revolt in 776, and, thanks to a poignant plea addressed to Charles in 785, Paul's efforts to secure his brother's release finally succeeded.[62] The epitaphs of Rothaid and Adelhaid, written about this time, were kept at Metz, where these little girls were buried. Both poems stress the ancestry of the girls' father.[63] Though Bertrada was not named in Rothaid's epitaph, the choice of burial-place was credited to her 'parents', and this is similarly hinted at in Adelhaid's epitaph. 'The cold style of commissioned pieces' is unsurprising, given that Paul wrote a generation after the girls' deaths and had not known their parents.[64] By contrast, Paul's epitaphs for the infant daughters of Charles and Hildegard, with their inclusion of female offshoots of the dynasty and the expression of heartfelt emotion, made emphatic and unconventional points.[65]

VIII. CHARLES'S *PUERITIA*

After the pope's return from Francia in 754, Pippin made good on his promises to fight the Lombards. Homecoming Frankish warriors, including Pippin, no doubt regaled their offspring with tales of victory and prowess, especially in bringing back huge amounts of gold and silver, valuables and tents from the 754 campaign, and in 756 besieging the Lombard capital Pavia, enforcing King Aistulf's surrender, and, again, carrying off quantities of loot.[66] There arrived in 757 at Compiègne an embassy from Constantinople bearing lavish gifts including an organ, which was what made most impression on the Franks, and (surely!) the nine-year-old Charles as well.[67]

Pippin's governmental ambitions and political practice can be read in the records of assemblies summoned by him in 755 at Ver, and at Verberie in 756, and at Compiègne in 757. The Ver meeting was a synod, involving 'nearly all the bishops of the Gauls'. If tranquil times were allowed him, said the king, his intention was to have the canons of church law more fully preserved and observed. Pippin personally attended sessions, and laid down some new regulations of his own.

> The lord king says that when he wishes that abbesses come to him on his orders once a year when necessary, with the consent of the bishops in whose dioceses these abbesses are located, she should not delay on her estates or elsewhere, but whether coming or returning, should travel as quickly as she can, and not to leave her convent without first sending a messenger to the king. And if the king tells her to come, she is to come. But if she is to stay in her convent, we must meanwhile improve the observance of the canons.[68]

In a supplementary synod, whose decrees no longer survive, Pippin ordered abbesses of royal convents to send in their accounts to the king, but if their convent were under episcopal direction, to send them to the bishop. Other decrees concern protection of pilgrims, the banning of simony, and the prohibition of any bishop, abbot or layman receiving bribes in any legal cases, 'for where gifts run rife, justice is voided'.[69] Already, Pippin was setting the scene for Charles's yet more active intervention in ecclesiastical law and life.

A decree of the council of Verberie (756), in its report of a difficult case centring on the position of a wife whose husband has had to depart from the marital home, reveals much about gender in lay social life:

> If a man, when unavoidable necessity compels him, flees to another duchy or province or follows his lord (*senior*) to whom he cannot betray his faith, and his wife, since she wishes to and can do this, refuses to follow him for love of her own kin, let her remain unmarried for the whole time that the husband whom she did not follow is still alive. For that husband who fled to another place when necessity compelled, if he cannot abstain, can receive another wife, after doing penance.[70]

The conduct of both man and wife is governed by secular norms; but a gender-divide is starkly drawn. A man must follow his lord and must not betray his faith; a wife can refuse to follow her husband 'for love of her own kin'. Canon law treats man and wife differently: he in his new surroundings can remarry after doing penance; she cannot remarry, but must remain unmarried for as long as her husband is still living. Behind these secular norms and canonical regulations seems to lie an actual case.

The *decretum* emanating from a combined synod and assembly the following year in the public palace at Compiègne, in twenty of its twenty-one *capitula* set out rulings of canon law on marriage, including the prohibited degrees of relationship, and penalties for incest and various sexual offences, and ended with a ruling partly reminiscent of that of Verberie but with a quite different – and even-handed – conclusion: 'If men flee to other countries because of feuds and leave their wives, neither husbands nor wives can [re]marry.' But among these *capitula* the odd one out is no. 9, which is presented as the account of a case, ending with a judgment:

> A *homo Francus* accepted a benefice from his lord (*senior*), and brought with him a vassal, and after that, the lord died and left that vassal there [on the benefice]; and after this another man accepted that same benefice, and so that he might have that vassal better [*sic*], he gave him a woman from the benefice and he had her for some time; and then he put her aside and he went back to the kin of his dead lord, and there accepted a wife there, and he has her now.
>
> It was decided that he should have the woman he took after the previous one.[71]

This case reveals interesting things about benefices and their transmission, vassals, lordship, and women. But none of those is my primary concern in the present context, which is that of Charles's life as a nine-year-old. Taking into account points made earlier about the location of palaces and their functions as both royal family-residences and places of assembly, and also about the appearances of sons with their fathers at public events as part of their training, it seems likely that by the age of nine and midway through *pueritia*, Charles attended assemblies, and in the course of informal discussion with his father and his father's counsellors, and with other kinsmen, asked questions about procedure and process, testimonies and decisions, and the final judgment stating how and why 'it was decided'.[72] Perhaps royal and high-born women, and girls who were prospective wives and co-managers of *beneficia*, or future abbesses, and who were members of the palace as an institution and community 'of people who dwelt therein', were also onlookers at assemblies, and anyway took a keen interest in cases like that recorded in Compiègne c. 9.[73] Charles could have learned much from his mother as well as from his father, and from senior kin of both sexes.[74]

IX. CHARLES'S *ADOLESCENTIA*: COMING OF AGE AND LEARNING TO FIGHT IN THE 760S

In a charter issued in 752, Pippin had granted his *mundeburdum* (a Germanic word meaning protection, routinely found in formulae, charters and capitularies) to the monastery of St-Calais in Maine. In 760, he strengthened this grant by associating Charles's *mundeburdum* with his own *tuitio*.[75] This may well have been linked with Charles's coming of age, for one form of Frankish law (*Lex Salica*) made twelve the age of majority, though in another form (*Lex Ribuaria*) that age was fifteen.[76] In any event, the occasion signified Charles's playing of a political role in Neustria, with the prospect of military action. In the 760s, the mobilizing of heavenly support for the Franks' wars became an ongoing priority.

In May 752, at Nierstein near Mainz, only a few months after Pippin's and Bertrada's consecrations as king and queen, Pippin had made a grant to Prüm, in which he and Bertrada refounded the monastery of Prüm by dedicating it no longer to the Virgin Mary and saints Peter and Paul, John and Martin, but to the Holy Saviour and the Virgin, and called on the monks to pray for the royal pair.[77] Prüm had been the foundation of Bertrada's grandmother (after whom she was called), and her father Charibert/Herbert. On 13 August 762, at the *villa publica* of Trigorium near Koblenz, in what was effectively a second refoundation, Pippin and Bertrada together gave a charter to Prüm, each subscribing it, and also having it subscribed and consented to by their two sons Charles and Carloman. As both spouses made substantial donations of their inherited properties to Prüm, this was very much a family affair.[78] In the charter's preamble written by Pippin's arch-chancellor, Baddilo, the king declared that 'divine providence had manifestly anointed us [the royal 'we'] to the throne of the kingdom', and he went on to include his wife along with himself in these extensive gifts to Prüm, 'for love of the Holy Saviour, and Mary the mother of God' as well as an augmented number of saints including John the Baptist, Stephen, Denis and Maurice. Pippin recalled how the couple 'put monks there to pray for the state of the Church and longevity of our kingdom and also of our wife and sons and the whole Catholic people': a statement of piety with a comprehensive reach which explains the summoning to Trigorium of nine bishops and eleven counts. Of Pippin's thirty surviving charters, only this one has such a lengthy witness-list.[79]

Pippin and Bertrada had 'placed in the church of Prüm' not only relics of Mary and the other saints but 'the relics of the sandals of Christ'. New research suggests that these had been brought to Francia by Stephen II and presented to Pippin and Bertrada, probably at St-Denis, in 754. At some point between then and August 762, the sandals of Christ had been taken to Prüm on the occasion of the fresh endowment. Other relics were outhoused, to Prüm's secondary establishments, St-Goar and Münstereifel, or sent as gifts elsewhere, as for instance to St-Riquier. The mother-house never changed its prime dedication – to the Saviour.[80] What distinguished Prüm thereafter was not only its specific connection with the royal dynasty and papal authority, but its possession of relics peculiarly associated with the living Christ and, via Rome, with the incorporation of the sandals into papal ceremonial.[81] The Trigorium assembly was special because of the cluster of ritual events: the public affirmation of the royal couple's patronage of Prüm through their placing there of the sandals of Christ, the association of this with Charles and Carloman's 'consenting' to their parents' gifts, and the wider consent given by the leading men of the Frankish church and kingdom. What explained the scale and timing of the assembly were Pippin's military priorities, and hence the need to mobilize heavenly support.

The 760s saw a significant shift of Frankish attention from Italy to Aquitaine, partly because the Lombard threat to the papacy had diminished with the death of Aistulf in 756 and the succession of Desiderius (757–74). The new king's first objective was to stabilize Italy by installing the Friulan noble Arichis as duke of Benevento in 758, arranging for the marriage of his daughter Adelperga to the new duke, and associating his son Adelchis with his own rule (in 759). Another aspect of this shift of attention was leaving Duke Tassilo of Bavaria to build up his princely power in that duchy, not least through his marriage to Liutperga, another daughter of Desiderius, in 763. In the 760s, Aquitaine not only dominates the narrative of Nibelung's Continuation of Fredegar, but crops up in early annals.[82] The wars there persisted from 760 to 768 (with an intermission during a famine in 764–5). Pippin's goal – the conquest of Aquitaine – evidently loomed in the king's mind as the necessary achievement of his reign: necessary because it repeated that of the Merovingians.

In 760, Pippin had subjected Duke Waifar of Aquitaine to violent tactics; and in 761, Charles and his brother Carloman had joined their father on campaign in Aquitaine, where several strongholds were captured.[83] In 762, Pippin, again with his sons, campaigned in Gascony and then captured Bourges.[84] There the bishopric's lands were divided between the bishop and various laymen of Pippin's choosing: an experience of power distribution and regional resource-management from which his sons could learn on the spot.[85] Whether this 762 campaign pre- or post-dated the Trigorium assembly is not made clear by any of the sources. My guess is that the assembly pre-dated – was even the precondition of – the campaign. With Frankish morale fortified, Pippin could move south into Aquitaine, where the taking of Bourges, the chief place in Berry, was a major triumph. Pippin was in charge, of course. But in light of what is known of royal family politics in this period, the sons can be credited with agendas of their own that included fraternal rivalry. War fostered ambition.

So did peace. In 763, Pippin held an assembly at Worms and 'gave counties to both his beloved sons'.[86] Triangulating from earlier Pippinid interests in regions west of the Seine and, more specifically, from Charles's protective rights over St-Calais in and after 760, scholars have surmised that Maine was a county put by his father into his elder son's hands. If this unruly border region provided a tough assignment for Charles, that could well have been Pippin's way of testing him.[87] In 763, Charles and Carloman together wrote a letter taken to Pope Paul by their father's envoys. The brothers expressed 'deep shame' at not having been able to send gifts of their own to the pope, because of the gifts' inadequacy or unavailability.[88] This episode, rather than being a diplomatic solecism symptomatic of youthful incompetence, could be seen as reflecting tension between father and sons, in which the abbot-envoys too played the roles of mediators, or partisans. Both Droctegang of Jumièges and Wulfard of St-Martin, Tours, controlled rich and strategic monasteries. They were Pippin's appointees. But the pattern of Charles's grants and confirmations in the charter-rich years of the 770s suggests some engagement with Neustrian institutions and office-holders continuing from the 760s, and possibilities for the forming of ongoing tactical alliances at court.[89] As for Pope Paul's reaction: he assured his 'most sweet and most beloved sons, most victorious kings', that the only presents he wanted were

> the joys of hearing about their well-being . . . The Lord chose you before all kings, appointed you as liberators of his holy, catholic and apostolic church, and deigned to anoint you as kings by the hands of St Peter. But may the almighty Lord . . . grant you victories from heaven, and subject all barbarian nations beneath your feet . . .

Paul's timely theme was the brothers' military success in Aquitaine.[90]

While Paul's letters dwelled on the needs of St Peter, and the Franks' duty to protect Rome, the receivers of these letters had other priorities. Paul and his advisers, who received news about the war in Aquitaine from pilgrims as well as from envoys, could have had no illusions about its realities. Nibelung minces no words. Not counting euphemisms like 'travelling through', there are over twenty-five instances of 'burning', 'laying waste', and 'ravaging' in the six pages that cover 760–67.[91] *Omnia vastaverunt* is devastating enough; but more terrible still are the passages where material losses are detailed:

> after almost the whole region was devastated, and many monasteries laid waste, [Pippin] got as far as Issoudun where the greater part of the vineyards in Aquitaine were located, and seized and destroyed it; and in so doing, he utterly destroyed and ruined nearly all of Aquitaine where the monasteries and the churches, the rich and the poor, got their wine. [In 767] Waifar's kinsman Remistanus, broke his oath to Pippin and again accepted Waifar's lordship; and he laid waste Berry and the Limousin which the king had acquired, and ravaged them so thoroughly that no farmer in that land dared cultivate any fields or vines.[92]

This was no war of battles between armies, though the Franks had skills in siege-warfare, while Duke Waifar and the Aquitanians loyal to him found an answer to the Franks' fortifications by seizing opportunities to raze walls and make strongholds indefensible.[93] What the wars achieved through six years of Frankish attrition, made more terrible by Aquitanian reprisals, was the wholesale destruction of a region and way of life for at least a generation. Such were the campaigns in which Charles and Carloman learned a form of the warrior's trade. In these circumstances, the competitive aspects of Frankish warfare loomed large, as warlords – including Charles and Carloman – and their followers vied for glory and wealth.[94]

X. 767–8: CONSTANTINOPLE, BAGHDAD, SAINTES AND ST-DENIS

In the decade before 767, communications between Constantinople and the West had been frequent, though intermittently recorded. Nibelung, the contemporary source, said nothing about an embassy from Byzantium; but, writing in the ninth century, the reviser of the *ArF* did (an exception to the rule preferring the contemporary to the later source). 'Then [in 767] the lord king Pippin held a great synod at the villa of Gentilly [near Paris] between the Romans and the Greeks about the Holy Trinity and the images of saints.'[95]

The annal contains quite a detailed account of Pippin's campaign in Aquitaine that year, largely drawing on Nibelung, though the focus is on religious questions. Within Pippin's close family, what took priority were political relations, and these were inseparable from dynastic concerns. Pippin wanted to talk with the Byzantine envoys about the proposal they brought for a marriage-alliance between his daughter Gisela and Emperor Constantine V's son, the future Leo IV – a prospect that evoked 'the pope's horror'.[96] The pope's anxieties were real enough. They faded fast, though, when the plan apparently ran into opposition from Pippin's chief men, perhaps including Nibelung (hence his silence on the embassy). Gisela's brothers, too, their standing enhanced by their military efforts, surely expected a voice in these discussions, as, in the previous generation, Pippin and Carloman had expected to be consulted when their sister Hiltrud's marriage was the issue (Aunt Hiltrud's scandalous precedent did not inspire imitation).[97] Even more likely to have been closely involved in these discussions was Gisela's mother, Bertrada. A royal daughter's marriage naturally concerned both parents; occasional bits and pieces of evidence show high-born mothers having a voice, and sometimes a casting vote, in their daughters' destinies.

This circumstantial evidence helps explain why though Nibelung was silent on the Byzantine marriage proposal itself, he was surprisingly loquacious on Queen Bertrada's activities in 767–8 (in the narratives of Childebrand there had been only a single previous mention of Bertrada, in the context of 751). For it was at this point that Nibelung, in a loop-back, mentioned that Pippin had in 764 sent envoys to Baghdad, the new Abbasid capital, residence of the Caliph al-Mansur (754–75).[98] They had returned three years later, in 767, escorting Saracen envoys to Francia. The party left Baghdad, travelled across the Mediterranean, and, bearing great gifts, docked at Marseilles, whence they moved north to Metz. There, at Pippin's behest, hospitality had been arranged for them for the rest of the winter. To meet the king, so busy that year in the wild fastnesses of Aquitaine, the envoys had to wait until he could invite them to an appropriately impressive and safe venue.

Bertrada appears in Nibelung's narrative after Pippin's return from the 767 campaign, when she crossed the Loire with him into Aquitaine, and the couple went to winter at Bourges. There he gave orders for a palace to be built for them (I take *sibi* here as a plural pronoun). After taking counsel with his chief men, Pippin left Bertrada at Bourges with 'remaining Franks and his faithful counts', and himself led a force to capture Waifar, who escaped to what was to prove his last redoubt – the forest of the Double in the Périgord. Pippin returned to Bourges where Bertrada was, and there they stayed for the rest of the winter (767–8) 'in the palace'.[99] He sent the army to winter in Burgundy and, 'with the counsel of bishops and clergy, solemnly celebrated Christmas and Epiphany at Bourges'.

In mid-February 768 Pippin summoned his army to Bourges, where he had Count Remistanus, Waifar's uncle, hung on a gallows, a disgraceful fate. Pippin sent Bertrada from Bourges to Orléans, where she took ship down the Loire to the fortress of Champtoceaux. From Bourges Pippin moved towards the river Garonne in the south-west.[100] According to the *ArF*, other significant people had already been captured by Pippin's men: they were Waifar's mother, sister and nieces, who were being held at Saintes. The capture of these high-born women dishonoured Waifar and can only have accelerated the ducal family's downward spiral. Pippin pressed on southwards to the Garonne. 'There he met Gascons (they live on the other side of the Garonne) who came to him giving oaths and hostages: they swore to him and to his sons Charles and Carloman that they would always be faithful.'[101] I take this to imply that Charles and Carloman were present there, with their father, in 768. By Easter he had rejoined Bertrada at Champtoceaux, where they welcomed, at last, the envoys from Baghdad. The stay was brief, it seems, for Pippin had yet to see Waifar hunted down to the death. He sent his *comites* (here meaning military household), his elite troops (*scariti*), and his faithful men (*leudes*), in four separate squadrons, for the kill. According to Nibelung: 'Meanwhile, and this happened, so they say, on the instructions of Pippin himself, Waifar prince of Aquitaine was slain by his own men. And King Pippin now acquired the whole of Aquitaine.'[102]

It was high time to prioritize the reception of the envoys from Baghdad.[103] Pippin had arranged for them to stay at Metz until he was able to invite them to Champtoceaux, where Bertrada was holding the fort, in time for Easter (10 April). She had also been performing what in the next generation would be seen as the pre-eminently queenly task of organizing the *honestas* and *ornamentum* of the king's residence.[104] Impressing the caliph's envoys was important for Bertrada as well as Pippin. There was a very good reason for Pippin's initiative in 764, and the Abbasid caliph's pursuit, through his envoys, of a diplomatic alliance in 767–8: namely, that both parties shared an enemy in the shape of the Umayyad ruler of Córdoba.[105] Religious difference was no obstacle at all to the pursuit of shared political interest. But the settings in which these negotiations occurred when finally the royal family met the envoys from Baghdad mattered a great deal. With a little imagination, the reader can conjure up this meeting – the exotic figures bearing the caliph's proffered gifts.[106] Some nine years later, Charles's own memories of 768 were surely stirred when he received Saracen envoys, not from Baghdad but from Zaragoza, Barcelona and Huesca (whose local rulers wanted Charles's support against Córdoba), and again, not on the Loire this time but at the source of the Pader, Paderborn, in Saxony, where Charles staged an impressive assembly of 'all the Franks, and Saxons from every part of Saxony and everywhere'.[107]

Similarly, to return to 768, the celebration of Aquitaine's conquest following Waifar's death demanded, and got, appropriate staging: 'Pippin came in triumph and victory to Saintes where Bertrada awaited him', having ensured that the *ornamentum* was suitable to the occasion. 'There', according to Nibelung in his Chronicle's penultimate chapter, 'the king dealt justice for the salvation of the *patria* and the benefit of the Franks.'[108]

It would have been hard to capture more succinctly the thrust of the capitulary issued by Pippin in 768, probably while he was at Saintes, probably between late April and early July, and now as the ruler of the *patria* of Aquitaine.[109] Perhaps Nibelung's intention was precisely to summarize this text. In his Chronicle, he had depicted a ravaged region, and people deprived of hope. Pippin's *capitula* promised a restoration. Pippin acted *sinodaliter*, or in a fitting manner for an assembly, summoning a council over which he presided. Complementing ecclesiastical decrees already issued, law would replace violence. The wrongs suffered by lay people would be righted. The poor and powerless were not to be burdened with unbearable demands. Plaintiffs were not to be prevented by force from coming before the king to lodge their grievances. No one should appropriate or extort anything from his fellow (*par*) while that person was bringing their case before the king. Benefices and precarial grants were to be held as they had been before. All people (*homines*) should have their laws, whether Romans or Salian Franks. After the years of war, the royal family looked forward to a new time of peace and justice.

It was not to be. Pippin, already ill, knew his illness was mortal. His legacy to Aquitaine, apart from the capitulary itself, was the appointing of a cadre of counts and judges. With Bertrada, Charles and Carloman, the sick king made his way northwards, via St-Hilary, Poitiers where he confirmed its immunity* in July, to Tours where he distributed alms, prayed to St Martin and sought intercession and forgiveness for his sins. The family and their large retinue finally reached St-Denis. Pippin remembered fondly the monastery *ubi enotriti fuimus*, and whose claims to the tolls of its annual fair he had defended against the count of Paris.[110] In his dying days, in a series of charters, he referred to the saint as 'his special patron', confirmed the privileges and the judicial immunity of the

---

* An immunity can be defined as an area legally exempted from interference of secular or church authorities, especially used to protect monasteries and convents from state or episcopal financial demands.

monastery, and gave lands to Abbot Fulrad.[111] In a last massive grant of the royal forest of Ivelines, he affirmed his desire for his body to be buried where the precious body of St Denis lay.[112]

Nibelung described Pippin's final arrangements for the succession:

[c. 53] Seeing that he could no longer evade death, he summoned all his chief men, and the Franks' war-leaders and counts as well as the bishops and clergy. And there, with the consent of the Franks, and his chief men and bishops, he while still living divided the kingdom of the Franks which he had held between his two sons Charles and Carloman in equal shares (*equali sorte*): that is, he ordained for Charles, the older son, the kingdom of the Austrasians, but for the younger son Carloman the kingdom of Burgundy, Provence and Gothia, Alsace and Alamannia. The province of Aquitaine, which the king had acquired, he divided between them. When all this had been performed, after a few days King Pippin, sad to say, died. Kings Charles and Carloman, the sons of that king buried him in the monastery of St Denis the martyr, as was his wish, with great honour. He ruled for 25 years.

[c. 54] After doing all these things, Charles and Carloman each came with his faithful men (*leodes*) to the chief place (*sedes*) of his own kingdom, and when each had held an assembly and taken counsel with their leading men, on Sunday 18 September, Charles at the town (*urbs*) of Noyon and Carloman at the city (*civitas*) of Soissons, on the same day and in the same way (*pariter*) was raised into their kingdom by their leading men and through the consecration of [their] bishops.[113]

Nibelung (or rather a hasty scribe on his staff) offered no date for Pippin's death and gave Sunday 18 September as the date for the consecrations, which according to all other sources took place on 9 October, St Denis's day.[114] Nibelung's work ended with a muddle.

Life went on. It was not Nibelung but Pope Stephen III (768–72) who left the record of the important fact that Pippin, perhaps sensing urgency in summer 768, had arranged the marriages of both his sons to noble Frankish women.[115] Both these women bore sons, Charles's wife, Himiltrud, in 769; Carloman's wife, Gerberga, in 770. Both little boys were called Pippin in a parity symptomatic of fraternal rivalry. Only in the case of Himiltrud does skeletal evidence survive to demonstrate the stature that was conventionally deemed a sign of nobility. She must have stood out alongside her husband: imposing figures making a regal pair, he 6′3″, she just under 6′.[116]

Grandfather Pippin lived to see neither of his grandsons.[117] Bertrada was more fortunate. She assumed a widow's veil and the title of *Deo devota*, 'a woman [often meaning widow] devoted to God'. She was also devoted to planning for the next generation and the one after that: for her sons, between whom Pippin's lands had been distributed equally; for her daughter Gisela, still with prospects of marriage; for her grandchildren; and for herself, as a senior player in family politics that were also 'international' politics, in a peace-making role recognized by the new pope Stephen.

More telling than all these concerns was Pippin's very last wish. The earliest evidence for it is a letter from his grandson, Louis, to the abbot of St-Denis, Hilduin, c.835. It was to the effect that 'our grandfather Pippin, such was his great humility, had given orders that once the course of his life was over he was to be buried in front of the doorway of the abbey-church, and he gave instructions for the inscription (*titulus*) on the tomb-slab'.[118] Humility was the royal quality most prized by Louis, true, but Pippin himself had given orders for it to be represented in the laying to rest of his corpse. Pippin, it could be said, felt much need, and had much cause, for a penitential posture. Kingship was a high office that tended to provoke low deeds and required much penance. Bertrada herself was complicit in those deeds. It would not have been surprising if the fates of his older brother, and that brother's sons, Pippin's own nephews, lay heavy on his conscience – and on Bertrada's. How fraternity and fair shares played out in the generation after Pippin, what followed in the way of foreseeable and unforeseen consequences, and how important to Charles was the memory of his father, are the subjects of Chapter 4.

4

Family Fortunes

I. THE RIVALRY BETWEEN CHARLES AND CARLOMAN

Pippin's division of his realm between his sons, based on the 742 division between Pippin himself and his elder brother, had been made and approved by the magnates of the two kingdoms respectively, and Charles and Carloman had been consecrated in parallel rites performed at two episcopal cities just a day's march from each other (see Map 4, p. xv). Separate but identical rites on different sides of the frontier could suggest some wariness and a sense of competition on the parts of the two young kings and their followers.[1] It's rightly been observed that in Nibelung's last chapter, there was a sense of the oneness of the Franks as a people, and the phrase *regnum Francorum* packed an emotional punch; while Pippin's assembly at Saintes early in 768 had its collective purpose in seeking the *utilitas Francorum* ('the best interests of the Franks').[2] Yet each successor-king had successfully laid claim to his *sors*, his lot or inheritance; and each expressed this by making a beeline for where very recently Pippin had visibly and concretely inhabited a palace in working order – at Aachen, for Christmas and Easter 765–6; and Samoussy for Christmas 766. Thus in 768 Charles celebrated Christmas at Aachen, and Carloman at Samoussy in northern France.[3]

Thanks to the survival of Charles's earliest extant charter, an original, it's possible to say a good deal about Charles's frame of mind during that first Christmas and first winter of his reign.[4] The charter was issued from Aachen on 13 January 769, and it was written by Charles's notary Hitherius, a former notary of Pippin's (he wrote five of Pippin's thirty extant charters: nos. 13 (753), 24, 26, 27 and 28 (these

93

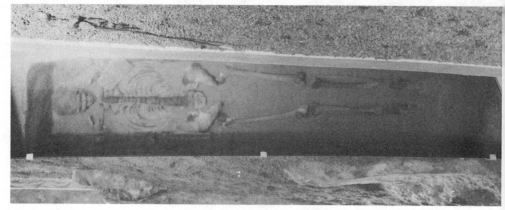

The skeletal remains of Himiltrud in the crypt at Nivelles.

Charles's charters: number of charters issued, by year, 769 to 813

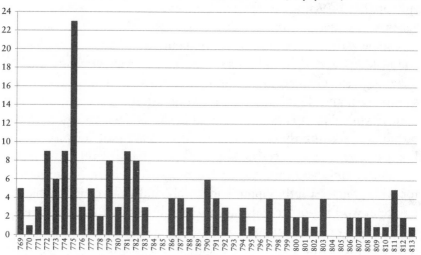

Note: graph excludes three charters that can be dated no more precisely than 777–797, and three that can only be dated to 774–800.

four all 768)) who joined Charles's service after Pippin's death. Pippin's title, used always at the beginning of his charters, had been *rex, vir inluster* ('illustrious man', an old Roman title of honour). Charles's title, opening this first extant charter, was *gratia Dei rex Francorum vir inluster*. Pippin's charters had never ended with a monogram; Charles's charters all ended with his monogram. Hitherius or a subordinate might have suggested these innovations, but neither title nor monogram could possibly have been introduced without Charles's say-so. The inspiration came from Byzantium via Italy. Hitherius and his colleagues had seen monograms at Pippin's court on the documents presented by Byzantine envoys in 757 and – especially – 767 when politics were higher on the agenda than religious debates.[5] The gap of over a year between Charles's Diplomas (aka Charters) 60 (March 770) and 61 (which lacks a notary's sign-off) or 62 (April 771 or July 771) has been explained, thought-provokingly, in terms of Hitherius's absence in Italy during that period.[6] How heavily must Charles have relied in the early years of his reign on those who had been close to his father, and on how few men an early medieval ruler could run a 'chancery'!'[7]

D. 55 is the earliest text to throw light on Charles's relationship with his brother after their joint-accession in October 768. It is a grant to the abbey of St-Denis of St-Dié, a small monastery in the Vosges of which Pippin had had possession (*vestitura*). Small though it was, it was economically valuable: a Roman road ran through its lands, there were salt-wells on the banks of the Meurthe just downstream from the monastery, and also rich veins of silver and iron in the valley of the Lièpvre.[8] The document insists that future abbots (*rectores*) of St-Denis must be there *praesentialiter*, in person, whenever the grant was confirmed. This suggests that Abbot Fulrad of St-Denis had come to Charles in person to request the grant – something in any case quite normal. It seems likely that Fulrad was with Charles when Hitherius or his assistant prepared the document. Fulrad had been an influential elder statesman in the days of Pippin, and he was in charge of an exceptionally rich royal abbey with far-flung lands. Fulrad might have felt a duty to keep the peace between the royal brothers: he had a strong vested interest in keeping on good terms with both of them. Yet the Vosges lay in Carloman's kingdom, and so did St-Denis.[9] Why then was it Charles to whom Fulrad applied for the grant of St-Dié to St-Denis? The likeliest reason is that Charles had struck a deal with the abbot. Fulrad struck a deal of his own with Carloman, who gave St-Denis two grants in February 769 and a further one in March. The grant of St-Dié to St-Denis removed any problems that might have arisen from rival claims on the part of the two sons of Pippin. *Both* Pippin's sons needed to keep close relations with St-Denis: not only was it the major Frankish cult-site, but its abbot had been Pippin's closest adviser – a power in the land. As a further sweetener for Fulrad, D. 55 mentions not only that Pippin was buried at St-Denis but that Charles himself planned to be buried there – implying that his claims to all Francia were still live in the longer run.

The terms on which St-Dié was granted by Charles were as follows: it was always to be staffed by between ten and fifteen monks from St-Denis working in relays or on temporary stints (*per vices*), and they were not to cease offering by day and by night psalms and masses and other petitionary prayers and special prayers (*peculiares orationes*) 'for us [i.e. Charles] and for our lord and glorious father'. It sounds as if what Charles wanted from these monks was *laus perennis*, non-stop prayer, as pioneered at St-Maurice d'Agaune.[10] Charles added that he had ordered the grant to be made by a written charter to be given to St-Denis so that 'from this day the *rectores* of that monastery should personally receive the little monastery of St-Dié to possess by our grace so that they should always keep it.' This seems to preclude any suggestion that the rights of St-Denis were somehow temporary.[11]

Charles's D. 55 and Carloman's D. 43 show interesting differences. In D. 55 Charles repeatedly highlighted his closeness to his father. Carloman's D. 43, his first extant charter, issued at the palace of Samoussy near Meaux (between Aisne and Marne) in January 769, was a confirmation of Pippin's and his predecessors' charters assigning the tolls of the fair of St-Denis to the monastery. As no more than a confirmation, it lacked the touches in D. 55 that connected Charles and his grant *directly* with his father. The equivalent connecting touch in D. 43 was not to Pippin but to Fulrad, who certainly received Carloman's confirmation-charter in person. There was no *gratia Dei* title here (though Carloman in D. 45 (March 769) started using it), and no monogram in D. 43 or any of Carloman's subsequent eleven charters. Had Fulrad's been the mind behind the monogram, it would surely have been more likely to have been first used for Carloman, whose man he was and in whose kingdom his abbey lay.[12] In the early years of Charles's kingship, Hitherius occupied the role of right-hand man. I think the mind behind the monogram was that of Hitherius.[13] A further comparison can be made between the places where Charles and Carloman issued their first charters. Both brothers were keen to have a *sedes*, a seat, where their father had sat, and to issue their first charters in places where their father had stayed. Some determined rivalry was going on.

Pippin had ordered Aquitaine to be divided between his sons. But Hunald, a kinsman (perhaps a son) of Waifar, had already begun to rekindle rebellion in Gascony and Aquitaine. Charles, though he had further to travel, moved first, and 'with a few Franks and the Lord's help' set about undermining Hunald's support. Carloman joined Charles south of the Loire at Moncontour in Poitou, not far from Chasseneuil, one of the main palaces of Aquitaine. The earlier version of the *ArF*, written up c.790, implies that Carloman left 'abruptly' (*iter arripiens*) and returned to Francia. The revised *ArF*, written up in the early ninth century, elaborates: 'acting on the wicked advice of his great men, Carloman refused to give his brother any help. The colloquium took place but, with no agreement achieved, Carloman returned to his kingdom.'[14] The strictly contemporary evidence of a papal letter (late 769/early 770) confirms the reality of the brothers' hostility to each other: Pope Stephen wrote to them to say that he attributed their 'division and discord' to the Devil's intervention – a common excuse; but at the time of writing they had assured the pope that they had abandoned their *rixae ac litigia* (quarrels and disputes) and resumed their former concord.[15] Stephen's letter, invoking Pippin's example, was a plea for the brothers' co-operation in securing the rights of St Peter, by using force against the Lombard king. Meanwhile Charles had moved fast and firmly into Aquitaine to regain the control Pippin had had in the Angoumois and the Périgord. In May, he was at Mornac, on the river Seudre, an affluent of the Garonne, on the northern edge of the wild and marshy forest of the Double, where Pippin had cornered Waifar and induced some of Waifar's men to kill their lord. In July, Charles was at the palace of Angeac on the Charente, some 15km west of Angoulême.[16] His moves carefully replicated his father's. Angoulême was refortified and restored to its status as the prime citadel of Aquitaine.

In 769, quite possibly at Saintes (located on a major Roman road, Saintes was an important site in this north-western part of Aquitaine), the capitulary Pippin had issued there early in 768 was reissued.[17]

Rosamond McKitterick has made a persuasive case for the genuineness of Charles's 'first capitulary', though she leaves open the possibility that the reissue was the work not of Charles but of Carloman.[18] That Charles was responsible seems to me much more plausible, given the points made above. Legislating was the clearest attribute of rulership. Evidence of Pippin's experience of it as a legislator survives from his time as mayor when, as *dux et princeps Francorum*, he issued the Capitulary of Soissons (2 March 744), and, more crucially, as king, when he issued four capitularies between 754 and 768.[19] Charles in his first capitulary (no. 19) used a lengthy title (for which there were to be parallels in the *Admonitio generalis* of 789 and a recently discovered capitulary of 798/9[20]): *gratia Dei rex regnique Francorum rector et devotus sanctae ecclesiase Defensor atque adiutor in omnibus*. My guess would be that Charles took with him a copy of his father's text, or alternatively, that locals had presented Charles with a copy of their own.[21]

In 768, after gathering a large number of Franks and the necessary equipment, Charles moved to the river Dordogne where he built a fort at Fronsac. From there he sent his *missi* (here meaning specially picked troops) to the Gascon leader, Lupus, with orders to bring Hunald and his wife to Fronsac. Lupus complied.[22] 'Having taken possession of Hunald, [the king] returned to Francia and christmased at the royal estate of Düren' (where Pippin had summoned a synod in 761), some 40km from Aachen.

Charles had done enough in Aquitaine to gain what can be termed 'control', allowing, that is, for limitations imposed by geography and poor communications.[23] According to Nibelung, the best contemporary source up to and including 769, Pippin had planned to divide Aquitaine between his sons. By 769, however, the plan had become a dead letter. The author of the early ninth-century version of the *ArF* asserted, twice-over within a couple of sentences, that 'the province of Aquitaine had fallen to the lot of the elder brother'. During the months between October 768 and May 769, Charles had decided to shove his brother out of the frame. Carloman is not documented again in Aquitaine. The confirmation of Pippin's capitulary in 769 was the work of Charles alone.[24] That confirmation was recalled by Charles himself in 789 in a capitulary addressed to *missi* (here meaning high-octane roving royal officials) in Aquitaine, when he asked for reports on what had been happening over 'these twenty years'.[25] There is, admittedly, no

other direct evidence of Charles's engagement with matters in Aquitaine during the next ten years. His grant of an immunity to St-Stephen,
Angers, which Bishop Mauriolus apparently received in person at Herstal in March 770, does indicate concerns with the border-zone of the
middle Loire valley.[26] The absence of evidence for any contact between
Charles and those who had accepted his rule in Aquitaine between 769
and 778 seems to signify local quiescence, the end of any further
stirring of a descendant of the ducal dynasty of Eudes and Hunald,
and, for Charles, an absence of trouble.

By this time, Charles and his brother had wrapped up some unfinished
ecclesiastical business. Pope Paul had died in 767. Stephen III, soon
after he became pontiff-elect (August 768), had sent Sergius, son of his
primicerius (chief adviser) Christopher, to Pippin and his sons with an
urgent request to restore order in Rome.[27] Control of the city had been
seized in a coup by a local warlord, Duke Toto of Nepi, who promptly
installed one of his brothers as pope with the name of Constantine.
By the time Sergius (he had been appointed papal treasurer) reached
Francia, Pippin had died. There is no record of the reaction of Pippin's
sons to news of the violence, appalling even to warlords trained north
of the Alps, that the military coup had unleashed in Rome. By August
768, a counter-coup had resulted in Constantine being deposed and
Stephen III's reinstatement. He immediately, once again, sent Sergius
as his envoy to Francia, with letters requesting that twelve bishops be
sent to a council in Rome. Charles and Carloman, keen to establish their
credentials as defenders of St Peter, and to carry out what would have
been among their father's last wishes, obliged. They sent, as requested,
twelve Frankish bishops to join thirty-eight Italian confrères at a council, tasked with 'restoring church order'. They ended their deliberations
with an endorsement of the veneration of icons, and then returned to
Francia.[28]

'It would have been in the new kings' interests to work together.'[29]
Given all that's known of intra-dynastic rivalry in this period, the
observation seems a shade anachronistic. Evidence of fraternal friction
is not hard to find.[30] Stephen III mentioned this explicitly, as did the
authors of both versions of the *ArF*, in different ways. In light of the
division-map of 768, the following can be considered Charles's bishops:
George of Amiens, Archbishop Lull of Mainz, Gislebert of Noyon,
Gaugen of Tours, Ermenbert of Worms, and Bernulf of Würzburg. And

these Carloman's: Archbishop Wilchar of Sens, Wulfram of Meaux, Tilpin of Reims, Archbishop Hermenar of Bourges, Erlolf of Langres, and Archbishop Ado of Lyons.[31] That the brother-kings each sent bishops says nothing about fraternal harmony. It could be read less as collaboration than as fierce competition for influence on the part of the kings and of their bishops too. The partition of 768 had meant that Carloman's share brought him a preponderance of archbishops. Each brother was determined to project himself as his father's successor, and to signal not just to his own faithful men, but to the pope and Italian confrères, the fidelity of his specially selected bishops.

II. CHARLES AND HIS BROTHER BOTH BECOME FATHERS

Charles's sights were reset between 769 and 771 because of changes in the configuration of the royal family. The first was that his wife Himiltrud gave birth to a son in 769. His parents gave him the name Pippin, clearly identifying him as the first-born in the next generation and Charles's likely successor.[32] The second change was that Carloman's wife Gerberga gave birth to a son in 770, whom the parents also named Pippin.[33] Fraternal rivalry could hardly have been more tellingly expressed. Not only did it put paid to any notion of concerted 'Frankish' protection for the papacy, or 'Frankish policy' in Italy: division between the kings also meant division between their followers.

III. CHARLES, HIS MOTHER AND THE DAUGHTER OF DESIDERIUS

A third change was that the grandmother of those two baby boys, the dowager queen Bertrada, so prominent in Nibelung's account of the last year of Pippin's life, resumed – or perhaps continued – a more active role in family politics. She had proven her skills as a queenly counsellor in 767–8. After Pippin's death, she had chosen to wear a widow's veil and to call herself a *deo devota* as a sign that she would never remarry. Widowhood could be a very significant phase in the life-cycle of a high-born woman, and Bertrada, now aged about forty, put herself forward as particularly well-qualified to act as a marriage-broker between Charles and a daughter of Desiderius of the Lombards.[34] Peace-making was a strongly gendered activity, and here Bertrada had shown form, taking care of her sick brother-in-law in 754, for instance, and hosting the Abbasid envoys in 767.

For both Charles and Carloman, Frankish 'protection' of the papacy posed huge logistical problems in practice. Absence in Italy raised risks of unrest at home, and for Charles there was the additional difficulty that his kingdom shared no frontier with Italy. In Rome itself, faction-fighting had become rife. Sergius, son of Christopher the *primicerius*, and pope-maker of Stephen III, had arrived in Francia shortly after Pippin's death and brought a first-hand but highly partisan account of events: Christopher with troops at his command fiercely resisted Lombard efforts, on the part of Desiderius and his agents, to remove him from power. The bishops who returned from Rome in the early summer of 769 brought eye-witness news of factional violence. With these conflicts Charles and Carloman aligned their rivalry from a distance: in Rome, Carloman's *missus* Dodo, 'with his Franks', which is to say, with a small army of Franks, became Carloman's proxy, while Desiderius, seizing a moment of opportunity in which Bertrada was only too glad to co-operate, became Charles's. If neither Charles nor Carloman made war in 770 or 771, that was not (or not only) because they considered the situation too risky;[35] still less because they shared a common goal. It was because they were running a proxy war in Rome.[36]

Desiderius was already the father of an adult son, Adelchis, and the father-in-law of two princes. Inspired, perhaps, by the sixth-century Italian model of Theoderic, king of the Ostrogoths, and his carefully constructed policy of dynastic marriages (as well as his martial prowess), Desiderius now aimed to acquire not just another son-in-law but a royal one, in the shape of Charles.[37] Like Theoderic, and also like his own immediate predecessors as Lombard kings, Desiderius saw potential benefits in good relations with the pope. With this multi-layered alliance constructed, Desiderius could have foreseen a quasi-imperial role for himself in the West as challenger to Byzantium. Charles, though, as Desiderius well knew, was central to the plan's success. This required a go-between; and Bertrada fitted the part perfectly.[38] As well as being genuinely committed to peace-making for religious reasons, she had a clear-eyed view, in the best traditions of Frankish noble matrons, of what made an advantageous marriage. For Bertrada, given the prospect of advantages that eclipsed any a Frankish noblewoman could offer, the chance to engineer Charles's marriage to Desiderius's daughter seemed irresistible. Charles's alliance not just to a mighty father-in-law but to three princely brothers-in law – Adelchis, Tassilo of Bavaria, husband of Liutperga, and Arichis of Benevento, husband of Adelperga – would leave Carloman outside a charmed circle.

Bertrada had apparently chosen to reside with Charles after her husband's death.[39] That she had a special fondness for her first-born is an inference emerging strongly in some retrospective, but near-contemporary, evidence, recorded shortly after Carloman's death, in a letter written to Charles by the Anglo-Saxon cleric Cathwulf, 'your humble servant' (*vester servulus*) in 774 or 775.[40] Cathwulf presented a list of blessings bestowed by the Almighty on Charles:[41]

> First: you were conceived from the dignity of the king and queen and in addition through their prayers, they who especially prayed God [for you] and most of all your mother, as it therefore pleased God, but you were born [and procreated] by God. O my king, consider carefully these words.
>
> Second, that you are the first-born. And receive this with God's blessing, according to Scripture: 'Every first-born [*primogenitus*] because he opens the womb is called holy to God.' [Exod. 13:2, and Luke 2:23]
>
> Third, that God preserved you in all respects from the plots of your brother, as it is spoken concerning Jacob and Esau [Gen. 25:19–35].[42]
>
> Fourth, that you shared the kingdom of the Franks with your brother.
>
> Fifth, not the least sign of your being blessed was that God transferred him [your brother] from this kingdom to another one, and exalted you to be above the whole kingdom, without any bloodshed.

To my mind, the person most likely to have given Cathwulf information about the parental, and especially the maternal, prayers that ensured Charles's conception, and his coming into the world 'as *primogenitus* . . . called holy to God' (points 1 and 2) was Bertrada.[43] (The birth of this royal child was of great public as well as private concern.) Point 3 says that 'God preserved you from the plots of your brother', citing the Scriptural analogy of Jacob and Esau; Point 4 adds, as further evidence of Charles's goodness, that he shared his kingdom with his brother; and Point 5 says, with perfect clarity and specificity, that

God transferred Carloman from this world to another kingdom (i.e. Heaven), thereby bloodlessly reinstating a single Frankish kingdom.[44] It would be hard to imagine a more frank account of consistent fraternal rivalry, even if Cathwulf wrote when it had become perfectly safe to write, and at a moment – the dedication of Abbot Fulrad's new basilica at St-Denis – when Charles was especially keen to highlight his association with the saint. After 769, thanks to divine intervention on 4 December 771 – the date of Carloman's death – the fraternal rivalry never quite flared into open conflict in Francia.[45] By the time Cathwulf wrote this letter, the issue of Carloman was no longer politically 'live', any more than was that of Carloman's sons. Cathwulf could be frank about the intensity of earlier fraternal rivalry, though he tip-toed round the possibility of uncle–nephew rivalry that menaced the next generation.

Meanwhile, vis-à-vis her second son, Bertrada combined shrewdness with tact and even some affection. In 770, en route for Italy, she visited Carloman at the fortress of Seltz, in Alsace.[46] Her itinerary must have been planned with Charles's approval for Seltz was in his kingdom, though near the border with Carloman's.[47] In the view of the author of the *ArF* reviser, writing some forty-odd years after the event, Bertrada was there *pacis cau*sa, 'for the sake of peace'.[48] From Seltz she moved east to Bavaria to visit Duke Tassilo, Charles's cousin and now his prospective brother-in-law too, before pressing on southwards.[49] The journey, however made, was long, though navigating some of the way down the Danube could have reduced the time somewhat. Perhaps Tassilo managed the staging of the encounter between himself and Bertrada to coincide with a large synod at Dingolfing, some 50km south-east of Regensburg, preparing the way for future co-operation.[50] Thence she continued south across the Alps to the Po valley, and on to Rome.

The course of the marriage-plan did not run smooth. It had presupposed papal support, but Stephen III, when he first heard rumours of it some time before Bertrada arrived in Rome, but not knowing yet which of the kings was to be the bridegroom, fired off to Charles and Carloman a letter of violent xenophobia laced with misogyny.[51] There was Scriptural authority for aversion to marrying out of one's *gens* (people), and the contemporary biographers of Stephen III's predecessors Paul and Stephen II, and, more directly still, in papal letters to the Frankish court, intermittently expressed strong hostility first to King Aistulf and then to Desiderius.[52] Iconoclasm and heresy were important elements here. A literalist reading of the Second Commandment could become a call to iconoclasm as promoted by the Byzantine Emperor Leo III (717–41). From the point of view of Rome it was necessary to insist on iconoclasm's heretical nature. (Had not the revered Pope Gregory the Great said that 'what writing presents to readers, a picture presents to the unlearned who behold, since in it even the ignorant see what they ought to follow, in it the illiterate read'?[53]) Papal Lives and letters alike often combined assertiveness with an acute sense of vulnerability. No letter can rival Stephen III's to Charles and Carloman in 770, though, in its extreme virulence towards the Lombards. 'It was *the* example of how [Lombard] ethnicity could be instrumentalised [by a panicky pope]':[54]

That Old Enemy [the Devil] strives to steal away the minds of the faithful through the weakness of their nature, and hence it comes about that what happened long ago to the first man who was placed in Paradise could be persuaded by the pestiferous blandishments of the weak nature of a woman to disobey the divine command, and thus stealthily brought the destruction of fearful death to the human race. And therefore, most excellent sons, great kings, you need to be all the more careful to resist the Old Enemy's savage efforts to catch anyone in the net of his arguments, the more we see him attack the hearts of the faithful in order to deceive them by his frequent snares.[55]

It has been brought to our notice – and we say this, be assured, with great grief of heart – that Desiderius, king of the Lombards, is understood to be urging your excellence that his daughter should be joined in wedlock to one of your brotherhood. And if such be the case, assuredly, this is particularly the Devil's contrivance and seen to be not so much the union of matrimony as a cohabitation of most wicked artifice, in as much as we know that many people, as the history of divine scripture teaches us, have strayed from God's commandments and through an unrighteous coupling with a foreign race fallen headlong into a great crime. For, most excellent sons, great kings, what sort of madness (*desipientia*), which is the least it can be called, is this that your illustrious people of the Franks, which shine with such splendour and high nobility, should be defiled – may this not happen! – by the perfidious and most foully stinking people of the

Lombards (*perfidae ac foetentissimae Langobardorum genti polluatur*), one in no way to be reckoned among the number of the peoples (*gentes*), one from which the stock of lepers (*leprosorum genus*) is known for certain to have sprung! Truly no-one of sound mind could even suspect that kings of such high renown might become involved in such detestable and abominable contamination, 'for what has light in common with darkness? What has the faithful to share with the unfaithful?' [2 Cor. 6: 14–15].

Furthermore, most gentle and most gracious God-instituted kings, you are already, by His will and decision, and by your father's order, joined in lawful marriage, having accepted, as illustrious and most noble kings, wives of great beauty from the same fatherland as yourselves, namely from that same most noble people of the Franks. On the one hand, it behoves you to be bound to love them; on the other, you most certainly are not permitted to cast them aside, to marry other wives or to mix in the consanguinity of a foreign race.

Moreover, there is none of your forebears – not your grandfather, nor your great-grandfather, nor your father – who took a wife from another kingdom or a foreign race, or who has seen fit to contaminate yourself or to deign to mingle with the horrible people of the Lombards – may God forbid! – as you are now being urged to pollute yourselves with that same frightful people. No man who took a wife from a foreign people ever remained unharmed by that. Remember, I beg you, how many and what sort of mighty men they were who abandoned the commands of God through marriages with foreign women, and then following the will of those foreign women fell into terrible excesses and suffered huge dangers. For it is wicked even to allow the thought to enter your hearts to take other wives beyond those you have and whom you certainly took first. It is forbidden for you to commit such a sin, you who hold to the law of God and reproach other men for doing such things. These are what pagan peoples do, but far be it from you to do likewise, you who are thoroughly Christian and 'a holy people and a royal priesthood' [1 Peter 2:9]. Remember, and consider, that you have been anointed with holy oil through the hands of the vicar of St Peter and sanctified by heavenly blessing.

The extreme language of Pope Stephen's letter suggests extreme anxiety, on the pope's part as well as that of his chief adviser Christopher, who was especially hostile to Desiderius. All the main players were under great pressure and their options were limited. At this point, the Lombard king was urging not just a marriage between his daughter and Charles, but also the acceptance of the Lombard alliance as a package, including his sons-in-law Tassilo and Arichis. Bertrada's visits to Bavaria and, via Lombardy, to Rome, sealed the deal and, as Stephen III now switched to a Lombard alliance, would soon seal Christopher's fate. In the *Codex Carolinus*, the first sign of that switch was a letter to Carloman, sent in the summer of 770.[56] The pope had not risked written details, but said he had given a detailed response orally, via Carloman's *missi* Abbot Berald and the lay magnate Audbert.[57] He also begged to baptize the infant son of Carloman and his queen and thus renew the relationship of compaternity between a pope as successor to St Peter and a Frankish king.

'In the summer of 770' is an unfortunately imprecise date, but it is the best scholars can suggest for a series of extraordinary events. They were recorded under the year 770 in three sets of more or less contemporary annals with a common source: 'Bertrada was in Lombardy at a formal assembly to negotiate with Desiderius, and a number of cities were returned to St Peter, and Bertrada took Desiderius's daughter back to Francia.'[58] Bertrada's mission was reported briefly in the *ArF* some twenty years after the event: 'The lady queen Bertrada journeyed to Italy . . .' and, with more detail of what Bertrada did at Seltz and in Rome, in the revised *ArF*, some forty years after the event:

> Bertrada, the kings' mother, after discussions at Seltz with her younger son Carloman, in the cause of peace, went to Italy. And when she had concluded the business which was the purpose of her journey and had worshipped at the thresholds of the holy apostles in Rome, she returned to Gaul, to her sons.[59]

The near-contemporary annals have the gist of the story. By the time the next extant letter of Stephen to Bertrada and Charles was written, later in 770, or early in 771 (the appearance of the queen-mother's name *before* her son's could signify her recently established rapport with the pope, as well as respect for her religious status), Bertrada was safely home in Francia, with Charles's new bride.[60] Mission accomplished. In this letter, Stephen had nothing to say about Desiderius's daughter. He thanked Bertrada and Charles profusely for sending their *missus* Hitherius with other *missi* (here implying a troop of armed men) to Benevento to arrange, presumably with Duke Arichis, now Charles's brother-in-law, for the acknowledging of St Peter's rights to properties in the duchy. Stephen ended by suggesting that Hitherius deserved huge thanks from Bertrada and Charles for his good work. The Lombard marriage-plan seemed to be working after all. Stephen's next and final letter in the dossier as it survives, also addressed to Bertrada and Charles, told them of a plot to kill him hatched by Christopher and his son, with the collusion of Carloman's *missus* Dodo 'and his Franks and certain most wicked accomplices'. Stephen 'afflicted with great sorrow' described the killing 'against our will and intention' of Christopher and Sergius by a Roman mob, and imagined the regret that Carloman would feel over Dodo's conduct. The pope ended with a paean of praise for Desiderius. They had now made an agreement whereby St Peter would recover his rights.[61]

The years 770–71 are exceptionally poorly documented, and this could well signify a cover-up. It was Einhard, writing nearly sixty years after these events, who reported that the marriage of Desiderius's daughter to Charles 'for reasons uncertain, lasted barely a year, and then he repudiated her';[62] and it was Einhard who then, by way of afterthought, said that Charles had a son by a concubine (he did not name her, nor did he say that she was in fact Charles's first partner), and that the son's name was Pippin, who 'though he had a handsome face, was a hunchback'.[63] The contemporary annalists said nothing about the fates of Charles's first two wives. They did, however, put it beyond question that the second wife was a daughter of Desiderius. Oscar Wilde wrote about another kind of family context, 'To lose one parent . . . may be regarded as a misfortune; to lose both looks like carelessness.'[64] Something similar could be said of wives. Himiltrud is absent from the sources from 771 to 792, when her son Pippin rebelled against his father and brothers (a story to be told later in this book), after having been consigned to the great convent of Nivelles – not necessarily such an uncomfortable fate for a royal cast-off – for just over twenty years.[65] Her disappearance from public life was the absolute prerequisite for Charles's Lombard marriage. Unfortunately for the bride, that is, Charles's second wife, her husband's priorities very soon changed and she too was repudiated.

Whatever Church law had come to prescribe over the centuries, marriage for elite men was in practice something that could be unilaterally ended, and the wife disposed of.[66] Changing political imperatives trumped any moral ones. In these respects, Charles in effect did what it suited him to do. There is too little evidence of marital practices in this time and place to know whether Charles's conduct was quite common or highly unusual. Heinrich Fichtenau observed that Charles had an unusually strong sex-drive.[67] More recent scholars have been more coy. As far as the evidence goes, no other early medieval king ever repudiated one wife after another in quick succession within hardly more than a year. Perhaps Charles was lucky to get away with it. After all, even if it was possible to 'lose' a wife who, like Himiltrud, was a noblewoman 'of the same [Frankish] people', Charles's repudiation of a great king's daughter, with inevitable damage to her and her family's honour, was a high-risk move. Why did he make it?

The first answer lies in the unexpected death of Carloman, at the age of twenty, on 4 December 771 at his favoured residence of Samoussy, whence his body was swiftly taken to Reims for burial in a fine sarcophagus.[68] Charles, as at previous crucial moments, moved fast. There is no way of knowing exactly when and where he got the news of his brother's death, and possibly, at the same time, information that the funeral was to be (or had been) managed by the bishop of Reims, and that Carloman on his deathbed had left six grants to Reims, the largest of them the estate of Neuilly.[69] Charles's known stopping-place before 4 December was Longlier, where he issued a judgment on 3 November.[70] Within days of Carloman's death and burial, Charles moved to Corbeny, on the border between his kingdom and Carloman's.[71] The author of the *ArF* reported:

> The lord king Charles came to the *villa* of Corbeny [just a few km north of where the Roman road from Reims to St-Quentin crosses the river Aisne], as did also Archbishop Wilchar of Sens and Abbot Fulrad of St-Denis, with other bishops and priests and counts Warin and Adalhard and other *primates*: these were Carloman's men. But Carloman's wife with some few Franks went to Italy. And the illustrious King Charles celebrated the lord's birthday at the *villa* called Attigny [previously in Carloman's kingdom].[72]

The later revised *ArF* gave more details:

> Intent on taking over the kingdom in its entirety, the king came to the villa of Corbeny, where he received those who came to him – Wilchar

bishop of Sitten [an error for Sens], the priest Fulrad, and many other
bishops as well as his brother's counts and great men, among whom the
most outstanding were Warin and Adalhard. Carloman's wife and sons
set out for Italy with a group of great men. But the king put up patiently
with their setting out for Italy, on the grounds that that was quite
pointless.[73]

The only other annalist to elaborate was the Chelles author of the
AMP, who followed up the mention of 'Warin and Adalhard and others of Carloman's leading men' with an addition:

> And they anointed the most glorious king Charles as their lord over them
> and he felicitously obtained monarchy (*monarchia*) over the whole king-
> dom of the Franks. But Gerberga, Carloman's wife, with her two little
> sons and a few leading men from the side of her husband Carloman, made
> for Italy and reached Desiderius, king of the Lombards.[74]

This is the only author to name Gerberga, or to mention an anointing of
Charles in 771 (it's possible that Wilchar of Sens, keen to show his
elevated archiepiscopal status, masterminded, or negotiated, Charles's
anointing here).[75] The author is also alone in using the term *monarchia*.[76] All these might be considered predictable Frankish themes. More
striking, and again unique to this author, is the explicit statement that
Gerberga and her sons and supporters 'reached Desiderius': a Frankish
theme with a vengeance. There were experienced Frankish aristocrats
such as Autchar, now in exile from the Frankish court, who were well-
versed in Italian politics. For Charles, the existence of his nephews at
the court of Desiderius was to be a matter of acute and persistent concern over the next two years and more. Desiderius's daughter compounded the problem, in so far as it seems extremely likely (though no
author attests this) that her repudiation entailed being sent back to the
royal palace at Pavia in what contemporaries could only have understood as the most blatant of insults to her and her family's honour: 'a
demonstrative act' indeed.[77] Insult and injury were now on show at
Pavia, but so at the same time was the abiding protective power of Lombard monarchy.

Einhard, though not very forthcoming as to why this second repudiation occurred, linked Charles's decision with Bertrada's departure
from public life. 'The divorce of Desiderius's daughter, whom Charles

had married at his mother's suggestion,' was, Einhard said, 'the only thing that ever caused discord between the king and his mother.' Einhard then assured readers that Bertrada grew old at her son's court 'in great honour' and, the failed marriage-project apart, 'was held in the utmost reverence'; and that 'she lived to see three grandsons and three grand-daughters in her son's house'.[78] But further pursuit of the question of Charles's motive(s) for rejecting his Lombard wife takes the story on into 772.

IV. CHARLES, HILDEGARD AND THE SAXON CONNECTION

Quite simply, Charles had hit on the idea of remarrying as soon as possible after repudiating his Lombard wife and dispatching her home to Pavia. And he had decided on a new bride: Hildegard, 'a girl of the most noble family of the Swabians [a synonym for Alamans]'. It took a noble to appreciate the virtues of noble lineages. In this case, the noble was Thegan, who wrote in 836-7 his *Deeds of the Emperor Louis* (Charles's son and heir). The scholar Walahfrid, also writing in the 830s, described Thegan as 'a Frank by birth, noble and sharp of mind, one who could not keep silent about what caused him grief: the dishonourableness of persons of low birth (*indignitas vilium personarum*)'. Thegan, after providing in chapter 1 a genealogy from St Arnulf to Charles, in chapter 2 provided a genealogy for Hildegard: 'The emperor [Charles] married a young woman of the most noble people of the Swabians, named Hildegard, who came from the kindred of Gotefrid, duke of the Alamans. He fathered Huoching, who fathered Nebi, who fathered Imma, who gave birth to Hildegard, the most blessed queen.'[79]

That neither Thegan nor Einhard mentioned Hildegard's father or his lineage points to her mother Imma's superior rank: she was, after all, directly descended from Duke Gottfried (*c.*679–*c.*735) and the Alamannic ducal line. Charters supply ample evidence that Hildegard's father was Count Gerold, a Frankish noble with extensive properties in areas of the Middle Rhine region that Carloman had ruled. Gerold and Imma's marriage was a classic case of the 'associations [made] between different peoples by affinities' of which Charles later wrote approvingly.[80] This particular alliance was calculated to integrate the Alamans into the Frankish realm, thereby healing the still-raw memory of the Alaman defeat at Cannstatt.[81] The offspring of this marriage, and especially Hildegard, born (probably) in 757, little over a decade after the battle, embodied reconciliation. After Charles married Hildegard early in 772, her parents gave estates to the great abbey of Lorsch in the Middle Rhine region, over which Charles later that year assumed the office of protector.[82] As for Charles's own calculations: now that his own brother was gone, Charles's new father-in-law was the obvious great man to fill Carloman's place in the political geography of the new 'monarchy'. Gerold could operate positively as a successor to Carloman, filling the informal but crucial role of a regional governor east of the Rhine without posing any risk that he might try to rival Charles.[83] Hildegard, a decade younger than her husband, seems to have slipped smoothly into *her* crucial role, of spouse and child-bearer, helpmeet and ally, without receiving much mention in annalistic despatches.

Charles seized another opportunity to entrench his supporters, and with them his own power, in lands that had only three months before belonged to Carloman's kingdom. The occasion was a legal judgment in a dispute between great men: Abbot Guntland of Lorsch and Heimrich, the son of Lorsch's founders. The abbot claimed that his brother, Bishop Chrodegang of Metz, had been given Lorsch by Heimrich's mother and grandfather. The case was heard before Charles and a panel of four counts and five *vassi* (here meaning men of rank performing service as public officials). Heimrich lost, and Guntland's claim to Lorsch was upheld.[84]

It was in (and after) 772 that Saxony began to feature in Frankish annals more prominently than ever before. Earlier Frankish sources too had had things to say about Saxony, but they said different things dating from very different times, with such long silences between scarce informative moments that anything like a story is hard to construct. After 772, though gaps remain, there is a more or less consistent interest in Saxony, especially in the *ArF*, until 785, and from 791 until 804. In the rest of this chapter, I first consider what can be known about Saxons and Saxony before 772, and how this can be compared with what is known about Francia and the Franks.[85] A recent scholar's verdict has been categorical: 'Saxon society and culture corresponded in no way to those of the Franks, and it was therefore difficult for the Franks to get a handle on this enemy.'[86]

That verdict can be justified up to a point, but it needs, I think, some serious qualification. Just as late Roman authors wrote about a people beyond the imperial frontiers called *Franci*, so writers before, during and after Charles's time endowed the Franks with a 'distinctive ethnicity', and a religiously authorized identity as a New Israel.[87] Modern scholars have homogenized 'the' Franks by supplying translations of texts by and about *Franci* with a definite article. Even after all that effort, bursting seams and fraying edges are not hard to spot in the day-to-day Frankish world. 'The' Saxons received a similar treatment, perhaps because the Franks wanted to depict them as having a strong sense of ethnic identity. In fact *Saxones* never constituted a distinctive or homogenous whole: there were different leaders of different subgroups, often living far from each other and without the regular political contacts that a mid-ninth-century Saxon source alleges, for instance, an annual pan-Saxon assembly at Marklo.[88] The archaeological evidence of pottery and military hardware shows a material culture very similar to that of the Franks.[89] It's possible to acknowledge this lack of Saxon homogeneity, and at the same time stress the similarity of the Saxons' material culture to that of the Franks. One event purportedly belonging to 775 but recorded in the latter years of Charles's reign reveals the dimensions of that similarity:

> The part of the army which [Charles] had left on the Weser, and which had pitched camp in the place called Lübbecke, acted incautiously (*incaute* – a strongly pejorative word in the Latin of this period) and was tricked and deceived by a ruse of some Saxons. For when Frankish foragers were coming back into their camp at about 3 p.m., those Saxons intermingled themselves with them as if they were their comrades (*socii*) and so got into the Franks' encampment. They fell upon those who were sleeping or half-asleep, and are said to have wreaked no little carnage on a great number of incautious men. But those who were awake manfully resisted the attackers and drove them back from the camp, and then they departed, after both groups were in such bad shape that they reached an agreement (*pactus*).[90]

This cautionary tale implies that Franks and Saxons looked so much like each other – *quasi socii* – as to be indistinguishable; and, further, that Franks and Saxons were ready to cut their losses by a negotiated stand-off.

Scholars have long claimed, though, that there was one respect in which Saxons differed not just from Franks but from all the *exterae gentes* (external peoples) whom Franks encountered, and that was their religion. On this line of argument, it was *only* (some) Saxons whom (some) Franks regarded as extremely pagan (*paganissimi*) in the time of Charles Martel.[91] In 772, there was no sign, as yet, that Charles considered the Saxons as 'natural subjects' who had to be forcibly converted.[92] Later in Charles's reign, neither pagan West Slavs like Wends, or Abodrites ('our Slavs'), nor pagan Avars, were subjected to this.[93] In texts, Frankish authors constructed Saxons as the 'Other' in ways that could not have been envisaged in 772.

Saxons had been recorded in sixth- and seventh-century Frankish histories, and that Saxon presence *then*, in earlier texts that were still read and copied, and in old songs and stories that were still sung and told in Charles's time, helps explain Charles's own focus on Saxony *now*, in 772.[94] Much about Saxony and Saxons will never be known. Theirs was not a literate culture, and so they left no records. What can be known historically comes from Frankish and Anglo-Saxon sources, largely from chronicles and saints' Lives. There is archaeological and place-name evidence, but mostly from the period before the mid-eighth century, and/or hard to date. With the *Chronicle of Fredegar* comes some usable evidence.[95] In 633/4,

> [the Merovingian king] Dagobert got news that the Wends were attacking the Thuringians [who belonged to Dagobert's realm]. Saxon envoys came to Dagobert requesting that he waive the tributes which they paid to support the king's household. They promised to fight the Wends at their own expense and promised to guard the Franks' frontier from their own side. After taking the Neustrians' counsel, the king agreed. The Saxons who had come with their requests, confirmed with oaths sworn on their weapons, as was their custom, what had been agreed on behalf of all the Saxons. But the promise was of little effect. The Saxons had the tribute which they had been accustomed to pay remitted on the king's command. They had been used to paying 500 cows per year as tax since the time of Chlothar I [511–61], and Dagobert abolished this.[96]

Matthias Springer points out that Saxon envoys are not likely to have spoken for 'all the Saxons', because 'in reality, it was always groups or sections of Saxons who regarded themselves as bound by agreement'.[97]

A second story about Saxons, this time involving not legal agreements but religion, and more specifically conversion to Christianity, comes much closer to Charles. The date is 744 and the protagonist is the mayor of the palace Carloman, older brother of Pippin (who had yet to become a father):

> When three years had elapsed, there was a Saxon rebellion, and Carloman again burst with his army into the Saxon border-zone adjoining his territory. There he took captive some of the inhabitants who seemed to be living on the borders of his realm, successfully took over part of the territory without a decisive military encounter, and after most of them were baptised, thanks to Christ's leadership, they were blessed by the sacrament.[98]

A third event is an episode that occurred in the sequel to Pippin's seizing of power in 751. The years 751 and 752 are a blank in both the *ArF* and the revised version; and it is tempting to guess that the explanation lies in the suppression of the bad news of unrest arising from the coup, partly because Pippin's half-brother Grifo was still causing the king difficulties (he had fled to Saxony, then Bavaria, then Gascony and finally to what are now the Swiss Alps, where he was killed late in 753).[99] But when the annalistic record was resumed, Saxony reappeared: 'King Pippin went on campaign into Saxony, and Bishop Hildegar was killed by Saxons in a fortress called Iburg; yet King Pippin emerged as victor, and he reached as far as the place called Rehme.'[100] Assuming that the post-coup unrest was quelled by 753, it looks as if Pippin took the first chance he could to launch a campaign into Saxony. He got impressively far north and east, to the Weser; and the *ArF* author thought the killing of Hildegar, bishop of Cologne, by Saxons in one of their fortresses was an event to publicize.

These stories provide spy-holes into Frankish views of Saxons formed before – sometimes long before – Charles was born, thus giving a sense of the context in which Charles learned about Saxons in the early years of his reign. In the rest of this chapter, and sticking close to Charles, I will attempt to reconstruct the events of 772 as forming a pattern.

Charles's priority was the reproduction of his branch of the family. He spent Easter at Herstal (29 March). His new marriage took place before 30 April.[101] Perhaps the date chosen was Easter Day itself. The couple and their new court now moved to the palace of Thionville for perhaps two months, making the most of palace amenities which would help ensure Hildegard's comfort and well-being. By early July Charles was at Brumath, just 17km north of Strasbourg in Alsace; thence, by road or river, the army followed the Rhine down to the episcopal *civitas* of Worms, where he held an assembly of laymen and clergy that provided political counsel as well as religious reassurance. When it became feasible to campaign in Saxony, which Pippin had made his first target after he had secured power, Charles again took the chance to follow in his father's footsteps.

There was, of course, a wider context. Encounters between Franks and Saxons were certainly not new in the two centuries before Charles's reign, but they were very infrequent. Chronicles and annals, as just noted, preserved memories; authors were plunderers of word-hoards; texts came to light in other texts. According to Einhard,

> There were incidents that could disturb the peace [between Franks and Saxons] on a daily basis, for our boundaries almost always touched theirs in flat, open country . . . Killings, thefts and fires never stopped happening in these regions. Such things made Franks get so irritated that they would no longer engage in tit-for-tat raids, but they decided to undertake a full-scale war. That war was waged against them with huge hatred on both sides, and it went on for thirty years without a break, but Saxon losses were greater than Frankish ones.[102]

Einhard probably exaggerated the border-raids. In the campaigning season of 772 military moves began in earnest when Charles and his forces left Worms. Perhaps they proceeded down the Rhine to a convenient affluent (the river Ruhr or the river Lippe) within striking distance of the Saxon ring-fort of the Eresburg, or going overland by the *Hellweg*, the great military road before and especially during Charles's reign.[103]

'Charles, after devastating the surrounding territory with fire and sword and depopulating it, captured the Eresburg, and reached the Ermensul, and destroyed that shrine, and took away all the gold and silver he found there.'[104] Though other annals mention the destruction of the 'shrine', or 'idol', only the *ArF* specifically says that Charles removed all the gold and silver. Charles and his men did not stumble by chance on the hoard at the Ermensul. Plunder was indeed the stuff that kept the political system working by carefully calibrated infusion and diffusion.[105] As if to underscore the divinely approved outcome of what was in effect a raid, the *ArF* author inserted a biblically authorized miracle. Suddenly, after a severe drought, a dramatic mid-day downpour amazed the snoozing troops.[106] Then Charles pressed on, again in his father's footsteps, 'all the way to the Weser [where] he arranged an assembly involving Saxons and Franks, and he received twelve hostages before returning to Francia'. Such formal arrangements showed similar customs and procedures operating between parties already quite familiar with them.

The 772 attack was something new, though. The destruction of the sacred shrine, and the scale of the loot the Franks carried off, signalled a step-change: from living with frontier irritants to prosecuting a fiercer war at a distance. Charles's thinking was strategic. The distribution of the plunder would cement old loyalties and win new ones. It would make possible a different war: a war against the large and well-led army of a rich Lombard kingdom with fortified cities that made Saxon forts look puny, and against a Lombard king who was holding Carolingian princes in an Italian tower, and controlling the alpine passes that led directly down into Italy. Charles now had the resources in men and materiel to put paid to conflict between rival Carolingians – that is, between him and his young nephews and their supporters. Intra-familial conflict was a much more dangerous Achilles heel than any frontier dispute. If Hildegard had been impressed by her husband's palace amenities, then Charles's new father-in-law, Gerold (I) and perhaps also his new brothers-in-law, Gerold (II) and Udalrich, were now, in July and August 772, no less impressed by his ability to supply a quick fix of plunder.[107]

More interests were involved than just those of the new in-laws. An old in-law, Tassilo, whose mother, Charles's aunt Hiltrud, had occasioned her share of family scandal, could have felt nothing but dishonour-by-association when his wife Liutperga learned of her sister's repudiation. Charles's new wife, as a member of the sprawling Agilolfing family, was as high-born as Tassilo, and there were complicated kin-relationships between Agilolfing branches. From the *Life* of Abbot Sturm of Fulda, a text written post-814, some historians have spun a story of the holy man engineering a rapprochement between the ex-brothers-in-law.[108] In this case, as often, the chief concern of the author of a saint's life was to give a puff to the saint. A better reason for thinking that Tassilo preferred to swallow the insult is that he had other priorities of his own in 772. One was to reinforce his existing ties to Desiderius by taking his son Theodo to Rome to be baptized by the pope at Whitsun (19 May), thus establishing a relationship of *compaternitas* similar to that of earlier popes with Frankish rulers. Then, while Charles was busy defeating Saxons, Tassilo 'overcame the Carantanians (later known as Carinthians)', a Slavic people on Bavaria's south-eastern frontier. This victory was recorded in annals written at Regensburg and at Salzburg.[109] In Frankish annals, competition between Tassilo and Charles continued to be recorded in a subdued hum: in fact relations between these cousins remained a major theme in Charles's life-story through to the mid-790s, ending only in the political extinction and monastic confinement of Tassilo and his family in 794.

Authors of Bavarian annals noted another change in 772: the succession of Hadrian as pope (on 9 February). Hadrian, from a noble Roman family, had been brought up in the papal court and had become a seasoned politician.[110] Like Charles, he was capable of responding fast to new circumstances when convinced this was necessary; his first political acts as pope were to recall important exiles – clerical and military – and to free captives of similar rank. Desiderius too was a fast responder. He immediately sent *missi* to the new man on the papal throne with a message of friendship, to which Hadrian replied equivocally that he too was keen on peace, but could not trust the Lombard king. The pope's instincts were sound, only now they inclined him to delaying tactics: Desiderius had reneged on every promise he'd made about the return of cities (i.e. territories) to papal control, especially in the case of Ravenna whose archbishop sent *missi* to Rome where they beseeched Hadrian 'in floods of tears to try to recover the cities or it would be impossible for them to live'.[111] Within a few sentences, the author of Hadrian's *Life* revealed the truth:

> The wife and sons of the late Carloman king of the Franks, together with Autchar, had taken refuge with Desiderius . . . who was trying hard to make good his contention that the sons of Carloman should assume the kingship of the Franks [and] . . . was trying to entice the pope to come to see him, hoping to stir dissensions in the kingdom of the Franks. [112]

Hadrian, now in temporizing mode, temporized. He sent envoys to Ravenna and to Constantinople, and then a whole series of envoys to

Desiderius 'beseeching him to come to his senses (etc.)'. Finally he sent envoys to Charles at Thionville, where Charles and Hildegard were spending winter (after having celebrated Christmas at Herstal) and awaiting the birth of their baby.[113]

V. CHARLES AND HILDEGARD GET THE POPE'S MESSAGE

Everyone now knew, if they had not yet guessed, that Desiderius intended to realize the maximum dynastic capital embodied in the princes in the tower. Given the speed rumour travelled and the efficiency of communications, Charles and Hildegard, wintering at the palace of Thionville, could not have been surprised to hear that a *missus* named Peter had arrived from Hadrian. Peter had had to travel by sea via Marseilles, then by land north to Francia because Desiderius had ordered the closure of roads and passes in Lombardy. Before Peter uttered a word, and partly because papal messages were quite predictable, Charles and Hildegard and the court knew what his message would be:

> He came to urge the glorious king and the Franks, for the service of God and the rights of St Peter and the relief of the church, against King Desiderius and the Lombards. Charles took counsel with the Franks, and . . . it was decided that what Hadrian's *missus* requested should be done.[114]

Charles's next move was south-eastwards, to Geneva. More *missi* were sent out to summon a large army to assemble there. From Geneva Charles's route to Lombardy would cross the Mont Cenis. Soon Charles would be following in his parent's footsteps again, this time Bertrada's. But her travelling days were over. Hildegard's were soon to begin, and she would follow her husband to Italy.

5
Charles in Italy

I. SOURCES AND SILENCES

This chapter is about Charles's first journey to Italy, its purpose and its outcome, which I'll argue was not planned before, but evolved while he was en route for Pavia. It was not until the siege of Pavia was well under way that a series of largely unforeseen events led to the crystallizing of Charles's decision to seize the Lombard kingdom. Before I present my argument, I'll first revisit some source problems and, quite briefly, present some rethinking about the campaign's geographical contexts, for Charles's quick grasp of the landscape was a prerequisite to military success.

In the previous chapter, I noted that these years are poorly documented. Gaps in the archive are sometimes accidental: worms attack parchment; leaky roofs result in water-damage. The *Codex Carolinus*, as will be obvious by now, is a key source for the period 739–91.[1] It contains no letters written between 771 and late 774. In modern times, archivists in the pay of governments 'weed' the records, that is, withhold from the public for extended periods of time, or actually destroy, documents considered especially 'sensitive'. In 791, when Charles ordered the *Codex Carolinus* to be compiled, there could have been reasons to weed the papal letters received at his court in the preceding twenty years. The weeding process might indeed have begun before 791. My suggestion is that Charles masterminded a cover-up for this period, 771–4. According to Einhard, Carloman's widow 'for no reason at all, spurned her husband's brother, and placed herself and her children under the protection of Desiderius'.[2] Einhard was writing in 829, that is, nearly sixty years after the event. In his *Life* of Charles were layers

The Great St Bernard pass.

of elision and innuendo, and (to borrow 2017's phrase *du jour*) 'alternative facts'. Later in this chapter, I revisit those princes in the tower.

Charles's charters offer a considerable compensation for gaps in
other sources. They constitute particularly important sources for these
early years, for, as the table below shows, they are more plentiful than
they were to become later in the reign.[3] Their distribution is uneven in
several ways, some accidental, some for which explanations can be suggested. Because in each charter the standard procedure of the royal
notaries was to note place, as well as date, of issue, there is evidence for
Charles's itinerary to supplement and cross-check the *ArF*'s year-by-
year mentions of where the king spent Christmas and Easter.[4] Thirty-
three of Charles's 164 extant charters dated from the years between
769 and 774, and fifteen of those were issued either in Neustria or for
Neustrian recipients.[5] Later in Charles's reign there was to be a marked
reduction in the proportion of charters issued in Neustria or for Neustrians, as compared with those issued in or for other parts of Charles's
much-extended realm, especially east of the Rhine. In the 770s, while
the distribution of charters varied greatly, the trend was for an increase
in both overall numbers and the Neustrian element therein.

Year	Charters per year	Neustrian element[6]
769	5	4
770	1	1
771	3	2
772	9	1
773	6	2
774	9	5
775	23	15
Total	56	30

The Neustrian element reflects not just the exceptional richness of
the St-Denis archive but a significant continuity. Neustria, with its
roots in the Merovingian as well as the Carolingian past, remained
Charles's comfort-zone, epitomized by the palace of Quierzy on the
Oise, which he followed his father (yet again) in making his preferred
residence in these years.

With the brief *Life* of Stephen III (768–72) and, especially, the
action-packed narrative of cc. 1–44 of the *Life* of Hadrian (772–95),

the Book of the Popes (*Liber Pontificalis*) comes into its own as a key source, covering the years 772–4 in remarkable detail. The letter of Cathwulf retains its unique value, not any longer as evidence for Charles's conception, birth and youth (see Chapter 4), but for his activities in Italy in 773–4. The *ArF* are (the point is blindingly obvious but worth repeating) not contemporary, and they are highly tendentious, but they offer basic and sometimes verifiable information about Charles's whereabouts and, suggestively, the plans behind those. From a sixteenth-century version of a well-informed eighth-century Bavarian source can be gleaned evidence on Tassilo of Bavaria which is valuable, not least because it and the *Life* of Hadrian are mutually reinforcing (see p. 190 below).[7] All these sources, though without exception produced by churches and churchmen, allow secular persons and priorities to emerge more clearly, and usefully qualify traditional historiography representing religion as *the* central theme of the Carolingian period.

My second preliminary is to suggest how geography might have formed Charles's mental landscape. His childhood had been largely spent in the pleasant regions transected by the Oise, the Aisne and the Seine, where old Roman cities, major monasteries and Roman roads made transport and accommodation relatively easy to manage for royal stewards and quartermasters. As an adolescent Charles had become acquainted with the old cult-site of his family at Prüm, learned to hunt in the Ardennes with its rough terrain, rolling hills and often vertiginous descents, and acquired the arts of war in Aquitaine south of the Loire, in the wild regions of the Double and the Périgord and south-west to the formidable rivers Dordogne and Garonne. Once king, he had travelled further north and east of the Oise and the Aisne, crossing the mighty Meuse to stay at Aachen, an old Roman fortified site, and then heading west again to Rouen, another Roman *civitas*, before settling unfinished business in Aquitaine. Thereafter he was back in the Meuse region, at Düren and Liège, and in 770, the Rhineland, where he stayed at Worms and Mainz, then in 771 at Valenciennes on the Scheldt, again within the old heartlands of the family, at Corbeny near the *civitas* of Laon and thence to Attigny on the Aisne, and Herstal on the Meuse.[8] The Saxon campaign of 772 took Charles to Worms, then across the Rhine and east to the river Weser, and back to Francia to winter at Herstal interspersed with prolonged stays at the palace of Thionville on the meandering Mosel. That river was then (if the poet

Ermold's comments on the Rhine in the 820s can be extended to its affluent), as it is now, flanked by fine vineyards on the steep slopes overlooking the river. All these were sites and scenes of Charles's childhood and youth.

II. CHARLES CONFRONTS THE DYNASTIC PROBLEM

The message brought by the pope's envoy to Thionville had done more than make Charles aware of the threat posed by Desiderius to 'the service of God and the rights of St Peter'. Once Carloman's young sons had arrived with their mother at Pavia, possibly as early as February 772, the pope's officials had known that Desiderius's mind was set on persuading Hadrian to travel to Pavia to consecrate the boys as joint-kings of the Franks – a direct, total challenge to Charles – meaning that the pope would thereby enter into a form of *compaternitas*, spiritual co-fatherhood, with Desiderius.[9] The band of Carloman-loyalists accompanying the princes, chief among them Autchar, would have been only too happy to help engineer this outcome, performing their duty of fidelity to the sons of their dead lord.[10] Hadrian, who needed time to establish himself and his relatives in control of Rome, preferred to postpone any decision about Carloman's sons as a way to keep options open: he could indicate to both Desiderius and Charles that some kind of deal was still on the cards. In Charles's mind, where the Saxon campaign took precedence in 772, the next priority was to get his nephews into his custody by offering a deal to Desiderius. If that could not be managed, then a campaign into Italy it would have to be.

The year 773 brought a momentous change in Charles's horizons. As in 755 and 756, when Pippin might have had to talk some leading Franks into trusting that his high-risk game was worth the candle, Charles in 773 won round waverers by bringing them 'into his counsels'. That summer, after sending out *missi* through his land to summon his *fideles*, he gathered a great assembly at Geneva in the southernmost reaches of his kingdom, where his plans won the backing of the Frankish elite. Charles was familiar with such large rivers as the Loire, Meuse and Rhine, and with such imposing hills as the Auvergne and the Süntel, but he had never seen such an expanse of water as Lac Léman (Lake Geneva), nor rivers plunging through high mountain gorges, nor snow-capped mountains like the Alps. From Geneva, Charles's route led south in the direction of Lombardy.

Geneva, though a bishopric since the fifth century, seldom features in early medieval sources, so it's worth asking why it was the chosen venue. Strategically situated on an important route used by transalpine pilgrims and traders in holy things, Geneva was a communications hub all to itself. Its documented profile in ecclesiastical geography was quite small, but it was close to places that loomed very large. At the other end of the lake, and just a few kilometres south on the route into the Alps, was the great abbey of St-Maurice d'Agaune, and a little further east again was the bishopric of Sitten (aka Sion). That both cathedral and monastery were held by the same man, Wilchar (d.786), 'put an end to any possibility of opposition between abbot and bishop!'[11] Wilchar was a man already with a brace of other bishoprics, archbishop of Sens and bishop of Mentana in Italy, and was the former bishop of Vienne, archbishop of the province of the Gauls, de facto successor to Chrodegang of Metz (d.766) and a leading power in Francia. Wilchar had a good deal to do with Charles's creation of a new archbishopric at Tarentaise, comprising the four dioceses of Tarentaise, Sion/Sitten, Maurienne and Aosta: in essence an ecclesiastical frontier-march that straddled both sides of the Alps, thus penning Desiderius – and Carloman's sons – within Italy.[12] Last but not least, Wilchar was *persona grata* at Rome, a figure widely known and an active envoy first for Pope Paul I, then for Pippin and Charles. At Corbeny in December 771, it was he, together with Abbot Fulrad, who had led the *fideles* of the dead Carloman to recognizing Charles as their one and only king, and perhaps also consecrated him.[13] Autchar, with a similar history of papal and royal service, chose to accompany Carloman's widow and sons to Pavia. Perhaps Wilchar and Autchar were not just fellow-*fideles* of Carloman (though after his death they chose different allegiances), but each other's kinsmen? Each an influential figure, near-coevals, together they formed a transalpine political axis over four decades.

III. THE EVIDENCE OF THE *LIFE* OF HADRIAN

Historians have different views on Hadrian's *Life*. According to one school of thought, its author was writing twenty years after the events described, hence *c.*795/6, soon after Hadrian's death on 26 December 795, but basing his account on 'strictly contemporary written records', which were 'generally reliable'. To others, however, the author was writing 'nearly contemporaneously with the events . . . in the 770s'.[14] There is something to be said for both views. But writing that is contemporaneous need not be reliable; nor should the fact that it provides unique information and has internal coherence make a text plausible, let alone reliable. The *Life* of Hadrian is longer, and has much more circumstantial detail, than any other *Life* in the *Liber Pontificalis*. Its readability is seductive: authorial comment is highly tendentious, and unique material is hard to test or gainsay. There's a hero – Hadrian – and there's a villain – Desiderius. Only a very few modern historians of Lombard Italy have a good word for Desiderius. Hadrian by contrast has elicited historians' sympathy, inflected often by confessional allegiance. This is reflected in the historiography.

There are some statements in the *Life* which seem to me to be acceptable because they are borne out by other sources: for instance, the author highlighted the arrival of Carloman's 'wife' (meaning widow) and her sons in Lombardy early in 772 to take refuge with the king of the Lombards. Not supported by other sources, but plausible nevertheless, is the author's statement that Desiderius was scheming for 'Carloman's sons to assume the kingship of the Franks', and hoped 'to persuade the holy pontiff to travel to him to anoint Carloman's sons as kings of the Franks'. Equally plausible is the author's comment, with satisfaction, that Desiderius 'failed to divorce the bountiful pontiff from the charity and attachment that the Christian king, the great Charles, had towards him'.[15] The narrative continues with the grudging remark that Desiderius 'with obstinate courage (*pertinax audacia*)' left his palace [at Pavia] 'along with his son Adelchis and the Lombard army, and with him the wife and sons of the late king Carloman, and Autchar', and then tried to come to Rome without the pope's knowledge, sending on ahead three high officials in hopes that they would be able to arrange a meeting, which Hadrian flatly refused, 'unless he [Desiderius] first fulfils our side's entire lawful rights'.[16] There is a certain consistency in the statement that Desiderius continued his journey towards Rome. It is entirely credible that Hadrian fortified the city, sent three trusted bishops to warn the king to depart, and never again to enter papal territory, 'neither he, nor any of the Lombards, nor Autchar the Frank either', and finally threatened excommunication for any who disobeyed. That Autchar appears yet again as an important player adds credibility to this exchange. The author's next comment looks more subjective: Desiderius, after getting as far as Viterbo, 'now withdrew immediately and returned home in great perplexity'.[17] 'Astonishingly, Hadrian's gambit paid off', is one historian's comment.[18] Modern judgements on both these characters tend to be extremely partisan. How is a historian to test claims as between the two *partes*, translatable as 'sides'? 'Perplexity' was Desiderius's state of mind in the opinion of the author of the *Life*. Perhaps, though, Desiderius was not so much 'perplexed' as increasingly anxious to keep custody of Carloman's sons in a Pavian tower, and his reliance for that on their de facto guardian, Autchar.

A recent analyst has raised some methodological questions, the answers to which in my view clarify matters and are to be taken very seriously.[19] First, when was the *Life* written? A distinction must be made between cc. 1–44, which offer a detailed narrative from 772 to 774, and cc. 45–97, which cover groups of papal donations and building projects over the years 772 to 792. Even in the short period of overlap, it is necessary to differentiate one type of short-term project from another, longer-term one.[20] Another question is of genre: is a papal *Life* a biography, that is, an account of the personal traits and experiences of an individual? Or is each *Life* an exemplar of a stereotyped model?[21] Then again, the author's presentation of Charles's relationship with Hadrian takes no account of the problem that the two protagonists were at cross-purposes where the big issue of property-rights was concerned. When Charles visited Rome in 774, Hadrian had his officials read out to him a promise of 'restorations' purportedly agreed by Pippin twenty years previously at Quierzy.[22] Charles told Hitherius to produce another promise of donation on the model of the earlier one (*ad instar anterioris*): not, accidentally, an ambivalent phrase. When promises to 'restore' or 'return' property were made, the principals were often arguing about different things. This becomes clear from the slightly later evidence of Hadrian's letters (the *Codex Carolinus* resumes play at the end of 774). Hadrian had in mind whole territories, whereas Charles or his *missi* were claiming rights to estates within larger regions or in the environs of cities.[23] Something similar had occurred when Desiderius (or his envoys) argued against Hadrian or

Charles (or their envoys). The papal archive may well have been, as Walter Ullmann thought, its 'storehouse of ideological memory'.[24] Uncertainty entered when it came to this property or that: archival practice could be haphazard, and always much depended upon local knowledge and memory.[25] In short, the so-called Donation of Quierzy was the very reverse of a watertight legal or lawyerly document. Much of this section of the *Life* was less fact than fiction.[26]

IV. CHARLES'S MOVES IN 773

Carloman's death in December 771 had changed everyone's calculations – Charles's most of all. Unlike some modern historians, however, Charles also recognized what had *not* changed. Only hindsight and teleology have allowed the Lombard kingdom to be represented as falling apart in 772/3. In a strictly contemporary view, Desiderius, Charles's former father-in-law, continued to rule a powerful kingdom, controlling internal communications, guarding his frontiers, fielding large armies when necessary and, as heir to the exarchate, putting effective pressure on many cities to accept his authority in northern and central Italy. The dukes of Bavaria and Benevento had not ceased to be sons-in-law of Desiderius. His son Adelchis was a formidable military figure in his father's regime. Above all, Desiderius still held aces in his hand at Pavia: at this point, he was determined that the sons of Carloman, under the protective eyes of their mother and of Autchar, would not be the objects of a deal with Charles.

Other influential figures, strategically located (see Map 6, pp. xviii–xix), were meanwhile engaged in the alternative option of dealing with Charles. Abbot Asinar travelled from Novalesa, just 37km south of the crest of the Mont Cenis pass, to Quierzy, where in March 773 he received from Charles a charter of immunity for his monastery, strengthening the privileges conferred by Carloman in 769 and 770.[27] Another charter, a damaged original lacking the final note of date and place, but recently dated on good grounds to 773, shows Charles negotiating an agreement further east, in Rhaetia, with Constantius, bishop and count of Chur.[28] In the style of a judgment, Charles announced 'to all our *fideles*' a treaty between himself and Constantius, whom he had established as '*rector* of the *populus* of the Rhaetians', and, further, that at the request of Constantius and the *populus* of his homeland, he was now taking them 'under his protection and defence so that they should not suffer any unjust disturbance from men who were outsiders (*homines extrinsecus*)', and 'so that we would keep law and custom as their forefathers had with our predecessors'. The Rhaetians in return should offer Charles *servitium* and *fides*, which in this context had military connotations. There was a backstory of long-ago agreements between Merovingian kings and mayors of the palace, on the one hand, and Rhaetians on the other, as well as more recent agreements with Carolingian rulers, including Charles himself. Formerly the 'outsiders' could have been Franks; in 773 the 'outsiders' seem more likely to have been Bavarians and some neighbouring Lombards under Tassilo's rule.[29]

The takers of the initiative in the case of both Novalesa and Chur were the abbot and bishop respectively, both hedging their bets against 'coming upheavals' in the region.[30] 'Coming upheavals' are liable to be predicted only by those who keep themselves exceptionally well-informed: Asinar and Constantius, in control of alpine passes, were certainly that. Pope Hadrian's appeal for Charles's help very early in 773, his envoy's itinerary by land and sea and again by land, and Charles's unhesitating response were the kind of news that reached Asinar and Constantius. Asinar was at Quierzy on 25 March, presenting his charter of immunity to Charles to sign; and it looks likely that two or three months later, petitioners from Chur waylaid Charles in Burgundy when he was already en route for Geneva.[31] Charles was concerned to protect his new interests in Rhaetia. He needed to ward off any Bavarian intervention in the frontier-zone between Friuli and Bavaria around Bolzano and Säben, in the upper valley of the Adige, north from Verona, and looking to the Reschen and Brenner passes that led to Bavaria.[32] He also wanted to cement a bond with the bishop of Chur. Its effects are still visible in the little cluster of richly decorated churches built between the 770s and *c*.800 – St Johann Müstair, Heiligkreuzkapelle Müstair, St Benedikt Mals, St Prokulus in Naturns – which Charles's patronage made possible.[33] The decisions of Asinar and Constantius, two wielders of power in alpine regions, invited collusions with Charles, whose eye was also on Lombardy. Charles's positive responses, in the Val de Suse and in the diocese of Chur, showed the strategic shrewdness of his longer view.

Some of the men closest to Charles's father, and whom Charles certainly knew in childhood, had taken part in Pippin's Italian campaigns in the 750s. Among them, almost certainly, was Pippin's younger half-brother Bernard (born *c.*730 to one of Martel's mistresses). A close kinsman, with at least a couple of decades' war-experience, Uncle Bernard was among those summoned to the assembly at Geneva.[34] So, plausibly, though more tentatively, were the four counts and five *vassi* who featured in the Lorsch judgment in 772. One was Count Ro(t)-land, and two of the *vassi* were Theuderic (possibly to be identified with the *consanguineus* of Charles mentioned as a military commander in Saxony in *ArF* for 782) and Alboin; it is tempting to identify these latter with the two counts who appeared, along with Bernard, in a judgment of 775.[35] The 'Hagino' of D. 65 (772), the 'Agino' of D. 102, and the 'Aginard' of D. 110 (these both 775) may represent one and the same count. The tally of identifications is small, but suggestive. Two other senior churchmen – the bishop of Le Mans and the abbot of St-Calais – are very likely to have answered a summons to Geneva, for both of them owed the king the military service of their warrior tenants, and both are documented as having been with Charles and his army in Lombardy in February 774. At Geneva, Bernard, one of a very few lay leaders to be mentioned in the *ArF*, had been given command of the second of the two parts into which Charles had divided his forces, with a view to a two-pronged advance. This was a tactic that Charles made his speciality. The plan was that Bernard and his army would move south by the Mons Iovis (its modern name is Mont Joux or the Great St Bernard), while Charles led the other part of his forces the more westerly route by the Mont Cenis.[36] That Bernard had had prior experience of alpine warfare back in Pippin's day could well explain his being given the tougher assignment: the altitude of the Mont Joux pass is 2,469m, that of the Mont Cenis, 2,081m. Charles (or Bernard) may well have ascertained from local scouts that the pass of Mont Joux was no longer being defended by Desiderius's troops, and that would tally with Aosta's having already come under Frankish ecclesiastical control (see p. 124 above).[37]

Charles had, meanwhile, sent to Rome three high-ranking envoys, Bishop George of Ostia and Amiens, Vulfard of Tours, 'abbot and counsellor', and a layman with the Lombard name of Alboin who, according to the author of the *Life* of Hadrian, was a favourite (*deliciosus*) of Charles.[38] (The 'international' character of Charles's inner circle then, and later too, is worth noting.) On their arrival at Rome, Pope Hadrian told them all about Desiderius's failure to withdraw from the lands claimed by St Peter. Hadrian sent the envoys, along with envoys of his own, back to Charles, who had by now reached Geneva, with a baleful reminder of what Pippin had promised St Peter. En route, the envoys 'deviated' for talks with Desiderius, but 'he refused to restore anything whatsoever'. Back on Frankish territory in or near Geneva, they again reported the talks' failure to Charles.

> And immediately the most gentle (*mitissimus*) and truly Christian (*et re vera christianissimus*) king of the Franks sent Desiderius his envoys, namely [. . . gap in the text] begging him to restore the cities and restore the Romans' rights. In addition, Charles promised to pay Desiderius gold and silver to the amount of 14,000 gold *solidi*. Yet neither entreaties nor gifts succeeded in bending his most savage heart (*ferocissimus* co*r*).[39]

V. THE PRINCES IN THE TOWER*

The juxtaposition of 'begging to restore cities' and 'promising to pay' money might suggest a deal: cash in return for St Peter's cities. The author of the *Life* continued:[40]

> Achieving nothing, the envoys of the Franks returned to their Christian king. [c. 29] Then the God-protected king, great Charles, mustered the full number of the troops of his kingdom of the Franks. Some of his army he sent to occupy all the mountain barriers [that is, passes that had been fortified]. With many mighty Frankish warriors, he came towards the Mont-Cenis close to these barriers, then waited with his forces at some distance inside the territory of the Franks. Desiderius and the whole number of the Lombard armies were waiting to put up a strong resistance at the barriers, which they had carefully strengthened by building various

---

* For those familiar with Shakespeare and English history, the suitability of the allusion to the fate of the only surviving sons of King Edward IV, imprisoned on the orders of their uncle Duke Richard of Gloucester, Richard III, in the Tower of London, will become apparent. An evocative picture of the scene – *The Two Princes Edward and Richard in the Tower, 1483* – by Sir John Everett Millais, 1878, is part of the Royal Holloway, University of London, picture collection. For 'the Tower of London', read 'a tower in Verona'. For uncles and nephews, see below, pp. 134–5.

walls. [c. 30] At the moment the Christian king of the Franks came close to these mountain barriers, he immediately sent his envoys to Desiderius again, asking the king as before to accept the amount of *solidi* mentioned and restore the cities peacefully. But the shameless king would concede nothing whatever. When he continued so obdurate, the Christian king of the Franks, desiring to get back St Peter's lawful rights, sent a message to the Lombard king that he need hand over to him no more than three sons of Lombard high officials (*iudices*) as security for the restoration of the cities, and he would immediately return home with his armies of Franks without causing any harm or engaging in battle. [c. 31] Even so, he failed to turn his evil mind.[41]

Was Charles, with this third offer, ready to throw in the towel? It was at this point, apparently, that the Franks' morale had collapsed: they 'were willing to return home the next day'. If so, Charles now risked the kind of frank resistance that Einhard hinted at in imputing to Pippin's noble followers back in 755/6 similar threats to go home.[42] The author of the *Life* of Hadrian laid less stress on any crisis of confidence, or even on Desiderius's wickedness, than, at this critical moment, on divine intervention – in effect, an Old Testament-style miracle:

> Almighty God, seeing the evil Desiderius's iniquitous perfidy (*perfidia*) and unbearable shamelessness (*intolerabilis protervia*), instilled terror and mighty fear into his [Desiderius's] heart, that of his son Adelchis and the hearts of all the Lombards. That very night, abandoning all their tents and gear, they all as a whole took to flight, though no-one was pursuing them. When the armies of the Franks saw this, they did pursue them, and killed many of them.[43]

It's time to recap on, and make sense of, this series of events. As late as early/mid-September 773, Charles, though he had come very close to military engagement with Desiderius, was still very keen to avoid open conflict. He had directed two armies to different alpine passes, and hence almost to the frontier between the Lombard kingdom and Francia, yet neither his army nor Bernard's had crossed that frontier. Charles remained set on negotiation rather than fighting. He chose to make a final offer. My own suggestion is that Charles offered cash, not to buy, as it were on Hadrian's behalf, Desiderius's return of St Peter's cities, but for another purchase entirely. Furthermore, he was prepared to make that offer twice over. And only then did he make a third and last, and much less impressive offer, in effect, to accept three high-born Lombard hostages.[44] This I interpret as symptomatic of his fearing to try too far the patience of *the Franks*.

What Charles sought to purchase was the custody of his nephews, the princes held at Pavia. Parallels for deals akin to hostage-taking can be found in the papal letters, but not (so far as I know) for the payment of cash. By any standards, though, 14,000 *solidi* (or bullion to the value of) was no ordinary amount. It was completely *extra*ordinary. In the present context, 14,000 *solidi* look to me like a pair of *wergilds*: the price of two princes, 7,000 *solidi* apiece.[45] *Wergilds* were man-prices in the laws of the Lombards and of the Franks, but the amounts specified differed according to status and circumstances. The only higher royal *wergild* I know of was that for an Anglo-Saxon king: 7,500 shillings (= *solidi*); an Alaman duke's *wergild* was 600 *solidi*; the *wergild* of a Frankish king's bodyguard (*antrustio*) was also 600 *solidi*. And the amount could be tripled in certain specially heinous cases, for instance of murder. In practice amounts were not fixed: a recent very helpful observation derived from a legal formula is that the amounts of *wergilds* were negotiable.[46] If Charles considered 14,000 *solidi* an excessively generous starting offer, he could have been hoping that Desiderius would settle for less. Or did Charles feel confident that his offer was one that Desiderius simply couldn't resist? If so, he underestimated one thing that was beyond price: the Lombard king's honour. What father does deals with the man who has repudiated his daughter? Only in Desiderius's absolute refusal did Charles finally understand this. The result was the decision to go, after all, for a conquest that would necessarily include one way or another getting control of the princes held in safe-keeping (say, in a tower?) at Pavia.

Divine intervention – God's sudden striking of terror in the hearts of Desiderius and Adelchis and their troops – was one way the author of Hadrian's *Life* presented a complete reversal of the military situation.[47] The same (or possibly another) author also gave a rational explanation of events: Desiderius had tried to block access to the Mont Cenis pass, but then became aware that his troops risked being trapped from the rear by Bernard's forces, which had crossed the Alps (and maybe already reached Aosta).[48] Desiderius therefore retreated as fast as possible to Pavia, where he strengthened the fortifications for a siege, and 'made ready to resist the armies of the Franks and defend his city with his Lombards'.[49] What Charles did not yet know, but would soon discover, was that Desiderius's son Adelchis had taken 'Autchar the Frank and Carloman's wife and sons with him and entered Verona, because that city is the strongest of all the Lombards' cities (*fortissima pre omnibus civitatibus Langobardorum*)'. Charles 'with all his forces, advanced on Pavia, and laid siege to it, surrounding it on all sides': a huge military operation for a city so large and with walls so strong.[50] Only then, at Pavia, did he learn that the princes were now being held at Verona, then as now a city of towers.

Two further urgent decisions, both of them driven by dynastic priorities, followed from Charles's decision for conquest. Of these, one was more urgent than the other. First, 'he immediately sent word to Francia and had his most excellent wife, Queen Hildegard, and his most noble sons, brought to him there at Pavia.'[51] His sons – Pippin, Himiltrud's son, now aged (probably) four and Charles the Younger, Hildegard's son, now aged (probably) two – embodied the future of Charles's branch of the dynasty, the alternative to the future of his nephews as kings of the Franks.

Charles had already celebrated Christmas at Pavia when his family arrived in the camp early in 774, Hildegard heavily pregnant. She was now sixteen, and this travelling with her husband would remain the pattern of the marriage.[52] Their daughter Adelhaid was born 'near the high walls of Pavia, while her mighty father was taking control of the kingdoms of Italy', as Paul the Deacon put it in the epitaph he wrote for this 'very little girl'. 'Hastening back over the Alps [presumably sent to a safer place, with her wet-nurse and a select retinue] to the Rhone valley, there she died, while her mother, far away, was heart-broken with grief.'[53] This epitaph, and several others for female Carolingians, were written for their tombs at Metz in 785/6. The poem, like its companion-pieces, was more than boilerplate. There was real feeling here, and the baby's epitaph, 'commissioned work' though it was, was not 'cold'. From the poet, Charles got what he had asked for, which was quite evidently a real expression of grief, albeit nine years after the event.[54]

Like the commissioning of epitaphs for dead princesses at Metz, Charles's bringing of his family to Pavia was a demonstration of dynastic cohesion under what his sister Gisela would later, in the year 771 of the annals she sponsored, term *monarchia*. That family, with all those who served its court, made an impressive show with its tents and gear, its nursery, travelling chapel and writing-office (with Hitherius, Charles's one-time envoy in Italy, resuming his role as chief notary) amidst cavalrymen and footsoldiers and the armed retinues of bishops and magnates.[55] Something like normality persisted: Bishop Merol of Le Mans and Abbot Rabigaud of St-Calais solemnly exchanged, at Pavia, properties they had in Maine in Neustria over 1,000km away.[56] They had 'seized an opportunity', as they put it, and had come to Italy armed with written statements about the properties concerned, and, said Charles, 'they showed us these to be read . . . and from them we understood [what they wanted approved]'. Charles ordered two copies of the exchange-document, signed them, and had them sealed and officially 'recognized' by his notary Hitherius on 19 February 774 'at the city of Pavia, publicly'. Rabigaud had come to Charles's attention in 770,[57] and he served the king again in 773–4.[58]

The second urgent decision was a military one. Since the armies of Bernard and Charles had evidently merged into one army, it had become possible for Charles to maintain the siege of Pavia while hiving off an elite force to be deployed at Verona:

> Charles left most of his forces at Pavia, and with a number of his bravest Franks moved rapidly towards Verona. As soon as he got there, Autchar and Carloman's wife and sons immediately handed themselves over of their own free wills (*propria voluntate . . . se tradiderunt*) to the most kindly (*benignissimus*) king Charles. Having received them, his Excellence went back to [the siege of Pavia]. Straightaway he sent out select bands of his warriors from his forces, and captured various of the Lombards' cities lying north of the Po and brought them under his power.[59]

Charles had succeeded in getting Carloman's sons into his custody, together with their mother and the grandfatherly figure of Autchar. That small family, which had cast its shadow over his own and continued to challenge his family's existence while the stalemate-siege lasted, had given up whatever claims they had cherished. They had surrendered.

In the chapters of the *Life* of Hadrian just quoted, it is not hard to spot an authorial quirk: the lavishing of superlatives on Charles's personal character. In c. 28, 'the most gentle (*mitissimus*) and truly Christian (*et re vera christianissimus*) king of the Franks' offered 14,000 *solidi*; in c. 34, 'Autchar and Carloman's wife and sons handed themselves over to the most kindly (*benignissimus*) king Charles'. In the remaining chapters of the *Life*'s historical section (cc. 1–44), the superlative *benignissimus* is repeatedly used to describe Charles (cc. 37, 38 and 39). 'The most gentle', 'the most kindly': in these epithets Charles might (if he ever did read, or had read to him, the *Liber Pontificalis*) have found himself eulogized.[60] The author protests too much. He does not say whether the princes were left (in custody? for safe-keeping?) in a tower in Verona, or taken back with 'the strongest Franks' to the camp outside Pavia. Given Verona's reputation for being uniquely strong, as compared to the security-risks of a camp in open ground, Charles's choice was a no-brainer. A moment's reflection on the fates of other princes in towers does not indicate good prospects for *these* princes: their fates were the fates of the offspring of junior branches in dynastic states. Where succession involves indeterminacy, it engenders uncertainty, insecurity, anxiety. Nephews were the classic rivals, and victims, of their paternal uncles. 'The history of monarchy is stained with the blood of close kin.'[61] The author of Hadrian's *Life* does not mention the princes again – nor their mother, nor Autchar. No other source – not Einhard, not the *ArF* – mentions them again. For the man who wears the crown, there are sleepless nights. The rest is silence.

VI. CHARLES'S FIRST VISIT TO ROME: EASTER 774

'By the high walls of Pavia', the siege went on. Did the tension become intolerable? I think, to use a modern idiom, that Charles did not 'do' intolerable. Easter, 3 April that year, was imminent. Hildegard (still grieving for her baby daughter's loss) and the little boys would have to spend it without him. By late March Charles had made another decision: to leave his family at Pavia, together with most of his troops, and, 'Easter being so close, and having a great desire (*magnum desiderium habens*), to hasten to Rome and the thresholds of the Apostles, with bishops, and abbots, and military commanders, that is, dukes and counts' leading their contingents in what was still a substantial army.[62] Travelling on still-usable Roman roads from Pavia, Charles crossed the Po to the Arno and then came through Tuscany. The distance to Rome would be some 600km:

He came so quickly that he presented himself at the apostolic thresholds on Holy Saturday, 2nd April [Charles's birthday – for him, surely, no coincidence]. News of his coming threw the pope into great bewilderment and consternation for the king of the Franks had come so unexpectedly. The pope sent all the high officials out to meet the king some thirty [Roman] miles [48km] from Rome . . . and there they greeted him with the standard.[63]

The initiative for Charles's coming to Rome was entirely his own. According to the *Vita* author, at this point – exceptionally – very specific about dates, Charles arrived in Rome on Easter Saturday, 2 April, and left on 6 April. During these six days Charles's mind underwent a sea-change as rapid as it was extraordinary.

Hadrian's consternation was understandable; from all he had heard, Charles was toughness incarnate. But Hadrian did not underestimate Charles's desire to seize a window of opportunity and to close a deal. The author of Hadrian's *Life* wrote truth when he identified Charles's 'great desire' to visit the thresholds of the apostles, and again, when his word-picture inscribed Charles's hard power. For modern secular-minded historians, this may look implausibly contradictory. For Charles and so many of his contemporaries, it was perfectly possible for the same mind to contain profound belief and smart calculation.

Charles at the age of five had ridden out to receive Pope Stephen II and led him to meet the rest of the royal family at Ponthion in 753; he had participated with his parents in a great relic-*translatio* at St-Germain-des-Prés in 755; and he had been present at another large ritual occasion on the installing of priceless relics, again with the family, at Prüm in 762.[64] The situation in 774, however, was different. Rituals related to the arrivals (*adventus*) and receptions (*occursus*) of imperial exarchs and patricians provided the precedents for the hastily organized welcome rituals of 1 April.[65] The leading men of Rome processed out to greet Charles with the banner (*bandora*) at Novae, some 45km outside the city.[66] As the now much augmented groups of Franks and Romans who had advanced southwards together down the *Via Flaminia* got to within a couple of kilometres of the city, *militia*-men from each of the twelve or fourteen companies of the civil regions of Rome came out from the city to greet Charles, and a procession of little boys came to throw palm leaves and olive branches on the road and chant ritual acclamations in front of him (did he perhaps at that moment think of his own two little boys?), while the pope sent out 'more crosses, that is, banners (*cruces id est signa*) to receive him, just like greeting an exarch or patrician'.[67]

Charles, his troops and personal retinue, with their large numbers of servants, together with the leading Romans and their entourages, now reached Rome. Map 10 (p. xxiii) makes it possible to visualize the city's late-eighth-century geography. A number of roads led into Rome, and most passed through gates. Charles would have come by the *Via Flaminia*, following in part the classic pilgrim route for people from north of the Alps, later known as the *Via Francigena* (the Frankish Road). Entry to the city was through the *Flaminia*'s north gate in the north-western part of the city walls. The pope's residence was on the Lateran Hill, on the south-eastern edge of the ancient city, not very near any gate. From the Lateran palace the pope would process to St Peter's via one important 'station' or 'stational church' to another, pausing to perform the liturgy at each. He would pass by the Colosseum, place of martyrs, and the old Forum, and a string of still-impressive but crumbling buildings (the *Liber Pontificalis* contains several accounts of accidents caused by falling masonry), and across the bridge over the Tiber that led to the long-since fortified Tomb of the Emperor Hadrian (later, and still today, known as Castel Sant'Angelo), and thence to the huge Roman basilica – formerly a palace of justice, long since con-verted into a church – where St Peter's relics were enshrined. This church and the pilgrim hostels that flanked it were outside the city, 'across the Tiber' (Trastevere) on the Vatican Hill.

Charles went directly from the Flaminian gate to the bridge across the Tiber, where he stayed on the night of 2 April in a hostel close to the great church. Charles had come as a pilgrim, not a conqueror. For him, access to the relics of St Peter imparted a special intensity to the visit to Rome. Though the author of Hadrian's *Life* does not say so explicitly, Hadrian's letters, and bits of lost letters from Charles embedded in Hadrian's replies, from the 770s provide plenty of evidence for Charles's faith in St Peter's intercessions with the Almighty. Given the situation at Pavia, Charles urgently needed those intercessions. It would be sur-prising if Charles had not also wished to pray, along with as many of his Franks as there was space for, in the chapel, right next to St Peter's, of St Petronilla, the *auxiliatrix* of the royal family (as Pope Paul had written in a letter to Pippin);[68] for to visit Petronilla's shrine was to assert not just the dynasty's legitimacy but also the Franks' political stake here as 'the new political partners of the papacy'.[69] In Charles's mind, the religious and the political were inextricably entwined.

At daybreak on Holy Saturday, Hadrian received Charles at the top of St Peter's steps and they embraced each other. Taking the pope's right hand, Charles entered the church to pray 'near the apostle's tomb'.

> The whole clergy and all God's servants the monks chanted praise to God and to His Excellency, loudly acclaiming, 'Blessed is he who comes in the name of the Lord' etc. And so the king of the Franks, all the bishops, abbots and high officials and all the Franks who had accompanied him, came with the pope close to the *confessio* of St Peter.[70]

Charles requested from Hadrian the *licentia Romam ingrediendi* ('permission to enter Rome' – he would need the entry-permit later that day). Pope and king, with the high officials of the Romans and Franks, then 'went down together to St Peter's body and ratified their oaths to each other'.[71] For Charles, this oath-taking on Peter's relics in a very confined subterranean space could not have been other than a never-to-be-forgotten experience. A strong emphasis on 'the spiritual nature of [Charles's] visit [to Rome]' is surely correct.[72]

That, however, was not *all* that was involved. Desiderius and Queen Ansa and their daughter, together with many Lombards loyal to them, remained within the walls of Pavia, and, while other loyalists were active elsewhere in the region, regnal power resided, still, in Pavia. The hoped-for taking of the city, and the ousting of the Lombard royal family, would involve some ideas for a new working relationship between the Frankish king and the pope, even if much uncertainty remained. The presence of Hitherius with his writing materials indicated the prospect of agreements in black and white concerning papal properties in various parts of Italy.

In his five-night stay, Charles never slept in the city, but returned every night to the environs of St Peter's. On Easter Day, king and pope, after celebrating the liturgy, feasted together at the Lateran palace. On Monday the 4th and Tuesday the 5th of April, Charles and Hadrian followed the usual papal Easter itinerary. On Wednesday 6 April, at St Peter's, Hitherius got out his parchments and pens.

First the pope gave Charles a copy of what he declared to be the agreement made at Quierzy by Stephen II and Pippin in 754. Charles had two copies made on the spot by Hitherius.

> [c. 43] Once the donation was made, and the Christian king of the Franks had ratified it in his own hand, he had all the bishops, abbots, dukes and counts subscribe to it. They placed it first on St Peter's altar, and then inside his holy *confessio* [the space in front of the altar above the saint's tomb], and both the king of the Franks and all his high officials handed it to St Peter and to his holy deputy Pope Hadrian, promising under a terrible oath to maintain everything included in that donation. The Christian king asked Hitherius to write out a further copy of the donation; and then, with his own hands, Charles placed it inside over the body of St Peter, beneath the Gospels which are kissed there, as a firm security and an eternal reminder of his name and of the kingdom of the Franks. Further copies of the donation, made in the writing office of the Roman church, Charles took away with him.[73]

The next two chapters of the *Vita*'s narrative give a detailed account of what purport to be the territorial dimensions of the 754 Donation of Quierzy.[74] As noted above, misunderstandings and disgruntlements seem to have ensued in 774 and for long after. There was evidently a large gap between the spin provided by the author of Hadrian's *Life* and what the visit to Rome had meant to Charles. It was the seriousness of Charles's position in March 774 that had drawn him to Rome. He believed that he and his armies, including those stuck outside Pavia, could be rescued from disaster by the prayers of St Peter and those alone. The means of rescue lay neither in law nor in politics but in the experience of contact, and of ongoing contact, with the relics of St Peter.

Popes had long known how to convey something of that experience, even if the beneficiaries did not come to Rome. Gregory I (590–603) had sent privileged recipients tiny pieces of cloth that had been in contact with Peter's tomb. In 770, a papal scribe had written in Stephen III's name a strongly worded letter of protest, which the pope had 'placed in the *confessio* of St Peter and offered the sacrifice and offerings to our God upon it', and then taken out the letter and sent it to Charles and Carloman.[75] On 6 April 774, Charles ordered Hitherius to write out a copy of the Donation allegedly made in 754.

Then Charles with his own hands placed it inside [the *confessio*] over St Peter's body, beneath the Gospels which are kissed there, as a firm security and an eternal reminder of his name and that of the kingdom of the Franks, and took away with him another copy . . .[76]

In leaving the document there, Charles manifested his trust in Peter's power to protect him and his people more securely than ever. The materiality of these proceedings was part and parcel of Charles's religion. The *confessio* of St Peter was, as it were, like 'a numinous oven, whence [as in 770] a letter emerged charged with holy power'. The document left in the *confessio* was 'like a battery on permanent charge'.[77]

This was not the only written text that worked on Charles's mind in the final fevered day of his stay in Rome. The Dionysio-Hadriana collection of canon law, compiled by a sixth-century monk called Dionysius and including the canons of fourth- and fifth-century councils and papal decretal-letters, had come to be widely used in the Latin Church. Hadrian had only just enough time to find a fine copy of the law-collection (hence thereafter it bore the double-name Dionysio-Hadriana) and to commission a scribe capable of composing a dedicatory colophon consisting of forty-five lines of acrostic verse (that is, lines in which the initial letters, read downwards, spell out a message) addressed to Charles, beginning

DOMINO EXCELL. FILIO CARULO MAGNO REGI HADRIANUS PAPA ('To the excellent lord and son Charles, the great king, Pope Hadrian [gives this]'):

> *Divina fulgens doctrina sceptra praecellit regni*
> *Origo regum felix semper genitura beata*
> *Molem perspicimus legis gratiam laudis habere.*
>
> . . .

The Donation had been customized as that of Pippin, Charles's father, at Quierzy back in 754; the Dionysio-Hadriana colophon customized the collection itself as the instrument of Charles and his offspring 'through future ages'. One copy of the Donation was to remain permanently in the *confessio*. Another copy of it, and also the manuscript of the Dionysio-Hadriana (with its new colophon), were portable, and were indeed carried north in Charles's personal baggage. It was not the urgency for negotiations over papal properties, or military considerations demanding a quick return to Pavia, powerful as these were, that now drove Charles's actions: these writings were in themselves formidable engines of holy power. The impact of the Dionysio-Hadriana on canon law turned out to be not only of enduring importance for Charles and ecclesiastical personnel generally, as the *Admonitio generalis* (789) would very clearly show, but it had profound effects on Charles's practice of government and the delivery of justice. These were long-term effects. In the immediate present, the colophon-poet, who perhaps considered the fall of Pavia a foregone conclusion, after praising the victories of Charles's father and commending his example, asserted that Charles had

> given back the gifts of old to his Mother the Church:
> great cities, territories, and various fortified places . . .

and ended with the wish that

> *by fencing in the Lombards' realm, you return your reward,*
> *the promised holy gifts to the church of Peter the key-bearer,*
> giving yourself more ample victory and honour as well,
> to reign along with your offspring now and in future ages.
> Observing these things laid down, never depart from the law.[78]

Hadrian might well have been expecting that the king would stay for a while in Rome, seeing more shrines and deepening his personal bond with St Peter. Instead, Charles abruptly left Rome on 7 April. There would be other times to visit Rome to pray at shrines and the thresholds of the Apostles. St Peter's property claims could (or would have to) wait. But what, actually, were Charles's plans? What options were available? The *Vita*'s author, writing in 775–6, had the benefit of hindsight: did he imagine that Charles left in vexation because Hadrian had not given him even a contact-relic of St Peter (such gifts had been bestowed by Gregory the Great on favoured patrons)? It was most probably for military reasons that, faith and morale recharged, Charles saw the need to return to Pavia as soon as conceivably possible. Experienced in siege-warfare, he well knew the risks involved. In the course of a long winter, besiegers were as liable as those who were besieged to become demoralized and to suffer from hunger or, worse, disease.[79] The Po river could flood and turn a camp into a quagmire. Frankish troops could get cold feet, as events not so long ago had shown, and make their own demands on their leader to strike a deal with their opponents (probably involving the transfer of a chunk of the Lombard royal treasury), and then head back north, cutting their losses.[80] What nerved Charles to decide otherwise? The answer was, I think, his memory of what had occurred in Rome and his faith in the subterranean battery on permanent charge. But even that faith, that heightened morale, might not have been enough, had not disease struck those holding out in Pavia:

> [c. 44] After Charles with his forces had returned to the river Ticino, he attacked and besieged the city of Pavia in strength. And since the wrath of God raged and stormed against all the Lombards in that city, and they were increasingly enfeebled by disease and death, so, by God's will, the excellent king of the Franks captured the city together with Desiderius king of the Lombards and all who were with him and subjected the entire kingdom of the Lombards to his power. And he took the aforementioned Desiderius and his wife back to Francia with him.

The *Vita* author, whatever else he made up, is unlikely to have invented the story of the epidemic in Pavia and its dire effects. There is also the testimony of Cathwulf, whose list of Charles's blessings ended with:

> Seventh, when your enemies fled, you crossed the Alps, and you captured the hugely wealthy city of Pavia, with its king, without any shedding of blood, and you also seized all its treasures.
>
> Eighth, you entered golden, imperial Rome, and you smoothly received from the King of Kings the realms of the Italians with all their precious things. In how many ways, after your enemies fled before your face, you stood out as the victor! And this too was exemplified concerning you what is read in the Psalms, though specially understood concerning Christ and David: 'I will pursue my enemies and I will capture them'.[81]

Annalistic accounts corroborate (and also correct) Cathwulf:

> And when the lord king Charles, returning from Rome, again reached Pavia, he captured that city, and also King Desiderius and his wife and daughter and all the treasure of his palace. And all the Lombards from all the cities of Italy made themselves subordinate to the rule of the glorious lord Charles the king and of the Franks. Adelchis son of King Desiderius fled across the sea and reached Constantinople. And then

Charles, after having subjugated Italy and set everything in order, left a garrison of Franks in the city of Pavia, and returned with his wife and rest of the Franks in great triumph with God's help.[82]

And [Charles and the Franks] brought King Desiderius with them as a captive to Francia.[83]

The city of Pavia was surrendered to the Franks, and King Desiderius was sent into Francia, and the lord king Charles after sending counts through all Italy, joyfully restored to St Peter the cities which he owned, and, after everything had been set in order, came swiftly into Francia.[84]

The story can be summed up as follows: Charles, imbued with new confidence, left Rome to save his family and his troops at Pavia. In his mind – and he thought strategically – there was a strong sense of there being no time to lose, complemented by an equally strong belief in the Almighty's power, mediated through Peter's intercession, to 'rage and storm against all the Lombards in Pavia'. Charles and his consolidated army, encouraged by the army's clergy, saw God's will in the catastrophe inside Pavia. The city's fall followed two months later. Those deaths from sickness were not fictions but signs. The *Vita* author credited an angry God, and ended his narrative with the Lombard kingdom's destruction. Charles himself gave thanks, and – being only human – embraced his wife and children with a huge sigh of relief.

VII. THE 'CONQUEST' OF THE LOMBARD KINGDOM

The escape of Desiderius's son and his flight across the sea to Constantinople, whenever it happened, became a factor in a now-total collapse of Lombard morale. That was why Charles could be said by Cathwulf to have taken possession of Pavia and its rulers 'without bloodshed'. Desiderius and his wife had been taken captive, and had (as Autchar and Carloman's widow and her sons had at Verona) performed at Pavia some such act of surrender as kneeling or being stripped of insignia, while from other cities local magnates came to offer gestures of submission.[85] Too little is known of Lombard royal inaugurations to do more than guess how Lombard elites publicly acknowledged Charles as their king.

This must have happened before 5 June, for on that day Charles displayed his kingship over the Lombards, and so the extension of his regality, by issuing as *rex Francorum et Langobardorum* a charter for an Italian beneficiary, the abbot of Bobbio. Assuming that the abbot came in person with a retinue, as would have been normal, and given that Bobbio was only some 80km from Pavia, via Piacenza by the rivers Trebbia and Ticino, Abbot Guinibald was perhaps quickest off the mark. This, anyway, is the earliest charter evidence for Charles as king of the Lombards. The 5 June grant was generous, and its beneficiary, represented by the abbot, was St Columbanus, a name to conjure with in Liguria and far beyond. At the request of the brethren, Charles 'in the palace of Pavia' gave to the monastery 'where St Columbanus lies buried', a piece of woodland, an estate and an 'alp' called Adra, 'a large site . . . in the Petronio valley'.[86] The issue of a royal charter in the palace was a public event. By then the palace had been 'set in order', and other elite Lombards were there to witness, and also to attest, the handing over of the document.[87]

There is only one other extant charter given by Charles at Pavia in 774 (the next one he issued there was in 781, on his way home from his second visit to Rome). This charter, dated 16 July, is much more interesting than the one for Bobbio six weeks earlier. Charles had presumably remained at Pavia meanwhile. Much had been happening during those six weeks: Charles had got on with 'setting things in order'. This charter started, as charters did, with the assertion that it was issued in the name of Charles alone. It soon made clear that the gift Charles was making was from 'our wife Queen Hildegard' as well. The recipients of the gift were the Franks' patron saint, Martin of Tours, and the living abbot of Tours and his successors, 'for the increasing of our [that is, Charles's and Hildegard's] shared reward'. What the couple gave was a perpetual gift to St-Martin and the church's congregation (that is, the monks/canons), for the provision of clothing, and also

> the island-fort of Sirmio, situated in Lake Garda, with its boundaries, publicly seen to pertain to the [Lombard] palace but which will henceforth belong to our fisc [i.e. the royal lands]; the monastery just below the fort, which was newly built by Ansa in honour of the Saviour, in its entirety; and also the Val Camonica with the forest of Candinum and as far as Dalanias, with the mountains and alps from the boundary of Trento

which is called the Tonale [pass], to the boundary of Brixen [in one direction] and the environs of Bergamo [in the other], whatever is within those boundaries which has been known for a long time past and is still known now to lie in that direction and to belong to that valley ... All of this territory has been publicly and at the palace given back, and will from henceforth fall within our fisc, and in a similar way in its entirety to what we have written about Sirmio, thus we have handed over these other [lands]. And we have also added the *xenodochium* [a guest-house for pilgrims, the poor and the sick, under episcopal supervision] built near Pavia in honour of Holy Mary [and other properties near Pavia].[88]

Strategic considerations operated here. The Val Camonica offered a route (as did the Valtellina) via the Tonale pass to Bolzano, thence via either the Reschen or the Brenner to southern Bavaria (see Map 8, p. xxi). For the time being (which was the timespan that mattered to Charles), St-Martin's territory resembled an ecclesiastical 'principality' under a Neustrian abbot.[89]

Other even more pressing considerations involved the symbolism of power. Before Desiderius's surrender, Charles and Hildegard and their sons could be seen as a new Lombard royal-family-in-waiting. After that surrender, Charles and Hildegard and their sons could take up residence in the Lombard palace as a new Lombard royal family replacing the old. In the Val Camonica charter, the topographically specific features seem to have been based on a documentary model from Lombard times, presumably tracked down by Hitherius in the palace archive and emended to suit the new times.[90] The grant showed Lombard royal power replicated and absorbed by the new Frankish rulers and a kingdom of two peoples visibly created. The (untitled) 'Ansa' in the charter-clause transferring the monastic island-fort of Sirmio was the high-born heiress and Lombard queen, devotee of the Virgin Mary, founder of the monastery on Sirmio and, some years before, founder of San Salvatore, Brescia, in her own name and using her own patrimony. Ansa had been a very active consort. Her name, stripped of royal dignity, or any other signifier, at the heart of the charter reminded those who saw or heard it of the rank and status she had now lost. Near the charter's beginning, Hildegard's name stood out as the bearer of a queenliness that was implicitly Frankish. Charles's new title embraced a double kingship, explicitly of Franks and of Lombards. Hildegard's rank and status were implicitly double too, linking her with the Frankish people into which she had married and also with the Lombard people which her husband now ruled.

The calculated re-use by the Frankish royal couple of the charter's Lombard model evoked the power of the new dynasty not just to overlay and suppress the old, or to supersede it, but to inherit it. Hence when Sirmio, from pertaining to the Lombard fisc passed into the Frankish fisc, Hildegard stepped into Ansa's shoes. The author of Hadrian's *Life* had used the phrase *ad instar anterioris* in reference to the borrowing at Rome of the alleged previous Frankish donation at Quierzy: the way the old Lombard fisclands were declared to belong to the fisc of the new ruling family, with its double kingdom straddling the Alps, could be understood as another case of power replicated *ad instar anterioris*. The distance between Francia and Lombardy, and the formal devolution of power in Italy to a sub-kingdom in 781 (see Chapter 7), precluded any practical continuity of Frankish-Lombard queenly management in the longer term. The spectral presence of such a continuity persisted in the *De ordine palatii*, written c.812 by Adalhard, Charles's cousin and de facto viceroy of Italy for much of Charles's reign (see Chapter 16).

In June 774, Desiderius and Ansa, with their daughter, were in custody in Pavia. Adelchis, their only son, had fled to Constantinople, and they were never to see him again (though in 788 he returned to Italy and made a last-ditch failed attempt at a restoration).[91] It seems to me likely that Charles and Hildegard went through a ritual installation as king and queen of the Lombards. True, there is no contemporary evidence at all in this case; but Archbishop Wilchar, who had been on hand to improvise Charles's consecration to a Frankish *monarchia* in December 771, could have been enlisted as consecrator again in 774.[92] If so, Charles and his family stayed in Pavia for at least a couple more months after staging the rituals and performing the legal acts that signified the removal from power of Desiderius and Ansa and the assumption of rule in Lombardy by Charles and Hildegard.[93] 'Setting everything in order' meant taking over the Lombard royal fisc, coming to terms, one by one and collectively, with members of the Lombard elite, and organizing 'the custody of the city of Pavia by Franks'.[94] An echo of Lombard defeat and nostalgic resignation can be heard in the comment of a Frankish annalist: 'As [the Lombards] themselves affirm,

they held sway for 214 years.'[95] A sense of Lombard identity nevertheless survived in the shape of a kingdom with much autonomy, most
obviously in having its own historic laws and legislative power, its own
army, and distinctive ecclesiastical traditions. The so-called 'conquest'
of Italy was not a conquest in any normal sense, for it was bloodless.
Charles's belated decision to extend his rule into Italy left the Lombard
kingdom as de facto largely separate, within an ever-growing *regnum*
of *regna*. Rooted in a more dense and continuous Roman inheritance
than any other early medieval 'barbarian' kingdom, Italy had a distinctive culture. It was grafted on to other 'barbarian' cultures, in particular
that of the Franks, by enthusiastic scholars like Paul the Deacon and
Paulinus of Aquileia who believed themselves to be, and indeed were,
Rome's heirs. In terms of the influence of intellectuals, but also in terms
of social relations and solidarities, shared religion and values transmitted through much peaceful intermarriage, the effect was to expunge
a sense of having been conquered, leaving, instead, a sense that the
'conqueror' himself had been conquered. The Lombard kingdom had
been ended without anything recognizable as a full-blooded conquest
of Italy.

Politically, there was more or less peaceful annexation. People writing in northern and central Italy tended to regard cities, or groups of
city-dwellers, as the basic political units below region-level. These were
run by local notables called *iudices*, and bishops too sometimes loomed
large. There were also dukes in Lombard Italy, but their importance
steadily diminished: by the end of Charles's reign counts had replaced
them.[96] Many counts had Frankish or Alamannic names, and there was
a good deal of intermarriage between elites. In Friuli, for instance,
Charles would replace some, but not all, local counts with Franks, a
story to be told in the next chapter. Through skills of man-management,
and deployment of kin (provided they were not too close), through
ruthlessness and determination, Charles had triumphed, and his family
remained a united one for the next seven years. During them, Italy did
not remain bloodless, any more than Charles's *regnum* (the word can
mean 'kingdom' or 'empire') remained a united kingdom. Charles needed
skills of negotiation and conciliation too. These were to be enhanced,
and more than once tested to near-destruction.

For the moment, in July or August 774, Charles and Hildegard with
their sons headed for Francia, taking with them the Lombard royal

treasure, together with Desiderius and Ansa and a daughter (whether this was Charles's ex-wife or the ex-abbess of San Salvatore it's impossible to say).[97] According to tenth-century annals, Desiderius and Ansa, were 'exiled' at the monastery of Corbie, where the ex-king appeared in the sources for the last time as 'occupied in prayers and fasts and good works until the day of his death'.[98] This was now an ex-royal family, but within it some were more definitively ex- than others, namely, the women – terminally expunged from memory and from the historical record.

6

Peace and War: 774–9

I. CHANGES IN THE SOURCES, 774–80S

Historians since the nineteenth century have considered annalistic sources, especially the *Annales regni Francorum* – the *ArF* – the central pillars on which to reconstruct the events of Charles's reign. In the years from 774 until 785, the court-centred *ArF* are dominated by the Saxon wars. As indicated earlier in this book, the annal-writers' main purpose was to highlight Charles's military exploits in Saxony and his efforts to convert Saxons to Christianity. In a genre by its very nature tendentious these annals are pre-eminently so, because they were being written with the benefit of hindsight in *c.*791 and at Charles's court for court-connected audiences. Some of the so-called 'minor' annals give unique details, indicating special contacts and particular production-contexts. The *Annales Petaviani* (named after an antiquary, Denis Pétau (d.1652), who owned a copy of them) belong in a group of minor annals that begin in 687 (with the victory over the Neustrians at Tertry of Charles's great-grandfather Pippin 'II'), continue in threadbare fashion, and then become fuller from the time of Charles's father, Pippin. The author(s) of these annals from 747 to 770 wrote a compilation of brief notes on Pippin, his sons and their offspring, in (or soon after) 770.[1] There's material in the *Annales Petaviani* not found in the *ArF* on Charles's dealings with Saxons and their conversion (see later in this chapter). 'Minor' annals, then, can be of major interest.

Understanding the Saxon wars of the 770s and early 780s presents more serious difficulties than does the *ArF*'s tendentiousness. Until the 790s, Frankish voices drown out others, or find only their own echoes. Truth to tell, there are no contemporary or even near-contemporary Saxon voices at all. Historians interested in Saxon social arrangements,

The pass of Roncesvaux.

or the origins of individual Saxon leaders, or Saxon contacts with other peoples to the north and east of them, find themselves clutching at evidential straws, or sharing a recent scholar's whimsical thought that Widukind (a Saxon leader first named in 777) could have dropped out of the sky.[2]

For the years covered in this chapter, other sources help give a bigger picture. The papal letters in the *Codex Carolinus* (see Chapter 1), after a gap between 772 and late 774 (for reasons explored in Chapter 4) regain a steadier flow, and information about events as viewed from Rome acquires a new salience, as the letters illuminate many dark Italian corners hitherto poorly lit. Then there are charters. From the single year 775, no fewer than twenty-three charters survive: an amount never matched again in the entire reign. Charters have been discussed relatively seldom in the story so far (though see Chapter 4, pp. 93-7), and they survive patchily:

776	3
777	5
778	2
779	8
780	3

For these years, charters provide very useful information about Charles's itinerary, and about the churches and, very occasionally, the individuals he favoured. In the sections that follow, the focus will be on, successively: Charles's continued involvements in Italy; the Saxon wars; Charles's moves to and fro across the Alps, as, first Saxon raiders, then Italian rebels, exploited his absences from Francia; the extension of Charles's interests to Spain and the aftermath of that reorientation; and, finally, in 779, a flood of light on a significant refashioning of Charles's government.

II. THE *CODEX CAROLINUS* CONTINUED FROM LATE 774

The good news is that the *Codex Carolinus* series resumes with no. 49; the less good news is that the letter can't be dated more precisely than 'late 774'. It is the first of Pope Hadrian's forty-nine letters to have been included in the collection.[3] Hadrian wrote in great agitation about the 'tyrannical and utterly shameless conduct' of Archbishop Leo of Ravenna

after Charles left Italy in July 774. According to the pope, Leo had ille-
gally taken control of nine cities in the province of Emilia, and also of the
Pentapolis – in effect, a good slice of the former exarchate of Ravenna
(see Map 9, p. xxii). Leo had told Charles that Hadrian himself had
authorized the takeover, but this was a tissue of half-truths and wishful
thinking. Leo had thrown out papal officials from cities in Emilia and
replaced them with his own men; still worse, he had been controlling all
the public offices in the city of Ravenna itself. Hadrian continued:

> What in the times of the Lombards we [the pope(s)] held in our power
> and clearly controlled and governed, now in your [i.e. Charles's] times,
> godless and wicked people are trying to take away from our power. They
> reveal themselves as your rivals (*emuli*, envious ones) as well as ours. *Et
> ecce!* [And now look!] Many who are our enemies are taunting and revil-
> ing us, and saying: 'What good did it do you that the people of the
> Lombards was destroyed and put under the yoke of the kingdom of the
> Franks? *Et ecce!* [And now look!] – not one of the promises made has
> been kept.'[4]

In late summer 775, Hadrian had received a letter from Charles to
say that 'Archbishop Leo had hastened to him'. In his response, Hadrian said no more about whatever else Charles might have conveyed.
Either Leo had taken the initiative in 'hastening' to Charles, and
Charles had not repulsed him, or Charles had taken the initiative in
inviting Leo. Hadrian continued:

> As truth is our witness, we very happily receive those who hasten to Your
> Royalty, since . . . a single love exists between us. And if the archbishop
> had sent us word that he wanted to go to your presence, we would with
> happy heart have sent an envoy of ours with him.[5]

The facts were that Leo had *not* sent Hadrian word of his wish to visit
Charles; and Hadrian's heart was *not* happy. This three-way exchange
seems to have little to do with 'a single love between us'. Charles was
egging on Leo to build up Ravenna's lordship at Hadrian's expense. It
would be based on the control of at least ten cities (see Map 9), and
backed by Charles. Early in 775, Hadrian had received a letter from
Charles to say that he planned to come to Rome in the October of that
same year. By October Hadrian was becoming very worried that this
visit was not going to happen after all.[6] He wrote to Charles:

We inform Your Excellence [i.e. Charles] that we have received a letter despatched to us by Patriarch John of Grado which reached us this very day 27 October 775; and we immediately at that same hour, that same moment – neither we nor the notary writing this have taken time off to eat or drink – have forwarded this to you with our apostolic words. We have been greatly distressed to discover that the seals on that letter have been tampered with. The whole thing was read by Archbishop Leo of Ravenna before it was forwarded to us. Your Most Excellent Christianness can see proven here how false is the faith of Archbishop Leo: he dared to open and read the letter before forwarding it, for no other reason than so that he could reveal all that was written in it – as surely everyone can see – to the Duke of Benevento and others who are our rivals (*emuli*) and yours. The archbishop has clearly told them everything.[7]

By November Hadrian had contacted Charles's officials at Pavia to confirm arrangements with the king's *missi* for Charles's visit. Hadrian received a reply to this effect: 'the king's *missi* are certainly not about to set out to visit you any time soon.'[8] It would take a while for Hadrian to grasp a certain truth in the comment of the *emuli*: 'What good did it do you that the people of the Lombards was destroyed and put under the yoke of the kingdom of the Franks?' It was becoming clear that Hadrian's often tenuous claims to restore papal control over what had long ago been papal estates were never going to materialize, and that his attempts to establish a mediatory role for the papacy in Italy were likely to fail.[9] Charles's *missi* would play a cat-and-mouse game with Hadrian, and meanwhile seek constructive engagements with protagonists in Italian politics at the pope's expense. Duke Hildeprand of Spoleto was the most important of Charles's new allies.[10] There is a near-hysterical tone in two of Hadrian's letters dating from December 775/January 776. Charles's *missi*, instead of going direct to Hadrian, had

deviated from the right road and proceeded to Hildeprand in Spoleto. They sent a message saying: 'We are just having talks with Hildeprand and will join you then', but later . . . for reasons unknown to us, they travelled from Spoleto into Benevento, leaving us in great ignominy and increasing the insolence of the Spoletans.[11]

In the next letter, Hadrian had persuaded himself that a huge conspiracy had been formed involving the dukes of Spoleto, Benevento, Friuli and Chiusi (Tuscany), and Adelchis, son of Desiderius, and the Greeks: 'They intend to occupy Rome, this city of ours, to strip bare all the churches of God, to steal the canopy (*ciborium*) of your patron St Peter and, God forbid, take us ourselves prisoner, and further to restore the king of the Lombards and to oppose your royal power.'[12]

In 776, Hadrian's tone was calmer, however. He now foresaw a new, more circumscribed but autonomous, position for the papacy in Rome and its environs. The news from Constantinople of the death of the Emperor Constantine V (on 14 September 775) marked the start of a process whereby imperial traits, for instance the right to mint coins, were adopted into the papacy's symbolic self-representation and projection.[13] By this time Charles, while still (thanks to Hadrian) in touch with affairs in central Italy, had already become deeply involved in affairs in Saxony.

III. SAXONS RAID BORDERLANDS: CHARLES SENDS IN TROOPS

There is no evidence of exactly when Charles became aware of a Saxon attack on the Franks' borderlands in Hesse, or when he decided to prioritize a counter-attack. His absence in Italy had left those borderlands vulnerable and 'unsecured by any treaty'.[14] Saxons had taken their opportunity in late 773. Some had advanced as far as Büraburg, a Frankish fort in northern Hesse, in which the locals took refuge from 'Saxon savagery'.[15]

Saxon efforts to burn down the nearby church of Fritzlar (consecrated by Boniface) failed, thanks to a miracle brought about by the power of the martyr-saint which 'struck terror into the assailants and put them to flight'.[16] So frequent were contacts between the Po valley and the Rhineland that it seems unlikely that Charles did not know of the Saxons' attack quite soon after it occurred.

Charles had preferred to finish off one campaign, involving the removal of two royal families (those of Carloman and Desiderius) and the 'setting in order' of Italian affairs, before embarking on a new one aimed at avenging the Saxon attack on Fritzlar the previous year. In August 774, Charles turned his full attention from Italy to Francia, and refocused it on a Saxon threat. He was ready to leave the Po for the

Rhine. A charter issued from Worms on 2 September for the monastery of Lorsch, only some 20km from Worms, suggests that Abbot Guntland was part of a communications network that kept the king in the loop even when he was far away.[17] Though Charles had brought his armies from Italy more or less intact, he could not have forgotten the threats of defection voiced by some of his own Frankish men before they crossed the Alps and put Desiderius and his frontier-guards to flight in September 773 (p. 131). After almost a year's gruelling stint in Italy, Charles was shrewd enough to reckon his men had earned some home-leave. There's no evidence of where he had resided when he stowed the Lombard treasure in large and sturdy war-chests and stood down most of his men, but his next stops after Worms were apparently Düren, some 40km east of Aachen, where he spent most of September, and then Ingelheim, which could be reached by old Roman roads still usable by horsemen.[18] At Ingelheim, Charles grouped selected men into four *scarae* (bands). 'Three *scarae* engaged in battle with Saxons and were victorious. The fourth did not fight but returned home unscathed with great booty.'[19] Charles could evidently count on the effectiveness of his picked men, even when he was not personally leading them; and the capture of 'great booty', when added to the Lombard royal treasure, would have amplified the royal hoard and boosted the morale of all concerned. Charles then made for Quierzy in Neustria, where he spent Christmas 774 and Easter 775.[20]

IV. CHARLES LEADS A CAMPAIGN INTO SAXONY, 775

The campaign into Saxony in 775, unlike that of 774, was led by Charles himself. It was exceptionally demanding. This passage from the *ArF* is worth quoting (in slightly abbreviated form) because it sets some of the patterns to be seen in later phases of the Saxon wars:

> Charles seized a fort at Hohensyburg and had the fort at the Eresburg rebuilt. He and his men advanced to the Weser, where Saxons were waiting for them on the other bank of the river. Charles forced a crossing, engaged with his opponents and defeated them. He divided his forces into two groups. One he led to the river Oker, where a local leader called Hessi

came with the Saxon Eastphalians and they gave hostages as it pleased Charles to demand, and they swore oaths that they would be faithful to Charles's side. Likewise when the king returned from there, the Angrarians came with Brun and their other leading men to the district of Bucki, and they gave hostages as the Easterners had done. Returning from there, Charles joined up with the army on the river Weser: they were holding the river-bank, as ordered. Saxons had fought a battle with them at Lübbecke, and victory had gone to the Franks who killed many of those Saxons. When Charles heard of this, he fell upon those Saxons a second time and inflicted no less slaughter on them, and won much booty from the Westphalians, who gave hostages like the other Saxons.[21]

The *ArF* author summed up: 'Charles had taken hostages, acquired abundant booty, and three times brought about carnage among the Saxons.'

A longer summing-up might go like this. Charles had first concentrated on forts, a key part of his strategy. He had then divided his forces into two armies, of which he led one (the leader of the other being unnamed). Charles had already used this tactic in 773 when he and his uncle, Bernard, crossed the Alps with their separate armies by separate passes; the author of the *ArF* mentioned here for the first time a three-fold division amongst Saxons – Eastphalians, Westphalians and Angrarians, and two Saxon leaders, Hessi and Brun, were named (neither is mentioned again). When Charles, after leading his first army to victory on the river Oker, returned to the second army stationed on the river Weser, he found them still at their posts, as ordered, implying he did not need to be there in person for his men to obey his orders. The second army had beaten the Saxons at Lübbecke. Charles beat them again and won 'much booty'; he then conducted negotiations and peace-makings through the demanding of hostages and the taking of oaths. Coming home with much booty was *the* sign of victory, and all three victories were credited to Charles. Many of these features recurred in the Saxon wars.

There were no 'average' years in the reign of Charles. Late in 775, an event occurred which is mentioned in none of the sources but can be calculated by reference to other events and later guesswork about dates: this was the birth of Hildegard's daughter Rotrud, named for her great-grandmother. Such an event was important enough in dynastic terms to warrant a celebration by family and court in a favoured royal residence. Charles, however, glad as he was to have a daughter to play a part in future family strategies, could not be part of that celebration. The news of a rebellion in Friuli set him moving rapidly south 'with a number of Franks' (implying a select force rather than a large one) to spend Christmas at Selestatt in Alsace en route to Italy.

V. THE CHARTER EVIDENCE OF 775, AND A RECENT HYPOTHESIS

For no other year in Charles's reign does the number of extant charters near anything close to that of 775. Twenty-three survive from that year, and for every month of that year save September, at least one charter still exists. After the travels and upheavals of 772–4, Charles in 775 veered between relatively long periods of stable residence and a relatively brief period of frenetic military activity. Eleven charters were issued at the Oise-valley palace of Quierzy where Charles apparently stayed between Christmas and Easter, with the exception of a visit to St-Denis in February where perhaps he visited his mother, and from then, with the exception of a visit to Thionville (some 120km from Quierzy) in early May, until the end of July.[22] This period of Neustrian residence registered continuity with both the reign of Pippin and, before that, the days of Merovingian rule. Further, a glance at the list of recipients of these charters indicates the now greatly increased extent of Charles's realm, of the catchment-area of beneficiaries, and of his own itinerary.

The monastery of Hersfeld in Thuringia was founded in 769 by Boniface's successor, Archbishop Lull of Mainz, who 'set himself up as abbot'. On 5 January 775, Lull received from Charles a grant of protection for his monastery, as well as giving the monks the right to choose their abbots; a second charter on the same day granted the valuable asset of saltpans on the rivers Werra and Weser, and, not long after, three further grants of tithes.[23] Later that year, grants or confirmations or favours of various kinds were received from Charles by the following:

Bishop Angilramn of Metz for his cathedral church
Abbot Fulrad of St-Denis[24]

Abbot Amico of Murbach, near Colmar
Abbot Manasses of Flavigny in Burgundy
Abbot Hitherius of St-Martin's, Tours[25]
Abbot Probatus of Farfa in Spoleto
Abbot Beatus of Honau in Baden
Abbot Sturm of Fulda
Abbot Asoarius of Prüm

The above pattern of grants has rightly been considered, in a neat résumé, 'a Carolingian church policy' combined with a series of 'attempts to regulate and control the church'.[26] From the beneficiaries' standpoint, all this could also be called something of a bonanza. By way of comparison, 37 of Charles's 164 extant charters date from the years between 769 and 775.

A different approach to these twenty-three charters was proposed in 2008 by Rosamond McKitterick, who offered a new suggestion about the way charters were issued. Scholars had previously held that charters were given by the king in person to beneficiaries who thus had to travel to wherever he was known to be residing. The new suggestion was that the charters issued from Düren in July, August and October 775

> would require [the king] to have been returning from the Weser river campaign, at least a ten-day journey, at regular intervals, before finally reaching the palace of Thionville [in November] . . . Rather than accepting the charters as an indication of the physical presence of the king, therefore, it is far more likely that we are seeing in many, if not most, instances the activities of the king's officials . . . The itinerary for these years is much more likely to have been simply from Quierzy to Düren to Saxony [then back to Thionville].[27]

The only other source for Charles's itinerary in 775, namely, the *ArF*, does not say when the army was summoned and when the king left Düren for Saxony: if he had done so in August or September, there would be no difficulty in pinpointing his return from campaign in late October, the date of DD. 104 and 105, and no need to suppose the king's 'returning [from Saxony] at regular intervals'.[28]

A second objection to the new hypothesis is more far-reaching and needs to be taken very seriously. Were it to be generally accepted that groups of the king's local officials issued charters, not only would that destroy the ground-rules of diplomatics (medieval charter-studies) as a scholarly sub-field, but it would require a total rethink of present understandings of how early medieval kingship worked. It would mean, as a leading German medieval historian put it, 'questioning an axiom of both diplomatics and the constitutional history of the early and high Middle Ages'.[29] It would also imply, I think, an inexplicable reduction in the performative and ritual aspects of royal action: areas in which Charles himself was interested, and which were variously elaborated in the course of his reign.[30]

VI. REBELLION IN FRIULI AND THE *NOTITIA ITALICA*

The rebellion, late in 775, led by Duke Hrodgaud of Friuli in north-eastern Italy had rapidly set Charles on the move again with 'all his most vigorous men' – and with a vengeance. Hrodgaud 'had betrayed his faith and broken all his oaths'.[31] He was rumoured to have 'stirred up many cities to defect to him', and 'aspired to kingship'.[32] Charles took the time it took to crush the rebellion definitively. Hrodgaud was killed. Charles spent Easter 776 (14 April) at Treviso. 'He distributed all the captured cities – Cividale, Treviso and the others which had rebelled – among Franks.'[33] It was characteristic of Charles to take the opportunity of being back in Lombardy to 'set matters in order' again, as he had in 774, but now not just by putting Franks in charge of captured cities, but also by legislating. The *Notitia italica*, dated 20 February, but without a year, has generally been dated to 776 on the reasonable grounds that Charles was in no position to legislate for Italy on 20 February 774.[34] A recent attempt has been made to claim the evidence 'ambiguous', and to connect the issue of a charter (D. 79, dated 19 February, outside Pavia, ratifying an exchange between two Frankish churchmen) with a legal assembly on the following day.[35] Charles was not yet *rex Langobardorum* in 774: he was acting as if in a corner of a foreign field that was for the moment Francia. But the terms of the *notitia* are all about *Lombard* problems. Of course it is *possible* that the *notitia* was produced 'to win over the local population' or as 'an invitation to transfer political allegiance' in February 774, and *possible* that it was 'a very practical and immediate response to the problems created by the presence of Charlemagne's army camped outside Pavia'.[36] But to my mind it is *probable* that this *notitia* was issued as an Italian capitulary by Charles acting as king of the Lombards (*Placuit nobis* . . . 'It has pleased us . . .' is a standard form in Carolingian Italian capitularies) when he was actually ruling over them and not in a camp during a siege.[37] He began, in a brief prologue, by recalling 'when men had had to sell their families into servitude', and he now declared that any charters made then, if found, should be made void and their children be 'as free as before'. Further,

> [c. 2] If anyone complains that their property has been sold at an unjust price, both parties are to come with estimators who will make a written assessment of what the price was *when the property was in a good state before we came here with the army*. If the price was fair, it shall stand . . . If the seller can prove he sold under threat of starvation, the sale shall be null and void . . . [c. 4] And *we command that in those parts where we and our army were, a just judgement should be made, as written above*; and we lay down this, that [in the case of] charters made in the time of Desiderius because of threat of starvation, or by some trickery, that that case should not be counted, but settled according to their law [my italics].[38]

Charles made a strong rhetorical point here, not contrasting bad times then with good times now, but acknowledging his own share of responsibility for bad times then, and at the same time showing that he was now intent on providing just government over his people 'according to their law'. In short, Charles presented himself as a man of magnanimity (a quality later stressed by Einhard!).[39] What the *Notitia italica* showcased was Charles's virtue. The contrasting of 'then' (*tunc*), when things were in a good state of repair, with 'before we came here with an army' (*antequam nos hic cum exercitu introissemus*), was a frank acceptance of responsibility. Charles's campaign into Friuli at the beginning of 776 ended with success not just in military and political terms, not just presentationally, but also, to give him his due (or at least the benefit of the doubt), *morally*. 'The time of Desiderius' had been no golden age ('men had had to sell their families into servitude'), but it was Charles's intent to restore a time when 'things were in a good state of repair'. His agents might have discovered that, in comparison with Francia, Italy showed 'a noticeably greater . . . concern to present voluntary unfree service as reciprocal in nature and not in principle dishonouring', while 'self-givers ... had a great deal of scope to present their own actions as an honourable gift of themselves, in the spirit of Christian virtue'.[40]

Before leaving Italy, though, Charles took out an insurance policy for keeping control there. He chose a select group of high-born Lombard hostages to take to Francia with him. The evidence for this is typically indirect, surviving in two very different types of source and dating from some years after 776. One is a public document, a capitulary issued at Pavia in October 787 in the name of Charles's by then ten-year-old son Carloman (now known as King Pippin of Italy), but actually a document sent to Pavia by Charles himself. It is headed, 'In the name of the Lord. Here begins a list of *capitula* about various legal rights, according to the document (*sceda*) of the lord Charles, our father'; and c. 10 begins: '*Placuit nobis de illis feminis quarum mariti in Francia esse videntur . . .*'

> It has pleased us, concerning those women whose husbands are evidently in Francia: our *missi* throughout our kingdom must make inquiries into this, whether they keep their rights in full, as has been the command of our lord king, or whether they do not keep them: if they do, fine (*et qui sic habuerit, bene*); but if they do not, then it is our will that our *missi* along with the count in whose area of responsibility they are must entirely carry out what our lord commanded.[41]

The thrust of this order is in line with the more general aims of the *notitia*: Charles had meant what he said. He intended his *missi* and counts to make inquiries, to obey orders about giving protection to those needing it, and he specifically wished the wives of Lombard hostages held in Francia to 'keep their rights in full'.

The second piece of evidence is a poem written by Paul the Deacon, brother of one of the Lombard hostages. Written in 'the seventh year after the *nova causa* [upheaval, disaster] generated so many sorrows', that is, in 782, and addressed either to Charles or to one of his counsellors, Peter of Pisa, the poem evoked the wretched situation of Paul's brother ('a prisoner in your land, with a heart full of grief, stripped and needy'), and was a plea for his release.[42] From this Lombard's point of view, 774 had not been the end of the disaster, and nor had 776. The brother's story did in fact have a happy ending; but, as Paul wrote his plea, his brother's time of sorrows was ongoing.

VII. CHARLES ATTENDS TO A PERSONAL MATTER

Charles spent Christmas and Epiphany in 777 at the palace of Herstal for the first time since 772 (when he had confirmed St-Germain's immunity at what was doubtless a great assembly).[43] For Charles Herstal became a relatively frequent residence, to be outstripped only by Aachen.[44] In January 777, at Herstal, Charles made grants to Lorsch at the request of Abbot Guntland and to Fulda at the request of Abbot Sturm.[45] On the back of D. 116 the draft of a manumission is inscribed in Tironian notes. The beneficiary was *Sigrada, ancilla nostra* ('our handmaiden), declared free 'by our hand, by a penny-throw according to *Lex Salica*', as described in a legal formula.[46] As Alice Rio points out, a patron's manumission – and what patron could have wielded more clout than Charles? – would 'protect more vulnerable freed women'. Noting parallels with later Carolingian rulers' manumissions of women, Rio adds that this 'perhaps reflected a prior or existing sexual connection'.[47] If so, this could suggest that Charles had sexual relations with *ancillae* or concubines during the same decades that he had a series of queens. Hildegard was his queen from 772 to 783. Given the number of her pregnancies, Charles may well have enjoyed sex with other women in those years, contrary to the impression given by Einhard that a series of queens was followed, when Charles was a widower, by a number of other women.[48] Sigrada may have been Charles's concubine, or a particularly faithful maidservant (a wet-nurse, for instance).[49] That Charles had a document drawn up to manumit her suggests a conscientious concern to protect an individual woman in his service.

VIII. CHARLES NEGOTIATES A SETTLEMENT WITH SAXONS

The author of the 776 annal had a story to tell of encounters in and around the Frankish forts of Eresburg and Syburg, in all of which the Franks came off best. As in 773, there was a miracle about a church, this time a church in a fort. Saxons were preparing to attack the

Christians in the fort when a miracle occurred: 'God's glory appeared manifest above the building that housed the Lord's church.' As in 773, the author used the labels Christians (here, four times) and pagans (once).[50] Charles had apparently returned to Worms from Friuli by the time he learned of all these events: an indication that they had happened very recently.

> He summoned the assembly to Worms, at which a decision was quickly made. He went with extreme speed (*nimia festinatione*) and so was able to surprise the Saxons by getting into their barricades and defence-lines, and striking such terror into them that they came from the whole region to the place called Lippspringe. There they all surrendered their fatherland (*patria*) by a pledge into their [the Franks'] hands, promised to be Christians, and subdued themselves to the rule of the lord king Charles and of the Franks. Charles, with the Franks, rebuilt yet again the Eresburg fort and another fort on the river Lippe. They came with their wives and children, a multitude without number, and were baptized and gave hostages, as many as the king asked for. And after the forts had been completed, and the Franks had stationed *scarae* in them to live there to guard them, Charles returned to Francia.[51]

Events in Saxony had turned out better than Charles could have hoped. The author of the *ArF* marvelled at the numbers to be baptized. All those seeking baptism, and all those hostages needing suitable minders, kept clergy and laity fully occupied. Several authors of minor annals amplified the picture: the numbers baptized acquired a plausible solidity as 'leading families';[52] 'Charles built a *civitas* which is called Karlsburg on the river Lippe', and 'a city was built by the Franks in the land of the Saxons which is called the fort of Charles and the Franks (*urbs Caroli et Francorum*)'[53] – a political statement if ever there was one. Spain had its Reccopolis, named after the seventh-century king Recceswinth; but the name to conjure with, and imitate, was that of Constantinople. Perhaps it was because Saxons burned down the new city only two years later that the Franks (it had been their city too) felt no urge to rebuild it.[54]

The *ArF* for 777 is unusually brief, in effect consisting of three statements. Its information is also exceptionally important – which makes it tempting to infer that something else was being suppressed by an author with the benefit of hindsight. The first statement was this:

a general assembly was held at Paderborn, in Saxony, for the first time. All the Franks gathered there and, from every part of Saxony whatsoever, the Saxons too. The exception was Widukind [unnamed hitherto]. He with a few others was in rebellion and took refuge in Nordmannia with his warrior-companions.

Significantly, the *ArF* author noted Charles's holding of an assembly in Paderborn 'for the first time', and also that Franks as well as Saxons were assembled there.

I shall return in a moment to the second statement (about Widukind), and give the third now:

A multitude of Saxons were baptized there and, in accordance with their custom, with their own hands they surrendered their freedom and their property as a pledge, to be forfeited if they should undergo a change of heart – such was their evil habit – and not maintain their Christianity and their fidelity to Charles, his sons and the Franks.

All this was a repeat of the surrenders of land and pledges of submission to Charles and the Franks, and the mass baptisms, of 776. What differed was the setting, the Saxony-wide area whence came those assembled, and a small but significant change in the wording of the oath, which was now taken not just to Charles but 'to his sons and to the Franks' as well.[55] Certainly, this was nothing new: it went back at least three centuries in the practice of oath-swearing, if irregularly. But now, in Charles's time, there was a stronger stress on the solidarity between the ruler and his *gens*, his Frankish people, and also on the continuity from one generation to the next that persisted, reassuringly, through dynastic succession. The second statement, brief and sandwiched between other, longer, passages about Saxons and Franks, was this: 'To this assembly there came also Saracens from Spain: namely, Ibn al-Arabi, and the son and son-in-law of Deiuzef (Yusuf), called Joseph in Latin.'

The author of the revised version of the *ArF* was writing more than a decade after the *ArF* author, and over (perhaps well over) two decades after these events themselves.[56] The reviser was much more interested in Saxons than the *ArF* author, and, drawing much more on hindsight, larded his narrative with comments on Saxon fraudulent promises and false vows. He named Sigifrid king of the Danes as the Northman to whom Widukind had fled, and also identified Widukind as 'one of the chief men of the Westfalians'. The reviser placed the Saracens' arrival at Paderborn at the end of the 777 annal (adding only the fact that the assembly ended, and the conventional mentions of where the king spent Christmas and Easter). Finally, the reviser left out the particulars about Joseph's son and son-in-law, but stated that Ibn al-Arabi had come 'with other Saracens, his associates, into the presence of the king, and had surrendered himself and the cities of which the king of the Saracens had put him in charge'. Contemporary annals add details, on the strength of information obtained in Spain in 778: Abu Taher and Ibn al-Arabi were 'kings of the Saracens' who ruled 'the cities of Huesca, Barcelona and Gerona'.[57]

Some of the history of eighth-century Muslim Spain is needed for the backstory.[58] Yusuf had been amir of Córdoba until 756, when he was ousted by Abd al-Rahman, the last scion of the Umayyad dynasty. When the Abbasids had taken over the caliphate from the Umayyads in 750 (and moved their capital to Baghdad), Abd al-Rahman had escaped from Damascus to Spain, taking several years before he established himself at Córdoba as amir. His hold on Muslim Spain was limited to al-Andalus in the south and south-west. He did not control Toledo or Zaragoza or the Ebro valley. Yusuf had died some time after 756, leaving sons and a son-in-law. (It was one of those sons and the son-in-law who were mentioned along with Ibn al-Arabi as present at Paderborn.) A late tenth-century historian writing in Córdoba recorded an alliance and revolt of al-Arabi, governor of Barcelona and Gerona, and al-Ansari, governor of Zaragoza, in 774, without, apparently, stating the outcome.[59]

Historians have accepted that the Saracen visitors to Paderborn had come on their own initiative: Yusuf's son and son-in-law to see if Charles would support their attempt at a restoration of their family; al-Arabi to defect from the nominal rule of the amir, and offer his city to the king of the Franks. Given what is known of communications networks – transmontane, riverine, or along still-usable Roman roads – those suggestions are conceivable. Given what is known of Charles's responsiveness, when it suited him, to others' requests, it is conceivable that this was another case in point. But an alternative possibility is also worth considering: namely, that Charles used his information networks and far-flung contacts to take the initiative himself in 777, to send out feelers and, in effect, to invite these potential defectors from the amirate to come to Paderborn. Charles had reason to believe he could close a deal which could benefit all parties, however temporarily. The Franks had a long military track-record of intervening against Visigoths, and more recent memories of successful efforts against Saracens.[60] An intervention in the Ebro valley was not a fantasy, but a potentially lucrative and politically advantageous plan. If presented as a defensive reaction to the actions of the Hagarenes (an alternative term for Saracens), even the pope could welcome it.[61]

Then there was the matter of staging. Charles had selected Paderborn as the location of that year's great Frankish assembly. He had planned for massed baptisms there, and the building of a church: 'And the Saxons came together for catholic baptism, and many thousands of those pagan people were baptized; and the Franks built a church there. Wherefore King Charles presently rejoices with John the Baptist, who also baptized, preaching baptism in the remission of sins.'[62] The contemporary author of the Petau Annals recorded a moment of eschatological elation when he likened Charles to John the Baptist. As 'thousands' of Saxon converts and a very large number of Franks looked on, the presence of exotic envoys (bringing, it goes without saying, exotic gifts) could only heighten the headiness of a hugely symbolic event.[63] The *coup de théâtre* that was the Paderborn assembly was followed by negotiations with the Saracen governors of cities and territories, and the making of plans for the construction of a cordon sanitaire in Navarre and the Ebro valley to protect the Franks' Spanish March. Charles was already planning the demonstration of power that a very large army comprising contingents from many different peoples would embody and represent in Spain. He spent Christmas 777, for the first and only time in his reign, at Douzy on the Meuse. Probably from this place, on the historic margins between the major provinces of the Frankish realm, Charles sent out summonses to 778's campaign.

Something of the Paderborn assembly's atmosphere of excitement persisted, heightened, into the winter at Douzy. Charles had invited the young Lombard scholar and cleric Paulinus (who would become bishop of Aquileia in, probably, 787) to join the court circle in Francia in 776, so the young scholar participated in the 777 assembly, and in the presence of the Saracen envoys watched the mass baptism of Saxons. At Douzy, Paulinus recited a panegyric seventy-two-line poem (*carmen*) to the court. It was entitled 'The Saxons' Conversion'. A few lines convey the impact the poet wanted to make on his audience and especially on the impressionable Charles:

> Charles the prince, girded boldly with gleaming arms . . .
> tamed this people through various blows and a thousand
>   triumphs and . . . crushed it down and subjected it to
> himself with brandished sword:
> he dragged the battalions of forest-worshippers (*silvicolae*)
> into heavenly kingdoms . . .
> Afterwards he poured over with the salvation-bringing
>   dew of baptism
> the untaught Christ-worshippers (*Christicolae*), and sent
>   them to the stars of heaven
> . . . and led the new progeny of Christ into the hall . . .
> May God grant that the clement prince, for so great a
>   reward . . .
> may taste the sweet pastures of honey-flowing life:
> pastures which our Redeemer already long since
>   promised by right
> with his own mouth to give to the Heaven-worshippers
> (*Caelicolae*).[64]

Now, perhaps for the first time, Charles grasped the power of poetry to influence politics.[65] It was a portent of further experiments in the creation of a courtly society.[66]

IX. CHARLES'S SPANISH CAMPAIGN, 778

In the army that Charles assembled were troops from the heartlands of Francia and from 'Burgundy and Austrasia, Bavaria and Provence and Septimania and parts of Lombardy'. Charles reused a tactic he had tried successfully in 773 and in 775: he divided his forces into two. The army of many peoples travelled by a more southerly route; Charles's Frankish army, probably augmented by an Aquitanian contingent, would travel via Chasseneuil and Pamplona, and the two armies would meet at Zaragoza. Why Chasseneuil, where no Carolingian is ever known to have stayed before then? Annal-writers seldom if ever mentioned a queen's pregnancy or a royal baby's birth, but they would, almost infallibly, mention where the king celebrated Easter. Chasseneuil was where Charles celebrated Easter on 19 April 778, according to the author of the *ArF*, who did not say that Hildegard was there too. A quite different writer who *did* show an interest in Hildegard was the so-called 'Astronomer', a court cleric who (as his nickname suggests) had an interest in astronomy, and who in 840 wrote the *Life of Louis the Pious*, the first twenty-one chapters of which covered Louis' life and reign in Aquitaine before 814. It was the Astronomer who recorded that Hildegard was staying at Chasseneuil that Easter, pregnant again, this time with twins – one of them the future Louis. Chasseneuil, the largest of the four royal palaces in Aquitaine, and presumably the most comfortable, was where Hildegard stayed while Charles went southwards with his army. The Astronomer continued: 'Charles crossed the Garonne on the frontier between the Aquitanians, and the Gascons whose land he had long since received in surrender. There Charles regulated matters as circumstances and advantage dictated.' At this point, the author, who evidently did not know quite when in his narrative to place this information, observed: 'Charles decided to overcome the difficulties of the Pyrenees and go to Spain.'

The Astronomer, writing over sixty years after these events, produced a fair sketch of Charles's actions in 778, drawing most likely on the memories of old comrades and courtiers. The *ArF* author retold early summer's events in Spain in a few lines (I abbreviate slightly):

> Charles came by way of Pamplona. His army and the other army converged at Zaragoza, as planned. There Charles received hostages from al-Arabi, Abu-Taher and many Saracens. After Pamplona had been destroyed, and the Spanish Basques and Navarrans subjugated, he returned to Francia.

This author had no more to say about the Spanish campaign. 'As understatement, this account is masterly to the point of mendacity.'[67] Was this the flipside of masterly tendentiousness? A defeat could not be elided or concealed when the audience at whom the account was directed, only a dozen years after the event, was Charles's court. The omission was deliberate. But the *ArF*'s reviser took a different view, as, later, did Einhard, and the Astronomer.

The annal's reviser, with longer hindsight, and information he had no interest in concealing, described a quite different outcome:

At the persuasion of al-Arabi, Charles then conceived the far from idle hope of gaining certain cities in Spain. After calling an army together, he set off, overcame the heights of the Pyrenees in the territory of the Basques, descended to Pamplona which he attacked and whose surrender he accepted.[68] From there, crossing the river Ebro by a ford, he advanced to Zaragoza, the principal city of those parts. Then, having received the hostages offered by al-Arabi and Abu-Taher and certain other Saracens, he returned to Pamplona. He razed its walls to the ground to forestall the possibility of future rebellion, and, deciding to withdraw, moved up into the pass across the Pyrenees. At the highest part of the pass, Basques lay in ambush. They attacked the rearguard and threw the whole army into great confusion and disorder. Although the Franks were manifestly superior to the Basques in both weapons and courage, they were neverthe-less made inferiors by the steepness of the terrain and the unequal nature of the battle. A considerable number of palace dignitaries (*aulici*) whom Charles had put in command of these troops were killed in this encounter. The baggage was plundered and the enemy promptly slipped away in all directions, because of their knowledge of the landscape. The pain of the wound he received overclouded in the king's heart a large part of what had gone successfully in Spain.[69]

The deaths of *aulici* – none of them named by the reviser – evidently made a deeply sad and memorable impression on Charles. Einhard's account in the *Vita Karoli*, as well as giving an account of events quite similar to the reviser's, adds some important further details – including three names:

He decided to invade Spain with as large an army as he could muster. After crossing the wild country of the Pyrenees, he received in surrender (*in deditionem*) all the towns and fortifications on his route, and turned back with his army safe and sound – except that in that same Pyrenean pass [as on the outward journey] as he was returning, it happened that he very soon experienced the treachery of the Basques. Dense forests stretching in all directions make this a good place for setting ambushes; while the troops were proceeding in a long column as the narrowness of the local defiles allowed, Basques had set their ambush at the top of the highest mountain, and they came rushing down from above onto the last part of the baggage-train and the troops supporting the rearguard, protecting those who had gone on ahead. Forcing these troops down into the valley below, the Basques joined battle with them and slew them down to the last man. They then plundered the baggage and, protected by the cover of the night which was beginning to fall, they scattered with all speed in every direction. The Basques were helped by the lightness of their armour and the nature of the ground on which all this was happening, whereas the Franks were made completely unequal to the Basques, because of the heaviness of their armour and the unevenness of the terrain. In this battle died the king's steward Eggihard, the count of the palace Anselm, and Roland, commander of the Breton March, along with many others. Nor was it possible to avenge this deed for the present because the enemy had dispersed in such a way that no report (*fama*) of the encounter could be found among the peoples (*gentes*) in the area wherever they were located.[70]

The consensus among historians has long been (and still is) that Roncesvaux was 'a military catastrophe',[71] and at least one distinguished historian thought that Charles's 'vanity and inexperience' were to blame for it.[72] An extension of that suggestion might be that the Paderborn assembly had gone to Charles's head. Historians differ in their assessments of the campaign itself: for instance, the razing of Pamplona's walls has been seen as foolhardy;[73] but the annal reviser saw it as tactically wise, because it would forestall the city's rebelling (*ne rebellare posset*) – a comment evidently implying that, in the reviser's view, at least, Charles planned to return to Pamplona.[74]

The reviser's account was infused by what used to be called (and perhaps still should be called) Carolingian rationalism.[75] It would be unreasonable to think Charles could have foreseen the ambush. Basques were mountain-men, experts in setting ambushes. The Franks were unfamiliar with such tactics. The mountainside up which the Frankish baggage-train moved was very steep and the terrain very uneven. With night coming on, visibility was poor.

Einhard partly shared this rationalizing view. His account in chapter 9 started with a very long sentence, whose penultimate phrase was 'he was returning with his army safe and intact', and whose last phrase begins *praeter quod* – 'except that . . .' The reader has the impression of an unspoken thought between the two phrases: 'all would have gone well – except that . . . it happened that . . . (*praeter quod . . . contigit . . .*)'. Human beings could not be blamed when contingency intervened. The Astronomer, though inserting plenty of allusions to divine favour, and claiming that Charles's campaign had been undertaken 'to bring help to the Church suffering under the yoke of the Saracens', could also adopt a rationalizing tone. In his account of the outward journey across the Pyrenees, he added some touches to the description of the mountain-topography – the density of the forests, the narrowness of the path – and the prosperous outcome (with several references to classical writers and such heroes as Pompey and Hannibal). When it came to the return journey, the Astronomer did not mention Basques but instead attributed the ambush to 'a treacherous, uncertain and changeable turn of fortune', and, a little later, to 'a misfortune [because of which] certain of the rearguard of the royal column were killed in those mountains'.

Charles's campaign was just that: a campaign. It was not a wild venture prompted by a sudden rush of blood to the brain at Paderborn, though there was more than a whiff of collective apocalyptic enthusiasm at the winter court at Douzy which followed that assembly. Charles took preparatory measures to minimize risk. (It is possible that he or one of his commanders had access to the work of the late-fourth/fifth-century Roman military expert Vegetius, author of a comprehensive manual *De re militari* (*On military matters*).[76]) The campaigns in Lombardy had been similarly planned. Had other things been equal, and but for the ambush, the Spanish campaign could have been a success both in retaining the interest of Saracen allies and acquiring Navarran plunder.[77]

Charles's responses to the experience of Roncesvaux were not defeatist. True, once back on the Frankish side of the Pyrenees, Charles did not concern himself with campaigning in Spain for the next twenty years. Nevertheless, his withdrawal was strategic. He rightly reckoned that neither the Saracen city-lords, endlessly involved in internecine conflicts with the amir of Córdoba and each other, nor the Basques in their Pyrenean fastnesses were likely to pose an offensive threat in the near future. In the meantime Charles had urgent matters to deal with in Aquitaine and in Francia, and – as he surely guessed – in Saxony. To these he very quickly turned. He headed back to Chasseneuil to see the baby twin boys and, together with Hildegard (whom it's not far-fetched to credit with an interest in dynastic histories), to give them names:

Clovis (Louis) and Chlothar (Lothar) – defiantly evoking two Merovingian kings who had triumphed in Aquitaine and Saxony. 'The *rex Francorum* hoped to bind his *gens Francorum* yet more closely to himself at this critical moment.'[78] These names were to be appropriated as pledges of the new dynasty's good fortune. Charles found little time to celebrate the twins' arrival, and did not linger in Aquitaine. Instead, he moved some 400km north-east to Auxerre.

There he got news which he might well have anticipated, for it was not a new story: 'Saxons finding themselves with an opportunity [had taken up] arms and advanced to the Rhine.'[79]

> He sent a Frankish *scara* to hasten at great speed to oppose those Saxons, but they got as far at Deutz and then plundered up the Rhine ... When they suddenly heard of Charles's return and of the *scara* sent against them, they withdrew to Saxony; but the Franks found their trail and pursued them to Leisa on the Eder in Hesse. Battle was joined and the Franks were the victors. A multitude of Saxons were slain there while those who fled returned to Saxony in deep disgrace (*cum magno contumelio*).[80]

In 779, another Frankish campaign was mounted into Saxony where local Saxons this time seemed likely to offer resistance.

> They did not prevail: they fled, abandoning all their defences. The way lay open for the Franks who went among the Westphalians and overcame them all. When Charles arrived at Vlotho [on the Weser near the Süntel hills], the other Saxons came there from beyond the Weser, gave hostages and confirmed their oaths.[81]

In 780 Charles himself came to Saxony, where, in the *ArF*'s reviser's phrase for all seasons, 'he settled everything . . .'

> He came to the Eresburg, and then moved to Lippspringe where he held the assembly. Then he went to the region of the Elbe, and on that campaign, all the Bardengau people and many of the people of the Nordleudi were baptized at Ohrum on the other side of the river Oker. The king reached the Elbe at the point where the Ohre flows into it, and there settled everything concerning Saxony and also the Slavs. And he returned to Francia.[82]

The two years, summer to summer, that followed the Spanish campaign were full of Frankish military action, all of it successful. Despite the misfortune that had struck down the rearguard, Charles had got the bulk of his army out of Spain safe and intact, materially un-affected. The loss of the baggage-train itself and whatever materiel the Basques took could be seen as relatively minor setbacks, when compared with the huge gain of the Lombard royal treasure (in 774), and (probably) loot that accompanied the hostages from Friuli (in 776). In short, the year 778 was not, after all, and with due respect to the judgement of that great historian F.-L. Ganshof, a year of 'extremely serious crisis' and of a 'failure' that 'almost transformed defeat into disaster'. Nor was 'the Carolingian state on the verge of collapse'.[83]

X. NAMES

The Astronomer, who had so carefully disambiguated the little twin boys born to Hildegard in 778, was interested in the phenomenon of twins:

> One of these was snatched away prematurely by death, beginning to die almost before beginning to live in the light, but the other had emerged safely from his mother's womb, and was being nourished the way babies are. They were born in 778. And when the one who gave promise of a vigorous constitution was reborn through the sacrament of baptism, it pleased his father to call him Louis.[84]

Unlike the Astronomer, writing over sixty years after the event, who mentioned the twins but named only Louis, Paul the Deacon, writing c.784, gave the names of *both* twins in his *Deeds of the Bishops of Auxerre*, with the extra information that Lothar lived for two years before dying in 780. Baby Lothar's epitaph indicated that he died soon after birth. As long as the dynasty lasted, both names continued to be chosen for Carolingian baby boys.

The Astronomer, after attributing the ambush at Roncesvaux to 'the treacherous turn of fortune' that caused 'certain of the rearguard to be killed in those mountains', added: 'Since their names are widely known, I have decided not to give them.'[85] This may have been yet another expression of Carolingian rationalism – interesting in itself, if true, for what it revealed of what was 'known' after a lapse of sixty years. A notable feature of religion in Charles's reign was concern on the part of the laity, not only elites but peasants too, to record the names of those bringing offerings of bread and wine (or corn and grapes) to church 'to bring consolation to the living'.[86] Among elites in this period, the commemoration of the dead individually by their own names also came to be widely practised, whether through being named *legibly* in annals or epitaphs, or through having their names recorded in Memorial Books kept in monasteries or cathedral churches, and read out *audibly* in the liturgy. Names were very often grouped by family for purposes of group-remembering, and this happened in Charles's case too.[87]

A class of male persons that acquired a profile in Charles's reign were officials who performed particular functions at court.[88] They were laymen (whereas counsellors could be laymen or churchmen) serving primarily in the palace or hall (*aula*) or in military commands. While *palatini* were current among the Franks long before Charles's reign, *aulici* appeared in 778 in the context of Roncesvaux. Of the three *aulici* named in Einhard's *Vita Karoli* (written, almost certainly, in 829), the historic existence of Eggihard is proven by his epitaph, and that of Anselm by his appearance in two of Charles's charters as count of the palace.[89] Of the 123 extant manuscripts, a whole large group, labelled 'B' by palaeographers, did not include Roland's name, but a much smaller group (labelled 'A' and descending from a slightly earlier manuscript tradition) *did* include his name. Roland's name appeared in the place of a mint-name on an early coin of Charles's reign, when a number of great magnates controlled regional coinages before Charles established his full authority over minting.[90] Finally, it's likely Roland the *aulicus* is the 'Count Rothland' mentioned in D. 66 of 772.[91] This trio, then, pass muster as men who actually existed and occupied the kinds of posts held by *aulici*.

The sources make clear that *aulici* were appointed by Charles personally; their service to the king was especially important, and their deaths in battle signified correspondingly painful losses for the king. The relationship between the king and each *aulicus*, like other vertical dyadic bonds – between lord and man, between nurturer and nourished – were peculiarly emotionally charged.[92] It was a matter of trust. The *ArF* reviser wrote – in words that deserve to be repeated: 'The pain of the wound the king received overclouded (*obnubilavit*) in his heart a large part of what had gone successfully in Spain.'[93] The late Tim Reuter persuasively dated the reviser's work to very near the end of Charles's reign. If this is right, and the reviser was writing at court on the basis of conversations with (among others) Charles himself, it is a plausible suggestion that the memory of Roncesvaux's psychological trauma and loss was present to Charles in old age – perhaps more present than it had ever been since 778.[94] The Astronomer's chief informant, Ademar, born, like Louis, in 778, surely grew up on stories of those who fell at Roncesvaux. Einhard, or someone in his circle, wrote in the names of Eggihard, Anselm and Roland. The Astronomer, Einhard's contemporary, affirmed in the second chapter of his *Life of Louis* that he had chosen not to give those names because they were so widely known. Those names, and the name of the site of the ambush on 15 August 778, would echo down the centuries, along with the name of Charles himself.[95]

XI. CHARLES OFFERS NEW RESPONSES TO CRIME AND FAMINE, 779

As 778 turned into 779, Charles wintered at Herstal. It was not a residence that had ever loomed large in his father's itinerary, though large tracts of land had been held by the family in that region.[96] In the early 770s it had become a preferred place for Charles, although not, I think, for such reasons as are implied in the delightful German word *Lieblingsresidenz*,[97] but rather, because of his campaign agenda in Saxony and the relevance to that of Herstal's location on the Meuse. Wintering at Herstal again signalled Charles's determination to persist with that agenda. In 779, five charters were issued from Herstal.[98] Altogether, Charles stayed eleven times at Herstal, making it the most stayed-at residence during the reign as a whole, Aachen apart. The choice to spend Christmas and Easter 778/9 at Herstal was driven by an urgent need less for crisis management than for a three-month-long deliberation about the state of the double realm, Frankish and Lombard. To borrow a little passage from the comparable context of the King-Duke William the Conqueror,

> At midwinter [1085], the king was at Gloucester with his council and held his court there for 5 days, and afterwards the archbishop and ordained men had a synod for 3 days . . . After this the king had great thought and very deep speech with his council about this land.[99]

I imagine Charles and his counsellors having 'great thought and very deep speech' at Herstal.

The result was a capitulary which a French legal historian termed 'a constitutive charter granted by Charles to all territories of the ancient Frankish kingdom'.[100] Charles had his father's example to go on (he reissued Pippin's capitulary of 768), but now he wished more generally 'to preserve the *capitula* which our father laid down in his assemblies and for his synods'.[101] Charles was keen to have these things written down. This capitulary, the first of Charles's own, was certainly important, both in terms of manuscript preservation indicating circulation (thirty-one manuscripts, of which nine were written in the ninth century) and in terms of the exceptional interest of its very varied contents. Topics covered ranged from the structure and managerial responsibilities of the church hierarchy (cc. 1–6) and the (new and universal) requirement to pay tithes (c. 7), to the prohibition of mutual oath-swearings in gilds while entry into mutual associations (*convenentiae*) which did not involve oath-swearing was allowed (c. 16) and sales of weapons outside the kingdom were forbidden (c. 20). The origins of this material were various: some echoed late Roman canon law and some late Roman imperial law. But the question that emerged most strongly was how the crime of robbery was to be dealt with. The king's chief concern was less with criminals than with the misdeeds or injustice of his own officers and agents operating at different levels, as three *capitula* show:

Robbers who are caught within the area of an immunity should be presented by the local judges of that area at the court of the count.[102] Anyone who fails to comply with this is to lose his benefice (*beneficium*: land or favour conferred as remuneration) and his office (*honor*). Likewise a *vassus* [a retainer, usually free and in receipt of a *beneficium*] of ours if he does not comply is to lose his benefice and his office. Anyone who has no *beneficium* is to pay the *bannus* [a fine to the king of 60 *solidi*, or 720 pennies].[103]

Concerning the judgment and punishment inflicted upon robbers: the synod has ruled that the bishops' testimony is equivalent to that of the count, provided there is no malice or ill-will and no intervention in the case except in the interests of seeing justice done. If the judge should maim a man [i.e. mutilate as a punishment] through hatred or bad intent and not for the sake of justice, he is to lose his office and is to be subject to the laws according to which he acted unjustly.[104]

If a count does not administer justice in his administrative district (*min-isterium*), he is to arrange for our *missus* to be provided for from his [i.e. the count's] household until justice has been administered there; and if a *vassus* of ours fails to administer justice, then the count and our *missus* are to stay at his house and live at his expense until he does so.[105]

Significant points arising here are the intermeshing functions of counts, operating in their counties, and *missi*, who are sent out from the palace to act as inspectors of counts and judges; and the crucial importance of intention on the part of these officers, especially judges who are lower-level agents. If they are found to be motivated by 'envy, hatred, or ill-will' (*invidia, odium, malum ingenium*) these officers will forfeit their offices. The most imaginative arrangements (c. 21) were those aimed at counts and their subordinate *vassi*. The count would be required by the king's *missus* to provide hospitality for him in the count's household until he delivered justice; and, at the next level down, if a *vassus* failed to deliver justice, he would have to provide hospitality in his household for both *missus* and count, who would then live at the expense of the *vassus* until that *vassus* could have another think ... Clunky though these arrangements may seem, they have a down-to-earth practicality about them. Counts and *missi* travelled with retinues. The *vassus* might find himself with a houseful of visitors and no time-limit on their stay (Lear's daughters spring to mind) – until the *vassus* did something to change what Charles in later capitularies would call his *conversatio*, his motives and his conduct.[106] There are striking con-tinuities of thought and practice between Charles's first capitulary and its early ninth-century successors.[107]

In March 779, also at Herstal, a special assembly was convened to deal with a serious famine. Unmentioned in either the *ArF* or the revised version, this 'great tribulation' was reported in the contemporary Mosel Annals (*Ann. Mos.*) and Lorsch Annals (*Ann. Lauriss.*): 'in this year [779] there was great famine and mortality in Francia. And the Lord King remained at Worms.' The Bishops' Capitulary, recently re-dated to March 778, along with the Herstal Capitulary itself, established relief measures for 'the starving poor'.[108] These measures were to be activated by St John's Day, 24 June, usually the beginning of the harvest season. The bishops set up arrangements for fasting and alms-giving to be provided by clergy, abbots and abbesses, and laity of different ranks and at different social levels, reaching down to that of local priests and local people. Counts, for instance, were divided into three categories: stronger, middling and lesser. The middling were 'moderately well-off office-holders'.[109] That meant that they were responsible for alms to the value of 120 pennies (half a silver pound). Fasting and alms-giving went hand in hand: those who fasted contributed the food they didn't eat for the relief of the starving. Scripture said, 'As water extinguishes fire, so alms-giving extinguishes sin' (Ecclus. 3:30). Such a major relief operation was apparently not beyond the means of this regime, or at any rate not beyond aspirations driven by Charles. Later in his reign, similar measures in times of tribulation in 792–3 and 805–6 would be proposed and legislated for.[110] It is impossible to assess with any precision how effective these measures were. A comparable situation occurred some 800 years later in Elizabethan England, in the winter of 1596, and similar measures were proposed 'for the relief of the poorer sort of people' across the country. In this case there is archival evidence at least in some localities that the plans were implemented and alms were provided.[111] I think it would be wise not to underestimate the capacities of Charles's *ancien régime*.

From Herstal, and the celebration of Easter on 11 April, Charles moved west to Compiègne, a palace where Charles is not previously recorded. It is a good guess that 'the business that had taken him there' (as the author of the *ArF* put it), revisiting the Oise valley where the Merovingians, and also Pippin and Charles themselves, had so often resided, and specifically residing at Compiègne where Pippin had stayed twice in the 750s, was fundamentally political.[112] It was a public performance designed to reassure the Neustrian Frankish elite that the king still wished to have their counsel and help; that Charles was still their king, would listen to them, would give them justice and be present to them.[113] Charles was already well aware that defeating enemies in the east would require troops not just from between the Meuse and Rhine but from the west as well.

Italy was never out of Charles's mind for long: on the way back to Austrasia from Compiègne, Duke Hildeprand of Spoleto came to meet him at Verzenay near Reims 'bearing great gifts' – a meeting which had evidently been planned. Charles received him graciously, gave him gifts, and sent him back to his duchy. Co-operation was working well. Now, though, '[Charles's] mind was set on a Saxon campaign', and, after wintering at Worms, he set off for Saxony again in 780. The campaign was another triumph for Charles. It followed the now usual pattern of burning and wasting Saxon territory, taking a lot of hostages, receiving oaths, and having large numbers of Saxons baptized.

There was time, nevertheless, for more forward planning with Italy in mind. In July at Lippspringe, Charles held his assembly and established his camp with sufficient amenities to receive Abbot Anselm of Nonantula, who had come a long way from his home monastery near the Via Emilia, not far east of Modena. Anselm had been the brother-in-law of the Lombard king Aistulf, Desiderius's predecessor, who, along with some Friulian nobles, had been a major benefactor of the monastery. Charles saw the strategic advantages of maintaining a close tie with it by confirming its property given by previous kings 'and by us'.[114] Now back in Francia, at Worms, Charles took stock – and took counsel.[115] The decision was made to travel to Rome, unsurprisingly 'for the purpose of prayer', but a second purpose was indicated by Charles's bringing with him Queen Hildegard and four of their children.[116] As in 773, family matters were on the agenda. They left the palace of Worms 'without delay', probably in October, and arrived at Pavia to celebrate Christmas. They had promised Pope Hadrian to reach Rome in time for Easter 781. They did not fail to keep their appointment.

Saxon sword.

7

The Family Deployed, '. . . all Saxony subjugated'

I. CHARLES AND HILDEGARD AND THEIR CHILDREN: WORMS AND ROME, 781

In 780 Charles decided the futures of his four surviving sons (little Lothar having died). 'He left Pippin and [Young] Charles at Worms' may not sound like a major decision. Neither the *ArF* nor the *ArF* reviser mentioned it; indeed the only writer to do so was the well-informed contemporary author of the Mosel Annals whose wording indicated that Pippin the first-born was regarded, still, as the special and senior son of Charles, recognized as such by the *aulici* at Worms, the major royal residence at this point in the reign.[1] Born (probably) in 769, Pippin was of age, or very nearly so. To be a first-born son, a *primogenitus*, was, as Cathwulf had emphasized, a status strongly approved in Scripture.[2] Young Charles, born in 773, was not yet of age. Charles had already made plans, along with Hildegard, which involved the other two sons and the family journey to Rome. The paired decisions concerning the two sons left at Worms and the two taken to Rome were tantamount to – though not referred to as such in the historiography – a division-project.[3] Provisional as such projects were, they offered road-maps for the future, and a 'spread bet' in case of disaster.

Charles and Hildegard had decided to bring with them to Rome four of their children: Rotrud (aged six), Carloman (four), Louis (three) and Berta (one).[4] The priorities of Charles and Hildegard as they travelled across the Alps to Rome 'for the purpose of prayer' at St Peter's shrine were the futures of Carloman and Louis. Charles came to Italy this time not with squadrons of battle-hardened Frankish warriors but with a small army of servants and nursemaids equipped with push-chairs.[5] And Hildegard was pregnant again. They arrived at Pavia to celebrate Christmas; and for Charles this surely recalled the events of 773–4, the siege of the Lombard capital and his rushed visit to Rome to meet the pope. Seven years on, priorities were different for both Charles and Hadrian.

Hadrian had had to wait much longer than he could have expected (he had started to wait in late 774) to see Charles revisit Rome.[6] Perhaps – and these are only guesses – Charles put his recent contacts, Duke Hildeprand of Spoleto and Abbot Anselm of Nonantula, to work in providing hospitality for the royal family en route from Pavia to Rome in the spring of 781. It was not until 15 April that Charles and Hildegard arrived at Rome (by then the queen was near to giving birth to her eighth child, Gisela, named for the baby's aunt, Charles's sister).[7] In 778, Hadrian had been repeating his territorial claims of 774, and excoriating assorted 'abominables' who seemed hell-bent on thwarting him: Beneventans, Neapolitans, Greeks, the patrician of Sicily.[8] By 781, Hadrian's sights were more limited (he was claiming no more than particular bits of land in a region near Rome), and his tones were more measured. He was also in charge of the liturgical arrangements required to effect the baptism of Carloman, and the anointings and coronations of Carloman and Louis as kings of Italy and Aquitaine respectively.[9] These rituals established spiritual ties of compaternity and commaternity with the boys' parents. Bonds of spiritual kinship with the Carolingian royal family had been constructed by Stephen II and Paul. Now Hadrian seized the chance to create similar bonds with Charles and Hildegard, and to repeat references to them in his letters. From 781 to early 783, which was as long as Hildegard lived, Hadrian wrote of her as 'most excellent daughter and spiritual *commater* (co-mother)', as well as addressing Charles as *compater*, co-father.[10] These were symbolic relationships, without implications for potential allegations of incest or, indeed, for political alliance. They were important for Hadrian, as they had been for several previous eighth-century popes. But it's possible to exaggerate an importance which varied with often misty circumstances.[11]

Clear-cut, by contrast, was the (re-)creation of two *regna*, kingdoms: for Carloman, that of the Lombards (soon to be called the kingdom of Italy); and that of the Aquitanians for Louis. Italy has been considered much the more important *regnum*. It was much more fully documented than Aquitaine and had the distinctive contours of a kingdom; for centuries, the Lombards had had well-known borders, and had been ruled by kings who gave laws and appointed officials to police them. Aquitaine was different, for it had been ruled not by kings but by warrior-dukes. Fortunately for Louis, his Aquitanian *regnum* was written up by the Astronomer as chapters 3–33 of the *Life* of Louis, on the basis of the memories of a fellow-Aquitanian, Ademar, which gave an insider's account of the region's government, life and culture.[12]

The baptism of Carloman had been long deferred: the baby boy born in 777 was now four years old, and the rite of baptism, both in canon law and in what is known of actual practice, was normally given to infants.[13] Why the delay in Carloman's case? It looks as if Hadrian was determined to perform *this* baptism in person, and so replicate with Charles the spiritual relationship of *compaternitas*, co-fatherhood, that Charles's father had had with popes Stephen II and Paul. Another reason for the delay was that Charles had had to take on such heavy commitments elsewhere between 778 and 781 that Hadrian's pressing invitations to Rome fell on deaf ears. Hadrian could only wait, determined that he and no other should baptize the third of Charles's sons who was now to rule Italy. Reviving in this new generation the compaternity bond between the dynasty and the papacy meant much to both Charles and Hadrian; and when Archbishop Thomas of Milan baptized baby Gisela in May, as the royal family were en route back to Francia, imitation was the sincerest form of flattery.[14]

The exceptional feature of the 781 plan was that Carloman's name should be changed to Pippin. There is a historians' consensus-view that Hadrian chose the new name because it evoked that of Charles's father, grantor in 754 of the Donation of Quierzy whereby Pope Stephen II had received an extensive 'patrimony', a *res publica*, in Italy. Two Frankish campaigns in the mid-750s had failed to force successive Lombard kings, Aistulf and Desiderius, to recognize the papacy's rights over these territories.[15] From 774, when the Donation of Quierzy was confirmed, Pippin was a name for the pope to cherish. In the years just after the Frankish takeover of the Lombard kingdom, Hadrian was still fighting these old battles against Lombard claims. At stake for the papacy in the name-change of Carloman, then, was the perpetuation of the spiritual bond. More than compaternity was (re-)created: Hadrian conferred the magic of legitimacy on this highly irregular situation.[16] For ordinary mortals, what was significant in Carloman's name-change was that there were now two (half-) brothers with the same name, two Pippins.

Why Charles and Hildegard had chosen the name 'Carloman' for their third son in 777 is not an easy question to answer. Though the name itself was well-established in the dynasty, the circumstances of the 'retirement' to a monastery of Charles's uncle Carloman in summer 747 (only months before Charles's own birth on 4 April 748) remained (and remain) unclear. The name had been overclouded (to borrow an apt word from the *ArF* reviser in another context) during the fraternal conflicts between Charles and his brother Carloman during the years 768–71, and thrown into even darker shadow after Carloman's death which, within a little over two years, left utterly obscure the fates of Carloman's sons. It is a striking fact that no other Carolingian king gave his son the name Carloman until some sixty years later, and even then, it would only be given to a boy far down the birth-order of a set of siblings or destined for a career in the church. Had the name carried shades of ill-omen for Charles? Had its re-use in 777 evoked feelings of regret, even guilt? Perhaps Hadrian hatched the renaming plan with Charles with the aim of making Carloman 'reborn' in the font of baptism and to give him a new 'clean' name. The contemporary and close-to-court authors of the Mosel Annals and the Lorsch Annals entered the same words under 781: 'King Charles went to Rome and his son was baptized there, the son who had been named Carloman but whom Pope Hadrian, after changing the name, called Pippin.'[17]

Hildegard approved the plan together with Charles. She too saw matters from her own personal standpoint. The future of Pippin the first-born was not her concern: after all, she was his stepmother, not his mother. She wanted to have *her* son become king of the Lombards, and to have him re-christened, as it were, with the name that resonated most loudly in the dynasty into which she had married. She as well as Charles was an interested party in the name-change: this becomes clear in the light of a piece of contemporary evidence, the dedicatory poem for an evangelistary – a book of Gospel readings – written by a scribe called Godescalc and now kept in the Bibliothèque Nationale in Paris. Charles and Hildegard commissioned it 'in the fourteenth year of his reign', that is, 781. The poem opens:

> Charles pious king of the Franks along with his excellent
> wife Hildegard
> ordered this exceptional work to be written.

The lord king of kings, glory of the heavens, Christ,
watches over their lives with his salvation-bringing name.

And near the end, the poem describes the baptismal renaming:

The co-father lifted from the blessed waters the
    white-clad child
reborn in the font and washed by holy baptism,
sprung from the famed line of Charles the prince,
the child Carloman, whose name was now changed to Pippin.

An accompanying picture shows an eight-columned structure around a
fountain of life within a paradisal scene, and art historians have interpreted this as evoking Cathwulf's columns supporting a just king and a just realm.[18]

A foil to Godescalc's poem is a set of *Laudes regiae*, liturgical acclamations sung in honour and in the presence of rulers in the Latin West and in this form, though related to other types of acclamations for the arrivals of potentates, or for triumphal processions. It is a distinctively Carolingian genre.[19] This set, now preserved in Montpellier, is among the earliest sets to survive, dated to between 783 and 792. It begins thus:

Karolo excellentissimo et a Deo coronato
magno et pacifico rege Francorum et Langobardorum
ac patricio Romanorum, vita et victoria!
Salvator mundi, tu lo iuva!
Sancte Iohannis, tu lo iuva!
Exaudi Christe!
(To Charles the most excellent and crowned by God,
great and pacific king of the Franks and the Lombards
and *patricius* of the Romans, life and victory![20]
Saviour of the world, help him!
St John, help him!
Hear O Christ!)

The second verse is:

Pipino et Karolo
nobilissimis eius filiis, vita!
Exaudi Christe!
(To Pippin and Charles

his most noble sons, life!
Hear O Christ!)

The third:

Pipino rege Longobardorum, vita!
Sancti Mauricii, tu lo iuva!
Exaudi Christe!
(To Pippin king of the Lombards, life!
St Maurice, help him!
Hear O Christ!)[21]

Carloman's name-change at first looks highly problematic, given that Charles's first-born Pippin was still very much alive. There are precedents or parallels for a prince's name being changed, but no case of a name-change resulting in two half-brothers having the same name at the same time.[22] Perhaps, though, not everyone at the time saw this as a problem at all. In the *Laudes* just cited, the two Pippins are hailed in consecutive verses, differentiated in ways perfectly clear to contemporaries. Whoever composed, chanted or heard these *Laudes* evidently saw no incongruity in offering them for two different Pippins, one after the other.

The decisions about the two kingdoms, Italy and Aquitaine, were put into immediate effect. Louis was taken to Orléans, where he made a ritual crossing of the Loire into his kingdom in some kind of portable chair, and his subsequent royal itinerary was between the four palaces of Aquitaine (of which Chasseneuil in Poitou was the chief residence). Pippin entered his Lombard kingdom and resided at Pavia. Each child-king was provided with *baiuli*, functionaries who acted as regents and tutorial advisers.[23] As each of the boys came of age, a fully fledged court and palace coalesced around him.

II. TASSILO MEETS CHARLES AT WORMS, 781

Tassilo, duke of Bavaria, born in 741, and Charles, born in 748, were first-cousins. There is a backstory to Tassilo's life which in this book has not yet been taken into account, though it has important implications for the way the *ArF* should be understood. So far, I have drawn extensively on the *ArF* without exploring the purpose of its author (or authors), their intended audience, or who commissioned them and when. It is high time to look more closely into why the historian who set out in the 1980s to review these questions, Matthias Becher, ended up with a new interpretation, published in 1993. Running through these annals, Becher realized, was a series of episodes, of which the first, in 757, represented Tassilo as publicly subordinating himself to his uncle King Pippin at Compiègne in an event that could well have been witnessed by the nine-year-old Charles.[24] What can be seen now – though for well over a century of modern scholarship it was *not* seen – as the simple method of comparing the *ArF* (and their dependent accounts, the revised *ArF* and the *AMP*) with the independent accounts in contemporary minor annals (the *Ann. Mos., Ann. Lauriss.* and *Ann. Petav.*), reveals that oath-swearings and a commendation '*in vasatico*' (into a vassal-relationship) were inserted into the *ArF*'s story of 757 at a significantly later moment – soon after Charles deprived Tassilo of his dukedom and imprisoned him in a monastery in 788.[25] In other words, it was only once Tassilo had been deposed and Charles had annexed Bavaria that the king commissioned a justificatory account of these events for the consumption of a wide and largely Frankish public.

The ongoing story of relations between Tassilo and Charles up to and including 781 was *not* one of Tassilo's increasing subordination to Charles. The two cousins ruled in a curious unsynchronized counterpoint to each other. It used to be thought that they were almost the same age, until, in a stunning piece of detective work published in 1973, the late K. F. Werner made a strong case for Charles's having been born in 747; and in 1992 Becher fine-tuned the argument by showing that Charles was born in 748.[26] Rather than being of more or less the same age, Tassilo was seven years older than Charles. When Tassilo's father, Duke Odilo, died in 748 and the mayor of the palace Pippin helped install young Tassilo in his father's place, Charles was a babe-in-arms; and when Tassilo came of age, Charles had only recently lost his first milk-tooth.

In the 760s, there is rich documentary material from Bavaria for Tassilo's founding and giving to monasteries and dealing justice in disputes over their property.[27] Not until the 770s would the same be true of Charles. Tassilo had married, probably in 763, Liutperga, a daughter of King Desiderius, and soon after Pippin's death in September 768, Tassilo went to Rome to forge a friendship with Pope Stephen III.[28] Charles married another daughter of Desiderius in 770: Charles and Tassilo may well have become brothers-in-law after Queen Bertrada, en route for Rome, had diplomatically attended the Council of Dingolfing where she witnessed decrees being laid down 'thanks to the action of the lord Tassilo, the *princeps*', and the Bavarian bishops and abbots signalled their solidarity by making a formal prayer-brotherhood nineteen-strong.[29] At Neuchingen in 772, a council issued more decrees, this time (mostly) *De popularibus legibus* ('concerning secular laws'), 'with the help of the *princeps*, lord Tassilo', and again, Tassilo entitled himself *princeps* and *dominus*. Charles gave or confirmed many gifts to churches in the early 770s; but he did not summon councils. For most of 771, Charles and Tassilo were still brothers-in-law: only late that year did Charles repudiate his Lombard wife, thereby risking a serious falling-out with Tassilo. The duke chose discretion over valour, and steered clear of vengeance. But contemporaries within Charles's own family, notably his cousin Adalhard, who withdrew from the court to the monastery of Corbie, made plain their disapproval of Charles's action.[30]

The relationship between the former brothers-in-law now became more obviously competitive. In 772, the year when Charles first campaigned in Saxony and destroyed the Irminsul, Tassilo sent his son Theodo to Desiderius and thence to Rome to be baptized at Whitsun by Hadrian, who thus made Tassilo his *compater*.[31] That same year, annalwriters at Salzburg and Regensburg registered Tassilo's victory against the Carinthians on his south-eastern border.[32] When Charles, in 773, was considering negotiations with Desiderius for the transfer into his own custody of his nephews, the Lombard king's protégés, Hadrian, steeled by Charles, refused to consecrate them as kings.[33]

> Duke Tassilo, his wife the Duchess Liutperga and their son Duke Theodo, out of special devotion for the salvation of their souls, sent a magnificent embassy . . . to Rome with very large gifts. King Charles would let only two of the envoys past, Bishop Alim of Säben and Abbot Atto of Mondsee . . . Tassilo was displeased and felt insulted that his cousin King Charles had refused to let his men through and was seized by great bitterness towards him. Charles, for his part, was anxious about Tassilo, who, he thought, was becoming too powerful. Tassilo was certainly at one with the Saxons, Wends and Huns, all of whom had long been sworn and mortal enemies of King Charles and all the kings in Francia.[34]

Charles and Tassilo competed to attract praise and advice from courtier-clerics in the 770s: Tassilo from an Irish scholar, Clement, probably in 772, Charles from the Anglo-Saxon Cathwulf in 775.[35] After Charles had captured Pavia, deposed Desiderius and become king of the Lombards in 774, both Tassilo and Charles devoted them-selves to expanding their territories, and to conflict-management on and beyond their borders, in careers that ran in parallel. In the hind-sight knowledge of 787–8, Stuart Airlie asked, 'What made Tassilo so dangerous?'[36] It could also be worth asking *if* and *when* Tassilo was dangerous. Tassilo and Charles seem to have treated each other in the 770s and early 780s warily. 'In a sense', to quote Airlie again, 'Tassilo was Charlemagne's "significant other".' Perhaps the onset of Charles's perception of Tassilo as an insidious threat should be dated to 773, and Airlie's 'in a sense' should be left ambiguous.

In 781, before Charles left Rome, he and his new *compater* Hadrian had thought up plans to bring Tassilo, also a *compater* of Hadrian, and Charles on to terms of respect for each other. The *ArF* and the revised *ArF* both reported Charles's return to Francia after April, adding that the pope sent two bishops, Formosus and Damasus, as envoys, as well as Charles's own envoys, Riculf and Eberhard, to Tassilo to remind him of the promises and oaths he had made to Pippin 'long before' (that is, in 757). Tassilo replied that he would be willing, *if* – a significant 'if' – Charles first sent him hostages, to meet the king. Charles agreed to this, and Tassilo appeared at Worms and took receipt of the hostages handed over by Charles.

> The lord king did not refuse this, and Tassilo duke of the Bavarians, presenting himself to the king at the city of Worms, there renewed the oaths and handed over 12 chosen hostages as pledges that he would in all respects observe with regard to the said king Charles and his faithful men whatever promises he had made to Pippin under oath.[37]

In a separate clause, hostages were brought by Bishop Sindpert (of Regensburg) from Bavaria and duly handed over at Quierzy. (Charles, perhaps not coincidentally, given that place's connection with his father, wintered at Quierzy in 781–2.[38])

One point about the 781 meeting deserves special attention in light of Becher's advice to compare the *ArF* and their dependent accounts with other annal-sets. Only the *ArF* and the dependent accounts asserted that in 781 Tassilo *renewed* to Charles the oaths given to Pippin in 757. The independent accounts – the Mosel Annals, Lorsch Annals and the *Annales Petaviani* – though they mentioned Tassilo, said nothing about any such renewal of oaths. Here, then, is another link in the *ArF*'s chain of argument leading to the submission of Tassilo at the Lechfeld (the river Lech was the boundary between Alemannia and Bavaria) in 787 and Tassilo's trial and fall in 788 at Ingelheim. The independent contemporary accounts, which present a much more independent Tassilo, are those to be preferred. In these, before Tassilo presented himself at Worms, he asked to receive hostages *from Charles* – and secured Charles's willingness to hand them over. This is the one and only time, so far as the records go, that Charles *gave* hostages as well as receiving them. Independent accounts emphasize an exchange of gifts. Such exchanges were not always what they seemed, and never equal. According to the Petau Annals, 'Tassilo presented great gifts to the lord king'. Supporting this account of the gift-giving at Worms is the testimony of Tassilo's chancellor Creontius (Crantz in German): 'The duke came to his cousin king Charles at Worms, and gave him great gifts of goods and money: in return the king gave him [Tassilo] even more.'[39]

An important insight into such exchanges is that they were competitive, and there was therefore 'a need to outbid'. But evaluating gifts was not then (any more than it is now) an easy matter, and outbidding may be inappropriate in certain contexts.[40] Creontius added: 'Charles received Duke Tassilo very honourably and treated him with great honour and respect. They concluded an eternal peace with each other.' The best assessment of the 781 meeting is that both parties gained much and hoped to gain more.

A further gift-arrangement made in 781, this time in Rome, was not directly to do with Tassilo, but belonged in the much wider network of inter-familial dynastic exchanges in which the daughters of rulers were involved. Of the daughters of Desiderius, two were still very active in pursuing the interests of their husbands, their offspring, and the peoples ruled by their husbands and offspring. One of these women was Liutperga, Tassilo's wife; the other was Adelperga, wife of Duke Arichis of Benevento.[41] Their brother Prince Adelchis, exiled in Constantinople, was ever-hopeful of a return to Italy. Charles had become increasingly au fait with Italian politics, and his own communications network had expanded to include Byzantium. Charles's father, in 767, had seriously considered arranging a marriage between his daughter Gisela to the son of Emperor Constantine V, the future Leo IV (775–80). It had come to nothing, however, and Leo too was now dead.

In 781, Leo's widow, the Dowager Empress Eirene, took the initiative in asking for Charles's daughter Rotrud as a bride for her son, the young Emperor Constantine VI (780–97). An embassy was sent to Rome, the hub of high politics, diplomacy and gossip, at a time when Eirene knew that Charles and the family – including Rotrud – would be there. The embassy included high palace officials and a scholar, Elissaeus; and 'after an agreement was reached and a betrothal was concluded, the officials left Elissaeus behind to teach Rotrud the language and literature of the Greeks and to instruct her in Roman imperial ways.'[42]

This interesting information comes from the *Chronicle* of Theophanes.[43] The only western contemporary to record this agreement was the author of the Mosel Annals, who, after reporting the anointings of Pippin and Louis, added: 'And the king's daughter Rotrud was there betrothed to the Emperor Constantine.'[44] From the *ArF* and *ArF* reviser, both writing after the idea of Rotrud's Byzantine marriage had faded and died, there was not a word on the subject. During the years from 781 to 787, it's a good guess that Rotrud's thoughts often turned to far-away Constantinople as well as to Rome. Charles and his eldest daughter (and perhaps, too, her aunt Gisela, wishing a better fortune for her niece than she herself had had) were seriously committed to the marriage-plan until 787.[45] Only with hindsight does the marriage look chimerical, and all that Greek learning seem sadly in vain.

III. THE ASSEMBLY AT LIPPSPRINGE: SAXONS, NORTHMEN AND AVARS

The annalistic record for the 780s needs a brief, but necessary, comment, because these were the years when there began 'a flurry of annal-making . . . somehow officially sponsored'. The argument of Roger Collins that this 'unprecedented spate' was 'encouraged' by Charles and his advisers at court is, in my view, compelling.[46] Perhaps the start of the 'flurry' could be dated a little earlier than 'the late 780s' and its end seen as overlapping with 'an attempt to promote a single "authorised" and centrally produced record in the form of the Royal Frankish

Annals (that is, the *ArF*)'. In what follows, a distinction will be maintained between what Becher calls the 'independent' annals, and what Collins calls the 'authorized' (or quasi-official) record.

The annal for 782 in both sets of records started with Charles's summoning a Spring assembly (or 'Mayfield') at Lippspringe, 'the place where the river Lippe rises'. After that, the two annal-groups diverged. The 'independent' annals continued with a remarkable piece of information: 'he established over it [Saxony] Saxon counts of the most noble birth.'[47] Another version of this event gives: 'Charles held a great assembly with the Saxons again, at Lippspringe, and appointed noble Franks and Saxons as counts over them.'[48] It might be that Charles was no longer overly concerned about Widukind and thought (wrongly, as it turned out) that matters in Saxony had been settled: perhaps the envoys of the Danish king Sigifrid had come to the Lippspringe assembly to negotiate with Charles a way of co-opting Widukind into the service of the Frankish regime, as many of the Saxon *primores* had already been.[49] It would be easy to imagine that assembly as an event where – though all the practicalities would remain to be worked out over time – counties were assigned and the names of the new counts publicly read out. German historians write of a 'county-structure' imposed by Charles, on the model of similar structures elsewhere in the realm.

The business of politics moved on with even greater momentum than usual, as is evident from the following charter trail from July to September: on 4 July Charles was at Düren, where he granted the church at Fritzlar to Archbishop Lull; on 25 July, he was at Lippspringe, where he confirmed remission of dues to the bishop of Trier in *haribergo publico ubi Lippe confluit*, 'in the public army camp where the Lippe flows out'.[50] Only three days later, on 28 July, he was at Hersfeld, 150km to the south-east, granting lands to the monastery recently founded by Archbishop Lull, and also confirming the estate at Schornsheim to Leoba, abbess of Tauberbischofsheim for 'so long as she lived' (she died two months later). Leoba, forty years older than Hildegard, had enjoyed a 'longstanding friendship' (*antiqua familiaritas*) with her, and Charles's grant may have been intended as a favour to the queen as well.[51] Charles was back in Francia at Herstal in August (he may have returned in July already), where on 18 August he settled a dispute between the monastery of Farfa (a group of monks had come bearing charters to make their case) and Duke Hildeprand of Spoleto (who did not come in person), in Farfa's favour.[52] Charles was staying at the palace of Gondreville on the Mosel south of Trier when, on 26 September, he granted an immunity to Bishop Geminianus of Modena.[53] Gondreville is some 100km south of Thionville where Charles and his family would winter in 782–3.

The 'authorized' annals foreshortened the sequence of events by implying that Charles's return to Francia followed soon after the Lippspringe assembly, and that his next decision was the sending of an army, composed jointly of Franks *and* Saxons, to fight 'a few Slavs'.[54] The charter evidence shows a longer chronology: it was only at the end of September or early October that news of Widukind's return from Nordmannia (the land of the Northmen, or Denmark) to foment another serious Saxon revolt and cause a Frankish military disaster, prompted Charles's swift return to Saxony. It looks as if Charles had banked on Widukind's remaining in Nordmannia, and so had inferred that the time was not yet ripe for 'turning' him.

There is a little more to be got from the independent annals. In comparing those with the authorized ones, historians have encountered problems. For one thing, the *ArF* and the *ArF*'s reviser offered – uniquely – accounts that were quite distinct yet somehow connected, each drawing on different sources of information or invention. Further, the reviser was a master of narrative, offering lessons at once political, military and moral: this too was a unique feature in the near century's-worth of authorized annals. The *ArF* account, relatively succinct at twenty-three lines in the Latin text, depicted an army consisting of Franks and Saxons led by Charles's senior officers (*missi*), Adalgis, Gailo and Worad, who had orders to attack 'a few Slavs', suddenly 'hearing en route that [other] Saxons had rebelled, combined to form a joint *scara* and rushed upon the Saxons without informing the lord king Charles of what they were doing'.

Was this statement intended to imply that had Charles been in a position to intervene, disaster could have been avoided? If so, was it therefore meant to be taken as a criticism of the *missi*? In a blatant distortion, the *ArF* author presented the outcome as a victory:

> The Franks fought bravely, killed many Saxons, and emerged as victors.
> And two of those *missi*, Adalgis and Gailo, fell there. Charles, hearing
> this, advanced there with as many Franks as he could quickly muster and

arrived where the river Aller flows into the Weser. Then all the Saxons once again assembled and subjected themselves to the lord king. They handed over all the malefactors who had most determinedly settled on rebellion (*rebellium maxime terminaverunt*), 4,500 of them, to be put to death. This was done – except for Widukind who escaped by flight to Nordmannia. When all this had been done, the lord king went back to Francia.[55]

The *ArF* reviser's account, at fifty-six lines, is much longer and more complicated, asking rather a lot of its readers and hearers, then and now. It deserves to be presented in full:

Charles summoned three of his officers (*ministri*) to his presence: Adalgis the treasurer, Gailo the constable, and Worad count of the palace, and ordered them to act as fast as possible taking with them East Franks and Saxons to repress the boldness of the stubbornly disobedient Slavs. After they had crossed Saxony to carry out their orders, these men heard that Saxons acting on Widukind's advice were preparing to make war on the Franks. They abandoned the route by which they had been intending to advance against the Slavs, and quickly marched with East Frankish troops towards the place where they had heard Saxons had gathered.

They were joined in Saxony by Count Theoderic, the king's kinsman (*propinquus regis*), with as many troops as he had been able to gather in a hurry in the Rhineland on hearing of the Saxons' rebellion. He advised the hastening officers (*legati*) that scouts should first ascertain as fast as possible where the Saxons were and what they were planning, and then, if the nature of the terrain allowed, he [Theoderic] and they [the *legati*] should make a joint attack on them. They thought his advice was praiseworthy, and they advanced together as far as the Süntel Hill, as it is called, on whose northern flank lay the Saxon camp. After Theoderic had pitched camp there, they crossed the Weser, as agreed with him, so that they could bypass the hill more easily, and they made their own camp on the river-bank.

But they were afraid, when they discussed matters among themselves, that if they had Theoderic with them in the same fight, the fame of victory would be transferred to his name (*veriti sunt ne ad nomen Theoderici victoriae fama transiret*); and they therefore decided to engage the Saxons without him, and, acting not as if they were taking on an enemy drawn up in battle-line against them, but as if they were pursuing a fleeing foe to seize booty, each man seized his weapons and charged with as much speed as he could muster, as fast as his horse could carry him, onto the place where the Saxons were standing in their battle-array in front of their camp. Just as this charge went badly, so the ensuing battle went badly: for in the engagement they were surrounded by the Saxons and killed almost to a man. Those who managed to escape fled, even so, not to their own camp but to Theoderic's, across the Hill. The loss to the Franks was greater than numbers alone, however, for two of the officers (*legati*), Adalgis and Gailo, four counts and as many as twenty other distinguished and noble men were killed, as well as the others who were in their followings and who chose to die at their sides rather than outlive them.[56]

Count Theoderic himself (or someone in his following) has been suggested as the teller of the tale.[57] Its lessons could certainly be read as a familiar part of the moral repertoire of faithful followers: one group of the king's men should not compete for glory to each other's destruction; men should follow their lord even unto death, in which they would find posthumous glory and a memory in song and story – the three *aulici* and their men at Roncesvaux come to mind; and the king would avenge the deaths of his faithful officers and comrades.

The rest of this story became one of crime and exemplary punishment. The *ArF* account can be abbreviated, thus: when Charles had learned of the fate of his *missi* and their men, he advanced to where the Aller flows into the Weser; and all the Saxons assembled and subjected themselves to Charles, and handed over to be executed all the evildoers – except Widukind, who escaped to Nordmannia – who were responsible for the rebellion, 4,500 in all. The reviser's account follows this, repeating the number 4,500, but putting great emphasis on the Saxons as perpetrators of a crime (*scelus*, and a few lines further on, *tantum facinus*) which had had to be avenged and for which the penalty was beheading.

A few further comments are à propos. One is that older generations of scholars, persuaded by a Marxist analysis of class war, blamed the nobility for selling-out the peasant rebels.[58] Another is that beheading was the normal penalty (*laesa majestas*) for treason in late Roman law and for heresy (breach of the Faith) in the laws of Christian emperors.[59]

A third is that the figure of 4,500 is suspiciously large, and its tidiness increases suspicion. It could well have resulted from a scribe mistakenly (or through deliberate inflation) adding a zero.[60] The basic story can be retained, however, and it's reinforced by the information by the author of the Petau Annals: 'Then with a great army (*exercitus*) the Frankish army-detachments (*hostes*) went into Saxony and the Franks slew a multitude of the men of the Saxons and led many Saxons captive into Francia.'[61]

IV. THE *CAPITULATIO DE PARTIBUS SAXONIAE*

The Capitulary about the regions of Saxony is one of the most puzzling texts that scholars of Charles's reign have to come to grips with. It survives in a single manuscript written in *c.*825 at Mainz.[62] Most twentieth-century historians have inclined to date it to 782, and a fairly recent fresh appraisal adds strength to the argument.[63] The Lippspringe assembly has been considered the context in which the *Capitulatio* was issued, on the grounds that what was then put in place was a 'structure of countships'.[64] Counts in Saxony, whether Saxons or Franks, were a new phenomenon without a tradition originating in late antiquity. Counts in Saxony, unlike those in Francia, were appointed by the king to a *ministerium*, an office, held from the king directly, rather than rooted in a locality or inherited lands. Saxon counts had more restricted powers in their counties (*pagus* or *comitatus*) than Frankish counts in theirs. A royal official (*missus*) in Saxony had the role of king's representative and agent implementing royal decisions, rather than a local judge.[65]

While the count featured as an important figure in the *Capitulatio*'s cc. 24, 28–31 and 34, no count appeared anywhere in the remaining *capitula*. By contrast, cc. 3–14 are largely concerned with the application of the death penalty for pagan acts and especially heinous crimes, and cc. 15–23 with ecclesiastical matters such as fines, penalties and burial practices. This arrangement of the material has struck some historians as indicating that the *Capitulatio* ought not to be treated as a single text but as a compilation of two, or three, separate texts.[66] This strikes me as plausible, but unprovable. For now, the *Capitulatio*, whether a single text or a compilation from older sources including the Old Testament and a slightly earlier text, the *Indiculus superstitionum et paganiarum* ('The list of superstitions and pagan practices'), is best dated to 782.[67]

Was it the *Capitulatio*'s promulgation at the Lippspringe assembly that provoked the Saxon revolt and its bloody consequences? It is certainly possible to stick with the scholarly consensus on this cause-and-effect answer. But an alternative question, still apparently unasked, is: did Charles and his advisers put together and issue the *Capitulatio* as a response to the revolt and the loss of his men, as described by the *ArF* reviser three decades after the event, probably on the basis of oral testimony? The *Capitulatio* could still be dated to 782, but, in view of the charter chronology, near the very end of the year, and issued at Verden as a prerequisite to the legal process of inquiry, condemnation and the exaction of death-penalties.[68] Charles and his advisers were driven less by practical considerations than by ideology. The *Capitulatio* was a deeply ideological text: here 'the rhetoric of paganism is used to contrast an assortment of practices and affiliations with the Frankish behaviour Charlemagne's court wished to promote'.[69] Vengeance was indeed the Lord's, but *not only* the Lord's: it was also Charles's vengeance for the deaths of Adalgis and Gailo, four counts, and so many other 'men of distinction and nobility'. Their deeds became part of a collective Frankish memory, recalled and commemorated long before they were recorded by the *ArF* reviser near the end of Charles's reign.[70] Collective Saxon commemoration may have existed too, focused on a place, Verden, and a shocking event; but only very much later did it surface in denunciation of Charles as 'the Saxon-slayer'.[71] Historians and archaeologists nowadays tend to agree that the *Capitulatio*, with its 'savage penalties' for cremating the dead, was aimed, 'less at Christianising Saxons', than at 'suppressing Saxon identity' by assimilating Saxons – especially elite Saxons – to 'the Frankish majority'. In fact, Saxon pagan practices of cremation and mound burial had long been in decline.[72]

After Verden, Charles made for a favourite residence in which he and Hildegard and their children could overwinter and begin a return to normality by spending Christmas 782 and Easter 783 at Thionville in the Mosel valley. Looking back to 783, the *ArF* reviser ventured a rare lyrical evocation of that year's 'mild and smiling spring'.

V. CHARLES AND AN EXEMPLARY JUDGMENT

Judgments made at large assemblies (*placita*) and involving high-status parties, lay or ecclesiastical, had long formed a special category of document in the Frankish kingdom: they were decisions on legal disputes made, usually, in one of the king's palaces by the king and a panel of counts and faithful men, and recorded by a notary of the count of the palace.[73] Only ten judgments of Charles survive, very unevenly distributed through the reign. In them – even more clearly than in charters because they are inherently adversarial – can be traced 'the imposition, challenge and final acceptance of a new relationship between central and local power under Charlemagne'.[74] The dispute (*contentio*) between the cathedral church of St Peter's, Trier, and the sons of Lambert was heard at the palace of Thionville on the Mosel in late 782.

> Our *missus* Wicbert together with the *scabini* [local judgment-finders assisting at the courts of counts and *missi*] and witnesses of the Mosel region came and reported to us about [the monastery of] Mettlach, because it was a thing of our property. Our grandfather the Mayor of the palace Charles [Martel] beneficed Milo [bishop of Trier] with Mettlach, and then our father King Pippin beneficed Milo with it and then Bishop Hartham [of Trier]. They said that Bishop Leodonius, father of Milo and Wido, had given it by documents to the church of Trier which is built within the walls of the city of Trier; and Milo, Leodonius's successor, had sent abbots to it from Trier, as Pippin had beneficed Milo's successor . . . Then there was a dispute between the *missus* Wicbert and the sons of Lambert, Wido, Hrodold and Warin. The representatives of St Peter's and the *scabini* said that Lambert had seized Mettlach by force (*per forcia*) with the power of King Pippin in a wicked way (*malo ordine*) and despoiled Bishop Hartham of it. Wido and his brothers said that their father Lambert had left it to them as lawful hereditary property (*legitimo alode*). And this was how they judged, that the possession of the property was in law and justice on the side of us and of St Peter's because Bishop Milo and Bishop Hartham had always had that monastery by the benefice of the Mayor Charles and of King Pippin. But Warin and his brothers

contradicted this, saying that the possession was theirs because their father Lambert had left them possessed of it as lawfully inherited property. For this reason, there was a great dispute (*magna contentio*).

Then we with our faithful men joined with all the *scabini* of the duchy of the Mosel who unanimously judged that [because] Wido and his brothers had never had any documents to vindicate their father's claims to the monastery against King Pippin, our lawful possession must be on the side of St Peter's. But since Wido and his brothers could produce no witnesses nor *scabini* [to attest] lawful possession, the judgment was handed down to them that they must restore in our presence with a solemn promise [what was owed] to the said monastery and to our side in the dispute over St Peter's, Trier.

This they did, and in person they made over through their *missus* the possession of the monastery to the side of St Peter's, Trier whose bishop is Archbishop Weomad, as has been judged by us and by our faithful men, and as we have been seen to have adjudged to St Peter's, by us and our faithful men Bishops Angelramn, Peter and Borno, counts Erhard [and 10 named others] and our other faithful men the *scabini* Thetfrido [and 43 named others] and the Count of the Palace Worad and as many other faithful men as possible who were there present. Archbishop Weomad will receive a written order (*preceptum*) and a vindicated judgment (*iudicium vindicatum*) concerning the monastery of Mettlach and the property and people (*homines*) pertaining to it and belonging to the side of the Trier people (*Treverenses*). And this we have done . . .[75]

Like many abbeys, Mettlach was the foundation of an aristocratic family, with, in this case, close associations to the bishopric of Trier. The bishops were chosen from the founder's dynasty, and the descendants of the founder did the choosing. Lorsch was a similar and slightly earlier case: it had passed from the founding family via the family's gift to Bishop Chrodegang of Metz, and a judgment made in Chrodegang's favour by Charles in late March 772, to a near-simultaneous de facto takeover by Charles himself when he granted Lorsch his *mundeburdium vel defensio* ('protection and defence') later in 772 or early 773.[76] Matthew Innes, having deftly noted the Lorsch parallel, summarized the outcome of the Thionville judgment as imposed by the ruler and accepted by locals.[77]

Charles Martel and King Pippin had granted out Mettlach in

benefice to successive bishops of Trier, 'out of Trier cathedral property' apparently.[78] When Trier tried to recover Mettlach, the sons of Lambert refused, and Charles's judgment went in Trier's favour. But, at the same time, Charles himself claimed Mettlach. His use of churches as benefices led to lordship (*dominium*) 'more focused and "proprietary" than general royal authority'.[79] The Church's military service to Charles had its roots in attitudes like these. His letter of summons to Fulrad, lay-abbot of St-Quentin, shows exactly how much was expected.[80] The lay-abbacies of people such as Alcuin and Angilbert were the – highly selective – grants of a king who, like his father, wanted orderly reform and faithful service at the same time.[81] Such abbacies were run by laymen with primarily military obligations to the king – hence modern historians' terms lay-abbot and lay-abbacy – and a dual arrangement developed whereby an ecclesiastical abbot managed the liturgical side while the military abbot operated alongside him: a practical solution combining orderly reform and faithful war-service.

It's appropriate to end this section by returning to the *magna contentio*. The record of the Trier judgment is so detailed that a modern reader is able not just to follow the process and the outcome, but to visualize the assembly as if he/she were there along with the king, the three archbishops, the eleven counts with the count of the palace and, last but not least, the forty-four *boni homines*, men of the region of Trier, each with his shiny new title of *scabinus* denoting an office and a duty sworn to by an oath, and bursting his buttons with pride. It was this sense of personal enlistment that signalled a new regime: a practice of empire, an engagement in trust, and a presence culture shaped, instrumentalized and lived out by Charles.[82]

VI. LAYING WASTE AND MOPPING UP

The executions at Verden did not end the Saxon wars. As Charles began to prepare for a new campaign, he got news of 'a general defection of them' (*omnimoda eorum defectio*) – meaning, Saxons. If the *Capitulatio*, in whatever form, had quickly become known in the region where resistance had been concentrated in the previous decade, it could have been calculated to arouse new extremes of hostility, not near Verden or in Angraria, but in Westphalia and the Süntel hills, and in the Weissgau between the rivers Weser and Werre.

Charles first attacked 'with a few Franks' some Saxons 'arrayed in battle-formation' at Detmold on the Werre: 'he manfully (*viriliter*) fell upon them and they as usual turned tail.' While waiting for more troops to join him from Francia, Charles got news that Saxons were assembling on the river Hase. Charles was, according to the *ArF* reviser, *commotus*, a term which, as used by Suetonius in two of his *Lives of the Caesars*, meant 'enraged'.[83]

In a second battle, 'An infinite multitude of [Saxons] were cut down, spoils were seized, and great numbers of captives were carried off.' And Charles's forces 'put them to flight as far as the Elbe' before returning to Francia.[84] Einhard claimed that these were the only two cases in which the king in person led his armies into battles in Saxony, and both these occurred within a single month.[85] These triumphs of personal leadership clearly impressed Einhard. (In fact, Einhard underrated Charles's capabilities as a war-leader, for he had personally led troops into battle at Lübbecke in 775, and again at Bocholt in 779, after which he had 'conquered all the Westphalians'). There is no mention of Widukind here, but his old supporters in that region could well have been involved in increasingly desperate resistance. The only sources to provide evidence of Charles's movements for late 783, or for the whole of 784, 785 and early 786, are the *ArF* and the revised *ArF*. From a period of thirty months, not a single charter survives. This was emphatically *not* business as usual.

In 784, the areas Charles first targeted were likewise in Westphalia. Severe flooding in that region, however, soon made Charles look in other directions. For the first time, he deputed major military responsibility that year to his son Young Charles, who remained in Westphalia engaged in mopping-up operations. Charles himself went eastwards into Thuringia and its northern borderlands with Eastphalia, making an encircling move to Steinfurt, thence to Schöningen, and finally traversing Thuringia again in a south-westerly move back to Westphalia. Father and son, both successful, returned to Worms at the end of the campaigning season. The Franks were becoming accustomed to winter-warfare. Charles decided on a short sharp mid-winter campaign in Westphalia, in the Weissgau and on the river Emmer, where he celebrated Christmas at the *villa* of Lügde, and then attacked Rehme, near Vlotho, on the Weser.

Then, severe flooding again caused a further change of plan: Charles based himself at the Eresburg on the river Diemel. This was the Franks' first great Saxon fort, constructed in 772, retaken by Saxons in 773, recovered and restored by Charles in 775, briefly evacuated by its Frankish garrison in 776 while Charles was absent in Italy, and then, on his return, rebuilt once more by 'Charles and the Franks'. Now in 785, he stayed at the Eresburg from Christmas through to June 'because of the very severe flooding'. He bade his wife and sons and daughters to join him there, rebuilt the fort and also built a church, and, while waiting for the weather to improve, celebrated Easter there.[86] The intensification of fighting in the preceding year had discouraged normal political transactions.

The flooding and persistent rain made living conditions hard for everyone. For the Westphalians, they became intolerable, and the outcome inevitable:

> Charles resided at the Eresburg and the Franks in the area round about, in huts. Then mobilizing the army from their tents, he came to Dersia [Hesse], and burned that region, and crossed the Weser and that same year destroyed the barriers and the defence-works of the Saxons. And then, with God's help, he acquired (*adquisivit*) the Saxons.[87]

For the Franks, morale was constantly being boosted by Charles himself:

> He sent out *scarae* on numerous occasions while he was staying there, and also campaigned in person. He despoiled rebel Saxons, captured their forts, made his way into their fortified places, and cleared the roads, while he awaited the arrival of suitable weather.[88]

The *ArF* reviser laid on the message with a trowel:

> Charles had his wife and children summoned and brought to him. Leaving an adequate garrison of loyal and steadfast soldiers with them in the fort, he himself went out with a swift-moving force to devastate the districts of the Saxons and plunder their estates, and he paid back the Saxons with an unquiet winter as he and the war-leaders he sent out went everywhere throwing all into confusion with killings and burnings. By ravaging throughout the whole winter in this way, he inflicted a huge disaster on nearly all the regions of the Saxons.[89]

In 785, after he had held his assembly at Paderborn, Charles was able 'to march about Saxony, going wherever he wished on open roads, meeting no opposition'.[90] Saxons looking out over their ravaged landscape saw a different tranquillity – that of death and destruction. Later in life, when Charles became acquainted with Augustine's *City of God*, he would begin to understand the perils, but also the potential, of an 'ordered tranquillity' – 'peace of a kind'.[91]

VII. QUEENS DEAD AND ALIVE

From Verden, Charles had returned to Francia in time to join Hildegard at Thionville for Christmas in 782, staying through to Easter (23 March) 783. They must have recalled a previous winter there a decade before, when the pope's envoy had arrived with an urgent request. Hildegard had been pregnant then, with the child who would be named after his father and great-grandfather, and who had by then reached the age of ten.[92] Hildegard was pregnant again. The baby was born in late April, but the birth was difficult or she suffered complications *post partum*. On 30 April she died at Thionville, aged twenty-five. The recording in the *ArF* of the date of the queen's death attested the impression her life made on contemporaries. On 1 May, Charles granted an estate near Metz to St-Arnulf's, 'for the soul of our most beloved wife, Hildegard the queen'. The wording was conventional enough; more unusual were the arrangements for perpetual lights at her tomb day and night, daily masses, psalmody and prayers, and the insistence that future abbots and custodians must never relinquish control of the property granted for this purpose.[93] A similar grant of royal properties belonging to the royal residence at Florence to the church of San Miniato, for lights and prayers for Hildegard's soul, probably belonged to Christmas 786 which Charles celebrated at Florence.[94] The baby, named for her own mother, outlived her by only forty days. At Charles's court in (probably) 784, Paul the Deacon wrote epitaphs for them both, commissioned by Charles. The genre dictated conventionality, but the baby's epitaph conveyed a father's anguish, while in Hildegard's the poet singled out her 'candour of soul and inner beauty' (*simplicitas animae, interiorque decor*) as rather more than merely conventional traits associated with her piety.[95]

Evidence for a queen's experience in the form of letters and court poetry becomes available only for the years after Hildegard's life ended. Her personality could be considered inaccessible. Yet in her case, one source may offer an alternative route: Notker the Stammerer's *Gesta Karoli*, the earlier part of which was written at St-Gall in 885–6. So far I have made very little use of Notker's work. There are connections, however, between Notker himself and Hildegard. Both were Alemans. At Notker's monastery, an oral tradition in the form of stories gathered around Hildegard and her family, and Notker set a few of these down in the *Gesta Karoli*.[96] One such story is worth presenting here. It concerns 'a bishop' (in fact, the archbishop of Mainz) who was a particular object of Notker's dislike:

> When the most warlike Charles was away on campaign . . . this bishop was left to take care of the most renowned Hildegard. When he began to be so over-excited by working closely with the queen, and so insolent that he became bold enough to ask her if he could borrow the golden sceptre of the incomparable Charles (who had ordered it to be made for his own ceremonial use) – so that he himself could carry it on feast-days instead of his episcopal staff. With a clever bit of deceit, Hildegard said she would not dare to give it to anyone but she would faithfully pass on the bishop's request to the king. When Charles came home, she laughingly told him about the 'mad' bishop's request. The king, highly amused, agreed to do what Hildegard had asked, and said he would do even more. When almost everyone of any importance from the whole of Europe had gathered in an assembly, Charles announced the bishop's request, adding that he himself hadn't been consulted! The bishop left in confusion.[97]

This typical Notker joke might just (though I'm not sure I'd bet on it) record a real-life episode, which not only denounces episcopal greed and ambition but preserves a memory of the royal couple's relationship.[98]

Little over two months after Hildegard's death, Charles's mother, Bertrada, died on 12 July. Again, her impact on contemporaries explains the record of her death in the *ArF*. Einhard, who could never have known Bertrada, wrote that, apart from the falling-out over Charles's repudiation of his Lombard bride, 'Bertrada lived with her son and grew old in high honour. She had lived long enough to see 3 grandsons and 3 granddaughters in her son's house.' Einhard omitted to say that Charles's daughter Berta had been named for her grandmother, nor did he mention Bertrada's episodic presence in the environs of the monastery of St-Denis, although he knew that she had been buried at St-Denis 'with great honour', beside her husband.[99] The two queens, the consort and the dowager, had in common more than closeness to Charles. As wives, they shared much of the ritual patterning of their respective husbands' lives, and accompanied them in their public acts. The two queens' experiences also differed in two important respects: Hildegard not only lived with but travelled with her husband when possible, whereas the record seldom indicates that in Bertrada's case; and, connected with that difference, was another, namely Hildegard's exceptional performance bearing children (nine babies in eleven years of marriage). In contrast, Bertrada gave birth to four babies in twenty-four years of marriage, followed by fifteen active years of widowhood and grandmotherhood. What Pauline Stafford called 'the inexorable unfolding of the female lifecycle' is something anyone interested in early medieval dynastic and family politics has to confront, and often lament.[100]

Within roughly six months of Hildegard's death, Charles had married again. The bride was Fastrada, daughter of Count Radolf, an East Frank whose family connections in the Rhineland, notably with Archbishop Riculf of Mainz, can be traced in charters. Some historians of nineteenth- and twentieth-century vintage (and it goes without saying that these are all men) have taken a very critical view of Charles's too-swift remarriage, as resulting from his pathologically uncontrollable sexual desires. Einhard twice (in succeeding sentences) framed Fastrada as responsible for the two revolts of Charles's reign, in 786 and 792, because of her 'cruelty', which contrasted so starkly, Einhard thought, with the gentle nature and kindness of Charles. Not so long ago, Johannes Fried nailed Fastrada as 'young, beautiful, and cruel – vampiric traits' (indeed!)[101] Other historians have pointed out that Charles had come to value greatly the duties performed by Hildegard as consort: a king needed a queen as much as a man needed a wife.[102]

There is something to be said here for a middle way. Charles had repudiated two wives one after the other after only one son had been born to the first wife. Fathering nine children within eleven years on his third wife may have pushed the limits of normality, even for the richest and most powerful man. Einhard presents details about Charles's wives, and then his mistresses, giving a sequential chronology of relationships that could have run concurrently. The manliness of early medieval warrior-elites included a lusty sexual appetite. Churchmen preached monogamy. Contradictory pulls, and tensions, were unavoidable, as the authors of advice-books for aristocratic men acknowledged.[103] Historians nowadays (often women) tend to a practical and practicable *via media*: Charles's strong sex-drive was exceptional enough to be remembered in a horrified monk's nightmare years after his death;[104] yet Charles also manifested concern and affection for both Hildegard and Fastrada.[105] That concern persisted after their deaths. In two charters, both issued in 787 and in Italy, Charles arranged for prayers to be said for 'us, our queens, and our children'.[106] The plural queens were the dead Hildegard and the living Fastrada. The formula may sound soullessly, even heartlessly functional, but it represented a moment of bridging and continuity.

Gender compounds the paradoxes in the otherness of the early medieval past. The nature of the sources makes it almost impossibly hard to capture how high-born women experienced lives that were at once private and public, yet the female lifecycle inexorably unfolded for women of all ranks (did Bertrada share with the women of her household the signs of her pregnancy in 747?), and female religious shared with laywomen the experience of menstruation and menopause (did the *antiqua familiaritas* between the old nun Leoba and the young but childbirth-worn Hildegard include conversations about bodily as well as spiritual things?)[107] Fastrada's eleven-year stint as queen will occupy sections of the next two chapters, and she gets a small but memorable part in the next section, below.

VIII. ATTIGNY, 785

In this final section of the chapter, I want to recapitulate the story of the Saxon wars so far, and then consider how and why it looked as if some kind of closure had been achieved. The wars had begun as classic border-disputes, pitting a stronger, more organized state against its more fragmented neighbours in occasional demonstrations of power by cross-border ravaging and the seizing of booty.[108] It was only in Charles's reign that a pattern of conflict became recognizable. Raids and battles were followed by the extracting of oaths of fidelity, conversions and mass baptisms, the explicit opposing of Christians to pagans, and frequent allegations of perfidy and rebellion. These came to form the main theme in the narrative of the *ArF*. Westphalia was the core area of conflict, though longer-distance raids further north and east became more frequent. Charles summoned his assembly to Paderborn for the first time in 777 and staged a performance of power in front of Franks and Saxons (except for Widukind), and envoys from Spain; he staged similar performances in 780 when he held his assembly at Lippspringe and marched north-east as far as the Elbe, and in 782, when again the assembly was at Lippspringe, with Saxons (except for Widukind), Franks, Danes and Avars constituting the audience and counts were appointed in Saxony. An unusually clear charter-trail makes it possible to see where Charles was, whom he favoured, and to whom he did justice in the months from July ('in the army-camp') to September 782. Rebellion followed, resulting in serious Frankish casualties; and late in that same year, Charles staged a spectacular event at Verden on the Elbe, combining a legal trial, at which an unbelievably large number of Saxons were condemned for treason and beheaded, with old-fashioned vengeance for the Frankish dead. In the following two years, 783 and 784, Westphalia was so ruthlessly ravaged and plundered that resistance there collapsed and Charles could travel 'on empty roads, wherever he wanted'.

Floods are memorable events, as anyone who has experienced one knows all too well. It was severe flooding that, according to the *ArF* author, impelled Charles to leave Rehme in waterlogged Westphalia and move to the Eresburg, 'where he bade his wife, the lady queen Fastrada to come with his sons and daughters to join him . . . for the whole winter'. Fastrada had stepped into Hildegard's combined role of queen and carer-of-the-family, but with the difference that she was the children's stepmother. Not all of them were in a position to answer their father's bidding: Rotrud might have stayed at Worms to mourn her mother and continue her Greek studies; Pippin king of Italy and Louis king of Aquitaine were residing at Pavia and (probably) Chasseneuil, respectively, with their new households. At the Eresburg, a 120-metre-high Iron Age hillfort strongly fortified by Charles and supplied with a church, louring steeply, over the river Diemel and its wintry rain-soaked landscape, the children present would have been Pippin the first-born, Young Charles, Berta and Gisela: two big boys, two little girls. Fastrada may well have already been pregnant, for the first time. The cycle was unfolding again. Einhard's chapter 19 reports that as soon as they were old enough, [Charles] had his sons taught to ride in Frankish fashion, to use arms, and to hunt. He made his daughters learn to spin and to weave wool, to use the distaff and the spindle, and acquire every womanly accomplishment rather than fritter away their time in sheer idleness.

It takes a bit of imagination to see the family at the Eresburg. Two historians have recently done just that in imagining speculation about the sex of Fastrada's unborn child.[109]

By the time Charles held his summer assembly in 785, he had complete freedom of manoeuvre in the Westphalian heartland of Saxony. Everyone knew it – including Widukind, who had seen the writing on the wall for rebels. It was Charles who took the initiative, making the move in Widukind's direction: he travelled from Paderborn to the Bardengau in the area near the mouth of the Elbe in north-east Saxony. From this point, the *ArF* reviser has a fuller story:[110]

Once there, he learned that Widukind and Abbio were in the region of the Saxons which lay across the Elbe [impossible to say when they had moved from Nordmannia] and he began to urge them, through Saxons in the first instance, not to hesitate but to put perfidy behind them and come over to fidelity to him (*ad suam fidem*). Conscious of their crimes, they were doubtful about committing themselves to fidelity to the king. But at length, after receiving from him the promise of impunity that they wanted, and obtaining from him the hostages for their safety that they had asked to be given, they came with Amalwin, one of his *aulici* whom the king had sent to escort the hostages to them, to appear in his presence at the *villa* of Attigny, and there were baptized . . .

The *ArF* author adds: ' . . . with their followers. And then all Saxony was subjugated.'[111] With this firm claim, the *ArF* author shows that his text was written before 795, when another Saxon revolt broke out. In hindsight, it can be said that a decade of peace in Saxony ensued.

That Charles made the first overtures to Widukind was profoundly significant, as was the fact that he had sent hostages, as he had previously done for Tassilo in 781. Charles recognized the moment as a tipping-point, and he was prepared to seize a great opportunity. Most significant of all, though, were the baptisms of Widukind and Abbio, and the additional fact, known, as so often, from minor annals (*Ann.*

Mos.; Ann. Lauriss.) that Charles raised them from the font, that is, became their godfather.[112] The spiritual relationship, like that of compaternity, could mean a great deal – or it could mean little. In this case, there is no evidence in the sources either way. But for once, absence is good evidence: the disappearance from the record of both Widukind and Abbio indicates that they stayed in Westphalia, making good their losses, and remaining faithful to Charles.[113] The genuineness of the Saxons' submission was affirmed by Charles in a letter to Hadrian late in 785, and hailed enthusiastically by the pope himself early in 786. Charles had announced that praises should be sung for a month and a day in thanks to God, and at Charles's request, Hadrian had

> sent forth orders into all our lands, those lying under the dominion of your spiritual mother the Holy Roman Church that under God's protection litanies are to be celebrated in those regions, as by us also on the 23 and the 26 and the 28 June which are, first the Eve of St John the Baptist, then the birthday of SS John and Paul, and also the Eve of St Peter the Apostle. And may your Royal Power likewise send word throughout all his territories and to those regions across the sea where the Christian people (*populus*) is to be found, for the performance of litanies for three days in this fashion. It is because Christian peoples (*gentes*) live so far away from your royal dominion that we have provided for the deferment of the litanies . . . We have also decreed the singing of praises to the Redeemer of the world that those peoples brought to the Christian Faith through your royal solicitude may, through your support, abide in it for all time.[114]

Some Saxons did rebel again, it's true, but not in Westphalia. In the final phase of the Saxon wars, the scene would shift to the far north and east of Saxony. For contemporaries, and still, for the author of the *ArF*, peace had broken out at last in Saxony.

The papyrus letter of Maginar.

8

Boundary-crossings

I. TROUBLE AT SAN VINCENZO, 783–4

Charles's military and political priorities, always inseparable from each other, were very obviously entwined in Saxony in 783 and 784. In the late summer of 783, he and his household had a further priority of a more personal as well as political kind: namely, his marriage at Worms to the East Frankish noblewoman Fastrada. With an empire to manage and multiple interests to attend to, Charles was inevitably bombarded with communications from near and far. A few of the thousands of letters written to him have survived, largely thanks to the compilers of the *Codex Carolinus*, especially those from Pope Hadrian. For the letters sent in the early 780s there are some tricky dating-problems. The consensus now is that no. 66, the shortest letter in the entire collection, was sent sometime between May and September 783, and no. 67 in February 784 (meaning that they post-date nos. 69–72, presumably as the result of an archivist's error). Dates of arrival are unknown. But the contents of no. 66 presuppose that Charles was already aware of trouble at San Vincenzo.

San Vincenzo was one of the three richest monasteries in central Italy (the others were Monte Cassino and Farfa). Thanks to excavations conducted in the 1980s and 1990s, it is now a very well-known and deeply impressive site.[1] Conflict arose partly from political tensions between Hadrian and Charles over contested claims to property in the duchy of Benevento, and partly from tension between Frankish and Lombard members of the monastic community. So important were communications with the Lombard kingdom's southern boundaries in the 780s that for Charles, wherever he was situated in Francia or Saxony, and however absorbed in the priorities just mentioned, Hadrian's letters were vital sources of information. Fraught relations between the incoming Frankish regime and indigenous Lombards had lain behind Hrodgaud's revolt in 776.[2] In 777, Duke Arichis of Benevento apparently offered no resistance to Charles's using his influence to secure the election of a Frank, Ambrosius Autpert, to the abbacy of San Vincenzo. But in December 778, Autpert was deposed (he died soon after) and replaced by a Lombard, Potho, with Pope Hadrian's support. Though Hadrian had been hostile to Desiderius before the Frankish takeover, his relations with Lombards further south were sometimes cordial. In 783, he wrote to tell Charles that three Frankish monks in the San Vincenzo community were accusing Potho of faithlessness (*infidelitas*) and demanding his deposition. Hadrian's brief letter made the case for Potho's defence:

> The whole community of St Vincent [San Vincenzo] have asked us [Hadrian] to make favourable representations on behalf of the abbot who has been unjustly accused to you, and has indeed been removed from the monastery . . . and brought before Your Royal Presence . . . His accusers will in no way be able to prove the charges of faithlessness towards Your Royal Potency because the charges brought against him are totally false . . . We beg that he [Abbot Potho] should be absolved as guiltless . . . and restored to his original office by your most merciful command and at our request.[3]

Evidently, Potho was already at Charles's court and, therefore, a boundary-crosser. Early in 784, Charles's mind was 'set on finishing off what remained of the Saxon war'.[4] The arrival at Charles's winter residence at Herstal of papal couriers with the formal report of the inquiry into Potho's conduct was welcome, nevertheless. For Charles, far from being a distraction, it could help confirm his control over San Vincenzo. The hearing had been held in Rome before a number of senior churchmen and also several high officials in the pope's service, including Hadrian's nephew Theodore, Theophylact, the papal librarian, and the chamberlain Stephen. The chief witness against Potho was the monk Rodicausus, apparently a Frank. His two vital bits of evidence were things he claimed to have heard from Potho's own mouth:

> When we had finished the liturgy of the sixth hour and according to custom were chanting the prophetic psalm [Ps. 54] for the safety of the king and

his offspring, suddenly the abbot got up and refused to go on chanting . . . [On another occasion] the abbot said to me, 'If I hadn't been so
concerned about the monastery and the Beneventan land [*terra Beneventana*], I'd have treated him [Charles] the same way I'd have treated a dog!'

Potho's alleged refusal to chant prayers for Charles and his family
was tantamount to treason. His alleged comments on Charles were
worse than insulting; they deeply dishonoured the king. Hadrian and
the other judges considered the witness unsound: they ordered him and
ten monks, five Franks and five Lombards, to take oaths of innocence
(alas, there is no record of those) and then the pope sent the ten monks
to Charles in Francia. Potho was deposed by Charles on 30 April 783.[5]

II. 'A BATTLE BETWEEN THE BAVARIANS AND ROTPERT AT BOLZANO', 784 OR 785

A glance at Map 8 (p. xxi) will show how Bolzano's location, on the
route from the Adige valley to the Brenner Pass and north-eastwards
into Bavaria, gave the town a new strategic importance after the Frankish annexation of Friuli in 774. Charles's success in suppressing
Rodgaud's rebellion in 776 confirmed that importance. After Duke
Tassilo's meeting with Charles at Worms in 781, no Frankish or papal
sources are available until 787. The Bavarian sources disagree on the date
of the battle: the Salzburg Annals place it under the year 784; the
Annals of St Emmeram, Regensburg, place it under 785, and identify
the combatants as 'Bavarians' and 'Hrodpert'.[6]

Creontius's information fills the gap between 784 and 785:[7]

Duke Widukind from Saxony, who attacked Francia, did great damage
to king Charles. For this reason, king Charles's chief man in Italy, the
above-named duke Rotpert, believed there was a plot instigated by duke
Tassilo in Bavaria, fell upon that land in the valley of the Adige, captured
the city of Bolzano, sacked it and left it burned to the ground. The Bavarians, seeking to revenge this, came to their city of Bolzano, repossessed
it and drove into Italy against duke Rotpert of Lombardy (now
Milan) . . . And duke Tassilo concluded an eternal peace with his neighbours the Huns. And duke Rotpert again invaded Bavaria intending to

capture the Bavarian city of Bolzano. Duke Tassilo sent his chief men there, Gewein and Iwein; they killed duke Rotpert and many of the enemy with him; the rest of the people all fled. And so the Bavarians won a great victory and much booty.[8]

There is no other information about Rotpert.[9] As Charles's right-hand man in Italy, Rotpert's suspicion of collusion between Bavarians and Saxons was a reasonable inference, and so was his assumption that an attack on the Bavarian border-city of Bolzano would gain Charles's approval. This region remained problematic for Charles until his conquest of Bavaria, after which the strengthening of Pippin of Italy's regime created a new geopolitical arc stretching from Friuli, the Norican Alps and south Tyrol, to Rhaetia.[10] What does seem likely is that after the debacle in 785 at Bolzano, 'the rift between Charles and Tassilo became unbridgeable'.[11]

III. A REVOLT 'MADE IN GERMANIA', 785–6

Einhard, as a good classicist, knew 'Germania' to have been the Roman name for the lands east of the Rhine. In his *Life of Charles*, he wrote of two conspiracies against the king: the only two in the whole of Charles's long reign. Awkwardly, Einhard mentioned them out of chronological order: first, that of Charles's first-born son Pippin (in 792); and second, without naming any leader, an earlier 'powerful conspiracy' (*valida coniuratio in Germania*) in 785.[12] This information, absent from the *ArF*, was included in the work of the *ArF* reviser, on whom Einhard clearly relied:

> This same year [785] across the Rhine, among the eastern Franks, and the author of which was Count Hardrad as was well-known, a very extensive sworn association (*inmodica coniuratio*) was formed against the king. But intelligence of this was swiftly brought to the king, who by his shrewdness soon laid to rest such a formidable conspiracy (*tam valida conspiratio*) before any great danger had occurred. Some of its leaders were condemned to the loss of their eyes, others to banishment into exile.[13]

The *ArF* reviser added a significant comment to his account of what caused the sworn association (*coniuratio*) in 792 of Pippin the first-born: 'certain Franks who asserted that they could no longer bear the cruelty of Queen Fastrada . . . therefore had conspired to bring about the king's death'.[14] Einhard, again drawing on the *ArF* reviser, wrote: 'It is believed that the cruelty of Queen Fastrada was the cause and origin of these conspiracies. And a conspiracy was therefore made against the king in both cases because he seemed to have consented to his wife's cruelty and thus dreadfully exceeded his usual kindness and gentleness.'[15] Since both the *ArF* reviser and Einhard were writing considerably after Fastrada's death, and no other source alleges her cruelty, it looks as if she was retrospectively made a scapegoat for the actions of others – especially those of Charles himself. Casting the blame on a woman (often in order to whitewash a man) is a common enough political tactic. In this case, context and timing need to be explored a little further.

Like the 785 revolt, Fastrada herself was *facta in Germania*. Her father, Count Radolf, was a Frank born east of the Rhine, and so was his daughter. Einhard pins down her lineage more precisely as 'of the people of the Eastern Franks, that is, the Germans'.[16] Among her family connections seem to have been Archbishop Riculf of Mainz, whose brother had estates near Frankfurt, in East Francia.[17] One way of explaining the revolt (and perhaps also of attributing it to Fastrada's cruelty) would be to suppose that there was a rift between noble factions, of course with landed interests, east of the Rhine. This is the impression given by the Lorsch Annals, also contemporary:

> An attempt at rebellion was made by some counts and also by quite a few nobles in parts of East Francia. They formed a sworn association and compelled everyone they could to rise up against the lord king. Such a deed filled many with fear. And when they realized that they could not carry through their abominable enterprise, and that the moment was inopportune, they were seized by sudden terror and sought out hiding-places everywhere. When he learned of this, the lord king, with his usual mercifulness (*clementia*), managing everything with wise counsel, ordered them to come to him. In due course, in August, he caused a great synod of bishops and an imposing general assembly to gather at Worms, and there he decreed that those who were convicted of being most powerfully implicated in this sworn association were to be deprived of their lands (*honores*) and their eyes, but those who had been innocently seduced into this sworn association he mercifully (*clementer*) absolved.[18]

Another set of annals, again contemporary, written at the abbey of Murbach in Alsace but sharing descent from earlier annals with a Lorsch connection (hence the name, *Annales Nazariani*, from St Nazarius, one of the patron saints of Lorsch), give what at first glance looks like an account of some other revolt, but on closer inspection seems more probably a version of the story of Hardrad's rebellion viewed from another perspective. The narrative deserves to be quoted in full. It falls into three parts, which I will consider in turn:

> Thuringians formed a plot to capture Charles king of the Franks by treachery, and to kill him; if they were unable to perpetrate this sin and most abominable crime, then they wanted at least to bring it about that they should not obey him or comply with his demands. This vile plan could in no way long remain hidden from the king, who, however, prudent and merciful as he was, bore it with the most extreme patience. And so, after a while, the said king sent a senior officer (*legatus*) of his to one of those Thuringians in the matter of the Thuringian's daughter who was betrothed to a Frank and known to have been betrothed according to the law of Franks, saying that he should hand the Frank's bride over to him at the appointed time. But the Thuringian, treating the king's commands with contempt, not only refused to promise to hand her over but also gathered almost all his Thuringian neighbours together and sought to defend himself from the king of the Franks.

The plotters were Thuringians, and they came from a people long since subject to the Franks. From a Frankish perspective, those who plotted to kill Charles were committing not only treason but a terrible sin. Their fall-back position was to refuse obedience to the king. Nevertheless Charles took no immediate action. 'After a while', Charles chose to intervene in a marriage-dispute involving a Thuringian woman and a Frankish man. The delivery of the bride within an agreed time was a requirement of Frankish law: when Charles insisted this be met, the woman's father refused to comply, instead enlisting the support of other Thuringians to reject Charles's demand. Disputes over betrothals between a man and a woman of different peoples were sufficiently frequent to have elicited legal measures to avert trouble, as, apparently, in the present case. Or perhaps the dispute and Charles's intervention came first, and the Thuringian plot against the king took shape as a consequence. Charles's intervention, or his officer's, may have been heavy-handed. The role of valiant protector of Frankish men and Frankish law was surely one no Frankish king could turn down. At this stage in the narrative, nothing was said of any specifically *East* Frankish involvement. Yet the second part of the story reveals exactly that.

> Now the king was mightily angered (*iratus est valde*) on hearing this and indignantly despatched against them some of his elite troops (*satellites*) who proceeded against them with shrewdness and boldness, devastating their estates and properties. Seized by fear, the Thuringians took refuge at the tomb [at Fulda] of the blessed martyr Boniface so that the king might, out of veneration for this saint and through his merits, forgive them the injury, treachery and plots which they had attempted to set going. Then the abbot of that monastery soothed them with peaceable words and sweet discourse, and through his own messenger (*nuntius*) informed the king of everything. The king therefore sent his officer (*legatus*) to them so that they should come to him with peace; and soon they journeyed to him and stood before him. The king for his part inquired of them whether what he had been informed about them, namely, that they intended his death, and if unable to effect that, to treat his commands with contempt, was true or false. They could in no way deny it, nor did they deign to do so. Indeed it is reported that one of them said to the king: 'If my comrades and associates had proved to be of my way of thinking, you would never again have been seen crossing to this side of the Rhine alive.' But the king, since he was most gentle and most wise above all the kings who had preceded him in Francia, put up with this with great moderation.

In this part of the narrative, the tone changes. The merciful Charles becomes the extremely angry Charles: he sends his men to devastate the lands of the plotters, whose terrified reaction is to seek refuge at the monastery of Fulda. The abbot, not named here, was in fact Baugulf, a former count in the Rhineland, whose older brother Wielant, and nephew Warin, were also influential in the orbits of King Pippin and, later, Charles. After taking over the protection of Fulda in 774 and granting it immunity from an outside power's intrusion and the monks' freedom to choose their abbot (DD. 85 and 86), Charles made sure that Baugulf succeeded Sturm as abbot in 779.[19] It was Baugulf who, after soothing the plotters' fears, 'sent his own messenger' to Charles to 'inform the king of everything'. But by this point, the Murbach writer depicted

Charles as having moved into moderate mode, taking in his stride a rebel's bare-faced cheek.

Baugulf, by soothing the rebels and at the same time betraying them, but always acting as a loyal officer to Charles, settled the plotters' fates. These were spelled out in the third and briefest section of the story:

> After some days had passed, therefore, the king sent those Thuringians together with his *missi*, some into Italy and to St Peter [i.e. to Rome], but some into Neustria and into Aquitaine, sending them to the tombs of saints, so that they might swear fidelity to the king and his sons; and this they are attested to have done. Several of them were arrested on their return journey from these places. Their eyes are known to have been torn out. But some reached the city of Worms and were arrested there and sent into exile, where their eyes are known to have been torn out. And all their possessions and estates are known to have been seized by the royal fisc. The king remains unharmed and safe, therefore, ruling the kingdom of the Franks and Lombards and Romans most excellently, because the King of the Heavens is proven to be his protector.

This third section prompts broader and deeper understandings of the revolt. As a political crisis, its broader context is to be found in the massive transfers of lands to churches, especially recently founded monasteries, in the two decades before 785. From the archives of the two great monasteries of Fulda and Lorsch, both east of the Rhine, survive well over 3,000 charters dating from Charles's reign and preserved in cartularies, 'charter-books', in which old documents were copied out.[20] Some 180 royal charters survive from Charles's reign, 97 of them from the years 769–83 inclusive. This means that just under 60 per cent of all Charles's charters date from the first fifteen years of his forty-six-year reign. A number of monasteries were given to Charles by their founders or founder-abbots. Lorsch itself had come into Charles's protection by a judgment of 772.[21] Hersfeld was transferred into Charles's hands by its founder in 775.[22] In 780, two counts saw their tithe income from Hersfeld property transferred to Charles 'through a precept of our authority'.[23] A royal judgment made by Charles in 782 brought Mettlach out of its founding family's control and into that of the Archbishop of Trier under terms that sounded as if the king could claim the property of the bishopric.[24] A man named Alpad found himself investigated in 790 by a pair of Charles's *missi*, one of whom was the abbot of the great Carolingian family-monastery of Prüm, and deprived of substantial estates which were found to have rightfully belonged to the king himself (Charles promptly handed them over to Prüm).[25] The monastery of Murbach seems to have come into Charles's hands c.780.[26] Charles 'did not found monasteries, he acquired them'.[27] These acquisitions did not come about simply because 'the aristocracy had a vested interest in a Carolingian system which eased the enactment of structural changes' (though there is a good deal to be said for such an analysis).[28] The aristocratic world was full of competition, and Charles's interventions, through his agents, in regional and local politics typically involved violence.

Men like Hardrad and his associates were driven by grievances. A charter, surviving as an original, in which Charles gave Fulda the estate of Rosdorp (Rossdorf) in Thuringia in 781 offers a case in point:

> We have granted to the monastery of the Saviour on the river Fulda where lies St Boniface, and where Baugulf is abbot, our estate called Rossdorf, which Hardrad gave by charters to that holy place, and afterwards our *missi* gained it by a judgment as being for our benefit (*ad opus nostrum conquisierunt*), and also what the monks got through earlier charters in dues and renders from the people (*conlata populi*) on that estate, and we have conceded it as a whole to that abovementioned holy place, and we have handed it over whole and entire to that abovementioned holy place for possessing in perpetuity.[29]

The gist is clear: Hardrad had given some land and rights to Fulda; Charles's *missi* successfully claimed these as being Charles's, and Charles gave them to Fulda. I am not the first to suggest that this Hardrad is the same man as the rebel of 785.[30] Some scholars have thought it suspicious that the Hardrad of D. 140 is not given the title 'count', and they have noted that there are quite a number of other Hardrads among the thousands of men named in the charters of Lorsch and of Fulda. There are also two places called 'Rossdorf' or 'Rosdorp', one in Hesse, the other in Thuringia. No-one can be absolutely certain of identifications on these points.

What matters in this charter is the detail about Charles's work-methods: the sending-in of *missi* to swing a judgment in a local court; the overriding of a local man's rights and gift; and the king's takeover of both the land and, by the re-donation of the gift, his acquiring the gift's spiritual benefits for himself. Charles did these things not by virtue of his lordship of Fulda, though no doubt the abbot was a willing enough ally, but by political intervention in the locality and the local society concerned, through what could be called conquisitive agents (borrowing D. 140's term): *missi* who did not arrive unaccompanied. The *satellites* whom Charles sent in fury against the rebels in 785 were men who 'in wise and trusty fashion (*sagaciter et fiduciater* [sic]), devastated their estates and properties'. *Missi* and their men could devastate too.[31] By 785, Charles had indulged once too often in local acts of high-handedness and violent suppression of dissent. A string of intrusions into the workings of local courts; the treatment of Saxons at Verden; the harsh decrees of the *Capitulatio de partibus Saxoniae* of 782; the insulting intervention in the dispute caused by the collapse of a marriage-alliance; and, worst of all for those east of the Rhine, the cruel punishments – blinding, exile, wholesale confiscation of property – meted out to the rebel leaders of 785/6; all these were signals of the wrong kinds of boundary-crossing. Some historians have found a final puzzle in the arsy-versy sequence of events: the rebels swore oaths *only after* having rebelled, and *only after* having sworn oaths of loyalty were they brutally punished by Charles's agents. But the function of the oath of fidelity here was a kind of test: an ordeal, interpretable as proof of guilt. A text well-known to Charles and his entourage was the *Chronicle of Fredegar*, and there could be found the story of Godin, who had allegedly plotted the death of a king: Godin was ordered by the king to travel to the shrines of saints and swear oaths of fidelity at each, 'so that, at a suitable place, the king could have Godin killed' – which is exactly what happened.[32] Logic was in the eyes of beholders.

Already in 779 in the Capitulary of Herstal, Charles had prohibited sworn associations: such prohibitions grew more frequent and peremptory. The *coniuratio* centred on Hardrad and directed against Charles himself, was, as far as can be known, the last of its kind in Charles's reign – the *coniuratio* of Pippin the first-born apart.[33] The fates of the rebel leaders in 785–6 were designed to promote trust, by showing the rebels' oaths to be false. The repeated use of 'proof' words – *conprobatur, noscuntur, cognoscentur* – leads up to a resounding *ergo*, a final *conprobatur*, and a confident assertion in the present tense: 'Therefore the king is safe and sound.' The sequence of events proves that God protects the king. The 785 revolt seems to me so significant precisely because it arose as a provincial reaction, compounded of many local reactions, against what had come to be – or were perceived as becoming – the political practices of the regime itself. In the aftermath of 785–6, Charles took time to reflect at length. He and his counsellors, in 789, came up with something that was old: an oath of fidelity for all, which had only briefly, if ever, been out of use.[34] Meanwhile, events of another kind were propelling Charles's contemporaries into other reflections, and Charles himself into deliberate *in*action.

IV. SIGNS AND PORTENTS

The revolt of Hardrad, and the appearance of alarming signs and portents in 785–6, have seldom been connected by modern historians. Contemporary authors *did* make the connection, however. The visibility of these signs ensured that they were widely reported in several sets of annals and in different regions, including places to which the rebels were sent to swear oaths of fidelity and undergo punishment: Italy and Rome, Neustria, Worms. Three Bavarian sources are informative: at Salzburg it was reported that 'the sign of the cross appeared on men's clothes. Hardrad betrayer of the fatherland made a great plot against the king.'[35] The author of annals at St Emmeram's, Regensburg, wrote, 'Hardrad made a wicked plan; and a sign [was] on the clothes of men.'[36] According to Creontius:

> Concerning the prodigious happenings of this time. [In 786] there was a great earthquake in the winter. And afterwards in May there came a great coldness. A deep snow fell; and the birds dropped frozen to the ground. Men picked them up in their hands, and found them in the woods dead upon their eggs. Various water-courses ran blood-coloured, and little black drops, burning-hot like a fire, fell upon people: when one drop landed on a bare hand the person died within hours; if it landed on his clothes, he did not die so quickly, true, but he was lucky to escape with his life. When this plague struck Bavaria, Duke Tassilo, on the advice of the Bavarian bishops and other wise men of the land, had a general fast ordered throughout the entire land; everyone including the prince himself had to fast, to strew ashes on his bare head, to go barefoot, to do public penance in church and to make confession. Then the plague ended.

Crosses also fell at this time. Many more wondrous happenings occurred at this time.[37]

In Francia, the author of the *Annales Petaviani* wrote:

There was no campaign that year, except that in the season of winter, Charles travelled to Italy with his army and came to Rome and from there reached Beneventan territory by God's help. A sign was sent upon the earth from heaven by God (*signum de caelo a Deo in terra*) in this year, and there was great terror.[38]

Also in Francia, the author of the Chesne Fragment reported:

Many signs are reported to have appeared this year. For the mark of the cross appeared on men's clothes, and blood flowed forth from the ground and out of the skies, and many other signs appeared, and therefore a mighty dread and fear overwhelmed people in a health-giving way so that many reformed themselves (*pavor ingens ac timor in populo salubriter inruit, ita ut se multi corrigerent*). And six days before the Lord's birthday there occurred such enormous thunderclaps and flashes of lightning that the churches in Widli [probably Witla at the mouth of the Meuse] were shaken and the sound was heard throughout almost the whole of Francia, and many men were killed; even the birds of the air were slain by that thunder. And a heavenly bow appeared in the clouds that night [Genesis 9:13–15]. And afterwards there was great mortality. And Archbishop Lull departed this life. Charles travelled to Rome, thence to Benevento.[39]

A further testimony is that of the author of the Lorsch Annals for 786:

In this year in December, such terrifying battle-arrays came to be seen in the heavens as had never before been manifest in our times; moreover the mark of the cross appeared on men's clothes, and some said they had seen it raining blood. Wherefore a mighty dread and terror seized the people. And afterwards there followed great mortality.[40]

These 'signs' were extreme weather-events that caused terrible suffering for human beings and birds. They included things that fell out of the sky: natural and supernatural, terrestrial and celestial. They occurred in time, with meanings beyond time: portentous as the rainbow in the cloud. They crossed boundaries: in particular, the boundary between a political event – Hardrad's revolt – in the present, and warnings for the future. Of the passages just cited, two were interpreted by their ecclesiastical authors as conducive to personal reform. The author of the Chesne Fragment wrote: 'great fear and terror . . . so that many reformed themselves'; and in Creontius's account of Duke Tassilo's more conventional and generalized instructions, confession and penance brought an end to plague.[41] Though the signs were various, common to all of them were meanings to be understood and acted upon.

There has been a recent burst of scholarly interest in the meaning of the Apocalypse for people in Charles's reign, and particularly in relation to his imperial coronation (in 800, see Chapter 13). A straight line has sometimes been drawn from 786 to 800. As James Palmer has pointed out, the line is *not* straight: search for 'signs' between those dates and you will find 'virtually none, so it is hard to see this as a part of an escalating pattern of apocalyptic signs related to a countdown'.[42] Nevertheless, it is hard *not* to see in and just after 785–6 a generalized anxiety, and also a particular anxiety among elites, clerical and lay, about the trend to arbitrariness and violence in Charles's governmental style and practice, not least in relation to Bavaria. From the events – and the mistakes – of 785–6, Charles learned much.

'Heaven and earth shall pass away . . . but of that day and hour knoweth no man, no, not the angels of heaven, but my Father only.'[43] These Gospel passages were surely familiar to Charles. He had learned something else, too, about the *management* of signs. That is to say: neither in the *ArF* nor in the work of the *ArF* reviser is there any reference to signs and portents in 785–6, and this silence seems most likely to have come about by a determined channelling, and suppression, of information in court circles in and after the mid-780s, when Charles and his advisers decided to make annals 'officially sponsored'.[44] The timing of this has implications for a personage whose role close to Charles was discussed earlier in this chapter: Fastrada. I am unpersuaded by the suggestion that she might have influenced the court annals' production.[45] I do think, though, that she had an important political role that can hardly be squared with her alleged cruelty.[46] She herself was a boundary-crosser, a soother of fearful persons on both sides of the Rhine, a negotiator, or manager, of faction, and a consensus-builder at court, whether at Worms, at Regensburg, at Frankfurt, or at Mainz. Her role was made easier by the fact that she had no son but only daughters, and by her willingness to act as substitute for

Hildegard, from her stay with Charles and some of his children at the Eresburg in 783–4 to her stay at Regensburg in 791–2.[47]

V. THE MISSION OF GEORGE AND THEOPHYLACT, LATE 786

Late in 785, Charles had requested the pope to organize litanies to thank God for victory against the Saxons and, early in 786, Pope Hadrian had gladly agreed to have these performed on three particular holy days in June; but at the same time he had asked Charles to collaborate by sending word to 'those regions beyond the sea [meaning the Channel and the North Sea] where the Christian people is to be found' to organize similar litanies. Hadrian had added: 'it is because Christian nations live so far removed from your royal realm that we provided for a time-lag [in implementing these orders]'.[48] It was no coincidence that Hadrian took account of the timing of Charles's co-operation and the distances involved. The pope was mindful of the original papal mission, back in 596, to far-away nations: Gregory the Great's sending of Augustine and his monks to convert the *Angli*. Bishop George of Ostia and Amiens was soon to remind Hadrian that since Augustine, no other *missus* had been sent 'except us'.

'Us' were Bishop George and his colleague Theophylact, bishop of Todi.[49] Charles's ties with Bishop George (recorded as active between 753 and 798 – the longest stint of any of Charles's trans-alpine experts) commended George as leader of the mission to England.[50] The choice of Bishop Theophylact of Todi in the duchy of Spoleto was closely linked with Charles's decision to visit Rome for a third time and to extend his journey further south into south-central Italy and the duchy in Benevento. Charles's political interests in these regions were obvious (and they will be considered presently). To accompany the *missi* (more familiarly known in the historiography as legates), Charles had also chosen an *adiutor* (helper): Abbot Wigbod of (probably) St Maximin's, Trier, and author (certainly) of an encyclopaedic *Commentary on Genesis* who was among the first to be drawn into Charles's scholarly circle.[51] These choices of personnel were no doubt discussed with and approved by Hadrian (by letter and through the spoken words of *missi*).

Fundamentally, though, the initiative behind the sending of a mission to England was that of Charles. If his hands were all over the political choices, Charles's ideological priorities were written into the canons of the councils held by the legates. Their report survives. Its introductory narrative is dated by Charles's reign-years. In the one surviving (and not fully complete) manuscript, the names of those attending are listed, and they include those of the top elite of laymen (known elsewhere as *seniores terrae*) as well as of bishops and abbots. In the final part of the letter-report George notes that the Mercian council was attended by Alcuin and Pyttel, identified as *lectores* and 'the *legati* of the Northumbrian king and archbishop', and that the council's decrees were read out aloud in not only Latin but *theodisc* – the vernacular.[52] One of those *lectores*, Alcuin, would have an astonishingly fruitful future in Francia, beginning in 786.

Before George and Theophylact had left Italy, they were aware that Charles himself had decided to set out for Italy. When he arrived at Rome in early January 787, the legates' letter-report was in Hadrian's hands at the Lateran. Coincidentally, a much lengthier and imposing set of decrees (in Greek) than those in George's report (in Latin) was being put together and discussed in Constantinople during these same months, preparatory to the holding of the Seventh Ecumenical Council, also known as Nicaea II. Nicaea was where the Emperor Constantine had assembled 318 bishops (by one traditional count) at the First Ecumenical Council in 325. However synchronicity did not spell communication when there was a very large language barrier in the way.

VI. 'A CLOUD NO BIGGER THAN A MAN'S HAND . . .'

This phrase from the Jewish Bible (slightly mistranslated in the King James Version) has become a standard allusion to any 'small, menacing omen'.[53] This was what had appeared on Charles's horizon in 785/6. Charles was enough of a connoisseur of signs to have censored those he did not welcome (as noted in the preceding section). In this case, the sign was a double one – an invitation and a non-invitation. In August

784, the Empress Eirene, since 780 the effective ruler in Constantin-ople, sent Pope Hadrian an invitation to an ecumenical council at Nicaea (an invitation to which he did not reply until October 785, accepting it on behalf of the envoys who would represent him); at the same time, there was *no* invitation to any Frankish bishop. Early in 787, if not before, Charles would have become aware that Rome was abuzz with news of both the invitation and the non-invitation.

Settling matters in Italy was more complicated than Charles had expected, in more ways than one. It is a good guess that he took the non-invitation as a snub from Eirene, and perhaps also from Hadrian (who made no move to enlarge the western contingent, and in none of his letters made any reference to the forthcoming council). With Charles, given his claim to some authority, and much interest, in mat-ters religious, the snub rankled. Contacts with Constantinople had been few and far between since Charles had agreed Rotrud's betrothal to the young emperor Constantine VI in 781; and no further discus-sions are documented between 781 and 786. Charles seems to have taken the initiative of suggesting a meeting between himself and Eirene's envoys in early 787, when he would be in southern Italy – a region with which Eirene's diplomats had frequent contacts. As things turned out, Charles's visit was very brief; but the short time he stayed at Capua in March was to be the window of opportunity. The only near-contemporary Byzantine narrative source is the *Chronicle* of The-ophanes. According to him (and, remember, he was writing after 810), Eirene broke off the betrothal in 788/9, much to her son's chagrin. What actually seems to have happened is that Charles broke off the betrothal in 787, at Capua. (There is no evidence that he brought Rotrud to Italy with him in 786/7, as he had in 781.) Charles's motives, probably mixed, included revenge for Eirene's ecumenical snub. No Frank was at Nicaea to hear the decrees read out in Greek. A Latin translation was made on Hadrian's orders, but it was seriously flawed because the translator was not bilingual, and worked from glossaries.[54] The consequence was that Charles commissioned a searing critique of the official conciliar text, which in his mind confirmed his own stand-ing as a qualified religious arbiter. The cloud no bigger than a man's hand had blown up into a storm which broke in late 790, with ram-ifications stretching to 792.

VII. CHARLES IN ITALY, 786–7

The context of Charles's third visit to Italy was his sense of continued basking in the glory of having pacified, or subjugated, the Saxons in 785, and then having turned to Brittany, with similarly cheering results in 786.[55] Brittany was considerably easier to pacify than Saxony, but had recently proved troublesome, as the Bretons, taking advantage of Charles's preoccupation with Saxony, refused to pay their customary tribute. Charles delegated command of a punitive campaign to Audulf, his seneschal, a Frank with connections in the Middle Rhine region who was later to become count in Bavaria.[56] Audulf dealt rapidly with the Bretons' 'contumacy' by taking their strongholds. He then brought hostages and large numbers of the Breton nobility to Worms, to pay their respects to Charles. As on previous occasions, Charles responded with some elation to a great assembly, complete with hostages and representatives of barbarian peoples. His perception was that all was peaceful, thanks to God's help. This was the moment, then, to go to Italy. In addition to the usual 'purposes of prayer' at Rome, Charles had two very practical objectives in mind: first, 'settling affairs in Italy'; and second, conferring with 'envoys of the emperor', as the *ArF* author put it. Everyone knew, of course, that the person in charge at Constantinople in 786/7 was not the emperor but the Dowager Empress Eirene.

Charles arrived in Italy in time to celebrate Christmas at Florence, where, as noted, he granted the church of San Miniato urban property belonging to the royal residence there 'for the soul of my most beloved wife Hildegard'.[57] He then moved as fast as possible to Rome, where Hadrian received him 'with the greatest honour' (and perhaps a smidgeon of embarrassment about his having not been invited to send representatives to Nicaea).[58] News of Charles's arrival at Rome had already reached Benevento: Duke Arichis tried to forestall any move further south on Charles's part by sending his son Romuald to Rome with great gifts and conciliatory words for the king – accompanied by a polite request 'concerning the king's coming (*adventus*), that he should not enter (*non introisset*) Benevento'.[59] The plan of 'settling affairs in Italy' was now redefined, as a result of discussions between the pope, the Frankish magnates and Charles himself: the king *would* 'come into (*advenisset*) Beneventan territory' – in context, a (not very grammatical) verb, with a darker tone than its corresponding noun. En route for Capua in February 787, Charles visited Monte Cassino, the monastery of St Benedict.[60] This was Charles's personal decision and the experience left a deep impression on him. There, in the place where his uncle Carloman had sought the monastic life, he was greeted by Abbot Theodemar, and by Paul the Deacon, not long back from Francia. Paul presented Charles with a copy of the model Homiliary on which he had been working for the past two years, adding dedication verses praising the king.[61] Charles made Monte Cassino the reciprocal gift of a confirmation of its privileges.[62] Later in 787, Charles, now back in Francia, would commend, in the *Epistola generalis*, the work of 'our friend and little client', Paul.[63]

For the moment, the focus of political action had moved further south, where 'of the states that contested power south of Rome . . . [t]he political centres of five were clustered in the middle of Campania: Capua, Naples, Benevento, Salerno, and Amalfi'.[64] After Charles's annexations of 774, and for the very reason that these five places had not been conquered but instead constituted a frontier region, the contest for power became more intense. Charles's previous two journeys to and in Italy had not taken him south of Rome. Now, on his third journey, crossing what for him was a new boundary, he entered the border-zone. 'While Charles had come to Capua, [Duke] Arichis left the city of Benevento and blockaded himself in Salerno.'[65]

The *ArF* author continued:

[Duke Arichis] thoroughly terrified, dared not meet the lord king Charles face to face; instead he sent *missi* and both his sons, Romuald, whom Charles already had with him, in effect as a hostage, and Grimoald whom Arichis still had with him, and offered many gifts and other hostages to comply with what Charles sought. Then the glorious lord king Charles along with his senior clergy and his other great men saw to it that that land [Benevento] would not be destroyed nor its bishoprics and monasteries devastated. He chose twelve hostages and a thirteenth who was the son of the abovementioned duke whose name was Grimoald. And after he had accepted the gifts, all the Beneventans swore oaths, including the abovementioned duke and Romuald. And the oft-named most pious king turned back and celebrated Easter with the lord pope in Rome.[66]

Charters confirm Charles's stay at Capua: Bishop David of Benevento came there to receive lands and a privilege of immunity on 22 March, and the community of San Vincenzo a similar grant on 24 March. Both these grants were significant favours to major religious institutions in Beneventan territory.[67] By 28 March Charles was back in Rome, where he granted lands and immunity to Monte Cassino and also, at an unspecified date, presided over a judgment in favour of San Vincenzo.[68]

Rome was the destination, probably in April 787, of *missi* sent by Duke Tassilo of Bavaria. They were Bishop Arn of Salzburg and Abbot Hunric of Mondsee, two of Tassilo's key agents, and their mission was to ask Pope Hadrian 'to settle a peace between the lord king Charles and Duke Tassilo'.[69] When Hadrian asked Charles for more information, the king replied that he had long wanted peace but had been unable to get it, and was now determined to agree a peace with Tassilo's envoys in the presence of the pope. The envoys refused on the grounds that they could make no peace-treaty on their own authority. The *ArF* author reports the pope's reaction at some length:

> Recognizing the unreliability (*instabilitas*) and mendacity (*mendatia*) of the *missi*, the pope immediately imposed a sentence of anathema on Duke Tassilo and his supporters should he fail to fulfil his sworn promises to the lord king Pippin and the lord Charles, likewise king. He called on the abovementioned *missi* to adjure Tassilo that he must not do anything other than be in all things obedient to the lord king Charles and to his sons and to the people of the Franks lest there ensue great bloodshed and harm to Tassilo's land. If that duke with stubborn heart should disobey the pope's words, then the lord king Charles and his army would be absolved from all danger of sin and whatever was done in that land by way of burning, killing, or any sort of evil would be the fault of Tassilo and his supporters, and the lord king Charles and the Franks would be innocent of all guilt therefrom. When the pope had finished speaking, Tassilo's *missi* were given leave to depart. The pope and the king bade each other farewell, and the king, after receiving blessing and completing his devotions, returned to Francia.[70]

Tassilo had learned that Charles was to be in Rome and timed the mission of his envoys accordingly.[71] A recurrent theme in the present book has been that communications between political players in

various parts of Charles's realm, and beyond it, were frequent and relatively rapid, and included a lot of grist to rumour-mills, especially those
at Rome. It seems to me quite likely that among those in fairly regular
contact with one another were the surviving daughters of Desiderius –
in particular, the wives of Duke Arichis and Duke Tassilo, that is, the
sisters Adelperga and Liutperga. There is a hint of this in the *ArF* reviser's comment on Charles's reason for intervening in Benevento, namely
that he already had the major part of Desiderius's kingdom of Lango-
bardia (Lombardy), and now wanted to have the lesser part too in the
form of Benevento. Pursuing such a line of thought, Charles could well
have believed he had special interests in another part of Desiderius's
familial empire – Bavaria. Hadrian's evident mistrust of Tassilo could
have gone back to the difficult years before 774 when Charles had repudiated his Lombard wife, Tassilo's sister-in-law. As for the pope's
opinion of Tassilo's *missi* as 'unreliable': well, Arn, at least, had shifted
his loyalty from Tassilo to Charles and back again.[72]

The *ArF* author, after mentioning Charles's second aim in going to
Italy, namely negotiations over Rotrud's betrothal, did not return to
this subject. The *ArF* reviser tacked on a very brief reference to it at the
end of his 786 annal, that is early in 787 (before Easter, which fell that
year on 8 April), after reporting 'the despatch of officers to secure both
the duke [Arichis] and the Beneventans by oaths', added: 'he held discussions with legates from the Emperor Constantine who had been sent
to him to endeavour to obtain his daughter. He gave them leave to
depart and then returned to Rome.'[73]

Charles's brief stay in the border-zone at Capua had apparently been
long enough for him to discuss with the emperor's legates the future of
Rotrud's betrothal-agreement – and to terminate it. The *ArF* reviser
noted under the year 788 that 'the Emperor Constantine, angered at
being refused the king's daughter, ordered the patrician Theodore, governor of Sicily, with his other military commanders to devastate the
land of the Beneventans'.[74] Theophanes, in his *Chronicle* under 788–9,
gives a different version of what happened: 'The Empress Eirene broke
off the marriage-agreement with the Franks, and married Maria [of
Amnia] to her son the Emperor Constantine, though he was very
grieved about this and unwilling, since he remained set on the daughter
of Charles.' The information in the western sources on date and context seems more plausible than the alternative offered by Theophanes.

Other griefs and grievances would soon arise from events in Benevento: meanwhile Charles's decision to prioritize Bavaria dictated a rapid departure from Italy.

VIII. CHARLES'S ROAD HOME VIA RAVENNA, 787

Sometime between late April and June, Charles travelled north-eastwards from Rome, with Grimoald as a hostage. Also in his retinue were 'many noble Lombards'.[75] En route to Francia, Charles almost certainly stayed at Ravenna.[76] Few sites were (and are) more memorably impressive. After viewing the former imperial capital's glories, Charles wrote to Hadrian asking that he should 'be assigned mosaics and marbles along with other items situated both on the floor and on the walls of the palace of the city of Ravenna'. Hadrian replied:

> We have, with very great love of Your Excellence, given effect to this assignment, and we have conceded that the mosaics and marbles and other items must be taken away from that palace because the church of your patron St Peter benefits every day from your many and good and laborious royal efforts, so that your plentiful reward will be ascribed in heaven.[77]

The language of assignment, concession and removal conveys a legal 'must' as well as a moral 'must', for in the later Roman Empire rights over *spolia* were an imperial preserve.[78] The context of Charles's letter suggests that he was giving orders which Hadrian had to obey.

The rest of Hadrian's letter consists in effect of a complaint about two horses sent to him by Charles. One the pope rather grudgingly described as 'useful'; the other had died en route. In future, Hadrian asked, could Charles please send horses 'distinguished in their bones and in the fullness of their flesh: horses which would shine to praise your name already bright with triumphs'? Here the discourses of law and gift-exchange appear in the same letter. Hadrian sounds an unmistakable note of resentment for an imputed slight, and implies that Charles had deliberately sent sub-standard gifts. In Italy, and early in 787, Charles had been determined to crack the whip on the Beneventans and to break his agreements with Constantinople if that was the price to be paid; since then, however, relations had soured. Hadrian's response to Charles's gifts may well have been, as Achim Hack infers, a demonstrative use of imperial rights. It was more than that, however: Charles demanded mosaics and marbles *from Ravenna*.[79] He had had the idea of getting actual *spolia* to create a palace at Aachen with an imperial look. By the time he wintered at Aachen in 788–9, he had got what he wanted.[80] Marbles and mosaics were material realities in a sharp focus: legalities could be left for later negotiation.

IX. CHARLES'S HOMECOMING TO FASTRADA AT WORMS

Carolingian annalists, normally impassive dealers in nouns and verbs, just occasionally allowed emotion (in the form of adjectives and adverbs) to enter their narratives. One such occasion is the *ArF*'s vignette of Charles's homecoming from Italy in the summer of 787: 'The most gentle king joined his wife, the lady queen Fastrada in the city of Worms, where they rejoiced and were happy in each other's company, and together praised God's mercy.'[81]

Charles's active sex-life is clear in the record of his prolific paternity, but other bits and pieces of evidence too imply that this was a couple who were genuinely fond of each other. Though Charles and Fastrada seldom travelled together, as Charles and Hildegard had done, after autumn 783 the king's homecomings were welcome to both partners. Worms, where they had got married, was the place where Fastrada, 'with Charles's sons and daughters, and the whole court (*comitatus*)', awaited Charles and his men in 787. The couple had been apart since (at the latest) November. A special reason for joy on Charles's return from Italy might have been that Fastrada was pregnant for the second time, and the couple's hopes for a son had been growing.[82] Perhaps, too, maturing plans to oust Tassilo from his duchy were connected in Charles's mind with a further project to earmark Bavaria for a future son – or even to Pippin the first-born, who had yet to be assigned a realm of his own. Royal family-planning was (and is) a frequent subject of discussion at any court.

When Charles was in Italy, Fastrada, pregnant or not, had royal business to attend to. The former royal chaplain Riculf had been consecrated to the archbishopric of Mainz on 4 March 787, during Charles's absence, implying that Fastrada had adopted something of a regent's role. Perhaps Riculf was part of her *comitatus* that summer at Worms.[83] Charles's gladness was more than personal. When he summoned that summer's assembly to Worms, he wanted to make political capital out of it by delivering a full report on his expedition to Italy to his assembled higher clergy and leading men.[84] This report (*adnuntiatio*), the sole surviving eighth-century instance of what in the ninth century would become a better-attested genre, was presented in terms of a taking-into-his confidence of the Frankish elite: those whom, after the previous year's revolt, Charles particularly wanted to reassure.

X. THE ECLIPSE OF 16 SEPTEMBER 787

The Annals of Lorsch begin their unusually brief entry for the year 787 with this event, an annular solar eclipse, for which the writer gives the precise date.[85] The court annals, as in 786, say nothing about this event at all. 'The day and the hour must also have given further food for thought because the day was a Sunday, an extremely rare occurrence, and the eclipse lasted for at least two hours.'[86] It was the first time in Charles's reign that such an eclipse had occurred. It was visible northwards of a line from Paris to Munich, and Charles assuredly saw it. There can be no doubt that the sight was awe-inspiring – but from all that's known about Charles, he was not one to tremble.

It was important for Charles to show that the borderlands of the realm were, or could be, 'settled', especially east of the Rhine, in the Alpine regions, and in Italy in the later eighth century.[87] ' "Peripheral vision" may assist in focusing our images of the centre.'[88] The peripheries in this case were the acquired *regna* surrounding the core. Charles used a mixture of force, negotiations, assertions of overlordship and a willingness to make alliances when 'imperial rhetoric . . . broke down at the frontier'.[89] When Charles and Avar princes exchanged envoys in 790, 'the issue between them concerned the borders (*confinia*) of their realms: where ought these to run? Contention and dispute on this matter was the seedbed and source of the later war.'[90] Contemporaries understood the terminology of boundaries (*fines*) and marches (*marcae*). Officials and faithful men in these zones worked along the grain of princely, aristocratic and ecclesiastical interests that were sometimes combined, sometimes in tension, with spasmodic efforts to enforce royal control. The toll-stations created by Charles along the eastern frontier, from the Elbe down to the Danubian lands, were sites of magnate and royal power at the same time.[91] In borderlands, landowners and monasteries were 'the earliest representatives of the Carolingian state'.[92]

XI. THE MISSION OF MAGINAR, 787–8

Maginar was among the most faithful of the eighth-century Carolingian kings' faithful men. He had been a monk of St-Denis before he became Carloman's notary (the only one whose output survives) in 768. After Carloman's death Maginar returned to St-Denis, where, in 777, he was the leading witness of Abbot Fulrad's testament. He and Charles's chief notary Hitherius (also an alumnus of St-Denis), seem to have accompanied Charles and Hildegard to Rome in 781, and, at Pope Hadrian's request, Charles sent both Hitherius and Maginar to conduct inquiries about lands allegedly belonging to St Peter, though Hadrian believed that 'perverse and wicked men' had deflected the *missi* from accomplishing their task in full.[93] When Fulrad died in 784, Charles gave the abbacy of St-Denis to Maginar. In 785, Hitherius and Maginar were again paired as *missi* and sent to Rome to seek Hadrian's advice on the penances to be imposed on the defeated Saxons.[94]

The politics of the border-zone had shifted. Charles's presence in March 787 had impelled Arichis to flee from Benevento, the capital city of the duchy, to Salerno on the coast. After Charles had left Rome for Francia in April or May 787 taking Duke Arichis's son Grimoald as a hostage, the duke had sent envoys to Eirene and her son 'promising that haircut and dress would conform to the usage of the Greeks', a symbolic way of acknowledging acceptance of imperial authority, hence, implicitly, rejecting any submission to Charles's authority. This was a significant blow to Frankish hopes of growing Beneventan loyalties. Arichis's repositioning vis-à-vis the Greeks also had limits, however: when he asked for Desiderius's son Adelchis to be sent to Italy with an expeditionary force to strengthen Beneventan efforts to annex the territory of Naples, the imperial response was that Adelchis would be sent with Greek troops, not to Arichis in Benevento, but to Treviso (in Friuli) or to Ravenna.

To the volatility of political allegiances, 'summer sickness' added another type of risk. August was a dangerous month, especially so in 787, and first Romuald, then Duke Arichis died within weeks of each other. Unmentioned in any contemporary narrative source, these deaths were lamented by Paul the Deacon, now back at Monte Cassino, in an epitaph written to comfort Arichis's widow, 'the most unhappy Adelperga', and to remind her that at least her second son and two daughters survived.[95] Those personal losses signalled less of a shift. Any contemporary familiar with Adelperga's political track-record knew she had nearly thirty years' experience of sharing rulership in Benevento and expertise in managing the Beneventan elite: Paul the Deacon had praised her as 'the emulator of her husband'. For now she was perfectly capable of holding the fort.

The big question in the minds of so many in Francia and Italy was, what decision would Charles make about Grimoald? Keep him as a hostage, or send him back to Benevento on condition that he would resist any Greek-backed expedition to restore Adelchis to power? Pope Hadrian was especially knowledgeable, so he assured Charles, on the subject of Grimoald: 'if you send him back to Benevento, it will be quite impossible for you to hold Italy without terrible trouble (*conturbatio*)'.[96] Hadrian continued, intriguingly, that he had received secret information from a south-Italian bishop about 'Adelperga's plan':

> as soon as Grimoald crosses the border into Beneventan territory she intends in a clever move (*ingeniose*) to take her two daughters with her and, for reasons of prayer, to travel to St Michael the Archangel at Monte Gargano and then go on to Taranto [in Apulia] where she keeps her treasures stored, since it's only some 80 Roman miles [130km] from Monte Gargano to Taranto.

Treasures fund wars. Charles had decided to return Grimoald to Benevento. Adelperga was aware of the unreliability of Greek promises of military help, and, now that Charles's decision had been made, she is very likely to have put the ducal dynasty's money on him too.

Meanwhile Maginar, Charles's trusted Italy-hand, had again been sent to Rome. The abbot's mission was to move into Beneventan territory, not so much to resume Charles's unfinished business there and to negotiate the recovery of lands claimed as St Peter's (and also some of Charles's) – though those were among his objectives – as more immediately to assess the extent of fidelity to Charles in the various parts of Beneventan territory. With very limited resources of men and material, Maginar was the leader of a small team of *missi*, operating a long way from home, and in a disputed border-zone. Only once there did he fully realize the difficulties of his assignment.[97]

Maginar had four colleagues with him. Atto, a deacon and abbot, whom Charles had sent to Rome in 779 to arrange for timbers from the Spoleto area to be sent to repair the church of St Peter's, and again in 779–80 to investigate Greek collusion with Neapolitans and Beneventans plotting the return of Adelchis to Italy. Charles's son Louis (in a charter of 794) called Atto 'his kinsman', and also 'a most faithful man of Charles and himself [Louis]'.[98] Godramn was a layman and, as an *ostiarius* (doorkeeper), a high official at Charles's court; his name indicates that he was a Frank.[99] The third was Joseph, another deacon, probably an Irishman, certainly a scholar and for that reason better documented (for instance in several of Alcuin's letters, one, sending news to the abbot of Clonmacnoise that his *vernaculus* (servant) Joseph was well, and another, in the 790s, asking the bishop of Chur to pray for Joseph's soul – implying that Joseph may have died in crossing the Alps). He seems to have been the youngest of the group, and perhaps even chosen for his sense of humour (one meaning of *vernaculus* in classical Latin was 'jester').[100] The fourth was Liuderic, a count, again with a Frankish name, but about whom no more is known.[101] Maginar himself, and the two ecclesiastical *missi*, Atto and Joseph, were Italy-hands, then; but for Godramn and Liuderic evidence of similar qualifications is a known unknown.

Mentioned among the forty-nine papal letters preserved in the *Codex Carolinus* from the years 774 to 791 are the names of twenty-five *missi* sent by Charles to Italy. Seventeen were clerics or abbots, and eight were laymen. They acted both as envoys and, sometimes, as local agents, and constituted a cadre of diplomatic experts specializing in Italian affairs, and with contacts in Italy. The nature of this communications network meant that *missi*, whatever written instructions they had been given on departure, had to take initiatives on the spot. The envoy's job entailed, to borrow an early-seventeenth-century English ambassador's ironic pun, having to 'lie abroad for the good of his

country'.[102] Charles I of England did not just send a man with a letter
to Spain: neither did Charles son of Pippin just send a man with a letter
to Italy, still less into Beneventan parts. Envoys travelled with followings, sometimes substantial ones, including scribes and men who were
good with horses. But that Maginar's group was poorly resourced is a
known known, because Maginar's own report survives.

It is a unique survival of what must have been a large genre, namely,
first-hand reports back to the king of *missi* or envoys.[103] The value of
this particular letter is confirmed by a clutch of Pope Hadrian's letters
dating from 787–8, which contain contemporary material complementing Maginar's report.[104] Surviving in the archive of St-Denis, the report
was written on papyrus, presumably supplied in Rome by papal archivists. It is fragile and the first and final sections have gaps (as indicated
by the dotted lines, see below).[105] 'Your Lordship' is Charles:

---- Your Lordship---

---- that is, Atto --- [it was agreed] between us that they [that is, Atto
and Godramn] --- [would enter] into the Beneventan border-zone (*in fine
Beneventana*) by way of Valva --- but we [Maginar, Joseph and Liuderic]
[would go by way of] Castel di Sangro. And if one group of us should
arrive first, they should await their companions (*pares*) there; and whatever we might have discovered on the journey there concerning fidelity
to you, we would let them know, and they likewise would let us know
[what they had discovered]. But Atto and Godramn arrived at Benevento
four days before we did. Now, when we had learned through those who
were faithful to you that these Beneventan men were not behaving as was
right, we immediately sent word to them [i.e. Atto and Godramn], and
we asked them if they thought it more sensible *not* to go on to Salerno
before they joined up with us at Benevento.

When we had crossed into the Beneventan border-zone (*dum in fine
Beneventana intrassemus*), we realized there was no fidelity towards your
excellence. Again we sent by our messenger (*missus*) [or: by a messenger
of ours?] with our letter, to Atto and Godramn, telling them to wait for
us there at Benevento, since the lord *apostolicus* [i.e. the pope] had warned
us that whatever we had to do, we should do as a single group (*communiter*), and that later, if they waited for us following the orders of the lord
apostolicus, and if we had found it possible to ascertain the fidelity of
those there at Benevento, we should proceed to Salerno. But if [these

Beneventans were] not faithful, we should decide, there, between ourselves to tell them [i.e. Atto and Godramn] by our messenger and letter that they must come to us so that there we should argue out what would be in the best interests of the lord *apostolicus* and yourself, as you told us to do. They [Atto and Godramn] told us that they were willing to wait for us and also willing for us to make our plans there before going to Salerno. But when [after travelling] through [lands of] those people who had no fidelity towards you, for God was against them, we reached Benevento, [expecting] to find our companions, and there plan how best to carry out your orders, they [Atto and Godramn], just one day before we arrived, had already moved off towards Salerno.

Now as a result we had got into a state of great distress (*magna tribulatio*) because we did not have our companions (*pares*) with us, and those who were faithful to you had let us know that if we went [to Salerno], the people there wanted to detain us until they were sure about what you wanted to do about Grimoald and about their *missi*. And they declared that if we did not give them a sure guarantee (*certam firmitatem*) that you would give them Grimoald as their duke and hand over to them the cities that you had given to St Peter and the lord *apostolicus*, they would absolutely refuse to carry out your commands, and would not hand us over [i.e. release us] but instead would detain us under duress (*fortiter*). But if we did promise that, then they would carry out any command you gave.

When we knew this, I, Maginar, pretended to be detained by an illness so grave that I was unable to go to Salerno. Meanwhile we had realized the ambush they had laid for us, and in order to get our companions back with us from Salerno, we sent a letter to Adelperga and other leading Beneventans to say that I, Maginar, had wanted to send there [to Salerno] Joseph and Liuderic and they had refused to go without me, and they should send us Atto and Godramn and twelve or fourteen Beneventan magnates, or however many they were willing to send. After that had been done, we would tell them what orders we had received from you [i.e. Charles] and so we would negotiate with them concerning your interests and the well-being of that land (*salus terrae illius*). After all that, if I, Maginar, could get my health back, I would go to Salerno with them. But if that were not to be possible, [then] Atto, Joseph, Liuderic and Godramn would negotiate again at Salerno about all these matters with the Beneventan magnates.

But Adelperga refused to send her magnates, and only sent Godramn
to us at Benevento. But since we found out from those whom we knew
to be entirely faithful to you (*vestri fidelissimi*) that they [Beneventans]
were intent on destroying us, we told Godramn everything about the
extent of unfaithfulness to you, and he likewise told us, and Godramn
wanted to go back to Salerno for Atto's sake, and we said it was better
that one man be detained than two --- [And] since we [now] knew all
these things and many other things about the extent of unfaithfulness to
you, at cockcrow, after staying there --- and having learned nothing about
what was in your interests, we withdrew without their agreement, and,
with the help of God and because of [our] fidelity to you, we fought our
way from your enemies through to the Spoletan frontier (*fines*) ---

Maginar's letter has been criticized by modern historians for its
poor Latin and general clumsiness. Maginar himself has been criticized
(I think, unfairly) for his inept diplomacy. He and his companions had
been given the tasks of assessing Beneventan fidelity and reporting their
findings. They did just that. The *missi* had encountered 'no fidelity
towards your excellence' and 'we travelled through lands of those
people who had no fidelity to you'. The pope had warned that 'whatever we had to do, we had to do as a single group . . .' Maginar had
done all he could to comply.

Atto and Godramn told us they were willing to wait for us [Maginar,
Joseph and Liuderic] and also willing to make our plans there [at Bene-
vento] before going on to Salerno . . . but when we reached Benevento
thinking to find our companions, they had already moved off to Salerno
just one day before we arrived.

An exercise that depended on acting *communiter* had fallen apart. It
was hardly surprising that Maginar, Joseph and Liuderic 'got into a
state of great distress because we did not have our companions with
us'. It became apparent to them, as well as to Atto and Godramn, that
the people in Salerno wanted to detain them by force because the Beneventans wanted guarantees that Charles would return Grimoald to
them. At the heart of the letter was a message to Charles: the return of
Grimoald was clearly the precondition of any fidelity whatsoever in the
Beneventan land.

Maginar's diplomatic illness ('lying abroad for the good of his country . . .') was a justified tactic (I like to imagine that he was comforted in his ordeal by Joseph's Irish jokes), as was his appeal to Adelperga to negotiate through leading Beneventans about 'the well-being of that land'. Her refusal was justified in the light of her own experience. Maginar rejected Godramn's idea of going back to rejoin Atto in Salerno. It turned out that Maginar's decision was correct. Hadrian, in a letter written at about the same time as Maginar's (or very shortly after), reported to Charles that Atto had sought asylum in the church at Salerno where he 'clutched the altar in terror', and that the Beneventans, smooth-talking dissemblers, had returned Atto direct to Charles, without his rejoining Maginar and the other three *missi*. Part of the explanation of Atto's special treatment may well have been his well-known kinship with Charles (or with Hildegard).

Charles sent Grimoald back to Benevento probably within weeks, certainly within months, of receiving Maginar's letter. It seems likely that Charles's decision was, if only in part, the result of having received the letter and hence grasped the situation in Benevento. Far from revealing a cock-up, therefore, Maginar's letter showed that the mission had fulfilled its objectives.

The return of Grimoald naturally had conditions attached: the coins and charters he issued were to bear the signs and symbols of his acceptance of Charles's authority. In the first four years of his reign, at least, his coins bore the images of both Charles and himself, and his charters acknowledged his position as subordinate to that of Charles.[106] During the months of Grimoald's stay as a hostage at the Frankish court, Charles had won his trust; and Grimoald had won Charles's. As the author of the *ArF* put it:

> There was war between the Greeks and the Lombards, that is, duke Hildeprand of Spoleto and duke Grimoald whom the lord king had placed as leader of the Beneventans, and Winigis together with a few Franks was sent to oversee everything they did. And with the Lord's help, victory was achieved by the Franks and the above-named Lombards.[107]

Theophanes added that Eirene had sent her treasurer John to oppose Charles if possible and to detach men from him.[108] She had also sent 'the former king of Greater Lombardy, Adelchis, along with the Patrician Theodore, Governor of Sicily. When battle was joined, John was captured by the Franks and put to a cruel death.'

The critical battle against the Greeks and Adelchis's men was fought and won by Grimoald and Hildeprand in Calabria. Its reverberations were important enough for the news to have reached Anglo-Saxon England, and thence Ireland.[109] Alcuin, in a letter written early in 790, informed his friend Colcu of Clonmacnoise about 'events in the world', and 'how by God's mercy his holy church in Europe enjoys peace, gains ground, and grows greater'. Alcuin reported a battle 'two years ago when the Greeks descended on Italy with a fleet but were overcome by the dukes [Hildeprand of Spoleto and Grimoald of Benevento] of the aforementioned king [Charles] and fled to their ships. Their dead are said to have numbered 4,000, and 1,000 were taken prisoner.' As it happened, the Irishman Joseph was a protégé of both Colcu and Alcuin, who, when revisiting Northumbria, had entrusted Joseph with his affairs in Francia (in which the procuring of well-chosen gifts loomed large).[110] If it's possible to imagine Joseph in Beneventan territory cheering Maginar with jokes as the old man was 'lying abroad' during his diplomatic illness, there's Alcuin's own word for it that Joseph made him happy, 'so often'.

The personal ties between these men, and their ability to mobilize contacts in various capacities in different parts of Charles's empire, calls to mind similar diplomatic communities in modern times. The role played by abbots and junior clergy in this cadre of men attested Charles's managerial skills and his capacity to retain loyalty. In Maginar, Charles made a very good choice, and Maginar in turn chose promising juniors and able lay adjutants who proved themselves, for the most part, good colleagues. Now elderly, Maginar had already earned his reward from Charles in the form of the abbacy of St-Denis, and he seems to have spent his last years there, after returning to Francia in 788. He died in the autumn of 790. Alcuin produced for him a serviceable epitaph which made no mention of his service to Charles. This was a competitive world.

The Tassilo Chalice.

9

Franks, Bavarians and New Thinking: 787–9

I. TASSILO'S SUBMISSION, 787

A scholar named Clement (historians still debate whether he was Irish or Anglo-Saxon), in an open letter written in 771 or 772 to his 'dearest and most beloved lord duke Tassilo' and also to 'the bishops and the noble and powerful men of the Bavarians', had compared the duke to Old Testament counterparts:

> May the Lord grant you victory over your enemies as he gave it to Gideon, war-leader of the people of God . . . May the Lord grant strength to our lord duke Tassilo, as He gave strength to Samson, war-leader of the people of God (*duces populi Dei*), who hunted down the Philistines.[1]

The context in which Clement read out the letter had presumably been the ducal court and/or a summoned assembly, and readings-out of it oft-repeated.[2] On 5 October 787, however, Tassilo's days of basking in Old Testament triumphalism came to a halt.[3]

With hindsight, the end of Tassilo's ducal reign can be seen to have begun at the summer assembly held at Worms in 787. The king, his sons and the Franks were in agreement about what were Tassilo's just deserts. They agreed equally strongly about Tassilo's breach of his sworn promise and the heinousness of his refusal to come face-to-face with Charles.[4] They agreed that a military solution was the only real option. Charles directed the assembling of three separate armies to converge on Bavaria. All three assembly-sites were strategic, making Tassilo aware he could be 'surrounded from all sides'. The sites were also symbolic. The first was the Lechfeld. The river Lech was the boundary between Alemannia and Bavaria, and the Lechfeld was the site of an important battle fought in 743 by the Frankish mayors Pippin (Charles's father) and Carloman (Charles's uncle) against Duke Odilo of Bavaria, Tassilo's father, and his Alemannic, Saxon and Slav allies: 'a triumph costing many Frankish lives' in a serious defeat, avenged only three years later, in 746, at Cannstatt.[5] The second site, Pförring, an old Roman fortress in the Alemannic/Bavarian borderlands some 60km from Regensburg, was a place from which Regensburg itself could readily be threatened. The third, Bolzano, was the location of a recent heroic Frankish defeat by the Bavarians which had yet to be avenged. Worse for Tassilo than a sense of his own vulnerability was the realization that

> the Bavarians were all more loyal (*plus fideles*) to the lord king Charles than to himself and recognized the justice of the lord king's claims, so that the Bavarians preferred to consent rather than to oppose. Hemmed in everywhere, Tassilo came in person, putting himself with his hands into the hands of the lord king into the position of a vassal (*in vassaticum*); he returned the kingdom entrusted to him by the lord king Pippin, and confessed that he had sinned and acted wickedly in all things. Then he renewed his oaths once more and gave twelve chosen hostages with his son Theodo as a thirteenth.[6]

The Chesne Fragment alone gives a precise date for Tassilo's submission: 'Tassilo arrived [at the Lechfeld] on 5 October and he returned the kingdom of the Bavarians to Charles and put himself and the kingdom of the Bavarians in the hand of King Charles.'[7]

The author of the *Annales Nazariani* was unique in giving precise details of a ritual event, the handing-over of a staff: 'Duke Tassilo of the Bavarians came to Charles at the Lechfeld and returned that fatherland (*patria*) to him with a staff (*baculus*) at whose head was carved the likeness of a man, and he became Charles's *vassus*.'[8] The staff symbolized Bavaria's autonomy as a *patria* or dukedom (as distinct from a kingdom) ruled by 'a war-leader of the people of God' (*dux populi Dei*).

II. POETIC JUSTICE

So often, the annalistic narratives are all there is to go on. Their tendentiousness and tunnel-vision hamper serious focus on cultural surroundings.

This is exactly where poetry can help. One of the earliest examples that survives (in a single incomplete manuscript datable to Charles's reign) was written by an anonymous Irishman at Charles's court. This was the context in which a small number of poets produced writings in a special genre but intended too for a wider audience: assemblies where consensus was formed and competition thrived. The first forty lines of the poem consist of a dialogue between the Poet and his Muse (alternatively understood as 'an interior monologue between two projections of a composite persona').[9] The muse tells the poet: 'the art of poetry will remain for all time', and adds that 'the great deeds of ancient kings shine forth in poetry, and present actions are told for future ages'. The poet, though he affects humility, uses 'interior dialogue' to make large claims for poetry, establishing it as a fitting genre for the court. The poet asks rhetorically in what circumstances conflict, past or present, has arisen?[10]

> Who has tried to break the great peace of the fathers?
> Who has changed exceptional peace into weapons in vain?
> What plague has touched the faithful servant so that
> he deserved
> to see the face of the Lord made sad?

These are the poet's answers:

> The slippery serpent 'the adversary' of Scripture
> [also known as 'Satan' in the Gospels] spewed
> poison from its mouth;
> it was the same snake who from its heart decreed
> for the wretched spouses [i.e. Adam and Eve]
> the mortal voices of death, who tore apart two brothers
> [i.e. Cain and Abel] with a savage wound;[11]
> . . . who broke the treaties of perfect peace,
> and instead fomented wars, and sowed quarrels.

The poet sets the peace-breaking and perfidy of his own times within the history of humankind since the Fall:

> This was the serpent, who, envious, broke the peace
> by which the outstanding King Charles and
> the famed Duke Tassilo were bound perpetually
> in a blessed law.

The serpent links biblical history and the world of 787:

> Rumour attacks, and contaminates the whole world;
> the perfidious one assails pure ears with these words:
> 'Tassilo sinned, because he abandoned the royal commands,
> and did not fulfil the service imposed on him by treaties.'
> These words rolled into Charles's excellent ears
> and rumour began to flit around the wide world;
> the king's presence was disturbed by these words
> and first of all he withdrew his pious ears from them
> and told everyone: 'This man really is entirely faithful to me
> and he seeks good fortune for the realms of the Franks.'[12]
> But frequent rumour confirmed to the king, and the
> whole earth shouted together: 'That duke is not faithful!'
> Finally, much disturbed by these voices,
> the most upright hero assembled his forces, put his ships
> on the bank of the Rhine which divides the lands of the Gauls
> from those of Germania, and he crossed the river
> with a favourable current and famous Germania trembled
> at such vast forces. But the king of the Franks, surrounded
> by thousands of tall men, and greatest of them, exults, a victor,
> in his ancestral weapons, and addresses his faithful war-leaders,
> and speaks thus: 'O royal people, which set out from the
> lofty ramparts of Troy and brought our forefathers to
>   land on these shores,
> the judge of the world handed these lands over to them,
> and he put the peoples of the Franks under equitable laws,
> he who from the stars shaped and ordained for them eternally
> these ample bounds, and the cities to be entirely taken, giving
> them all the maidservants and manservants who
>   owed them service.[13]
> But lately, an enemy has arisen in our regions,
> the envious serpent with a savage wound . . .'

The role of rumour in forming public opinion was well enough known to a poet whose audience was the court. If Charles was presented as overly trusting in his view of Tassilo, perhaps the poet endorsed the king's unwillingness to rush to judgment. Did the poet present Charles as simply unable to believe in Tassilo's perfidy, or was the king being shown as testing Tassilo by giving him a final chance to prove himself faithful? When 'the whole world shouted Tassilo's guilt', Charles, in the poet's story, had to listen to what his people told him. From that moment, Charles dominates the scene, first as the man of action mobilizing his ships on the Rhine and his troops in Germania, then as the orator, narrating the myth/history of the Trojans' coming from Troy to the West to inhabit the land and the cities and supply the working population that God had assigned them.[14] The serpent/Satan made a final appearance, and the missing section presumably recounted his defeat.

The poem continues (after two missing folios) for a further ten lines, which retrieve the opening theme of a great assembly and describe – in a neat inversion of the leading men's 'annual giving of gifts to the king' – the lord king's 'giving of lavish gifts to his servant the boy Tassilo', who responds with a pledge of lasting service:[15]

> . . . arm-rings made of gems and gold of massive weight.
> He is given a horse gleaming with trappings of gold.
> The boy is enriched with the finest gifts from his lord,
> as the king addresses these words to him in the
>   language of peace:
> 'Receive these pledges of your being for ever in our service!'
> Then, pouring the sweetest kisses on the king's knees,
> the duke uttered these swift words from his heart:
> 'O king, to thee may the gift of salvation in all things be given.
> But I shall forever pay to you the service I owe.'
> Having said this, he withdrew to the fortress with
>   the gift of the king.

The recurrence of the dialogue form and of the assembly and gift-giving themes produces a triple effect: of sacred history, of Trojan into Frankish history, and of history being enacted now, in the poem's present. Poetic licence allows the 'famous duke Tassilo' (who was actually seven years older than Charles) to become 'the boy', to be presented as the king's junior and subordinate: the Lechfeld encounter defines an extremely *un*equal relationship between lord and servant. Because the unique manuscript is mutilated, it's impossible to be sure whether the poet meant to end the story at 787 or had already planned a sequel in the form of 788's trial. On the evidence of this poem, a court, and an elite literate in Latin, already existed.[16] They had had good teachers, thanks to Charles's power to attract scholars to his entourage. An eminent specialist in this material shrewdly suggested that 'during stays in Italy, Charles gained impressions which enabled him to grasp something of the political power of poetry'.[17] In the 770s, Anglo-Saxons and Irishmen were already coming to Charles's court; then, in the earlier 780s, from Italy came the Lombards Fardulf, Peter of Pisa, Paulinus and Paul the Deacon. True, the poets' works were self-referential: these authors were 'strong personalities responding to the challenges of each other's verse' in 'coterie poetry'. Historians, of all people, should not underplay poets' capacity publicly to discuss political ideas found significant by contemporary elites. More than Latin literature 'emerged' at Charles's court.[18]

To ask what was poetry's 'function' is a legitimate and necessary question.[19] That function is rooted in poems' topicality, as *pièces d'occasion*, performed or recited at great assemblies of various kinds, ritual events that were also recent events.[20] There was always an audience, a public, which consisted of a more or less expandable elite, often of a particular people or regional group. The date of the Irishman's poem matters in so far as in 787 at the Lechfeld a Frankish audience was envisaged as the prime audience, consisting of lay *proceres*, leading men and their retinues, the *populus*, the *gens regalis*, at once secular and Christian, and (so the poems on the court in the 790s clearly indicate) including clergy as well. If there was a now-lost closing part of the Irishman's poem intended for 788, the consumers of the poet's message would have been Franks and Bavarians, Lombards and Saxons, together. The assembly-as-court that Charles summoned to Ingelheim on this occasion would not have been hard for the Irish poet to describe or imagine, nor its response to a call for judgment. The hindsight-driven prose of the narrative sources portrays Tassilo as having run out of road. Poetry, strictly contemporary as here, leaves open the possibility that Tassilo, still, saw alternative options.

III. THE *EPISTOLA GENERALIS*, 787

The *Epistola generalis* was a letter addressed by Charles 'to the religious readers (*religiosi lectores*) subject to our rule'.[21] The date has only recently been established as early 787 rather than later.[22] Charles began:

> Though God with his divine mercy can always guard us in our home and outside it, in war and in peace, even if human frailty may not be able to repay any of his favours, nevertheless our God, being of inestimable mercy, generously approves wills devoted to his service.

The letter continued with an arresting image:

> It is our responsibility to advance our churches to a better state and to repair by vigilant study the workshop of learning (*litterarum officina*) which now lies almost ruined by the laziness of our predecessors, and to summon to thorough knowledge of the liberal arts whomsoever we can, even by our own example.

Both the project and its timing were the direct results of the king's previous acquaintance with the Lombard scholar Paul the Deacon. Paul had spent time at Charles's court between 782 and 784.[23] In February 787, Charles, during his brief visit to the monastery of Monte Cassino, had the opportunity to reacquaint himself with Paul, who had resettled into the monastic life in 784/5. During that time, he had been able to compile a homiliary (a collection of homilies or sermons) in two volumes, a copy of which he now presented to Charles.[24] In the earlier of the only two extant copies of Charles's letter, it was accompanied by Paul the Deacon's poetic dedication of his Homiliary to the king.

There was a backstory. Charles had been inspired – as so often – by the example of his father. In the 760s, Pippin had asked Pope Paul I to offer training in the Roman liturgical plainchant to Frankish monks sent to Rome by Pippin's half-brother, Bishop Remedius of Rouen. The Roman chant was to be promoted in all the churches of the Gauls (i.e. the provinces west of the Rhine).[25] The young Charles would have registered this important change as it was happening. From this, he reminisced, had grown his concern, 'a long time ago now' (the date can only be a guess), to correct the errors introduced by scribes into the texts of the Old and New Testaments. For Charles, assuring authentically Roman chant and correcting Scriptural readings were complementary projects. He wanted to put his own mark on (*insignire*) his father's achievement by authorizing Paul's Homiliary.

For we [the royal 'we'] discovered that, despite correct intentions, the readings compiled for the night office by some men were labours lost and in no way suitable because they were set out without their authors' names and were full of countless ramifications of faults. We could not endure ill-sounding grammatical errors in divine readings during holy offices to resound in our days, and so we are directing our mind to re-form for the better the whole thrust of these readings.

Charles ended his letter: 'having thought over the text of all [Paul's Homilies] with our keen judgement (*sagacitas*), we confirm the said volumes by our own authority, and deliver them to your reverence to be read in the churches of Christ.'

Not many letters of Charles survive, and it has been argued that none of them is really his, but rather the work of a member of the staff of the palace writing-office, using a bureaucrat's stereotypical language.[26] The following traits in *this* letter suggest anything but stereotypicality:

> The 'workshop (*officina*) of learning' is an exceptional and memorable phrase in its likening of the artisan's labour to the scholar's.
> Charles *himself* is an example of someone who has mastered the liberal arts.
> Correcting scribal errors in Scriptural texts must be done perfectly (*examussim*, a rare word), and nothing else will do.
> Charles has 'long since' been busy assuring this correction.
> Charles intends to follow 'the example of our father Pippin'.
> Charles will 'put his own mark' (*insignire*) on Pippin's work.
> Charles will not tolerate faults and *soloecismi* (another rare word) *in our times*.
> Charles asserts *his own* 'keen judgement'.

What these traits *do* suggest is an author who is both egocentric and, at the same time, other-orientated and altruistic. It may well be true that Charles's letters were often written by secretaries or counsellors, though few such men can be identified before 789. This letter seems distinctive, though, not just in its exceptional details of style and autobiographical substance but also in the impetuosity of its flow. The king sounds as if he were dictating a series of ideas as they occurred to him, and these ideas tumbled from his lips rather than following any strict order. The importance of readings in the night office is made very clear and a monastic context therefore implicit. But it seems very likely that these readings were also designed to be used in churches where the audiences consisted of laypeople, and the *lectores* gave explanations of what they read out. A further inference would be that laity attending Sunday services were not only people of high status but could include local peasant parishioners.[27]

Charles had been deeply impressed by his visit to Monte Cassino, the quality of the community's life and the value of Paul's work. The king had grasped that homilies, in the hands of well-trained readers, were the best means whereby the Bible's meaning could be communicated correctly, and hence uniformly, to hearers. He had grasped, too, that his authorizing of Paul's Homilies was the most effective way to have them recognized and diffused as a standard text. The royal 'we', so often repeated in this letter, gave assurance not just of royal authorship, but of Charles's authorizing of a correct text and of correct readings. That so much of Paul's collection consisted of extracts from the homilies of Gregory and Bede, the two most authoritative of the early medieval Fathers, was a further guarantee of the brand. The *Epistola generalis* was Charles's 'earliest manifesto' for a religious reform in which reading-aloud from Scripture was central, and, for the vast majority of Christians, learning came from listening.[28] I think the *Epistola generalis* has been underestimated, partly because it was so brief, partly because its currency, as measured in numbers of manuscripts, was extremely restricted, and partly because its objectives were not fully set out. Despite those limitations, what comes across, clear and urgent, is the voice of Charles.[29]

IV. THE FATES OF TASSILO AND HIS FAMILY, 788

No fewer than five more or less full annalistic narratives deal with the fates of Tassilo and his family. Modern scholars argue over what happened in 788, still more about how the case against Tassilo was put together in the *ArF* from earlier material. According to that author, it was Bavarians who first accused Tassilo of breaking his faith to Charles:[30]

Then the lord king Charles summoned an assembly at the *villa* of Ingelheim, and Tassilo came there at the lord king's command as did also the rest of his *vassi*. And Bavarian faithful men began to say that, since giving his son and the other hostages and taking oaths, Tassilo, incited by his wife Liutperga, had not kept his faith safe but been seen to betray it. And Tassilo could not deny this, but had to confess that since then he had sent messages to the Avars, had urged the *vassi* of the said lord king to join him and had plotted their deaths. He had also ordered his men to make mental reservations when they were swearing oaths and to swear deceitfully (*quando iurabant, ut aliter in mente retinerent et sub dolo iurarent*). What is more, he confessed to having said that if he had had ten sons, he would rather lose every one of them than accept that the agreements (*placita*) should remain as they were or allow what he had sworn to stand. And he even said that it would be better for him to die than to live thus. And after he had been convicted of all these things, Franks and Bavarians and Lombards and Saxons and those from every province gathered at that assembly, remembering all his earlier evil deeds, and how he had even deserted the lord king Pippin on campaign, which in the German language is called *herisliz* (deserting the army), they saw fit to condemn the said Tassilo to death. But while they all cried out with one voice (*una voce*) that he should impose the death-sentence, the aforesaid most pious lord king Charles, for love of God and because Tassilo was his kinsman, was moved by mercy and obtained the agreement of those faithful men of God and of himself that he should not die.[31]

Questioned as to his wishes by the most merciful lord king, the aforesaid Tassilo requested permission to have himself tonsured, enter a monastery and do penance for such great sins that he might save his soul. His son Theodo was likewise condemned, tonsured and despatched to a monastery, while a few Bavarians who were still intent on persisting in hostility to the lord king Charles were sent into exile.[32]

In the *ArF*, Tassilo's fate is foreknown as long ago as 748/9: the year when Pippin had put Tassilo in charge of Bavaria 'by a favour' (*per beneficium*). There followed the oath-swearing of 757, the *herisliz* of 763, and the renewal of his oath at Worms in 781. These episodes in the *ArF* have been rightly interpreted as a retrospective construction of Tassilo's past which could justify the charge that the serial oath-taker was finally the most heinous of oath-breakers and deserters – and hence guilty as charged.[33] To connect the sequence of these events is to produce a kind of shadow-biography of Tassilo as 'Charlemagne's significant other'.[34]

Particularly damaging to Tassilo in 788 were two allegations. The first was that he had committed the crime of *herisliz*, deserting Pippin's army in 763.[35] This charge was historic. The second, highly topical, charge was that he and his wife Liutperga, 'hateful to God', had been colluding with Avars to oppose the Franks.[36] No Bavarian or Frankish source suggests an Avar threat in the 780s before 788, but when Charles crushed the Lombard Rodgaud's rebellion in Friuli in 776, sheer political geography had drawn the surviving rebels to the court of the Avar khagan. In 782, the khagan and the jugur of the Avars sent envoys to Charles's assembly at Lippspringe in 782 'supposedly for the sake of peace'.[37] Authors of Bavarian annals recorded, for 782 and 783, that large Avar armies came as far as the river Enns – the furthermost west they had come hitherto, 'but they did no harm'. As Charles's relations with Tassilo deteriorated, and as the Avars' power weakened and they began to regard any enemy of Charles as a potential ally for themselves, Charles himself became increasingly interested in the Danubian lands beyond the Enns.[38] The *ArF* reviser noted that Liutperga was a daughter of Desiderius and, as such, after her father's deposition and exile, had 'been constant and extreme in her enmity to the Franks'.[39] The claim itself was extreme but the gist of it was plausible enough.

Perhaps, even as late as 788, Tassilo thought he could negotiate an outcome that, whatever happened to him and his son Theodo, would leave his lands and treasure in the hands of Liutperga and her younger son and her daughters, Cotani and Rotrud – beyond Charles's control.[40] Perhaps Liutperga herself saw an analogy between hopes of salvaging her own future and the futures of her younger son and daughters, on the one hand, and, on the other, what her own sister, Adelperga, had succeeded in doing in southern Italy that same year.[41] If so, both Tassilo and Liutperga failed to take location and distance into account: there was a world of difference between Bavaria and Benevento.

The author of the *Annales Nazariani* gives some suggestive further details:[42]

[Tassilo came to Charles at Ingelheim.] Following this the king sent his officials (*legati*) into Bavaria in search of the wife and children of the duke. They carried out the king's orders conscientiously (*studiose*) and effectively (*efficaciter*) and brought all of these together with their treasures and household, extremely numerous (*una cum thesauris ac familia eorum copiosa valde*), to the aforesaid king. And when this had been done, the aforementioned duke was arrested by the Franks; his weapons were taken away and he was brought before the king. And when they spoke together, the king questioned him about the plots and treacherous schemes which, for a long time past, he had been attempting to set on foot with many peoples (*cum multis gentibus*). He was seen to be quite unable to deny these, and was therefore ordered, against his will (*invitus*), to be shorn of the hair on his head. But he implored the king, with powerful entreaties, that he should not be tonsured there in the palace, because of the shame and disgrace (*propter confusionem atque obprobrium*) in which he would be seen by the Franks. And the king, acceding to his entreaties, sent him to St-Goar [on the west bank of the Rhine just a few km north of Ingelheim], and he was there made a cleric, and from there was exiled to the monastery of Jumièges. His two sons, named Theodo and Theodbert, were both also tonsured and exiled. And the wife of the aforementioned duke, Liutperga by name, is attested also to have been exiled.

The author of these annals supplies information all his own. The thoroughness and efficiency of Charles's *legati* is reminiscent of that of the *satellites* who devastated the properties of the Thuringian rebels in 786. Similarly, Charles's having Tassilo disarmed before he was interrogated, and Tassilo's request not to be tonsured in the palace because of the shame and disgrace in which the Franks would see him, do not sound like literary touches: rather, they reveal an insider's acute understanding both of rituals of humiliation and of the effectiveness with which Charles deployed them. The terrifying face of kingliness was on display . . . yet also on display was the human face. Tassilo was Charles's cousin, after all; his sons were Charles's first cousins once removed (i.e. within the second degree of kinship), and his wife Liutperga had once been Charles's sister-in-law.

V. THE LETTER TO COTANI

Most annals were produced, year by year, a while after the relevant events. Poetry, though sometimes datable to particular moments, was distanced from them by stylistic artifice and classical borrowings. The hallmark of letters was their immediacy, for the genre's chief purpose was to purvey hot news or urgent requests.[43] Not long ago, the palaeographer Bernhard Bischoff discovered a letter in a collection of model-letters. It was sent by one of Tassilo's leading ecclesiastics (unnamed) to Cotani, the duke's elder daughter who was then in Bavaria, probably at Regensburg on the Danube. Apparently Tassilo still hoped to rescue his family from ruin, especially the womenfolk. Meanwhile, Cotani received the following (prefaced by a long and flowery salutation):

> I want to inform you, I together with my colleague whose name is Liut-
> prant, that he well and carefully and according to the will of the king,
> set out his case before the king, and concerning the indescribable problems
> (*de inenarrabilibus enigmatis*) about which you had spoken earlier, the
> colleague above-named spoke in detail to the king, in so far as you could
> best be pleased. But after this, you must be quick and ready to go away
> again (*post haec vero citote vos migratur*), and likewise the above-named
> priest with you, to western parts to see the king now. You must get pre-
> pared beforehand, for your servant who is to escort you, everything
> necessary to take [perhaps a reference to money, as in ducal treasures?].
> I inform you of this in the present letter, as an order, not as a request
> (*mando, non peto, per istas litteras*).[44]

The letter seems to describe a sudden change in Cotani's position: those pleading with the king on her behalf had not been able to sway his decision. That change is starker still as mirrored in the last sentence, with its shift in tone from polite report to brusque command: I give orders, I don't ask. Behind and beyond the unnamed letter-writer was the hand and power of Charles. Cotani had to leave Bavaria for Fran-cia, taking with her everything necessary to take. The letter lends credibility to the *Annales Nazariani*'s account of what Charles did to traitors. Only after Charles had got the women of the ducal family under his control, together with the 'extremely numerous household' of the duke and the treasure of the ducal dynasty, could he send his Franks to arrest and disarm Tassilo, and personally interrogate him. It was a far cry from the Danube to the Rhine, and still further to the peaceful Aisne and the convent where Cotani would pass the rest of her life.

Liutperga's position at Regensburg looks similar to that of her sis-ter Adelperga of Benevento, who had remained at Salerno with her daughters before moving south-east to the place where she had stored her treasure.[45] Perhaps Liutperga still hoped to keep control of the family silver and salvage something of the family fortunes. If so, she underestimated the implacable Charles. Her ultimate destination was a convent in Francia that no source identified. She may have died before 794; she was not mentioned in the very public decrees of the council held at Frankfurt in that year. Charles's court annalist had tagged her as 'hateful to God' (*Deo odibilis*).[46]

As for her daughters, they might not have thought their own fates so tragic. They ended up in well-endowed establishments whose abbesses, as well as other inmates, were often royal women: Cotani at Notre-Dame, Laon, on the Aisne, and Rotrud (named, like Charles's daughter, for their great-grandmother, wife of Martel), at Chelles on the Marne near Paris, whither she took a psalter (still surviving in the library of the University of Montpellier) made at Mondsee, near Salzburg in Bavaria, a monastery her father Tassilo had founded.[47]

The conclusion is inescapable: Charles, after the Lechfeld encounter, had systematically and ruthlessly planned the moves that led to Tassilo's overthrow the following year, in particular by persuading a substantial majority among the Bavarian elite to abandon their duke, even if 'a few Bavarians wanted to persist in their hostility to the lord king Charles'.[48] For the most part, the story of Hardrad's revolt in 786, including the role of Charles's trusty *satellites*, repeated itself in that of 788's effective *legati*.[49] True, dissenting voices echoed in the aftermath:[50] the exact dates of the tonsuring of Tassilo and Theodo were remembered, as were Agilolfing names, including some women's names entered in lists of those people to be liturgically commemorated, for instance, Rotrud and Cotani in the Fraternity Book of St Peter's, Salzburg, or Tassilo's birthday in Easter Tables (lists of dates of Easter). Signs and portents were added retrospectively in annals under 787; and the Chesne Fragment presented a whole alternative version of the years 787 and 788. Old loyalties and old names became less and less audible, however, as pro-Carolingian voices drowned them out. The echoes did take some time to die away; and the conquest of Bavaria in the early 790s was to prove a lot more complicated than Charles could have foreseen.[51] Nevertheless, the outcome was definitive: the destruction of the old dynasty meant the end of the ducal line and the end of the old duchy of Bavaria. Einhard put it like this: 'Tassilo was summoned to the king's presence and was not allowed to go back home afterwards. The government of the province over which he used to rule was entrusted from that moment onwards not to a single duke but to counts.'[52]

VI. SETTLING MATTERS IN BENEVENTO, FRIULI AND DANUBIA

Charles's priorities altered after 787. For one thing, he vindicated his own judgement that his former hostage Grimoald, once back in Benevento, could be trusted to keep his word to the king: with strong support from Duke Winigis of Spoleto and a small but effective contingent of Franks, the combined Lombard-Frankish force inflicted a heavy defeat on the Greeks. Adelchis, now over thirty and a distinctly Old Pretender, withdrew from Italy to Constantinople, never to return. In north-eastern Italy, in Friuli, another Frankish force had attacked Avars in the region and driven them out. Bavarians, who were now Charles's faithful men in his expanded realm, formed part of a combined Frankish-Bavarian army that defeated Avars in the Ybbsfeld south of the Danube and downstream from Lorch. Finally, another army of Bavarians loyal to Charles and officered by Franks took on an Avar force determined to revenge earlier losses. The result was that 'with the Lord's help, victory fell to the Christians'. Huge numbers of Avars were killed on the battlefield and many others drowned in the Danube. Charles, who had not himself been involved in any of these encounters, went to Regensburg in person. There, on 25 October 788, he explained in a charter that 'those malign men Odilo and Tassilo our kinsman had taken away Bavaria from our realm, but we have restored it to our rule ... and also granted the monastery of Chiemsee to the church of Metz, of which Angilramn, who governs our palace chapel, has charge.'[53] He had 'ordered the Bavarians' territories and frontier-regions so as to make them safe from the aforementioned Avars, and from there went to the palace of Aachen where he spent Christmas and then Easter [19 April 789]'[54] This was the first time that Aachen had been termed a palace. Charles had chosen it as the place where a small team of priests and scholars would set to work on a comprehensive agenda of correction through admonition. Things had been moving on since Charles wrote the *Epistola generalis*.

VII. THE *ADMONITIO GENERALIS*

'No other capitulary of Charles seems to have been so clearly formulated and structured, or so demanding, as the *Admonitio generalis*.'[55] Thus thought Michael Glatthaar, the scholar mainly responsible for the recent superlative edition of this text. Many have been equally impressed.[56] Another view, however, could suggest a rather different judgement – of a very rich yet more disparate production, 'demanding' because formulation and structure are *not* so clear. One of the findings reported by Glatthaar in his introduction is that the *Admonitio generalis* was the work not of an assembly (as I among others had mistakenly thought) but of a small committee.[57] Audible, unsurprisingly, are the different voices of scholars and counsellors, and, occasionally but very distinctly, of Charles himself. After a standard brief invocation of the reign of Christ, Charles began:

> *Ego Carolus* – I, Charles, by the grace of God and by the gift of his mercy king and rector of the kingdom of the Franks and devoted and humble helper of the Holy Church, to all the ranks of ecclesiastical piety and dignitaries of secular power, in Christ the Lord and eternal God, the greeting of eternal peace and blessedness.[58]

In the prologue Charles together with his 'priests and counsellors' addressed his bishops as follows:

> Therefore it has pleased us to ask Your Sagacity, O shepherds of Christ's churches and leaders of his flock and brightest luminaries of the world, so that you strive with sedulous admonition . . . to bring the erring sheep back within the fortress of the Church on the shoulders of good example and exhortation, lest the wolf who lies in wait should find someone transgressing the sanctions of the canons or infringing the teachings of the Fathers of the universal councils – perish the thought – and devour him. Let Your Holiness [here, a collective noun for the bishops] be fully assured that in this labour and exertion Our Diligence [the royal 'we'] is co-operating with you. Therefore we have also sent our *missi* to you, so that, with the authority of our name, they may correct, together with you, those things that must be corrected . . .
>
> . . . For we read in the Books of Kings [2 Kings 22–3] how the holy Josiah, by visitation, correction, and admonition, strove to recall the

kingdom which God had given him to the worship of the true God. I say this not to compare myself with his holiness (*non ut me eius sanctitate aequiperabilem faciam* [in the first-person singular]) but because it is our duty . . . to follow the examples of holy men . . . Therefore, as said above, we have seen fit to indicate certain articles, so that you may apply your-selves to recalling these with whatever others you know to be necessary for you, in order to preach both the one [i.e. what we have indicated] and the other [i.e. what you know to be necessary] with equal devotion. Do not omit, and thereby fail to preach with pious zeal, anything that seems to Your Holiness advantageous to the people of God.[59]

Charles's bold *ego*-start could well have been inspired by the similar *ego*-starts of the Lombard law-giver King Rothari in 643, and, nearer to home, of Charles's uncle Carloman in opening the *Concilium Germanicum* of 742 and, especially perhaps, that of his father Pippin at Soissons in 744.[60] The prologue's strong emphasis on preaching, which returns forcefully later on in the *Admonitio*, picks up a major theme in the *Epistola generalis*. Then there are significant pointers to at least two of the counsellors who contributed to the *Admonitio*. 'Therefore' (*Quapropter*) is an Alcuinian tick.[61] The allusion to King Josiah is not accompanied by a quotation from the Vulgate; and Josiah is never men-tioned in any work of Alcuin. In fact, among the writers in Charles's reign, only Theodulf in his great poem about justice and against bad judges, mentions Josiah:

> What mattered first and foremost for you, O Josiah, was observing
> the Law and this raised your famous name to the heights.
> You are the one who removes the impious monuments of
>   ancient crime
> and as far as you can renews the ancestral laws . . .[62]

Though this was written a decade later, Theodulf was almost certainly at Aachen in 789 and wrote a stinging poetic critique of (bad) bishops at just the time the *Admonitio* was being targeted at bishops.[63] As a sharp historian with a nice sense of humour recently observed, 'Josiah did all manner of things, *except* "visiting, admonishing and correct-ing" '.[64] Charles, by contrast, demanded of his bishops that – with his help and co-operation – *they* do those things.

The *Admonitio*'s first section, consisting of *capitula* 1-59, draws very heavily on the Dionysio-Hadriana collection of canon law, a copy of which Pope Hadrian had given Charles at Rome in March 774. The Dionysio-Hadriana carried the combined authority of the sixth-century canon-law compiler Dionysios, and of Hadrian himself.[65] Without that book (or another copy of it) on the committee-table at Aachen, the *Admonitio* would not have been thinkable. Most of the *capitula* come from the decrees of fourth- and fifth-century church councils, with, for instance, the first twenty *capitula* in the following clusters: Nicaea (325), with cc. 1–6; Antioch (341), with cc. 7–13; and Laodicea (fourth-century), with cc. 14–20. The selecting of these first twenty *capitula* looks eclectic, as does their ordering in the *Admonitio*. Juxtapositions may have had their own logic, though: for instance when 'forbidding women to go to the altar' (c. 17) is adjacent to 'prohibiting sorcerers, enchanters or enchant-resses' (c. 18). Others are harder to explain: for example (from later in the first section), 'the false names of martyrs and uncertain shrines of saints are not to be venerated' (c. 42), next to 'a wife cast aside by her husband is not to take another during her husband's lifetime' (c. 43).

The *Admonitio*'s *capitula* fall broadly into subject categories: in the first twenty, for instance, episcopal authority and the maintaining of diocesan boundaries (cc. 3, 7, 9, 10, 11), and the authority of metro-politans over bishops and of bishops over auxiliary bishops, and twice-yearly meetings of the metropolitan with bishops (cc. 8, 10, 13). The status of metropolitans (cc. 10, 13) is taken as a given: it had already been declared at Pippin's Council of Ver (in 755) and again at Charles's Council of Herstal (779).[66] There is some connection, too, in the con-cern to prevent contamination: contamination by women in the houses of priests or clerics (c. 4), clerics' self-contamination by going into tav-erns (c. 14), and contamination by women going to the altar (c. 17), but the *capitula* dealing with these topics are not juxtaposed. Similar clus-ters, and lack of juxtapositions, recur in the later section of the *Admonitio*. The new edition of the text, and the editor's invaluable notes, allow today's general reader to make their own surmises about links and disjunctures, and the question of whether or not this text, as a collective production, has a 'written-by-committee' flavour.

After c. 59, a short but significant bridging-passage, unnumbered, starting in the first-person plural and addressed to the *dilectissimi* (the bishops), summed up the *Admonitio*'s contents to this point: they were *magis necessaria*, 'especially necessary' (l. 205). Attention was drawn to, on the one hand, the dangers of anathema for contravening the canons of ecumenical councils and, on the other, the rewards of felicity and peace-loving unity. The passage ended with a 'Therefore' and an *ammonitio* [sic] about the Last Judgment. A single sentence then differentiated the preceding *ammonitio* from the remaining *capitula*, which were declared to be *nobis utilia* 'useful for us' (l. 214). The prologue's phrases *nobis necessaria*, and *vobis necessaria* (ll. 26 and 37), and l. 205's *magis necessaria*, pulled together the work so far. The voices of both Charles and Alcuin are audible in this passage.

What came next was a basic change in the *Admonitio*. In the earlier section (cc. 1–59), the Dionysio-Hadriana had been the primary source. The later section, instead, offered a rich melange of Scriptural texts, many selected from the law-books of the Old Testament, and brief extracts from a few patristic and hagiographical works, together with several earlier bits of Carolingian legislation, and (another clue to Alcuin's influence) passages from the letter-report of Bishop George of 786. Most but not all of the Ten Commandments were included. Exceptionally, in the latter part of c. 67, the fifth commandment was tagged 'to be preached with great zeal (*cum magno studio*), "Honour thy father and thy mother" '.[67] Some *capitula* in the later section recapitulated those in the earlier: c. 64 was a much extended version of c.18; c. 68 a much extended c. 2. Most of the later section was concerned with topics that would feature very largely in Charles's capitularies and, a decade or so later, the first episcopal statutes. The *Admonitio* was a positive portent of things to come. The injunction that liturgical chant was to be Roman chant (c. 78), and a firm and detailed prohibition on Sunday work (c. 79), ended this second section of the *Admonitio*.

From this point on, with the last *capitulum* 80, the format changed to address the *dilectissimi* in the second-person plural, the numbering of *capitula* was abandoned, and the *Admonitio* became a series of *Items* which were commands: priests must preach in conformity with the canons; the Lord's Prayer and Creed must be taught and preached on; the resurrection of the body was to be preached, and mortal sins preached against; love of God and neighbour were to be preached, as were humility and almsgiving, and preparation for the Last Day, for 'ye know not day or hour . . .'; and a final 'Therefore' enjoined such preparation. The word 'preach' was repeated ten times in these closing lines, ll. 393–420. These repetitions were reminders of the theme of the

Admonitio as stated at the beginning: 'Therefore we [the royal first-person plural] have sent our *missi* to you [bishops], so that, with the authority of our name, they may correct, together with you, those things that must be corrected . . .' The effect (if a touch of anachronism is pardonable) resembles the final restatement of the theme in the Goldberg Variations: at once an end and a new beginning.

To compare the *Epistola generalis* with the *Admonitio generalis* is to be struck by similarities. First, there is *ego*-mode in both epistle and *adnuntiatio*. Then, there is a terrific sense of urgency: in the letter, Charles's words tumble over themselves; in the *Admonitio*, the top- and tail-parts resound with Charles's own voice. There are echoes in both of Charles's profound respect for his father. Finally, there is the emphasis on preaching, and on bishops' preaching, in both. There are also striking contrasts. The most obvious is the difference between two genres: between the *Epistola*'s originality, freshness and brevity, and the derivative long-windedness of the *Admonitio*. The *Epistola* has the look of a private message, Charles's personal communication, without a formal date or place of issue, whereas the *Admonitio* was a group effort – and, thanks again to its recent editor, clues to the significant input and influence of Alcuin and (to a very much lesser extent) Theodulf, and Bishop George's letter-report, are easy to spot.[68] The *Admonitio* ends formally with a final record of date and place: 'Aachen in the public palace, 23 March 789, in the 21st year of our reign, the edict for the *missi* of the legation.'

It's recently been claimed, a shade optimistically perhaps, that the *Admonitio generalis* 'could be translated as "a sermon to all" '.[69] In the *Epistola*, Charles could never have aimed at anything like comprehensiveness of audience or programme. In the *Admonitio*, where the intended readership of no fewer than forty-two *capitula* is termed 'all', many of these *capitula* seem far more narrowly targeted.[70] There are also surprising omissions, as the *Admonitio*'s editor points out: no mention of monetary payments as penalties for sins, no mention of asylum (by contrast with the *Capitulatio de partibus Saxoniae* of 782), and – most surprisingly, since it appears in George's letter-report and had been a topic dear to the heart of Pippin – no mention of tithes.[71]

The most striking contrast between Charles's *Epistola* and the *Admonitio*, however, is the minuscule number of manuscripts of the *Epistola* – effectively, one – and the thirty-six of the *Admonitio*.[72] In the case of the *Admonitio* manuscripts, there can be only one explanation for this very large number, namely the impulse given by Charles himself: initially, his ability to set so many scribes to work at Aachen to make the requisite copies, and so quickly, and then to marshal such a large number of those copies to be despatched to so many different destinations, and so many bishops, also with resources for disseminating the copies. Out of the thirty-six, one, probably the oldest, dates from the very end of the eighth/beginning of the ninth century, and thirteen date from the ninth century. Charles was evidently set on achieving to the maximum what would in the contemporary anglophone academic world be termed outreach, impact and knowledge-transfer. Nor would everyone necessarily agree that anachronism was involved: at least one distinguished medieval historian has recently written of Charles's 'commitment to knowledge and education' and his making of his court 'a headquarters of knowledge organisation such as the world had not seen anywhere before. Its most recent heirs are modern government ministries of education and research.'[73]

Summing up the *Admonitio*'s character and purpose without using anachronistic terms and ways of judging is *not* easy. Modern historians have been strongly – and not wrongly – impressed by the *Admonitio*. Its praises resound in all of the recent studies of Charles's reign.[74] The voice of the *rector* was 'demanding' all right, but for today's general reader of the *Admonitio* (and, happily, there still are such readers), 'clearly formulated and structured' are not the first words that come to mind. Many of its *capitula* were aimed at 'all', but, as noted above, they dealt with quite specific topics which only ecclesiastics could have tackled. In the *Admonitio*, the laity are seldom seen, let alone heard. When they appear, their doings are entangled with those of clergy.[75]

Probably all historians (the present writer included) need to take more fully into account the *Admonitio*'s context, the place of secular law and custom in this late-eighth-century thought-world, and the men and women who inhabited it. To contextualize is to qualify. How could Charles have thought to reform 'society' without including and enlisting his great men and his local representatives, and, in the villages and on estates, the *patresfamilias* and *matresfamilias* (for alongside the 'little patriarchs' were *matres*) with parental and godparental responsibilites?[76] The context of the *Admonitio* embraced capitularies, and would very soon embrace episcopal statutes. These other genres reveal new connective dimensions of that thought-world.[77] Whoever drafted c. 63, for instance, knew a lot about oaths and swearing falsely:

> Beware perjury, not only on the holy gospel, or on the altar, or on saints' relics but also in everyday speech (*in communi loquella*); for there are some who swear by love and truth, taking care to avoid an oath in God's name, and who do not know that God's name is the same thing as love and truth, the Apostle John saying that 'God is love . . .' [1 John 4:16] And whoever has to swear on the saints . . . is to realise that he will render account to God for each single oath, wherever it takes place, within a church or out-side . . . And whoever shall have once committed perjury is thereafter neither to be a witness nor to enter upon sworn obligations . . .'[78]

Charles had recently wrestled with problems of oaths and perjury in the case of Hardrad's supporters in 786, and Tassilo and his supporters in 788. In Italy and the border-zones, the king had encountered the high risks of faithlessness. During these military and political crises, Charles's men had endured some narrow squeaks. At Aachen in 789, those drafting the *Admonitio*'s c. 63 could connect with real-life experiences.

VIII. 'WHY THESE OATHS ARE NECESSARY'

The 'Double Edict for sending out of tasks for *missi*' (Capit. no. 23) and the 'Capitulary of the *missi*' (no. 25) were both linked with the *Admonitio*.[79] The text of the first oath-formula issued by Charles was an item, c. 18, in the Capit. no. 23: '*Sacramentum fidelitatis* . . . Thus I X promise to my lord the king Charles and to his sons that I am faithful and shall be so all the days of my life without fraud or evil design.' Capit. no. 25 survives in a single copy, but in the same manuscript as no. 23, the Double Edict, which survives in sixteen copies. Both no. 23 and no. 25 are now securely dated to 789. No. 25 has an explicit con-nection with 'a great disturbance' involving unfaithful men:

> 1. Concerning these separate *capitula* in which the lord king gives orders to his *missi* as to how they must hear and do these oaths. As to why these oaths are necessary, they have to explain, first, that it derives from ancient

custom, and second, that these unfaithful men recently plotted a great disturbance in the realm of the lord king Charles, and they conspired against his life, and when questioned, they said that they had not sworn any oath of fidelity to him.[80]

The 'great disturbance' can hardly be anything other than Hardrad's revolt. It had taken three years for the relevant inquiries to be made, and Charles had now determined on action, throughout the length and breadth of his realm. He spelled out in detail who was to swear, and how and why. He spelled out which office-holders were responsible for implementing the arrangements. He spelled out exactly how he himself was to be involved, making crystal-clear that the buck stopped with him:

2. How that oath must be sworn by bishops and abbots and counts and by royal *bassi* [for *vassi*] bishops' administrators, archdeacons and canons.

3. Clerics that go by the name of monks but have not yet completely changed their way of life and those who still hold to the Rule of St Benedict must only promise by word and in truth, and about them their abbots must bring these cases to the lord king.

4. Then advocates and vicars, hundredmen and priests who live outside communities and monasteries, and the whole generality of the people, from the age of youth at 12 years until old age, who are able to attend assemblies and fulfil and keep the orders of their lords, whether they are men of the county, or the men of bishops or abbesses or counts or other men, and men of the royal estates (*fiscalini*) and free men (*coloni*) and men belonging to churches and *servi* who have been given benefices and hold offices or who have been granted the post of a vassal by their lord, and are able to have horses, weapons, shields and lances and swords and short-swords: all are to swear. And the *missi* are to take with them lists (*breves*) of the names and numbers of those who have sworn, and counts likewise the names and numbers of all the hundredmen, both those born in the county and those who have come from elsewhere and been commended in vassalage.[81]

If anyone has fled from their county and gone to another county and refused to swear, they must know that they will be reported on the list, or have sent pledges, or been brought in person before the king, and kept under guard, or if willing to stay in the neighbourhood they must swear like the others.

5. The *missi* are to explain that it has been reported to the lord king that many bring complaints that their law has not been kept, and that it is completely the king's will that each man should have his law fully kept, and if anything has been done to someone against their law, that that is not the king's will nor done on the king's orders. But if that has happened, let the count or the *missus* report it to the lord king and he will make amends for it in full. And everyone is to be asked individually by name what is his law. And let *missi* not carry out their investigations without the count being there, unless the count is serving the king elsewhere or kept by illness from attending.

6. The *missi* together with the counts in whose administrative areas they are working must be ready to carry out the duties they owe, so that all together (*generaliter*) must come this year prepared for war to help the king as ordered, and let them keep the peace in the fatherland while they are travelling through it, and he [the king] intends to let them know by letter about his will as regards when and where they must assemble.

Whatever this particular scribe's linguistic limitations, the king's orders are clear when you take into account the combination in communicative practice of the written word with oral speech. Reinforcing the commands of the king and his agents is the back-up of royal letters. Equally remarkable is the comprehensive remit indicated by the word *generaliter*.[82] 'All must swear' (*Omnes jurent*). Exactly how the oaths are taken is not spelled out here, but is assumed on the basis of customary arrangements that *are* spelled out in a legal formulary datable to *c.*700, but evidently still being copied and still in use in the eighth century:[83]

King [A] to Count [B]. Since, with the unanimous consent of our great men, having decided that our glorious son [C] should rule in the kingdom of [D] therefore orders you to summon the *pagenses* (men of the county), Franks, Romans and men of whatever other people, and have them assemble in appropriate places in cities, villages and strongholds, in order that they should swear fidelity and submission to our excellent son and to ourselves in the presence of our *missus*, the illustrious man [E] whom we have sent out from our side for this purpose, in the places of the saints and on the relics which we have sent there through the same *missus*.[84]

Charles's military campaigns have already received a lot of attention in this book so far, and there will be more to come. For the moment,

Capit. no. 25 reveals in particularly valuable detail how, in 789, Charles demanded military service and from whom, and how central oaths were to the gathering of locals for the army every year. *Missi* organized the swearing of oaths by *pagenses* on relics supplied by the king. There is evidence from the early/mid-ninth century of these events actually occurring as prescribed: oaths taken, names written down in lists, reports taken back to the king, contingents assembled and led to the rendezvous.[85] The king was at the centre not just of power but of an efficient communications system: one that worked through oral messages and, very notably, through written lists and letters as well. Officers knew what was required of them; men came armed as necessary, to be counted and inscribed on lists. Clergy were there to help organize the ritual. All these things together were Charles's answer to the question presupposed in Capit. 25: 'why are these oaths necessary?'

The Rhine–Mosel confluence at Koblenz, near St-Goar.

10

The Regensburg Years

1. 'THE FRANKS WERE QUIET'

'*Franci quieverunt*.' This is the shortest annal in the mainstream annalistic record of the eighth century.[1] The non-event for 790 was recorded because for the Franks a year without a campaign was highly unusual. There was just one precedent in the *ArF*, for 765, and the annalist was a little less laconic: 'Pippin held his assembly that year at Attigny, and he made no other campaign (*nullum fecit aliud iter*).' That the word *iter* meant 'journey' as well as 'campaign' also tells something about the Franks. Writing in the early 840s, the Astronomer wrote that in 790 King Louis of Aquitaine had come to the Worms assembly that year 'on his father's orders, on his own, not with an army (*simpliciter, non expeditionaliter*)'.[2] The *Annales Mettenses Priores* said: 'Charles, attending to the internal needs of the kingdom (*utilitates interiores regni*), took no army anywhere this year [790]', as if these were somehow alternatives (or as if excuses had to be made . . .).[3] Charles also called an assembly to Worms in the summer of 790, when envoys from the Avar khagan came to Worms to argue the toss about boundaries.[4] 'Quiet' was a relative concept. Before the assembly disbanded and without any campaign ensuing, 'contention and dispute' between Franks and Avars created 'the seedbed of [the] war' that broke out the following year.[5]

II. FAMILY PLANS: CHARLES, THE YOUNG CHARLES AND HIS BROTHERS

Charles had already turned his mind in 781 to plans for the next generation. The anointments and coronations of Carloman/Pippin and Louis at Rome, and the betrothal of Rotrud also at Rome, had, Charles hoped, settled their futures while they were still in the nursery. His two eldest sons, Pippin the first-born and Young Charles, who remained to be provided for, stayed at Worms in 780–81.[6] The Young Charles, born in 771 or 772, was first mentioned in the *ArF* as campaigning with his father in Saxony in 784 when he had recently come of age at twelve. The king decided to attack the Eastphalians, leaving the Young Charles with a *scara* to confront the Westphalians. Taking the initiative, the king's son 'emerged victorious with the Franks'.[7] In 786, the king's crushing of Hardrad's revolt was signalled by the rebels' 'swearing fidelity on saints' relics to the king and his children (*liberi*)'.[8] It is an interesting fact that from 787 until the end of Charles's reign, the clauses in his charters where prayers were sought for him and his family, which up till then had used the standard terms *progenies* or *proles* for 'offspring', started to employ instead the word *liberi*, which in Roman law meant legitimate offspring produced within marriage, whereas *proles* could signify children by any sexual partner.[9]

The king, at any rate, saw the need to revisit the family plan. The author of the contemporary Annals of St-Amand wrote, under 789: 'the king's son Charles received a *regnum* beyond the Seine'.[10] The author or patron of the *AMP*, identifiable (I think) as the king's sister Gisela, noted that the king granted his namesake 'the *ducatus* of Le Mans'.[11] It was at this point, 790 but *sine anno* in 'Gisela's story', that her nephew was identified for the first time as '*primogenitus*'.[12] There was a precedent to this lordship: it was the region, 'parts of Neustria consisting of twelve counties', that Charles's father Pippin had assigned his half-brother Grifo in 748.[13]

According to the author of *Gesta of the Abbots of St-Wandrille*, written up in (probably) c.840, the Young Charles asked for King Offa of Mercia's daughter Ælfflæd in marriage.[14] This need not mean that the suitor acted against his father's will: father and son could well have agreed the plan, to coincide with the giving of the *regnum* across the

Seine. There's no sign of hostility between father and son at this point, or indeed at any time later. The Young Charles had already served as his father's right-hand man in Saxony, and he continued to act as a faithful adjutant throughout the 790s. *Regnum*, anyway, more often meant 'an area ruled' rather than a kingdom, and that was certainly so in this case. The sequel in Frankish sources confirmed that, for the Young Charles was not made a king in 789 or 790, and stayed only briefly beyond the Seine. What the *Gesta* author did state explicitly, though, was the cause of the *dissensio* that ensued, namely, that Offa's response had been to make the Young Charles's marriage to Ælfflæd conditional on King Charles's daughter Berta being handed over in marriage to Offa's son Ecgfrith (the verb *tradere* neatly captures the handing over of the woman as gift). The *Gesta* author continued:

> King Charles, for a short time, was enraged (*commotus*) and ordered that no-one from the island of Britain and the people of the English was to reach port in Gaul for commercial purposes. But Abbot Gervold prevented this from happening thanks to his admonition and his supplication.[15]

No more is heard of the abortive double-marriage-plan, stymied by Offa's insistence on the acquiring of Berta as a bride for his son. The notion of kings Offa and Charles as being somehow of equal rank and status has rightly been called by a sceptical historian 'a figment of the collective imagination of historians of Anglo-Saxon England'. In another context, that same sceptical historian, noting that the *Gesta* were written up thirty to forty years after the event, could suggest that the proposed marriage-alliance 'may be a figment of the *Gesta* author's imagination'.[16] Figment or no figment (and I'm inclined to see fact, not fiction), it was one thing for Rotrud to have been betrothed to an East Roman emperor, quite another to trade Berta as a bride to an Anglo-Saxon kinglet.[17]

A good test of the *Gesta*'s plausibility is that the dating and details fit with the date of Alcuin's Epistle 7, indisputably of early 790, and sent from York to his Irish friend Colcu. Alcuin dealt with, among other things, the fall-out from recent dissension between King Charles and King Offa which had resulted in a trade-embargo on both sides. The *Gesta*'s details also chime with the date of Alcuin's Ep. 9, late in 790: at this time of writing, in Francia, Alcuin was still ignorant of the reasons for the dissension – or perhaps he decided diplomatically to keep silent about them. Alcuin's Ep. 9 referred to dissension between men who had been 'friends in times past' (*olim amici* does not translate as 'old friends'), which could fit well with a 787 dating for the plot allegedly hatched – and vigorously denied – by Charles and Offa to depose Pope Hadrian, as revealed in *Codex Carolinus* 92.[18]

What really interested the author(s) of the *Gesta* were stories about conscientious abbots in the past and the rulers who protected them. Gervold, one of the most able and best-placed to oversee cross-Channel traffic, served as Charles's superintendant of tolls (*procurator*) at Quentovic near the mouth of the river Canche. Gervold was said to have been addressed in many letters from Offa of Mercia as 'dearest friend'.[19] Offa's 'friend' will appear later wearing his Frankish toll-taker's hat.[20] True, the *Gesta* are not strictly a contemporary source, but they are in a general way a plausible one, not least thanks to the circumstantial detail they offer in relation to the Young Charles's marriage-proposal and cross-Channel contacts, but also showing the value of the protection Charles extended over St-Wandrille's property and the documentary evidence for this.

The Young Charles did not remain 'beyond the Seine' for long: according to the *AMP* author, he attended the Worms assembly 'in summer' 790, though nothing is said about his brothers. The usually well-informed author of the Mosel Annals made no reference to the Young Charles's presence but did mention that the assembly had been attended by 'Pippin king of the Lombards and Louis king of the Aquitanians'. The *ArF* author added that when that assembly was over, Charles made a river journey from Worms down the Rhine to Koblenz and then north-east up the Main and back, 'lest he should be thought of as becoming sluggish through inactivity, or wasting his time'.[21] Forming in Charles's mind were the strategic considerations that would underlie the Avar war of 791 and his canal project just two years later.

Information is so sparse on the relationships between Charles and his sons, and his sons with each other (especially the half-brothers Young Charles and Pippin son of Himiltrud), that it's worth squeezing as much juice as possible from another text written c.840. The author was Wandalbert, a noted scholar, whose monastery, Prüm, was a place of dynastic memory for Carolingians and those who kept the record. The small monastery of St-Goar was a dependent house of Prüm. According to Wandalbert's *Miracles of St Goar*, in a chapter entitled,

'The Emperor Charles in danger because of something hidden' (*De Imperatore Carolo ob dissimilationem periclitato*), Charles took his two elder sons along with him on his Rhine journey in 790:

The emperor went from his palace at Ingelheim to the fort sited at the confluence of the Mosel and the Rhine [Koblenz] where he decided to stay for the night, while his sons Charles and Pippin followed him, each in a separate boat. When he had reached the monastery of the holy confessor [St Goar] by boat, Abbot Asuerus [of Prüm] came to meet him and asked if he would come out to St-Goar and make an offering of a 'charity' (*caritas*), to use the everyday word, at the saint's cell. The emperor refused his presence [i.e. refused the chance to visit], and turning round he signalled with his hand to his son and namesake that he [the Young Charles] should leave his boat at the church so that he could go and pray, while he [the emperor] himself would continue on his journey as decided. When the Young Charles had disembarked, the emperor's other son Pippin who was coming along in his boat behind his brother, thinking that this boat was his father's which he could see had been driven onto the river-bank, got out of his own boat and went to join him in the church [of St-Goar] not knowing that this was his brother. There in the church, because there had been for some time many serious dissensions and rivalries between them, it was by the inspiration of divine mercy and with the support of the merit of the most holy confessor [St Goar] that they now came together in brotherly concord and a pledge of friendship. They had something to eat and drink, and then speedily and happily they came to the place above-named [Koblenz] which they had begun by heading for with their father, and they and every one of their men arrived there safely. But after his sons had disembarked, and while the emperor had remained on his own boat with his own men and was [still] wanting to make for the place above-mentioned, suddenly a very thick cloud completely covered him and that cloud was followed by an extremely dark fog, so that they missed their way on the river and neither the emperor nor any of his companions and not even the steersman himself had any knowledge or sight of where they were, or where they were going or whither to steer the boat. Thus, when they were exhausted and in difficulties after being on the water for what remained of the day, after the emperor had acknowledged his fault [of not having offered a 'charity' and having refused the chance to visit], and began to pray to St Goar for much of the [next] day and night was coming on, they came onto the adjacent shore a little more than three miles from the place which they had intended to reach, and the emperor was forced to spend that night there without any necessities. Next day, such was his [sense of] sin that he publicly testified to what he deservedly experienced in danger on the river, which differed so greatly from the comfort of the journey and the amenities of the royal residence. What had happened to him had not happened in vain: rather, he had revisited St-Goar and [felt] the deserved penalties he had suffered for contempt of the saint, and in his grief he had weighed up the penalty of a humble petitioner [which was] to vow himself and to promise most firmly that never would he come to that neighbourhood, no matter how much of a hurry he was in on some great journey, without turning aside [to the cell of St-Goar]: he who had experienced such danger [wanted] to ask those who thought themselves negligent to experience something like it, rather than wanting revenge on them. After vowing all this, he sent 20 lb. of silver and 2 palls of pure silk to the cell [of St-Goar]; and never again in his whole life did he neglect for any reason whatsoever what he had vowed.

Wandalbert did not fail to back up the story's veracity by adding: 'the steersman of Charles's boat is still alive and it is he who has passed on all this to me.' As a little coda to the piece, Wandalbert added to the same chapter another miracle, as if it followed directly from the rest of the events recounted above:

> Concerning the cure of Queen Fastrada in the same place. The wife of the above-mentioned prince (*princeps*, i.e. Charles) was tortured by the pain of a most excruciating toothache, and she had come to that place to find a remedy for her pain, and immediately, as a suppliant, she was made free from her illness. The emperor therefore gave the estate called Nassau to St-Goar and it has to this day remained part of the rightful property of that place.[22]

The Prüm author recorded these miracle-stories not only for the edification of his readers (and hearers), but because they concerned royal-family matters. That the Young Charles and Pippin had been on very bad terms for some time, and that at St-Goar they buried the hatchet, are bits of information found only here. The significance of this material has only recently been grasped.[23] 'Dissensions' about the respective positions of a king's sons in the line of succession were everyday realities. Pippin was the older, and the first-born. But in (probably) 784, Paul the Deacon, writing at Charles's court, had mentioned – in an awkwardly worded passage – that Himiltrud was a concubine, not a lawful wife;[24] and in 786, the decrees issued in Northumbria by George of Ostia and his colleagues, who included as their 'helper' Charles's special appointee the Frankish scholar Wigbod, had laid down that an anointed king's heir must be the child of a lawful marriage.[25] It looks as if the Roman-law distinction between the offspring of a lawful wife (*liberi*) and the offspring of a sexual partner (*proles*) was beginning to matter in the 780s in a way it had not necessarily done previously. Reports or rumours of the unexpected pledging of friendship between Charles's two eldest sons are plausible because they fit the date, 790, and the Rhine journey reported by the *ArF* reviser. For those at court, and, more widely, for members of the elite, rumours could indicate that all previous bets were off. The mere thought of Pippin son of Himiltrud and the Young Charles dining at the same table raised possibilities of new political alignments, and of Charles's envisaging new options on Bavaria's future. As for the story of Fastrada's cure, the timing fits 790.[26]

What the story of St Goar's miracle tells of Charles's religious mentality is plausible too. It attests the king's fear in a very dangerous situation, his realization (or rationalization) of his refusal to visit the saint's shrine as a serious sin of contempt for the saint, and his faith in the powers of St Goar to work for him: after all, the *cella* of St-Goar was where, on 6 July 788, Tassilo had been tonsured, in private, and hence permanently excluded from power in Bavaria. After the king's escape from such danger, it was to Prüm, one of the Carolingian family's key powerhouses of prayer, that he turned to receive remission for his sin of negligence towards the saint, to Prüm that he promised lifelong devotion, and to Prüm that he assured patronage, protection and 'charity' (everyone knew what that meant). For Wandalbert, the half-brothers making peace with each other was nothing short of a miracle. For Wandalbert again, the series of particular events involving Charles were not mere commonplaces to pad out a well-honed example of the genre of miracle-stories, but divinely approved interventions in earthly affairs. St Goar's miracles can be compared with the one at the *translatio* of St Germain where Charles had lost his first milk-tooth. There was an element of entertainment as well as edification in these stories, as with *carmina*, the songs and tales of ancestors. There could be scene-stealing on the part of a seven-year-old when Charles lost his tooth in the midst of a great ritual event. The forty-two-year-old Charles felt exposed to serious dangers in navigating the whirlpools of the Rhine Gorge in 790, and river-boatmen and pilots still know about these even today. Such things were remembered by those who experienced them and those who told of them, not just to their own generation but to the next as well. These stories stood the test of time. The king now turned more resolutely than before to 'the world beyond the Rhine'.[27]

III. 'THE PALACE OF WORMS . . . BURNED DOWN THROUGH AN ACCIDENT AT NIGHT'

The palace at Worms had become one of Charles's most frequent places of residence in the 780s (he stayed there in 781, 783, 784, 786, 787 and 789), though only in 789 did he overwinter there. In this decade, his marriage to Fastrada, whose family connections were in the middle-Rhine region, and the use of riverine communications (especially the Rhine), explain the residence-pattern. Only this once during Charles's lifetime was the burning-down of a palace recorded, in 790. There is a fruitful comparison to be made of reactions to this event with the ways authors reported other events of 786: in both versions of the *ArF* for that year, there was a suppression of any information about signs and portents, by contrast with the attention paid to these by other contemporary sources. Here in 790, the burning-down of the palace might have been expected to elicit comment; but all that's recorded is the event itself (and the sources don't quite agree on the extent of the damage). I have been struck by the authors' apparently rationalistic approach to what might otherwise have given rise to supernatural explanations: the burning-down of the palace simply happened 'by accident at night'. A comparable approach will be discussed below in reference to the prolonged heavy rain that *naturaliter* put paid to Charles's canal project in 793.[28]

Just as there were times and places for miracles, and for signs and portents, so there were other times when the interpretation of events needed to be managed by Charles and his counsellors in ways that suppressed the supernatural. That, despite the fire, Charles and his court still stayed at Worms and overwintered there could have been read as determined belying of doom and gloom. This was, after all, the very time when a major campaign, perhaps the most risky Charles ever embarked on, was about to start – the war against the Avars. It was an age of faith: it was an age of reason. Rationalism and faith, paradoxical as it may seem, coexisted in court culture.[29] For now, it's worth noting the two-fold consequences of the burning-down of the palace of Worms. First, Charles, drawn eastwards in any case by the military threat posed by the Avars, in 791 transferred his court to Regensburg, where what had been Tassilo's major palace now became Charles's, and what had been the main ducal scriptorium, the monastery of St Emmeram's, was now at the disposal of Charles's scholars. Secondly, simultaneously, Charles pressed ahead with the construction of a new major residence at Aachen, where the building of a great church preceded, and was complemented by, the building of a great palace.[30]

IV. THE AVAR CAMPAIGN AND EQUINE PESTILENCE

The Avar campaign dominated the annalistic record in 791. Three more or less detailed different contemporary accounts, and a fourth, a little later, by the ArF reviser, complement each other. The ArF author(s) described the gathering of the host at Regensburg, the discussions of Franks, Saxons and Frisians and the collective decision to carry out the campaign 'in view of the immense and intolerable evil which the Avars had perpetrated against the holy Church and the Christian people (*populus christianus*), and for which they had not managed to obtain satisfaction through *missi*'. The ArF narrative damned the Avars and exaggerated their military power at the same time: their skills in equestrian tactics and archery were still formidable. The Avar polity, its heart in what is now western Hungary and in the steppe-lands east of the Danube, had in fact been growing weaker for some time, however, in part because of internal strains and rivalries, in part through the gradually increasing pressure of the Franks' expansion in Friuli and Carinthia with the enhanced military power of Pippin's kingdom of

Italy.[31] In 791, after moving rapidly east to the river Enns, Charles decided that the army should perform litanies and celebrate the solemnities of the mass for three days, seeking God's help for the safety of the army and Christ's aid for victory and vengeance (*pro victoria et vindicta*) against the Avars. The report added details of military action, and, thanks to Christ, the success of his people (*populus suus*).

The *ArF* reviser added other details: the 'exceptionally powerful' nature of this army, its division into two, one force led by Count Theoderic, Charles's kinsman, and the Treasurer Meginfrid (both leading commanders, mentioned twice more in this annal) on the north bank of the Danube, the other by Charles himself on the south bank, and the supplies and baggage taken by boats down the river; the litanies were also mentioned. The *ArF* reviser, writing some twenty years after the event, was the only source to mention that the force led by the king suffered a severe reverse: 'so great an equine pestilence (*tanta equorum lues*) that barely one-tenth of so many thousands of horses survived'.[32]

Such a pestilence had not hitherto been recorded in the Frankish world. In recent years, historians and veterinary scientists have made it their combined business to throw light on these terrible losses, and I shall return later to this research. For the moment, what needs to be addressed are the consequences for not only the Franks but the Avars too. The breeding and training of mature horses were key to the military success of both Franks and Avars. There are no Avar written sources, but the one Frankish source just cited indicates the huge problem these losses posed for Charles and his commanders. It's been calculated that the equine population would have taken three years to replenish itself. Meanwhile, the increased use of riverine transport went some way to meeting the emergency. The silence of the strictly contemporary sources can hardly have been coincidental: Charles, as with the signs and portents of 786, coped in part by suppressing information, in part by maintaining calm as a default position. There is no further mention of equine pestilence in the sources for the rest of Charles's reign.

The Lorsch Annals gave rather different details of tactics (the division of the army into three) and strategy (Charles's troops 'moving around that land (*terra*) for 52 days, burning and wasting it and taking spoils without measure or number and a multitude of captives, men, women and children'), but did not mention Charles's litanies. The

Chesne Fragment, brief and largely following the Lorsch Annals, did include a mention of the litanies. All these accounts, and others, stressed with particular relish the ravaging, the spoils, and the captives.[33] Annal-writers evidently attached varying significance to the performance of litanies for the safety of armies in war. Such liturgical texts, of late-Roman origin, were important props to military morale.[34]

V. CHARLES'S LETTER TO FASTRADA, SEPTEMBER 791

A piece of writing in a quite different genre supplies more evidence of litanies. It is a uniquely personal letter of Charles and it survives in a formulary collection. Formulae are generally stripped of all specifics, but in the formulary copy of *this* letter, though names are omitted, some very interesting specifics have been left in.[35] First, Charles gave a report on the campaign against the Avars. He passed on news from 'our beloved son', who in the context must be Pippin of Italy, about the Italian border-regions;[36] and he also retailed news of a successful campaign further north which, on Charles's orders, had moved into Avar territory on 23 August, and gone on to win a great victory in which a list of anonymized *fideles* did outstanding service. Charles then described 'three days of litanies' which he and his army had performed 'so that God will grant us a successful expedition'. Here dates have been left in: 'Monday 5 September and Tuesday and Wednesday'. This performance involved fasting and almsgiving on the part of several types of people, clergy of different ranks, and laity: large numbers, evidently, requiring a lot of organization.[37] 'Our bishops (*sacerdotes*) decreed that only those not hindered by age or infirmity were excused fasting and abstinence from wine' – but there was a buy-out clause covering three categories of men (reminiscent of the three categories devised by the bishops in the Second Capitulary of Herstal of March 779):

> for those who wanted to be free to drink wine during those three days, the greater and more powerful men (*maiores et potentiores homines*) should give one *solidus* for each day, and the less powerful (*minus potentes*) according to their means, and a man who could not give more

but wanted to drink wine (*qui amplius dare non potebat et vinum bibere volebat*) should give at least one *denarius*.[38]

Litanies had been performed before.[39] Charles's father Pippin had reminded Bishop Lull of Mainz that God sent 'tribulation to punish our sins' but then sent the wondrous consolation of a tremendous harvest: the king suggested that every bishop perform thanksgiving litanies in his diocese, probably during normal processions, without fasting, but with everyone giving alms and feeding the needy.[40] The linking of the king's *iniustitia* with divine punishment, and the special responsibility of the king towards God, appeared in Cathwulf's letter to Charles of *c*.775. As just mentioned, in March 779 litanies were decreed by the combined efforts of king and bishops during a terrible famine in Francia. In early 786, Charles had announced one- or two-day litanies, and Pope Hadrian had sent orders 'into all our lands, those lying under the domination of the holy Roman Church ... Christian peoples far beyond your royal dominion', decreeing three-day litanies on 23, 26 and 28 June, and asking Charles to back them.[41] The two-fold aim of both king and pope that year was to give thanks to God for bringing peoples to the faith (the Saxons seemed to have capitulated in 785) and to beseech God to drive away sickness and pestilence and avert the threats of fearsome portents throughout 786 (there had been a serious rebellion earlier that year).[42] The public enacting of supplication, penance and thanksgiving was not new, then. Nor was it merely medieval. Almost exactly 700 years later, in the deep midwinter of 1596, Elizabeth I decreed fasting and alms-giving in England – and churchwardens' accounts show that these acts were (sometimes, certainly) actually performed.[43]

The recipient of the king's letter of September 791, and organizer of the litanies in possibly the third week of that month (and evidently at Regensburg), was Charles's queen, anonymized in the formulary but well known to historians: Fastrada. The letter was addressed thus:

> *Dilecte nobis et valde amabili coniuge nostrae ill.* [anonymized in the formula] *regine.* To our beloved and very lovable wife . . . the queen. We desire by this letter to send a loving greeting to you (*tibi*) in the Lord, and, through you, to our darling daughters (*dulcissimis filiabus nostris*) and to the rest of our *fideles* who are staying with you (*tecum commorantibus*).

After the report part of the letter, the king continued:

> And because of this, it is our will that, along with [anonymized] . . . and
> [anonymized] . . . and the other *fideles*, you should consider [the verb is
> in the second person singular *considerare debeas*] how the same litanies
> should be performed there. As for you yourself, according to what your
> ill-health allows, we commit [all the above] to your judgement. And we
> have been surprised that no messenger and no letter from you has reached
> us . . . from Regensburg [since we left Regensburg?]. And so it is our wish
> that you write more often to us about your health and about whatever
> else you decide. And again we send you much greeting in the Lord.

Whatever else is obscure, the assignment given to the queen is clear:
she is entrusted with prime responsibility for the litanies, believed to
bring 'a happy and successful outcome to the war', and involving co-
operation with *fideles*, lay and ecclesiastical (the community of St
Emmeram's, and its busy scribes), and the participation of a great many
others. The task in hand could hardly have been more important as far
as Charles was concerned. Chris Wickham's incisive commentary on
the letter to Fastrada captures perfectly 'the mixture of military action
and religious ritual . . . [and] the ecclesiastical and moralizing edge to
political practice' that the litanies reflect.[44] What he underestimates,
though, is the mixture of the personal with the political: he does not
mention that Charles sent warm wishes to his most sweet daughters
(*dulcissimae filiae nostrae*), referred to Fastrada in the salutation of the
letter no fewer than four times in the second person singular, and ended
by insistently asking for news of Fastrada's health. To my mind, a personal relationship, and a strong emotional bond, is in evidence here.

There is also a reminder of 787, when Fastrada had been left at
Worms with 'the sons and the daughters and the entire court which
[the king] had left with them' (*filiosque ac filias et omnem comitatum
quem apud eos dimiserat*), when he was in Italy.[45] Here again the queen
played a vitally important role in minding the family and the *familia*.
The sons on that occasion were Fastrada's stepsons Pippin son of
Himiltrud and Charles, Hildegard's eldest son. In 784, the names of
the royal family as it then was had been entered in the Salzburg *Book
of Life* (in which the names of the dead were commemorated), probably
at the bidding of Bishop Arn of Salzburg: Charles, Fastrada, Pippin
son of Himiltrud, and Charles, Pippin and Louis – the three sons of

Hildegard – and Rotrud, Hildegard's oldest daughter.[46] In September 791, the family-members with Fastrada were probably Pippin son of Himiltrud, certainly Louis, her own daughters, and probably some of her stepdaughters residing at or visiting court. Fastrada had remained at Regensburg, staying in what had been Tassilo's palace with those members of the court who had not gone on campaign with Charles.[47] These must have included the owners of the two names anonymized in the manuscript, evidently leading counsellors of the queen at this point.

One of these was almost certainly Bishop Sindpert, who attested a document at Regensburg on 1 September, and died on 29 September, possibly also at Regensburg.[48] The other might have been Gerold, brother of the late queen Hildegard and hence maternal uncle of Louis and his sisters, as well as Pippin of Italy and the Young Charles. Gerold was appointed by Charles, at a date not exactly known, to be *praefectus* of Bavaria after Tassilo's removal. Gerold's first documented entrance there was as the first-named of Charles's lay *missi* in a charter, dated 20 September 791, issued at a judicial assembly at 'Lorch on the river Enns' where Charles's army was encamped, some 200km east-south-east of Regensburg.[49] Perhaps Gerold was despatched from Lorch to Regensburg with Charles's letter, helped Sindpert with the planning and performance of the litanies, and then brought back news of them? That would have made a round journey, including litanies accomplished, theoretically possible within a fortnight, given a more or less usable Roman road – and less if using a boat on the Danube.

With a little imagination, the reader can visualize the litanies as fronted by an exceptionally strong line-up of Charles's family, featuring Fastrada as being a careful guardian of the offspring of her predecessor as queen, perhaps with their uncle in a powerful supporting role. There was no sign of a 'wicked stepmother' here; that piece of negative stereotyping appeared well over a decade after her death in the charge of cruelty made against her by the *ArF* reviser, and more decades later still by Einhard.[50] As a capable stand-in for her husband, Fastrada (assuming all went according to plan) projected to Franks and Bavarians alike the replacement of Tassilo's ruling family and court by Charles's, his litanies and victories by Charles's, as signs of divine approval in present and future. Achim Hack has imagined that Fastrada was suffering from terrible toothache throughout the performance.[51] If so (and whatever her illness), she staged a triumph of her own.

VI. A COURT BEFORE AACHEN

Before the Aachen palace, there was a court, an *aula renovata*, a court renewed, in which the 'essential preconditions of the post-793 court, the earlier formation of the individuals who were among its participants and commentators become . . . a mould which has fused with its casting. But the mould and its making have a history of their own.' Thus the late Donald Bullough.[52] His account of the preconditions illuminates the reign of Charles's father and the first two decades of Charles own reign, when Italian scholars put in so much of the spadework for the court's renewal. Worms, 'the Carolingians' last urban residence', may well have been, in 790, home to the writing of the 'Court book-list'.[53] Bullough observed that the period 791–4 saw 'a new breed of scholar-counsellors . . . set Charles and his policies in new directions; and in doing so completed a new remoulding of the Court' in the old ducal palace at Regensburg.[54] There, in 791, the compiling of the *Codex Carolinus* was commissioned by the king from Bishop Angilramn of Metz, and in that same year, very probably, the *ArF* began to be written up contemporaneously.

VII. THE 'BIG COUNCIL' AT REGENSBURG AND THE PROBLEM OF HERESY

Charles had stayed at Regensburg through the winter of 791–2. At the top of the agenda of the 'big council' he summoned to Regensburg in July 792 was the 'Adoptionist' heresy being preached in the Pyrenees by Bishop Felix of Urgell.[55] Trained in the traditions of the Spanish Church and in the theology of the Greek Fathers, Felix had acquired a profound understanding of, in particular, the meaning of Christ's 'emptying of himself, taking the form of a *servus*' ('slave' or 'servant'; Philippians 2:7). The accusations of heresy levelled by Alcuin of York and Paulinus of Aquileia against Felix resulted in part from a failure to understand such terms as 'emptying' and 'adoptive'. These are sometimes, and with justification, treated as linguistic issues.[56] But there was more to it than that, as John Cavadini has shown. Felix's view was that Jesus was a *servus* because of his *natural condition*. It was 'a condition of his nature' that he had another, spiritual, birth and made such a birth available to all. Felix pictured Jesus

> gathering together the sins of humankind onto himself in 'the likeness of sinful flesh', going into the water [of baptism], and then on his ascent from the river presenting to God a renewed humanity with himself as its Head . . . The final moment of the saving mediation itself [is] when Jesus presents us all to God washed clean of sin because of our incorporation into his renewed humanity.[57]

In his *Confessio* of orthodoxy, Felix spoke of himself as 'vanquished by Alcuin without force and through reason'. Subtle and original theologian as he was, Felix may have spoken with just a touch of irony. Still, both men in their debates displayed humanity.[58]

Not officially on the agenda at Regensburg was Charles's response to the Greek second Council of Nicaea in 787 and to the pope's reception of that council's decrees. As over Iconoclasm, linguistic problems similar to those embedded in the Adoptionist controversy had already arisen; political dangers lurked as well. Men from Septimania (southwest France) and Aquitaine raised fears of heresy's diffusion.[59] Charles, flanked by his son Louis, now of age, fielded a formidable ecclesiastical team: Abbot Benedict of Aniane, Abbot Atto of St-Hilary's, Poitiers; from Italy, King Pippin and Bishop Paulinus of Aquileia; and a strong Bavarian contingent including Arn of Salzburg, Atto of Freising and Waltric of Passau, and key abbots; and two of Charles's closest counsellors, Angilbert and Theodulf.[60] When Felix had confessed error, Angilbert was given the job of escorting him to Rome to present himself to the pope, and also with taking a first draft by Theodulf of Charles's response to Nicaea II.[61] The strongest impression left on the Bavarians, and (so the timing could suggest) on the large army assembled at Regensburg from several *regna*, was the burning, at Charles's command, of heretical adoptionist writings.[62] The public ceremony, inspired by the law and action of Roman emperors whose successor Charles now claimed to be, was enacted in the collective presence, and with the authorization, of Charles and two of his sons by Hildegard. The atmosphere at Regensburg was of deepening political fears across a broader front: Saxons, aware that Avars were thirsting for revenge after 791's defeats, now allied with them.[63] Bavaria was too close for comfort to Pannonia, and Charles prepared for intensified hostilities.

Across the years 787–94, Charles's political and diplomatic sights never ceased to include Francia. For the meantime, however, his focus was on Bavaria and strategically linked Italy, and to a lesser extent Byzantium. There were indeed some basic continuities of principle and policy throughout Charles's reign.[64] Yet one of his most notable traits was a capacity to switch ideas in new directions in response to new conjunctures. Max Weber metaphorically called such switchers 'pointsmen' or signalmen. Charles himself was a real-life signalman; and some of those he deployed have some claim to the name. Angilbert, Theodulf, Alcuin, Adalhard – all effected redirections in person and through texts.[65]

VIII. THE REVOLT OF PIPPIN SON OF HIMILTRUD, ?EARLY AUTUMN 792

Pippin's *conjuratio* was one of the two big rebellions and most serious crises of Charles's reign.[66] Its exact date is debatable: the contemporary author of the *ArF* said 'during the summer', the author of the Mosel Annals said autumn, Einhard said winter. Late summer/early autumn sounds most likely. As to where: there are several pointers to Regensburg as the epicentre. The nearest-to-contemporary evidence, that of the Lorsch Annals, made it just about as clear as it could have been to a public versed in Old Testament history that Pippin's plot was aimed

> against the life of the king and of his sons by a lawfully wedded wife, for they intended to kill the king and those sons and Pippin sought to reign in the king's place, like Abimelech in the days of the Judges of Israel, who slew his brothers, 70 men, upon one stone, and reigned in the place of his father Gideon but with wickedness and not for long.[67]

The Lorsch annalist was well aware that Pippin was the son of Himiltrud, Charles's first wife, and that Pippin's targets were his father and his half-brothers, sons of Charles's third wife Hildegard. What the Lorsch writer did not quote, but his readers well knew, were the chapters from the Book of Judges that identified Abimelech as Gideon's favourite son whose key supporters were his mother's brothers. On a close reading of the annal-writer's syntax, it also appears that Pippin acted closely with someone else, and that that someone was his mother.[68] Himiltrud made an unexpected comeback onto the political stage as she, and (to be inferred) her brothers, as well as her son, at last confronted the sons of Hildegard, who were also the stepsons and protégés of Fastrada. These royal women, dead or alive, were the poles around which politics revolved, and pre-existing rivalries between the women's natal families could be expected. Himiltrud's natal family were Pippin's chief supporters, and they were Franks. Pippin had supporters in Bavaria as well; and seizing Bavaria may well have been his initial, even primary, aim, precisely because it offered a perfect opportunity to cut out his rivals, his half-brothers. For Pippin, during the high summer of 792, the risk from the offspring of Hildegard had become intolerable – and also removable. He found himself, perhaps for the first time in a long time, positioned to resolve his problems at a stroke, as all three of Hildegard's sons were together with their father in the palace of Regensburg. Their removal would leave Pippin as sole ruler of the Franks and the Lombards and the Aquitanians, as well as the Bavarians.

Notker of St-Gall's testimony is late, and has the ingredients of a good yarn, but he sets the scene of the plot firmly in St Peter's cathedral in Regensburg very near the palace.[69] Notker does not name 'the cleric who hid under the altar' and whom the conspirators made swear not to betray them; but the *ArF* reviser not only names the cleric as 'the Lombard Fardulf' but adds that he was given the monastery of St-Denis as a reward for keeping faith.[70] Once the conspirators had left the church, according to Notker, the cleric headed straight for the palace and gained access to Charles thanks to the good offices of the womenfolk who looked after the queen and her daughters.

> They heard a knock at the door, found the wretched cleric, barred the doors again, and with much laughter and chattering pulled their skirts over their faces and tried to hide in corners. The emperor who was no fool and whom nothing under heaven could escape, questioned the women closely . . . When he learned that the man who had knocked at the door was only a shorn tramp, clumsy and acting strangely, clad only in shirt and pants, and asking to speak with Charles, he ordered the man to be admitted. He fell at the emperor's feet and revealed everything.[71]

Altogether more sober, and datable to 791–2, is an entry in the list of persons to be prayed for in a Bavarian Sacramentary, probably

produced at the behest of Bishop Adalwin of Regensburg who succeeded Sindpert and is first recorded in office on 22 July 792. The list
runs: 'Karalus rex, Fastraat regina, Pippinus rex, Ludiuuic rex, Hrod-
rud, Adaluni episcopus [Regensburg], Atto [Freising], Pipinus rex,
Karalus, Arn, Uualtrih episcopus [Passau]; and [two other Bavarian
bishops]'.

These 'odd jottings in a discarded mass-book', have made it possible
to identify the second King Pippin as the son of Himiltrud, and the
untitled 'Karalus' as the eldest son of Charles by Hildegard, and to
explain the ordering of the list in terms of 'uncertainty regarding the
older brothers' territorial claims and claims to the succession, as
compared with those of the younger Pippin and Louis'.[72] Another explanation might be the timing of entries in whatever jottings preceded the
list: the first five names (Charles, Fastrada, Pippin of Italy, Louis of
Aquitaine and Rotrud) were of those present at the July council; but
the older brothers appeared at the assembly that followed. True, nothing is known of the Young Charles's whereabouts in these critical years,
but the mention of him in Adalwin's list could conceivably mean that
he was present in Regensburg in 792, in other words that the king had
wished to stage, there and then, a united family front.

The plot's betrayal not only put paid to the hopes of the conspirators
but doomed many of them to death. Even though some high-born
office-holders – two at least are identifiable: Bishop Peter of Verdun and
Count Theodold of Chambly in the Oise valley – were involved, Charles
was able to suppress the plot.[73] He could summon an assembly of the
Franks and others, and the army gathered for the 792 summer campaign may still have been on the scene, where

> the whole Christian people judged and sentenced both Pippin and those
> who had consented with him to loss of inheritance and life. On some this
> sentence was carried out; but as for Pippin, since the king did not want
> him to be put to death, the Franks judged that he must bow himself to
> God's service . . .[74]

That matters were not settled quickly or definitively has been inferred
from the fact that Charles's sons by Hildegard steered clear of Regensburg in 793.[75] That is quite possible; but a complementary explanation
might be that the king was keeping them at a distance for his own
political benefit. He was able to hand-pick key personnel: the sons'

maternal uncle Gerold, since 788 prefect of Bavaria, would take care of the Bavarian clean-up with the help of co-operative bishops.

Himiltrud disappeared from the written sources at this point. The only other evidence of her is skeletal. She was buried at the convent of Nivelles, founded by St Gertrude back in the seventh century, and thereafter a Pippinid family-house. Her remains are on display in the convent crypt, with a metal plaque apparently of tenth-century date identifying her by name.[76] Though the exact date of her death is unknown, her bones indicate that she died aged between thirty-five and forty, and was nearly six feet tall.[77]

IX. THE ASSEMBLY IN REGENSBURG IN ?SPRING 793

Charles had one more large piece of political business to complete in Bavaria: the exemplary rewarding of those who had remained loyal to him. He wintered in Regensburg and stayed there during the early months of 793. The Lorsch Annals recorded an exceptional assembly there:

> That winter, the king again held an assembly at Regensburg, and when he had identified his faithful men, bishops, abbots and counts who had been there with him, and the rest of the faithful people who did not join Pippin in that most wicked plot, he rewarded them abundantly with gold and silver, silk and numerous gifts.[78]

The emphasis in the above sentence should be on the words '*did not join*'. Charles knew who his *fideles* were. In all the accounts of political relationships in Charles's reign, this is one of the most telling comments on loyalty, and the rewards thereof. 'To requite service, and especially armed service, was one of the most important functions of early medieval kings.'[79]

X. THE RE-COINAGE OF ?EARLY SUMMER 793

At some point between autumn 792 and autumn 793, probably early summer 793, Charles and his counsellors decided to carry out a 'renewal of the coinage', involving the production of new, heavier (1.7g) silver pennies bearing 'the monogram of [the king's] name'. The composition of one particular coin-hoard found on a pass across the Alps – one post-reform coin, thirty-seven pre-reform (as well as a number of other coins including a Muslim dirham issued at Tunis in 789/90 (AH 173) – points to the date of the re-coinage. Manuscript evidence complements that of the coins: the lay notary and scribe Wandalgar copied out a collection of three large legal texts – Roman, Frankish and Alemannic – and he noted the date on which he completed his work, 1 November 793. An illustration in his manuscript, just at the point where the Roman law text (the Breviary of Alaric) deals with the counterfeiting of coins and the terrible penalty that offence carried (*damnatio ad bestias*, being thrown to wild beasts), shows a man holding on high a coin with Charles's monogram, evidently representing a *novus denarius*.[80]

Among the probable short-term effects were increases in the value of coins paid to the king and members of the elite, and in the volume of payments made to squads of labourers.[81] Along with such deflationary effects probably went increased profit-margins for minters who were royal officials as well as for local magnates, and indeed for the king himself who could choose to apply his cut to public spending.[82] More significant in the longer run were the regulations made at the Council of Frankfurt in 794.[83]

Why summer 793? Was Charles not busy enough with damping down the aftermath of the previous year's rebellion, with further military action, with plans for a canal linking the Danube and Rhine, with supervising the completion of the *Opus Caroli* and with preparations for the arrival of papal envoys known to be en route for Bavaria? This astonishing cluster of political, ideological and technological projects-in-progress amounted to an imperial programme into which Bavaria was firmly locked.[84] For the local population as well as for Charles and his close advisers, 793 was surely a summer to remember.

XI. THE LABOURS OF THEODULF AND THE VOICE OF CHARLES

Exactly *when* Theodulf completed the *Opus Caroli* is unknown. According to the scholar best-qualified to make a good guess, 'sometime late in the summer of 793, presumably, Charlemagne presided over a gathering at which the completed work was read, while his comments were recorded in the margins'.[85] *Where* Theodulf completed the *Opus Caroli* was very probably the monastery of St Emmeram at Regensburg.[86]

The purpose of the *Opus* was to rebut the decrees of Nicaea II, and especially 'the errors of the Greeks'. Theodulf and other scholars at Charles's court were unaware that the Latin translation of those decrees was deeply flawed, and the errors of the Greeks were ascribed to 'the arrogance of their rulers': Emperor Constantine VI and his mother the Empress Eirene had claimed that 'God co-rules with us'.[87] The translation had been made by scholars at Rome whose knowledge of Greek was very poor. Just as with the failure of Franks and Romans to comprehend the Greek texts which underlay the theology of Bishop Felix's Adoptionism, so linguistic incompetence stymied the efforts of Theodulf to grasp the meaning of the decrees of Nicaea II.[88] 'Without skilful translation mutual incomprehension became only too evident ... The entire council was bedeviled by inaccurate and in some cases intentionally incorrect translations.'[89] This is a Byzantinist's view. Its mirror-image is the view of an expert on Theodulf: 'The Latin version [of the Nicaea II decrees] sent to [the king] was ... a monument of inadequate translation. Its garbled nature gave rise to outrage among the court theologians.' Theodulf sincerely believed that Eirene had convened the council 'to promote the superstitious adoration of images', and that 'heresy ... required a response'.[90] The pope saw things differently, in a way that deeply disappointed Theodulf.[91] As far as 'the ecclesiastical sphere' was concerned, Nicaea II 'normalized' relations between Hadrian's papacy and Eirene's empire.[92]

In the political sphere (if spheres can really be kept separate), Charles was a realist. A few years before, he had put up with Eirene's snub in not inviting any Frankish bishops to the Council, and now he wanted Theodulf to complete his labours on the *Opus Caroli*. That meant finding patristic testimonies to truth. Theodulf, well-acquainted with the Latin Fathers, placed particular intellectual reliance on 'my Augustine, nay rather, God's labourer'.[93] The working copy was subjected to revisions – hundreds of them – by other scholars in Charles's employ. A fair copy, since lost, was sent to Hadrian's Rome; but the working copy apparently remained in Germany, and reached the Vatican Library only in the sixteenth century, where it remains.[94]

Any reader or hearer of Theodulf's massive *opus*, and its revisers, cannot but be deeply impressed. What of Charles's response? The Tironian notes that survive in the margins of the Vatican manuscript were the work of scholars at Charles's court who had been trained in the esoteric knowledge of this shorthand system, and, once the manuscript was in Charles's archive, would have been able to interpret them.[95] Thanks to nearly a century of brilliant scholarly detective work, and some ensuing fierce debates, it was finally established by, above all, the late Ann Freeman, that these notes represented the spoken comments of Charles himself as he responded to a reading of Theodulf's work at an assembly of scholars at court.[96] Twenty-nine different words or short phrases were used; of those, one – *bene* – was used twenty-four times and another – *optime* – ten times, while fifteen others were used only once. In no case, however, was the comment out of place: on the contrary, each showed Charles's understanding and approval of what was being read out. Normally the comment precedes the series of explanatory examples that follow in the text; sometimes the comment comes later on, or at the end.[97]

Two comment-words are particularly interesting. *Rationabiliter*, 'according to reason', was used twice, and both times aptly. In *Opus Caroli* I, 19, Theodulf, following 2 Cor. 3:6, contrasted 'the letter which kills with the Spirit which gives life'. This was to be understood as condemning Greek exegesis which stopped at the literal sense without grasping the spiritual sense.[98] Theodulf offered more examples: 'we are not the carnal Israel, but the spiritual Israel'; and proceeded to contrast the Old Testament – *in illo* ('in that one') – and the New Testament – *in isto* ('in this one'), ending with:

> in that one the people of Canaan were promised a kingdom and a wealth of bodily things, in this one is promised eternal life and the kingdom of heaven; in that one a land of milk and honey [Exod. 3:8], in this one a celestial fatherland which the eye has not seen nor has the ear heard [1 Cor. 2:9].

At this point is the marginal comment, *rationabiliter*. It summed up Charles's response to Theodulf's typological interpretation of Scripture throughout his work: every Old Testament example prefigured one from the New.[99] The word makes a second marginal appearance at II, 17, a short chapter where the Scriptural citation is attributed to St Paul: *Probate spiritus an ex Deo sint* ('test the spirits [to find] whether they are of God'), and again, *Noli credere omni spiritui, sed proba mentem*

('Believe not every spirit, but test the mind').[100] The marginal *rationabiliter* appears at the beginning.[101] This too is a rationalistic response to a Scriptural injunction to test before believing: it also responds to what some scholars have considered a distinctively Spanish element in the court culture of the Carolingian Renaissance.[102]

Syllogistice was a comment Charles only used once, in reference to a syllogism in which 'image' was differentiated from 'similitude' and each of those from 'equalness' (*aequalitas*). Charles knew what a syllogism was, and how its theses produced inferences that led to a conclusion. His comment on a particular passage of Augustine was perfectly apt.[103] The implications of these echoes of Charles's voice are far-reaching: he had acquired a basic grasp of the liberal arts, and of Latin, at some time in his boyhood (*pueritia*), a life-stage which Einhard would claim was, in Charles's case, undocumented.[104] But then, every connoisseur of Einhard knew (and knows) that he had form when it came to being economical with the truth.

XII. FAMINE 792–3 AND THE CANAL PROJECT

In 793, the author of the Mosel Annals noted a severe famine, followed by appalling events: abominations (*immundiciae*) and cannibalism, 'called forth by our sins': 'And in the spring of that year, there appeared in various places in the realm, in fields and woods and marshes, a vast abundance of false corn (*falsa annona, innumera multitudo*) which people could see and touch, but no-one could eat.'[105] Was this a sign? In the Rhineland area affected, famine caused massive shock and distress. Charles registered the urgent need. He responded like a pointsman who, with biblical exemplars in mind, and also *rationabiliter*, even *syllogistice*, had received an extra-strong prompt to charity and, in response to that need, undertook new forms of action on a scale unprecedented.

Charles's project for a canal to link the river Rednitz, an affluent of the Main (and thence the Rhine) and the river Altmühl, an affluent of the Danube, is documented in a number of contemporary texts.[106] Two of these are the *ArF*, the so-called 'original' version, and the version of the *ArF* reviser. The 'original' version, now better-termed 'contemporary', has this under the year 793 and the beginning of 794:

The king in autumn-time made a journey from Regensburg with boats to the great ditch between the rivers Altmühl and Rednitz, and there papal envoys were presented [to him] with large gifts. There a messenger reported that the Saxons had again broken their faith. Thence via the Rednitz he reached the Main by a boat journey, and celebrated Christmas at St Kilian's at Würzburg. [794] Easter was celebrated at Frankfurt.[107]

The reviser has this:

And when [the king] had been persuaded by certain men who claimed to be expert in this matter, that if ditches capable of carrying boats were to be dug out between the rivers Rednitz and Altmühl, it would be possible to navigate very readily between the Danube and the Rhine since one of those rivers flowed into the Danube and the other into the Main, he came without delay to this place, and his whole court with him (*cum omni comitatu*), and after he had gathered a great multitude of men, spent the entire autumn on this project. Thus a ditch was dug between the afore-mentioned rivers which was 2,000 paces [i.e. some 10,000 feet, or 3km] in length and 300 feet [90m] wide. But in vain. For because of the con-tinual rain and the bogginess of the land which was in the nature of things (*naturaliter*) completely waterlogged, the work that was being done could not hold firm, given the excessive wetness, and as much of the earth as was excavated by the diggers during the day slid back again and sank into the soil during the night . . . He returned to Francia and celebrated Christmas at St Kilian's on the banks of the river Main, but he spent Easter at Frankfurt on the same river, where he had also wintered.[108]

Three further accounts should be considered, all certainly or very prob-ably contemporary. The *Annales Laureshamenses* have:

And the lord king, after spending Easter at Regensburg, in the summer had wanted to get to Francia by boat, and had given orders that a certain canal should be made between two rivers, namely the Altmülh and the Rednitz, and had stayed at that place for a long time. But the king, with Christ's help, came from that place to Francia and reached Frankfurt by boat, and stayed there for the winter.[109]

The *Annales Guelferbytani* (so-called 'Wolfenbüttel Annals') have: 'From [Regensburg], he came by boat into the Salafeld to the great ditch; and as winter was starting, he came to Frankfurt with those boats, both dragged overland and also travelling by the rivers, and there he stayed.'[110] The *Annales Mosellani* have:

> [In 793 the king] resided there [at Regensburg] for almost the whole year, except that at about autumn-time he moved to a certain canal which he had begun to construct between the river Danube and the river Rednitz, and there he pressed on in determined fashion with the project above-mentioned, and he remained there for almost the whole of the remaining part of that year, except that a few days before Christmas he went to St Kilian's leaving the above-mentioned project unfinished, and there he celebrated Christmas and the end of that year and the beginning of the next.[111]

These accounts clearly describe the same project. The Lorsch, Wolfenbüttel and Mosel Annals may be as (nearly) contemporary as the 'original' *ArF*. The differences in details have something to do with an author's sources, and/or place of writing. The Mosel Annals, for instance, give unique evidence for the project as an *aquaeductus*, an engineering construction to carry water on arches (think Pont du Gard) or in a channel or canal dug in the ground (think Central Arizona Project); its purpose either to bring water to urban populations or arid zones, or to allow waterborne traffic. The same annals uniquely attest the project's abandonment.

The Wolfenbüttel Annals, with local information, uniquely mention the Sualafeld as the canal's general location and uniquely report first the dragging of boats across land, then travelling by river to Frankfurt.[112] Unlike the *ArF*, the Mosel Annals continue with an account of a terrible famine in 792–3, location unspecified but familiar to the author, as well as of an attack (on Septimania) by Saracens from Spain (other annals mention Saxon attacks too). These threats put the project's abandonment in context.

The context and preconditions for Charles's plan become much clearer when the consequences of the annexation of Bavaria in 788 are taken into account. For some three years, from 791 to 793, Charles resided more or less continuously in Bavaria, at the former ducal palace at Regensburg, with his queen Fastrada and various of his offspring. Ecclesiastical gatherings dealt with various causes of concern, including Adoptionist heresy, and helped Charles to establish close relationships with bishops and abbots whom he needed in key posts and whose spiritual services he required. Avar hostility required a military response, and Charles both called on clergy for spiritual support and deployed leading laymen to help govern Bavaria and fight the Avars.[113] In 791, Charles used the Danube and the Roman roads running along its northern and southern banks as a major route into Avaria:[114] his forces were split into three, on the northern route a Frankish army led by Theoderic and Meginfrid, on the southern route, a second Frankish army led by the king himself, and a third force of Bavarians travelling in boats on the Danube.[115] Charles granted, in c.791, to the monastery of Herrieden in the Sualafeld, on the river Altmühl, three properties in the *terra Avarorum ... ex parte subjugata* ('partly subjugated land of the Avars'), Bielach, Melk and Grundzwita.[116] This presupposed thinking ahead in Avaria, to more complete subjugation, and to mission. Linked-up thinking in the Sualafeld between king and monastery was also in Charles's mind, and this has some relevance to the canal-building project he embarked on in the summer/early autumn of 793.

Three other comparable projects in the long eighth century supply contexts for that of Charles: the Danevirke on the Danish border of what centuries later became Schleswig-Holstein; Offa's Dyke on the English–Welsh frontier; and the Great Fence of Thrace.[117] Though military and defensive purposes, including the fixing of boundaries, were sometimes involved, the most important common feature was a political one. It took a political anthropologist, James C. Scott, in *Seeing Like a State*, to sense the double-edged impact of such prestige projects in ancient and modern times. In each case an ambitious ruler sought to enhance his power by mobilizing men on a hitherto unknown scale, commandeering their services, and making their demands acceptable to their subjects.[118] To enhance their power and technological capacity, rulers in early medieval times too undertook these huge projects to demonstrate their authority and prestige, often producing miniaturized applications of coercive power at the level of local landscapes within which these great works were meant to be seen.[119] The chief preconditions, then, were an ideology of state-building, and a rulership style.[120]

Two features of Charles's project distinguish it from the other three just mentioned. In the first place, both this project, and its political context, were well-documented at the time, whereas the textual sources in the other three cases are next to non-existent, and that inevitably weakens the case for ideological change. Secondly, and more important, Charles's project demonstrably relied on pre-existing practices and developments of complex engineering technology.[121] It was, in short, about a lot more than digging ditches, fundamental as that was. There is much evidence, in Bavaria and elsewhere, for pre-existing expertise in hydraulic engineering, notably in connection with the building of mills and their ancillary installations – leets, dams, weirs, mill-races and mill-ponds. 'Those who claimed to be knowledgable in such matters' may have included *agrimensores* (land-surveyors), whose skills had been transmitted from late antiquity.[122] They also included mill-builders, for whom monastic and secular lords provided capital and impetus.[123] Other hydraulic works in Charles's period included protective ditches at Regensburg, and extensive systems of water-supply at the palaces of Aachen and Ingelheim and the monastery of St-Denis.[124]

Modern historians have estimated that Charles's project employed 6,000 men for some three months.[125] Various motivations have been proposed. Fortunately, there is no need to choose *between* motives: Charles had in his head at one and the same time a number of motives. He was certainly interested in riverine traffic and trade, and especially so in a year of desperate famine in certain localities.[126] He was concerned in a general way about economic performance on his own estates, and on the lands of others, especially those who held benefices from him (the new coinage was in part designed to bring in more revenue for the king, and for elites).[127] In the early 790s, Charles also had military aims in view, as problems crowded in, both on the margins of the realm and at its heart. The campaigns of the early 790s had proved the value of waterborne forces and pontoon bridges. In 793, to bring the entire court in boats from Regensburg to the site of the canal was certainly a propaganda exercise but it was also a practical decision. At the end of that year, the court beat a retreat northwards – using boats. Ideological considerations, too, were never far from Charles's mind. The arrival – surely by appointment – at the digging-site of papal envoys bearing gifts was calculated to impress the envoys as well as to enhance the king's prestige and show his authority in Bavaria. Prayers and penances boosted morale, thereby helping to bring victory over the Avars in 791. If there was no mention of those in any annal for 793, that was because the aims of the canal-project were conceived in terms less of military needs than of providing more rapid communications and facilitating food transfers to large numbers of people. Charles was 'pressing ahead sedulously with the task above-named' (*praefato operi sedulus insistens*).[128] 'Sedulously pressing ahead' had its limits. 'Seeing like a state' meant, among other things, grasping how problems might occur *naturaliter*. Charles saw December 793 as a moment to cut his losses and stop groping in wintry murk. At that moment, perhaps the annal-writer, who attributed the diggers' problems not to any sign or portent or divinely sent chastisement, but rather to exceptionally rainy weather over many months, represented not just the writer's own view but that of Charles and his experts too.

There was more than met the eye to Charles's seeing like a state in the early 790s. The state that inspired him was the Christian Roman Empire: a very large state that depended crucially, like all empires, on management of food supplies. The spectre of famine dogged 'the biological *ancien régime*'.[129] The late antique Mediterranean world, notorious for the variability of its harvests due to climatic conditions, was liable everywhere (save Egypt with its guaranteed Nile flood) to suffer 'harvest shocks'.[130] Christian communities, as pagan ones had done before them, sought supernatural protection from 'hail, mildew, hurricanes, locusts, so that none of these plagues may attack this estate and the fruits that are all found there'.[131] The emperor's responsibility to protect and help all those under the empire's law was universally recognized.[132] The imperial virtue of *clementia* had been commended *c.*400 by the pagan poet Claudian as that 'which alone closes the gap between the gods and us'.[133] Augustine thought Christian emperors could be 'called happy if they compensate for whatever severe measures they may be forced to decree with the gentleness of mercy and the generosity of benevolence'.[134]

'Harvest shocks' were also a hazard in Charles's world, and there too the ruler's obligation to give help to the hungry was considered divinely imposed. Both the Lorsch Annals and the Mosel Annals mentioned a serious famine in Charles's realm in 792–3, first observable in Beneventan territory (*famis validissima*), then in Burgundy and Francia (*famis valida*), resulting in many deaths. Both these sets of annals mention first the famine, then, immediately after, Charles's canal-project. The Mosel Annals' author described 'a famine so great that it worsened during the months from later 792 and into 793', thus prompting the author to anticipate, exceptionally, the events of the following year.[135]

Juxtapositions in annals often seem intended to suggest causal connections. This is a striking case in point. It was – at least in part – because of this series of acute harvest shocks in regions which Charles considered of especial importance, that he made the decision to embark on the construction of the *fossatum magnum*. In other words, in addition to whatever economic and military considerations entered the frame, the project's raison d'être was to bring food-supplies as quickly as possible from a region unaffected by famine to famished Francia.

Euergetism, the performance of good deeds for public benefit, had motivated leaders and leading citizens in the Greco-Roman world. Euergetism worked in Charles's world by his enlisting of the service hierarchies of ecclesiastical and secular office-holders.[136] This had already become apparent in 779. The Second Capitulary of Herstal, which scholars formerly categorized as a set of episcopal *capitula*, has now been recognized as 'ecclesiastical and secular regulations combined, yet also differentiated', to cope with relief in 'this present famine' and 'for the starving poor' (*pauperes famelici*).[137] In 792/3, Charles's canal-project connected public works and public benefit, and pointed ahead to the Council of Frankfurt in 794.

Saxons, Saracens, Northmen and the Council of Frankfurt: 792–4

I. TROUBLE FROM SEVERAL SIDES

The evidence presented in the previous chapter focused on Bavaria and lands east of the Rhine. This chapter begins by focusing instead on problems affecting other, more northerly peripheries of Charles's realm. Annal-writers in 792 reported attacks by Frisians and Saxons.[1] The author of the Lorsch Annals railed against those peoples who had

> like a dog returning to his vomit [Prov. 26:11] reverted to paganism
> (*reversi sunt ad paganismum*) . . . breaking faith with God as well as with
> the lord king who had provided them with so many good things,
> and . . . sending their *missi* also to the Avars, they presumed to rebel, first
> against God, next against the king and the Christians.[2]

The positive notion of 'the faithful men of God and the king (*fideles Dei et regis*)' had here been spectacularly turned into a negative. Though scholars still argue about the identity of the author/patron of these annals, there remains a possibility, I think, that he was Ricbod, abbot of Lorsch from 784 and archbishop of Trier (791–804), who had strong contacts with the court but offered his own distinctive view.[3]

In 793, Charles had received 'two highly unwelcome reports from different parts of the world'. One report, recorded in the *ArF* and by those annals' reviser, had been brought to Charles in the autumn at the site of the great ditch by a *missus* who told of a 'general defection (*omnimoda defectio*) of Saxons'.[4] So serious was this that Charles 'abandoned his campaign in Pannonia while concealing the magnitude of the loss'. However general was the defection, some Saxons, especially in the north-east, were willing to attempt yet another bid to

The new coinage, 793.

recover their traditional freedoms. A second unwelcome report, recorded (surprisingly) in the Alamannic Annals, came from the Septimanian frontier: 'William [count of Toulouse] had fought Saracens at Narbonne and lost many men there and killed a king (*rex*) of theirs and a multitude of Saracens.'[5]

Another set of annals now enters the evidential frame: the *Chronicle of Moissac*, whose archetype was written contemporaneously in Septimania.[6] The archetype's author, showing a strong and well-informed interest in the politics of that region, added to the Alamannic Annals' information by saying that Hisham, amir of Córdoba (788–96) had known that Charles was preoccupied with beating the Avars in eastern Bavaria (more proof of lively communications in and beyond Charles's realm) and therefore seized the opportunity to attack Narbonne, 'torch its suburbs and capture many Christians and much booty'. Hisham had intended to lead his forces to Carcassonne, but William and other Frankish counts came out against them and engaged in a bloody battle at the river Orbiel, where

> the greatest part of the Christian people fell that day, though William himself fought bravely. But seeing that he could not hold them since his comrades (*socii*) abandoned him and fled, he broke away from them. And the Saracens collected the spoils and returned to Spain.[7]

Partly thanks to William's power-base and extensive political network in the south-west, religious houses in the region received support not just from the local aristocracy but from Charles himself.[8]

Raids by Northmen posed a new threat to Alcuin's Northumbria: the monastery of Lindisfarne off the Northumbrian coast was attacked on 8 June 793. Alcuin wrote from York to Bishop Higbald of Lindisfarne (who was also abbot), sharing his horror at this event: 'They desecrated God's sanctuary, shed the blood of holy men around the altar, laid waste the house of our hope, and trampled the bodies of the saints like dung in the streets.'[9] At the very end of a letter full of blood and guts, calls to repentance and appeals to Heaven, Alcuin abandoned his rhetorical fortissimo and struck, incongruously, a pragmatic note:

> When our lord king Charles returns home after subduing his enemies by God's mercy, we intend, with God's aid, to go to him. And if then we can provide help in any way about the boys [*pueri*, i.e. the child oblates or

young monks] who have been carried off by the pagans into captivity, or about any of your urgent needs, we shall diligently attend to putting such help into effect.

Charles had contacts of his own with Northmen already, and knew where in Scandinavia trading-centres were located.[10] Alcuin evidently hoped to get Charles to activate these contacts: in other words, to negotiate the ransom of the captive boys.[11] By 793, however, it was no longer so easy for Alcuin to enthuse, as he had done in 790, about the Church's 'prospering and growing in the regions of Europe, thanks to the numbers of Saxon and Frisian converts'.[12] Later in 793, Alcuin left Northumbria for Francia, never to return.

II. THE COUNCIL AT FRANKFURT:
CONTEXT AND TEXT

Inhabitants of 'the regions of Europe' knew they were under threat on several fronts. Charles's determination to mount a co-ordinated defence lay behind his summoning of another big council (*synodus magna*) in 794, reminiscent of the Regensburg council in combining 'a general assembly of his people' and 'a council (*concilium*) of bishops' working to a shared agenda.[13] The choice of Frankfurt was strategic. It was a hub of riverine and Roman-road communications, making access relatively easy, especially for participants from areas north of the Alps.[14] Remains of Roman occupation were visible in the local landscape, and documentary evidence shows the economic arrangements that had made it possible by the end of the eighth century for a substantial royal residence to be sustained by peasant holdings farming hundreds of acres.[15] By Easter 794 (24 March) Charles's plans were well underway; prospective participants had been notified, with instructions to reach the site in time for the council to begin formally in June. Frankfurt, undocumented till now, hit the written record. The earliest charter Charles issued from Frankfurt was for the monastery of St Emmeram, Regensburg, where Theodulf and his team of scribes toiled over the *Opus Caroli*.[16] Charles confirmed the jurisdiction of Bishop Dulcissimus of Ceneda in Friuli over carefully specified lands.[17] Pope Hadrian had sent two legates to represent him. (One of them was Theophylact of Todi, who in 786 had been Bishop George's colleague on the mission to Anglo-Saxon England.) Abbot Anianus of Caunes travelled from Septimania to Frankfurt with his monks: for them and for the recently founded monastery, Charles issued a grant of protection in July 'in the Frankfurt palace'.[18] Alcuin, perhaps colluding with Northmen rather than braving them, had arrived from Northumbria.[19] The Council assembled 'at the beginning of summer'.[20] Bishops from Francia and Bavaria, and Italy, were present, but because the extant documentation consists of a capitulary rather than a full set of conciliar *acta*, their names are not recorded. It was the *ArF* reviser who noted that 'the heresy of Felix was condemned and a book against it composed on the joint authority of the bishops, who all subscribed it with their own hands'.[21]

The short preface to the Capitulary of Frankfurt itself stated that 'all the bishops and *sacerdotes* of the kingdom of the Franks, and of Italy, Aquitaine and Provence, were gathered together with divine favour, by apostolic authority, and at the command of our most pious lord king Charles in the 26th year of his *principatus*.'[22] Later, claims would be made for an attendance of 300 bishops, from 'all the provinces'. This figure was much inflated: there were only some 130 bishops in the entire Frankish Empire, bar northern Italy.[23] It was, nevertheless, as the *ArF* author said, a 'great council', directed and animated by Charles.

III. THE ILLNESS AND DEATH
OF FASTRADA

There was, I think, another reason for Charles's choice of venue. Fastrada had been at Frankfurt since at least Easter. Her queenly performance at Regensburg had impressed. She proved able to hold court on her own, in a social sense and in a judicial sense too:

> when Fastrada the queen of our lord Charles had come from Bavaria to winter at Frankfurt, Hortlaich was slain in her presence by mischance because before this Hortlaich had slain a man named Ruotmund, and for this reason all his property which he had at . . . had been resumed into the public fisc.[24]

This episode had evidently occurred before Charles arrived, and Fastrada had settled the case. More than just an adjunct or ornament to her husband, she had assumed at Frankfurt, in Charles's absence, political importance in her own right. Once Charles had joined her, the council's siting was settled. The participants came to Frankfurt not only because Charles was there but because Fastrada was too.[25]

Fastrada's illness proved fatal. 'There Queen Fastrada died' in the middle of the summer dogdays on 10 August.[26] She was buried with honours at St Alban's, Mainz on 12 August after her body had been brought there by boat. Archbishop Riculf, probably her kinsman and ally, presumably officiated in his own church.[27] Her epitaph was written by Theodulf. Its brevity may come as a surprise, by contrast with Hildegard's lengthy one:

> *Inclita Fastradae reginae hic membra quiescunt,*
> *De medio quam mors frigida flora tulit;*
> *Nobilis ipsa viri thalamo coniuncta potentis*
> *Sed modo caelesti nobilior thalamo.*
> *Pars animae melior, Carolus rex ipse remansit;*
> *Cui tradit mitis tempora larga deus.*
> (Here lie the renowned remains of Queen Fastrada
> Whom cold death carried off in mid-flowering.
> Noble herself, she was wed to a powerful man,
> But now, nobler still, she is married to a heavenly bridegroom.
> The better part of her soul, King Charles is still with us;
> To whom may merciful God grant a long life.)[28]

The citation from Ovid at line 5 (*pars animae melior*) is given a twist that disparages her and elevates Charles in both the Latin version and in the English translation: *Pars animae melior, Carolus rex ipse remansit,* 'The better part of her soul, King Charles himself is still with us'.

Einhard's assertions about Fastrada's cruelty have predisposed older generations of scholars to disparage her; and the brevity of Theodulf's poem has been interpreted as the result of his dislike of the queen. Neither reading is acceptable. Charles himself commissioned Theodulf to write the epitaph. The late Franz Staab's solution to the conundrum was to revisit the punctuation at lines 4–5. Try placing a comma instead of a full-stop after *thalamo* in line 4, a full-stop after *melior* in line 5 and, again in l. 5, a comma instead of a semi-colon after *remansit*. The result connects Fastrada with Christ as her heavenly bridegroom, and clearly differentiates the royal widower, Charles.[29] A likely explanation for the epitaph's brevity is that it was destined to be an inscription on a stone slab or gravestone: Riculf, as well as Charles, wanted St Alban's in Mainz to house Fastrada's remains.[30]

IV. CHARLES 'SUDDENLY SURGING' TO CONFRONT HERESY AT FRANKFURT*

The eye-witness testimony of Bishop Paulinus of Aquileia captured a memorable moment:[31]

> On a certain day, while all the bishops had taken their seats in the hall of the sacred palace, and the priests, deacons and all the clergy were standing around them in the shape of a crown, a letter was brought into the presence of the *princeps* aforementioned: it had been sent by Elipand, archbishop of Toledo and territory adjoining, the author of this whole irregular business. When the letter had been read out in public on the king's orders, the venerable *princeps*, suddenly surging from his royal throne (*statim surgens . . . de sella regia*), took his stand on its step, delivered a long speech about the matter of Faith, and then added: 'How does all this look to you? From the year before this one, when from the boil of perfidy this plague began with swelling madness to bubble up and spread more widely, so much error has become rooted in these [Pyrenean] regions, far away though they are on the extreme boundaries of our realm: error which must be cut down by the censure of Faith with every possible means.'[32]

Though Paulinus, leader and spokesman of the bishops of the kingdom of Italy, was hardly in a position to lecture anyone on verbosity (*prolixus sermo*), he preserved a vignette of Charles at Frankfurt: a physical force radiating energy, a man of power loudly demanding his hearers' response to his interrogative barrage.[33]

The first item in the Capitulary, and the substance of c. 1, was the condemnation of 'the abominable heresy of Elipand, bishop of Toledo, and Felix bishop of Urgell, and their disciples, who, with wicked opinion, asserted adoption in the Son of God'.[34] The assembled bishops

---

* My translation of *statim surgens*, 'suddenly surging', is idiosyncratic but gives a sense of Charles's physical dynamism.

'rejected and unanimously denied adoption, and decreed that this heresy must be wholly eradicated from the holy church'.[35]

The Capitulary's second item was

> the recent question of the synod of the Greeks . . . concerning the adoration of images and in which it was set down in writing that they judged anathema those who did not devote worship and adoration to the images of the saints as to the Holy Trinity. Our above-mentioned holy fathers completely rejected and scorned such adoration and worship and agreed in condemning it.[36]

A strong theme in the Franks' self-representation since the 740s had been their special status vis-à-vis other peoples, as 'immune from heresy'.[37] In Charles's reign, followers of so-called Adoptionism and allegedly icon-adoring Greeks lent themselves to being classed as heretics; and, in what was for Charles a virtuous circle, it became easy to take on the role of a Christian Roman emperor in the line from Theodosius and Justinian as defender against heresy of all those peoples and provinces over whom he ruled. In the preface to the *Opus Caroli* (written by Theodulf), Charles declared himself 'at God's command, king of the Franks and with God's help ruler of the Gauls, Germany and Italy and the provinces adjacent to those'. At Frankfurt, 'the most pious lord king Charles in the 26th year of his *principatus* gathered together all the bishops and *sacerdotes* of the kingdom of the Franks and of Italy, Aquitaine and Provence'. Since one way of defining an empire in early medieval times was as 'rule over many provinces', these statements already rang with an imperial tone.[38]

V. CLOSING THE CASE OF TASSILO

It was six years since Tassilo and his family had been unceremoniously removed from power in Bavaria. Tassilo himself had personally requested not to be publicly tonsured in a ritual of humiliation before being consigned to a monastery. A similar fate had been visited upon his wife Liutperga, his two sons and his two daughters. Tassilo did not remain long out of Charles's mind. On 3 January 791 at Worms, Charles had responded to a request of Abbot Fater of Kremsmünster, a monastery founded by Tassilo in 777 in the easternmost part of Bavaria, some 35km from Lorch on the Danube and a similar distance from the Enns. Fater had shown Charles the original document of Tassilo's endowment. Already, it was clear that because of Tassilo's absence, locals in Bavaria were engaged in land-clearance using Slav immigrant labour, without ducal licence. As Fater put it, '*now*, the monastery's hold on Tassilo's endowment could in no way be thought firm or stable'.[39] Fater could well have foreseen that the campaign Charles planned for the coming year would involve his army going all too near Kremsmünster, as indeed it did.[40] Fater's request evoked swift action from Charles. He took Tassilo's charter and, using a royal notary, incorporated its words into a new one of his own. In that case, Charles was indeed Tassilo's successor.

Pippin son of Himiltrud had gathered some Bavarian support for his revolt. After the rebels had accepted defeat, Charles needed to show willing in 'the integration of Bavarian property-owners into Carolingian hegemony'.[41] Obviously that was bound to be a long-term process. Meanwhile, though, the king wanted a more comprehensive, public and ceremonious statement to the effect that integration was already under way. Frankfurt provided the opportunity for just such a statement, with text in triplicate.

Heretics and icon-adorers had been condemned in cc. 1 and 2. Item 3 was 'a *capitulum* decided upon concerning Tassilo, previously duke of Bavaria, and the cousin of the lord king Charles'. It described how the king had stage-managed Tassilo's confession and renunciation and Charles's own demonstration of forgiveness, grace and loving-kindness.

> He stood in the middle of the most holy council, and begged forgiveness for the offences (*culpae*) he had committed, both what he had committed in the time of the lord king Pippin against him and the kingdom of the Franks [note that these are unspecified here], and those offences he had committed later, under our most merciful lord king Charles, in which he had proved himself to have been a betrayer of his own faith. He was seen to ask, with a humble request, that he might receive pardon from the king, and for his part, he manifestly put aside, in a sincere spirit, all anger and embitterment, and whatever with his own knowledge he had perpetrated against the king. Furthermore, he abandoned and renounced and, to avoid all future dispute, surrendered irrevocably all rights and allodial

property [i.e. inherited property, held by a person in full right] whatsoever in the duchy of the Bavarians which ought lawfully to have belonged to him or to his sons or daughters, commending all these to the king's mercy. And our lord, therefore, moved by mercy, forgave the afore-mentioned Tassilo with a willing spirit the offences he had committed, and fully granted this graciously and with charity and was seen to have received him with loving-kindness so that hereafter he would remain secure in God's mercy. He ordered that three copies should be made of this *capitulum* in identical wording: one to be kept in the palace; the second to be given to Tassilo to keep with him in the monastery; and the third he ordered to be kept securely in the chapel of the sacred palace.

This has been interpreted as another show-trial to follow up that of 788. But, in fact, the synodal setting and staging, and the quasi-penitential tone of the proceedings, strongly indicate that Charles was presenting something new that he was in a position to impose.

The contemporary author of the Lorsch Annals offers a different take from that of Charles and his advisers: 'Tassilo came to this synod and there he made peace with the lord king (*pacificavit ibi cum domno rege*), renouncing all the power he had in Bavaria and transferring it to the lord king.' This author, who had connections with the court but was not writing to Charles's orders, assigned Tassilo in 794 more agency, suggesting active conciliation, and concern for conflict-avoidance in the future.[42] This could not be described as a show-trial, or even a political quick fix. It was an exceptional performance.

Neither the court-based author of the *ArF* nor the annals' reviser had a word to say about Tassilo's appearance at Frankfurt in 794. 'The sources' distorting mirror' had much to answer for.[43] But so did Charles, since the silence of the *ArF* in 794 can only have occurred on Charles's orders, leaving the *ArF*'s record of 788 to stand as a fair account of crime and punishment. The *Capitulum* differentiated between a historic offence against Pippin – the abandoning of the army (*herisliz*) in 763 – and a recent, specific and heinous betrayal of faith to Charles in 788.[44] Here was the finale of generations of struggle between two powerful families, Agilolfings and Arnulfings.[45] Here, at the same time, began a new phase in Charles's expansionary project: one which presupposed the integration of Bavaria into Charles's *regnum*, and, even more striking and innovative, Charles's control of the media on which integration depended. Though Tassilo's myth proved lasting, especially in Bavaria, his history ended at Frankfurt.

VI. THE REST OF THE FRANKFURT AGENDA

Grain prices

One of the most surprising features of the conciliar decrees of Frankfurt is Charles's legislation on grain prices in c. 4:

> No one, whether ecclesiastic or layman is ever, in time either of abundance or of scarcity to sell corn at a higher price [than that now established]––

> 1d. per measure of oats
> 2d. per measure of barley
> 3d. per measure of rye
> 4d. per measure of wheat

> But if anyone wants to sell in the form of bread––

> 1d. for 12 wheat-loaves, each weighing 2 lb.
> 1d. for 15 rye-loaves, each weighing 2 lb.
> 1d. for 20 barley loaves, each of 2 lb.
> 1d. for 25 oat loaves, each of 2 lb.

> But for the grain stocks of the lord king, if this be sold––

> 2 measures of oats for 1d. [i.e. a half-penny per measure]
> 1 measure of barley for 1d.
> 1 measure of rye for 2d.
> 1 measure of wheat for 3d.

What this meant was that the king sold his grain at prices at least a quarter lower than those stipulated above.[46]

> Whoever holds a benefice of ours is to take diligent care that . . . none of the *mancipia* belonging to that benefice dies of hunger. And the benefice-holder is to sell whatever is surplus to the needs of those dependants, according to the above law.[47]

Famine was clearly the context here. As soon as Charles came up with capitularies of his own, he was keen to require and regulate public services.[48] In 779, in the Capitulary of Herstal, to the duties of prayer and supplication on behalf of the king and the army of the Franks was added relief 'of the present famine', while monetary payments were to be given by bishops, abbots and abbesses as well as counts and *vassi dominici*, to provide alms for the *pauperes familici*, 'the starving poor'. This theme recurred in subsequent *capitula* as well. The Double Capitulary for the *missi* was the immediate follow-up to the *Admonitio generalis*: it was issued at Aachen on 23 March 789, and widely disseminated. Its thirty-seven *capitula* covered a very wide range of topics, from the form of the oath of fidelity 'which men have to swear to us and our sons' (c. 18) to the requirement of universal Sunday church-attendance (c. 25) and the prohibition of such practices as baptizing bells and hanging invocations against hailstorms up on poles (c. 34).[49] Famine was not an issue between 780 and 792, but widespread *tribulatio* and suffering struck again in 793–4. The Frankfurt *capitula* were aimed at, *inter alia*, relief for the starving poor.

The coinage reform

A strong case has recently been made for dating the coinage reform legislated for at Frankfurt in July 794, to between late 792 and late 793. The grounds for the re-dating consist of numismatic and manuscript evidence, and historical context.[50] In c. 5 of the Capitulary of Frankfurt, Charles's *novi denarii*, new pennies, were mentioned for the first time. This 'confirmed or elaborated' measures already decided on at Regensburg. It also provided 'additional financial resources' for the king's current and future projects.[51]

C. 5 made obligatory the use of the new coinage, and penalized anyone who rejected it. It presupposed a circulation 'through every city and every trading-place'. Its impact, though hard to document in the short term, is traceable through economic and social relations in the longer term.[52] A strong ideological message, already purveyed long since in Late Roman law, was reinforced in a collection of legal texts copied out in 793, specifically in passages directed at corrupt officials and those who issued false coins.[53] Pitted against those is *nostrum edictum*, 'our edict', with the reference clearly to the royal 'we'.

Points of canon law

Cc. 6–10 recorded deliberations and decisions made by king and synod together on points of canon law and judgments. Cc. 6 and 7 echoed Charles's earlier capitularies; cc. 8, 9 and 10 recorded decisions made in particular cases – one of them, c. 9, that of Bishop Peter of Verdun. Accused of treason through complicity in the plot of Pippin son of Himiltrud in 792, Peter had sworn 'in the presence of God and his angels', and, with two or three others, that 'he had not conspired against the life of the king, or ever been unfaithful', but he had been unable to provide witnesses to the oath and so chose 'one of his men' to undertake an ordeal to prove, vicariously, the bishop's innocence, which the man successfully did. The synod granted pardon to the bishop on the grounds that someone who faced the ordeal did so of his own will (*spontanea voluntas*), without orders from king or synod. Despite the synod's constant appeal to canonical tradition, Frankish churchmen in the eighth century were in practice finding their own solutions to political problems.

789's legacy embedded in 794's legislation

In the wake of the *Admonitio generalis* of 789 came two other documents. One was the *Duplex legationis edictum*, a summary list of thirty-seven points, of which cc. 1–16 were exclusively concerned with monks and the monastic life and largely borrowed from the Rule of St Benedict, while cc. 17–37 contained a mix of clerical, monastic and secular measures, including (c. 18) the formula for an oath of fidelity to be given to Charles and his sons. The other document was a ten-point memorandum for Charles's *missi* in Aquitaine, mentioning in the very brief prologue that these *missi* had been charged with organizing oaths of fidelity. Thereafter the text consisted of Pippin's Aquitanian capitulary of early 768, which Charles had re-issued in 769, and three *capitula* from the 779 Capitulary of Herstal, all these put in as a checklist to answer Charles's question, 'how have our own edicts been observed?' 'Learning to use capitularies', as Jenny Davis engagingly puts it, presupposed the existence of texts in this legislative format. There were indeed a few Frankish capitularies before Charles, but it must be said that in Charles's reign the Franks were slow learners, compared with the Italians.[54] This limited the material on which those present at Frankfurt in July 794 could draw.

The Capitulary of Frankfurt turned out to mark a further steep rise in the learning-curve. The opening cc. 1–5 dealt with what Charles prioritized as major issues of religious teaching and political and governmental strategy; cc. 6 and 7 highlighted the importance of bishops in delivering justice and stabilizing the Church in the realm; cc. 8–10 dealt with particular legal cases, and the final two, cc. 55 and 56, were the result of exceptional interventions by Charles himself to secure the services and ongoing support of leading ecclesiastical advisers and his personal teachers, Archbishop Hildebald of Cologne and Alcuin.[55] The remaining forty-four *capitula* were overwhelmingly drawn from the *Admonitio generalis* (thirty) and other capitularies produced in 789 (seven, including c. 15 quoted from c. 7 of the *Duplex legationis edictum* and c. 26, which referenced c. 2 of the *Breviarium* of the Aquitanian *missi*).[56] Finally there were eight new *capitula* (cc. 12, 17, 26, 29, 38, 47, 52 and 54), to which I'll return.

It was entirely in keeping with Charles's efforts in having the *Admonitio* compiled and diffused in 789 that the Frankfurt synod included so many of the *Admonitio*'s *capitula*, and that these insisted so firmly on ecclesiastical action, and especially, if not always explicitly, the action of bishops, abbots and abbesses. To say that Frankfurt 'reveals the enormous extent to which the Church . . . had come to serve as an instrument of power of the king' is certainly one way of looking at all this. But the historian who recognizes Charles's power also appreciates 'what a diligent defender of the faith he himself was'.[57]

Amplifiying c. 42 of the *Admonitio*, 'To bishops. Further, that false names of martyrs and uncertain shrines of saints are not to be venerated', are the voices that resound most loudly in the corresponding c. 42 of the Frankfurt *capitula*:

> That no new saints are to be venerated or invoked and no shrines for them are to be put up at roadsides; but those alone are to be venerated in the Church who have been deservedly chosen on the authority of their *Passiones* (Accounts of the deaths of martyrs) or their *Vitae* (Lives).[58]

Who controlled the shrines? 'Sanctity could be an effective agent in the reinforcement of power only if there was a genuine belief in its efficacy.'[59] In the case of the convent of Chelles, for example, the power reinforced was not only that of the saint(s) but also that of Gisela, sister of Charles, custodian of an exceptionally large relic-collection, and proponent of dynastic power through the family narrative, the so-called *Annales Mettenses Priores*.[60] Part of Charles's own power resided in his own relic-collection, from which he dispensed choice gifts to those in charge, episcopal or abbatial, at Sens and St-Riquier as well as Chelles.[61] 'Control' is a diffuse notion whence power, easily tapped into, easily seeps out. Charles, an alert observer of the contemporary scene, did not need a crystal ball to foresee the scale of the growth of relic-acquisition and relic-transfers in the years after 794, and the role of bishops and abbots in these, as interested parties.[62]

Innovations

Another side of Charles's religion emerges in the eight new Frankfurt *capitula*: 'new' because they make their first appearance here. Take c. 52: 'Let nobody believe that God can only be prayed to in the three languages [i.e. the languages of Scripture, Hebrew, Greek and Latin], because God can be adored and man listened to in every language if he asks for things that are just.'

This last phrase 'seems to represent ethic, inner meaning and right intention in Charlemagne's concept of prayer'.[63] To infer Charles's personal religion from a *capitulum* in a set of synodal rules and regulations may be an imaginative bridge too far; but there is enough evidence that Charles *had* a personal religion, and a voice of his own, to tempt me, at least, to find and cross that bridge, and hear that voice, a voice that has echoed in preceding chapters, and will echo again, only more loudly, in the final chapters of this book.

Then there is c. 54: 'Concerning churches that are built by free men, it is permitted to give these away, or to sell them, provided they are not destroyed as churches but the churches' services (*honores*) are performed every day.' This is pragmatic, and respectful, and says something about the religion of such free men in Charles's world.

Frankfurt c. 47 is another of the 'new' *capitula*, presented here partly because a gender-loaded statement is always worth investigating, and partly because, if not exactly echoing the *Admonitio generalis* c. 74 there is some connection, indicating – yet again – the importance of the *Admonitio* for Frankish canon law in and after Charles's reign.[64] *Admonitio* c. 74 is addressed to bishops and abbots:

> To bishops, to abbots. It has been heard that certain abbesses, against the custom of God's holy Church, give blessings by the laying-on of hands and making the sign of the cross on the heads of men . . . Know, most holy fathers, that this is to be utterly forbidden in your dioceses.[65]

Frankfurt c. 47 could be seen as condemning conduct similarly forbidden: 'Concerning abbesses who live neither in houses of canonesses nor follow a nuns' Rule, bishops must hold inquiries and report [these women] to the king, so that they can be deprived of their office (*honor*).'[66] Co-operation between king and bishops and a shared hard line were the prescribed solution to such irregularities.

An abbess, possibly suspect ('it has been heard . . .') as a wielder of authority, perhaps an exception that proved the rule, was one of Charles's contemporaries and well-known to him. This was Leoba, a confidante of his wife Hildegard. Leoba's hagiographer recalled that when a terrible storm threatened her church, in which she and her nuns and all the local people had taken refuge,

> she rose from prayer, threw off her cloak, boldly opened the church-doors and, standing on the threshold made the sign of the cross opposing to the fury of the storm the name of the High God, stretched out her hand to heaven and thrice invoked Christ's mercy . . .

and God came to their aid, and the storm was stilled.[67]

VII. WAS FRANKFURT 'A HIDDEN FAILURE'?

It is possible to regard Frankfurt as something of a damp squib after the pyrotechnics of 789. Compare and contrast the thirty-six manuscripts of the *Admonitio generalis* with the two manuscripts of the Capitulary of Frankfurt! Yet some of the most important capitularies are extant in only one manuscript: no. 25, the *Capitulare Missorum* with its vivid evocation of the mechanics of an oath-swearing; no. 26, the *Capitulatio de Partibus Saxoniae*; no. 29, the *Epistola de litteris colendis*; no. 33, which F.-L. Ganshof christened 'the Programmatic Capitulary' of 802; and no. 32, the *Capitulare de Villis*. In what Marc Bloch called 'the residue of the fortuitous', scarcity of copies may be inversely correlated with what a scholar rates as a manuscript's importance.[68] Partly because it drew on other much more widely circulated texts, especially the *Admonitio generalis*, partly because other conciliar texts – those of Reisbach/Freising (799) and Salzburg (802/3) – and the *Chronicle of Moissac*, cross-referenced it, the Capitulary of Frankfurt retained its place in canonical tradition.[69] Because Hincmar of Reims drew on it and some other texts received at or sent out from Frankfurt in 794, it had an afterlife in the ninth century.

Frankfurt's very last two *capitula*, cc. 55 and 56, turned out to be immensely significant. In c. 55, Charles announced that he had arranged, with papal agreement, that Archbishop Hildebald of Cologne should remain permanently at the court (de facto the king's main residence was now Aachen) to meet the needs of the church (*propter utilitates ecclesiae*) as head of the royal chapel. Though seldom at Cologne, Hildebald had many books copied for the cathedral library. Largest and greatest was the copy of Augustine's *Commentaries on the Psalms* made at Hildebald's request by the nuns of Chelles, who were fine copyists. The archbishop was something of a polymath, interested in chronological calculations, and in the architectural calculations involved in getting a fine new cathedral built at Cologne. He was Charles's *familiarissimus pontifex*, the closest to him of all his bishops.[70]

Even closer to Charles at this time in his life was Alcuin. Charles's acquaintance with Alcuin had begun when they met in Parma in 781: Alcuin was on the return-journey from Rome where he had collected the *pallium*, the symbol of office, for Eanbald, the new archbishop of York, and Charles and his family were heading Rome-wards to negotiate with Pope Hadrian the establishment of kingdoms for his two younger sons. Alcuin played a key role in the legatine mission masterminded by Charles in 786, and then he was recruited, via the good offices of Bishop George of Amiens, to join Charles's court. He stayed for a little over three years. For Alcuin, those years were formative, and creative. He learned the ways and means of the court, as it moved from one Frankish palace to another, and he experienced, with some relief perhaps, Charles's absences in Italy and in Bavaria. He wrote poetry, and biblical exegesis; in the winter of 788–9, at Aachen and again at Charles's beck and call, he wrote most of the *Admonitio*; after the court had spent Christmas at Worms, he returned, early in 790, to York, to his *patria*, where for another three years he tried to navigate the treacherous currents of Northumbrian politics, with little success. A letter to Gisela early in 793, responding to one from her assuring him that their *familiaritas* and bond of love remained ever-firm, begged her for the protection of her prayers now that he was about to embark on the crossing of the stormy sea.[71] Eventually he returned to Francia and a quieter life at an unrecorded place, perhaps not far from Chelles.[72] He sent a string of agonized letters of admonition to various Northumbrians, following the Viking raid on Lindisfarne of 8 June 793, advising kings and laity as well as clergy to repent and reflect.[73]

Charles recommended Alcuin to the synod at Frankfurt, and saw to his enlistment into the prayer-brotherhood of the bishops, on the grounds that he was 'a man learned in ecclesiastical doctrines'.[74] Charles was a shrewd appraiser. Many modern historians of medieval philosophy have rated Alcuin as 'not at all a thinker in his own right'.[75] What was wanted, though, was a great teacher – and a teacher of laymen, including Charles himself. In 794 Alcuin wrote *De Rhetorica* in the classical form of a dialogue.[76] The speakers were called 'Karlus' and 'Albinus' (Alcuin's nickname). It was intended as a basic textbook, therefore part of the Trivium, the lower stage of the student's curriculum. Alcuin drew heavily on the works of two Roman authors, Cicero (106–43 BC), whose *De Inventione* ('On the Composition of Arguments') was, speeches and letters apart, the earliest of his writings, and Julius Victor (fourth century AD), whose *Ars Rhetorica* ('The Art of Rhetoric') was strongly influenced by the rhetorician Quintilian (d. *c.*AD 95).

In the *De Rhetorica*'s opening words, put into the mouth of Karlus: 'God led you, and brought you back [to Francia], O revered master Albinus.'[77] Between them, God and Charles had ensured Alcuin's presence in 794 at Frankfurt, where the writing of the *De Rhetorica* could start. Karlus as a character in a dialogue should be differentiated from the historical Charles. Nevertheless, given the similitude between the two, it could be said that Alcuin made Karlus a stand-in for the king. Karlus begins by saying that he wanted to question his teacher about the rules of the art of rhetoric,

> for I remember you once said that the strength of this art lay entirely in dealing with public questions (*civiles quaestiones*) . . . We are constantly having to busy ourselves with questions of this kind; and it seems ridiculous not to know about the rules of an art when the necessity of using it confronts us every day.[78]

Following more or less word-for-word an origin myth told by Cicero in his *De Inventione*, Albinus retells a 'once upon a time':

> People wandered about, doing nothing by the reasoning power of the mind and everything by sheer brute strength . . . At a certain point in time, there was a great and wise man who understood how much capacity for the highest things inhered in the minds of humankind if only someone were able to elicit it . . . By force of reason he collected human beings into one place instead of being scattered . . . and he assembled them all together and led them into everything that was useful and honourable. At first they protested, but then they listened eagerly, and because of his reason (*ratio*) and eloquence (*oratio*) they listened more attentively, and from being savage and brutal they became gentle and mild.[79]

Karlus was the avatar of 'the great and wise man'.

After explaining that the objective of rhetoric is the art of speaking well, Albinus continues: 'Rhetoric is concerned with public questions (*civiles quaestiones*)', and Karlus in next to no time has grasped rhetoric's remit: 'concern with legal cases and public questions'.[80] The rest of the dialogue sets out a series of categories and types of questions, and, using examples from biblical and classical history, Albinus differentiates between the just and the unjust. Further on, he explains how to arouse emotions, how to elicit sympathy in an audience, and how important is the role of style (*elocutio*), of being fluent and open (*facunda, aperta*), and of using figurative terms because they expose meaning more clearly.[81] Karlus, following Cicero, deems memory 'the noblest part of rhetoric', to which Albinus responds that 'if memory could not be trained to be the storehouse of thoughts and experiences, the speaker's other talents will come to nothing . . . Delivery (*pronuntiatio*) must be in accord with the speaker's subject, and so too must bodily gestures, and [what would nowadays be called] his look.' Karlus sees 'how necessary it is that training at home (*domesticus usus*) should begin to provide what a public assembly (*publicus conventus*) will later require.'[82]

Finally, the Christian religion must celebrate virtue: 'religion is an attribute of justice which is a disposition of the mind to give each his due. The worship of God, the laws of humanity, and the principle of equity in all of life, are preserved in this virtue.'[83] The dialogue ends where it began, with Albinus's assertion that 'this dialogue of ours had its origin in the changing abilities involved in civil questions, and finished in changeless stability.' The last word is Karlus's and takes the form of a rhetorical question: 'Who could dare to say that we have talked in vain?'[84]

Alcuin's *De Rhetorica* is a work curiously seldom cited or discussed in modern scholarship until very recently. Of its twenty-six extant manuscripts, twenty date from the ninth and tenth centuries.[85] Rhetoric was about more than style or look: its basic meaning was the *vis persuadendi*, the power of persuasion, and it was to be used in public speech about civil questions, where men used the knowledge of speaking not correctly (*recte*) but well (*bene*).[86] This immediately introduced an ethical dimension. 'The art of speaking well (*bene*) . . . is concerned in public questions . . . as can be inferred from natural disposition of the mind.'[87] 'According to Julius Victor . . . "civil affairs", defined as those matters on which everyone with any intellectual capacity can speak and judge . . . [could] cover anything in fact, which is open to accusation, defence or simply debate over its equity and utility.'[88]

Alcuin's knowledge of rhetoric and its uses was not just acquired from residence in Francia and readings of Cicero and Julius Victor. He was himself an experienced assembly man in Anglo-Saxon contexts, through participation at Northumbrian moots and synods, including the well-documented Legatine Synod of 786. Charles too had several decades of assembly experience behind him. Working on the *De Rhetorica* brought teacher and king together in thinking hard about the art of persuasion. In 794, that art met life. Rhetoric was key to the discourse of assembly politics, as practised in Charles's reign (and in Francia for generations before that): 'politics [were] conducted *through* assemblies and . . . *at* assemblies'.[89] Frankfurt, I infer, inspired Alcuin to write *De Rhetorica*. The collaboration between 'Karlus' and 'Albinus' might have been imaginary, but the work itself contributed something to Charles's real-life practice of assembly politics, especially once Aachen became a more regular place for king and court to reside. After his imperial coronation, legislative activity gained a new scale and momentum.[90] These are trends to be explored further. But to end this chapter, I would like to answer the question posed in the heading above: 'Was Frankfurt a hidden failure?' Johannes Fried has not put this as a question: rather he has stated it as a fact: 'A Hidden Failure: The Synod of Frankfurt'.[91] I would like to answer my own question with a resounding 'No'. And I hope that with a little help from Alcuin among others, I have explained why.

12

The Beginning of the End of the Saxon Wars: 792–9

This chapter will begin with some recapitulation. In 785, the author of the *ArF* entry that year had ended with the words *et tunc tota Saxonia subiugata est* ('and then the whole of Saxony was subjugated'). Did Franks breathe a sigh of relief at this news? Did they at the same time mutter to themselves that subjugation might not be a stable state, and that the phrase *tota Saxonia* could give a false impression of homogeneity? In the autumn of 793, Charles had received news of a 'wholesale defection of Saxons' (*Saxonum omnimoda defectio*).[1] Neither the *ArF* author nor the reviser offered further comment – and yet the news blasted the hopes of 785. Wholesale defection may not have come as much of a surprise to Charles and his court in Bavaria. Rumours crossed borders easily. And yet, unfaithful Saxons in Rüstringen on the northern frontiers (in modern Friesland) were one thing; unfaithful Saxons in the area south of Paderborn (in modern North-Rhine Westphalia) were quite another. The *ArF* author (now writing contemporaneously) described events in the wild north and noted conflict not just between but *within* peoples in 792: 'Saxons killed Franks on the river Elbe, near the sea, on Friday, 6 July';[2] 'Saxons, Slavs and part of the Frisians (*Fresi ex parte*) rebelled.'[3]

Writing 'the Saxons' and 'the Franks' (as you might write 'the Vikings') is misleading in another way, because it implies that Saxons, or Franks, were, or thought of themselves as, homogeneous. They were, on the contrary, internally divided or separable. The identity of a group, or a *gens*, was *variously* represented by the men and women who belonged to it, and it was expressed orally.[4] When Einhard highlighted Charles's wearing of the *vestitus patrius*, 'the clothing of his [Frankish] fatherland', was he by any chance criticizing those Frankish aristocrats

The church at Aachen.

who *didn't* wear it?[5] On the subject of cultural difference between Saxons and Franks, the dictum of a modern historian, already quoted, is worth repeating: 'Saxon society and culture corresponded in no way to those of the Franks, and it was therefore difficult for the Franks to get a handle on this enemy.'[6] A single anecdote from 775, in which Saxons and Franks are juxtaposed, raises immediate doubts about the dictum's accuracy. To recall, and summarize very briefly: Saxons sneaked into the Frankish camp along with a group of Frankish foragers one summer-day at siesta-time and then started slaughtering the snoozing Franks. The inference surely is that those Saxons and Franks did not look very different, or act very differently, from each other, whether in terms of dress, facial hair or weapons.[7] That inference is further strengthened by studies of relevant archaeological material and displays of recent finds in great German exhibitions.[8]

Historians continue to argue over ethnic identities in the early Middle Ages.[9] In the case of Saxons in the eighth century, the lack of written evidence provided by Saxons themselves is a problem. A written narrative about Saxons was constructed by Franks, all of them churchmen. The most striking presentation of the narrative in the 790s was written by the author of the Lorsch Annals. His voice echoed the concerns of the court in the late 790s about how Saxons were to be dealt with. This chapter will explore how relations between Franks and Saxons evolved between 792 and 799, when Charles saw the prospect of a *Christianus populus* unfolding, and being given meaning and impetus by the formation of a court.

In 794, a Saxon campaign had had to be postponed. By August 794, however, the 'great assembly' at Frankfurt was over, and Queen Fastrada had died and been buried. Charles without delay announced plans for a two-pronged attack on Saxony, one *turma* (cavalry-battalion) to be led by himself, the other by his namesake, the Young Charles, who had perhaps already been at Frankfurt with his father. In the event, the Saxons targeted by Charles and his son declined battle and gave hostages (*obsides*) and oaths instead. Charles returned to Aachen, and for the first time since 788 wintered there. This set the pattern for 794-5, 795-6 and 796-7. In 797-8, breaking the emerging pattern, 'Charles in November entered Saxony', presumably with an army, 'and spent the whole winter settling affairs in Saxony'. In 798-9 he wintered at Aachen again.

I. THE PATHOLOGICAL VOCABULARY
OF ANGER

In a stimulating article in a volume entitled *Anger's Past*, a German scholar argued that 'the principal sources for the history of Charlemagne . . . have no place for royal anger. Just the opposite.'[10] It's true that the *ArF* author dwelt on Charles's mercifulness (*clementia*), and his gentleness (he was frequently described as *mitissimus*, most mild): these were stock items in the ideological toolkit of Charles and his son Louis. In some other texts, however, Charles was shown in real-life circumstances displaying anger, especially when confronted by opposition. How else to describe his reaction in 786 to Hardrad's revolt: 'mightily angered' (*iratus est valde*)? Or his meting-out of condign punishment of rebels by blinding them?[11] Or his response to the discovery in 792 that a very large number of the most noble Franks, younger men or older, were in league with his rebellious son, Pippin son of Himiltrud, after which 'some were hanged, some beheaded, some flogged and exiled'?[12] Or in 798 his being violently angry (*graviter commotus*) on getting news of the killing by Saxons of his officer Gottschalk?[13] Or in 801 his sending of a wrathful letter to Alcuin and the Tours community accusing *them* of anger?[14]

From 795, a vocabulary of devastation began to spatter the annals. Though annal-writers did not say in so many words that Charles was angry, the vocabulary of violence indicated as much. Perpetrated by Charles and his armies in the 790s, acts of violence exceeded in scale and frequency anything that had gone before. They were depicted not as impetuous but as deliberately and coolly calculated to destroy the Saxons and their land. Changing vocabulary reflected a changing strategy, which first manifested itself in 795. Charles and his advisers had realized that internal strains within the Avar regime were widening into civil war. The Avars' leaders, the khagan and the jugur, were reported slain by their own men, and a third-level next-in-command, the tudun, sent envoys to Charles at Lüne near Bardowick, near the Elbe, 'to surrender his land, his people and himself to the king and to accept the Christian faith at the king's command'.[15] Charles had correctly diagnosed the dissolution of the Avar polity, and this had repercussions for relations between Franks and Saxons.

The author of the Lorsch Annals provided a new diagnosis of his own in 795:

> Unfaithfulness arose – from where it habitually did – on the part of the Saxons.[16] When the king wanted to campaign against other *gentes* [i.e. Avars and Slavs] they [i.e. the Saxons] did not join him in full strength (*pleniter*), nor did they send him the support he had ordered. Then, after he had realised their faithlessness yet again, the king marched against them with his army. Some from the Saxon side came to meet him and completed their campaign with him, giving their support, and he and his army reached the Elbe. But others around the marshes of the Elbe and in Wihmodia did not come in the full numbers promised (*pleniter non venerunt*) . . .
>
> Then all came to him, except those just-mentioned and those living across the Elbe: they had not come in full numbers (*pleniter*) up until now, because they had killed King Witzan of the Abodrites who had been Charles's man (*vassus*) and did not think they would be able to return to Charles's grace.[17] The others all came peacefully, promising to obey his orders, and so the lord king trusted in them again, and did not put any of them to death deliberately, so as to retain their trust [in return].[18]

From arguing over Saxons' willingness to join the king's army and asking whether they had 'come in full numbers', another strategy evolved, and a new pattern of war, made visible by the author of the Lorsch Annals also in 795: 'the lord king, residing at Bardowick, took from there such a multitude of hostages (*obsides*) as was never taken ever in his time nor in his father's time nor in the days of the kings of the Franks.' This new strategy centred on the taking of hostages and captives, and the rounding-up of deportees. The strategies were used as alternatives in 795, but over the next few years, hostage-taking and deportation increasingly became the preferred route to crushing Saxon resistance.

II. PATHOLOGICAL DEVASTATIONS AND BURNINGS, 795–8

In the earlier phase of the Saxon wars, the military operations had been sieges, skirmishes and battles; objectives had been the seizing of fortifications and the taking of spoils (*praeda*).[19] The outcome of those campaigns had often been that hostages were given, sometimes termed 'select' hostages by historians because they were few and of high status. In the years 795–8, the words that recur insistently and starkly in the vocabulary of the annal-writers are *vastare, devastare, populare, cremare, incendere*, all meaning 'devastate' 'ravage' or 'burn'; and the object of these verbs was usually land (*terra*), which was taken to included appurtinences – farms, barns, crops, livestock. In 795, the author of the Petau Annals wrote that '*Karolus . . . venit in Saxoniam omnemque terram illam vastavit*' ('Charles entered Saxony and laid waste the whole land'); in 796, the same author wrote: '*cum providentia et decertatione vastavit Saxonia*' ('he laid waste Saxony with forethought and decisiveness').[20] Altogether, between 795 and 798, this writer used the words *vastare* and *devastare* six times and *subjugare* (crush) and *succendere* (burn) once each. The tally for the Lorsch Annals between 796 and 798 was 'burning and laying waste' (*incendere, vastare*), three times, once each year.

III. THE NEW WARFARE, 795–8

In 795–8, when annal-writers mentioned Saxon aggression or resistance, it was increasingly located much further east and north, in the marshy coastal regions of Rüstringen, Wihmodia, Hadeln and the Bardengau on the lower Elbe, and east of it in the *Transalbiana regio*. Here were Frisians, *Nordliudi trans Albim sedentes* or *Transalbiani Saxones*, neighbours of Slav peoples, the Abodriti and Wilzi. Hostilities continued on an annual basis in these northern regions. The broader changes just noted emerged with exceptional clarity in the record of the Lorsch annalist(s) for 795–8, partly thanks to the concerns of the patron of these annals. The changing patterns and new strategy are worth looking at more closely.

The Lorsch writer's account showed the extent of divisions *between* Saxons. Though an oath of fidelity included an obligation to provide a given number of fighting-men, in practice the commitment was not always honoured, and a local leader's following was in any case 'loose and fluid'.[21] Witzan's status as Charles's man (*vassus*) presumably entailed such conditional terms. Saxons who were geographically marginalized in the far north and north-east, and had failed to deliver their quotas, risked a royal reprimand or worse.

The Lorsch writer (or his probable patron, Ricbod of Trier) may well have shared the views of others on the necessary treatment of Saxons in these years (variants on the themes of ravaging, burning and laying waste); but this author presented a line of his own when it came to hostages, captives and deportees. In the passage just quoted on p. 323, he exclaimed over 'the unparalleled number of hostages' taken in 795.[22] In 796, the author of the Petau Annals reported Charles 'taking great booty and receiving hostages' in the Dreingau in the south of Westphalian territory, suggesting Westphalian efforts to broker an agreement through hostages.[23] The Lorsch writer observed that: 'Charles moved around the land of the Saxons where there were rebels, burning it and laying it waste, and from there he took away captives, men, women and children, and spoils, an abundance without number.' Then, when Charles entered Saxony in 797 and reached the region of Wihmodia (the region between the rivers Weser and Elbe):

he and his army wasted and burned that *pagus* (county). And finally, there came to him all the Saxons from all the remote places and dark corners where they were living; and he carried off from there either hostages or as much as he wanted from them, and then did the same with the Frisians.

The next year, 798, saw Charles at Bardowick in summertime with his army:

And people there all delivered themselves into his hands and he took from there as many leading men (*capitanei*) as he wanted and as many hostages (*opsides* [*sic*]) as he desired.[24] Meanwhile our Slavs who are called Abodrites joined together with the lord king's *missi* against Saxons living to the north of the Elbe. They ravaged and burned their land. And those Saxons there gathered themselves together in a single force (*in unum*) and the two sides fought a great battle with each other, and although the Abodrites were pagans (*fanatici*) yet the faith of the Christians and of the lord king aided them and they had the victory over the Saxons, and 2,901 fell before them in that fight.[25]

The last report in the Lorsch writer's sequence followed the meeting of Charles with the pope at Paderborn in July 799:[26]

And the lord king took from Paderborn a multitude of Saxons with women and children, and settled them through various regions of his dominions, dividing their lands among his faithful men, that is, bishops, priests, counts and his other vassals (*et collocavit eos per diversos terras in finibus suis, et ipsam terram eorum inter fideles suos, id est, episcopos, presbyteros, comites et alios vassos suos*).

The vocabulary of pathological devastation – *vastare, devastare, populare, concremare* – speaks for itself. But there was more to this penultimate phase of warfare in and around Saxony. The attack on the Avars' great Ring, or stronghold, first by Duke Eric of Friuli in 795, then, definitively, by Pippin of Italy in 796, had given Charles, who now ruled Bavaria, a golden opportunity to extend his realm eastwards and south-eastwards, and for Pippin to share those spoils. The Avar collapse resulted from both unforeseeable and foreseeable problems. First, there can be discerned a gradual weakening of the Avar polity in the course of the eighth century; an obscure process patchily documented in the years immediately before the 790s. In 791, the *ArF* reported a terrible equine epidemic in which 10 per cent of the Franks' horses died. Modern researchers on veterinary history have noted that such epidemics were highly contagious and that the Avars' horses were likely to have been just as badly affected as those of the Franks. The blow to the Avars was all the heavier, though, because the cavalry was the key component of their armies. Charles's stud-farms were capable, it's been calculated, of renewing the Frankish equine forces in three years, but for the Avars, given the scale and duration of losses, the cavalry may well have been much harder to replenish. Additionally, the distribution of power between the Avars' leaders tended to produce internal conflicts between rivals and between chief and men: in 796, both leaders were killed by their own followers.[27] A replacement khagan and his leading men seem to have opened negotiations with Charles later that same year. Charles and his ecclesiastical advisers, with Paulinus of Aquileia and Arn of Salzburg in the vanguard, were already enthusiastically gathering resources for a missionary effort (with a strong element of competition between these two prelates) in Pannonia and Carinthia, while Alcuin supported his long-time friend Arn from afar:

the brave army that goes with you is sent for your security and protection – a plan which comes, in a way, from the Huns themselves (*et hoc consilium quodammodo ab ipsis processit Hunnis*) . . . It was a strong and stable kingdom for a long time. But it has been conquered by One who is stronger, in whose hands are all the powers of kings and kingdoms . . . If

His grace has regard to the kingdom of the Huns, who could dare to draw back from ministering to their salvation?[28]

In late August 796, Alcuin wrote to assure Charles that

Christ has brought the Hunnic peoples (*gentes populosque Hunnorum*) who have long been feared for their ferocity and might, beneath your warlike sceptre to His honour, and with prevenient grace has bound their necks, haughty for so long, to the yoke of faith, pouring the light of truth on minds long blind from ancient times.[29]

The question of whether Saxon help was needed in these regions had become irrelevant. In the years 797-9, Charles organized systematic deportations of Saxons, to be 'settled . . . through his various dominions', while the lands they left were 'distributed among his faithful men'.[30] Charles was well aware of the slowness of progress in Christianizing Saxony: the Lorsch writer's comments showed the king's determination to provide the material resources for this, and for the collaboration of bishops and counts on the Frankish model. Alcuin's letters point towards a different ideology and strategy of mission which he had crafted for the Saxons (never forgetting that the Old Saxons were his kin). Now, in the late 790s, Charles and his counsellors (especially Alcuin and Meginfrid) intended to apply this strategy to the Avars.[31]

IV. ON THE SAXON FRONTIER

On and across the Saxon frontier, parallel to the annalists' story of material devastation is a very much less well recorded story of the experiences of individual Saxons and their families. The very slim dossier consists of two charters of Charles issued from Aachen, and a petition to Charles's successor, Louis. Each has the unique quality of making audible an individual voice. The first of the two charters is worth quoting in full:

A Saxon named Adalung, when other Saxons in his neighbourhood acted faithlessly against the king, preferred to keep his faith to Charles rather than to stay with the others who were faithless. He went to a village called Vulvishanger which at that time was inhabited by both Franks and Saxons. He wanted to stay there with these people, but he was completely unable to do so. He then moved on again, this time to a place called Waldisbeck situated between the rivers Weser and Fulda. There he cleared and took possession of a part of the forest of Bocchonia.

When Adalung died, he left this property to his son Bennit.

> Then Bennit approached Our Clemency and made a request to Our Highness that he should confirm a precept of Our Authority in respect of him, so that he and his heirs in perpetuity could hold and possess it peacefully without prejudice to anyone. We could not deny this request. Let it be known that we have granted and confirmed it in all respects. We therefore command that none of our faithful men, present or future, should presume to despoil or disquiet Bennit or his heirs in respect of this property, which in their language is termed a *bivanc*. But let it be lawful for them through this precept, to have and possess this land for all time, just of the dimensions as his father had it and as he bequeathed it to his heir in heredity. To ensure this document's authority, and to preserve that through time, we have ordered that it should be sealed with our ring, as below.

This charter survives in the original, as written by the notary Suavis, standing in for the chancellor Ercanbald and evidently well-trained in legal language.[32]

A second charter, the last to survive from Charles's reign and, again, in the original, also concerned property in the forest of Bocchonia, between the Werra and Fulda rivers. It had been cleared and owned by Hiddi, who bequeathed it to his son Asig, Charles's faithful man, also known as Adalrich. It had been confiscated, incorporated into the royal lands (the fisc) by Charles's *missi* and thus put at Charles's disposal (*ad opus nostrum*) and made part of the inheritance of the late Duke Gero.[33] 'But because of the faithful service of Asig and his father's petition, we have conceded the property to him and his heirs to keep.'[34]

These charters are the tip of what was once a documentary iceberg. Lay archives tended to lack the longevity of ecclesiastical ones.[35] They suggest that, however many the law's delays, Charles was seriously concerned to get justice done.

The third document, the petition, dates from *c.*815, very early in the reign of Charles's son and successor, Louis the Pious. The petitioner (never named) and his sister complained that they had been deprived of their inheritance in Saxony as a consequence of events that had occurred when their father, Richard, and uncle Richolf, who were Christians, had been serving Charles loyally, but some of their relatives and neighbours who hated Christians had plundered their houses and destroyed them completely. Sometime after this, Charles sent Richolf as a *missus* across the Elbe along with three counts, one of them named Gottschalk, and a fifth man. 'All were slain on the same day because they sought to defend their Christianity.' Richard then went to Charles to tell him what had happened. While he was en route, Richard's wife was abducted by the very same men as had killed the royal *missi*. Richard managed to rescue his wife and they fled to his [or her?] maternal inheritance. The petitioner continued: 'Following a *transmigratio* from Saxony done on the emperor's orders, they [the petitioner's parents] had been led away into different parts (*per partes*), through many distances, they stopped for some time (*commorantes*), alienated from their own land (*a propria abalienati terra*).'[36]

The petitioner, whose father had meanwhile died, requested that that land be returned to him and his widowed mother and his sister by the new emperor. The date of this family disaster can be retrieved because the *ArF* reviser described, under the year 798, how Saxons across the Elbe killed Charles's officers (*legati*) who had been sent 'to do justice there', one of whom was named as Gottschalk. 'News of his killing made King Charles violently angry (*graviter commotus*). He collected his army, took up arms against the defectors, and, as the avenger of his legates' deaths, laid waste with fire and sword the Saxon lands between Weser and Elbe.[37]

The outcome of this plea is unrecorded; but whatever it was, it seems likely that, as in the two cases dealt with by Charles, long periods of time were liable to elapse before wrongs were righted. A tart but telling recent comment on the case behind the petition is that *transmigratio* was a euphemism for *deportatio*.[38]

V. POPULATION TRANSFERS, 795-9

The Lorsch Annals writer was not the only one to record population transfers, but he showed a particular interest in them across those five years. He was also well aware this was not a new phenomenon but one that could be traced back to 'the days of the Frankish kings' and had been put to use by Charles himself at Bardowick in 795.[39] It could have been traced back very much further, in fact, had the annalists known more Hellenistic and Byzantine instances.[40] I summarize the evidence in the Lorsch Annals:

> *Obsides* and *captivi* 795–9 (The subject was Charles in all cases)
>
> In 795, the verbs used were *ferre* and *ducere*. The persons carried away or led away were termed *obsides* (hostages).
>
> In 796, the verb was *ducere*, and the persons *captivi*, further specified as *viri, mulieres et parvuli* (men, women and little ones).
>
> In 797, the verb was *ferre* and the persons were *obsides aut de ipsis quantum ipse voluit* ('hostages or of those as many as he wanted').
>
> In 798, the verb was *ferre*, the persons were *capitanii quos voluit* and *de opsidibus quantum ei voluntas fuit* ('the chief men whom he wanted, and of the hostages as many as he wanted'), and *de ipsis Saxonis quos voluit, et quos voluit dimisit* ('of the Saxons those whom he wanted and he dismissed those he wanted [to dismiss]').
>
> In 799, the verbs were *ferre, collocare* and *dividere*, the persons were termed a *multitudo Saxanorum cum mulieribus et infantibus* ('a multitude of Saxons [taken away] with their women and children'), placed *per diversas terras in finibus suis* ('through various lands within his boundaries'), and the division was of *ipsa terra eorum inter fideles suos, id est, episcopos, presbyteros, comites et alios vassos suos* ('that land of theirs, between his faithful men, that is, bishops, priests, counts and others of his free men who served him').[41]

It's been rightly pointed out that the lands divided among Charles's *fideles* would not have been deprived of their workforces, for if they had been, the estates themselves would have been of little value to their owners, at least in the short run. Charles was 'not interested in guilt or innocence when it came to deportations. He wanted to deprive the land

[Saxony] of its elite.'[42] To clarify the point: what Charles wanted was to remove those of the Saxon elite who still resisted. The existence of noble factions explains how, in Saxony as in Bavaria, it was possible for Charles to divide and rule through the selective distribution of favour. An example of Saxon-on-Saxon division and double-dealing to rival that of 782 occurred in 798 when, after Saxons suffered a heavy defeat, 'some of the survivors negotiated with Charles for peace-terms, and the king received hostages, including those whom *primores* (chief men) of the Saxons designated as the most perfidious'.[43]

As in the *ArF*, the revised *ArF* and other annals, *obsides* is the word most often used in the Lorsch Annals over 795–8, in preference to *captivi*. *Obsides* were of higher status than *captivi* and those who gave them were more likely to be able to negotiate terms.[44] The king 'took away' hostages from Saxony in each of the years 795–8, but no destination is specified until the entry for 799, as noted above, when the multitude of Saxons 'taken away . . . were settled by Charles through various regions within the boundaries [of his realm], and the lands they left were divided among Charles's *fideles*.' In 802, according to the *ArF*, '[Charles] sent an army of Saxons against the Saxons across the Elbe, and devastated [them]'. The clearest evidence of population transfers, deportations or resettlements thus comes in the 790s, with one exception which came at the end of that period and will be discussed presently.

VI. THE *CAPITULARE SAXONICUM*, OR THE SECOND SAXON CAPITULARY

The *Capitulare Saxonicum* was very different from the *Capitulatio de partibus Saxoniae* of 782. For a start, its introductory statement declared itself issued by Charles at Aachen on 28 October 797, 'with the unanimous consent of all the assembled bishops and abbots and counts, and from their various districts, Westphalians and Angrarians as well as Eastphalians'. Its opening broadside was to the effect that just as any Frank disobeying the king's command had to pay a fine of 60 *solidi*, any Saxon had to pay exactly the same fine (c. 1). Compensation payments rather than death penalties were the rule. Nothing was said about tithe-payments. Fines were to be paid over, as customary, to the inhabitants who had delivered judgments in local courts, but if a case had been brought to the palace for settlement in the king's presence, fines paid in compensation were to go to the king (c. 4). If a king's *missus* was killed, the killer must pay a three-fold compensation (c. 7). In c. 9, 'since the lord king has announced his wish to establish, with the consent of the Franks and of faithful Saxons, a heavier fine for infringing his command as regards enforcing public order and [dealing with] feud and major crimes, he may order the 60 *solidi* doubled'. In c. 10, the king declared that 'if a criminal takes refuge with the royal power, the king should decide whether he should be put to death or removed, with wife and family and possessions, outside the district, or settled in a frontier-area'.[45]

Processes of accommodation in Saxony south and west of the Elbe, however poorly documented, go far to explaining why the tone of 797 was so different from that of 782. But the fundamental difference was that whereas only five out of thirty-four *capitula* of the 782 *Capitulatio* mentioned the king, the hand of Charles lay heavy on the 797 *Capitulare* (the king appears in five out of the ten *capitula*). A postscript decreeing what should constitute a *solidus* as a unit of value among the Saxons, distinguished Bortrini, i.e. Westphalians, from Northerners, thus:

> the Bortrini must give 40 bushels of oats for one *solidus*,
> and 20 bushels of rye; but those to the North must give 30
> bushels of oats for one *solidus*, and 15 bushels of rye; the
> Bortrini must give one and a half *siccli* of honey for a *solidus*,
> but those to the North must give 2 *siccli* for a *solidus* [and]
> likewise of winnowed barley they are to give the same amount
> as of rye for one *solidus*.[46]

These equivalents are not really comparable to the prices per measure for different types of grain and weights of bread in the Capitulary of Frankfurt, c. 4. Those were a way of price-fixing.[47] The *Capitulare*'s postscript seems to mean, though, that if foodstuffs were being supplied to the king as a substitute for *solidi* due, they would need to reflect relative values at least roughly, as well as reflecting the availability of agricultural/natural resources (oats, rye, honey).[48] 'The differences would even out because the Bortrini had to give more grain per *solidus* than the Northerners, whereas the Northerners had to give more honey.'[49] In 795-8, hostile Saxons were coming to be encountered predominantly in the regions near the mouth of the Elbe and beyond it. As Charles's forces pushed further north and north-east, they saw with their own eyes economic disparities reflected in the cultivation of oats, rye and barley, rather than of wheat (which is unmentioned in the postscript) and the harsh conditions experienced by dwellers in swampy and marginal land 'on the borders of the ocean'.

On 28 October 797, Charles's bishops, abbots and illustrious counts, and Saxons from the various districts, who had been assembled at Aachen to hear the *Capitulare* announced, would not have been surprised to know that war hadn't ended; but they had reason to hope that it was the beginning of the end.

VII. WARLEADERS AND WARRIORS, 793-9

Charles himself had been the Franks' pre-eminent warleader from the very start of his reign. In 774, his uncle Bernard (Pippin's half-brother) had proved an able lieutenant;[50] from him, Charles would have learned the advantages of sharing command and co-ordinating tactics. As the family-cycle rolled forward, the king, as well as continuing to plan and often personally command campaigns in Saxony, delegated military responsibilities to his sons, a new generation of warleaders. In 796, Charles had despatched Pippin to lead what proved to be the final campaign against the Avars.

> He reached the place where the kings of the Avars had been accustomed to reside with their princes and which in our tongue is called *Hringe* (the Ring). He took abundant treasure from there, sending it to his father; and later he himself arrived in Francia with his army and great treasure from the Avars. And King Charles himself stayed this year in Saxony with his [other] two sons, Charles and Louis.[51]

In the next chapter, royal family matters will be considered in detail. In the rest of this chapter, having signalled the contributions of all three of Charles's sons by Hildegard reported in the annals for 796-8, there will be more to say about Charles's warriors, and then about his evolving court.

Hildegard's sons were now, in the mid-790s, seasoned warleaders: Pippin with experience of generalship in encounters in Avaria; Young Charles in the special brand of sword-and-fire warfare in Saxony; and Louis in the tactics of fighting in the Midi and the Spanish March. For the ensuing years, there is good evidence to support the military skills and prowess of all three.[52] From their father's standpoint, his sons' loyalty and competence could hardly be faulted. From the sons' standpoint, Charles had proved himself a good father by giving them plenty of training and experience in war and in arranging for the intercessions that could bring victory.[53] For a noble or free-born youth, becoming a warrior was to enter a new life-stage.[54] At higher-status levels, in local society in a family setting, magnate households were the training-grounds. The affective ties that bound were made here and, later, in the course of army service where peers (*pares*) supported one another.[55]

Only the *ArF* reviser told the story of Count Theoderic, Charles's kinsman, who first appeared in these annals in 782, then re-entered the frame in 791,[56] and made a final appearance in 793: a typical small selection of fragments from which it's hard to construct even a rough sketch of a biography. In 793 Theoderic was bringing troops (*copiae*) through Frisia when they were intercepted by Saxons in the district of Rüstringen on the Weser and destroyed (*deletae*). Hearing of the disaster that had befallen Theoderic and his men, Charles abandoned his planned expedition to Pannonia, while he disguised the magnitude of this loss (*magnitudinem damni dissimulans*).[57] The suppression of this disaster as described by the *ArF* author, surely at Charles's behest, could be interpreted as an effort on the king's part to lessen the shock experienced by the court;[58] on an alternative reading, the silence could reflect an effort to conceal knowledge of it from the Avars.[59] I take the loss of Theoderic and his men to be one that Charles personally took so hard that dissimulation was needed.[60]

The names of very few of Charles's military commanders are recorded in the annalistic evidence of the 790s. Count Theoderic was exceptional in appearing thrice in the revised *ArF*. With Theoderic in 791 went Meginfrid, Charles's treasurer, when they co-ordinated tactics on the Danube campaign.[61] Theoderic's son, Count William of Toulouse, is known to historians thanks to a brief but enthusiastic notice in the Aquitanian *Chronicle of Moissac* of William's exploits in 793 on the river Orbiel near Narbonne, as well as two mentions in the *Life of Louis* whose author, 'the Astronomer', relied on an Aquitanian source.[62] After a small group of the king's officials had been sent across the Elbe 'to do justice' in 798, Charles sent his officer Gottschalk as his envoy to the Danish king. Local Saxons killed most of the officials and also intercepted and killed Gottschalk. Furiously angry at the news, Charles, 'as the avenger of his officers, laid waste that part of Saxony'. In the reaches of what's now Schleswig-Holstein, not far from the modern German frontier with Denmark, Charles's general Eburis, commanding the right wing in the Abodrites' battle-line alongside Duke Thrasco (appointed to his dukedom by Charles), defeated the Saxons' northward push, and survived to tell the tale of 4,000 enemy slain.[63] The following year, 799, two of Charles's *palatini* – Duke Eric of Friuli, 'after so many deeds accomplished successfully', and Gerold, governor of Bavaria (brother of the late Queen Hildegard) – were killed in separate incidents of local resistance: Eric in what's now Croatia; Gerold in battle against the Avars, probably in what's now western Hungary. These locations signposted the eastern/south-eastern extent of Charles's empire at this point, and, at the same time, a reaching of limits.[64]

By the 790s, Charles had succeeded in generating a strong sense of solidarity between himself and his senior officers and younger followers *in palatio suo militantes*.[65] According to the *ArF* reviser, Charles never ceased to lament those who had fallen at Roncesvaux in 778.[66] In 798, Charles was the avenger of his slain officers.[67] In 800 or 801, Alcuin wrote to Charles to tell him that he had heard with sorrow the news of Meginfrid's death in Beneventan territory in 800, and to intimate that the brethren of the Tours community would be praying for his soul. The naming in the *ArF* of outstanding warriors like Theoderic and Gottschalk, Eric and Gerold could be compared with the mentioning in despatches of soldiers in twentieth-century wars.[68] Epitaphs, like that of Eggihard the royal steward, killed in 778, and Alcuin's entering of Meginfrid's name, along with that of 'Karlus', in the Durham *Book of Life* after his death, and (probably) in a list of those to be prayed for at Tours as well, would similarly perpetuate the memories of these men.[69] Recalling memories of comrades was something that bound courtiers together.[70]

In the final section of this chapter, I will consider how far Charles had got towards the making of a court during the 790s while so much military action was ongoing. Preparation for the warrior's calling was not all there was to the lives of the king's sons. He had also encouraged them (and their sisters) in their acquisition of an education in liberal arts, and ensured they had good tutors and advisers. He had made provision for them (and their sisters) to be included in charter-formulae for prayers.[71] In the annal for 787, the *ArF* reviser used *comitatus* in the sense of 'court'. When Charles returned after his brief sojourn in Italy that year, he found at Worms '*uxorem Fastradam filiosque ac filias et omnem comitatum quem apud eos dimiserit*' ('his wife Fastrada and his sons and daughters and all the court dignitaries whom he had left with them').[72] David King might have chosen 'retinue' to translate *comitatus*: thereafter he translates *comitatus* as 'court'. Interestingly, this passage continues: 'and he decided to hold the general assembly of his people there' (*generalem populi sui conventum ibi habere statuit*). What connection was perceived between court and assembly, and in what sense these could be differentiated, have been penetratingly discussed by Daniel Eichler.[73]

VIII. THE MAKING OF A COURT, 794–9

There was one exception to the new pattern of the court's being centred at Aachen for the long overwinterings in the years 794–9: the *ArF* reviser in the annal for 797, uniquely, registered Charles's overwintering in Saxony, '*sumpto secum comitatu suo*', 'bringing his court with him'. *Comitatus* had come to signify *aula regis*, the king's court.[74] When Charles wanted to display the efforts of his engineers at work on the canal planned to link the Danube and Rhine in 793, he went to the site '*cum omni comitatu . . . ac magna hominum multitudine congregata totum autumni tempus in eo opere consumpsit*' ('with all his court . . . and with a great multitude of men gathered together he spent the whole of the autumn in that project').[75]

In 797, determined to end the Saxon wars once and for all, Charles went into Saxony and 'took his court with him. He made an encampment there which the locals still call the camp of the war-assembly . . . and he gave orders to his sons Pippin and Louis to come to him there.'[76] The camp became the court.

Central to court life was the reception of envoys and gifts. Charles 'received, and then dismissed, embassies from the Avars who had been sent with *magna munera*, and an envoy from the king of the Asturias who brought him *dona*.[77] And he spent Christmas and Easter there.'[78]

The 'camp of the war-assembly', having begun as the gathering of the host, could shape-change into a palace, which Hincmar of Reims, born within a decade or so of the making of the Aachen palace, defined thus: '*Palatium . . . regis dicitur propter rationabiles homines inhabitantes, et non propter parietes insensibiles sive macerias* [for *materias*]' ('The king's palace is called a palace on account of the rational people who inhabit it, and not because of its walls or its building-materials, which cannot feel or sense').[79] In short, the palace was an assembly of thinking, feeling, rational and responsive *homines* – human beings.

When Charles sent one of his officials, the notary Ercanbald (in post in 778, and still going strong, as arch-chancellor, in 813), to Louis at one of his Aquitanian palaces on government business, the report Ercanbald brought back to Aachen was that he had seen Louis sitting as a judge for three days a week.

> His father is said to have been so happy that he burst into tears, so great was his joy, and said to those who were there in attendance on him: 'My companions (*sotii*, for *socii*), let's rejoice that we're surpassed in the wisdom of an old man by this young man!'[80]

Apocryphal as this story may be, and written down decades after Ercanbald's visit (the Astronomer wrote Louis' biography *c.*842), it is easy to imagine its being told orally to audiences of 'companions' at court.[81] This was surely the way Louis would have liked to be remembered: a son who had the edge on his father. And Charles did have a notary called Ercanbald, who was mentioned by Theodulf in his poem on the court in 795, served as chief notary (arch-chancellor) from 797 until 812, and in 801 took care of the elephant which had arrived from Harun al-Rashid via North Africa and Pavia, and was now preparing for its new life in Francia.[82]

Alcuin seems to have taken the lead in giving nicknames, often borrowed from classical authors, and Roman or biblical history, to denizens of the court.[83] Erchanbald, for instance, was 'little Zacchaeus'.[84] The moniker was a kind of entry-card. One nickname, though, was very much more than a nickname: it was the name of David, greatest of Old Testament kings and, as an ancestor of Christ, a leader in war and peace, a maker of marriage-alliances, a poet and a patron of poets, conveying the significance of a role-model for Charles. (Needless to say, the poets did not mention the sins and sorrows of the biblical king.) Nicknames occurred often in the poems and letters that were the media through which *palatini* and *aulici* communicated with each other and reassured themselves (and each other) of their continued membership of the court's charmed circle. They could continue to belong *in absentia*, often many years after retirement.[85]

Alcuin had only briefly been in Francia, in 786–90: a period of three-and-a-half years, during which Charles's household was itinerant.[86] He overwintered at Aachen in 788–9, working on the *Admonitio generalis*, but left Francia for Northumbria early in 790. He made contacts with several leading scholars, especially Arn, a priest at the Frankish monastery of St-Amand, then abbot there from 778; in 785, without giving up the abbacy, Arn was appointed bishop of Salzburg. Any contacts Alcuin had with Arn in these years were by letter.[87] He returned to Francia to be present at Frankfurt in the summer of 794, and left again in August 796. It is hard to find evidence of Alcuin the teacher at court during the first of these stays. Poems and letters already presupposed a fair amount of Latin literacy in the court milieu; but the most likely window for a crucially formative teaching-phase presented itself in 794–6. Alcuin's *De Rhetorica* belonged here, as did his *De vera Philosophia*, which drew heavily on Boethius's sixth-century *Consolation of Philosophy*, and also, perhaps, the *Dialogue* between Alcuin and the young Pippin king of Italy, a brief work for teaching schoolboys basic Latin, spiced with a few jokes and riddles, almost entirely borrowed from a second- or third-century Roman author. It's not easy to pin down any teaching-time spent by Pippin at his father's court. The end of the *Dialogue* reveals, in a little *coup de théâtre*, that Pippin was a distance-learner:

ALCUIN: *Quid est tacitus nuntius?* (What is a quiet messenger?)

PIPPIN: *Quem manu teneo.* (The one I hold in my hand.)

ALCUIN: *Quid tenes manu?* (What are you holding in your hand?)

PIPPIN: *Epistolam tuam, Magister.* (Your letter, Master.)

ALCUIN: *Lege feliciter, fili.* (Read it with profit, my son.)[88]

Pippin, of course, had had his own court at Pavia since 781. There he inherited traditions of public debate, and learned from such experienced counsellors as Paulinus of Aquileia, a fine Latinist. It was a start.

Alcuin was keen to keep in touch with Charles's sons. He expected the future to be theirs. In a letter written in 796, the year of Pippin's marriage, Alcuin enjoined Pippin: '*Laetare cum muliere adoliscentiae tuae, et non sint alienae participes tuae*' ('Rejoice in the wife of your youth, and let not your partners be foreigners'). This is a straight quotation from Proverbs 5:18, 20 (which, to my mind, puts paid to any debate over whether or not Pippin's first sexual partnership was of marriage or concubinage: clearly, the partner was a wife, and a Frankish woman, and nothing else would have been suitable or, in this context, plausible).[89] Alcuin preceded this with a small *speculum principis* ('Mirror for a Prince'):

> Strive to adorn your nobility of birth with nobility of conduct, and aim to fulfil God's will and honour with all your might. May ineffable dutifulness exalt the throne of your kingdom and increase its boundaries and subject the peoples (*gentes*) to your power. Be generous towards the poor, kind to pilgrims, devoted in Christ's service, treating honourably God's servants and churches, and may their zealous prayer aid you. Be worthy in your way of living, chaste in body.[90]

Pippin's first military action, at his father's behest, was in 787. He was present (and perhaps came of age?) at the Worms assembly in 790, where he participated in planning the future of the family. Stints of military action ensued in 791–3. Only during his Christmasing at Aachen in 794–5 might there have been time for him to benefit from face-to-face conversation with Alcuin. Maybe Alcuin's *Mirror* was persuasive enough to have left its mark on his life thereafter.

Only one letter from Alcuin to the Young Charles remains of what once was probably a much larger correspondence. It is not more securely dated than 793–800.[91] It contains another little *Mirror*, this time warning that '*munera* [gifts also known as bribes] can blind the eyes of the wise and subvert the words of the just' (Exodus 23:8, and cf. Ecclesiasticus 20:29), and also asking to be allowed often to send the young king a message of admonition, adding, 'Your brother Louis, a most noble youth, asked me to send him letters of admonition frequently, and this I have done and, God willing, shall go on doing.'[92] Though Alcuin claimed to have received many requests from Louis for letters of advice, not one such letter survives. Fortunately, the Astronomer has a good deal to say about Louis' youthful conduct and training, and about his relationship with his father.[93]

Charles's biographer Einhard joined the court in the early 790s, during the Regensburg years, when he was in his early twenties. It's certainly tempting to see a link between the complaints expressed by Charles in the *Epistola de litteris colendis* (the model copy of which was sent to Abbot Baugulf of Fulda in 787) and Einhard's appearance at court.[94] Einhard, who was not a monk and was never to take holy orders, was already a well-trained charter-scribe by then, and as such favoured by Baugulf.[95] He had just the skills, knowledge and experience to appeal to the king. When Alcuin returned to Francia in 794, Einhard was there in Charles's entourage. He was lucky enough to be taught by Alcuin at the palace school until 796, when Alcuin was retired to Tours, but perhaps had not been taught at that school for long enough (less than two years) to have formed a close personal relationship with the Master. In the late autumn of 796, 'the larger part of the Avar treasure in 15 carts, each pulled by 4 oxen, carrying loads of gold and silver and precious robes of silk', trundled into Aachen.[96] Einhard can be imagined there among the bedazzled crowd.

Thirty years or so later, Einhard was telling a kind of truth when he claimed that 'no-one could write about these things [i.e. Charles's life] more truthfully than I could, for I was present and knew them by the witness of my own eyes, as they say.'[97] Einhard identified Charles's most striking character-traits as *magnanimitas* and *perpetua constantia*: 'greatness of soul and perpetual firmness of mind'.[98] These were qualities that enabled Charles to take the longer view, to judge correctly the distinctive institutional weaknesses of the polities of both Saxons and Avars, and to choose reliable commanders. Having got his hands on an unlooked-for quantity of movable wealth, Charles transferred to Francia and to Italy all those 'treasures accumulated over such a long time' (*congesti ex longo tempore thesauri* – Einhard's phrase expressed his wonderment), and then distributed it to a large yet discriminatingly selected number of recipients (it seems that Charles's new wife, Liutgard, had a hand in the selection) outside as well as within his own realms.[99]

> Human memory cannot record any war against the Franks that left them richer and more enriched: indeed, until that time they had seemed almost poor (*pauperes*) but they found so much gold and silver in that palace, and so much valuable booty was taken in the battles, that the Franks might be thought to have justly taken from the Avars what the Avars had unjustly taken from other *gentes*.[100]

There would have been a larger and fuller *aula renovata* even without the Avar treasure (think how much had been achieved in the late 780s and early 790s!), but renewal would have gone much more slowly, the Aachen church and palace taken a good deal longer to be built, aristocrats been less happy with Charles's distribution of rewards, and further imperial expansion less attractive. *With* the Avar treasure Charles had the wind in his sails.

In the years from 794 to 799 (and after 800 too), letters formed an important genre of communication between court, on the one hand, and warleaders and district officers in the field on the other.[101] From Aachen and, later, Tours, Alcuin wrote to prominent laymen, responding to requests for practical advice and moral guidance. The six letters of this type that survive, one of them to a count and his wife, all contained little *Mirrors*.[102] Here again was plentiful evidence of distance learning. There were also letters to multiple recipients when a committee of experts needed to be put in touch with each other via multiple messengers, rather than gathered at the court. In a letter of 798, Alcuin, enclosing his latest broadside against Felix of Urgell, asked Charles, then in Saxony, to have this work copied and then to act as a distribution-centre of the copies, sending them to the pope, Paulinus, bishop of Aquileia (nicknamed Timothy), Ricbod (nicknamed Macarius), abbot of Lorsch and archbishop of Trier, and Theodulf (perhaps nicknamed Zebedee), bishop of Orléans; and for each of these to reply to the king (presumably with comments) for himself.[103] The court could be a virtual community, as well as a physical one, finely landscaped – as Charles's Aachen was – with park and water-features.[104] In the eyes of Alcuin the *magister*, more important than letters to adult laymen was the training-up of the young in wisdom, for, as Solomon knew, 'it is through wisdom that kings reign and law-makers decree what is just' (Prov. 8:15-16):

> Lord king, exhort all the young men in your excellence's palace (*iuvenes quosque in palatio excellentiae vestrae*) to study wisdom in all zeal and by daily practice so that they advance in it at the age when they are flowering (*aetate florida*).[105]

Young men in the palace held in their hands not just the making of the court, but the future practice of empire. Over the 790s, the court became more visibly and tangibly a place of power. A German historian has identified three modes of power's working: '*Macht bei Hofe, Macht über den Hof, Macht durch den Hof*' ('power at court, power over the court, power through the court').[106] Exactly what these phrases mean, so another German historian has averred, 'defies clear definition' – which is to signal that looking for an institution might be a vain quest. Not long since, Rosamond McKitterick took a different tack in what is in effect a series of refreshingly practical approaches to 'the court', or rather 'a number of royal courts', via the question of itinerant monarchy and the implications of itinerancy for 'the system of Carolingian government as it was developed under Charlemagne'.[107] McKitterick's insights on the royal court are never less than fresh and shrewd, as, for instance, when she pries into the relationship of palaces and mints, or palace and court, or contrasts (rather than compares) Ottonian with Carolingian rulership. The priorities and practices of war and warriors surely affected the routes and rhythms of the court. Today's Anglo-Saxonists no longer imagine kings travelling about consuming such resources as beer and bread-and-honey from royal estates. If the Frankish realm is the one in question, scale and contingencies, especially military contingencies, matter; and what determine both scale and contingencies are – rather than regard for 'system' or 'systematic development' – very often family matters, and life-cycle.

A little cluster of Alcuin's letters, dating from 796, throws light on how royal counsellors dealt with a major policy decision, namely, what to do about tithes and, specifically, in the just-conquered kingdom of the Avars, in the light of experiences in Saxony. Alcuin wrote to Arn as if conveying something already well-known: 'Tithes, so it's said, have destroyed the faith of the Saxons.' Thanks to this cluster of Alcuin's letters, it is possible to understand how Charles and his advisers set about tackling this problem. Four times in the first section of Ep. 107, Alcuin mentioned a plan (*consilium*):

> Hope of a plan has not failed me, nor has there been delay in reaching a collective decision. But your joining the king's campaign [against the Avars] to test the truth of the matter has now, for the present, been settled . . . This plan (*consilium*) has, in a way, come from the Avars themselves . . . May we, then, see you returning . . . with a clear plan (*cum certo consilio*). I beg you, as soon as you return, to let us know about what is your plan (*per tuum consilium*).

Alcuin continued:

> The Avar realm for a long time was stable and strong (*stabile et forte*).
> But God Himself is still stronger ... And if God's favour looks down on
> the Avar realm, who is there who could dare to withdraw himself from
> the duty of care (*ministerium*) for their salvation?[108] ... Beloved
> brother ... be a preacher of true religion, not an exactor of tithes. For
> the new soul must be fed with the milk of apostolic piety, until it's strong
> enough to accept solid food [1 Cor. 3:1–2]. Tithes, it's said, have under-
> mined the faith of the Saxons. For what purpose do we force on the necks
> of the ignorant (*idiotae*) a yoke that neither we ourselves, nor our breth-
> ren, have been able to put up with?[109]

In 795, Alcuin had sent from Aachen a pair of letters to Duke Eric of
Friuli and Archbishop Paulinus of Aquileia.[110] He urged both to consider
how Christian mission to the Avars could be taken forward, pointing out
to Paulinus that he was ideally placed geographically to carry out this
work.[111] After his move to Tours in August 796, Alcuin wrote to Charles to
congratulate him on his victory over the Avars, and to persuade him that it
was now necessary to provide devout preachers to such a very new people.

> After considering all this ... may you look ahead to provide with a wise
> plan (*sapiens consilium*). Consider whether it would be better to impose
> the yoke of tithes on unlearned peoples (*rudes populi*) ... in such a way
> that tithe-payments must be exacted in full from every household, one
> by one, or to ask instead whether the Apostles sent into the world by
> Christ to preach would have required the exaction of tithes or instead
> made demands in some other way.[112]

Alcuin, in other words, was suggesting options, and a gradualist
approach. Just as the *Capitulare Saxonicum* of 797 represented a 'new
plan' compared with the *Capitulatio* of 782, so Alcuin, in the light of
experience, was urging that past errors not be repeated in a missionary
church, and that the Avars might be seen less as a problem than as part
of a solution. It helped, of course, that Alcuin had close personal bonds
with these correspondents.

With no-one were his bonds closer than with Meginfrid the chamberlain (or treasurer), the recipient of Ep. 111. In fact, Epp. 107 and 110 (to
Arn and to Charles) were complemented by Ep. 111.[113] Taking his text
from Matthew 25:15–21, the parable of the talents, Alcuin played on the

different meanings, financial and moral, of talents (*talenta*) in the sense of abilities but also a kind of coin, and *pecunia* (money). It was a parable well-chosen for a treasurer. Alcuin went on in the vein of St Augustine: faith could not be forced but had to be voluntary. Changing tack, he quoted St Paul who commended the expounding of the Gospel free of charge (*ut evangelium sine sumptu exponam*, I Cor. 9:18).[114]

> Let the teachers of the Faith be preachers not plunderers (*praedicatores non praedatores*). Let them trust in the goodness of Him who said, 'Do not carry a money-bag or a purse' (*Nolite portare saccellum aut peram*, Luke 10: 4). I have written to you in this way so that those who want to hear your counsel (*a te consilium*) can benefit from your admonitions. May the best-beloved David be made aware of these things . . . He has fewer helpers than he needs; yet I think no-one in the world has better men than he does. May he teach, advise and train them. And you [Meginfrid], most faithfully administering his treasuries and keeper of his counsels (*servitor consiliorum*) and devoted helper, do his will manfully! . . . There are priests who work for material rewards and for honour in this world. Forgive me for saying so (*ut cum pace dicam*) but these men are deprived of the power of binding and loosing . . . I tell you, dearest friend, the harvest in the Christian people is great, but in some places there are no reapers. You, now, ask the lord of the harvest, that is, my beloved David, to send workers to his harvest.[115]

Meginfrid, as one of Charles's highest functionaries, was ideally placed to act as Alcuin's go-between to the king. Here Alcuin was advising the treasurer not to rely on tithe-income in planning royal expenditure.

Communications between provinces and court worked well. When a letter from Alcuin arrived at the palace, it would be passed from hand to hand, discussed between Charles and his counsellors, and plans thus formed from shared counsels (as described in Ep. 107), while points omitted from Ep. 111 could be supplied in Ep. 110. These three letters, Epp. 107, 110 and 111, could be read, and still are best read, serially. Together they reflect Alcuin's insistence that tithes had no place in any apostolic model. If forcible tithe-taking offended Alcuin and his fellow-counsellors theologically, it troubled them too on practical grounds, as it still troubles historians who try to visualize the landscapes of mission. Nevertheless, in the light of Ep. 111, it seems likely that Meginfrid kept the issue alive at court; and the deluge of legislation in the form of capitularies, synodal decrees and episcopal statutes kept tithes on the agenda of reform.

A strangely wonderful phenomenon of the late eighth century, evoked by Charles's interest in late antique culture, and the centripetal pull exerted on elites of an *aula renovata*, was the production of poetry in many classical forms and genres. Latin was the *lingua franca*. The leading figures were Angilbert, a Frank, Theodulf, a Spaniard and Alcuin, a Northumbrian – plus the anonymous writer of the Paderborn Epic, who may have been Einhard, or Angilbert, or someone else entirely. The poets were jacks-of-all-trades: courtiers, envoys, teachers, managers of resources and of men; and they competed, competition being a characteristic of courts.

Each of the three leading poets produced a vivid evocation of court life: Angilbert in (probably) 795, Alcuin in 796 and Theodulf also in 796. All three poems conveyed praise of Charles and a triumphalist feel – this was 796, after all! Each name-checked a number of others (including their rivals) at court, holders of high offices, clerical – Erchanbald, Riculf and Hildebold – and lay – Eppin-Eberhard the cup-bearer, Audulf the seneschal, and Meginfrid the treasurer/chamberlain. All three poets mentioned or alluded to women at court. Angilbert praised his beloved Berta, Charles's daughter, and mother of Angilbert's two sons. Alcuin, discreetly and without naming her, alluded to Gundrada, his spiritual daughter (and Charles's biological one), and signalled both her learning and her piety by urging her to star-gaze and praise God who arrayed the heavens with stars. Theodulf's bravura performance celebrated Charles's victories. He named more people than did either Angilbert or Alcuin: the royal women figured largely, Charles's wife, his daughters, his sister. It takes a specialist in eighth-century Latin poetry to capture the intense feeling and sensibility of the palace as poems passed from hand to hand, and private reading led on to public recitation in what Peter Godman has imagined as 'an atmosphere of fun and malice . . . flattery and satire'.[116] The *Paderborn Epic*, also known as *Karolus Magnus et Leo Papa*, written in 799 or soon after, was a remarkable *pièce d'occasion*.[117] In a famous passage on the preparations for the royal hunt, the poet managed to mention even more royal women than did Theodulf. Berta was given special attention, not least because she so strikingly resembled her father.[118]

The large accretion of wealth that ensued from the capture of the Avar Ring – the khagan's vast fortress-palace – hugely impressed contemporaries. Its investment in and at Aachen, combined with the elite's pride in the revived poetic culture of imperial and late antique Rome, gave Charles's regime a new lease of life, the court a new élan.

Lateran Mosaic with St Peter,
Pope Leo and King Charles.

13
Interesting Times, Dangerous Times

I. POPE HADRIAN: HIS DEATH AND HIS EPITAPHS, 795–6

Hadrian died on 16 December 795, after a pontificate of almost twenty-four years: exceptionally long, and exceptionally well-documented until 791, when the *Codex Carolinus* stops. The years 791–5 are very patchily covered, in the later chapters of Hadrian's *Life* in the *Liber Pontificalis* and the early sections of his successor Leo III's *Life*, which consist exclusively of lists of donations to local churches. Florian Hartmann, author not of a biography of Hadrian but of a series of brilliantly insightful studies of his pontificate, makes two important points in a short summing-up. The first is that the quality of Latinity in papal Rome, as well as its manuscript output, declined markedly on Hadrian's watch, during which there also occurred a 'laicization' of the Lateran patriarchate in institutional and cultural terms. The second is that Hadrian himself exemplified these trends.[1] The assertion by the author of Hadrian's *Life* that this pope was 'multiply strong in spiritual exercises' can't be taken to mean that he was 'unusually well-educated'.[2] Hadrian's attention was focused on secular business, and his characteristic priorities were those of a Roman noble: wealth, good connections, impressive building projects and ritual splendour. He can be plausibly situated, as Hartmann situates him, in the world portrayed in his letters, his *Life*, or the Donation of Constantine (see below). Hartmann's appraisal of the relationship between Hadrian and Charles is epitomized in the title of his chapter 6: '*Kooperation im Konflikt*' – which needs no translation.[3]

News of Hadrian's death reached Aachen quite early in 796. For the

honour of writing the pope's epitaph on parchment, there was predictable competition.[4] The choice was, equally predictably, that of Charles.
At least three competitors are known: an anonymous writer (who won't
be dealt with here), Alcuin and Theodulf. Alcuin's submission won.
Most epitaphs, if you think about it, are conventionally appreciative, and
focus on the deceased. This epitaph, written in SQUARE CAPITALS, is
'the earliest instance of accomplished Carolingian classicizing monu-
mental capitals',[5] and Alcuin offered a double focus – on the deceased
and on Charles himself. The first sixteen of the forty lines are largely
elegant boilerplate, appropriate for a great prelate. The Rome connection
is mentioned twice, in ll. 1 and 14. At l. 17, Charles claims authorship of
the epitaph and it becomes clear that the entire poem is his. At l. 17 is his
name, followed by his expression of grief in l. 18, and the next two lines
ask for him to be remembered by Hadrian, and assure him that his mind
will always follow Hadrian when he has reached heaven:

> Post patrem lacrimans **Karolus** haec carmina scribsi
>   Tu mihi dulcis amor, te modo plango, pater.
> Tu memor esto mei, sequitur te mens mea semper
>   Cum Christo teneas regna beata poli.
> (Weeping after a father, I Charles have written these lines.
> You, father, sweet love for me, I now weep for you.
> Remember me, my mind is always following you,
> May you hold heaven's blessed realms with Christ.)

In ll. 23–6 Charles links himself with Hadrian even more securely (I
have bolded the salient words to indicate this):

> Nomina iungo simul titulis, clarissime, nostra,
>   'Hadrianus **Karolus**', **rex ego** tuque pater.[6]
> Quisquis legas versus, devoto pectore supplex,
>   Amborum mitis, dic, miserere deus.
> (Our names I join together with our titles, most illustrious one,
> 'Hadrian [and] Charles', I king and you father.
> Whoever reads these lines, suppliant with devout heart,
> Kindly for us both, say, God have mercy.)

Lines 33 and 34 resume the theme of the two being joined in heaven
where Charles as son joins Hadrian as father:

*Tunc memor esto tui **nati**, pater optime, posco,*
 *'Cum patre', dic, '**natus** pergat eat iste meus.'*
(Then, I beg you, best of fathers, remember your son.
Say, 'Let the son join his father, and this is mine.')[7]

Contemporaries would no doubt have considered this a finely wrought epitaph, expressing Charles's love for and tears for the deceased. Einhard, in the chapter of his *Vita Karoli* on Charles's care for his children, after praising his 'greatness of spirit', said:

> he bore the deaths of his sons and daughter *less* patiently [than that might have led people to expect], and his love, which was *not* less, compelled him to tears. When news reached him of the death of the Roman Pontiff Hadrian whom he held as outstanding among his friends, he wept as if he had lost a brother or dearest son.[8]

Einhard's comments too were conventional in depicting love and tears. What was *not* conventional in Alcuin's epitaph of Hadrian was Charles's self-representation as author and his own centrality, not just at the epitaph's poetic heart but in visual terms too. Let your eye scroll down the poem and it will be caught by the word *Karolus* at the centre of l. 17, and then again at l. 25 with *Karolus rex ego*. The *placing* of words in epigraphic contexts, which were without punctuation, had an impact on viewers who were also readers.[9]

What's also exceptional about this epitaph is not just its survival, and in two media, parchment and stone, but how much is known about it. The author of the contemporary Lorsch Annals described its making in a way uniquely and convincingly authentic, as is the case with this author's information discussed in earlier chapters:

> that winter [795] the supreme pontiff lord Hadrian of holy memory, died. The lord king, once he had ceased his [normal period of] mourning, asked that prayers be said for him throughout the whole Christian people within his lands and sent an abundance of alms for him [to Rome] and ordered an epitaph, written in gold letters on marble, to be made in Francia so that he might send it to Rome to adorn Hadrian's sepulchre (*ebitaffium* [sic] *aureis litteris in marmore conscriptum iussit in Francia fieri ut eum partibus Romae transmitteret ad sepultura summi pontificis Adriani ornandam*).[10]

The researches of Jo Story and her colleagues from the sciences of petrology, palaeontology, geochemistry and geology have established that the 'black marble' stone for the slab was quarried in the valley of the Meuse at Sclayn near Namur (in modern Belgium).[11] How it was transferred to Rome is a question not yet answered. But there it still is, in the portico of St Peter's in the Vatican, imposingly high on the wall yet rather too high for the visitor without binoculars and a good knowledge of Latin to make out the visual ideological message.[12]

The epitaph composed by Theodulf also survives.[13] Experts on Carolingian poetry seem to agree that Theodulf was a more original poet than Alcuin; and, without being expert, I tend to agree. It too is wholly written as if by Charles. The effect is in some ways similar to that achieved by Alcuin, but at ll. 11–16, Theodulf inserts a startling passage:

> *Quem cum dira dies non exhibitura sequentem*
> *Eripuit vivis, res patuitque mihi,*
> *Protinus agnovi veteris vestigia luctus.*
> *Morsque parentum oculis est revocatus meis.*
> *Taedia Pippini sensi venientia morte,*
> *Bertradamque dolor, pro dolor, iste refert.*
> (When the dire day, not destined to allow another,
> Carried off [my spiritual father] from the living,
>   and the thing was known to me,
> I instantly recognized the traces of an old sorrow
> And the death of my parents was recalled to my eyes.
> I felt the woes that were to come with Pippin's death,
> And this grief, O grief, brings back Bertrada too.)

Theodulf presents Charles's loss of Hadrian, his spiritual father, as summoning back to his mind's eye the loss of his earthly parents. One particular line sounds especially heartfelt: *Bertradamque dolor, pro dolor, iste refert.*

The flashback may be a poetic conceit. If Theodulf imagined Charles's loss of his spiritual father jolting memories of the loss of his earthly father and mother, did the poet also recall his own refugee experience of losing parents and somehow transfer it to Charles?[14] It's impossible fully to capture Theodulf's intention, or, even, to know whether he and Charles colluded. At a number of points in his life, Charles seems to have consciously imitated his father's acts, and followed, literally, in his footsteps.[15] As for his feelings for Bertrada, Einhard depicts her grand-motherly happiness in her son's household in the years between 771 and 783.[16] She had been dead for over a decade when Einhard joined the court; and, as usual, Einhard in his *Vita Karoli* cites no witness evidence other than his own. Could Theodulf really offer a glimpse into Charles's mind? Could a twenty-first-century psychotherapist recognize the way the death of a father-figure brings back memories of the deaths of par-ents? Theodulf could have been aiming more prosaically at an evocation of dynastic continuity. In the poetry of Charles's reign, there's nothing like these lines anywhere else. Charles might have considered Theod-ulf's work 'a little too personal'.[17] He may simply have preferred Alcuin's visual centring of *Karolus*, and the representation of king and pope as 'joined'. This would not have been the only public monument from the late eighth century to project a message of collaboration.

II. CHARLES'S LETTER TO
OFFA OF MERCIA

Charles had wintered at Aachen in 795–6 and there he took delivery of a large amount of the Avar treasure at or shortly after Easter (3 April that year). The letter was written in late April or early May, when news of the assassination of the king of Northumbria on 18 April could have reached Aachen. Who was responsible for writing Charles's official let-ters is seldom clear.[18] In this case, though, the vocabulary and style can almost certainly be ascribed to Alcuin, who was still resident at Aachen until August. In the letter's salutation, Offa is addressed as *frater caris-simus*; in the first few lines he's addressed as *frater dilectissimus*, and there are three appearances of *caritas*, Alcuin's signature-term. *Amici-tia* is there too, and *concordia, pactum* and *foedus* ('alliance') drive home a message. Relations between Charles and Offa had not always been amicable, but Charles was determined to make them so now.[19] Recalling an old treaty, he would make *this* treaty 'flower in the fruit of *caritas*'. The initiative had in fact been that of Offa who in recent times had sent letters on topics of shared interest. Charles's letter responded to a series of points Offa had raised: a 'businesslike' approach.[20]

Peregrini, pilgrims, were the first subject requiring Charles's attention, as they had also attracted Pippin's. Addressing toll-collectors, Pippin had decreed: 'You are not in any circumstances to detain pilgrims at crossing-points or ferries, and you are not to demand from any pilgrim false charges on their bag, and you are not to ask for any tolls from them.'[21] Charles in the *Admonitio generalis* decreed similarly but more insistently:

> It seems to us proper and respectful that strangers (*hospites*) and pilgrims (*peregrini*) and poor people (*pauperes*) should have hostels established at various places by monks and canons, for the Lord himself will say on the great day of reward: 'I was a stranger and you took me in' (Matt. 25:35).[22]

Capacity to care for *peregrini* was signalled as 'a sort of litmus-test of the ruler's competence and of the state of public order'.[23]

Charles had also 'learned by experience that certain persons in pursuit of profit not religion (*lucra sectantes non religioni servientes*) fraudulently mingle with *peregrini* for the purpose of trading'. Such persons, if found, would have to pay tolls at the right places. Charles's tone here is hardly fraternal. The salutation had already signified a disparity: Charles was a king twice over, 'of the Franks and of the Lombards'; and, following in his father's footsteps, he was also the '*patricius* of the Romans'. Offa was simply 'king of the Mercians'.[24] Connoisseurs of diplomatic exchange appreciated these niceties.

When Charles turned to his second point, about traders (*negotiatores*) coming into his realm from Offa's, he affirmed his commitment to protecting them: 'unlawful oppression' would be dealt with by 'our judges' and 'honest justice'. Here there was indeed a show of reciprocity: 'our traders if they suffer injustice anywhere within your rule (*potestas*) should appeal to your justice, so that no disorder can arise between our subjects'. In so far as there were echoes here of the laws of Christian Roman emperors, Charles combined a fraternal tone with that of a higher authority.[25]

The third point was a particular one, concerning Odberht, also known as Eadberht, formerly king of Kent: having now become a priest Odberht was ultimately under papal jurisdiction, yet, as an exile, he was under Charles's protection. Charles showed tact and caution in leaving judgment to the pope.[26] He returned to the safer topic of trade, but here again he had the upper hand: what Offa had requested were 'black stones', i.e. quern-stones, or Roman *spolia*, or (most likely) marble from the Meuse valley (the type used for Hadrian's epitaph), but the condition attached was that Offa must ensure that Mercian exporters reverted to producing the long cloaks that they used to send to Francia and which Charles (a big man) much preferred instead of the shorter ones they had recently been sending. 'Short cloaks' were indeed the subject of one of Charles's jokes, as transmitted on the monastic grapevine to Notker of St-Gall and written up in his *Gesta Karoli* in the 880s. Charles had noticed that the Franks had taken to wearing short cloaks because they were more suitable for fighting in battle, but later realized that Frisian traders were selling these short cloaks at the same price as the larger ones. Charles, with his near-the-knuckle humour, picked up on the material values of clothes-items:

> After that, he ordered that at this price no-one should buy from them any but the larger cloaks, very broad and very long. 'What's the use of these little napkins?' he asked. 'I can't cover myself with them in bed. When I'm on horseback I can't protect myself from the wind and the rain. When I go off to empty my bowels, I catch cold because my backside is frozen!'[27]

The final part of Charles's letter went beyond fraternity. Charles treated Mercia and Northumbria as satellite states: he had sent 'a suitable charitable offering from our dalmatics and copes' to every one of the fifteen bishops in these kingdoms (i.e. he'd sent fifteen sets of vestments) for the salvation of Hadrian's soul, and asked Offa to order generalized intercessions for Hadrian's soul. He differentiated his own relationship to the late pope from Offa's: for Charles, Hadrian was *pater noster* (as the epitaphs declared); whereas for Offa, Hadrian was 'someone who loved you', *amator vester*. In addition, Charles had sent to the archbishops of Canterbury and York 'something from our worldly treasure granted to us by Christ', and to Offa himself 'a Hunnic sword-belt and sword, and two lengths of silk'. These were rich gifts that no mere king could possibly match. The Avar hoard put Charles in the imperial league.

III. THE DONATION OF CONSTANTINE, OR THE *CONSTITUTUM CONSTANTINI*

This text was much discussed and much debated in the central and later medieval period. Whether it was regarded as so important in the eighth century is another kettle of fish. Its mid-eighth-century authors' aim was to bring to bear on their own world the imagined past of the fourth century, the age of the Emperor Constantine and Pope Sylvester. In their first section, the authors worked from a vivid fiction, the fifth-century *Acts of Pope Sylvester*.[28] In the second part of the Donation, the authors forged what purported to be Constantine's decree gifting 'the western provinces' of Christendom to the pope. Though the label 'Donation of Constantine' is anachronistic (belonging to later medieval periods), I keep it because it is well-known to Anglophones (and because the abbreviation CC for *Constitutum Constantini* can be confused with the acronym for the *Codex Carolinus*).[29]

After beginning in the manner of a decree, the text swiftly became a lengthy doctrinal statement or Creed (cc. 1–5), then turned into Constantine's autobiographical account of being struck down by leprosy, the pagan priests' suggestion that bathing in the blood of innocent children would cure his sickness, his compassion for the grief of the children's mothers, and his refusal of the 'remedy' (c. 6). Saints Peter and Paul then appeared to Constantine in a dream, told him to seek Pope Sylvester, who had fled the emperor's persecution, and promised that baptism by Sylvester would cure the emperor's leprosy. Awakening, Constantine summoned Sylvester, who imposed penance on him. Penance done, Constantine renounced paganism, was baptized by Sylvester, cured from leprosy and given the post-baptismal anointing. Sylvester explained to Constantine the power given by Christ to St Peter, and the emperor accepted Peter and his deputies as his intercessors with God (cc. 7–11).

The next section consisted of Constantine's forged decree, which I summarize:

> The pope shall have supremacy over Antioch, Alexandria, Constantinople and Jerusalem and all the church of God in the whole world. The holy law shall rule where St Peter was martyred. Constantine has built within the Lateran Palace a church with a baptistery to be the head and summit of all churches. He has also constructed the churches of Saints Peter and Paul. He has conferred on these churches, in order to provide lights, estates in the east and in the west, and various islands, to be administered by Sylvester and his successors. We concede our imperial Lateran Palace, a diadem, and a tiara, the collar, and all the imperial raiment, the same rank as those who preside over the imperial cavalry, the imperial sceptres, spears and standards, banners and imperial ornaments, all the advantages of our imperial position (cc. 12–14).

The text enumerated the clergy and their powers and dignities, from the different officials to the clergy's rights to horses and 'saddle-cloths of whitest linen' to the senate's right to wear 'goats'-hair shoes'. Constantine decreed that the pope would have the right to receive into the church any noble who wished to become a cleric (c. 15). The pope could wear the diadem, but could not wear this over the clerical crown, that is, the tiara. Constantine (moving back into autobiographical mode) described how he placed the tiara on Sylvester's head, and holding the bridle of Sylvester's horse he performed the service of a groom, and decreed that the pope could wear the tiara in all processions (c. 16). Returning to decree-mode, Constantine handed over to 'Sylvester the universal pope' the palace, the city of Rome, and all the provinces, districts and cities of Italy or of the western regions to the pope and his successors (c. 17). Constantine transferred his power and his kingdom to the regions of the east, and would build in Byzantium a city in his own name.

> Where God has established the head of the Christian religion, it is not right that an earthly ruler should have jurisdiction (c. 18). All this we have confirmed and we decree that no-one must disregard what has been conceded to the holy Roman Church and to all its pontiffs. Anyone who violates this shall be bound over to eternal damnation (c. 19). And this imperial decree we confirm with our own hand and place over the body of St Peter, promising to preserve inviolably all its provisions (c. 20).[30]

Although very little is known about who was aware of, let alone read, this document in the eighth century, a key piece of evidence is a brief passage in a letter of Hadrian to Charles in 778:

> Just as in the time of the Blessed Pope Sylvester, God's holy, catholic and apostolic church was raised up and exalted by and through the bounty of the most pious Constantine of holy memory, the great emperor, who deigned to bestow power in these western regions upon it, so also in these most happy times in which you and we live, may the holy church of God – that is, of St Peter the Apostle – burgeon and exalt and continue ever more fully exalted, so that all peoples who hear of this may be able to proclaim, 'Lord, save the king! And hear us when we call upon you' [Ps. 20:9]: for behold, a new Constantine, God's most Christian emperor, has arisen in these times . . .[31]

The references to Constantine in this letter have suggested to many historians that some notary or notaries in the papal curia knew about the existence of the Donation, and that it was actually produced in the curia in the second half of the eighth century.[32] The fact that a St-Denis manuscript datable to the tail-end of the eighth or very early ninth century includes a copy of the Donation, made during the abbacy of Fardulf (792–806), establishes its terminal date.

Though the earliest copy was written in Francia, a good case can be made for the forged Donation's having originated in Rome.[33] The details of the Donation, perhaps especially the chapter on the Roman clergy, suggest intimate knowledge of Rome and curial privileges there; and the Donation's vocabulary of power and protection is that of the Roman curia.[34] An important point is that Fardulf of St-Denis was a Lombard, and that he and his two predecessors had all served Charles in Italy.[35] Thanks to the *Codex Carolinus* sequence from 739/40 to the 770s, it is possible to track not only the envoys, many of them long-lived, who helped produce and then carry communications to and fro across the Alps, but also the evolving articulation of papal ideology through frequent contacts with the Franks.[36] Hadrian's letter of 778 did not emerge from nowhere, and it certainly led somewhere. The Donation crystallized the idea of a dual regime, of papal power backed by (and thus heavily influenced by) imperial power. This was to assume visual form in the later 790s (see section XI below), and would continue to have an immense impact in later centuries.

IV. BUILDING PROJECTS I: CHARLES AND AACHEN

Charles had been thinking about and planning for an Aachen palace as early as 768, perhaps, but certainly in the 780s. The site was not virgin territory: the overwintering of 788–9 necessarily involved more than camping out. The project materialized more fully from 794–5 onwards as Charles opted for 'becoming sedentary'.[37] The annalistic text that registers this was written, more or less contemporaneously, not in Francia but in Aquitaine – the *Chronicle of Moissac*. After reporting the return of Frankish officers to Aachen from an earlier Spanish campaign, the author continued:

He had established his seat there [at Aachen], and he built a church of extraordinary size there; he made its doors and the balustrade of the gallery of bronze and constructed that church, as regards the rest of its adornment, with such great care and honour as was possible and fitting. He also built a palace there which he named the Lateran, and he collected together his treasures from the separate realms and ordered them to be brought to Aachen. But many and great were the works he made in that same place.[38]

This rather detailed account accords with some of what can still be seen at Aachen. Recent archaeological work on the church, its precise location and its relation to the palace, the use of dendrochronology and examination of important internal details, including the marble *opus sectile* (inlaid) floor beneath the wooden seat of the throne, have contributed to greatly enhanced knowledge of the church's dating, and have enabled scholars to appreciate the speed at which the church was completed.[39] The builders used a larger number of models than realized hitherto, enabling many further influences to be identified, including those of the Holy Sepulchre at Jerusalem constructed by Constantine, and the Golden Octagon at Antioch, in addition to several more churches in Europe. The system of measurements used for the palace church has been reappraised, and linked with new research on 'the new Solomonic Temple' at Aachen. Interdisciplinary scholarship across the fields of archaeology, epigraphy, numismatics and historical textual analysis has, in short, transformed understanding of this astonishing building.[40] And that was only the church! Other researchers concentrating on what is in some sense the other wing of a diptych have focused on the archaeology of the secular buildings, and have connected the entire layout of church and palace in their townscape.[41]

In addition to all the research summarized above, much exploration has been recently undertaken on a broad and comparative approach to the relationships between big buildings and organizational headquarters, religious and secular, and their economic resources and management in medieval landscapes and townscapes. Without such resources and management, there could have been no Aachen palace, nor sustenance for (to borrow Hincmar's phrase again) 'the rational people who live therein'. Palaces are places from which power emanates and is exercised. Aachen emanated power through its design and architectural style, through gardens, parks and forests, through relics and altars, through ceremonial entries, and through rituals whereby rulers were made.[42] One ruler, Charles, was laid to rest in the Aachen church and there his remains still are.[43]

Aachen was an old Roman site, but one reconstituted and rebuilt by Charles. In that sense, it was a new place, which accumulated new power and new practices of power, not least religious. At Aachen, Charles planned an association of church and palace (in that order). Because he lived to see the church's completion but not that of the palace, it would have been easier for contemporary observers to watch Charles planting and nurturing and 'growing' legitimacy through his new church. It was no palace chapel (though it's still often mistakenly called a chapel) for the private use of ruler and *palatini* only. The church was a parish church, and the parish included the members of the elite who resided there along with ordinary parishioners.[44] When Charles suspected that some would-be godparents did not meet the requirements of knowing the Lord's Prayer and the Creed (on which depended, in the course of time, teaching these to their godchildren), he tested them publicly. They blushed for shame. He gave them a second chance to learn.[45] The Aachen church was not just one place, but the most important place, where Charles engaged in the practice of power and conveyed messages of power. In that church was inscribed a poem whose message, once translated and transmitted orally, could reach as many as 7,000 parishioner-hearers.[46] It is still there written around the wall of the gallery, below the bronze balustrade of the central octagon:

> *Cum lapides vivi pacis compage ligantur*
> *Inque pares numeros omnia convenient,*
> *Claret opus Domini, totam qui construit aulam,*
> *Effectusque piis dat studiis hominum*
> *Quorum perpetui decoris structura manebit*
> *Si perfecta auctor protegat atque regat:*
> *Sic Deus hoc tutum stabile fundamine templum*
> *Quod Karolus princeps condidit, esse velit.*[47]
> (When living stones are joined in a bond of peace,
> And by equal numbers all things are harmonized,
> Let shine the work of the Lord who built the whole hall,
> And bring into effect the people's pious efforts

Whose structure of perpetual beauty will endure
If the maker protects and rules the things he has made:
Thus may God will this temple to be safe with stable foundation
Which Charles the prince built.)

The first line echoed the injunction of 1 Peter 2:5 to local believers: 'Let yourselves be built as living stones, into a spiritual temple.' Visit the Aachen church, walk to the centre of the octagon, look up and around you: the message is about the ruler's power, yes indeed, but also about the limitations of that power. Charles on his throne was not visible to those on the ground floor of the church. *This* church, then, was not built as a theatre of royalty – it was built of 'living stones joined in a bond of peace': a congregation. 'The message being conveyed was that, however close to God, the ruler was nevertheless just a layman.'[48]

V. LEO III: HIS ENEMIES AND HIS FRIENDS, 796–9

The author of the *Vita* of Leo III began, as each Life in the *Liber Pontificalis* did, with a mention of the pope's parentage. The author of Hadrian's *Vita* had been exceptional: for the first time a *Vita* had begun by asserting that his subject was 'a very distinguished man, sprung from noble ancestry and born to influential Roman parents'. Leo's *Vita* began with no such claims: 'he was brought up and educated in the treasury of the patriarchate and was spiritually trained in all the Church teaching'. Responsibility for the recruitment of boys for such training ultimately rested with the pope in office – in this case Hadrian, who evidently did not confine appointments at junior rank to the nobility.[49] The rest of the opening chapter of Leo's *Vita* is conventional, as is chapter 2 on his election, ordination and early performance, though one sentence stands out: 'For his clergy he greatly increased the stipend for priestly functions', which took the form of gratuities on important feast-days. Leo attested his sympathies with non-noble ranks. This Life continues that of Hadrian in consisting 'almost entirely . . . of extracts from registers recording [papal] expenditure on [Rome's] churches, which virtually take the place of history'.[50] There are 113 chapters in

Leo's *Vita*, and only cc. 11–26 could be considered 'history' as in the contingency of political decisions and events.

Leo, like his predecessor (and like his successor-but-one Paschal I), was intent on making history in another sense: imposing a new form of papal power by literally constructing the papal city.[51] 'Construction' included the development of liturgy and ritual performances, and, to sustain these, finance and administration. The writers of the 'official' annals, the *ArF* and the reviser, are very brief – still more so the authors of the Lorsch Annals and other 'minor annals' – but at least they report, as the *Vita* does not, that the first thing Leo did on his election was to let Charles know about it:

> He quickly sent his legates [here meaning 'senior officials'] to the king with the keys to the *confessio* of St Peter [i.e. the area in front of the altar above St Peter's tomb], the standard (*vexillum*) of the city of Rome and other gifts, and asked him to despatch one of his leading men to secure the Roman people's fidelity and subjection by oaths (*fides et subjectio per sacramenta*). Angilbert, abbot of St-Riquier, was sent for this purpose and through him the king also despatched to St Peter's at this time a large part of the treasure which Duke Eric of Friuli had brought him from Pannonia this same year.

Eighth-century popes no longer notified the Emperor in Constantinople of their election, they notified the Frankish king. Leo III did more: the symbolic act of sending keys and standard to Charles signified a historic change. The Late Roman history of the symbolic handing over of city-keys to conquerors had been revived in the eighth century. After the Lombard king Aistulf's submission to King Pippin in 756, the keys of Ravenna and of some twenty cities and fortresses in the exarchate were taken by Abbot Fulrad of St-Denis to Rome and laid on the *confessio* of St Peter.[52] The message was clear: an acknowledgement of Rome's authority.[53] Key-traffic in the reverse direction too had long carried symbolic force of a quite different order: papal gifts of keys to the *confessio* of St Peter had been dispensed liberally by Gregory I; and in the late 730s Gregory III had twice sent such keys to Charles Martel.[54] A (?the) *vexillum Romanae urbis* had not been mentioned in any text before Leo III's gift. Neither Roman nor Frankish authors say anything more about Leo's pontificate after 796 until 799.

Leo's keys-and-standard inaugural message had an important corollary:

that the purpose of Angilbert's mission to Rome was 'to secure the Roman people's fidelity and subjection by oath'. The implication was that Charles's position vis-à-vis Rome was to be formally recognized; the Romans' 'subjection' necessarily publicly performed *now* as it had not been before. Leo was well aware that Hadrian's kinsmen still held commanding positions in the government of Rome. He was no less aware of his own deficiencies in that department: lack of resources, lack of powerful kin. The silence of papal sources on the three years between spring 796 and spring 799 can be explained in terms of the need for Leo to re-present and embed the Romans' fidelity and papal power in the city. Charles's preoccupation with events elsewhere, in and around his expanded realm and in far-off locations, explains the silence of Frankish sources on Leo's doings.

VI. CHARLES, BYZANTIUM AND EIRENE'S COUP, 797–8

'On 15 August 797, the emperor Constantine VI was terribly and irrevocably blinded by the will of his mother and her counsellors, with the intention of killing him. In this way his mother Eirene took power.'[55] Thus recorded Theophanes, writing nearly twenty years after these events. Relations between Eirene and Charles had become cool after the breaking-off by Charles of the young emperor's betrothal to Charles's daughter Rotrud in 787. In 788, Eirene had sent an army of Greeks to southern Italy; and, to operate further north in Lombardy, a force led by Charles's one-time brother-in-law Adelchis, son of Desiderius, in a now-or-never enterprise to recover an Italian kingdom: an enterprise that failed. She had also sent a treasurer to cover costs, together with the governor of Sicily and his chief officers to ravage the Beneventans' lands.[56] Eirene had grasped the importance of sea communications, and of the island of Sicily, but for the moment she had other priorities: building projects, including a new palace and various churches and charitable institutions, to stir popular support, and working to retain the loyalty of senior churchmen and, even more essential, the military.[57]

Probably in the spring of 797, Constantine VI made an attempt at contact with Charles. An envoy named Theoktistos arrived at Aachen from Governor Nicetas of Sicily, bringing also a letter from Constantine – for whom it was too late. His mother's efforts (and to be fair, there is only Theophanes' word for this) resulted in 'the way she took power' on 15 August 797.[58] Violence, and in particular blinding, were long-practised ways of taking power in Byzantium.[59]

Communications between Eirene and Charles seemed to have picked up after this. It was Eirene who took the initiative. In 798, her envoys Michael, the *patricios* of Phrygia, and a priest named Theophilos, arrived at Aachen bearing a letter for Charles: their mission was to secure the release of the brother of Patriarch Tarasius of Constantinople, Sisinnius, who had been among those taken prisoner in Benevento in 788.[60] Charles, having played a long game, agreed to Sisinnius's release. The mission's success, from Constantinople's standpoint, naturally improved Charles's relations with Eirene. Both of them had important interests to attend to in Sicily and in the wider world of the Mediterranean, as well as in the Balkans and the Veneto.[61]

Sometimes an unprepossessing bit of text can be elevated to the dignity of a key piece of evidence. This is what occurred in 1949, when a German scholar (re-)discovered a 'Memo' in a collection of notes on computistics (calculations of dates) made for Archbishop Hildebald of Cologne probably put together in 805 from a model written in 798:

> These are the years from the beginning of the world ... up to this 31st year of the reign of king Charles – this is the year when he received hostages from Saxony, a third of the population, and when *missi* came from Greece to hand over the empire (*imperium*) to him – down to the year 5998 which corresponds to the year AD 798, and whoever isn't pleased with this, let him sweat, and read, and count better.[62]

From this can be inferred that first, the computistic expert was calculating on a Spanish dating-system that started at 5,200 years before the birth of Christ; secondly, the Apocalypse, the end of time, would come 6,000 years after the beginning – adding 5,200 to 798, the expert worked out how near he was to the end; thirdly, the expert was struck by the coincidence in 798 of the transfer of a third of the Saxons and an offer 'from Greece' (thus, from the Empress Eirene) of *imperium*; and finally, the scribe had his own wry sense of humour.

Imperium could mean various things, from 'empire' to 'command' (as a noun) to 'rule of some lands' (in this case, in Italy, or perhaps the northern Balkans). In recent decades, most scholars have plumped for the interpretation 'lands'.[63] Alcuin, thanks to his many correspondents, had been able to look at a big picture early in 790, when his gaze extended from the Frisians in the north, to the Hagarenes (Saracens) in Africa and Asia Minor.[64] In the late 790s, thanks to a conjuncture of scholars' computational speculations and apocalyptic fears with two peculiarly shocking events (and a hyperactive rumour-mill in Rome), another big picture began to shape itself in Alcuin's mind.

VII. CHARLES AND THEODULF, 798–9

Theodulf's first appearance in the sources as bishop of Orléans came in a letter of Alcuin written in July 798.[65] Directly after this, Charles appointed Theodulf as a royal *missus* to southern Burgundy and the lower Rhône valley and what was then called Septimania (or, to use Roman/ecclesiastical terminology, the provinces of Lugdunensis (Lyons and its environs), Viennensis (Vienne and its environs), and Narbonnensis Prima and Seconda). The journey of these *missi* took three to four months, and then they dictated their report to a scribe. Late in 798/ early 799, Theodulf wrote a 956-line poem reflecting on his experience. What had first struck him particularly hard was the ubiquity of litigants offering bribes (*munera*).[66] Then he castigated unworthy judges, urging them never to accept bribes, but to pay special attention to the poor and needy. The final section of the poem expressed his horror at the cruelty of human judgments and penalties.[67] Nearly thirty years ago, Larry Nees suggested a connection between Theodulf's poem and Charles's imperial coronation.[68] Reform was the linking theme. Theodulf's commitment had impressed Charles, and in 801, Leo promoted Theodulf to the rank of archbishop.[69] In a letter to Theodulf himself after Charles had left Rome, Alcuin reported the words of 'Candidus, our son, your faithful servant', who had just returned from Rome:

> With what a free voice (*libera vox*) you [Theodulf] brought forth your proof-texts! how much you impressed those you encountered, whether persons high or low! how conscientiously you pursued your ecclesiastical business . . . ! 'Cry aloud, spare not, lift up thy voice like a trumpet!' . . . 'Set the trumpet to your mouth like an eagle over the house of God!'[70]

Alcuin surely had in mind the role of the parrhesiast, that is, someone who speaks truth to power, which ancient authors had admired. At

Rome, Theodulf had assumed that role, and become the most effective advocate for Alcuin's solution to the problem of judging the one who could not be judged.[71]

Important though Theodulf's voice was in Rome in early December 800, his writings had been influential since the late 780s, from his poem *Ad episcopos* (To the bishops), probably dating from 788, and his contribution to the *Admonitio generalis* (March 789), through to the *Opus Caroli* in 793, the poems of the mid-790s to the epic-sized *Ad iudices* (To judges) of 798–9.[72] True, these works were written for courtiers, for ecclesiastical and secular elites who were at the same time holders of public office such as counts and *missi*, but it was precisely in those circles that ideas and ideals of reform and *correctio* reverberated. They were transmitted on parchment, passed from hand to hand, and orally, through public recitation. They were conveyed artistically as well, to an audience consisting of Theodulf's clerical entourage and retainers, other high-status visitors and those serving on the estates of the bishop's lordship, in the Germigny apse mosaic of *c*.806 depicting the Ark of the Covenant that Theodulf commissioned.[73] The sociologist Max Weber used the metaphor of a track-changer or signalman on a railway, 'determining down which of several tracks social development would proceed'. Another sociologist, Michael Mann, suggested 'amending' Weber's metaphor to ' "moments" of tracklaying, and of converting to a new gauge. In these moments we find an autonomy of social concentration, organization, and direction that is lacking in more institutionalized times ... [These sources of social power] are "the generalized means" through which human beings make their own history.'[74] The 790s were such a moment, and Theodulf was the signalman.

VIII. THE *DE VILLIS* CAPITULARY

'The steward ... was a very hard-worked man, and when one reads the seventy separate and particular injunctions which Charlemagne addressed to his stewards one cannot help feeling sorry for him.'[75] I admire Eileen Power's empathy for the stewards, but I find it hard to feel sorry for them. They were highly valued royal servants, charged with such important responsibilities – minutely set out in Charles's *De villis* capitulary – as the minding of hostages (c. 12), the provision of key military supplies (c. 30) and equipment (cc. 42, iron tools, 62, shield-makers, 64, war-carts and weapons, 68, barrels), and engaging with local markets whenever possible (cc. 8, 9, 32, 39). The mentions of the queen at cc. 16, 27, 47 and 58 throw a useful sidelight on her contribution to the running of the royal household and its economy.

C. 16 prescribes:

> It is our wish that whatever we or the queen (*nos aut regina*) may order any steward (*iudex*) or whatever our officials, the seneschal or the butler (*sinescalcus et butticularius*), may order them in our name or in the name of the queen (*de verbo nostro aut reginae*), they shall carry out in full as they are instructed. And whoever falls short in this through negligence, let him abstain from drinking from the moment he is told to do so until he comes into our presence or the presence of the queen (*usque dum in praesentia nostra aut reginae*) and seeks forgiveness from us. And if a steward is in the army, or on guard-duty, or on a mission, or is away elsewhere, and gives an order to his subordinates and they do not carry it out, let them come on foot to the palace, and let them abstain from food and drink until they have reasons for failing in their duty in this way; and then let them receive their punishment, either in the form of a beating or in any other way that we or the queen (*aut quomodo nobis vel reginae*) shall decide.

C. 27 prescribes that

> our houses are to have continuous watch-fires and guards to keep them safe. And when our *missi* and their retinues are on their way to or from the palace, they shall under no circumstances take lodging in the royal manor houses, except on our express orders or on those of the queen.

And c. 47 that

> our hunters and falconers, and the other servants who are in permanent attendance on us at the palace (*qui nobis in palatio adsidue deserviunt*), shall throughout our estates be given such assistance as we or the queen may command in our letters (*consilium in villis nostris habeant secundum quod nos vel regina per litteras iusserimus*).

The fourth and last clause to mention the queen, c. 58, is worth citing a little more fully:

> When our puppies are entrusted to the stewards, they are to feed them at their own expense, or that of their subordinates, that is, the mayors or deans, or cellarers, so that they in their turn can feed them from their resources – unless there should be an order from ourselves or the queen that they are to be fed on our estate at our own expense. In this case, the steward is to send a man to them to see to their feeding and is to set aside food for them; and there will be no need for the man to go to the kennels every day.

This potentially queenly role too has its own significance. Puppies are part of the domestic scenario of so many representations of royal (or even presidential) family life, right down to modern times. Like children, these creatures will grow up, and have a future. The queen, meanwhile, can play a quasi-maternal role, if she so wishes, as a feeder of little ones, while the kennel-man takes a day off.

The distinction between unacceptable and acceptable gifts, c. 3, echoing that of Theodulf in his poem on justice, helps fix the date of *De villis* to 798.[76] Charles's seventy injunctions in the capitulary were outnumbered by the seventy-two different species of plants that every steward was to grow in his garden (while enumerating the varieties of fruit-tree species . . .). The nutritional importance of garden-produce in this period was recognized by Charles and his contemporaries, and, increasingly, by archaeologists and historians.[77] Edward Gibbon mocked Charles for concerning himself with such humdrum matters and showing no sense of proportion: 'I touch with reverence the laws of Charlemagne . . . They compose not a system, but a series, of occasional and minute edicts, for the correction of abuses, the reformation, of manners, the economy of his farms, the care of his poultry, and even the sale of his eggs.'[78]

Charles's concern was not with detail for its own sake: he recognized the crucial importance of establishing a system (*pace* Gibbon) of provisioning the palace, and a cadre of officials (*iudices* and *maiores* and other *ministeriales*) to run it. He had got the measure of the logistical changes required when the court became settled at Aachen, and of the human resources now available in the shape of literate and numerate stewards.[79] These changes were quite new; the burdens of itinerancy on managers of palaces and royal abbeys dwindling to become a thing of the past. Charles was very interested indeed in the hunting reserves in the Aachen landscape, and the yields of forests scattered throughout the royal estates generally – making available meat (fresh and preserved) for a much enlarged court.[80] He had grasped the need for the best communications possible, and the best cavalry: as is evident in *De villis*, cc. 13, 14 and 15, that meant rearing the best horses. Above all, Charles was determined to rule as a responsible lord, earning the trust of his dependants. He also urged stewards and *maiores* to set an example to others (c. 36, this in the context of paying tithes). The people for whom I feel a twinge of sorrow were the women textile workers. Their workshops were to be well-organized, 'with houses, rooms with fireplaces, and huts with screens', but there is a mistrustful note in the instructions for these dwellings 'to have good fences all around them, and strong doors, so that the women can perform properly the tasks we assign them' – as if both king and steward had to cast shades of the prison house on the female workforce.

IX. THE ATTEMPTED COUP AGAINST LEO III, AND ITS CONTEXT, 799

Nothing in the *Vita* of Leo, nothing in the *ArF* or the revised annals, quite prepares the reader for what is to come on 25 April 799. Here, in summary form, is the account of the *Vita* of Leo, cc. 11–15:

(Ch. 11) Leo had come out of his palace, Paschal [one of Hadrian's nephews] came to meet him and hypocritically asked his pardon for not wearing clerical dress. Leo pardoned him. Campulus the treasurer, travelling in Leo's retinue, conversed with him. Some malign men, armed, awaited him outside the monastery of Saints Stephen and Sylvester. Suddenly they leaped out and rushed him to the ground, Paschal at his head, Campulus at his feet.

(Ch. 12) All those around, unarmed and scared of the weapons, turned to flee. The ambushers [again] threw him to the ground. They cut his clothes off him and tried to put out his eyes and blind him totally. They cut off his tongue, leaving him – so they thought – blind and dumb in the middle of the street. Later they dragged him to the monastery's *confessio* and in front of the altar they tried again to put out his eyes and cut out his tongue, then beat him with clubs and left him half-dead and drenched in blood, and kept him in the monastery under guard.

(Ch. 13) Afraid Leo might be rescued, Campulus and Paschal ... made him come to them by night and took him to ... the monastery of St Erasmus, where they locked him up ... But it happened that, through God's foreknowledge and action, Leo recovered his sight and his tongue was restored to him so he could speak.

(Ch. 14) When God displayed this miracle through his servant [Leo], Albinus the chamberlain and others of the faithful secretly rescued him and took him to St Peter's.

(Ch. 15) Leo had gone to the hall of St Peter's, where straightaway Winigis the glorious duke of Spoleto came with his army to meet him. When he saw Leo able to see and speak, he took him to Spoleto. Hearing this, the faithful from the cities of the Romans came to him; and along with some from those cities and bishops and priests and Roman clergy and leading men from the cities, Leo set out to visit His Excellency the Lord Charles, king of the Franks and Lombards and patrician of the Romans.

This summary of the *ArF*'s much briefer version occupies six lines (as does that of the Lorsch Annals):

> During the Greater Litany [25 April] Romans seized the pope and blinded him and cut out his tongue. Sent to a place of confinement, he escaped through a wall at night, reached the lord king's officers who were then at St Peter's basilica, namely Abbot Wirund of Stavelot and Duke Winigis of Spoleto, and was escorted to Spoleto. The lord king crossed the Rhine, set out for Saxony, and encamped at the place (*locus*) called Paderborn.[81]

Both the *Vita* of Leo and the *ArF* were written some time after the event. The first reports would have gone by couriers to reach Charles, probably in the second half of May, at Aachen where he was prolonging his winter-residence, hosting a Council and a theological debate between Felix of Urgell and Alcuin, and planning a campaign into Saxony. The reports were shocking – but were they surprising?[82] Given the recent history of violent conflict in eighth-century Rome, those in the know – curial officials and their aristocratic kin – would present the first reports to reach Charles at Aachen in curial news-speak. Three letters of Alcuin, one written in 798 and two in 799, conveyed various understandings of what had happened and what should now be done. Responding in November 798, to Archbishop Arn's carefully worded message that Leo was 'suffering outrages from the children of discord',

Alcuin assured Arn that he had been 'warmed into life again with joy to know that Leo could still serve God'.[83] Early in 799, referring back to Arn's previous letter of 798, Alcuin reported that he had just received another letter from Arn mentioning

> certain complaints about Leo's conduct (*mores*) and your own danger because of the Romans. But I did not want that letter to get into the hands of anyone else, so Candidus alone read it through with me, and then it was put on the fire so that no scandal should arise from the carelessness of the man who looks after my correspondence.[84]

In June 799, writing to Charles, Alcuin described how disturbed he was by 'the manifold wickedness of the ungodly . . . among the greatest and the highest' – *quod metuendum est valde* – this is a situation greatly to be feared:

> Until now there have been three *personae* [authorities] in the world: one is the apostolic sublimity which has been wont to govern the see of the blessed Peter, and your reverend benevolence has taken the trouble to inform me of what has happened to him who was the rector of that see. The second is the imperial office (*imperialis dignitas*) and secular power (*saecularis potentia*) of second Rome [meaning Constantinople, or, by metonymy, Byzantium]: the report spreads everywhere of how unchristian was the way in which the governor of that empire was deposed, not by outsiders, but by his own people and inhabitants of his own city (*proprii et concives*). The third is the royal office (*regalis dignitas*) to which you have been ordained as the rector of the Christian people by Christ's dispensation, surpassing the two dignitaries just mentioned in the excellence of your power, the lustre of your wisdom and the loftiness of your dignity as a ruler. Behold, upon you alone rests the entire health, deteriorated as it is, of the churches of Christ![85]

Charles had let Alcuin know what had happened to the pope and apostolic sublimity (see below). Alcuin's personal reactions were of alarm at the prospect of 'dangerous times' foretold in two particularly alarmist Scriptural texts (Alcuin himself had included these in the *Admonitio generalis*).[86] Apocalyptic speculation was evidently of interest in some quarters, and especially in Spain. Charles himself, though he ordered a copy of a book on the prophecies of Daniel, seems not to have had in his library the standard apocalyptic texts; and in 793 he had taken steps to dampen down panic over famine. In 799, Charles's reaction to the news from Rome about the attack on Pope Leo, and his narrow escape, was calm and practical: he made for Paderborn and awaited Leo's arrival. These different responses are mirrored in modern historians' varying reactions to 'dangerous times'.[87]

Though Eirene had reaped political rewards from the Council of Nicaea in 787 and restoring the veneration of icons, her coup put her own position in jeopardy. A mother's killing of her son was universally viewed with horror. Patriarchy and good old-fashioned misogyny ensured that a woman ruling in her own right was viewed as monstrous in Byzantium as it was in the West. Dowager-regents were acceptable, just, because they were time-limited. Before Eirene, there had never been a female *basileus* (emperor), and there would never be another. Few scholars take seriously Theophanes's claim that Charles offered Eirene marriage, and to my mind it goes beyond the bounds of credibility. Her offer of 'lands', if credible at all, looks like a rather desperate effort to save her position.[88] Diplomatic exchanges in the cause of 'peace' were a more plausible route to political survival.

In August 799, to Arn, Alcuin referred to Leo's *aemulatores* (enemies) who

> are planning to charge him with adultery and perjury and then arranging for him to purge himself of these charges by . . . a most solemn oath, and by a secret plan then persuading him to lay down his pontificate without an oath and retire to a monastery.[89]

Alcuin's reaction to the plans of Leo's *aemulatores* was to tell Arn: 'If I stood at [Leo's] side, I should reply on his behalf, "Let him who is without sin cast the first stone".'

Leo's rapid recovery from the violence of the attack could not but raise another question: was it indeed a miracle? Theodulf addressed this in a poem to Charles, evidently written after April 799 and before late December 800:

> You are a protector of wealth, avenger of wrongs,
> > bestower of honours.
> Whatever you do is done by the facilitation of God.
> You are the weapons of bishops, the hope and defence of clergy.
> Through you the priesthood maintains holy laws.

I am in error if Pope Leo himself did not experience this,
As my poet's pipe will now briefly sing again:
His people wickedly ejected him from city and office,
Whom they prepared for death, not life.
But your kind pity, king, embraced him,
Who comforts, soothes, warms, nourishes and adorns
Him whom a furious man despoiled of tongue and sight
Of sacred vestments and holy orders.
Peter restored the things with which malicious Judas
  absconded . . .
A rebellious band followed with Judas as an example . . .
The crowd denies these were taken, denies they were restored,
Yet says it wanted these to be removed.
A miracle that they [i.e. tongue and sight, vestments and orders]
were returned, or could not be taken away!
But it's a matter of doubt which is more to be wondered at.
(*Est tamen in dubio, hinc mirer an inde magis.*)[90]

In that last line, *Est tamen in dubio*, Theodulf voiced a widely held view, yet left open the possibility that the attack on Leo was, if not a miracle, an attempt that failed. The rest of the poem is a panegyric to Charles, ending with an assurance that clergy and people badly wanted to see him in Rome (but also to come by way of Orléans, the see to which Theodulf had recently been appointed – this poet, like others, lost no opportunity to angle for a personal favour). Perhaps Paschal and Campulus 'miscalculated and bargained on getting Frankish support'.[91] When it came actually to getting Frankish support, however, Leo proved the smarter operator.

Alcuin, to judge by his letters, was a genuinely charitable man.[92] He emerged with credit from the insinuations of the *aemulatores*. He found the requisite legal argument against their plan to charge Leo in canons issued in the name of Pope Sylvester (in fact the canons were forged during an early-sixth-century dispute, but Alcuin believed they were genuine, and of which he may have had the only copy) declaring, 'the apostolic see judges but cannot be judged'.[93] Yet more important for his credibility, he won the moral argument. It was Alcuin who imagined himself standing beside Leo, and remembering Christ's words: 'Let him who is without sin cast the first stone' (John, 8:7).

X. PADERBORN, 799

It was already known that Charles planned to campaign that year in Saxony, but he was still at Aachen on 13 June. Soon after that, the war-assembly was held under Charles's leadership, but with the Young Charles and Pippin of Italy at his side, at the confluence of the Rhine and the Lippe at Lippeham. The army then moved to Paderborn, and from there Charles sent his namesake on ahead with his troops further into Saxony, while he himself, with his son Pippin and the rest, awaited Leo's arrival in July or August at Paderborn: a place in which Charles had already invested a good deal of political capital, and where he had impressed and conciliated Saxons when summoning assemblies there in 777, 783 and 785. In 799, probably in mid-September, Pope Leo himself arrived at Paderborn.

The only detailed account of Leo's reception to have survived was in the form of an (incomplete) epic poem, *Karolus Magnus et Leo Papa*. The poet described, as it were in a flashback, how Charles, while taking a nap during a hunt, had had a terrible premonitory dream: that Pope Leo had been attacked and mutilated by a Roman mob, but that Heaven had repaired his face with new light, and he had then fled to seek help in Spoleto, and thence travelled north to Saxony where Charles and his army waited. The entire army were astounded to see him . . . Charles, recollecting his dream, had no doubt of what was to come. While the Young Charles battled Saxons further east, his brother Pippin rode out to greet the pope. There was a meeting between Charles and Leo.

The date of the poem is still debated. Some experts think it could have been written as early as 799; others prefer a date in 800 or later. Its details are sometimes read as tantamount to facts, although not every scholar would go that far. Two interesting details are not to be found in the poem but come, instead, from an unusually well-informed annalistic source: Leo brought with him to Paderborn no fewer than 203 of his Roman counsellors (*consiliatores*), and *missi* from the Empress Eirene were also present.[94] Leo's stay was surprisingly brief: probably little over two weeks.[95] It was a long way to come for a fortnight's break. But Leo wanted to return to Rome quickly: assuming that the 203 counsellors accompanied Leo back to Rome, that would have given him a head-start in restoring stability there, with time to continue his building projects. Charles might have welcomed Eirene's apparent continuing interest in diplomatic contacts in the cause of peace. But he also had to respond strategically to potential frontier-problems resulting from the deaths of two important *palatini*: Governor Gerold of Bavaria (his erstwhile brother-in-law and – so far as can be known – a loyal official for nearly thirty years) killed fighting the Avars, and Duke Eric of Friuli, killed in an ambush by townspeople in Croatia.[96] These were sensitive zones for Byzantium too.[97]

Charles would have taken heart from the arrival of a monk from Jerusalem late in 799, bringing blessings from the patriarch and relics from the site of the Lord's resurrection which he had sent to the king: 'Christmas was celebrated at Aachen; and when Charles gave the monk leave to depart, he gave a priest from his palace, Zacharias, to go with him, to whom he also entrusted his gifts to be delivered to those reverend places.'[98] Meanwhile, Charles seems to have been unsure of how to cope with the situation of the pope in Rome. Both parties needed time, and time was what they got: roughly a year elapsed between Leo's arrival back in Rome on 29 November 799, and Charles's arrival at Rome on 25 November 800. That was to be an exceptionally busy year for both king and pope.

XI. BUILDING PROJECTS II: LEO AND ROME

Leo's building projects on the Lateran Hill had been begun before 799. The author of his *Vita* includes, at cc. 3–6, lists of Hadrian's donations to Roman churches between 792 and 795, and then, at cc. 7–10, Leo's donations during the years 796–9. Of these the most important, completed in 797–8, was

> the *triclinium* (dining-hall) built in his own name in the Lateran patriarchate, greater than all other such (*triclinium maiorem super omnes triclineos*) and adorned on a wondrous scale . . . He adorned the apse-vault and the apse with mosaic, and on the two other apses he painted various representations on the marble construction.[99]

Part of the Lateran Palace, much altered and restored on several occasions (including, especially, 1743) survives today. Coloured pen-drawings and sketches by church historians of the second half of the sixteenth century also survive of the painted and mosaic representations.[100] The apse mosaic showed the risen Christ telling his Apostles (Matt. 28:19–20):

> *Euntes ergo docete omnes gentes, baptizantes eos in nomine patris et filii et spiritus sancti, docentes eos servare omnia quaecumque mandavi vobis. Et ecce ego vobiscum sum omnibus deus, usque ad consummationem saeculi* (Go ye therefore, and teach all nations, baptizing them in the name of the Father, and of the Son, and of the Holy Ghost: Teaching them to observe all things whatsoever I have commanded you: and, lo, I am with you always, *even* unto the end of the world. [King James Version])

This, the fundamental message of universal mission, now 'projected a role for the pope as ruler' which connected with that envisaged in the *Constitutum Constantini* (Donation of Constantine).[101] To the viewer's left, in a scene wholly reconstructed in the eighteenth century, Christ handed a standard to a kneeling Constantine and two keys to a bearded figure clad in liturgical tunic and the scarf (*pallium*) denoting papal authority – St Peter or his successor, Sylvester; to the viewer's right, St Peter handed the *pallium* to the kneeling Pope Leo, and standard to 'the Lord King Charles'.

A second, smaller *triclinium* was completed by 800, which Leo called by his own name, the Leonine. It was a banqueting-hall able to provide seating-room for 130 people and was a social space as well as a showcase for the pope as host. In Charles's own lifetime, the audience for the mosaics reached thousands of guests and visitors to Rome and the Lateran Palace. Alterations and restorations notwithstanding, it's not too far-fetched to imagine Charles, when he came to Rome in 800, viewing these scenes and connecting these images of historical actors with himself, with Leo, and with Christ's command. Both Charles and Leo envisaged, and completed, the greatest building projects of the early medieval Christian West, at Aachen and at Rome. Because 'the intervisuality of architectural style' also involved intertextuality, Charles's and Leo's contemporaneous appreciation of 'the power of the visual' left an unexpectedly potent effect on political ideas in the early medieval West.[102]

XII. ROYAL FAMILY MATTERS, 799–800: GISELA AND CHARLES'S SONS

On 13 July 799, within some six weeks of the Aachen court's hearing the news of the attack on Pope Leo, there was a royal family gathering there. Charles himself was keen to leave for Lippeham and Saxony, with at least two of his sons, to prepare for the Paderborn meeting. What – or who – determined his decision to stay a little longer at Aachen? On 13 July, Gisela, Charles's sister, had come there from the abbey at Chelles where she lived as a *Deo devota* (a quasi-widowed state), to transact family business at Aachen. The business was in two parts: the granting of two extensive clusters of properties in Artois and Vermandois (both in northern France) to the monastery of St-Denis, and Charles's confirmation of the grant. Gisela had inherited or acquired these lands and they were therefore hers to give, following the injunction (by now standard in donations) of Matt. 6:20, 'Lay up for yourselves treasure in Heaven.' The beneficiaries were to be the monks and the lands would now become the ecclesiastical property of St-Denis, with alms and donations. Charles's confirmation is a copy kept in a cartulary (book of charter-copies) of *c*.1200.[103] Gisela's charter survives as an (only slightly incomplete) original.[104] She identified herself in the opening sentence as *nobilissima regis filia Pippini et Bertredane regine*, and in her final attestation as *nobilissima filia Pippini regis*. Beneath her *signum* (that word was followed by a cross) and attestation were those of her three nephews: Young Charles, Pippin and Louis, in that order, each identifying their *signum* and cross as of 'the most noble son of the most outstanding lord king Charles'. Gisela seems to have brought along her own *cancellarius* or notary, Winerad, who had prepared the document and signed it.

More than a family occasion, this was a *royal* family occasion. The Young Charles had been invited, or summoned, by their father to be ready for the campaign in Saxony; hence his presence at Aachen in June. Gisela's charter documents Pippin's presence at Aachen. Only the *Karolus Magnus et Leo Papa* poet mentions Pippin's presence at Paderborn, whence he had gone from Aachen with Charles and his namesake. The only evidence for Louis' presence at Aachen is Gisela's charter; and there is no evidence for his being at Paderborn. Taken together, these and other details support the impression that Charles's sons were summoned as and when required by their father.[105]

At this point no source reports any sign of friction between the brothers. They could have relished the Aachen meeting as an opportunity to discuss future plans with their father, and his and their counsellors. Gisela, their aunt, and Charles too, must have approved their acting as attesters of her donation. The nephews might have regarded her presence as conciliatory: she was after all a senior and powerful figure at the family's heart, glad to present herself at Aachen as such. It's not necessary to infer that the family-meeting was entirely happy, however. Three brothers might not have meant a trio of what contemporaries called *pares*, peers, but instead have resembled a little hierarchy, as their attestations did on the parchment page, with the first-born at the top.

Gisela was based at Chelles, probably the most influential, as well as among the most learned, of the high-born women for whom that house was home. The so-called *Annales Mettenses Priores* may have been written at Chelles, thanks to the patronage of Gisela herself. Alcuin rejoiced to call Gisela his friend, and a woman 'potent in words'.[106] If (and this can be no more than a guess) Gisela commissioned and supervised the production of the *AMP*, she seems to have ensured that her eldest nephew received a warm write-up in these annals, where Young Charles was called *primogenitus*, *nobilissimus* and *dilectus*, and a record of his victories was noted.[107] Though the Aachen meeting in July 799 might well have revealed relationships and preferences within the family, it masked tensions too. Young Charles's position within the family was to change dramatically in 800, as will become apparent in the pages below.

In mid-March in 800, Charles left Aachen and 'conducted a thorough survey (*perlustravit* – a technical administrative term) of the coastal region adjoining the Gallic ocean, because piratical Northmen were infesting the sea at this time . . . He saw to the building of a fleet, and organized fortifications.'[108] He then 'went on a tour of inspection (*circuivit* – another surveying term) of his estates and also of the bodies of the saints . . . until after reaching Rouen and crossing the Seine he came to Tours where the body of St Martin rests.'[109]

He had celebrated Easter at St-Riquier, where Angilbert, 'close to the king and his most intimate counsellor', was lay-abbot.[110] If Picardy and the lower Seine, Neustrian lands between the Seine and Loire, were the territories that Charles had had carefully surveyed, it looks as if they had been identified (again) as forming the kingdom of the Young Charles, now on the agenda for his formal anointing to that realm at Rome on 25 December. Charles did not reach Tours alone: 'his sons Charles and Pippin were already with him, and his son Louis arrived there too'.[111] This was the second meeting of the three brothers and their father within a year.

In the ninth century, the anonymous author of the *Life of Alcuin* told a little story about a significant moment at that Tours meeting: Alcuin had prophesied that the heir to Charles's empire would prove to be Louis, 'because of his humility'.[112] Another version of the story was that Paulinus of Aquileia had come to the meeting. First the Young Charles had marched into the church with a large retinue; Paulinus, on finding out who this was, had interrupted the service, and the Young Charles had to leave the church. The same thing happened with Pippin, who came and went. Finally Louis entered, knelt at the altar and prostrated himself, then, with tears in his eyes, implored Christ's help. Paulinus told him he could attain his father's rank 'because of your piety'. Later Paulinus told Charles what had happened, adding, 'If God wants to choose a king of the Franks from your family, it will be Louis.'[113] Two rather different versions written up by different authors at different times point to a story with a common root: uncertainty over the succession. Another pointer in that direction is the claim that that summer Charles summoned Louis 'to accompany him to Italy, but very soon after, changed his mind and told him to remain at home'.[114]

XIII. LIUTGARD: *CONCUBINA* OR *REGINA*?

There had been an extra reason to choose Tours as the rendezvous in 800: Charles had 'gone to St Martin' for the sake of prayer, because his wife (*coniux*) Liutgard was in poor health, and so he stayed there for some days with her. Her husband and her three stepsons were at her deathbed when she died at Tours on 4 June, and was buried there.

Einhard had a list of Charles's wives and concubines: Liutgard was not clearly assigned to either category, though he made it clear that after her death, Charles had only concubines.[115] Earlier generations of historians were happy to call her a queen. Recently, however, it's been pointed out that though Alcuin wrote to or about her in eight letters (several not very precisely dated), Liutgard was never called queen in any of them. Neither was she identified as a requester of any of Charles's charters, nor mentioned as the object of prayers in any monastery. She featured in the annalistic record only once – when she died and was buried.[116] The poets, by contrast, celebrated her fulsomely, and as queen (*regina*) – it could of course be argued that poets were prone to exaggerate. It could also be argued that none of those Alcuin letters (except the last, which consoled Charles for her death) was written after 798. A plausible explanation for Liutgard's not otherwise having been called queen in prose was that she was not indeed a queen before 798, but in the betwixt-and-between position of a bride-in-waiting, a woman not yet endowed (given a *dos*, a dowry) for marriage. The situation was rectified by the making of an endowed marriage. The years between late 794 (after Fastrada's death) and 798 constituted a trial-period, and as the letter-evidence shows, a very active period, which was concluded by a lawful marriage that made Liutgard an *Ehefrau*, a wife.[117] In the end, these legalistic considerations can be taken seriously and yet set aside in favour of realistic ones: Carolingian royal marriages always had something provisional about them, 'a certain libertinism', and were (as the historical record shows) rather frequently subject to disputes resolved (if at all) by being recognized as 'questions of power rather than of Christian morality'.[118]

It would be unfair, given the poetic evidence, to leave Liutgard in limbo. That evidence, though scarce, is telling. It bears out the signal significant importance of Liutgard's consistent performance as a mediator, a go-between, a facilitator, a person who would wish to put Alcuin's mind at rest about the king's whereabouts, and go the extra mile to take her step-daughters to the Carolingian dynastic shrine of St Gertrude at Nivelles.[119] Her posthumous reputation can be left in the hands of Theodulf:

> O powerful queen, glory of the great monarch,
> Auspicious and beauteous light of the people and of the
>   order of priests:
> May God in heaven preserve you for long ages,
> May you profit the people and the Church of God . . .
> You labour night and day in His service
> And ever raise His name on high.
> Though beautiful in appearance, more beautiful still in spirit,

So that it remains in doubt which supersedes which.
Beautiful in command of words, but more beautiful in action,
Only you are victorious in both . . .
Grant me, O queen, a balsamic liquid
So that the ointment of chrism may suffuse the realm.
Then may the harvest of supreme reward redound to you
When the same baptismal balm will confer the name of
    worshipper of Christ.[120]

Striking here is the repeated reference to chrism – consecrated oil –
linking it in one context metaphorically with a queenly anointing that
could only have evoked the consecration of Charles's mother Bertrada
a half-century before, in the other, with baptism and a 'harvest of
supreme reward'. The poet seems to place Liutgard as already in heaven,
able to act an intercessor with the Almighty for the people and Church,
and actively engaged in promoting mission. It's tempting to associate
Theodulf's epitaph for Liutgard with his epitaph for Hadrian scarcely
five years earlier, with Charles's mother a connective presence in both.

    After Liutgard's death and burial at Tours under St-Martin's care,
Charles took an unexpected route back to Aachen, by way of Orléans and
Paris – the first and only time that he had stayed at either city as king. In
the heyday of the Merovingian rulers, both had been *sedes regiae* (royal
seats), and Paris (specifically St-Denis) a favoured burial-place. Charles's
father Pippin had reverted to Merovingian custom when he chose St-Denis
for his tomb. In 778, Charles had chosen Merovingian names for his twin
baby boys, Louis and Lothar. These two Neustrian *sedes* were interesting
choices for Charles to make his staging posts in 800, perhaps signalling
future plans for the *primogenitus*. From Aachen, it was only some 200km
on old Roman roads to Mainz, where Charles had summoned his summer
assembly. From Mainz to Ravenna with an army was another proposition
entirely: Roman roads were available, but the distance was five times
longer than that from Aachen to Mainz, and there were the Alps to cross.
Charles had already visited Ravenna, in 787, and had got the measure of
Theoderic's imperial city. In 800, Charles seems first to have planned to
take all three of the Young Charles, Pippin of Italy and Louis of Aquitaine
with him; but he had second thoughts about Louis, who was despatched
back to Aquitaine.[121] Leaving Mainz, '[Charles] went with an army to
Ravenna, and then, after waiting for 7 days, directed his march for Rome,

sending Pippin [king of Italy] with the army to undertake the campaign against the Beneventans and plunder . . .'[122]

The army was to be Pippin's, then. Charles headed south from Ravenna with Pippin and the army as far as Ancona. From there Charles turned south-westwards to cross the Apennines and head for Rome, presumably with his son and namesake (though the author of the *Vita* of Leo mentions the Young Charles's presence in Rome only in December). What next? Some 700 years later, the apologists of another Charles (the Emperor Charles V) adopted the motto *plus ultra* – 'still further'.[123] In 800, that thought – or something like it – was uppermost in the minds of both Charles and his namesake.

XIV. PERSPECTIVES ON CHARLES'S IMPERIAL CORONATION, 800/801

According to the *ArF* author, Charles reached Mentana, *c*.20km from Rome, on 23 November, and Pope Leo was waiting there to wine and dine him 'with honour'.[124] Leo had had the choosing of that day: it was the feast-day of St Clement, the first of the apostolic fathers, and believed to have been consecrated by St Peter himself. The last time a pope had come out from Rome to meet an emperor, he had come 10km.[125] In doubling his journey, Leo was sending an unmistakable message: the new emperor was to be in a different league from previous ones. Leo then went back to Rome, and from there sent the banners of the city to be distributed to 'the squadrons of foreigners and citizens' stationed along the route where Charles on a (no doubt superb) horse was acclaimed by *laudes*. Leo, accompanied by clergy and bishops, received Charles, who had dismounted from his horse, at the steps of St Peter's on 24 November 800.[126]

There is no mention of the size of Charles's retinue, although it was surely large enough to look like an army. The papal retinue (*pontificale obsequium*) that had escorted Leo back into Rome on 30 November 799, as detailed by the author of Leo's *Vita*, was likewise large: two archbishops, four bishops and a bishop-elect, and three 'most glorious' counts, each assigned his own *obsequium* of thirty to fifty horsemen, plus grooms and servants.[127] When Charles arrived at Rome a year later, he came with a baggage-train which had transported across the Alps a silver table, and various vessels of fine gold for the service of that table [weights of these not given], a gold crown with large jewels which hangs over the altar [of St Peter's *confessio*] weighing 55 lb., a large gold paten with various jewels with the inscription 'CHARLES', weighing 30 lb., a large chalice weighing 58 lb., a gold-rimmed chalice weighing 37 lb., and another large gold-rimmed chalice weighing 36 lb. [and other items whose weights aren't specified].

The weight of those objects for which weights are given was almost 100 kilos.[128] These were gifts fit for St Peter.

The question remained of what was to be done about the pope. It was decided, a week later, that a synod was the correct forum. It would take place in the large Lateran *triclinium*, and Charles would preside (as he had presided at the Frankfurt Council). The options were that Leo be tried on the basis of the testimony of his enemies (Paschal, Campulus, *et al.*), or that he be permitted to take an oath instead, to purge himself of any alleged misdeed. Alcuin had already advanced the legal argument that 'the apostolic see could judge, but could not be judged'. Among those who spoke in support of that argument was Theodulf: and thanks not least to Theodulf's *libera vox*, it was agreed that Leo could not be tried.

Three weeks later, on 23 December, the plenary synod resumed: Leo took his oath. That same day, Zacharias, whom Charles had sent to Jerusalem a year earlier, and two monks arrived at Rome bearing the keys of the Holy Sepulchre and the standard. On Christmas Day, in St Peter's, Leo crowned Charles and the new emperor was acclaimed 'by the whole people of the Romans'. Because the author of the *ArF* dated the beginning of the year from 25 December, the date was 801.

Einhard muddied the waters: claiming the privilege of the eye-witness courtier, he wrote, 'At first he [Charles] was so averse to [receiving the name of emperor] that he said he would never have entered the church that day, even though it was a most important feast-day, if he had known the pope's plan beforehand.'[129] There is still some mileage in the idea that Charles (or Einhard) employed the old clichés of unworthiness and hence refusal of office.[130] It's also the case that the order of events (coronation before acclamation) did not accord with 'Roman' (Byzantine) tradition, and hence might have displeased Charles (and/or Einhard). But there is plenty of evidence that Charles and Leo between them, with help from their counsellors, carefully planned and stage-managed the

sequence of rituals. Any argument to the contrary simply can't be sustained. That evidence is to be found in the three main sources for the event, and the most nearly contemporary with it; and since each of these offers a different take, each is best considered in turn.[131]

First, then, there is the *ArF*:

> That same day [23 December], after the pope had sworn his oath of purgation before the whole people in the church of St Peter, Zacharias [a priest from the palace] returned to Rome from the east with two monks . . . The patriarch of Jerusalem had sent these men with Zacharias to the king, bearing, as a sign of his benediction (*benedictio*), the keys of the Lord's Sepulchre and of the place of Calvary, and also the keys of the city [of Jerusalem] and of Mount Zion, with a banner . . . Charles celebrated the Lord's Nativity at Rome. And the count of years changed to 801. And that very same day, when the king rose from prayer before the *confessio* of St Peter, Pope Leo placed a crown on his head and he was acclaimed by the whole people of the Romans: 'To Charles *augustus*, the God-crowned great and pacific emperor of the Romans, life and victory!' And after the acclamations (*laudes*), he was saluted by the pope in the customary manner of ancient emperors, and the name of *patricius* was abandoned and he was called emperor and *augustus*.
>
> A few days later, he ordered those who had overthrown the pontiff the year before to be produced. They were tried and sentenced to death in accordance with Roman law as guilty of high treason. But the pope interceded with the emperor on their behalf and they were granted their lives, and not mutilated, but banished into exile [in Francia].[132]

Planning and timing were (and are) of the essence in any great ritual event (or series of events), as both Charles and Leo were well aware. The arrival in Rome from Jerusalem of Zacharias and his companions, with the keys and the banner, was timed to a tee – that is, for 23 December, two days before the coronation itself on 25 December: an all the more remarkable success, given the time and distance involved. Leo swore the oath of purgation in St Peter's, and later that day, Zacharias arrived with keys and standard. The coronation was timed for Christmas Day, and the first day of a new year and (in the view of a few contemporaries) a new millennium.[133] In the ritual process at St Peter's, it preceded the acclamations, according to the *ArF*; but no-one seems to have raised the issue of 'constitutional implications'. Within 'a few days' of the coronation, Leo's enemies were condemned by Charles acting as judge according to Roman law.

Second, there is the *Vita* of Leo III:

On 23 December, in the church of St Peter, there assembled all the archbishops, bishops, abbots and all the Franks in the service of that same great king, and all the Romans. In that same church, and in the presence [of all the above], Leo said on oath in a loud voice, 'I have no knowledge of these false charges . . . and I do not admit to having committed such crimes.' . . . On 25 December, they all assembled again in St Peter's. Then the venerable pontiff with his own hands crowned [Charles] with a very precious crown. Then all the faithful Romans, seeing what love Charles had for the holy Roman church and its vicar, exclaimed [with this acclamation]: 'To Charles, most pious Augustus, crowned by God, great and pacific emperor, life and victory!' . . .

And there too, the most holy bishop and pontiff with holy oil anointed Charles's most excellent son Charles as king that same Christmas Day.

After the celebration of Mass, the serene lord emperor presented . . . [and there follows in the same c. 25 the list of gifts quoted above].

Afterwards, when those wicked evil-doers Paschal and Campulus had been brought into the pious lord emperor's presence, with the noble Franks and Romans in attendance, and they were all satisfied about their evil plotting and action, Campulus turned on Paschal and rebuked him: 'It was a bad moment when I first saw your face, because it was you who first put me in this danger.' The others . . . each damned each other and thus proved their guilt. When the pious emperor realized the extent of their cruelty and wickedness, he sent them into exile in regions of Francia.[134]

Again, sequencing was all: on 23 December, Leo's oath as to his own innocence was the prerequisite of two inaugurations, one after another. On 25 December, Leo crowned and acclaimed Charles as emperor, and 'on that same Christmas Day', Leo anointed with holy oil Charles's son as king. The Young Charles's being anointed king is mentioned, uniquely, in the *Life* of Leo III. This anointing ritual in St Peter's in Rome connected the Young Charles with the dynasty's double-stranded traditions of king-making, through unction and/or coronation, in 751, 754, 768 and 781.

The third source, the Lorsch Annals, is the most nearly contemporary, but the author and/or patron (Ricbod is the best guess as to his identity) was someone who preferred a line of his own:

> Because the name of emperor was at that time in cessation in the land of the Greeks and they had a woman's rule (*femineum imperium*) among them, it seemed to the pope and to the Christian fathers and to the rest of the Christian people that they ought to give the name of emperor to Charles, king of the Franks, who was already holding Rome where the Caesars had always been accustomed to sit, and holding the other seats too: Italy Gaul and Germania . . . King Charles himself was unwilling to deny their request, and so, in all humility . . . that same day, the Nativity of the Lord Jesus Christ, he received the name of emperor with the blessing (*consecratio*) of the Lord Pope.

This author was more ambitious than the others. Rather than a narrative, he produced arguments. To legitimate Charles's acquisition of the name of emperor, he argued, first, that Eirene's assumption of *imperium* (and even, though seldom, the title of *basileus* (emperor) rather than *basilissa* (empress)) meant that there was an imperial vacancy. Charles's contemporaries in East and West were willing to agree: feminine rule was a contradiction in terms. Within less than two years, Eirene had been deposed in a palace coup. She was replaced by the imperial treasurer, Nikephoros, who soon had to take the role of military commander. A sequence of male emperors (the next two were military men) continued during the rest of Charles's reign: the vacancy argument was no longer operative, and the experiment with female rule was never to be repeated in Byzantium. The two other arguments remained good, however, both inherited from antiquity. Rome was where the Caesars ruled, and Charles now had authority in it; and, on the definition of an empire as a bundle of provinces, each with its own seat (*sedes*) or capital, Charles already ruled an empire. These arguments were timely; and, on the assumption that they were put forward in Rome early in 801, the timing of their presentation was perfect.[135]

From 801, Charles used the title *Carolus serenissimus augustus deo coronatus magnus pacificus imperator Romanum gubernans imperium qui et per misericordiam dei rex Francorum et Langobardorum* ('Charles most serene augustus, crowned by God, great peacemaking emperor governing the Roman empire and also by God's mercy king of the Franks and of the Lombards'), which could be termed wordy. The rather fuzzy formulation *Romanum gubernans imperium*, which had long been current in parts of Italy, came into use in Charles's documents very quickly.[136] It embodied a significant evasion: it was a substitute for 'emperor of the Romans', a title Charles never used.[137] Once matters were settled with the eastern empire in 812, there were two emperors: one, emperor of the Romans, in Constantinople; the other, just plain emperor, based in Aachen, which had never been among the seats of the ancient Caesars but was, instead, a new place of power.

XV. ALCUIN'S NETWORK

Alcuin's letter to Gisela and Rotrud early in 801 thanked them for the news in the letter Gisela had just sent him: 'I have received this with joy, thanking God for the exaltation of my most excellent lord David, and also that the pope is doing well, and that the envoys arrived from the Holy City [Jerusalem].'[138]

Alcuin's 'little sons' (*filioli*), that is, his former students, several of whom had been acting as his eyes and ears in Rome, had already left Italy, as Candidus had; others were still there 'with Pippin' in Benevento; and others sent letters home with Anglo-Saxon travellers or pilgrims.[139] Gisela had not mentioned the Young Charles's less dazzling 'exaltation'. Alcuin was already in the know, writing to the young man: 'I have heard that the lord pope has conferred on you, with the consent of the most excellent David, the name of king and a crown of royal dignity. I am rejoicing greatly about the honour of your name and of your office (*potestas*).'[140]

Assuming Alcuin's informant had accurately described the Young Charles's anointing, the crown was a metonym for name, office and ritual. Alcuin added a little 'mirror of princes' for the new king, commending the conduct of Solomon, quoting Exodus 23:8 on the perils of *munera*, gifts that could be bribes, and assuring him that he had received from his father, 'rector and emperor of the Christian people', the best possible examples 'in the palace (*domus*) in which you were nurtured', and would receive blessing from the Almighty so long as he strove to imitate his father's *mores*.

The Young Charles's kingly title was not amplified by an ethnic signifier: no contemporary ever called him king of the Franks.[141] His moves after his anointing in Rome are completely unrecorded in the annalistic sources between 800 and 804. It seems likely, though, in light of the surveying of Neustria in 800, and the young king's anointing in Rome, that his Frankish kingdom was up and running. Theodulf, who had been on good terms with Alcuin in 800, wrote a poem to the Young Charles most of which was a panegyric to him; but the opening section contained a little innuendo aimed at one of the Young Charles's retinue, Osulf, nicknamed 'Corydon', a man of small stature and apparently gay.[142] There is a sense in these years of sparring under way, both between the brothers (two of whom had not shared the blessings of an upbringing in their father's household), and between their partisans. For the moment, Pippin was active on the Beneventan frontier, while Louis (who had missed the opportunity to see Rome) was in Aquitaine planning the capture of Barcelona – a victory achieved in the autumn of 801.[143] No 'divisions of realms' were in immediate prospect, but there were straws in the wind.

14

Fin de siècle – début de siècle: Romanum gubernans imperium

I. LEAVING ROME

The last extant document in which Charles was entitled *rex Francorum et Langobardorum et patricius Romanorum* ('King of the Franks and the Lombards and patrician of the Romans') was a judgment made in Rome by Leo at Charles's request on 4 March 801. There had been a long-running dispute between the bishop of Siena and Bishop Aribert of Arezzo. Aribert took the chance to present his case to Charles, and hoped Arezzo's rights would be confirmed.[1] Charles, determined that the case be settled, asked Leo to 'make peace according to canonical authority', and that was exactly what happened. 'It had the distinct advantage of underscoring the papal power the king was in the process of trying to restore', while the bishop of Arezzo got 'the new emperor's confirmation of his rights', and Charles himself 'enforced the judgement': game, set and match.[2]

In his next extant document, also a judgment involving ecclesiastical parties, Charles used the new, rather more wordy title of *Carolus serenissimus augustus deo coronatus magnus pacificus imperator Romanum gubernans imperium qui et per misericordiam dei rex Francorum et Langobardorum.*[3] By then Charles had left Rome, on 25 April, after 'setting everything in order there'.[4] (Theodulf remained there a little longer, examining manuscripts and mosaics with a view to a project of his own.[5]) Charles, travelling via Spoleto (where he was lucky not to be harmed by a serious earthquake on 30 April) and Ravenna, was at Bologna near the end of May, and at Pavia in June. It is tempting to link this place and date with Charles's issue of the *Capitulare Italicum* of 801, with its reference to *provinciae disponendae* (provinces to

The noble warrior with his sword.

be 'governed' or 'looked after') as the reason why he had come to Italy.[6] At Pavia, the news reached him that envoys from the Abbasid caliph Harun al-Rashid had landed at Pisa, bringing rich gifts including – wonder of wonders – an elephant.[7] Even this did not detain or divert him, though he sent the notary Ercanbald to Liguria to arrange for a fleet to be ready to receive the elephant, and the other gifts. By 24 June Charles was at Ivrea, heading rapidly across the Mons Iovis (by the Great St Bernard pass) into Gaul, and thence to Aachen. Charles had his own special reasons for hastening north: at Aachen work was proceeding apace on the church and the palace. Aachen had never been among the seats of the ancient Caesars but was to be, instead, a new *sedes* in the heart of Francia. Did Charles ever wonder whether he would see Rome again? He had 'set everything in order there'. Aachen was now his goal and the focus of his attention: the place where new laws would be made and new things done, a new place of power, of *nova antiquitas* and *antiqua novitas*. On balance, there was more new than old.

II. A LOCAL DISPUTE: ALCUIN AND THEODULF, 801–2

Charles's two closest counsellors, between whom relations had been very good in 800, became locked in dispute early the next year over the right to sanctuary of a criminous cleric. To be involved in a dispute was not necessarily a mischance for these counsellors of the emperor. A dispute was a performance that gave *potentes* an opportunity to star in tilting at each other. The cleric belonged to the church of Orléans (Theodulf's church since 798), and, after being imprisoned for his crimes or sins, escaped and fled to Tours to seek sanctuary in the church of St-Martin (Alcuin's base since 796). The legal aspects of the case have been admirably covered in recent research.[8] There is more to be said, though, about both the local context and its wider social and political ramifications. Letters from Charles are very rare, but in this case a crucial piece of evidence is a letter from Charles in which his voice echoes very audibly. The letter has its own particular macro-context in the new emperor's agenda of delivering justice; its micro-context is the middle Loire valley – where rivalries had raged in Merovingian times and would rage in the ninth century too, for this was economically and strategically a key region in the Frankish world.[9]

Modern scholars have depicted the cleric as small fry. A closer look suggests otherwise. His offences were great enough for Theodulf to have been alerted to his 'many sins and serious crimes') and for him to have been put in chains; the cleric's contacts were such that he managed to escape from Orléans and find refuge at the church of St-Martin; and once there, his social standing was such as to make it possible for him to send a letter to the emperor requesting access to the imperial presence. Charles, having learned more about the dispute and giving due attention to who the disputants were, and being now firmly set on imperial government, sent one of his imperial *missi*, Teutbert, to sort out the problem. Teutbert took nineteen days to wrap up his inquiry ('he flogged whom he wished, he put in chains whom he wished; he put on oath whom he wished; he summoned whom he wished to your presence'), and this could be compared with the much briefer sittings described by Theodulf in his account of his stint as a *missus* in the Rhône valley and Septimania in 798. 'Local' did not mean trivial: it very often meant seriously complicated.

Just five letters constitute all the evidence there is, yet these five letters yield much. It's clear that both Theodulf and Alcuin were exaggerating not just the sin or crime, but also the problem of disorder and the consequent need for justice in the shape of law-enforcement. In the first letter, Alcuin responded to what he rightly saw as a threat to his own position. He wrote post-haste to two of his *filioli* ('little sons'), Candidus (aka Witto) and Nathaniel (aka Fridugis) who were at Charles's court, sending them instructions to 'throw themselves at the feet of my lord David, and beg him to summon the bishop [Theodulf] and also to find a place for [me to] defend and debate with him'.[10] Alcuin was all for remembering that 'mercy rejoiceth against judgment' (James 2:13) and that 'If we say we have no sin, we deceive ourselves and the truth is not in us' (1 John 1:8). He also sent the *filioli* some useful citations from the Theodosian Code (and derivatives) covering incarceration and asylum, prefaced by a timely reference to Constantine 'who once baptized, began to legislate', as well as commending to 'my lord David, the most Christian emperor', some relevant passages from Merovingian church councils.[11]

Once the man from Orléans had escaped to Tours, it became a

different kind of problem: a social and political one that was now more than local because Charles was directly involved. Theodulf, as a recently-promoted archbishop, was powerful enough to deploy a small army. Alcuin lacked any such resource, and the bishop of Tours was a broken reed (Alcuin thought him *simplex*, that is, artless, or dim). In another letter, perhaps to Archbishop Hildebald of Cologne, Alcuin gave an eye-witness account of what was in effect an urban riot.[12] When the men from Orléans tried to extract the escaped prisoner from his asylum at St-Martin's, they started fighting the men of Tours. There was fear, there was tumult, there was noise, and a huge crowd, especially of poor folk. The *infantes*, boy-oblates (always another potential source of disorder), 'joined in the affray on a foolish impulse', though they later acknowledged having been wrong to do so. Of the *vassi* of the church of St-Martin whose duty was to protect the church and calm the disorder, only one, Alcuin grumbled, 'was with me at that hour'.

Charles himself addressed Alcuin and the St-Martin's community. His letter began like this, without greeting or preamble:

> Yesterday when a letter came from you to me, another letter came from Bishop Theodulf, complaining of the dishonour suffered by his men, and not only them but also the bishop of Tours, and a contempt for our imperial orders . . . Of the two letters, yours was much the more bitter and full of rage (*iracundia*).[13]

Charles's own language then turned full of rage. '*Valde miramur*', he wrote,

> We are absolutely amazed that you alone should think fit to go against the decision of our authority . . . We could not possibly be more amazed (*in hoc satis mirare nequivimus*) that you preferred to hear the criminal's entreaties instead of our commands.

Charles finally addressed the brethren (his plural *vos* could include Alcuin too):

> You know very well, you of this monastery called servants of God (would it were true!), how often and by how many your way of life has been criticized, not without reason. Sometimes you call yourselves monks, sometimes canons, sometimes neither. We chose a suitable master for you and invited him from a distant province. He could have taught you the

right way of life . . . But it turned out otherwise . . . The Devil has found you to be his agents in sowing discord . . . You who have shown contempt for our orders, whether you call yourselves canons or monks, must come and give an account of yourselves and clear yourselves of these accusations.

Why had Charles written so harshly to Alcuin and the brethren? The new emperor was now operating in imperial mode, determined to assert his authority over provincial rivals in the Loire valley, just as Merovingian kings had done, but much more effectively. Both Alcuin and Theodulf had been appointed to important institutional posts in the region, Alcuin in 796, Theodulf in 798. Alcuin was in fact not an ordained abbot but a lay-abbot; Charles himself had given St-Martin's to Alcuin. A lay-abbot was a *potens* – a magnate and manager of magnates; and Alcuin was in charge of an exceptionally rich church. The arrangements at St-Martin's were not unusual in the later eighth century, but they were, let's say, irregular[14] ('sometimes you call yourselves monks, sometimes canons, sometimes neither').

St-Martin's was a major shrine in Latin Christendom, packed with pilgrims and traders who supplied their needs, and also with crowds of the urban poor and people who relied on the early-ninth-century equivalent of benefits (*matricularii*, meaning, people eligible for relief). When armed men from Orléans on the Loire some 100km upstream swarmed (or perhaps navigated furiously) down to Tours and threatened to disturb, even desecrate, Martin's shrine, the situation was liable to erupt in violence. As Alcuin wrote in the context of this very dispute: '*Illud etiam commune est omnibus ubique, quod moleste ferant suos dehonorare sanctos.*' ('It's common to everyone everywhere that people take it very badly when their saints are dishonoured!')[15]

How was Alcuin to respond to the emperor? It had to be with contrition. He told his own version of the story again, but displaced blame on to the bishop of Tours, *simplex* as he was and quite unable to cope with a fracas. He then blamed the tumult on the *vulgus indoctum*, the unlearned crowd, 'inclined as they always are to act improperly and without counsel, and liable to run to take up their cudgels'. He blamed the *infantes* who had joined in the affray, 'acting on their own foolish impulse', and, so they swore, no-one else had encouraged them to act that way. Alcuin added that he had sent them to 'your presence, and it will be possible to hear from them what they did'. Finally, on a rather more positive note, Alcuin asked Charles to consider that St-Martin's prayed for him, and that St Martin himself had always been honoured in the kingdom of the Franks and by their kings. 'If you mark our sins, Lord, who shall stand?' (Ps. 130:3) 'And so we say to you, "If you mark our sins, Lord Emperor, who shall stand?"' – especially as the most praiseworthy thing about emperors had always been that they show mercy (*clementia*) to their subjects. Alcuin's final reference was to the Emperor Titus, who famously said that 'no-one should leave the emperor's presence sad'.[16]

The consequence of the dispute was that the particular episode was rapidly followed up by legislation in the form of a capitulary *legibus additum* (i.e. added to *Lex Salica*) of 803.[17] This required the count to impose large fines on anyone who committed a crime within an ecclesiastical immunity under royal protection.[18] If anyone tried to enter such an immunity and resisted the count with a body of armed men, the count was to refer the case to the king or *princeps*. If anyone sought refuge in a church he was to be given refuge in the yard of the church, and it was not to be necessary for him to enter the church, and no-one was to presume to take the asylum-seeker away by force, but he must confess what he had done and be led by the hands of *boni homines* before a public inquiry (*discussio*).[19] In the flood of capitularies issued by Charles in 802–3, this was one of the most often-copied, and well over half of these manuscripts were copied in the ninth century.[20] One tenth-century manuscript included a brief account of the circumstances in which the capitulary was publicized: in this case by Count Stephen in the public court of Paris before the *scabini*, 'and all consented together, saying that they were willing to observe [the additions to the law] at all times and forever'.[21] Charles's decision on a case, followed soon after by a capitulary issued by him on the basis of that decision, was to become a pattern: 'a norm in a book'.[22]

Alcuin wrote to Archbishop Arn in 802, praising Charles for his concern for the *norma rectitudinis*, perhaps hoping to build bridges with the emperor.[23] It was too late: Alcuin, old and ill, regretted having had to leave his 'little cell' at Aachen:

> O my cell, my sweet beloved dwelling,
> Forever and ever, O my cell, farewell . . .

In you the gentle voices of teachers could once be heard expounding
    with hallowed lips the books of Wisdom.
In you at set times holy praise of God
Resounded from peaceful minds in peaceful words.
For you my cell, I now lament with tearful poetry;
Groaning I bewail at heart your decline . . .
The old man now leans wearily on his staff.
Why do we wretches love you, fugitive world?[24]

Alcuin died on 19 May 804. Theodulf, perhaps twenty years his junior, and anything but weary, was about to engage with his own new projects and with the emperor's new demands.

III. GOVERNING AN EMPIRE: PRESCRIPTION – CHARLES'S AGENDA IN 802

Before 802, Charles's output of capitularies had been low: on even the most generous number of those in the standard nineteenth-century edition, a dozen or so. In the single year of 802 alone, the count would be fourteen. What had happened to produce this extraordinary increase? It was not just a spin-off from Charles's imperial title, though implicit in that title was a newly urgent concern with law and justice. Nor was it generated just by the excitement of receiving the priceless, symbolically charged and pre-eminently princely gift of an elephant. Charles and his advisers had put a set of new governmental and educational goals on their agenda.

The modern word 'agenda' immediately brings to mind something written, but intended to produce action. There is a tension here that Matthew Innes translates as 'a strong opposition between written law as authoritative text and customary [i.e. unwritten] law as local practice'; or as another opposition between 'capitularies as disembodied statements of royal policy . . . and a complex web of communication and negotiation binding together, and in important ways defining, polity and society'.[25] A similar tension, or even something approaching a contradiction in terms, is suggested by Steffen Patzold's 'norms in the book', and by his subtitle, 'reflections on the value-claims of the so-called capitularies'.[26] The late F.-L. Ganshof called the largest of the 802 capitularies, the *Capitulare missorum generale*, 'programmatic', and that too echoes the idea of an agenda.

Charles had explained 'why oaths are necessary' back in 789, and he had required general oath-swearings.[27] In 802, he wanted a new kind of oath that didn't just set out positive aspects of fidelity but demanded, negatively, avoidance of anything that damaged the emperor's rights and assets.[28] These points were set out in the first nine *capitula*. The duties of clerical and monastic personnel were dealt with in *capitula* 10–24, the obligations, positive and negative, of lay officials and lay-persons generally in *capitula* 25–40. Charles especially abhorred the sin of incest, and spelled this out in a capitulary reminding all of a particular case within living memory.[29]

Charles took a strong personal interest in deciding which advisers to involve in the details of drafting, and in getting drafts approved in detail (*nominatim*). Drafts, once approved, were circulated by royal *missi* who, when taking final copies to provincial meeting-places, needed Charles's permission to leave the palace with them.[30] Drafting by committee usually ends up privileging the voice of the chair. In c. 75 of the *Admonitio generalis*, for instance, the voice of Alcuin had politely urged *clerici* to decide whether they were monks or canons, and Charles approved this wording;[31] thirteen years later, the voice of Charles fiercely berated Alcuin and his *congregatio* on the same subject.[32] Had Charles grown more testy with age? There was more to it. Once the text had winged its way from Aachen, it became possible for a *missus*, or someone with a fresh pair of eyes, at a place far from Aachen, to revise, modify, amplify and make alterations in a capitulary-draft. All this explained why, given a manuscript culture, there were so many differences in the various copies, and, conversely, why a fair number of capitularies, including the *Capitulare missorum generale* (Capit. no. 33), have survived only in single copies. This was chance, not serendipity.

The General Capitulary for the *missi*, issued in spring 802, after a general prologue (c. 1) with some special reference to the functions of *missi*, devotes a further nine *capitula* to the new oath of fidelity. The most important points Charles had to make were in cc. 2 and 3, where he first affirmed the empire-wide reach of the new oath of fidelity – 'all over the age of twelve' – and then continued:

[2] It is to be expounded publicly to all, in such a way that every person can understand, how important and how many are the matters which that oath comprehends – not only, as many have hitherto thought, fidelity to the lord emperor as regards his life and not bringing an enemy into the realm for hostile purpose and not consenting to, or remaining silent about, another's infidelity towards him, but that all should know that oath to contain the following meaning within it:

[3] First, that everybody is personally ([in] *propria persona*) to strive, to the best of his understanding and ability, to maintain himself fully in God's holy service, in accordance with God's command (*preceptum*) and his own promise (*sponsio*), for the lord emperor cannot himself provide the necessary care and discipline for each person individually (*singulariter*).[33]

This emphasis on individual responsibility had always been the key element in oaths to the king;[34] and it recurred in the General Capitulary in the hugely enlarged context of empire. Charles's preference for the personal touch was tinged here with a note of regret that contacts *singulariter* were less often feasible than before, yet at the same time more necessary for those charged with administrative office and accountable directly to Charles: his bishops, abbots and counts. (A similar note would be struck when Charles personally chided would-be godparents at Aachen, the parish church for locals, high and low, for their inability to recite the Lord's Prayer and the Creed: proof-texts of Christianity.[35] Very seldom does evidence survive of such an encounter between Charles and those for whom he knew himself responsible to God. There's a further glimpse in a little sermon, '*de periculo principum*', in a sermon-collection preserved in an early-ninth-century Bavarian manuscript. 'The more power a man has, the more responsibility he must bear for others, the more he must keep his *sponsio* to God.'[36] The preacher, surely, had in mind the *sponsio* to the emperor introduced in the spring of 802. A Bavarian charter dated 10 August 802 offers another glimpse, referring en passant to that same *sponsio*. These surviving fragments can be set within a much larger whole. It was not only *principes* who had to bear responsibilities and obey God's *preceptum*: it was each person individually, including *principes*, and including Charles.

In the *ArF*, no mention at all was made of the 802 spring assembly and the agenda-setting capitulary, nor of the October assembly at

Aachen. It was the author of the Lorsch Annals who saw fit to report October's 'universal synod':[37]

> In this year the lord Caesar Charles stayed quietly at the palace of Aachen with the Franks; there was no campaign. But mindful in his mercy of the poor people who lived in his realm and who could not enjoy their rights to the full (*et iustitias suas pleniter abere non potuerant*) he was unwilling to send out his poorer vassals from within the palace to do justice, on account of bribery (*de infra palatio pauperiores vassos transmittere ad iustitias faciendum propter munera*), and rather chose from within his realm archbishops and other bishops and abbots, together with dukes and counts, who no longer had need to receive gifts to the prejudice of the innocent (*qui iam opus non abebant super innocentes munera accipere*). These he sent throughout his whole realm, that they might do justice to the churches, the widows and orphans, the poor and the whole people. And in October he gathered a universal synod at the aforenamed place . . .

The decrees of the popes were read out; then to the abbots and monks was read out the Rule of St Benedict; then the canons were read out to all the ecclesiastics. They were to amend all faults and shortcomings.

> While this synod was being held, the emperor also assembled the dukes, the counts and the rest of the Christian people, together with men skilled in the laws (*cum legislatoribus*) and he caused to be read out all the laws in his realm, each man's law expounded to him and emended wherever necessary, and the emended law written down. And he declared that the judges should judge in accordance with what was written down (*et ut iudices per scriptum iudicassent*) and not accept gifts (*et munera non accepissent*), and that all men, poor or rich, should have justice in his realm.[38]

In 802, what especially worried the Lorsch writer was bribes (*munera*), and the propensity of *iudices* to accept them. In 799, Theodulf in his great poem on justice had worried at even greater length.[39] Some 1,400 years before the counsellors of Charles, the author(s) of the Book of Exodus had warned: 'Judge justly, ye sons of men, not with bribes, "for bribes blind the hearts of the wise and subvert the words of the just" [Vulgate, Exodus 23:8, *Nec accipies munera, quae etiam excaecant prudentes, et subverteunt verba justorum*].' One solution to that problem was to stop sending out as *missi* from the palace lesser and junior royal servants (*vassi pauperiores*) and instead appoint members of the administrative elite: 'archbishops and other bishops and abbots, together with dukes and counts, who no longer had any interest in receiving gifts to the harm of the innocent (*qui iam opus non abebant super innocentes munera accipere*)'.

It was not as if abolishing bribes was *only* a matter of replacing 'poorer retainers on the make' with 'great landowners and leading churchmen' whose wealth enabled them 'to rise above the inevitable low hum of honourable social exchange'.[40] For Theodulf, it was a matter of *discretio*, moderation, hence, a moral matter for an individual's decision. He explained just what that meant for such *missi* on their tours of justice:

> . . . I am willing to take small things willingly,
> Things not offered by any cruel hand, but by his [Charles's]
>   beloved hand:
> That is, the fruits of trees and of a flourishing vegetable-garden,
> Eggs, honey, bread, and what the horses eat.
> We have eaten tender chickens and little birds
> Whose bodies are small but good to eat.
> O happy is all virtue as long as it means *discretio*,
> The nurse of virtues, moderating her, adorning and
>   nourishing her.[41]

Another type of text conveyed a very similar ideal of moderation. These were the *tractoriae* or permits of the Roman Empire, whose public agents, like Charles's *missi* (hard-riding messengers), were entitled to daily requisitions from local officials when travelling on state service: 'fresh horses, and fodder, bread, wine and beer, meat, chickens and eggs, and condiments'.[42] *Tractoriae* worked similarly in Charles's empire (the evidence for them is scanty, but such is the nature of things as highly disposable as an undergraduate's library pass). A state which carefully met an official's needs with sufficient for an overnight stay viewed *munera* as excessive, and so forbade them. Such a state saw the delivering of justice by judges through written law as a way of diffusing norms. One agenda fed into another: with Theodulf's poem, the keeping of everyone's *sponsio*, the careful reading of the General Capitulary, and capitularies in general, it was a case of 'only connect'.[43]

IV. EADBURH'S STORY

Charles's jokes, as transmitted by Notker of St-Gall, have about them
a whiff of unreliability, because, though there is a plausible line of oral
transmission, they did not come from the horse's mouth. The story of
the West Saxon queen Eadburh has better credentials. Its original context lay in Wessex in the years between 786 and 802. According to the
Anglo-Saxon Chronicle, under the year 786, 'King Beorhtric succeeded
to Wessex'. The genealogy that precedes the 'A' manuscript of the
Chronicle says that 'Beorhtric succeeded [Cynewulf] and held the kingdom [of Wessex] for 16 years'. The *ASC s.a.* 789 says 'Beorhtric took
to wife Eadburh, daughter of King Offa'. Beorhtric's death is recorded
in *ASC s.a.* 802, 'and Ecgberht succeeded him'. So far, Eadburh's story
is an Anglo-Saxon one.

Asser in his *Life of Alfred*, written in 893, says that the people of
'that land', i.e. Wessex, were interested in knowing how the custom had
arisen whereby the wife of the king of Wessex was not called 'queen',
but only 'the king's wife'. A manifest anomaly tends to attract, and be
explained by, a story. In this case, the story was recorded almost a century later. Asser was nevertheless careful to stress that his source was
Alfred himself: 'he still often tells me about it, and he likewise had
heard it from many reliable sources, indeed to a large extent from men
who remembered the event in all its details.' Asser's knowledge came
by way of telling and hearing on the basis of multiple memories.

A brief résumé of the next phase of Asser's story about Eadburh
moves the scene from Wessex to the Continent. After her marriage, she
started behaving badly, loathing every man her husband liked, doing
things hateful to God, denouncing all those whom she could before the
king, and thus depriving them of life by either trickery or poison. This
happened with a young man very dear to the king, whom she poisoned
when she could not denounce him before the king. Eadburh had meant
to give the poison to the young man, not the king, but the king by mistake took it first, and so both of them died. Eadburh could no longer
stay among the Saxons. 'She sailed overseas with countless treasures,
and went to Charles the very famous king of the Franks (*famosissimus
Francorum rex*).'

Charles's Aachen was the scene of the next part of Eadburh's story, and Asser clearly regarded it as well worth telling:

> As she stood in the front part of the upper gallery (*ante solarium*) bearing many gifts for him, Charles said to her: 'Choose, Eadburh, between me and my son who is standing with me in this upper gallery (*in solario isto*).' She, replying foolishly and without thinking, said: 'If the choice is left to me, I choose your son – because he is younger than you.' Charles laughed and said: 'If you'd chosen me you'd have had my son – but you chose my son, so you won't get either of us!'

The sequel was evidently seen as still more entertaining:

> Charles did, however, give her a very large convent of nuns (*magnum sanctimonialium monasterium*), where she stopped wearing secular clothes and dressed as a nun, and performed the office of an abbess for some years (*perpaucis annis abbatissae fungebatur officio*). But just as she had acted wildly (*irrationabiliter*) in her own country, she behaved even more wildly (*irrationabilius*) among another people. When in the end she was caught publicly having sex with a countryman of hers she was thrown out of the convent on Charles's orders, and shamefully spent the rest of her life in poverty and misery, so that she ended up in Pavia begging every day, with only a slave boy to keep her company (as I have heard from many who saw her) and died a wretched death.[44]

Is there any truth in this story? First, West Saxon king's wives were not called queens, and, later in the ninth century, some people were asking why this was so.[45] Secondly, the chronology of Eadburh's career is plausible: her husband did die in 802, to be succeeded by Ecgberht, who had fled to Francia in 789 and had sought protection from Beorhtric at the court of Charles at Aachen.[46] The Young Charles had been close to his father in the later 790s, and had been anointed king on the same day that his father was crowned emperor. Unfortunately, there is no evidence for the Young Charles's whereabouts between 801 and 804, but his presence at Aachen during at least some of those years (during which he perhaps nurtured a Neustrian kingdom) is very probable.

Assuming that Eadburh fled as fast as possible to Francia, she arrived at Aachen in 802 or 803, and found both the emperor and his son there to receive her 'in front of the *solarium*' (or 'in the front part of the *solarium*'). Mayke de Jong, in her insightful paper on 'The *solarium*', differentiates the upper storey of the church from that of the palace, and notes the view of architectural historians that 'the *solarium* was situated in a two-storey building that intersected the stone gallery (*porticus*) connecting church and *regia*', while pointing out that 'archaeological evidence is missing'. She signals a passage in the *Life of Hadrian* which could constitute an analogous arrangement to that at Aachen: ' "a tower [in the papal palace] adorned with wondrous beauty" and serving as living quarters [which] must have been on the outside of this structure'.[47] This would fit very well the context of Eadburh's arrival 'with many gifts'. Here, indeed, was a *solarium*, and not a throne, as the standard translation of Asser misleadingly says (twice).[48] There is enough evidence to claim the story of Eadburh's foolish reply to the emperor's question, and her ensuing fate, as a memory of events. Charles's laughter and his rejection of Eadburh resonated, decades later, with Welsh and Anglo-Saxon audiences. I think this was an authentic Charles joke, which, like some of those recounted by Notker, hinged on humiliation and cruelty. It evidently also mined a seam of misogyny in the culture at Charles's Aachen – and at Alfred's court in the 890s.

V. GOVERNING AN EMPIRE: PRACTICE – THE *PLACITUM* AT RIZANO, 804

Charles's empire produced many more documents than had any regime in western Europe since the end of the Roman Empire. Encounters on frontiers, whether internal or external, were especially liable to generate documentation. Agendas were followed by decisions, which can sometimes be shown to have been followed up by actions. Provincial demands of multiple kinds evoked responses from the centre. Juxtaposing documents or texts of different genres can reveal hitherto unlooked-for examples of cause and effect – as when the dispute between Theodulf and Alcuin over a case of asylum, conducted entirely through letters, led to the production of a capitulary on the issue, establishing a legal norm.

The *placitum* (assembly) at the Istrian town of Risano (or Rizano) shows both some of the difficulties of governing this empire, and the resourcefulness of Charles, his advisers and his agents in addressing these difficulties. The *placitum* took place within local and regional institutions and structures which were disputed between Franks and Greeks. It was as recently as 788, with Charles's takeover of Bavaria, that Istria had ceased to belong to the Byzantine Empire and had come under Frankish rule. Emerging clearly in the record of the *placitum* are strains and stresses of various kinds: between generations, when the *parentes* looked back to the days of Greek rule and their offspring had to cope with new Frankish ways; between locals and immigrant Slavs disputing land-rights; between ecclesiastical and lay authorities arguing over privileges; and, most fundamentally, between military institutions established since late Roman times and upstart would-be dynastic lordships.[49]

When it comes to accounts of disputes, a good question to ask is, who made the record? The answer in the Risano case is Patriarch Fortunatus of Grado. Fortunatus's predecessor and kinsman, Bishop John, had been murdered (probably early in 803) by two dukes with power in the Veneto, Joannes and Maurice. Pope Leo III bestowed the *pallium*, the woollen scarf denoting archiepiscopal rank, on Fortunatus and entitled him 'Patriarch' in a letter from Rome dated 21 March 803, thus signalling the enhancement of Fortunatus's rank and snubbing the murderous dukes. At the same time, Leo made overtures to Charles and the Franks. Charles had spent Christmas and the winter at Aachen, and was still there on 13 June.[50] The *ArF* reported

> that three envoys from the Emperor Nikephoros, who had deposed Eirene [in 802] had come to the emperor [Charles] in Germania on the river Saale at Salz [in the north-western borderlands between Franconia and Bavaria], bringing gifts and messages to Charles from the new emperor Nikephoros, and they [the envoys] received a written peace-pact from Charles.[51]

The next link in the document-chain is Charles's grant of immunity to Patriarch Fortunatus of Grado, made on 13 August 803 at Salz.[52] Fortunatus had brought Charles 'gifts, a pair of ivory doors of wondrous workmanship'.[53] Charles issued another charter at about the same time (though the date is lost) to Fortunatus as 'patriarch of the Venetians and Istrians', to whose church he now also granted freedom from tolls on four ships.[54]

Today's experts on early medieval Istria suggest that the Frankish-Greek agreement in 803 (also known as the peace-pact of Salz) involved 'spheres of influence', putting Istria in the Frankish zone rather than the Greek one.[55] Charles had co-ordinated the meeting with the Greeks and Istrians at Salz. From there, still thinking strategically, he travelled, via the Böhmerwald (where he indulged his enthusiasm for heavy-duty hunting in which the prey were 'aurochs and other wild beasts'), to Bavaria and Regensburg. There was some less strenuous hunting in Bavaria while he awaited the arrival of troops he had previously sent to Pannonia. Once these troops had arrived back at Regensburg, he summoned a large assembly, including Avars and Slavs who 'subjected themselves with all that they possessed to the emperor's dominion'. And then, 'after settling all necessary matters in those parts, he took the route through Alemannia, passed through Worms and reached the palace of Aachen in the winter, and celebrated Christmas there'.[56]

Salz was no sideshow, then: it was in conversations there that Charles and Fortunatus had come up with the idea that royal *missi* should be sent to hold a *placitum* in Istria, and that the plan be co-ordinated with King Pippin of Italy. (It's worth adding, since there's been some historiographical confusion, that the meeting at Salz had nothing to do with the ending of the Saxon wars: that was a fiction put about by the anonymous 'Saxon poet' c.890.[57]) Charles's re-orientation of his priorities towards the south-east and the Adriatic meant, among other things, allaying the social and political conflicts in Istria referred to above. The emperor and Pippin identified three suitable *missi*. The first was Aio, a Lombard from Friuli who had probably sided with Duke Rodgaud in 776 against Charles and fled to the Avars; he had then been taken prisoner by Pippin in 796, and was pardoned by Charles at Aachen on 2 February 799, with the proviso that he remain faithful ever after. (In 809 Charles confirmed the property-rights of 'his faithful and beloved Count Aio' so that his inheritance could be divided between his three sons.[58]) The second of the *missi*, Cadaloh, an Alemannic aristocrat, appeared in a number of documented transactions in Alemannia from 790 onwards, but only in the reign of Louis the Pious was he mentioned as 'in charge of the March of Dalmatia'.[59] The third of the *missi* was a priest, Izzo, perhaps identifiable as attached to the great monastery of Farfa, which received a confirmation of its lands from Charles on 13 June 803.[60]

The name of Fortunatus, well-known in the region, wealthy and politic, trusted by the pope, comes up repeatedly in the *placitum* of Risano, and the scribe of the document acted 'on the order of my lord the most holy patriarch Fortunatus and the glorious Duke John [of Istria]'. His efforts on behalf of his church and (it must be said) himself were only part of the context of the *placitum*. The church of Grado's customary dues and traditional arrangements needed clarifying; the regional military and Duke John were engaged in power-struggles; and, finally and most vociferously, the local notables of Istria wanted the chance to voice their and the people's resentments against Duke John. The last of these interestgroups is the most interesting: 172 *capitanei* were empanelled by the *missi* conducting the inquiry (*inquisitio*) 'to swear on the gospels and the relics of the saints that they would tell the truth about all they know about everything on which we made inquiry of them'.

The list of complaints was long (it took up almost three-quarters of the document), and gave details about the impositions and particular acts of violence perpetrated by the duke, his sons and daughters and son-in-law.

> You have interrogated us about the acts of violence (*forcia*) that Duke John inflicted on us, which we know, and we are telling the truth . . .[61]
>
> When that man [Duke John] comes on his way to perform military service to the Lord Emperor (*quando ille venerit in servitio domini imperatoris*) or lead his own men, he takes our horses and leads away our sons with him by force and makes them pull the pack-horses for nearly 30 miles or more, and then takes those all away and makes [our sons] go back home alone on foot. But he leaves our horses in Francia or gives them as presents to his own soldiers.
>
> He announces to the people (*Dicit in populo*): 'Let us gather our gifts for the Lord Emperor, as we were used to do in the time of the Greeks, and let a *missus* [chosen] from the people come, together with me, and hand over the gifts in person to the Lord Emperor.' Now we have collected them with great joy. But when it comes to setting off [to the Emperor], he says: 'It's not appropriate for you to come: *I* shall act as intercessor for you with the Lord Emperor.' So he goes with *our* gifts to the Lord Emperor and gets honour for himself or his sons as if they've earned it. And we are left in great oppression and grief (*in grandi oppressione et dolore*).[62]

It's at this point that the complainants (who include the *populus* as well as the *capitanei*) express their sense of 'oppression and grief' with such anguish.

The very next year, perhaps (the date of the relevant capitulary is uncertain), Charles ordered as 'something to make known to everyone', that 'whoever presents horses as gifts for the ruler (*dona regia*) shall have the donor's name written on each of them'.[63] The requirement that donors of horses have their own names attached to their gifts seems a credible response to the cheating of magnates: in Istria, the presence of the *missi* and their holding of public hearings may have acted as deterrents to Duke John and his kinsfolk, and though there's no evidence of the effects of Charles's order, it had a characteristic ring of practicality. His keen appreciation of the military usefulness as well as the value and symbolic significance of horses was shared with his faithful men (and, judging from court poetry, with the womenfolk as well as the menfolk of his family).[64]

Duke John climbed down, the *missi* upheld the Istrians' rights, and the agreement made at Risano stuck, as becomes clear from a confirmation charter made early in the reign of Louis the Pious.[65] The outcome of the Risano case in the short run meant that Charles's and Pippin's authority was asserted. The eleventh-century *Historia Veneticorum* recorded the visit of a Venetian duke, Beatus, to Charles at the end of 805, but also recorded Beatus's visit to Constantinople in 807 to acquire the title of *hypatus* (consul). This looks symptomatic of a 'bidding-war' between Franks and Greeks.[66] The rivalry continued until 812, with regional control continuing to oscillate thereafter.[67]

VI. HOSTAGE MANAGEMENT, MAINZ, 805

In the summer of 804, Charles 'led an army into Saxony and transported (*transtulit*) to Francia all the Saxons who lived beyond the Elbe and in Wihmodia, together with wives and children, giving the districts across the Elbe to the Abodrites'.[68] The *Chronicle of Moissac* under that year tells a similar story of population transfer and dispersal 'within the kingdom, where [the emperor] saw fit'.[69] The removal of the Saxons from Transalbingia enabled Charles to hand over that area to the Abodrites, getting the support of their leaders and setting up a king over them. With hindsight, and writing nearly thirty years later, Einhard knew this to have been the high point, and also the end, of both the Saxon deportations and the Saxon wars:

After defeating all those who offered resistance, and subjecting them to his power, he transported 10,000 men who lived on both sides of the river Elbe, with wives and children, and distributed them in many groups here and there throughout Gaul and Germany. The war which had lasted for so many years ended on this condition imposed by the king and accepted by them [i.e. the Saxons], that they would reject the worship of demons and abandon their ancestral rites, receive the Christian faith and the sacraments of religion, and, united with the Franks, be made one people (*populus*) with them.[70]

Bits and pieces of evidence suggest the variety of forms of transfers of human beings. Hostages are mentioned in the Capitulary *De villis*, at the end of the eighth century.[71] The *Divisio regnorum* of 806 suggests high-status hostages 'given as sureties and distributed by us [i.e. Charles] through various places to be kept under guard (*ad custodiendum*)' had become part of a system by then.[72] More light is thrown on the taking of Saxon hostages by a list made, probably, in 805 at the monastery of Reichenau. Listed are thirty-seven sons of named Saxons of evidently high status, who were to 'come to Mainz and be received by Bishop Heito [of Basel, and a former Reichenau monk] and Count Hitto', each of them having been brought there by the man – in most cases a count or bishop – who 'held/has held' them (*habuit* is the verb in every case) or, in other words, has acted as their 'minder'. Each hostage had been held already before the summons to Mainz.[73] When the young men on Bishop Heito's list had been taken as *obsides* can only be surmised, but it seems likely to have occurred on one or more occasions post-dating 794.

The *Indiculus obsidum Saxonum* (the title is that of a modern editor) was in three sections, each preceded by the name of a group:[74]

Westphalians (*De Westfalahis*)
Bishop Haito and Count Hitto are to receive them.
[Then there is a list of 10 men's names, each, save the first, with the name of the man's father and that of the man who 'holds' him.]

Eastphalians (*De Ostfalahis*]
[Then 15 names]

Angrarii (*De Angrariis*)
[Then 12 names, with some holders' names missing, and at the end:]
There are 37 in all.
THESE ARE TO COME TO MAINZ IN THE MIDDLE OF LENT.

The scribe who wrote out all the above had been trained at the Ale-
mannian monastery of Reichenau, and 'Waldo abbas', one of the
'holders', can be identified as the abbot of Reichenau.[75] Almost all of
the lay 'holders' named were Alemans (only one or two can't be identified), and all three of the churchmen who were 'holders' were Alemans.
The 'receivers' at Mainz were both Alemans. The elite of what had
once been an independent ducal territory now presented themselves as
officials in the service of Charles.

As for the hostages: the Westphalians, Eastphalians and Angrarii
were varieties of Saxons. All these hostages were Saxons and sons of
Saxons. Very probably, the date was mid-March 805. The year before,
804, was the year when Saxon resistance ended, and in 805, when
Charles sent his eldest son and namesake with three separate detachments of troops to attack the Wends, one of the detachments consisted
of Saxons.[76] This points to an 805 date for the hostage-list. These
Saxon hostages and their Alemannic 'holders' were being taken to
Mainz, where the bishop and the count would tick them off the
abbot's list.

Perhaps Charles had decided to release these hostages because the
Saxons had surrendered in 804, and so could be trusted to fight with
the Franks against Slavs and others; but there is no evidence of such a
plan. A more plausible scenario would cover other and longer-term
situations: since the population transfers of the later 790s, aristocratic
Saxon hostages had been distributed through the empire's regions and
placed with 'holders' or minders. There are a couple of pieces of
evidence to support this: one, in the *De villis*, states that no steward
must commend one of Charles's hostages on a royal estate to someone
else (i.e. with the result that the 'holder', Charles, would lose control of
them);[77] and another in the *Divisio regnorum* (806), where Charles,
planning for the future holding and guarding of his hostages as sureties
(*credentiae*) in different post-division kingdoms, forbids one king to let
hostages return to their homeland (*patria*) without the consent of his
brother-king from whose kingdom they had been removed. Rather,
in the future, 'one brother-king should offer mutual assistance to
another in receiving hostages'.[78] All this implies that hostages were a
high-value currency within the empire, that Charles had always controlled their movements closely, and that he intended his successors to
do likewise.

Apparent here is Charles's gift for assessing and exploiting human resources: he had mobilized the Alemannic aristocracy to effect the integration into his 'Frankish' empire of a new generation of Saxons. The 'holders' of these Saxon hostages were nearly all Alemans, but two originated from elsewhere. These were Wala and Einhard, both Franks with large amounts of property in Middle Francia.[79] Other regional elites – presumably – would have been mobilized too, though lists comparable to that of Mainz have not survived. What has survived is the case of a West Frankish 'holder', Archbishop Wulfar of Reims (803–16), documented by the eagle-eyed Flodoard in the mid-tenth century: 'Proof of how great was the confidence placed in Wulfar by the emperor Charles was that he handed over to him 15 illustrious Saxon hostages whom he had brought across from Saxony and entrusted them to be minded (custodiendos) by Wulfar.'[80] Charles himself was directly involved in a system whereby Saxons, especially young Saxons, were 'held' by members of the lay and clerical elites of other regions in their respective households, and brought up to be educated in fidelity to God and king.[81] When Hrabanus Maurus, a former student of Alcuin, adapted Vegetius's late-fourth-century military manual for 'modern times', he interpolated into Vegetius's account of training in the Roman army a brief comment on '[what happens] today: youths are brought up in the households of magnates'.[82] The relationship between hostage and 'holder' or 'minder' resembled that of *nutritus* and *nutritor* in aristocratic Frankish society, where something like fosterage was normal.[83] Einhard, famously, called Charles his *nutritor*.[84]

In the case of the Saxons, there was a special bonus: the hostages were brought up in Christian Frankish ways, forsaking their ancestral paganism, and able to assimilate to, and be assimilated by, the Frankish elite. Charles understood the significance of individual as well as mass conversion. A contemporary annal-writer noted after one occasion involving 'many thousands of gentile peoples', 'The king rejoices with John the Baptist, who also baptised, preaching . . . the remission of sins.'[85] When Einhard wrote that 'the Saxons had abandoned the ceremonies of their fathers and accepted the sacraments of the Christian faith and religion and were united with the Franks and became one people with them', he was describing the most spectacular sign of a process of acculturation.[86] In the years after 800, Charles and his counsellors set out to preach the word about the meaning of baptism.

VII. PIPPIN IN ITALY, LOUIS IN AQUITAINE: DEVOLUTIONARY VARIATIONS

Pippin's kingship began formally in 781 when he was aged five. The government operated under a regency council of *baiuli*, tutors or advisers: Adalhard, abbot of Corbie, born *c*.751 and a cousin of Charles; Abbot Waldo of the monastery of Reichenau, whose position gave him a strategic transalpine role;[87] a Lombard, Duke Rotchild, in charge of the military; and Abbot Angilbert of St-Riquier, one of Charles's leading ecclesiastical officials. The Lombard kingdom had its *sedes* (notably Pavia, Verona and Mantua), a long history of government *from* the palace, and centripetal traditions drawing elites *to* palaces to seek justice. From the time of his takeover of the Lombard realm, Charles had maintained a strong interest in Italy, an interest attested by sixteen capitularies.[88] The first of these, the *Notitia italica* of 776, was the work of Charles himself, characteristically both determined to settle affairs in the acquired kingdom and keen to conciliate the people 'in those parts' by providing justice for them 'according to their law'.[89] A second intervention, in Pippin's name but actually an item on a list provided by Charles, provided for the legal protection in Italy of the wives of Lombard captives being held in Francia.[90] Another item of administrative law that worked in a similar direction was issued in Pippin's name (he was still under-age), but at Charles's behest, when local Italian authorities were required to ensure that properties in Italy that had been given to the late queen Hildegard were now to be *'descriptae per breves'* (surveyed and described in lists), and the lists to be taken to 'the king'.[91] The *Capitulare italicum* of 801 was issued by Charles (Pippin was of age, but far away on campaign, whereas Charles himself may still have been in Italy). Charles presented himself here as successor to the Lombard kings, insisting on army-tax, and threatening deserters with death. Another capitulary, datable to between 802 and 810, shows Charles addressing Italian *missi* across a range of subjects including frontiers (*marcae*), information on 'what our neighbours in frontier-zones have been doing off their own bat (*per se*) especially in recent years', and forbidding *marchiones* (marquises, frontier-commanders) to 'receive men who are fleeing from their lords (*seniores*)'.[92]

These capitularies reflect Charles's interventionist way with Italy. If further proof were needed, it's to be found in a letter sent by Charles to Pippin between 807 and 810:

> Charles most serene augustus crowned by God, great and magnificent *imperator* governing the Roman Empire, and also through God's mercy king of the Franks and of the Lombards, eternal greetings in the Lord to our most beloved son, the glorious king Pippin.
>
> It has come to the ears of our clemency that some dukes and their subordinates, *gastalds* [royal officials], *vicarii*, hundredmen and other officers, falconers, huntsmen and others living in and travelling around various territories, are receiving hospitality and post-service not only from free men but also in the churches of God, namely monasteries of men and of maidens, and hostels (*senodochia*) and in various local communities (*plebes*), and from servants of the church ... and further, imposing labour-services and cartage-service on them, and imposing many oppressions (*multae oppressiones*). Therefore, beloved son, we send you this letter so that you can make inquiries into all this, and if it is true, take measures to correct and amend it ...
>
> We have also heard that certain men of ours and yours are saying that certain *capitula* which we ordered to be written in the law throughout a number of places, because we did not declare these things to their attention in person, are therefore refusing to obey or consent [to them] or accept them as law. But you know very well how and in what terms we spoke to you about these *capitula*, and therefore we warn (*monemus*) your lovable belovedness, that you should make them known throughout the whole realm committed to you by God, and order them to be obeyed and carried out, in particular [the] command we have decreed about bishops and priests who have been killed ... Farewell dearest son.[93]

Charles referred here to the familiar misdeeds of officials and administrators, and to their familiar excuses or pretexts for disobedience: the law was written, and oral messages were no substitute. This was also a personal letter from father to son, calling to mind commands that had been transmitted both by voice and by writing: 'you know (*tu nosti*) how and in what terms we [the royal 'we'] spoke to you about these *capitula*' – with the strong implication that Pippin had failed to publicize these written orders and decrees throughout the realm. The father's complaint raised the question of how far the written could outperform oral communication. Charles made many interventions in Pippin's Italian realm. The problem of imposing orders on men of power did not go away – but those sixteen capitularies, some extant in many manuscripts and widely circulated, reflected the serious efforts of Charles and Pippin between them to impose their demands on their officers in Italy.

Louis' rule in Aquitaine is much less well-documented than Pippin's in Italy. There are virtually no charters or capitularies.[94] The Astronomer, writing Louis' *Vita* in *c*.841, relied for Louis' early life on the memories of Ademar, 'a noble monk' who 'was the same age as Louis and had been brought up with him', had served as Louis' envoy to Charles (in 801), and, a seasoned warrior at the age of twenty-five, had fought as right-hand man to his commander, William of Toulouse, at a battle against Saracens near Saragossa.[95] The Astronomer's testimony, at second-hand from Ademar's oral memoirs, is a rich source of information on both governmental and military matters. In the 770s, Charles had gained first-hand experience of Aquitaine; in the 780s and 790s, Charles's priorities often lay elsewhere, and Charles himself never returned to Aquitaine after 778.

Louis, aged about three, had been taken from Italy to Aquitaine in 781, straightaway after his anointing at Rome, and his father had then appointed a *baiulus*, Arnold, with colleagues (unnamed), to teach and protect the child-king, and with other *proceres* to advise him on the affairs of the state (*res publica*).[96] In 786, Charles had summoned to an assembly at Paderborn Louis and a group of boys of his age,

> all dressed in Gascon fashion, with a circular cloak, a shirt with long, wide sleeves, baggy leggings and spurred boots, each boy carrying a throwing spear in his hand. His father was delighted – it was he who had organised all this . . . And [Louis and his companions] returned to Aquitaine for the winter.[97]

Paternal stage-management early on signalled Charles's wish to ensure Louis' acculturation into his Aquitanian realm. In 791, when Louis was fourteen, he was summoned first to Ingelheim, then Regensburg to be girded with a sword by his father in a ritual coming-of-age. This was followed by his father's sending of him with his older brother Pippin to Italy to taste his first serious military experience, before being summoned back to Bavaria (where the rebellion of Pippin son of

Himiltrud had recently been crushed). In what the Astronomer depicts as an appraisal interview, Charles demanded why Louis found himself living in 'such straitened personal circumstances' (*tenuitas in re familiari*) that he could not offer even a present (*benedictio*) without being asked for one.[98] Charles's response to Louis' plight was to send two *missi*, Willibert, later archbishop of Rouen, and Count Richard, the overseer of his estates, with orders to bring back into public control what had previously served the needs of the state (*res publica*), after much filching away of properties by local aristocrats. As part of this reordering, Louis himself (now back in Aquitaine) decreed that there should be four palaces, all of them in the northern part of his realm: Angeac, Chasseneuil, Doué-la-Fontaine and Ébreuil-sur-Sioule. Louis would stay for one year in each in turn. In so far as Louis itinerated, his journeys seldom took him far from these northerly sites.

Louis took an important decision on his own initiative in 796 when he redressed what was apparently a longstanding grievance. Until then, the *plebei*, the commons, in effect the peasantry, had had to pay a fodder-tax to support the military. Now Louis, 'reflecting on the penury of those who paid and the cruelty of those who exacted payments', put an end to this imposition. 'This displeased the *viri militares*.' Louis' solution was to provide the warriors with oats and hay out of his own resources, that is, with public supplies of fodder.[99] At the same time and clearly related, was Louis' freeing of the men of the Albigeois from the tributes of wine and corn they had previously had to pay into the public cellars and barns.[100] These concessions were of strategic importance in the particularly vulnerable areas on the borders of Septimania. The military measures mentioned a little earlier in the *Vita* as datable to 787, and later, in the 790s, were part of a more general process of reorganization of public resources, economic and military, in Aquitaine.[101] The rather disconnected feel of these chapters stems, arguably, from the memories retailed by Ademar. Thanks to the Astronomer's reliance on his Aquitanian witness, the evidence is at least sympathetic.

The absence of evidence for Aquitanian elites travelling to palaces has been lamented in a recent notable study, and these southern aristocrats chided for 'not communicating' with the ruler or 'the centre'.[102] The *Hispani*, immigrants from Spain who found protected lands in the south-west of Aquitaine, and leaders of reformed monastic communities who travelled to Aachen for patronage, were exceptions that proved the rule.[103] To look for an answer to the problem of uncommunicative elites, it's not enough to fall back on lack of evidence. Monastic complaints about *pravi homines* (wicked men) – aristocrats who were greedier and more out of control than those further north – don't really provide compelling explanations for a huge north–south cultural divide. The differences were more specific: neither the Franks' treatment of Aquitaine and Aquitanians in the reign of Pippin, nor Charles's installing of Franks into Aquitanian countships in 778, could easily have been forgotten. Displacements, and resultant resentments, died hard.

The dangers of attack from the south into Aquitaine required recurrent responses from the Carolingian regime. In 797 the Muslim ruler of Barcelona put his territory ceremonially into Charles's hands; and in 799,

> Charles sent Louis with an army to besiege Huesca. Bypassing Barcelona, he attacked Lerida which he took and destroyed. Leaving it in ruins, he wasted and burned other towns and advanced to Huesca. The fields of the city were abundant with standing corn, and the troops cut this down, wasted and burned; everything found outside the city was consumed by the devouring flames.[104]

In 804, after a six-week siege Louis' armies captured Barcelona, and the victorious king staged imposing rituals for his *adventus*.[105] The next year, the territory around Tarragona was ravaged but the city itself remained untaken. Similarly, Tortosa was targeted, and the countryside ravaged, but the city withstood siege. Louis prepared a further expedition into Spain,

> but his father stopped him going there in person, because he [Charles] had just then given orders that boats were to be built on all the rivers leading into the sea against the incursions of the Northmen, and commanded Louis to act similarly with regard to the Rhône, Garonne and Loire. But Charles sent Louis his *missus* Ingobert who was to represent the person of his son and to lead the army in their joint stead.[106]

The Franks again planned to attack Tortosa, this time using prefabricated portable boat-parts and clever methods of re-assembly to cross the Ebro. But 'some Moor' having a swim, evidently a local, had detected bits of barley in a lump of horse-dung in the river and, smelling a clue to Frankish horses, alerted Tortosan scouts, and the siege soon had to be called off.[107] Charles again sent one of his own *missi*, Heribert, to take charge of another attack on Huesca, but this too failed.[108] There was a final attempt (though not explicitly stated by the Astronomer) to avenge the defeat at Roncesvaux back in 778 by trying to outsmart the Basques: the outcome for the Franks was a planned retreat, with some Basque captives held only until the Frankish army had crossed the pass back to Francia.[109] Some of these efforts were masterminded by Charles, and recorded by the reviser of the *ArF* as well as by the Astronomer. Others were organized by Charles's *missi*. Only Barcelona and its comital territory was a real success: a permanent annexation for the Carolingians.[110] It could be argued that Charles's backing for Louis was somehow half-hearted, or deliberately obstructive. I think, rather, that this was an instance of a well-known adage: that too many cooks spoil the broth. Charles attempted to bring into Aquitaine the Young Charles, then Pippin of Italy, then first one then another of his own *missi* to help Louis, but plans misfired. Distances were too great, campaigning landscapes too varied.

The Astronomer, and his key informant, teller of tales and Louis' standard-bearer at the siege of Barcelona, were neither of them unbiased. Nevertheless, a tale which amounts to a paean of praise for Louis sounds plausible: it evokes Louis' concern for religion during the years of his rule in Aquitaine. He was concerned for 'the spiritual health' of laity as well as clergy, and especially for those who practised the meditative life. After listing the large numbers of monasteries of which Louis was the patron, the Astronomer concluded that 'the whole kingdom of Aquitaine is adorned as if by bright-shining lamps (*veluti quibusdam lychnis totum decoratur Aquitaniae regnum*)'.[111]

A woman shall have the last word: she is anonymous, but clearly was an Aquitanian aristocrat and a widow, in desperate straits because of the rapacity and violence of Charles's own *missi*, hand-in-glove with the local bishop. At a date very probably in the early ninth century, she sent to the palace the following letter (which survives as a form-letter in the Formulary of Bourges) appealing for justice:

> I have not been able to present in person any defender, except to show the charter of protection of your royal clemency, and that did me no benefit because they [the men who claim to have been your *missi*] have thrown me out of my inheritance by a wicked plot and the worst of

ill-will. And so I, your handmaiden, have come in all haste to throw myself at your feet so that your mercy will decide to help me . . . (*Ego alium defensorem presentialiter manifestare non potui, nisi vestrae regalis clementiae cartam mundburalem ostendi, et mihi nihil profuit . . .*)

The letter was addressed not to Louis but to Charles. No evidence survives of any response, or any sequel.[112]

Devolved regnal power could work well, but the lengthier the distance of relevant communications, the higher was the risk that regional and local power would subvert regnal power; *munera*, in both senses – bribes and gifts – were rife, but sometimes, at the same time, trust held and justice prevailed. 'Heaven is high and the emperor is far away' was an adage in ancient China: it is still to be heard in China today. It's tempting to infer from the patchy evidence that Lombard Italy had a deeper and longer-term experience of effective dispensing of justice in local courts than did Aquitaine; but the available documentary description is so much thicker in Italy than in Aquitaine that any judgement risks being skewed. Jenny Davis has argued persuasively that effective practices of management and discipline are attested in Charles's devolved regime. In the end, it comes down less to any solidly objective measure of effectiveness by means of such written evidence as survives, than to a subjective assessment of individual rulers and their agents, and of the strength and warmth of personal relations between the emperor and his sons. On the whole I hope that the present book generates a degree of optimism. Anecdotes, letters and scraps of letters, rumour, gossip and hearsay (*rumor, fama, auditiones*) are the earlier medieval historian's lot. We make do and mend.

A small section of the *Breve commemoratorium* (*The Short Report*), 808.

15

The Aachen Years

1. CHARLES'S MEETINGS IN FRANCIA, WINTER 804–5

In the imperial years, the authors of the *ArF*, and of other annals too, had different preoccupations from before: diplomatic relations loomed large, and Charles's hunting activities, though not mentioned every year, were more frequently noted. Thus for 804, 'Charles returned to Aachen after the autumn hunting'. Next, disturbing any new pattern, came some surprising news: 'in mid-November, the emperor was told that Pope Leo wished to spend Christmas with him at whatever location might be possible.' If the author's wording here seems opaque, his account of the pope's motive, a few lines later in this annal, is even more tantalizing. Charles had 'been told' that Christ's blood had been discovered the previous summer in the city of Mantua, and had asked the pope to investigate the rumour (*fama*). 'Seizing the opportunity to leave, the pope first travelled to Lombardy as if to carry out the investigation, but then suddenly left, and came all the way to the emperor.' The thread can be picked up at the point where Charles, at Aachen, first heard of Leo's wish to visit:

> he immediately sent his son Charles to St-Maurice [d'Agaune] with orders to receive [the pope] with honour. The emperor himself set out for Reims where he received Leo and conducted him to the *villa* of Quierzy, where he celebrated Christmas, and then to Aachen. The pope stayed with him for eight days, and then returned to Rome.[1]

This curious disjointed narrative reflects, firstly, the concerns of the pope. Leo needed to 'seize the opportunity' to visit Francia, apparently using the smokescreen of the inquiry into what had occurred in Mantua in order to conceal his real intentions. The pope's position in Rome, once Charles had left in 801, was as vulnerable as before to local faction. Now, though, Leo also had to cope with rivalries between *duces* in north-east Italy, the old animosity of the exarchate of Ravenna, and episodic intrusions of the agents of two imperial powers, Frankish and Byzantine. In 804, Leo did not wait to be invited by Charles: instead, he invited himself for what he expected would be a visit lengthy enough to allow the firming-up of Charles's assurances of protection and support.

Leo's initiative in making the journey north stirred new questions in Charles's mind. He would need to choreograph Leo's visit. The Young Charles was now some thirty-two years old, a seasoned warrior and very capable leader. After his anointing at Rome on Christmas Day 800 (801), his whereabouts are undocumented for three years. In November 804, his father assigned him the high-profile role of escorting Pope Leo from the borders of Francia. The meeting of the Young Charles and the pope was to take place at St-Maurice d'Agaune, something over 800km from Reims. The emperor's mind had ranged back to 753, where as a five-year-old he had been staying at Thionville with his parents when news came that Pope Stephen II had crossed the Alps by the Mons Iovis (Great St Bernard) pass and was heading north. King Pippin sent Charles with a retinue of the realm's chief men 'nearly 100 miles' (*c*.160km) to meet the pope and escort him to the palace of Ponthion. Now in 804 Charles would send his namesake and *de iure* first-born son to perform a similar office fifty years later, for Pope Leo. (Pippin son of Himiltrud, incarcerated in a monastery since 792, had long since forfeited any rights to the title of first-born.) The emperor also recalled his own visit to St-Maurice in 773, when, en route for the most momentous border-crossing of his life, he took the road over the pass to Italy and the annexation of the Lombard kingdom in 774. Now, thirty years on, Charles was pondering the future division of his realms, and the strategic importance of the three major alpine passes in enabling the three successor-kings to have access to Rome and so share responsibility for protecting the Holy See.[2]

In Charles's mind these memories were connected with events much longer ago in a Frankish dream-time, and also with events of his own adult life, as when he planned his own meeting with Pope Leo in

December 804 at Reims. The symbolic origin of the Franks' kingdom as a Catholic Christian one was firmly located at Reims, where, in 508, Clovis had been baptized a Catholic by Bishop Remigius.[3] The fortunes of the see, and hence of St Rémi (as he came to be known), had fluctuated under the early Carolingians. Pippin had neglected Reims, but Charles's brother Carloman had favoured it, and when he died on 4 December 772, he had been buried in the ancient basilica of St-Rémi outside the walls of Reims.[4] Bishop Tilpin (c.748/9 or 751/4–94) had been promoted to archiepiscopal rank in 779 by Pope Hadrian.[5] Charles kept the see vacant for nine years (from 794 to 803) and seems never to have visited Reims until 804. The author of the *AMP* stressed the joy and veneration with which Pope Leo was welcomed at Reims.[6] In pondering succession plans, memories of his brother, long-dead, and his nephews, long-disappeared, surely recurred to Charles's mind, and then were stifled or repressed, to surface publicly in c. 18 of the *Divisio* of 806 (see p. 434).

From Reims, emperor and pope had travelled some 100km to celebrate Christmas at Quierzy, a favoured residence in the earlier decades of Charles's life and reign. Pippin and his family had met Pope Stephen II there in 754, when the king had agreed to defend St Peter's lands from the Lombards. Charles himself had visited Rome in 774 and had been reminded by Pope Hadrian of Pippin's promise at Quierzy, and shown what purported to be a text of it. Hitherius, Charles's notary, had made two copies of it there and then, one of which had been left on St Peter's body on 6 April 774.[7] Half a century after Pippin's promise had been given, did Charles consider the Donation of Quierzy a fiction successfully imposed upon the world?[8] Regardless of facts on the ground, or the failure of territorial restitutions to materialize, I don't believe Charles could ever have forgotten that day in St Peter's *confessio*. Long since etched in his own memory, that moment was now, in 804, reawakened in the emperor's mind when he spent Christmas with Pope Leo at Quierzy. They did not linger there for long. Instead they pressed on to St-Médard, Soissons, where Charles's father and mother had been consecrated to the kingdom in 751: another ritual event in which arguably Charles himself had participated, and which he may have recalled.

Charles, apparently without warning, left the pope and his retinue at the abbey of St-Médard while he himself travelled the 100km or so south-east of Soissons to the convent of Chelles where his sister Gisela had long resided. To leave Leo and his retinue looks like a kind of exclusion, perhaps disguised as a fraternal visit to Gisela who was in poor health. Charles had decided – perhaps many weeks earlier – to hold a *colloquium* at Chelles, because he wanted to consult Gisela (and other kin and counsellors) on a pressing familial matter: the succession. This was a subject in which Gisela had a stake, since she seems already to have had a preference for the Young Charles as *primogenitus*.[9] The word *colloquium* denoted a high-level political meeting.[10] In this case the aim was to begin hammering out a consensus on the division of Charles's realms. It was also a discussion in which the emperor evidently did not want the pope to be involved: hence his being parked at St-Médard. Once the meeting was over, Charles asked the pope to join him at Quierzy where they celebrated Christmas together *cum summa exultatione*. Finally, Charles escorted Leo to Aachen. Leo had heard much of the new palace location, but had not yet seen it. By now, there was a lot to see. Nevertheless, Charles gave Leo short shrift in time-terms. To travel from Rome to Aachen and back and be offered no more than an eight-day stay was surely an almighty snub for Pope Leo.

The central figure in Frankish military action during 805 was the Young Charles.

The emperor had sent him on a high-profile campaign against the Bohemians. 'He devastated all of their land and killed their leader (*dux*) whose name was Lecho.'[11] The *AMP* author gave a much fuller, even propagandistic, account:

> The emperor sent his army with his son Charles into the territory of the Slavs called Bohemians, ordering the army to penetrate the region by three routes: he commanded the section of the army with his son King Charles to move through the eastern part of Francia and Germania, so that it might fall upon the aforementioned Slavs after crossing the Hyrcanian Forest in Bohemia. A second section he sent through Saxony, so that, together with Saxons and innumerable Slavs, it might burst upon the Bohemians from another direction after crossing the aforesaid Forest from the north. And he ordered the armed force of all Bavaria to invade the same region from a third direction. Coming from all sides to the

Bohemian plain, all the leading men of different peoples (*universi principes diversarum gentium*) arrived in King Charles's presence. These countless hosts pitched camp at no great distance from each other. After receiving the order from King Charles and their princes who were with him, the whole army invaded that region. But [other] Slavs, taking themselves to the forest and inaccessible places, showed no aspiration at all for combat. For forty days the region was wasted and burned, however.[12]

Notable here is the presence of 'innumerable Slavs' with the Young Charles's forces, and later, the arrival of 'all the princes of different peoples' in the king's presence. Slavs in that region, for whom discretion proved the better part of valour, would not forget their region's forty-day burning. The *AMP* author repeated at this point a phrase recorded under the year 710 about the treatment meted out to his enemies (Alamans, as it happened) by the Young Charles's great-great-grandfather Pippin, the father of Martel: 'the region was burned (*incensaque regione*)'. The author of the *Chronicle of Moissac* added interesting details about the Young Charles's campaigns in 805, deploying three separate armies in the region between the Elbe, Saale and Ohre, and in lands on both sides of the Elbe, and in the Erzgebirge, against other western Slav peoples, the Wends and the Daleminzi: the Young Charles led a Frankish force, Audulf and Werinhar led Bavarians, and a third army consisted of Saxons. 'King Charles returned victorious to his father in Francia.'[13]

The emperor spent that summer in 'hunting and other pleasures', and travelled through the forest of the Vosges to Champ, where the Young Charles was received back from the campaign by his father. The two of them seem to have continued the hunting together, before wintering at Thionville. There is no clear evidence that King Charles returned at this point to the Neustrian kingdom apparently planned by his father in 800. The kingdom of Italy had been assigned to Pippin, with its *sedes* in Pavia and Mantua, just as the four Aquitanian palaces had been assigned to Louis. The Young Charles, curiously, remained unmarried: he had a military household but not, it seems, a *sedes* of his own. Perhaps he was biding his time until the dimensions of his prospective kingdom had been settled. The notion that he was gay, and therefore uninterested in marriage, seems to me anachronistic and not worth serious consideration.

II. A LETTER FROM CHARLES TO A BUSY BISHOP, LATE 805

The third great famine of Charles's reign struck Francia late in 805, after a disastrous harvest. Charles, in a letter to a bishop, vividly described the famine and attributed it to sin. The bishop was Ghaerbald of Liège (785/787–809), in whose diocese Aachen lay. Proximity to Charles offered Ghaerbald the benefits of access; on the other hand, the bishop's situation can never have been very comfortable, especially not during and after 802's huge burst of administrative activity. Ghaerbald had already received a wake-up call in the form of a letter from the emperor, castigating the shortcomings of would-be godparents, and the bishop relayed this letter to his priests.[14] Late in 805, Charles sent another letter to 'Bishop Ghaerbald and all those committed to you by almighty God and our command'.[15] The emperor, having discussed matters with his secular and ecclesiastical *fideles*, had decided to instruct the bishop that because of exceptional needs, to be spelled out below, three fast-days, on 11, 13 and 15 December, were to be observed by everyone, remembering that as the Lord says, 'Ask and it shall be given unto you, seek and ye shall find . . .' (Matt. 7:7). Details of further fast-days were given, and then these were followed by details of the especially severe and urgent circumstances (*necessitates*):

> sterility of the earth everywhere and beyond the normal, and imminent danger of famine, extreme weather damaging the crops, pestilence, and wars of pagan peoples on our borders . . . And we can most certainly gather from those external signs (*ab his exterioribus*) that we are forced to endure so many evils outwardly (*exterius*) because we are in no way pleasing the Lord inwardly (*nos per omnia Domino non placere interius*). And therefore it seems to us entirely right that each one of us must strive to humble his heart in the truth, and on whatever occasion he is caught having offended God in act or thought, must cleanse himself by penance and grieving with tears, protect himself as best he can and guard himself from such bad things in future . . . And may God turn (*convertat*) each one of us to the observing of his commandments and . . . since He knows we lack them – to bestow on us the good things we are unworthy to have,

and grant that we may deserve to be numbered among His members, that is, as parts of the body of the holy church, and deem us worthy to bring it to peace, to unite it and to rule it and protect it from all evil; for we are bound in that unity and it is so that we may deserve His grace that we have decreed these fasts and prayers to be performed by every one of you.

Also, after reading this letter, cause it to be read again (*relegere*) before all, and widely transmitted (*tradere*), so that all can understand for what urgent and severe need these things are being done. And, all of you, direct yourselves to your baptismal churches and send men who are good at inter-preting and explaining (*interpretes*) who can expound everything, as said above. And act in this way also for all the monasteries in your diocese.[16]

In Charles's mind and in the actions he took, outward and inward were intimately connected: sin could be cleansed by fasts and prayers, and error repelled by the observance of God's commands.[17] Charles was also aware that the Almighty did not always apply the sanctions at His disposal.[18] The letter would have been drafted with counsellors' help and dictated by Charles to a scribe. Through its emphatic cadences, however, could (and can) be heard Charles's urgent, demanding voice.[19]

III. ACCOUNTING FOR AN ABSENCE OF CHARTERS, 804–5

Charles's charters (154 in all, excluding documents best classed as judg-ments) have been cited frequently in the course of this book because of their exceptional usefulness in reconstructing the narrative of the reign and the life of the emperor. The charters' distribution across time is, however, frustratingly uneven. Jenny Davis's work is especially helpful for making it possible to compare the distribution of capitularies against charters in the imperial years.[20] Highs can be readily explicable. For instance, the twenty-nine charters issued in 774–5 following the suc-cess of the Italian campaign and its follow-up, and a notable run of five charters for the monastery at Hersfeld (DD. 35, 36, 49, 50, 51 – all of these originals) in 775, or the nine charters issued in 781 during and after Charles's second journey to Italy. Harder to explain is, for instance, the low (three charters only) of 788. Hardest to account for is the fact that for the years 784, 785, 789, 793, 796, 798, 801, 804 and 805, no charters at all survive; and only eighteen survive over the whole of the imperial years of 801 to 813.

Numbers of charters detailing land-grants of ninth-century Carolingians *after* Charles are much higher than the numbers for Charles's forty-six-year reign. Of all Charles's 154 charters, 142 were gifts to ecclesiastical institutions. Charles founded no new monasteries, and only ten existing houses were beneficiaries.[21] The location and timing of some of his gifts of property suggest that strategic considerations were often uppermost in his mind: Fulda was situated on the borders of Saxony, Nonantula lay on a key route south-east from the Po valley.[22] The Aachen church (it was the church of the Aachen parish) was a special case: its endowment came from Carolingian fisc-lands in the vicinity.[23]

The bulk of Charles's charters were issued at palaces, and, from the mid-790s, increasingly often at Aachen. There is no strong correlation of grants with seasonality, that is, with assemblies gathered in early summer for war. The assembly Charles summoned at Thionville apparently lasted from December 805 to February 806. Two factors limited its size: seasonality and famine (the worst kind of *tribulatio*).[24] From the weeks at Thionville, only one charter survives: Charles gave a single *mansus* (a peasant holding!) to Prüm, together with the fine owed by Abbot Tancrad for confirmation of gifts to churches made by Maginfred, now deceased, an unfree servant (*servus*) of Charles. Though Maginfred's loyal service was something the emperor wished to reward, the legalities had to be gone through posthumously.[25] That only one of Charles's charters survives issued at Thionville could also be the result of other recipients' (unquantifiable) losses of documents. In any case, many fewer charters were issued in the imperial years. With only one exception, the total number of Charles's charters issued between 807 and 813 (again, excluding judgments), is twelve, all issued from Aachen. This would indicate a rate of fewer than two per year. The exception – that is, the only charter surviving from this period and *not* issued from Aachen, was issued in 810 at Verden.[26] What was Charles doing at Verden on 12 August 810? Fortunately the authors of two sets of annals between them supply the answer. The *Chronicle of Moissac* has: 'The emperor Charles went across the Rhine with his son King Charles and through Saxony to the place called Verden.'[27] While the Annals of

St-Amand have: 'The emperor Charles went into Saxony with an army of Franks and held the assembly (*placitum*) there in Verden. And the Wends came there, and he gave them a king.'[28]

Was Charles's memory of events at Verden twenty-eight years before – the so-called 'bloodbath' of 782 following Widukind's rebellion – working overtime? Was his presence at Verden wholly or in part an act of remembrance? In the end, where did the charters go in the late-imperial years? It looks to me like a non-question. Judgments and dispute-settlements, forfeitings and restitutions of property were the preferred solutions to the problems that came up.[29]

IV. THE CAPITULARY OF THIONVILLE, EARLY JANUARY 806

Charles had left Aachen for Thionville in July 805. With hindsight, it can be inferred that he was making advance arrangements, perhaps including some enlargements to the palace and amenities for wintering there, as he did from December 805 to February 806. The Young Charles, after devastating Bohemia in the summer campaign of 805, joined his father in late summer to hunt in the Vosges, and then spent 'some time' at the convent of Remiremont on the river Mosel, also in the Vosges region, and from there it was a journey downriver of some 250km to Thionville.[30] In time to celebrate Christmas, Emperor Charles and King Charles were joined by kings Pippin and Louis. Presumably each ruler brought his court – perhaps a scaled-down group, because of the famine.

The assembled company at Thionville was exceptional in significance if not in size. Much preparation had gone into it. In the early days of January, Charles presided over the formal sessions which considered a total of thirty-eight items, or clusters of items, which, once approved, he issued in the form of a 'double capitulary', that is, one split into ecclesiastical and lay (or 'general') sections, both addressed to *missi*.[31] It survives in an unusually large numbers of manuscripts: the ecclesiastical section in twenty-four, the 'general' section, in whole or part, in thirty manuscripts, of which no fewer than fourteen date to the ninth century. Both sections were (in whole or part) included in the capitulary-collection of Ansegis, abbot of St-Wandrille, made in 827 at the behest of Louis the Pious. This meant that they were even more widely copied.[32] Both the circumstances of the Thionville assembly, and the wide and rapid diffusion of its Double Capitulary in the years following 806, raised two questions about royal agents which Jenny Davis posed as follows: 'How did Charlemagne try to control them? Did these aristocrats ostensibly serving the king [or emperor as he now was] actually function as accountable agents?'[33] I suggest some answers below, in section (vi).

In the ecclesiastical section, some notable items reflected Charles's particular interest in the standards of liturgical performance of cantors (royal agents indeed) and the maintenance of disciplines necessary to those, such as calendrical calculations, and chanting 'according to the manner and practice of the Roman church', whose traditions were particularly cherished at the school of Metz and whence Charles now ordered trained cantors to return to their home churches.[34] Charles, conscious of the risks run by 'laymen newly withdrawn from the [secular] world', ordered that such men 'were not to be sent out [from monasteries] on [secular] business until they had fully learnt their [new] law by living it', and that 'those who abandoned the secular world in order to serve their Lord – and then did neither – must choose between living the canon's way or the monk's way'.[35] There were echoes here of Charles's letter of 801/802 castigating Alcuin and the Tours brethren for not clearly differentiating between canons and monks.[36] The ecclesiastical section ended with *incestuosi*, people guilty of incest: 'they are to be tried according to the canons, and not let off because of anyone's friendship (*amicitia*)'.[37] Charles characteristically connected two of his deepest concerns: incest and injustice.

In the general section, addressed for good measure *Ad omnes generaliter*, Charles and his advisers revisited a number of themes. First they had to consider the situation they all found themselves in: *tribulatio* – famine.[38] This was spelled out in c. 4: 'In this present year because of the shortage of food, each person is to help his own people [i.e. dependants] as best he can and is not to sell his corn at an excessively high price, and no foodstuffs are to be sold outside our empire (*foris nostrum imperium*).'[39]

Linked together in cc. 5, 'concerning not bearing weapons within the country (*infra patria*)', and 7, 'concerning traders', were armsbearing and feuds:[40]

[c. 5] If someone is engaged in a feud, an inquiry is to be made into which party is hostile to their being reconciled, and let them be compelled to reconciliation, even if they are unwilling; and if they refuse reconciliation in any other way, they are to be brought before to our presence. And if after reconciliation, one man kills the other, he is to pay composition for him and to lose the hand by which he perjured himself, and also pay the emperor's bann.[41]

[c. 7] Concerning traders (*negotiatores*) who travel in the lands of Slavs and Avars: [six named trading-places are listed, together with the names of the *missi* in charge of them:] in the region of Saxony as far as Bardo-wick, Hredi; at Scheessel, Madalgaud; at Magdeburg, Aito; at Erfurt, Madalgaud again; at Forcheim, Lorch, and Regensburg, Audulf; at Lorch, Warner. Traders are not to take weapons and mail-shirts to sell: if caught carrying those things, they are to hand over their entire stock, half of it going to the palace, the other half going to the *missus* and whoever dis-covered the offence.[42]

A capitulary fragment dealing with other high-value tradable items provided a spy-hole into some shady deals which Charles wished to expose and ban:

Concerning trade, it is to be commanded above all that no-one should dare to trade at night in gold and silver vessels, slaves, jewels, horses and livestock except living animals and the fodder they need if they are travel-ling, but each trader is to engage in their business during daytime and before witnesses.[43]

Tim Reuter commented, 'We must, then, think of a very large-scale circu-lation of goods on this level of gift-giving and tribute-payment, which ran largely parallel to and independently of the normal "economic" circula-tion of goods (though there were naturally interfaces between the two),' and added that 'the prohibition of night (i.e. secret) sales was perhaps intended not only as a general measure against fencing stolen goods, but also to try to prevent feuds arising over the possession of such items.'[44]

One or two more topics discussed and agreed at Thionville are worth highlighting. Oaths on Charles's agenda were closely linked to conspiracies. The oath of fidelity to the emperor had loomed large in 802 in the 'programmatic' capitulary, and Charles returned to the subject at Thionville: 'Concerning the oath, that fidelity is not to be promised by oath to anyone other than to ourself and to each man's own lord (*senior*) with a view to our advantage and that of his lord.'[45] Before an assembly audience drawn from many parts of the empire, Charles took the opportunity to reinforce the impression made by the new oath of 802 on as many *seniores* as possible, and to underscore the analogous relationships between them and 'ourself', Charles, and between men and their *seniores*.

At Herstal in 779, armed retinues had been banned, as were mutually agreed associations (*gildonia, convenentiae*) if made by oath-swearings.[46] Again, and more urgently, at Frankfurt in 794, swearings-together and conspiracies (*conjurationes et conspirationes*) were not to be made, and where found, were to be destroyed.[47] At Thionville, Charles confronted anyone making a conspiracy, or confirming a conspiracy with an oath, with three possibilities:

> If evil has deliberately resulted, those involved are to be condemned to die, and those abetting them are to flog each other or slit each others' noses; but if no evil ensued, the penalties are flogging each other and shearing-off each others' hair; but if free men made a conspiracy confirmed by striking hands, they must either swear with trusty oath-helpers that they did not get involved with any evil intent, or, if they cannot do that, they must pay compensation according to their law (*suam legem componant*).[48]

Charles finally decreed, 'No conspiracy is to occur in our realm henceforth – with or without an oath.' In the second and third scenarios, the penalties were heavier than those of Herstal and Frankfurt, but they were exemplary rather than brutal.

To return to where this discussion started, accountability is dealt with in c. 12:

> Concerning advocates: that corrupt (*pravi*) advocates, subordinates of counts (*vicedomini*), deputies of counts (*vicarii*) and hundredmen are to be removed, and that such men are chosen as have both the knowledge and will to judge and settle cases justly. And if a corrupt (*pravus*) count is found, he is to be reported to us.[49]

Being reported to the emperor might have struck a corrupt count as a fearsome prospect, comparable to the reaction of a negligent steward in a similar situation.[50] For a count, or a steward, to be reported, then summoned to the palace and to the emperor's presence, threatened a terrible loss of face – a public humiliation. Rules and expectations operated at the various levels in comparable ways: between the emperor and one of his *seniores* (lords) between a *senior* and one of his men, and, across a wider status gap, between the emperor and one of his stewards.[51] Hierarchical as this world was, it was also full of reciprocities: Charles asked his stewards 'not to think it harsh for us [that is, himself, Charles] to make the [above-mentioned] demands, because it is our wish that they should likewise be able to make all sorts of demands of their subordinates without their feeling hard done by'.[52]

V. THE *DIVISIO REGNORUM*, FEBRUARY 806

This document was an exceptional response, in form and in substance, to exceptional circumstances. Formally, it began as if it were a diploma, or very solemn charter: it invoked the Holy Trinity, and addressed 'all', then in an *arenga* (a preamble) provided context and purpose – both 'of the highest importance concerning the empire's destiny and in the most solemn form', as Ganshof put it, adding: 'the exception that proved the rule'.[53] The date of its issue was not provided, as it would have been in a normal charter; it is known from a set of brief annals copied at the monastery of St-Gall in the ninth century. 'In AD 806 in the 14th indiction, in the 38th year of Charles's reign and the 8th year of his rule as emperor, on Friday 6th February, his realm (*regnum*) was divided between his sons, how much each would have after him [i.e. after the emperor's death].' The *ArF*'s account of the event is unusually detailed:

> The emperor held an assembly (*conventum*) with the leading men and the great men of the Franks concerning the establishment and preservation of peace between his sons, and with the division of his realm into three parts, so that each of them would know which part he must defend and rule, should he outlive his father. A testamentary deed concerning this partition was drawn up, and confirmed on oath by the great men of the Franks (*iureiurando ab optimatibus Francorum confirmatum*) while imperial regulations (*constitutiones*) were made with a view to the conserving of peace. All these mandates were put down in writing, and sent

in the care of Einhard to Pope Leo so that he would subscribe them by his hand. The pope read all these things, and gave his approval, and subscribed them with his own hand.[54]

Einhard may well have had a role in the plan and its writing, as well as the taking of a copy of it to Rome.[55] The phrasing of the document's *arenga* is inflected for a moment by the Latinity of Lucan, an echo, in another context and with a contrary message foretelling the outcome of the battle of Pharsalus: '*Tanti peribunt ut omne genus hominum omnibus seculis reparare non possit*' ('so many will perish that the whole human race through all the ages will not be able to renew [itself]').[56] Here, absorbing the classical voice, is the paternal voice of Charles:

> The Divine Mercy, at whose bidding the generations moving towards death are renewed by the successions of the generations (*cuius nutu ad occasum tendentia secula reparantur per successiones generationum*), has enriched us with a great token of His compassion and blessing by giving us three sons, and through them has confirmed our own prayers and hopes concerning the kingdom, and has lightened our fears of being forgotten by a hostile posterity . . .

Johannes Fried's rendering, via German into Peter Lewis's English translation, offers a different reading: 'God's clemency would, over the course of the succeeding generations restore to health the current *saecula* (times), which were racing headlong to destruction and downfall', followed by Fried's comment (in Lewis's translation): 'Charlemagne was not seeking to dispel eschatological fears entirely but rather to compel them to succumb to the Christian message of hope.' I do not read any eschatological reference in Charles's words; rather, what Charles is presenting is God's renewal of human life as children succeed parents.

The preamble also contains a substantial contribution to Frankish political ideas, influenced by the Christian Roman and imperial past:

> This also should be known to you, that we desire to have these our sons, by the grace of God, as co-rulers of the realm given us by God (*regni a Deo nobis concessi consortes*) while we are alive, and after our death, to leave them as heirs to our empire and kingdom conserved and preserved by God. May we not leave them any contention of strife and dispute by

thinking in terms of a whole realm in a confused and disorganized way! But in dividing the whole body of the realm into three parts one of which each of them must protect and rule, we have had [each] portion surveyed and marked out (*describere et designare fecimus*) – in such a way that each shall be content according to our order, and strive, by God's help, to defend the bounds of our realm which are extended to frontiers with foreign peoples (*alienigenae*), and to guard peace and love (*pax et caritas*) with his brother.[57]

Charles's insistence on 'peace and love' was that of a Christian Roman emperor. Having 'each portion surveyed and described', Frankish-style, was built into the plan of 'three portions', as it had been into his plan for Young Charles in Neustria in 800.[58]

As well as a vision of empire, Charles had a thoroughly down-to-earth view of its now vast resources, as attested in the last sentence of c. 4, relating to transalpine passes which offered access-routes to Italy. Divisions of the Frankish realm in the eighth century, though, had been based on the principle of equal shares: *aequa lance* ('by equal right', literally, 'by equal weight'). Charles chose 'a radical departure' from Frankish tradition.[59] In this new generation, the sons would not have equal shares but one of the three, the eldest, Charles's namesake, would have the lion's share. Perhaps (and this is a characteristically interesting suggestion of Johannes Fried's) it was Alcuin from whom Charles had sought an 'expert opinion' before 800, and recommended, '*optime natus et hereditatem legitime consecutus . . . magnam debeat hereditandi gerere Domino miserante fiduciam*'.[60] The lion's share, the *hereditas*, measured by the quantity and quality of royal lands and royally protected churches, and approved by the Franks and their oaths, was Francia: it was to go to the Young Charles. Theodulf, in a pair of strikingly political poetic interventions – '*Quod potestas impatiens consortis sit*' ('Power is impatient of a sharer') and '*Ad Carolum regem*' – rather clearly voices support for the Young Charles.[61]

In the *Divisio*'s twenty *capitula* were the details. First came the territorial partition:

[c. 1], the whole of Aquitaine and Gascony, parts of Burgundy, and Provence, Septimania and Gothia, we have assigned to our beloved son Louis; [c. 2], Italy, which is called Lombardy, and Bavaria as held by Tassilo [except for two estates in the Nordgau], Alemannia south of the

Danube, then from the Danube's source as far as the Rhine at Engen, then upriver towards the Alps, is to belong to our beloved son Pippin; [c. 3], whatever of our realm lies outside these boundaries, that is, Francia and Burgundy, except the part assigned to Louis, and Alemannia, except the part assigned to Pippin, Austrasia and Neustria, Thuringia, Saxony and Frisia, and the part of Bavaria called Nordgau, we have granted to our beloved son Charles. In this way, Charles and Louis will be able to have a route into Italy to bring help to their brother, should such necessity arise: Charles by the Aosta valley, which belongs to his kingdom, Louis through the valley of Susa, and Pippin may have exit and entry through the Norican Alps and Chur.

Then, allowing for the demise of one or another brother, Charles specified the fall-backs:

[c. 4] If Charles dies before his brothers, the realm is to be divided between Pippin and Louis as it once was [in 768] between ourselves and our brother Carloman, Pippin to have Carloman's share, Louis to have ours.

If Pippin predeceases Charles and Louis, then they are to divide Pippin's kingdom with the easterly parts going to Charles, the westerly to Louis.

If Louis predeceases his two brothers, Pippin is to have that part of Burgundy which we included in his kingdom, along with Provence, Septimania and Gothia as far as Spain, [while] Charles is to have Aquitaine and Gascony.[62]

The next two *capitula* can be summarized:

C. 5: If a son should be born to any of the three brothers, and the people (*populus* [meaning, the aristocracy]) should wish to choose him to succeed his father as heir to the kingdom, it is our will that the boy's uncles agree to this and let their brother's son rule that portion of the realm.

C. 6: To achieve our will of lasting peace between them, we have ordered that none of our sons should presume to invade the boundaries or frontier-regions (*terminos vel regni limites*) of his brother's kingdom, nor cause strife therein nor to threaten the frontier-regions (*marcas*), but rather to help his brother against his enemies within the country (*infra patriam*) or against external nations (*contra exterae nationes*).[63]

These *capitula* signal, in the one case, the political reality of aristo-cratic power, in the other, the contestable presence of boundaries and frontiers as danger-zones.[64]

The next three *capitula*, cc. 7–9, limit the mobility of men across regnal frontiers, whether to deter anyone seeking an alternative royal lord, or to deter a royal lord from receiving a man from a brother's kingdom, or in search of benefices from a different royal lord after the emperor's death; while c. 10 allows a free man to commend himself to another lord only after his royal lord has died.[65] Of the next three *capitula*, c. 11 limits transfers by gift or by sale of immovable property from one brother-king to another, but c. 12, by contrast, allows 'lawful requests for women in marriage from one kingdom to another, as cus-tomarily occurs (*sicut fieri solet*)', and insists on

> the lawfulness of women's being given and received reciprocally and for the peoples (*populi*) to be united with each other by marriage-relationships (*adfinitates*); and such women are to have power (*potestas*) over their prop-erty in the kingdom they have left although they must live in another kingdom because of the association with their husband (*propter societatem mariti*).

In c. 13,

> concerning hostages (*obsides*) given as sureties (*propter credentias*), and sent by us to various places, we will that the king in whose kingdom they [now] reside should not permit them to return to their homeland (*patria*) without the consent of the brother from whose kingdom they have been taken; instead, in future, help in receiving hostages should be mutually given if one brother asks this reasonably of his brother; and the same rules are to apply to those exiled for crimes.

In c. 14, again,

> concerning boundaries and border-zones, [Charles determined that] if hard cases or arguments or disputes arise between the divided parts of the realm such that they cannot be settled or resolved by the testimony of men, then . . . the will of God should be sought by the judgment of the cross* and not trial by battle or duel.[66]

---

* In a judgment by cross, the accuser and the accused stood on either side of a cross and stretched out their hands horizontally: the one who first lowered his arms was declared guilty.

The tone was still firmer in c. 15:

> But above all, we order and command that these three brothers accept together (*simul*) the care and defence of the church of St Peter, just as it was accepted by our grandfather Charles [Martel], our father of blessed memory Pippin, and since then, by us, so that they strive to defend it, with God's help, and cause it to have its rights and honour.

And in c. 16, Charles again added a fail-safe clause, that 'if these orders were to be infringed through accident or ignorance, we command that [the brothers] strive to amend matters as quickly as possible in accordance with justice, lest by delay the harm done might greatly increase.'[67]

The family preoccupied Charles in the last two substantive *capitula*. His daughters took precedence, in c. 17:

> With regard to our daughters, that is, the sisters of our aforesaid sons, we command that after our demise each shall have licence to choose the brother under whose protection and defence she wishes to place herself. And whoever among them wishes to choose the monastic [i.e. convent] life, she may be permitted to live in honour under the defence of the brother in whose kingdom she will have chosen to live. If, however, any among them should be sought in marriage, justly and reasonably, by a suitable man, and if married life should be pleasing to her, she is not to be denied to him by her brothers, provided that the will of both the man, in his request, and of the woman in her consent, should be honourable and reasonable.

Finally, in c. 18, Charles took thought for his grandsons:

> that is, the sons of our aforesaid sons, both those already born to them and those still to be born, it has pleased us to command that none of our sons should under any circumstances cause any of them accused before him to be put to death or be corporeally mutilated, or blinded, or tonsured against his will without lawful trial and inquiry. Rather, it is our will that they be honoured by their fathers and uncles and be obedient towards these with all the deference (*subiectio*) fitting in such a blood-relationship (*consanguinitas*).[68]

These two *capitula*, in different ways, go to the very heart of the family politics of the Aachen years. In c. 17, Charles, who had not permitted any of his daughters to marry, planned that after his demise, his legitimate daughters – Rotrud, Berta and Gisela (by Hildegard), and Hiltrud and Theodrada (by Fastrada) – would be in a position to opt for the convent life or to marry. Rotrud predeceased her father, while Berta is unlikely to have chosen either option, since her illegitimate twin sons by Angilbert (see below) were already born by c.800. The choices of Gisela, and of Hiltrud (who had already borne an illegitimate son by a Count Richwin before 811), are unknown; Theodrada became a nun after her father's death, if not before it.[69] As things turned out, it was left to Louis to deal with some of his sisters' choices in 814. It seems an exaggeration, though, to say (with Johannes Fried) that Charles in 806 'feared the worst' for his daughters when he ordered 'in great anxiety' that they be given options in the event of his demise.[70]

Fear and anxiety were à propos, by contrast, when it came to the 'positively hair-raising provisions' in c. 18 for the protection of royal nephews.[71] Recall c. 4, where it was stipulated that

> should Charles who is the eldest, predecease his brothers, the part he has been holding should be divided between Pippin and Louis, in such a way that Pippin should have that portion which our brother Carloman had [in 768], and Louis should take over that part which we ourselves took as our share.

The 768 partition was bound to evoke memories of 772, when Charles had reunited the realm by adding the dead Carloman's share to his own, and had left his nephews to a fate unrecorded (though I have likened it to that of the English Princes in the Tower in 1483).[72] Could c. 18, then, be recognized as 'a very belated flicker of a guilty conscience'? This was Walter Schlesinger's suggestion, put briefly and with a light touch, yet all too near the knuckle.[73] As expressed in c. 18, this was more a dreadful warning about uncles and nephews than about a grandfather and his grandsons.[74] Given ninth-century life-expectancies, men and women were lucky to live to see their grandchildren (Charles, again, was an exception who proved the rule).

VI. 'RE-READ YOUR CAPITULARIES', MARCH 806

Charles and his sons, counsellors and *fideles* did not stay long at Thionville. Pippin and Louis left for 'their allotted kingdoms'. Charles and his namesake travelled by boat downstream via the Mosel and the Rhine to the palace of Nijmegen, where they observed Lent and Easter. The *ArF* reports the emperor's return to Aachen with the Young Charles, whom he sent first on another successful campaign against the Sorbs (a Slav people), and then on further laying-waste of Bohemia as in 805. In the western Mediterranean, naval forces under orders from Pippin had variable success in 806 against Moors and Saracens.[75]

At Nijmegen in March, Charles had issued two further important capitularies. One reprised such familiar themes as the responsibilities of *missi* (cc. 1, 3), the meanings of oaths (c. 2), and the regime's responses to famine by, for instance, imposing price-controls (cc. 17, 18), bolstered by Scriptural and legal admonitions (cc. 11–16): Charles was keen to address problems in the area of the new Nijmegen palace itself, where the activities of counts and local *fortiores* (stronger men) were 'causing many evils to neighbours' (cc. 6–8).[76] The second, apparently conceived as an addendum in four *capitula*, urged counts to spurn hunting in favour of holding courts and assemblies to do justice, and to pay especially close attention to military duties *infra patriam vel foris patriam* ('within and outside the fatherland'), and gave more detailed instructions to *missi* about inspecting both benefices (including churches) and allods (inherited lands) 'held by our men or others' men to ensure their good management'.[77] It's absolutely clear that, in terms of capitulary production in Charles's reign, 802–3 saw something analogous to a great wave on a tidal-river;[78] but it's no less clear that the current continued to run strongly in the years from 806.

Part of that current, and closely connected both with Bishop Ghaerbald of Liège and local *missi*, was the injunction, '*Nunc autem admonemus vos, ut capitularia relegatis!*' 'Now we admonish you to re-read your capitularies!' This might have been the motto on regimental capbadges distributed by *missi* to counts. It was a group of *missi* who wrote a letter to a count (unnamed), and Ghaerbald who preserved that letter in a dossier of related documents compiled, among other reasons, as a record of the activities of *missi* in the region covered by the bishop's authority (Ghaerbald's authority is explicit in c. 1 of the letter below).[79] The original three *missi*, Rado, Fulrad and Unroc, were linked by bonds of locality (*in istis partibus*, here meaning Picardy and Vermandois) and kinship;[80] Rado had stood down because of ill-health, and the emperor himself had chosen two replacements: Adalhard, abbot of Corbie, and Hrocculf, both from the highest ranks of the aristocracy.[81]

> Our lord has commanded us to report to him truthfully in mid-April which of the things that through his *missi* in recent years he has ordered to be done have been done, and which left undone, in his realm, so that he may render appropriate thanks to those who have done them, and repay with such deserved chastisement as shall please him those who have not . . . And we admonish you now to re-read your capitularies, to recall the duties with which you have been charged orally . . . All the ensuing *capitula* should be taken as prefaced by the words 'we command and admonish . . .'

Capitula 1 and 2 are very general: they demand obedience from the counts and their subordinates, and fair judging in accordance with the law and justice. The next five *capitula* are specific:

> 3. Next, that you list the names, however great the number, of those who are rebellious or disobedient towards you and refuse to heed you in accordance with the law or justice, and either send the names to us beforehand, if that is necessary, or inform us of them personally when we meet, so that we may take such action regarding them as our lord has commanded.
>
> 4. Next, that you must most certainly see to it that if you are in doubt about anything in the whole set of commands . . . which our lord commanded of you in written form or orally, you must speedily send us a *missus* of yours with a good grasp of relevant matters so that you grasp everything properly and then, with the Lord's help, put it into effect.
>
> 5. Next, take the utmost care that you, so far as you can manage it, or anyone else in the county for which you are responsible (*in vestro ministerio*), don't allow yourself to be caught in such a bad plan as this, that you say, 'Keep quiet until those *missi* have moved on, and after that let us do justice between us for ourselves', and for that reason allow those cases to remain unjudged or dealt with only very belatedly; but instead, make every attempt to deal with these cases before we arrive – [6] because if any such bad plan is made between you, or cases that you could have dealt with yourselves are delayed, whether by negligence or by wickedness, until we arrive, be most certainly assured that we shall have very strong grounds for taking action against you.

7. Then, read this letter and re-read it many times and keep it safe, so that here will be evidence, both for us and for you, as to whether you have done what is written in it, or not done so.

Making all due allowance for exceptional circumstances – the proximity of Liège to Aachen, and the exceptional zeal of Bishop Ghaerbald – this letter, which is unique, documents the ordinary: a working relationship between a team of *missi* and a count (or counts). In showing officials warts and all, it offers three good reasons for inferring that Charles's government did in fact work. First, *missi* had ways of ensuring counts' accountability through a combination of checks and threats, carrots and sticks (especially evident in c. 2). Second, because *missi* and counts, under the watchful eye of the diocesan bishop, inhabited the same jurisdictional landscape, it was not difficult to make direct contacts, using the written and spoken word, with others involved in the system at local and regional levels. Third, looming over the region was the palace – the lord emperor, his close advisers and his officials, both senior and junior. It was the imperial communications system, and an emperor willing and able to monitor it personally, that enabled the practice of government effectively to function in a way that fostered trust at and between all levels.[82] 'Re-read your capitularies' said it all. Every injunction of *missi* to a count went to the heart of Charles's practice of empire. As for accountability, the answers to Davis's questions were – rightly – positive.

VII. THE ROYAL FAMILY, ITS BRANCHES, AND THE AACHEN COURT

Einhard's *Vita Karoli* is uniquely informative about Charles's family. In these imperial years, the family at Aachen was growing, not to say sprawling. In a conventional genealogy the eldest of Charles's sons, Pippin son of Himiltrud, appears top-left in the row. He had been in effect incarcerated at Prüm since 793, and nothing more is heard of him until the mention of his death, at Prüm, in 811. Next in the genealogy's row is the Young Charles, eldest of Charles's sons by Hildegard: his military exploits after 801 were punctuated by visits to Aachen, and that was where Theodulf located him in a poem written *c*.806.[83] Unsurprisingly in today's culture,

historians have raised the question of the Young Charles's sexual orientation, given the fact that he never married. It isn't at all clear that sexual
orientation was a major factor when medieval diplomatic marriages were
being discussed. If, when his father was planning a Neustrian *regnum* for
him in 790, the Young Charles himself had taken the initiative in negotiations to ally himself with a daughter of Offa of Mercia, he seems to have
rather quickly turned in the opposite – easterly – direction, where he foresaw political advantages in ensuing years.[84] As far as sexual orientation
goes, Theodulf's poems are all there is to go on. In his poem on the court
datable to 796, he mocked Osulf, along with 'Nard' (Einhard) and Ercam-
bald (the chief notary), for their small stature: 'If joined, their three feet
could belong to a single table.'[85] In a poem of 798, Theodulf ridiculed
three Greek eunuchs who were envoys at Aachen:

> The little Greek Potiphar, unpopular perhaps with the ladies
> Armed to no purpose and waging no war
> Accompanied by his associates Bagao and Egeus,
> Out of these three decrepits not one man is made.
> I think they are not voluntarily faithful in ladies' chambers,
> But the fierce hand of the physician forces them to keep faith.[86]

Osulf turns up again in the guise of the lovely shepherd of Vergil's
Second Eclogue ('O Corydon, Corydon . . . !'), in a poem dedicated to
the Young Charles and now thought to date from 806.[87] The recent find
of a longer version of this poem shows that the butt of Theodulf's humour
was Osulf, evidently a member of the Young Charles's entourage.[88] In a
pastiche of Vergil, Theodulf addressed Osulf in another guise:

> O Mochanaz, my pipe is coming to the end of this song;
> What are these whom my persistent love urgently scourges?
> O Mochanaz, Mochanaz, what are these fields that you are
>   so happy in?
> What are these fetters that bind you, tell me, I ask you,
>   O you who move so fast?[89]

'Mochanaz' was a transpyrenean term for a Saracen catamite. Later in the
poem, the Young Charles's father, grandfather and great-grandfather
were invoked to beat Mochanaz with sharp scourges. Since Mochanaz/
Corydon/Osulf was a former student of Alcuin, the teacher became the
object of Theodulf's attack for failing to guide his beloved boy. The

poem was certainly not attacking Young Charles, who was its addressee and an object of praise throughout.

> I ask that you load your slave with double fetters . . .
> With these chains your great-grandfather, grandfather
>   and father
> Binding the crowds, earned the throne of the realm.
> Then they scattered more haughty battalions,
> By battle they subdued more territory to their rule.
> But to you, great youth, go greetings and wishes forever
> That the Lord of heaven nurture, protect and adorn you,
> That you may follow in brilliance the paternal succession
> And, with God's help, hold in your hand the sceptre of rule.[90]

But the Young Charles died on 4 December 811, after his younger brother Pippin had died on 8 July 810 (and there were rumours that the death of Pippin son of Himiltrud in his monastery in 811 was no co-incidence, for it ruled out any belated challenge to Louis' now sole claims).[91] To return to the rest of the royal family: Charles's successive wives and queens have been discussed in earlier chapters, and there will be more to say about Pippin of Italy and Louis of Aquitaine as sub-kings. Charles's daughters Rotrud, Berta and Gisela, whose mother was Hildegard, and Hiltrud and Theodrada, daughters of Fastrada, had shared the limelight in Theodulf's court-poem of 796 with Ruod-haid, who was mentioned before Hiltrud and Theodrada.

> As their father sits down, let his excellent daughters offer him
> Charming kisses, as duty and dear affection demand.
> Berta gives roses, Rotrud gives violets, Gisela lilies.
> May each of them offer choice nectar and ambrosia.
> Ruodhaid brings apples, Hiltrud corn, Theodrada wine:
> Their appearances differ, but their beauty is one and the same.[92]

Of Ruodhaid's mother, Einhard said she was a concubine but added that he 'could not remember her name at the moment'.[93] Otherwise, Einhard listed separately the concubines Charles took after the death of the childless Liutgard in 800. They were Madelgard, who bore a daughter named Ruothild; Gerswinda, whose daughter was called Adaltrud; Regina, who produced two sons, Drogo and Hugh; and Adelind, whose son was named Theoderic.

Einhard did not tell the whole story. He did not mention four grand-sons born to three of Charles's daughters by Hildegard. The first and second, twins named Nithard and Hartnid, were, probably, produced in 800 by Berta from her relationship with Angilbert, a Frankish noble who had been brought up at Charles's court. Angilbert had been *primi-cerius* (chief administrator) of liturgical affairs at the court of the young Pippin of Italy, in the later 780s a student of Alcuin and a gifted poet, then in the 790s an important envoy and Italian expert. Now distinctly middle-aged, Angilbert withdrew from mainstream political life to St-Riquier to create a major religious centre there at Charles's command.[94] The third grandson was born to Rotrud by an unknown father, who could hardly have been other than high-born, and this son was named Louis.[95] The fourth, named Richbod, was born to Hiltrud, perhaps from her liaison with Count Richwin.[96] Both Louis and Richbod were put into monasteries – the best, naturally: St-Denis in Louis' case, St-Riquier in Richbod's – and became regular abbots (i.e. they followed the Rule of St Benedict).[97] There is no real evidence for the identity of young Louis' father. He is generally said to have been Count Rorigo, a Neus-trian aristocrat. It seems very unlikely that baby Louis, Rotrud's son, or indeed any other of Charles's twelve grandchildren (Pippin of Italy had a son, Bernard, born c.796, and five daughters; and Louis the Pious had two children by a concubine, a daughter Alpais and a son Arnulf, both born in the mid-790s) was named without their grandfather's say-so.[98] Why 'Louis'? Baby Louis had of course an uncle Louis, the future emperor Louis the Pious, born in 778 and king of Aquitaine since 781. In whichever year the grandparental name-choice was made, its mean-ing was surely a subject of speculation for Charles's contemporaries (as it still is for modern readers).[99] In 810, Charles was still at Aachen, plan-ning a campaign against the Danish king Godofrid, when Rotrud died on 6 June, perhaps at Chelles where she often stayed with her aunt Gisela, or perhaps at Aachen.[100] She was thirty-five.

> Charles reacted to her death with much less equanimity (*minus patienter tulit*) than might have been expected of someone who possessed such greatness of spirit, and because of his deep love for [his daughter and sons] which was no less remarked on, he was compelled to tears.[101]

A suggestion was offered some years ago that Rotrud might have died in giving birth to this child.

From these details emerges a picture of Charles himself remaining sexually active until he was over sixty (in all he fathered nineteen children, including five by concubines), and a court containing household living-quarters and aristocratic households in the environs of the palace itself.[102] For one exceptionally inspired and imaginative historian, it's proved possible to go further and visualize a court fizzing with sexual energy, where

> at least seven daughters born to Charlemagne [were] renowned for their vivacity and teasing games they played around the court . . . daughters so alluring, young and vivacious [that] . . . he was determined not to give them to any other foreign princes or even to any of his own magnates as wives, but rather always to keep them close at hand; but for precisely this reason, they were to bring him dreadful misfortune. Einhard alludes to these problems but does not go into detail . . . Charlemagne's court was thus at the same time devout and full of erotic intrigue . . . A court, perhaps, in the emperor's innermost image?[103]

Einhard and Alcuin between them evoke the masculine sociability of the Aachen baths, when 'over a hundred men might be in the water together', and when serious all-male conversations – about interpretations of Scripture, for instance – could be engaged in. Johannes Fried's picture sticks in the mind. Rightly, he wants to probe the limits of the thinkable. Where in this scene were women? 'Could women not bathe? Or was there a dedicated ladies' bathing day? Or a separate pool for them?' These are not frivolous questions. As in ancient Rome, or Byzantium, or the Islamic world, men and women bathed (if they bathed at all) separately.[104] From those quintessentially courtly genres, letters and poetry, it's not always wise to infer too much.

During the Aachen years, after 800 when there was no queen, some of the women at the court exercised what could be called influence if not power. The emperor issued an order to the effect that *missi* and counts 'were not to dare to compel the *homines* of our sons and our daughters' – implying that such *homines* were especially privileged and that *missi* and counts accounting for themselves to the emperor directly in such cases (as in many others) caused bottlenecks at Aachen.[105] On the other hand, the emperor's daughters were in a position to lessen the tensions that might otherwise have existed at court between father and sons.[106] They sometimes inhabited social spaces shared by men and women – notably, churches, including the Aachen church, but they sat separately.[107] To my mind, Fried exaggerates a bit in claiming that 'the court was characterized by strangely erotic and homoerotic goings-on'.[108] What Einhard may have suspected, or insinuated, went on at court may not have been imitated elsewhere.[109]

When it came to his children's education, Charles's priorities were what would nowadays be called gender-blind: 'he believed that both sons and daughters must first be instructed in the liberal arts which he himself had studied.' These were grammar, dialectic and rhetoric (the *trivium*), and arithmetic, geometry, astronomy and music (the *quadrivium*).[110] The gender-specificity of certain activities at court, by contrast, replicated Frankish practice generally:

> when his sons had reached the right age, he made them learn to ride, hunt and handle weapons according to Frankish custom (*more Francorum*). As for the girls, he ordered them to learn to work wool with distaff and spindle so that they didn't become idle and lazy, but devoted themselves to this work and to be trained in every virtuous activity.[111]

At the Aachen court, a second branch of the royal family was represented: these were Charles's cousins, the offspring of his father's half-brother, Bernard. Adalhard and his half-brother Wala had careers during Charles's lifetime that included stints at his court.

Adalhard also served at the court of Pippin of Italy at Pavia (with Verona and several other cities as outliers) as his chief adviser during the 780s, and intermittently thereafter, 'to mould with justice and discretion the realm and its king, the younger Pippin, into the status of a commonwealth devoted to the cultivation of religion'.[112] Wala had ties to the imperial court in the Aachen years, when he was 'celebrated in the senate and in military service strongest in discretion'.[113] His younger brother Bernhar was a monk at Corbie, where his fraternal bonds supplied good contacts with Aachen. Of the two sisters of this family-branch,

> Gundrada [the older] clung fast in constant attendance on her brothers, and although the virgin was friendly to the king (*virgo familiarior regi*), and although she dwelled amid wanton heats of the palace and charms of the youths, even amid caresses of delights and blandishments of passion, she alone was worthy to bring back the palm of modesty.

Alcuin had already in c.801 urged her to be 'an example of all goodness to the other virgins in the palace' and to be 'prudent in counsel, patient if abused'.[114] Apparently palace life had space for a small cohort of chaste women, whose spiritual leader was Gundrada.

At Charles's court, the formalities of charter-issue sometimes included the name – in Tironian notes, or Carolingian bureaucratic shorthand – of the powerful personage whose influence had secured the issue of the charter. In the very last extant charter of Charles's to be issued (on 9 May 813), because it survives as an original and not in a cartulary copy, the name of its requester, written in Tironian notes, is readable. According to the editor, Mühlbacher, it is 'Gundradus'. Given the difficulties of deciphering Tironian notes, it's possible that the last syllable is a feminine. If that is the right reading, and no other 'Gundradus' is mentioned in any of Charles's charters, then the influential requester was not an *ambasciator* (a male requester) but an *ambasciatrix* (a female one) – Gundrada.[115] Its beneficiary was the faithful man Asig (*Asig fidelis*), once an exile, now restored to imperial favour and power in the land. Asig's heir gave the property to Corbie. If she did act in this capacity, then Gundrada herself was a power in the land.[116] Her sister, Theodrada, 'had married but later soon embraced the second degree of chastity [i.e. chaste widowhood]'.[117] Paschasius celebrated the siblings' sweet quintet, 'the harmony sounding in concert together'.[118] The members of the second branch of the family seem to have coexisted comfortably enough with the first, to each others' mutual benefit; and only in the very last months of Charles's life did signs of conflict appear. A quite different account of the two branches' relations has been put forward, on the hypothesis that Theodrada married Pippin of Italy; but this discounts the view that such a marriage would have been incestuous by any contemporary standards, and so I am inclined to reject it.[119]

Stuart Airlie's assessment, based on vast knowledge of what could be called the mature Carolingian court (in fact a generic model that could fit anytime and anywhere between c.800 and the mid-tenth century), was this: 'On a political level, the distance between the court and the regions could be abolished. The court was the kingdom.'[120] The years between c.805 and c.813 showed Charles's court operating in some ways that were new: at once pulling power centripetally into its orbit, and radiating power out from itself, primarily by the issuing of capitularies and the deployment of *missi*.[121] Members of the royal family in the maximal sense, that is, including Charles's cousins, were beneficiaries and exercisers of the court's centripetal pull.

The evidence that historians rely on for these years is different from that of the 790s and the years immediately around 800. After 19 May 804, when Alcuin died, there are no more of his letters or poems to show the passing scene. The flow of poetry to and from the court had slowed since the 790s. Angilbert had apparently moved the active centre of his life to St-Riquier, where he faithfully carried out the building plans and cultic activities demanded, and supported, by the emperor.[122] Still, Theodulf, though now shouldering episcopal tasks, continued to write powerful verse;[123] and a young poet, Moduin (nicknamed 'Naso' after the classical Ovid), sounded a strongly optimistic note of 'Golden Rome's renewal' at the Aachen court. Ancient poetic genres were revived and cultivated at Pippin's court in Italy, too.[124] The interests of new audiences at the Aachen court were catered for by writers on rhetoric, theology, astronomy and philosophy, and also by the annal-writers who provided much detail on contacts with foreign courts and foreign parts, complete with borrowings from classical histories and epic poetry. Both Theodulf and Moduin referenced the Roman poet Lucan.[125] These scholar-courtiers took intellectual pursuits extremely seriously: indeed a striking feature of the inheritance of Rome was the range of books studied and disciplines cultivated.[126] A comparison of the Byzantine and Muslim worlds with Charles's project shows how distinctive that project was: driven by a 'community of the realm' that consisted of not just educated elites but 'little patriarchs' of and in households within hearing distance of 'the voice of Charlemagne', 'moralized politics' were theirs for the practising. Despite the famine of 805–6, despite military setbacks, despite the deaths of key Carolingian family-members cut off in their prime, 'optimism and confidence' were to be found in the imperial court of the Aachen years. Aachen itself – its church and its palace, its rites and rituals and its distinctive sociability, its aristocrats and their townhouses (as evoked by Notker) – did much to develop those sentiments.

The court was a textual community. It was also an oral one – and, up to a point, an emotional one.[127] It's as well to consider a plurality of communities within the plural spaces of the court. Fried's comments just noted on Charles and his men in the baths at Aachen are à propos. Fridugis (nicknamed 'Nathaniel' by his teacher Alcuin) sent an open letter to '*omnes fideles et domni serenissimi principis Karoli in sacro palatio consistentes*' ('all the faithful staying in the sacred palace of the most serene prince Charles'). It was about the substance of nothingness. These *fideles* sound like laymen (if not necessarily the great men (*proceres*) assumed by the nineteenth-century editor):

> the question of nothing had been agitated for a very long time (*diutissime*) by very many people and they had left it incompletely examined and impossible to have [it] explained . . . I have cleaned away what was clouded and brought it back into the light..

The letter's short title in the manuscript is: 'The Emperor Charles's question . . .' Fridugis's answer, presented in the form of a syllogism – 'every *nomen finitum* [finite name] signifies something, *nihil* [nothing] is such a *nomen*, therefore "nothing" must really exist' – did not find favour with a modern philosopher: 'it gives a distinctly unfavourable impression of the mental powers of its author'. But the modern philosopher added, 'negative concepts continued to perplex men at the palace even after they had digested Fridugis's opinions'.[128]

What was happening at Aachen was the recovering of Aristotelian dialectic and its application to theology.[129] The interrogatory emperor, and Alcuin and Fridugis between them, had set the ball rolling on universal questions, and they were promoting *examinatio* and *discutio* among an interested lay group. Nothing quite like this had happened for centuries, and it would not really recur outside episcopal schools before the high Middle Ages. A second letter, dated to 811 and also written in response to the emperor's questioning on a difficult topic, was that of the Irish scholar Dungal on the subject of eclipses.[130] Dungal knew that two had occurred the previous year, 810, and it was being suggested that they foretold the deaths of Rotrud and Pippin of Italy. Dungal denied any such link. He used late antique *scientia* (learning), which he knew forearmed human beings with *praescientia*, to explain the astronomical conjunctures accounting for the phenomena seen in the heavens. Dungal's audience would have consisted of the emperor not just as patron but as an intellectual, and, beyond that, of not just Charles but an audience listening to a public reading of a late antique text that would be understood by themselves, *palatini* or *aulici*:[131] 'a court that not only wished to see itself as learned but *was* so'.[132]

It's possible to identify another text-community within the larger community of the court, and alongside an elite or learned community. This was a group of lay people, men and women, who had a rather garbled knowledge of certain texts and some learning experiences of their own. The existence of this group is to be inferred from a single manuscript, now in Paris, and dated to the beginning of the ninth century.[133] The manuscript contains some Merovingian legal texts; two brief sets of questions-and-answers (or, dialogues) on the Trinity and on Philosophy; a set of early ninth-century capitularies; *leges* (laws); and miscellaneous additions in a later hand ending with form-letter no. 7 from the Formulary of Bourges. Sandwiched between the early laws and the capitularies are the two question-and-answer sets, which have recently been edited, translated and commented on by David Ganz.[134] Here is the second of them:

Q: What is the beginning of virtue? A: Not to do evil. Q: What is the advance of virtue? A: To do good. Q: What is the fullness of virtue? A: To persist in good. Q: What is the etymology of virtue? A: The just order of love (*amor*).

Q: What is the justice of love? A: That you love (*diligas*) God for Himself above all things, yourself because of Him, your neighbour as yourself, all things that are because they are made for this is loved (*diligatur*) for the praise of the Lord. This is the justice of love. Q: So will bodily beauty be something to be loved (*diligenda*)? A: Yes, it deserves to be loved (*diligi*) by you so that you can praise it together with God whose creature you are.

Q: So, I act out of love of the body? A: That is a perverse kind of love because you love badly what is good when from it you would rather hate yourself when you love that from which you perish. Q: Can someone born live for ever? A: Who can be born from what is immortal? Q: Can anyone *not* sin? A: One who can be born without sin. Q: What is sin? A: Contempt for a divine command. Q: What is the nature of contempt? A: Pride! For anyone who is proud despises his Lord's command and whatever else he does, he sins ... Q: So, why do I love quarrelling? A: Because you don't know reason. All quarrelling derives from discord. Reason pays learning (*scientia*) its due, and preserves peace. Q: So, I love a woman? A: Therefore you love death. For as someone says, 'One who loves his wife rather eagerly is an adulterer ... All love, whether great or small, of another man's wife is shameful [but so is excessive love for one's own wife].'[135]

Q: So, a woman means death? A: Not because she is death, but because she is the cause of death for through her we enter into death. Remember this true opinion, 'By a woman was made the beginning of sin and through her we all die.'[136] Q: So, a woman should be hated? A: Because of sin, not because of nature. Therefore I hate the flaw yet love the creature, for she too is a human being (*ipsa homo est*) and God's handiwork is good . . .

The text is unusual, certainly. Its editor leaves open the question of audience: it could have been thought apt for the schoolroom, or usable in the instruction (Donald Bullough thought) of 'older *pueri* (boys) or the less talented *younger adolescentes* (youths)'.[137] The editor worries about the text's Latinity and finds the section on the virtues 'very elementary'. He adds that 'the quality of the spelling must raise the question of how far this text could have been understood by anyone'.

The discussion of women, their beauty, their sin, their nature and their status as divinely made human beings touched on interestingly sensitive points. It may not be too far-fetched to imagine a lay gathering in some informal social space within the palace where people with different languages and levels of linguistic skill could get the gist of conversations, in which women and girls as well as men and boys participated. Maybe Charles himself – interested in the liberal arts and in their availability to the young of both sexes, keen on the dialogue form, and willing to entertain new ideas – sometimes dropped in on these discussions, and was heard to mutter '*bene!*'

A final word on Charles's sex-life and the atmosphere of the court. On these topics, distinguished historians have expressed rather shocked views:

Charlemagne's own conduct diametrically contradicted Christian doctrine on marriage. His practice of keeping several women at the same time and his arbitrary repudiations of at least two of them stood in direct violation of church teaching . . . Like the Merovingian kings, Charlemagne lived a polygamous life in which relationships were not strictly defined in legal terms.[138]

My own view is that Charles's conduct was probably similar to that of other elite males, and that polygamy is not, in this context, the appropriate term.[139]

VIII. THE *FILIOQUE* DISPUTE AND THE *BREVE COMMEMORATORIUM*

Christian theologians had agreed in the fourth century on a statement of belief (a Creed, from *credo*, 'I believe') which said that the Holy Spirit proceeded from the Father. It nevertheless became the practice in many parts of the Church, especially in the West, to say in the Creed that the Holy Spirit 'proceeded from the Father and the Son (*filioque*)'. There were arguments, but they did not seriously disrupt Church unity until there came a context, and a man. The context was the Holy Land in the eighth century and early ninth: an exceptionally severe earthquake brought down the 'New' Church in Jerusalem in 749, the establishment of the Abbasid caliphate in the Near East in 750 brought orders (not least from Harun al-Rashid) that newly built churches be destroyed, and Christian monasticism in Palestine generally suffered more from the arbitrary exactions of local authorities than it did from excessive demands for tribute from *dhimmis* (non-Muslims living in the caliphate).[140] The man was a Greek monk named John, formerly of the monastery of St Sabas; along with Frankish monks from the Mount of Olives, he was in the Church of the Nativity at Bethlehem to celebrate Christmas in 807 when he became aware that the Franks, when chanting the Creed, had uttered the word *filioque*. He there and then accused them of heresy and tried, unsuccessfully, to expel them from the church. The Frankish monks told John what to do: '*Sile, frater! Quodsi nos dicis haereticos, de sede sancta apostolica dicis heresim!*' ('Shut up, brother! If you call us heretics, you're saying what the holy apostolic see says is heresy!')

On 2 January 808 in the Church of the Holy Sepulchre, the Frankish monks and the archdeacon of the Jerusalem Church tried to establish what had happened at Christmas, and 'declared their conformity with the beliefs of the patriarchate and the Holy See'. The Frankish monks sent a letter to Pope Leo in Rome to tell him all this, and Leo received this letter in spring or summer 808.[141] He then wrote a brief report to Charles at Aachen with a 'please see attached', which was the letter of the Frankish monks. To publicize the situation in Rome, presumably later in 808, Leo had two large silver shields put up in St Peter's, inscribed with the Creed in Latin and in Greek, and a third disk with the same Creed, in Latin, at St Paul's-without-the-Walls: the text of the Creed did not include the word *filioque*.[142] Leo in the brief report to Charles had also mentioned that two men had returned from Jerusalem to Rome bringing him a letter from Patriarch Thomas. Their names, he told Charles, were those of '*fideles servientes vestri, Agamus et Roculfus*'. McCormick comments that these two were 'very possibly' the men responsible for 'traipsing about the Holy Land', tasked with the compilation of a *breve commemoratorium* (short memorandum) in 808.[143] To my mind, McCormick's case for these two being Charles's envoys is absolutely convincing: Agamus may be unknown but Roculf is familiar to anyone interested in how Charles got and kept his aristocracy on board.[144] McCormick's case is still more convincing in that it conveys vividly the 'operational style' of Charles's government in the imperial years.[145] The *missi* needed information above all, and they worked with questionnaires developed in the late 790s when the measuring of the parts and wholes of estates and *regna* were becoming standard practice.[146]

The increasing number of contacts in the late 790s and, especially, the early ninth century between the Aachen court and both Constantinople and Baghdad, generated knowledge of, and interest in, Christian communities in the Holy Land. In these years too, Einhard, in Charles's entourage, was in a position to share Charles's concerns. In 803, Charles was in Bavaria, with envoys from Jerusalem along with him.[147] In 807, an envoy from the king of the Persians came to Aachen 'with two monks, George and Felix, envoys of the Patriarch Thomas of Jerusalem – George is abbot of the Mount of Olives, he is from *Germania* by origin and his actual name is Egilbald.'[148]

'Charles kept the Persian envoy and the monks with him for some time, then sent them to Italy telling them to wait till it was time to sail.'[149] Information from the patriarch and from George and Felix was what immediately lay behind Charles's decision to send his *missi* to the Holy Land in 808. Their findings about the state of the Frankish religious houses there were presented in a form and 'operational style' similar to that of comparable investigations in Charles's realm (Archbishop Leidrad's survey of religious communities in the Lyonnais survives).[150] McCormick's edition, with translation and commentary, has made this extraordinary material widely available for the first time.[151] Einhard put Charles's efforts nicely in context:

[Charles] was very enthusiastic in supporting the poor (*pauperes*), and in that spontaneous generosity (*gratuita liberalitas*) which the Greeks call alms (*eleimosina*), so much so that he made a point of not only giving in his own country (*patria*) and his own kingdom (*regnum*), but overseas as well, when he discovered that there were Christians living in poverty (*in paupertate*) in Syria, Egypt and Africa [meaning the Maghreb]; and at Jerusalem, Alexandria and Carthage he shared the sufferings of their penury (*penuriae illorum compatiens*) and made a habit of sending them money (*pecunia*). The reason he zealously strove to make friendships (*amicitiae*) with kings beyond the seas was that he might get some help and relief to the Christians living under their rule.[152]

A brief extract from the *Breve* shows that the *missi* knew their business:

On the holy Mount of Olives, 3 churches: one, the Ascension of the Lord, priests and clerics 3; a second, where Christ taught his disciples, where there are 3 monks, 1 priest; a third, in honour of St Mary, 2 clerics, hermits who reside scattered in their cells, 11 who sing the psalms in Greek; Georgians, 4; Syrians, 6; Armenians, 2; Latins 5, one who sings the psalms in Arabic. Along the steps, when you go up to the holy mount: 2 hermits, one Greek, the other Syrian. At the top of the steps in Gethsemane, 3 hermits, a Greek, a Syrian and a Georgian; in the valley of Jehosaphat, 1 hermit.

A monastery of 26 women, of whom 17 nuns who serve at the Holy Sepulchre are from the empire of the Lord Charles (*de imperio domini Karoli*); 1 recluse from Spain; in the monastery of St Peter and St Paul at Besanteo [this is the Frankish monastery on the Mount of Olives]: 35 monks; at St Lazarus in Bethany, 1 priest; at St John which the Armenians hold, 6 monks.[153]

To Einhard's comments on Charles's motivations, it's worth adding another point; namely, the particular importance to Charles of the prayers for him and his empire offered up to the Almighty by the Frankish monks and nuns on the Mount of Olives.[154] That seventeen nuns served at the Holy Sepulchre is especially interesting, for they would have found their inspiration in the fourth-century examples of Roman ladies who went on pilgrimage to visit St Jerome in the Holy Land (some of them then stayed, as apparently Egilbald stayed to become a professed monk by the name of George). Two of the women nearest and dearest to Charles were his sister Gisela and his daughter Rotrud, who resided at the convent of Chelles near Paris: they were certainly inspired by the fourth-century women-pilgrims, for when in 800 they gently grumbled to Alcuin (he was then living at Tours) about his delay in sending them his commentary on the Gospel of St John, they reminded him that Jerome had *quickly* sent the Roman ladies Paula and Eustochium the books they wanted, 'all the way from Bethlehem to Rome – and the Mediterranean is a lot wider than the Loire.'[155] These women had their own operational style.

Having perused the *Breve commematorium*, and discussed the evidence with Agamus and Roculf, Charles was as good as his word – despite an inevitable delay: an agenda item at a Council at Aachen in 810 was, '*De elemosina mittenda ad Hierusalem propter aecclesias Dei restaurandas*' ('About the alms that have to be sent to Jerusalem for restoring God's churches').[156] 'Alms' in this context meant money (as Einhard also knew), and the *Breve* itself provided the detailed data on building repairs to enable the costings to be made, and the money sent.[157] The death of Harun al-Rashid in 809 caused another bout of violent conflict in the Holy Land. New financial burdens were heaped on the churches in Jerusalem, and these events perhaps lay behind the timing of the Aachen capitulary of 810. Knowledge of Charles's efforts was part of what lay behind demands made, from time to time, throughout the ninth century by Carolingian and West Saxon rulers for financial aid for the Holy Land.[158]

Charles himself summoned up more efforts once the *filioque* dispute of 807–8 (the successor of many earlier arguments, as noted) had brought events in Jerusalem to his notice. He acted vigorously and fast: no sign here of slowing-down. A council was summoned to Aachen in November 809 (after the autumn hunting). The author of the *ArF* noted that the issue had been raised by 'a certain monk in Jerusalem called John'.[159] To reach a decision, Charles first commissioned five expert opinions from Arn of Salzburg, Theodulf of Orléans, Heito of Basel, Amalwin of Regensburg and Abbot Smaragdus of St Mihiel's.[160] These were taken to Rome by two special *missi*, Bishop Bernhar of Worms and Abbot Adalhard for discussion with the pope. The Frankish experts were determined to keep the *filioque*; Pope Leo was content that it remain in practice in

Francia, but did not want to change the Creed of the Romans and Greeks (and there were many Greeks in Rome). The Franks were chided for not having got authorization for the *filioque*, but nothing was done to prevent their continuing the tradition they knew. The Frankish experts had had the opportunity to give an impressive demonstration of their theological expertise. Charles's handling of these proceedings showed an expertise all his own – in treating his experts with respect, and also treating the pope with deference and at arm's length. Leo was well aware that the Creed chanted in the Aachen church included the *filioque*. By now, pope and emperor understood each other.

IX. THE LOSSES OF 810

The year seemed to begin promisingly. Envoys from the Muslim potentate Amrus, who now controlled Zaragoza and Huesca, had arrived at Aachen late in 809 with promises to put that region under Charles's dominion. Charles was keen to follow this up, but events in the western Mediterranean prevented any further pursuit of the plan. Moors with a very large fleet subjugated the island of Corsica. In the Adriatic, King Pippin had better news to send to Aachen:

> driven by the perfidy of the doges of Venetia, he gave orders for an attack on the Veneto by land and sea (*terraque marique*). Once Venetia had been subdued and the surrender of its doges received (*subiectaque Venetia ac ducibus eius in deditionem acceptis*), he sent a fleet to ravage the coast of Dalmatia, but Paul, the governor of the Ionian Islands, arrived with an eastern [i.e. Greek] fleet to aid the Dalmatians, and the royal fleet returned home.

The peace-overtures between Greeks and Franks broached early in 809 were therefore stymied.[161] The concern of Charles, and Pippin too, with naval warfare had begun to predominate in the *ArF* record during these years. So far, 'on both land and sea' Pippin had acquitted himself well.

Charles's sister Gisela died at Chelles *c*.810, perhaps around the same time as her niece Rotrud, who died on 6 June 810 aged thirty-five.[162] Rotrud may have died at Chelles where she often stayed with her aunt, or at Aachen. Just over a month after Rotrud's death, Charles got news of the death, on 8 July, of Pippin of Italy. Einhard took it as showing what special proof Charles gave of his love for them all when, after their father's death, he decreed that his grandson [Bernard, now aged thirteen] should succeed his father and that his granddaughters [all five] should be brought up among his, Charles's, own daughters.[163]

Einhard, economizing on words, went straight on to describe Charles's reactions to the deaths of both Rotrud and Pippin and also of the Young Charles the next year in a single sentence covering all three. The economizing somehow heightens the impact of the tears.

Another death shocked the emperor in 810. It occurred when Charles had summoned an exceptionally large army, and had crossed the Rhine at the place called Lippeham to await the troops who had not yet arrived. 'While he stayed there for a time, the elephant sent to him by Aaron [Harun], king of the Saracens, suddenly died.'[164] Only a few lines later, after reporting 'the arrangement of matters in Saxony', did the annal-writer add:

> On this campaign, there was such a pestilence of cattle (*pestilentia boum*) that it was almost the case that not a single beast was left alive for such a large army but all died, to the last head. And it was not only there [in Saxony] but throughout all the provinces subject to the emperor that death raged most savagely amongst this type of animal.

Charles and his veterans recalled the terrible horse-plague that had raged in Sabaria in 791 and caused the emperor to revise some of his plans for action in the mid-to-late 790s.[165] What they now had to experience was an even more distressing pestilence – of cattle, and people. A little set of annals written at Fulda early in the ninth century (and seldom cited) has the following sequence of events for 810:

> *Mortalitas bovum maxima pene in tota Europa, nec non et hominum plurimorum, et Hruthruda filia imperatoris et Pippinus filius eius. Imperator venit in Saxoniam. Eclipses solis 2. Kal. Decemb.*
>
> (An extremely huge mortality of cattle in almost the whole of Europe, and also of very many human beings, and Rotrud the emperor's daughter and Pippin his son. The emperor came to Saxony. An eclipse of the sun on 2 kal. Dec.)[166]

The layout of this entry could indicate that Rotrud and Pippin were among the human victims of the pestilence, and perhaps Gisela too died then. It's been suggested that the elephant may have perished in this same outbreak.[167] Very recent research has shown that in the early Middle Ages, and specifically likely in 809/810, was a disease that 'jumped species', from measles in people to rinderpest in cattle.[168] No pestilence of this type, so far as is yet known, struck the Carolingian realm between its inception in 751 and 808. The elephant – Abul Abaz – 'died of a sudden death' (*subita morte periit*) in the summer of 810. He was not one of a herd, but a single specimen of his kind (and for Charles's enemies a terrifying one) and a singular victim. If only Einhard had recorded Charles's feelings as the elephant died in the camp on the Rhine.

As in 791, so in 810 did Charles continue the round of imperial duties: the reception of foreign envoys, the making of treaties with Greeks and Spaniards and of peace with the new Danish king, Hemming, nephew of the deceased Godofrid. In this year, wrote the *ArF* author, in the empirical deadpan tones commended by Dungal, the sun and the moon were both eclipsed twice, the sun on 7 June and 30 November, the moon on 21 June and 15 December. Charles lost two, and probably three, of his closest relatives in this one year. In response, the default mode at court, whatever might betide, was of calm and collectedness.

A small section of the cut-marble inlays (*opus sectile*)
in Charles's church at Aachen.

16

'Charles, by the bounty of divine grace emperor and augustus . . . to his beloved and honourable brother Michael glorious emperor and augustus'

I. DIPLOMACY AND WARFARE

In the years after 801, diplomatic relations loomed larger than ever before in the *ArF*, for reasons that had as much to do with status and honour as with maintaining the historical record. In and after 806, each annal tends to get longer. The authorial eyes scanned the geographical range extending from the northern frontier-zones to the Mediterranean and from Iberia to the Near East, with Franks and Greeks encountering each other in the Adriatic and on the Dalmatian coast. Encounters were, as had been those with the Empress Eirene, 'for the cause of peace' or putting an end to hostilities.[1] In chapter 4 of the *Vita Karoli*, Einhard promised to write about '[Charles's] deeds inside and outside [the kingdom]', following the model of each life in Suetonius's *Lives of the Caesars*.[2] In chapter 16, Einhard concentrated on diplomacy, 'the gaining of glory through the offerings of friendships by other rulers and peoples' by means of letters, embassies and gifts. Charles had begun the exchange of envoys with the caliph Harun back in 797, sending envoys with gifts to the Holy Sepulchre and to the place of the Lord's resurrection in Jerusalem. Harun had responded by granting Charles 'that sacred and salvation-bringing place, so that it would be formally assigned to his [Charles's] control (*potestas*)'. Harun also sent back lavish presents from the East. Here, naturally, the elephant loomed large.[3] Even more wonderful gifts arrived in 807:

> various tents, some of astonishing size and beauty, a brass clock constructed with marvellous mechanical skill, in which the passage of the twelve hours depended upon a water clock with twelve little copper

balls . . . and twelve horsemen, one of which would emerge from one of twelve windows . . .; also two brass candelabra of extraordinary size and height: all these things were handed over to the emperor in the palace at Aachen.[4]

The Franks' relations with the Greeks remained difficult, unsurprisingly, given the long history of snubs and misunderstandings. The competition for authority in southern Italy which had marked the late 780s and early 790s continued. In the years after 800,

> after [Charles] had taken up the name of emperor, they [the Greeks] suspected that they [the Franks] might want to seize their empire . . . For the power (*potentia*) of the Franks was always suspect to the Romans and the Greeks. Hence there's a Greek proverb: 'ΤΟΝ ΦΡΑΝΚΟΝ ΦΙΛΟΝ ΕΧΙϹ, ΓΙΤΟΝΑ ΟΥΚ ΕΧΙϹ.' '[If] you have a Frank as a friend, you won't have him as a neighbour.'[5]

In 804, 807 and again in 809–10, Greeks and Franks vied for control of Istria and Venetia (Venice and the Veneto).[6] On the whole, and as long as Pippin of Italy was alive, the Franks kept their end up in the Adriatic. In October 810, Charles made a peace-treaty with the Byzantine emperor Nikephoros (802–11) conditional on yielding Frankish claims to Venetia.[7] The deal was confirmed at Constantinople by Charles's envoys, Bishop Heito of Basel and Count Hugh of Tours, who in the emperor's name 'established such a firm treaty with the Franks that no source of any trouble might remain between them'.[8]

When Nikephoros was killed in a disastrous battle against the Bulgars in 811, his son-in-law Michael succeeded him, and it was he who gave the two Frankish envoys leave to depart, sending with them to Aachen three envoys of his own, Bishop Michael and two high military officials.

> They confirmed the peace Nikephoros had initiated, received Charles's written agreement to it (*scriptum pacti*) in the Aachen church and acclaimed him with *laudes* as is their custom, in Greek, that is, calling him emperor and *basileus*. When they came to Rome on their journey home, they received another copy of the same agreement for the second time from Pope Leo in the church of St Peter.[9]

The sound of Greek *laudes* in the Aachen church was surely music to Charles's ears. This agreement was sealed on the Franks' side by the issue of a new imperial portrait coinage.[10] Given the very small numbers of finds of coins of this issue, it looks as if the whole exercise was symbolic and propagandistic rather than economic. Exchanges of letters, like the one whose opening salutation provides the title of the present chapter, attested the fraternal relationship between the emperor Charles and the emperor Michael.[11]

Warfare too featured strongly in the *ArF*'s record of the years 806–13, often as a counterpoint to peace-making. The *ArF*'s report of the assembly for 'the establishing of peace' and 'the maintenance of peace' in the *Divisio regnorum* was followed by details of the Young Charles's campaigns against Sorbs, Slavs and Bohemians, and of Pippin's sending of a fleet to Corsica 'against Moors who were ravaging the island'.[12] There are many more references than before to naval matters (the word 'fleet' recurs at least nine times in various contexts).[13] Pippin of Italy's campaigns in Venetia and the northern Adriatic were waged 'by land and by sea'.[14] In 807, the emperor 'sent Burchard, count of the stables, with a fleet to Corsica to defend it from Moors who had been plundering there in recent years'. Though a Frank was nominally in charge, it looks as if Burchard was operating out of Genoa.[15] Those Moors had had a bad season of it, and, according to the *ArF* writer, they began to fear divine retribution 'for having abducted 60 monks from the island of Pantellaria and sold them in Spain'. Charles personally bought back some of the monks, who were able to return to their monasteries.[16] The Greek governor of the Ionian islands, stationed in Venetia with a fleet from Constantinople, made a peace with King Pippin and a truce to last until August 808.[17]

In that year, 808, the focus of the *ArF* shifted from the Mediterranean to northern lands. Four years before, King Godofrid of the Danes had promised to meet Charles, but had reneged on his promise. Charles was not one to be fooled twice: now having news that Godofrid and his army had entered Abodrite territory, Charles sent his son and namesake to the Elbe to forbid any assault on Saxony. Though Godofrid's men had taken severe losses, 'heavy tributes had been imposed on two thirds of the Abodrites'. The Young Charles threw a bridge across the Elbe and attacked the Slavs (Linones, Smeldingi) to the east who had defected to Godofrid, ravaging their lands, and returning with his troops unscathed.[18] Later that year, the emperor sent his commanders to build two forts on the Elbe and to garrison them against the Slavs.

A little dossier of ten of Pope Leo III's letters, all written to Charles, kept in the archive at the emperor's behest (rather as the *Codex Carolinus* letters were selected and compiled, kept and copied on Charles's orders), survive in a unique manuscript datable to the second quarter of the ninth century.[19] The letters throw interesting sidelights on diplomacy, warfare and local government – and the fuzzy lines between these – in Italy and in the northern world. In Letter 2, sent sometime after April 808, Leo reported that he was in need of consolation and that, after God and his saints, he had 'no-one to console him but Charles'. He then complained about Charles's *missi*:

> If Count Helmengaud, your and our *fidelis*, and all your other *missi* too who have come into these regions, had told you about everything we suffer every day, we think it would all be loathsome to your ears. We don't know if it was by your orders that your *missi*, who came to do justice, brought with them many men and established them in various cities. For everything that the duke set in position by us was accustomed to do in the way of taking fines for various cases and which he [the duke] paid over to us every year in the customary way, these men of your *missi* have now been taking into their own hands as proxies. And they have taken many taxes from that same people. And because of that, the dukes are quite unable to pay over the contributions they owe *us*. It seems to us very serious if we are telling you things that are loathsome to you.

Leo now turned to the subject of the exiled King Eardwulf of Northumbria, and his restoration, thanks to the co-ordinated efforts of himself and Charles.

> We are, however, very grateful for all the good things which you have performed for love of St Peter concerning our *missus* whom we have sent to the people of the English in the regions of Britain . . . But that what you intimated in your letter had happened, that is to say, that King Eardwulf had been thrown out of his own kingdom, we already knew from Anglo-Saxons themselves. That was the reason, especially, that we sent our *missus* because of that evil deed. Great joy came into our heart because your goodness sent his *missi* and they escorted him [Eardwulf] to you. We are delighted that he is still alive and still your *fidelis* and that his *missi* have been sent to us.[20]

In Leo's letters, it seems to be taken as read that *missi* come with military retinues, otherwise recognizable as small armies. This would be just as true of the two Frankish high officials, Rotfrid the notary, and Abbot Nanthar of St-Omer, sent to rescue Eardwulf. These men sound rather like Ercanbald the arch-chancellor and Abbot Fulrad of St-Quentin: secular figures or 'lay-abbots' – the sorts whom today's slang would label 'heavies', employed to use violence to maintain order, or in Eardwulf's case, men fit and able to re-establish a king.[21]

Leo added an *embolum*, an annex or postscript, to Letter 2:[22]

Because of the love and fidelity I have for you, I can't keep silent. Bishop Jesse [of Amiens], your servant, can perform another kind of service for you. He does not seem to us to be suitable to carry out the office of a *missus* through different lands (*per patrias*) nor to be summoned to serve as a counsellor. We ask your mercifulness to think about this in a merciful way ... About cases involving bishops ... we suggest that you ask your *fideles* [counts] Helmengaud and Hunfrid this question: when they were absolved by us and met in Ravenna and were invited to dinner on Palm Sunday by the archbishop, what readings and what admonitions did they listen to before the table (*mensa*) itself in the season of Lent when all pray to God that they be worthy to emend their sins. But the things they heard there, it would be disgraceful for us to intimate to you in writing.[23]

Leo's letters reveal what most other sources do not: the complicated, often dislocated, coexistence of different sources and layers of authority in northern and central Italy. In letter 2, Leo viewed the visits of *missi* sent from across the Alps as violent incursions that disrupted customary systems of payment for local administrators. He dared (and this must have taken some courage) to tell Charles that the bishop of Amiens was *non idoneus* – unsuitable – to act as a *missus* or a counsellor. In the final lines of that letter, the old smouldering rivalry between Ravenna and Rome burst into flaming allegations of unseemly conduct at Archbishop Agnellus's dinner-table.

Warfare has a way of insinuating itself into any serious account of Charles's regime. In classic papers, Tim Reuter put forward two views; first, that warfare brought in profits in the forms of plunder and tribute which sustained Charles's political support and were the motor of his empire, and second, that these methods became unprofitable in the imperial years, when lay aristocrats revised their cost-benefit calculations.[24] These views have been criticized on two grounds. First, that the wealth-production generated from within the empire was maintained well into the mid-ninth century; and second, that Avar treasure was the exception that proved the rule – in other words, that the boost of treasure was temporary, and that the most important factor in sustaining the empire was neither plunder nor tribute but ideology/religion.[25] There is still a good deal to be said for Reuter's view, especially where moveable wealth is concerned. Inflows of such wealth continued to occur spasmodically during the imperial years, and the use of coinage did have some effect on the ways surpluses were transferred, as the *De villis* indicates.[26] As for 'the end of expansion': at the time of Charles's death, his empire was still expanding in what had been Slav and Avar territory and in Istria, despite the concessions Charles had had to make in Venetia and Dalmatia.[27] There was expansion too in what would become Catalonia and in Navarre.[28] In 812, the amir Hakim (aka Abulaz) of Córdoba sought and got an agreed three-year peace with Charles.[29] Duke Grimoald of Benevento likewise made a peace, 'and the Beneventans paid 25,000 gold *solidi* under the name of a tribute'.[30]

Defensive warfare in frontier-zones emerged as Charles's priority in the imperial years. In 808 and 809, the pressures of Danish attacks, again – as in Venetia – by land and sea, aroused new efforts on the Franks' part: on the Elbe, the Young Charles's bridge and fortresses, and beyond the Elbe new fortifications on the river Stör constructed by Count Egbert. In the end it was luck that saw off the Danish threat in 810: Godofrid was murdered by one of his own military retinue (*quidam suus satelles*), and Godofrid's nephew Hemming made peace with the emperor in 811:

> Twelve *primores* from each side and each people, Franks and Danes, met on the river Eider at the place called . . . [gap in MS] and the peace was confirmed by mutual oaths given in accordance with their usage and custom. And the *primores* on the Franks' side were these:
>
> Count Wala son of Bernard, Count Burchard, Count Egbert, Count Theoteri, Count Abo, Count Osdag, Count Wigman.
>
> And on the Danes' side: Hemming's brothers Hancwin and Agandeo . . . and then others . . . Osfrid, Warstein, Suomi, Urm, another Osfrid son of Heiligen, Osfrid of Schonen, Hebbi and Aowin.[31]

Disputes within the Danish royal kindred were to bedevil the Danes for a generation and beyond, while relations between Franks and Danes ran more smoothly. They could, it seems, communicate with each other, culturally and, up to a point, linguistically.

All these diplomatic and military activities in frontier-zones added up to a track-record of overall success for the emperor. The most impressive evidence that Charles was in earnest about keeping frontiers secure lies in a string of capitularies issued by him between 802/3 and 811. First, Charles was able to grasp the different needs of different zones and, at the same time, to conceive all these as 'interlocking facets of a single puzzle of immense complexity'.[32] With all this in mind, and with the help of his counsellors, Charles could now work out the practical measures and detailed local arrangements. Perhaps more than ever now, he was aware of a double legacy: one from the Roman Empire, of whose achievements he had read and which he'd seen with his own eyes in many landscapes, and the other from his father, who had forbidden Frankish troops to ravage *infra patriam*, that is, while they were within the boundaries of the homeland, and from whom he had learned about the fundamental importance of the bonds that kept comrades-in-arms (*pares*) together.[33]

Charles had evidently addressed the need for such a clear and detailed agenda as part of the great output of 'reform' capitularies produced when he was settled back at Aachen.[34] The earliest of the military capitularies, in 802/3, detailed what contingents needed in the way of victuals ('flour, wine, pork . . .'), tools (hand-mills, adzes, axes . . .), military equipment ('lances, shields, bows and arrows . . .') and transport (carts).[35] Military matters did not monopolize the agenda: the emperor's surveillance extended geographically into the counties and sociologically down beneath the top governmental elite and the elders: '*homines boni generis . . . qui inique vel iniuste agunt in praesentia regis ducantur*' ('men of good family who act wickedly or unjustly are to be brought into the king's presence [where their fate would be decided]').[36]

Next came a letter (printed in the standard edition as a capitulary), dated to mid-April, 806, from Charles to Fulrad, abbot of St-Quentin:

> Be it known to you [*tibi*] that we have arranged to hold our general assembly this year in Saxony, in the eastern part, on the river Bode at the place

called Stassfurt. Wherefore we command you that you must come to the aforesaid place with all your men (*homines*), well-armed and well-equipped, on 17th June, which is seven days before the Mass of St John the Baptist. And you are to come with your men to that place equipped in such a way that you can go from there with the army to whichever region we shall command – that is, with weapons, implements, and other military material, provisions and clothing. Each horseman (*caballarius*) is to carry shield and spear, long-sword and short-sword, bow, quivers and arrows, and your carts are to contain implements of various kinds: axes and stone-cutting tools, augers, adzes and trenching tools, iron spades, and the rest of the implements an army needs; and provisions in the carts for three months following the assembly, and weapons and clothing for half a year. And this we command absolutely that you see to it that, whichever part of our realm the direction of your march may cause you to pass through, you proceed to the aforesaid place with good peace (*cum bona pace*), that is, that you presume to take nothing except for grass, firewood and water. And the men of each of you should march along with their carts and horsemen and each is to be with them at all times until they reach the place aforementioned, in such a way that the absence of their lord (*dominus*) gives his men no chance for wrong-doing.

As regards your gifts which you have to present to us at our assembly, send these to us by mid-May to whichever place we have come. If the direction of your march shapes up so that you can present the gifts to us in person on your route, this is something we would greatly wish for. See to it that you show no negligence in any of this, if you want to keep our favour.[37]

Fulrad was not an abbot in the mould of St Benedict, who back in the sixth century had written the *regula* (Rule) imposing a *regular* life on monastic communities. Fulrad looks more like a powerful lay magnate to whom Charles had given a monastery and its lands to run on condition that he organized its military service and offered valuable and useful gifts (horses, for instance).[38] The last sentence of Charles's letter – in its scarcely veiled threat of retribution if Fulrad's job was not well done – meant what it said. Modern historians have invented the term 'lay-abbot' for such a man, who would be documented later as operating in tandem with a regular (Rule-following) abbot.[39] Fulrad was one of the earliest known: a military man of the secular world with a large stake in a religious institution. In the letter to Fulrad, there is an echo of Pippin's capitulary of 768, and more than just an echo of the capitulary of 802/3 which first set out a whole new version of organization for war.[40]

In the capitulary 'on mobilization of the army' (808), Charles responded to reports of failings that had been brought to his attention the previous year: 'Whoever is found neither to have helped his comrade-in-arms (*par suus*) to perform his army service nor performed it himself is to pledge payment of our *heribann* [the 60 *solidi* fine for neglecting army-duty].' *Missi* armed with checklists were now to be sent to make further inquiries about pretexts or bribes given to excuse men who stayed at home with the permission of their lords (*domini*), and if such abuses had occurred, those men would be required to pay 'our fine'.

Multiple copies of this capitulary were made for *missi* and counts, with the chancellor (*cancellarius*) keeping a master-copy.[41] The Capitulary of Boulogne 'which is on the coast' (October, 811) listed a raft of penalties for non-performance of military service, ranging from fines to penal servitude to capital punishment for desertion (*herisliz*). Charles was addressing, in particular, counts, imperial *vassi*, and lords of free men. His decision was that any imperial *vassi* 'known to have benefices but who are still staying within the household should remain at home with the lord emperor yet they should not retain with them their *vassalli* [in this context, *vassi* of lesser rank] in their households but permit them to go [in the army] as *pagenses* (men of the counties, or more familiarly in English, shires) with their count'.[42] There were separate lines of command: between lords (*seniores, domini*) and their followers, and counts and the men of the shires. There were also complicated arrangements for allocating troops to serve on different frontiers, assuming in each case a three-month march to the frontier taking their own supplies, and living off enemy country during campaigns, as well as a customary system for calculating the amounts of victuals, arms and clothing that would be required for each regional contingent until the frontier was reached.[43]

Two clauses mention *pares*:

[c. 5] If someone from among those holding a benefice from the prince (*princeps*) should fail his comrade-in-arms (*par*) when he is going on campaign against public enemies and refuses either to go or stay with him [in the army], he [his comrade-in-arms] is to lose his office (*honor*) and his benefice . . . [c. 6] No-one in the army is to invite his comrade-in-arms (*par*), or any other man, to drink. And whoever is found drunk in the army is to be segregated in such a way that he may have only water to drink until such time as he acknowledges that he has done wrong.[44]

Here was a set-up designed to promote mutual discipline and morale. The notion of *pares* as comrades-in-arms (sometimes the term used is *socii*) underpinned a system, widespread and taking a variety of forms, whereby a group of men co-operated to support another man who would perform military service on the group's behalf: a system of selective service that bore heavily on free men but worked to strengthen the bonds between *pares*.

The permutations included: 'if one man has two *mansi* and another man has one *mansus* [a peasant holding], they shall join together and one shall equip the other, and the one who is better able shall come to the army'; or 'of those who have a half-*mansus*, five shall equip a sixth'; or 'if the campaign is against Avars or Moors, five Saxons shall equip a sixth'; or 'if campaigning against Bohemians, two Saxons shall equip a third'; or 'he who has only one *mansus* shall be joined to one of three who have the same and shall help him and he shall go alone, and the three who have helped him shall remain at home'.[45] Holders of *mansi* and half-*mansi* were clearly peasants.[46]

On Reuter's argument, the system's introduction seems to have been timed to coincide with, and cope with, the end of the empire's expansion. Expansion did not end, though; it was more strategically focused on the northern and eastern frontier-zones of the empire, and specifically on Istria, Dalmatia and the Adriatic.[47] Rather than plunder and tribute, it was bonds of loyalty and reward that remained the prime attractions for fighting-men. More economic demands were imposed by the powerful on the *pauperes* (the poor) and the *pauperiores* (the even poorer) among the free peasantry, and more demands were made on defence; but these were offset by further stratification of the peasantry and the appearance, however patchy the evidence, of a peasant elite.[48]

Charles was the heir of Rome, drawing on Roman traditions of public works, including fort-building, watch-service and bridge-work.[49] Charles was also the heir of his father: he cared about the *pares* in the troops he summoned.[50] The leader's military policy of selective service could never even have begun to work without his wish to evoke a sense of comradeship among the led – a sense of parity.[51] This was an idea that spanned social classes and social contexts. Court intellectuals were aware, thanks to Pope Gregory the Great, that the pastor and the believers were *in sui comparatione equales*: Alcuin, in his moral handbook on virtues and vices, reminded Count Guy of Brittany that 'entry into the kingdom of heaven was available equally (*aequaliter*)', while Theodulf warned judges that 'whoever is in charge of those lacking power (*pauperes*) must be most gentle / for you know that you are by nature equal to them (*teque his natura noveris esse parem*)'.[52] The words of the teachers reached *missi* and counts.

The reports of *missi* came to the palace. The only such report to have survived (and there surely must once have been many more) is from 811, and headed: 'Reasons why men often neglect their military obligations'. It begins:

c. 1. *In primis, discordantes sunt.* Firstly, they don't agree. They say that bishops, abbots and their advocates don't have control over their clerics and others. Likewise, counts say they have no control over their *pagenses*.

c. 2. Poor men/less powerful men (*pauperes*) complain that they're deprived of their property – and they make the same complaint against bishops, abbots and advocates as against counts and their hundredmen.

c. 3. They also say that, if a man refuses to hand over his own property to [the sort of men above-mentioned], those men look for chances to do harm to the *pauperes* and make the *pauper* go on every single call-up until he's completely impoverished or sells his property while others who have handed over their property stay at home with no trouble.

c. 4. [They say] bishops, abbots and counts let their free men stay at home because they have special duties as falconers, huntsmen, toll-takers, receivers of *missi* and their retinues.

c. 5. Others say that they use force on *pauperiores* [the even poorer or even less powerful] to make them go in the army, but they let those who will give them something stay at home.

c. 6. The counts say that some people in their counties don't obey them and refuse to fulfil the emperor's commands, saying they are answerable to the emperor's *missi*, not to the count.

c. 7. There are others who say that they are the men of [king] Pippin and [king] Louis and then when other people have to go to the army, say that they are going on the service of their lords (*domini*).

c. 8. There are others again who do not go and say that their lords (*seniores*) are staying at home and their duty is to go with their lords wherever the emperor orders – and there are those who, for this reason, commend themselves to other lords whom they know won't be going in the army.

c. 9. Above all, they say that people in the counties are becoming disobedient to their counts and running to the *missi* more often than they used to do before.[53]

Officials and *potentes* did not operate in serried ranks; they were split into different interest-groups, and worked at different levels in different localities. *Missi* had the emperor's ear, but so too did counts, when spoken to *singulariter* (individually) as Charles demanded, also in 811.[54] Rather than a diagnosis of a system in crisis, I see one of carefully gauged checks and balances. From the standpoint of Charles and his counsellors, encouraging *pagenses* to run to *missi* instead of counts was a very good way to keep counts in line, re-reading their capitularies. In the end, the doing of justice was a co-operative business: 'cases unjudged by counts are dealt with by *missi*, and . . . our *missi* are to hold their courts with those counts four times in the month and in four places acceptable to the counts as ones where they can meet together'.[55] How these arrangements worked on the ground is obscure, though it's possible to imagine how great a part was played by negotiation at local levels.[56] But the *ArF* for 811 gives the impression that they *could* and *did* work, and the explanation centres – predictably – on the emperor in action, restoring and inspecting:

> The emperor, in order to inspect the fleet which he had ordered to be assembled the year before, went to the maritime city of Boulogne where the ships had assembled. He restored the lighthouse established there in ancient times to guide the passage of seafarers and arranged for a fire to be lit on the summit at night. From there he went to the river Scheldt to the place called Ghent and inspected ships for the same fleet . . .[57]

II. 'WILLS AND A DIVISION': CHARLES'S TESTAMENT AND ITS ATTESTERS, 811

According to Einhard, in the final chapter, 33, of his *Vita Karoli*,[58]

Charles had decided to make wills (*testamenta*) in which he wanted to make his daughters and his children by concubines his heirs to some part of his property, but he had begun on this project too late and was unable to finish it. Three years before he died, though, he made a division of his treasures and his money and his clothing, and other movable property, in the presence of his friends and officials (*ministri*). He called on them to bear witness that after his death the distribution he made should be carried out by their support. He wanted everything in the division he had made of his property to be summarized in a *breviarium* (short document).

The procedure recalled the *Divisio* of 806 in so far as it could be considered a *testamentum* (will) ratified by Frankish magnates, confirmed by their oaths, and recorded in writing; and the vocabulary echoed that of the 806 *Divisio*, with a *constitutio* (an imperial regulation) and an *ordinatio* (ordinance). The will followed in part the model of the *breviarium* or statistical survey, as described by Suetonius in his *Life* of the Emperor Augustus. It detailed Charles's description and division of treasures 'found that day in his chamber', but it did not say what day. The intent ascribed to Charles was 'to free his heirs from all doubt and know clearly what belonged to them and be able to share their property by a suitable partition (*competens partitio*) avoiding litigation or dispute' (another echo of 806).

Far from being strongly influenced by such high-flown ideology as inhered in the Donation of Constantine, the *breviarium* evoked the materiality of the movables as did more or less contemporary wills. What Einhard put together for the emperor and for other readers was an idiosyncratic text: a distinctive account of Charles's patriarchal charity and piety framed in learned number-symbolism.[59] The movables in his treasury (*camera*) were divided into three parts: one to be left intact, the other two were to be divided in twenty-one parts to be given for charitable purposes, 'because there are 21 metropolitan cities in Charles's empire' (these are listed). Twenty-one strong-boxes had been made ready, each kept separate from the rest, and filled with assorted valuables of gold and silver, precious stones and royal vestments, and labelled separately 'and set aside under seal (*sub sigillo*)'. This represented a huge structural investment in the Carolingian Church.[60] The first part – now the third part – was to go on Charles's expenses as long as he lived, 'or after a voluntary renunciation of the affairs of this world (*aut voluntaria saecularium rerum carentia*)'.

Renunciation, then, was a possibility Charles allowed for – an opting-out of secular life and a transferring of that life's responsibilities to his heirs. After his death the third part would be divided into four: the first to be added to the first two parts; the second to go to his sons and daughters and to the sons and daughters of his sons, to be distributed to them in a just and equitable way; the third, in accordance with the custom common among Christians, to the poor (a further giving of alms); and the fourth to the menservants and maidservants on duty at the palace. The church property belonging to the chapel was to remain entire and undivided.* The books in Charles's library were to be sold and the proceeds given to the poor. Of four precious tables of great symbolic significance, one silver one with a representation of Constantinople was to go to St Peter's Church at Rome, a second silver one with the likeness of the city of Rome was to go to Ravenna; the third silver table plus a fourth (golden) one were to be added to the portions to be devoted to his heirs and to alms.[61] All these gifts reveal or confirm Charles's religious preoccupations and priorities in 811.[62] The destinations of the first and second silver tables (a depiction of Constantinople for Rome, and a depiction of Rome for Ravenna) signal something else too: Charles's sense of irony.[63]

The document was to be subscribed by the following:

Archbishops Hildebold of Cologne (c.787–819), Riculf of Mainz (787–813), Arn of Salzburg (797–821), Wulfar of Reims (803–16), Bernoin of Besançon (811–29), Leidrad of Lyons (799–816) and John of Arles (811–16).

Bishops Theodulf of Orléans (c.798–818), Jesse of Amiens (799–836), Heito of Basel (806–23) and Waltgaud of Liège (809–31).

Abbots Fridugis of St-Martin's, Tours (804–34), Adelung of Lorsch (804–37), Angilbert of St-Riquier (794–814) and Irmino of St-Germain-des-Prés (?811–before 829).

Counts Wala, Meginar, Otulf, Stephen, Unroch, Meginhard, Hatto, Richwin, Edo, Erchangar, Gerold, Bero, Hildegern and Roculf.

---

* The word *capella* here signifies 'the ecclesiastical equipment belonging to the royal court'.

This list, dated securely, offers some firm identifications, especially of ecclesiastics. As for the fourteen laymen, there are some interesting possible identifications. One feature that stands out is the apparent absence of a *secundus a rege* (second after the king) during Charles's long reign. (In this respect, the contrast with Louis the Pious and his favourites is striking.) In the very last years, perhaps, Wala, Charles's cousin, came close. Predictably on the list of the holders of countships were scions of the highest aristocratic families. Count Stephen of Paris was the son of Count Gerold of Paris, and other Gerolds, perhaps including the one listed along with Stephen, flourished in the Rhineland and within the support-network of the monastery of Lorsch in the late eighth century.[64] Otulf has been identified with the Frank Audulf, who became prefect in Bavaria and married into a noble Bavarian family.[65] Hatto could be the same man as the Count Hitto who, together with Bishop Haito (Heito), was assigned to receive the Westfalian hostages at Mainz c.805.[66] Unroc and Roculf have usually been assigned to the same kin group, known to modern historians as the Unruochinger.[67] Another kin group, whose characteristic leading-name was Megin-, had two of its men attesting: Meginar and Meginhard; and it seems likely that had a third member, Meginfred the treasurer, survived the fevers of central Italy instead of dying in 801, he too would have attested in 811.[68] Another name could indicate Charles's wish to have an attester representative of a distant frontier-zone: Bero (Bera), count of Barcelona. Richwin (Richoin), thought to have been the count of Padua but I think better identified as the count of Thurgau (on Abbot Waldo's patch), probably fathered the last of Charles's bastard grandsons, Richbod, whose mother was Charles's daughter by Fastrada, Hiltrud.[69] Most of the attesters on the 811 list can be linked personally with Charles in one way or another as close and trusted advisers or agents, or, in Richwin's case, the lover of Charles's daughter. A network of multiple bonds of kinship, lordship, geographical proximity, trust and loyalty, formed over decades, supported the organizational arrangements of Charles's regime.

III. THE VOICE OF CHARLES, 802–12

The imperial years marked a very distinct and significant phase in a long life and a long reign. Two of the scholars best qualified to assess the nature of the imperial years – F.-L. Ganshof and Heinrich Fichtenau – made their assessments in 1947 and 1948. Their post-war situation, and the experiences their world had recently undergone, inevitably influenced their judgements of Charles's imperial years. They were both pessimistic. In the Conclusion to this book I shall explain why I can't share that view. But here I want to use two short texts dating from 811 (classed as capitularies by nineteenth-century editors) to propose a different and more optimistic judgement: that in these two texts, it's possible to hear 'the voice of Charlemagne'.[70]

In the first, the voice was heard by 'our bishops, abbots and counts, addressing each group one by one (*singulariter*)'.[71] Charles's questions were uncomfortable, but he was confident that answers could be found.

> *Hic interrogandum est acutissime, quid sit quod apostolus ait* [2 Tim. 2: 4]: *'nemo militans Deo implicet se negotiis secularibus', vel ad quos sermo iste pertineat.* (This question has to be put in the most probing way, what it is that the Apostle said, 'Let no-one fighting for God mix himself up with the affairs of this world', and to whom is this manner of speaking addressed?)[72]
>
> *Quod nobis despiciendum est, utrum vere christiani sumus. Quod in consideratione vitae vel morum nostrorum facillime cognosci potest, si diligenter conversationem coram discutere voluerimus.* (That it is something for us to attend to, whether we are really Christians. That in considering of our life and our habits, it can very easily be known, if we want to discuss seriously in each others' presence.)[73]

In the second of the two capitularies, Charles spoke in a particularly direct, unmediated fashion.[74] It started as a harangue, continued as a wide-ranging series of reflections on the conduct of clergy, and culminated in a summons to 'every single one of us' not only to self-inspection, not just to confronting the reality of evil in the world, but to living out New Testament values in an exemplary way.[75]

There are other capitularies from this period that show just how deeply Charles wanted to go in this process of probing and exposing. A famously impatient response of the emperor was to one of his *missi* who was asking him *yet again* to say if it was possible for anyone to free himself from servitude by using false evidence. Charles answered: 'we have given you orders ubiquitously [meaning, repeatedly] that it's *quite impossible* for anyone to free himself from servitude by using false evidence!'[76]

Another *Admonitio* from Charles, to be delivered and diffused by his *missi*, began with the Creed, continued like a general sermon, but then shifted the register to the household: 'Husbands, love your wife and do not say shaming words to her; govern your homes in goodness, go together often to church.'[77] Capitular admonitions of Charles delivered in the Aachen palace in 810 included: 'Concerning the common people: let every man keep control of his juniors so that they obey, and agree better and better to, imperial orders and commands'; and 'Each man must be responsible for correcting himself and his household (*familia*).'[78] There was to be no buck-passing. A message clearly voiced as the first requirement of the Programmatic Capitulary was issued at the beginning of 802:

> Everyone must take personal responsibility for striving, in accordance with God's command and his own promise [*sponsio*, as in baptism] to maintain themselves in God's holy service, because the Lord Emperor himself is not able to provide the necessary care and discipline (*cura et disciplina*) for everyone individually (*singulariter*).[79]

Finally, a capitulary which now, after some serious scholarly doubts, appears to have been a product of Charles's imperial years, but was reframed by Louis the Pious in 829.[80] It contained an interestingly diverse set of *capitula*, including one about lordship:

> That no-one is to abandon his lord (*senior*) after he has accepted the value of one *solidus* from him, unless [and here is a remarkable set of four conditions] the lord seeks to kill him, or to assault him with a stave, or to debauch his wife or daughter, or to take away his inheritance.[81]

There seems to have been a venerable tradition of a lord's signing-up a warrior into his retinue by the handing-over of a *solidus* (the Anglo-Saxon equivalent was a shilling). This was not a hire-fee but a gift and therefore honourable. As for a lord's actions that could justify his man abandoning him, these were not just deeply dishonouring but, in the case of 'seeking to kill', potentially fatal. Here, and in a number of other *capitula* in capitulary no. 77, Charles exposed some deeply rooted Frankish values and social practices otherwise unattested in the sources for the reign. Capitularies made Charles's voice audible.

IV. THE DEATH OF THE YOUNG CHARLES

Charles was at Aachen when he heard the news that his eldest son and namesake had died, on 4 December 811. The place of the Young Charles's death is unrecorded. Whereas his younger brothers were buried in splendid tombs (Pippin at Milan, Louis at Metz – both these monuments can be seen today), for the Young Charles there is no known tomb.[82] No poet wrote his elegy.

The Young Charles's activities, nearly always military, for the years 804, 805, 806, 808 and 810 are well-documented.[83] His sustained track-record of successful campaigns beat that of his younger brothers, and post-800 was well-publicized in the *ArF* and in the *Chronicle of Moissac*. Nothing at all is recorded of him in 811, however. Perhaps he had a near-death experience in the pestilence of that year and never properly recovered. According to Einhard, Charles wept 'when his two sons and daughter died'. This may well have been true – though Einhard had cribbed a version of the idea from Suetonius's *Life* of Augustus.[84] The Young Charles's death, given the many campaigns he had successfully fought at his father's behest, and how often he was to be found at his father's side, would surely have been the heaviest loss the emperor had ever had to bear. He had been assuming his namesake's succession, and meanwhile the Young Charles had been content to await marriage and paternity and leave the timing to God. A Saxon poet (*Poeta Saxo*), writing *c*.890 at Korvey, had another explanation:

> *Hunc in Francorum sibimet succedere regnum*
> *Disposuit, si non aliter Domino placuisset.*
> It was the Young Charles that [the emperor] planned to
>   succeed him
> in the realm of the Franks, had it not pleased God to
>   plan otherwise.[85]

The Saxon poet's comment on the mysterious ways of the Almighty prompts a brief retrospective on this-worldly relationships within Charles's family, and especially between Charles and his sons. With the single exception of Pippin son of Himiltrud, the eldest of them, Charles's sons gave him their loyalty and were his willing comrades in war and (though much less well-documented) peace. Succession-planning and devolution involved collaboration. With all of his children and close family members for whom evidence is available – and indeed scattered through this book – there were deep emotional as well as pragmatic and political bonds. There is, of course, a good deal of idealizing in Einhard's *Vita Karoli* and (to be considered presently) in Adalhard's *De ordine palatii* ('On the governing of the palace'), but there are enough ways of looking at the everyday realities of Charles's life to show that his rulership style was more sociable and associative than controlling, more naturally familiar than aloof.

V. NEW PROSPECTS FOR BERNARD OF ITALY AND LOUIS OF AQUITAINE, 811–13

Bernard was the eldest of King Pippin of Italy's six children, and the only boy. He was born in *c*.797. His grandfather Charles, after the news had reached him of Pippin's death in July 810, had declared Bernard his father's successor. No strictly contemporary source said Bernard was illegitimate: only Thegan, writing his *Gesta* of Louis the Pious in *c*.837, alleged this, in the aftermath of Bernard's revolt and death in 817.[86] Charles had Bernard's five sisters sent for and brought up at Aachen with his own daughters.[87]

Adalhard, Charles's cousin and a monk at Corbie since 771 (becoming abbot there a decade later), had been the young King Pippin's *baiulus* (tutor/adviser) in the 780s.[88] From Alcuin's letters, Adalhard can be seen as one of Charles's leading counsellors, and probably accompanied Charles to Rome in 800.[89] In 809, he had been deputed, with Bishop Bernar of Worms, to take to the pope the decisions of the Aachen Council on the *filioque* question. He had arrived at Rome early in 810, but no sooner got back to Francia in the summer than the Aachen court learned of Pippin's death. Adalhard had plenty of experience of running matters in the kingdom of Italy; Charles trusted him, and, according to a local Corbie tradition, as a sign of exceptional favour gave Adalhard a relic of the True Cross.[90] And so, early in 811 Adalhard returned to Italy as de facto regent, with counsellors who were also Italy-experts. In 812, Charles sent Bernard to Italy under the protection of Wala, Adalhard's younger half-brother.[91] At some point in 811–12, Adalhard arranged the betrothal of Bernard and Cunegunda, an Italian noblewoman of the powerful Supponid family,[92] and in January 813 Bernard, now of age, took on the responsibilities of government.[93]

With the deaths of both the Young Charles and Pippin of Italy, Louis of Aquitaine was now in line to inherit the whole empire, except Italy. According to the Astronomer, Louis now felt 'the hope of obtaining all (*spes universitatis potiunde*) growing within him'.[94] He sent his chief falconer, Gerric, to consult with the emperor 'on various matters', which might have included arrangements to have Louis' succession finalized and presented publicly in ritual form.[95] Gerric, in the palace awaiting the emperor's response,

> was advised by *Franci* and *Germani* alike that the king should come to his father and stand close at hand to him . . . since his death might not be delayed much longer . . . Most of Louis' advisers thought this a good plan, but Louis, with loftier judgement, delayed action, lest by taking it, he should make his father mistrustful (*suspectus*).

In fact it may be the Astronomer's rather heavy-handed account itself that makes *Louis* sound mistrustful. There is nothing to suggest a contrast, to Louis' detriment, with the relationship between Charles and his namesake. On the contrary, Louis and his father are likely to have colluded in the summons to Aachen. There Charles 'kept him by his side throughout the summer, and instructed him on all matters he thought he needed to know . . .'[96] On 11 September Charles crowned Louis in the Aachen church, and made him co-sharer of the imperial title (*consors imperialis nominis*), and, on the same occasion, invested Bernard formally with the rulership of Italy and the title of king.[97]

Another of Louis' biographers, the poet Ermold, writing in exile at Strasbourg *c.* 827 in an effort (successful) to secure his return to imperial favour, produced versions of the speeches made by Charles and by Einhard at the Aachen assembly in September 813. These poetic confections conveyed a flavour of actuality, as Charles expressed his confidence in Louis and in Christ:

> Listen to me, my leading men, nurtured by my support,
> For I am going to tell you things we know to be true.
> While there was energy in my youthful body,
> I exerted myself in war and the pursuit of power . . .
> Now my blood grows sluggish and cruel old age makes me slow . . .
> Children born to me have died and, sad to say,
> With their duties done, they now lie buried . . .
> But Christ has not abandoned you, Franks, he has left behind
> From my offspring a worthy son . . .
> You have seen the many trophies he once sent me for his
> Conquest of the Moors: the king, weapons, captured people.
> O Franks, from your faithful hearts, give me your advice.
> I shall at once carry it out.

To which Einhard, who was 'in high favour with Charles, and also wise, clever, full of goodness', responded:

> O emperor, celebrated on high, on land and sea,
> You who now bestow your imperial name upon your son,
> There is nothing we can add to your plan . . .
> All of us, high and low, desire the rule of your son![98]

VI. ADALHARD'S DE *ORDINE PALATII*

Long travelling just under the name of Hincmar of Reims, a short treatise (*libellus*) written by Abbot Adalhard of Corbie, almost certainly between 810 and 814 and in Italy, was given substantial additions at the beginning, and a few revisions elsewhere, by Archbishop Hincmar of Reims in 882. The work was presented as an *Admonitio* to the young King Carloman of the West Franks (879–84). Hincmar affirmed that the core-work was Adalhard's, and that as a youth he himself had seen it and copied it, presumably at the court of Louis the Pious, sometime between 822 and 826.[99] It was a work of political science, unique for its time (and for long after too). In it, Adalhard did not moralize, he analysed; and, though he spent two important stints in Italy during the

780s and in 810–14, most of his political career, oscillating, as it did, between court and monastery, was played out at, and in close contact with, Charles's court between c.790 and 810.[100] (In 822, Adalhard wrote for his monastery a set of *Statutes*, which displayed an excellent knowledge of economic management and a fine grasp of detail.[101] To write not just one but two works on the theory and practice of organizations was a phenomenal achievement.)

The palace Adalhard saw in his mind's eye was that of Charles, which is where he lived and worked for most of his adult years. The *De ordine* described a system of interlocking parts and defined fields of responsibility, linked by effective lines of communication. This work and this system were required by the circumstance of 812/13, when Louis was girding up his loins for ruling an empire and perpetuating the Carolingian moment.[102] The *De ordine* was divided into two parts. The first was about the palace and the structure of its organization and personnel: here Adalhard enumerated the various palace officers and their duties, including the queen on the list. The second was about the empire and the process of running it: this part was even more remarkable, because it explored the governmental workings of empire. The interests of far-flung realms and border-zones had to be represented by a careful distribution of offices at court; good intelligence was required especially in frontier regions, given their sensitivity; particularly necessary was the delegating of responsibilities so that regional officers only forwarded matters to the ruler for decision when these could not be dealt with locally; last but not least, senior officials were bound by a commitment to confidentiality.[103]

The system was also a style of government: at small winter meetings the ruler made decisions with counsellors; at large summer meetings, 'outdoors if the weather was set fair', men spoke their opinions frankly, 'the more influential to frame counsel, the less important men to hear that counsel and sometimes to deliberate on it, and to confirm it, not because they were forced to do so but from their own understanding and freely-expressed opinion.'

There was an element of *familiaritas* 'when the king listened to the counsellors' debates', and another, rather different kind of familiarity

> when the king was occupied with the other assembled people, receiving gifts, greeting important men, swapping stories with people he didn't see

often, expressing sympathy with the old, sharing their pleasures with the young, involving himself with spiritual as well as secular affairs.[104]

Thanks to Tim Reuter, 'assembly politics' is the term that has entered mainstream historical discourse. Along with it, and no less mainstream these days, has come the term 'consensus politics'.[105] Thanks to Adalhard, a linguistic and conceptual tool-kit has become available to modern students of medieval polities.

Despite Adalhard's originality, there is no evidence that his work was diffused. It was not only time-required but, as it turned out, time-bound. This was explicable in terms of a series of accidents: Adalhard's stalled career and consignment to a monastery in 814; Hincmar's death in 882; the apparent end of the Carolingian moment. The *De ordine* is extant today in a single sixteenth-century paper copy, saved from total loss by an alert antiquarian. It's quite possible that Charles never saw the *De ordine*, for during the years of its writing, Adalhard was far from Francia, though his mind was stamped with impressions and memories of Aachen. In 813, Charles had other preoccupations. A lasting memorial to the achievements of what Charles could not have known (though he perhaps suspected) was to be his last year, were the preparations – in which he was closely involved – for the five councils of May–June 813.

VII. FIVE COUNCILS, 813

Charles had been pushing through this project for years, but especially since 811, when he had raised questions with bishops assembled at Aachen.[106] He had sent out questions to bishops (and also priests) about the performance of the liturgy of baptism in that same year, and received no fewer than sixty-one replies.[107] He was indeed 'an old man in a hurry'.[108] Five separate councils were held in 813 at places far distant from each other – at Arles, Reims, Mainz, Chalon and Tours – but all working to a single timetable (May and June) and (largely) to a single plan, based on a questionnaire sent from Aachen, and also taking into account the 811 agenda.[109] The text of only one of the councils' decrees supplied numbers of participants: this was Mainz, with thirty bishops and twenty-five abbots. The only documented compiler of a set of canons was Theodulf of Orléans, who wrote up the canons of

Chalon. The impulsion to correct was as strong as ever.[110] A great assembly met at Aachen to put together all five councils' decrees in a single collection, including all sixty-seven canons. No copy of such a composite work survives, unfortunately.

One of the decrees of Tours concerned free men in the Touraine who claimed that they had been disinherited of property their kin had given to a church: the bishops referred to local custom (*usus apud nos*) whereby such men got the property back in usufruct (that is, they had rights to the yields of these estates). According to the bishops, this worked greatly to the benefit of the claimants. Charles was especially troubled about this. The bishops (who seem to have got cold feet) wisely replied: 'We have aired these matters in our assembly – but whatever action our prince wants to be taken, we with willing hearts will follow his command.'[111]

Collaboration between prince and bishops was well-maintained. On Charles's part, there was no sign of diminished insistence. He presided, insistently, over the great assembly of September 813, when Louis and Bernard were ritually installed in their respective posts.[112] 'After this, Charles sent Louis back to Aquitaine, and the lord emperor held on to his realm and title, just as he deserved.'[113] Charles was still hale and hearty enough to hunt *more solito* (as was his usual custom), according to Einhard, in his favourite Ardennes hunting-grounds later in 813, returning about the first day of November.[114]

VIII. PORTENTS, THE *ARS MORIENDI*, CHARLES'S DEATH AND BURIAL; THE NEW REGIME

It was because Einhard found so many portents (*prodigia*) in Suetonius's *Lives of the Caesars* that he wanted to find analogous portents for Charles. He claimed that Charles himself perceived these as warnings of approaching death. Astronomical phenomena, the collapse of a building, the burning-down of a bridge, the falling of a fireball out of the sky – all these and several other extraordinary events had parallels in Suetonius. Einhard gave most attention to an event that had occurred back in 810, when Charles's horse stumbled and fell and the emperor was thrown violently to the ground 'so that the clasp on his cloak broke and his sword-belt came off'. Einhard found another portent in the

Aachen church. An inscription runs round the circular space in the lower part of the building (still to be seen, though restored in the nineteenth century), which names the church's builder as Charles, and ends with the words *Karolus princeps*.

> Some people noticed that during the last year of his life, only a few months before his death, the letters of the word *Princeps* had become so faint as to be barely visible. But Charles either scorned those things or took no notice of them, as if they had nothing whatsoever to do with him.[115]

Einhard, having said that Charles perceived portents as warnings of approaching death, reversed that view. Charles reacted to the prospect of his own death as he had to the loss of his children, with fortitude. After Louis' departure from Aachen, Charles became ill with a fever and took to his bed. Einhard describes him monitoring the course of his own illness:

> Charles prescribed for himself abstinence from food, as he always used to do in case of fever, thinking the illness could be driven off, or anyway lessened, by fasting. He also had a pain in his side which the Greeks call pleurisy, but he kept fasting, keeping up his strength only by very infrequent drinks. He died on 28 January, on the seventh day after he had taken to his bed, at 9 a.m., after taking Holy Communion.[116]

The tone of Thegan, later to be the biographer of Charles's son and heir, was quite different:

> The lord emperor began to do nothing else but devote himself to prayers and almsgiving, and to correcting books. In the last days before his death he had with the help of Greeks and Syrians excellently corrected the four Gospels of Christ which are assigned the names Matthew, Mark, Luke and John. In the following year [814] in the month of January, fever overtook the lord emperor after bathing. His weakness grew worse by the day . . . After the seventh day he began to struggle much with himself (*postquam laborare nimis secum coepit*), and he ordered his Archbishop who was the very closest to him (*familiarissimus pontifex*), Hildebald, to come to him and give him the sacraments of the Lord's body and blood to strengthen him for death. After this, he struggled in infirmity that day and the following night. On the next day, as the sun was rising, knowing what was going to happen, he stretched out his right hand with what

481

strength he could, and made the sign of the blessed cross on his forehead and over his chest and over his whole body. Finally, drawing his feet together, extending his arms and hands over his body, he closed his eyes, very gently singing this verse: 'Into your hands, Lord, I commend my spirit' (Luke 23:46). Immediately after this, in old age and in the fullness of days, he departed in peace. On the same day, he was buried in the church which he himself had built at the palace of Aachen.[117]

The *ars moriendi*, the art of dying, is often thought to have been a practice of the late Middle Ages, and later. Certainly there was no pre-scribed form of it in the early Middle Ages. Yet someone whose death in 735 was described in detail, in a letter that circulated widely, was Bede. The letter was written by an abbot of Wearmouth and Jarrow named Cuthbert, who in writing to Bishop Lull of Mainz had called himself 'Bede's disciple'. Contacts were close between Mainz and Jarrow. Cuth-bert reported that Bede, when he was dying, was translating into Old English the Gospel of St John. He was just one chapter short of com-pleting this when he asked another monk to write to his dictation . . .

> Six hours later, the boy who was helping him said, 'Dear master, there is only one sentence left.' And he said, 'Write it', and after a little, the boy said: 'There! now it is written.' And he replied: 'Good. It is finished.' And upon the floor of his cell, he breathed his last.[118]

Charles's *familiarissimus* Hildebald and other ecclesiastics at court knew of the account of Bede's death. Bede the gospel translator was the model for Charles the gospel corrector. Given Charles's contacts with Greek scholars and his strong interest in sending alms to Christians in Syria, it's entirely plausible that Greeks and Syrians were Charles's helpers in his last weeks.[119]

Who buried Charles? Einhard's account can only be called economical with the truth. He described a series of procedures: 'The body was washed and prepared in the solemn customary way . . . carried to the church . . . and buried . . . There was doubt as to where he ought to be buried because while alive he had given no instructions about this.'[120] Einhard misleads. Although at the beginning of his reign, Charles had envisaged burial at St-Denis, he had since then based himself firmly at Aachen and founded the church there. Though Einhard's wording – 'Finally (*tandem*) the minds of everyone settled . . .' – suggests quite prolonged uncertainty, the delay was in fact minimal: Charles was buried the day he died. According to the Astronomer, 'the funeral was taken care of by the children and leading men of Charles at the palace'.[121] Since Louis, the only surviving adult son, was far away in Aquitaine, and since Charles's other sons were still quite young, it looks as if 'the children' must have been his daughters. A further circumstance was obviously crucial here: in Francia, as in many other parts of Europe, tradition prescribed women's responsibility for the washing and laying-out of the dead.[122] Charles's daughters were entirely prepared for providing this last service to their father.

The church was exceptional in being neither a monastic shrine nor a cathedral. It was the parish church of Aachen, hence a baptismal church, open to women as well as men who might come to the *sedes regni*, 'the capital seat of the realm'. The earliest reference to the church in the making was in Alcuin's letter recalling a conversation with his *famula fidelissima*, very probably Liutgard, when they shared their admiration for the marble columns.[123] The church's main altar, on the ground-floor, was dedicated to the Blessed Virgin; the altar in the first-floor gallery was dedicated to the Saviour. Charles's father had been buried at St-Denis *in portico ecclesiae* (the entrance-way): Charles was buried beneath the west entrance to the Aachen church. Charles had abandoned his earlier plan to be buried at St-Denis; his self-modelling on his father yielded to his desire for burial in the new and wondrous church he had built for himself.

The new regime was not established immediately. According to the Astronomer, 'there was the greatest fear that Wala, whom the emperor had held in the very highest standing, might perhaps undertake some mischief . . .'[124] Louis had, it seems, foreseen problems. He was not on the spot. Those who were, and in control, were the daughters of Charles, perhaps aided by Charles's mistresses as well as leading male figures such as Hildebald and Wala. The Astronomer adds that Louis had already summoned an assembly – 'as if by some presentiment' – for 2 February, the feast of the Purification of the Blessed Virgin, also known as Candlemas. At Orléans, Theodulf prepared an *adventus* (a ritual entry) for Louis.[125] If Louis had been unable to manage the funeral itself, he was able to stage his *adventus* at Aachen on the thirtieth day after Charles's death and funeral, which in religious and liturgical terms was the crucial day for the first commemoration of the dead.[126] Charles's death could be represented as legitimizing his son's succession. On that thirtieth day, and in that place, the son paid the expenses for his father's funeral.[127]

One further important detail marked out Charles's burial: on the likeliest scenario, his body was laid in an antique marble sarcophagus that had been brought to Francia from Italy and been carefully prepared in advance.[128] The probable context for the arrival of the sarcophagus was the bringing across the Alps of a number of Roman marbles in the second part of Charles's reign. Einhard supplied the text of the epitaph carved on the arch constructed above the wall-niche, or *archisolium*, which housed Charles's tomb below ground.

SUB HOC CONDITORIO SITUM EST CORPUS KAROLI MAGNI ATQUE ORTHODOXI IMPERATORIS, QUI REGNUM FRANCORUM NOBILITER AMPLIAVIT ET PER ANNOS XLVII FELICITER REXIT. DECESSIT SEPTUA-GENARIUS ANNO DOMINI DCCCXIIII, INDICTIONE VII, V. KAL. FEBR. (UNDER THIS TOMB LIES THE BODY OF CHARLES, THE GREAT AND ORTHODOX EMPEROR, WHO GLORIOUSLY INCREASED THE KINGDOM OF THE FRANKS AND REIGNED WITH GREAT SUCCESS FOR FORTY-SEVEN YEARS. HE DIED IN HIS SEVENTIES IN THE YEAR OF OUR LORD 814, IN THE SEVENTH INDICTION, ON THE TWENTY-EIGHTH DAY OF JANUARY.)[129]

Perhaps Einhard gave the details because he himself had written the epitaph. But he said nothing about the sarcophagus. Charles would not be outdone by his long-dead brother Carloman, laid to rest in 771 in an imposing antique sarcophagus at St-Rémi, Reims.[130] The highlighting of imperial grandeur was a key motive in Charles's pre-mortem acquiring of the sarcophagus.

Nearly twenty years ago I inferred that Einhard, who, once Charles was gone, could express his disapproval of the emperor's closeness to his daughters, did not mention the sarcophagus because it was not his choice, but that of Charles's daughters. Louis no doubt shared Einhard's view. The sarcophagus, which is still on display in the Aachen treasury, and which depicts the abduction of Proserpina by Pluto, god of the Underworld, packs a powerful visual punch. It may well have Christianized the pagan myth as symbolizing the soul's ascent to heaven. But there is something more specific here, to be connected with St Augustine's marked interest in the Proserpina story in *The City of God*.[131] A key theme of Book VII is 'the need to uproot and extirpate depraved and ancient opinions which the long-continued error of the human race has implanted deeply and tenaciously in the dark places of the soul'. In chapter 20, Augustine discusses 'the rites of the Eleusinian Ceres', goddess of grain and fruits. To summarize: Ceres lost her daughter Proserpina, who signi-fied the seed's fertility, when she was carried off by Orcus (the Romans called him Pluto) and imprisoned in the Underworld during the winter months. This event was celebrated by public mourning. When fertility returned, there was joy at Proserpina's return. Augustine began the myth's allegorization into a triumph of the soul's resurrection over death: part of the process called *interpretatio christiana*, whereby pagan rites and stories were given a Christian meaning. Charles and his well-educated daughters had some, perhaps extensive, knowledge of *The City of God*: it seems plausible, then, to infer their familiarity with the alle-gory. Modifying my earlier suggestion that the daughters chose the sarcophagus themselves, I now think that they and their father together chose it, and planned some time before for its use at Aachen.

Louis, after arriving at Aachen in triumph, very rapidly removed the *coetus qui permaximus erat femineus*, 'the crowd of women which was very large'.[132] Charles had arranged for several of them to reside in wealthy convents, and his wishes were carried out. Now Louis would be master in his own palace and his own empire: his father's heir in charge of a new regime. He would reside, increasingly often, at other palaces. Charles remained at Aachen, in his sarcophagus. When it was opened, long years later, Charles's body turned out to have been wrapped in a shroud of beautiful gold and Tyrian purple silk, made in Constantinople, with a pattern showing a charioteer in a four-horse chariot. Was it Charles's *familiarissimus pontifex* Hildebald of Cologne, or Charles's daughters, who had been storing that silk against the day when Charles needed it?

Not long after January 814, a monk at the Italian monastery of Bobbio (which had been founded by St Columbanus, d.615) wrote a *planctus*, a lament, for Charles. After capturing Pavia, taking over Lombardy and assuming the kingship, Charles had made Bobbio a lavish gift of woodland and the estate of Montelongo in a charter in which he en-titled himself, for the first time, king of the Lombards.[133] The lament's twenty stanzas express sentiments that are largely generic yet not merely conventional. I have chosen eleven of them to convey the breadth and depth of the poet's vision and the sheer range of those whom he thought had been affected by Charles's death.

From the rising of the sun to western shores
A lament beats breasts.
Alas for me who am wretched.

Beyond the seas huge sadness touches men in battle-line
With extreme grief.
Alas for me who am wretched.

Franks, Romans, and all believers,
Are stabbed with sorrow and great trouble.
Alas for me who am wretched.

Children, old men, glorious bishops
And married women, lament Caesar's loss.
Alas for me who am wretched . . .

O Christ, you who govern the hosts of heaven,
Grant peace in your kingdom to Charles.
Alas for me who am wretched . . .

Woe to you, Rome and to the people of Rome,
Now that Charles, greatest and glorious, is lost.
Alas for me who am wretched.

Woe to you, Italy, the uniquely beautiful,
And woe to all your honoured cities!
Alas for me who am wretched.

Francia, who has suffered terrible injuries,
Has never suffered such grief till now.
Alas for me who am wretched . . .

O Columbanus, restrain your tears
And pour out prayers to Lord for him –
Alas for me who am wretched.

– 'Father of all, merciful Lord,
Give him a place most glorious.
Alas for me who am wretched.

Receive into a holy citadel with your apostles,
O thou Christ, Charles who loves you.'
Alas for me who am wretched.

By Way of Conclusion

Just because this book *is* a biography, I have kept the focus, as far as possible, on the course of Charles's life. I have been attentive to ongoing trends and changes in the world that surrounded him, his responses to those, and to the contingencies that occurred around him and sometimes ambushed him, and the social structures that framed his life. I have kept to a chronological sequence: a life through time.

In the early seventh century, Bishop Isidore of Seville (*c.*560–636) in his encyclopedic work, *The Etymologies*, transmitted the knowledge of Antiquity to early medieval Europe. In Book XI, ii, *De homine et portentis*, 'About human beings and portents', Isidore identified six ages of man, expanding on these in thirty-seven sections. The six ages were:

Age	Years
Infantia	0–7
Pueritia	7–14
Adolescentia	14–28

In Charles's time, the first three ages were identified in terms quite commonly used, and their meanings were fairly precise. The next two ages were seldom named as such, and were *im*precise:

Iuventus	28–50
Gravitas	50–70

And finally came

Senectus	70 +

Senectus too was a term quite often used, though not in any very specific sense: it meant, in general, old, or aged. In fact, only very seldom did a man (especially a layman of elite status and therefore obliged to engage in warfare) survive to anything approaching seventy or over and thus enter Isidore's sixth age. Charles himself died at sixty-five, in what Einhard wrote of as old age: *senectus*.

Einhard's *Vita Karoli*, c. 4, put a spoke in any subsequent biographer's wheel by denying knowledge of any evidence, written or oral, about Charles's *nativitas, infantia vel etiam pueritia* ('birth, infancy or even boyhood') though he said, near the end of the *VK*, that Charles had been imbued with the Christian religion *ab infantia*, 'from infancy'. The term *adolescentia*, defined by Isidore as youth, or young-man-hood, was associated with the acquisition of military skills. *Iuventus*, meaning the age of a mature soldier or officer, spanned the years from twenty-eight to fifty, while *gravitas*, denoting the authority and dignity of a man of much experience in public affairs, stretched from fifty to seventy. The terms *adolescentia, iuventus* and *gravitas* do not feature in Einhard's *Vita Karoli*, nor are they at all common in other texts of the period.

Interestingly, Charles's life fitted, more or less, into Isidore's six-age scheme. In Chapter 3 of this book, Charles makes his entrée, in a series of five appearances: first in *infantia* (section i) when at the age of three he (probably) witnessed his parents' consecrations in 751 and certainly (section iv) rode out nearly 160km to escort the pope to the palace of Ponthion in 753; then as a boy in *pueritia* witnessing the ceremony of translating St Germain's remains to a new tomb in 755 (section v), and (probably) participating in assemblies and informal discussions with his father and his father's counsellors later in the 750s (section viii), and then as a young man in *adolescentia* (section ix) with his parents and younger brother attending and formally consenting to the re-founding of the family monastery of Prüm in 762. In the course of the 760s, he learned in Maine and in Aquitaine the arts of war and peace, and (taking the end of *adolescentia* to last until the mid-770s) after his father's death, he continued these learning-processes in Saxony and Lombardy. The years from the mid-770s through to 798 completed the age of *iuventus*, in which Charles demonstrated his maturity, his acquisition of the skills of military and governmental leadership, and the pushing outwards of territorial expansion in Slavic regions and in Danubia. *Gravitas*, the age of authority and dignity embodied in the role of judge or count, entailed maximum administrative and legislative activity, and took Charles to the threshold of *senectus*, and death. Isidore's six ages can provide a useful framework for today's historians.

I have left until now a brief discussion of some foundational historiography, especially pertinent to Charles's imperial years. Two scholars, the Belgian François-Louis Ganshof (1895–1980) and the Austrian Heinrich Fichtenau (1912–2000), both writing shortly after the Second World War about Charles, his empire and his reign, are both still much read. Both reached very wide audiences because their major works were translated into English – Ganshof's in 1971, Fichtenau's in 1968. My own generation, and the present one, owe these historians huge debts. Had Ganshof not attended so closely to the two capitularies Charles produced in 811 as wake-up calls for religious and lay elites to examine their souls, their full significance would not have been appreciated, and nor would the significance of what Ganshof christened 'the Programmatic Capitulary', had his articles on institutions and government not laid bare the astonishing dimensions of that reforming programme.[1] In a paper published in 1947, however, Ganshof had already set out arguments for what he had become convinced was *l'échec de Charlemagne*, 'Charlemagne's failure': 'When declining years limited [the emperor's] powers of intervention', wrote Ganshof, 'the symptoms of disorganisation and disintegration increased ... The state of the empire in 814 was one of profound malaise.'[2] And in a paper published in Switzerland in 1948, Ganshof diagnosed, not 'failure', but 'decomposition':

> During the years 801–814 ... the Carolingian state experienced as never before ... the symptoms of ... malfunctioning of the public service, arbitrariness and extortion ... One has only to read the capitularies ... [There was] a great deterioration ... when [Charles's] physical and mental powers started to fail.'[3]

In the last sentence of that 1948 paper, Ganshof added: 'It was an empire already far advanced on the road to decomposition ... in 814.'[4] Ganshof, to ground his analysis, had found a powerful analogy, in which the organic, physical decay of the ruler's own body mirrored the decay of the body politic.[5]

In this case, the analogy was false: Charles in his sixties remained a keen huntsman and swimmer.[6] Einhard mentioned many portents, but no signs of Charles's deteriorating physical or mental powers until his last months. It seems that illness and *senectus* became visible only then. The *ArF* author noted that Charles went hunting in the Ardennes in the summer, but suffered from gout, and so returned to Aachen to convalesce. Einhard reported that 'at the very last stage of his life when he was now being oppressed by both illness and old age (*iam et morbo et senectute premeretur*)', Charles in August 813 summoned his last surviving legitimate son from Aquitaine to Aachen, and there, at a great assembly on Sunday 11 September 'he crowned Louis co-emperor with a golden crown'.[7] Einhard added: 'After that, as usual, though weakened by age, he went out to hunt not far from Aachen, and passed the rest of the autumn in this exercise.'[8] It is hard to infer decomposition from Charles's activities in 813, let alone to extend that back to the preceding decade.

In *Das Karolingische Imperium*, published in Switzerland in 1949, Heinrich Fichtenau was fundamentally pessimistic about Charles's efforts to pull together an inherently unruly 'great empire' (*Großreich*):[9]

> The aging emperor was forced to continue to govern with the help of the nobility who had made his rise to power and greatness possible. There was no change in personnel – the basic condition of all reform. He tried to strengthen the loosened ties between ruler and ruled through a renewal of the imperial oath . . . [and] there was one spiritual weapon, which Charles recognised and had already tried to use during the first part of the crisis: it was to win back the grace of an estranged God through fasting and prayer.[10]

But Fichtenau thought these efforts ultimately in vain. 'The Carolingian humanists moved . . . in a Christian atmosphere. But Christianity was not offered in its fullness but only, as it were, in an abridged edition.'[11] My own view is that Fichtenau underestimated the changes in personnel and effectiveness of Charles's efforts at reform.[12]

Why did Ganshof miss any ray of optimism when looking back on the decade after 802, and why did Fichtenau strike such a pessimistic note in *Das Karolingische Imperium*? I think, in part at least, it was because both were writing amid the still all-too-visible ruins and horrors of the immediate post-war years. By 1950, the mood had changed and European integration was on the agenda. This was the year in which some leading European politicians decided to award the

'Charlemagne Prize' to a public figure or body 'distinguished by their outstanding work toward European unity or cooperation between its states'. The ensuing decade saw the formation of the basic institutions of the European Economic Community and, by the 1970s, of the European Union – whose icon Charlemagne had become.[13] His acquisition of an 'iconic' status came to represent a quite other kind of significance: a 'longing for Charlemagne'.[14]

During Charles's lifetime his annexation of Lombard Italy had huge consequences in terms of transfers of knowledge and power. Because the Lombards were direct heirs to so much of Italy still visibly Roman in landscape, law and culture, their experience had much to teach the Franks. Charles, and the men who served him, learned from Lombards how to exercise power locally and at a distance. The turns-of-the-wheel in dynastic succession signalled change that Charles could plan for (as he did, spectacularly, in 806 and 813) but hardly control. As with Charles's Italy, so with Charles's Francia: the choice of key personnel, and their management once appointed, required a communications network that functioned well. There is plenty of evidence that Adalhard's treatise reflected governmental realities, not figments of an overheated imagination.

In the course of the ninth century, and what is nowadays known to historians as the post-Carolingian period, a thick mythic layer was overlaid on the world Charles had left and which was steadily being reconfigured in the ninth and tenth centuries. Now, in the twenty-first century, the historiography is transforming views of the Carolingian Empire, and judgements on Charles, in ways Charles himself could never have imagined.

Charles was a practical, down-to-earth man with a down-to-earth sense of humour (his jokes show that): someone of whom a French-speaker, had there been such a person in the eighth century, might have said *'se sentait bien dans sa peau'*, 'felt good in his own skin'. This was a consistent trait, evident from his early childhood on, through his boyhood and adolescence, and thereafter throughout his life. It enabled him not only to be an effective leader in war but to manage and adapt institutions, form and apply administrative practices, and create and sustain bonds of loyalty that worked well in peace. Through Charles's long life, threads and continuities can be traced and found to recur as Charles himself recalled memories of his parents and his kin and his own past. It was not Charles but an idiosyncratic poet who, in the so-called 'Paderborn Epic' early in the imperial years, fleetingly represented something like a Roman vision of Europe. Charles himself had no such vision, no truck with teleology.

In the imperial years, bombarded by communications and knowledge transfers from all over his empire and from many peoples far beyond it, Charles learned of attacks from Saracens and Moors in the Mediterranean in 806 and 807, and attacks from Denmark in 808 and 809. He personally demanded information from the Holy Land about the state of churches there in 808. There were always administrative problems in need of solving and rectifying, and from 801 onwards, Charles devoted near-obsessive efforts to administrative detail.[15] He experienced unforeseeable, sad, contingencies: the deaths of three of his children, Rotrud and Pippin in 810 and the Young Charles in 811.[16] He wept, but continued to govern and plan and organize.

There was so much that was going right: expanding efforts at control 'on land and on sea' in 810; promises kept – as in checking that the money to be sent to the Holy Land churches in 810 was sent;[17] painstaking care taken over the questionnaires sent out to bishops in the autumn of 813;[18] the question of the succession – every dynasty's bugbear – resolved satisfactorily in August 813 (but as in all such cases, only *pro tempore*, for the time being).[19] Charles's attitude to signs and portents was as down-to-earth as his sense of humour. He would ignore these when it suited him, and otherwise take them seriously. I have tried to show these aspects as complementary rather than contradictory. I have *not* tried to follow Charles's post-mortem influence in the reigns of his son and grandsons, nor to trace the construction of stories nor the making of myths about him in subsequent times, though I am well aware that other scholars have thrown much light on these.[20]

Within a decade of Charles's death, the monastic community at the Reichenau had produced, in prose and in poetry, the story of a monk's vision of Charles in the afterworld, being tormented by a beast gnawing at his genitals to punish him for his sins – obviously of a sexual kind – in life. This is the story with which Johannes Fried chose to begin his recent book on Charles: 'Rain, pouring rain. A man was standing in the deluge, at the foot of the Mountain of Purgatory.'[21] The story had an upbeat ending: the visionary was assured by his next-worldly guide that 'Charles's sins would be effaced by the mass of his good deeds and that he would joyously enter the place the Lord had set aside for him'. Needless to say, the story never was for popular consumption, but rather for a monastic audience that, to judge from the number of manuscripts, was extremely limited. Though the story's relevance to the mid-820s is clear, it does not belong to the biography of Charles.

My quest, first and foremost, has been to trace a life in time. I have tried to grasp the complex personality of this exceptional man, and the experiences and memories that helped to form it. I have also tried to offer readers as much of the evidence as possible, and convey it as clearly as possible. What emerges most clearly is Charles's driving energy, his consciousness of the divine blessing that powered it, and his trust in his faithful ones (*fideles*) who, thanks not least to Charles's religion, had come to share that consciousness.[22] The biographer looks for his/her subject's agency: in this case, the agency's source was crystal-clear to the subject himself. In one of his last letters, a diplomatic one to the Byzantine Emperor Michael (811–13), Charles affirmed that Christ had deigned to establish long sought-after and always-desired peace between the eastern empire and western (*'in diebus nostris diu quaesitam et semper desideratam pacem inter orientale atque occiden-tale imperium'*) – long sought-after indeed, and deeply satisfying to Charles himself that peace was so soon to come (as it did) 'in our days'.[23] In practice, and of necessity, Charles focused on what was happening in the here and – especially – the now.

What I hope to have conveyed in this book is something of his multifarious impact on his contemporaries, on his days, and on his world. As a historian, I have necessarily looked backwards. But I have not, I hope, looked teleologically for what was coming, as if that was foreordained: as if, in my bones, I believed Charles was the Father of Europe. That would indeed have been a vain quest. *My* quest has been of a different kind. I have made a journey towards the Other. I have not found him – that would be ridiculously too much to hope. But perhaps I have got nearer to him – and encouraged new generations of historians to get nearer still.

Notes on the Illustrations

p. xxxvi Bronze equestrian statuette of Charles

Debate has centred on the rider's identity: Charles, or his grandson Charles the Bald (r. 843–877). Donald Bullough nearly fifty years ago made a strong case for Charles, the subject of this book. The master bronze-worker was inspired by a late antique equestrian image of the emperor Marcus Aurelius, Theodosius, in Rome, and the similar statue of Theoderic brought from Ravenna to Aachen in 801. The image recalls the riders depicted on the miniaturized triumphal arch made by Einhard in his capacity as silversmith, sometime in the 820s, for the monastery of St Servatius Maastricht (whose lay-abbot he was), and representing Constantine and Charles. Not until the twentieth century did this masterpiece get the place in the Louvre that it deserves. (Bullough 1975; Gaborit-Chopin 1999.)

p. 34 The tomb of Abbot Willibrord at Echternach

Charles's grandparents had been patrons of Willibrord (d. 739). Shortly before 750, the abbot's remains were moved from a too-short marble sarcophagus to a miraculously elongated one, which was placed to the side of the main altar inside the monastery church, enclosed by sculpted stones forming a chancel. The priest celebrated mass facing the congregation and beside the altar, making the tomb visible and accessible. Echternach became a major pilgrimage site. (Alcuin, *Vita sancti Willibrordi* c. 25; Dierkens 2009.)

p. 66 The River Oise at Quierzy

The residences of mayors and of kings acquired a quality that modern historians have called *palatialité* or *Pfalzlichkeit*. They were places of government but also of sociability. Quierzy was the highest navigable point on the River Oise, not far from major Roman roads linking Soissons to Noyon and to Cambrai. Excavations at Quierzy in 1916–17 revealed traces of a large hall, brightly painted walls and ceramics, concentric walls around the enclosure and, nearby, a monastery, possibly serving as a palace-church. In the 750s through to the 770s, Quierzy was a favoured Carolingian residence, prompting the suggestion that Charles himself may have been born there. (Weise 1923; Lohrmann 1976; Barbier in Renoux, ed., 1995.)

p. 94 The skeletal remains of Himiltrud in the crypt at Nivelles

Charles married his first wife, Himiltrud, of noble Frankish birth, shortly before Pippin's death. The couple's first child was born *c*.770. Charles repudiated her in late 771, perhaps immediately sending her to the great Carolingian convent of Nivelles. She was still alive and active in 792, but the year of her death is unknown. Her remains in the crypt of Nivelles, indicating a woman aged 35–40, were identified in the 1970s by the presence in the grave of a tile inscribed 'Himiltrud died in Christ on 29 May' (I, though not all scholars, accept the identification with *this* Himiltrud). (M. Hartmann 2009: 97, 205–6)

p. 120 The Great St Bernard pass

Charles first ventured into Italy in 773–4. He initially tried to negotiate with King Desiderius of the Lombards, but it soon became evident that there was no alternative to crossing the Alps. The obvious route took the most experienced part of his forces, under the command of Charles's uncle, across the Mons Iovis (later known as the Great St Bernard Pass), while Charles himself took the slightly less demanding route via the Mont-Cenis. The two armies joined up, and their Lombard opponents fled before them back to Pavia. This turned out to be a crucial point in the reign. (Bachrach 2013)

p. 150 The pass of Roncesvaux

Charles's Spanish campaign of 778 was at one and the same time a high-risk affair and a well-planned strategy. Einhard's account stresses tactical difficulties that could not have been foreseen. The politics of the Spanish March were hard for the Franks to read: local rulers within the Umayyad Amirate travelled to Francia to make their own risk-assessments, and manufactured opportunities for working within the amirate when those became available. The larger part of Charles's army returned safely to Francia. His reaction to the loss of the rearguard was as much as anything a personal one – he had somehow failed his most trusted men. A lesson had been learned. Collins 1999: 66–8.

p. 180 Saxon sword

Saxons and Franks have often been contrasted, as if one ethnicity and culture was very different from the other and, in the end, a superior Frankish society triumphed over an inferior one. 'Ulfberht' swords used to be cited as symptomatic of the Franks' technological superiority. More recently, archaeologists have shown that Frankish and Saxon material cultures were technologically very similar. That these societies integrated remarkably fast owed much to Charles's vision. They became, as Einhard remarked, 'one people'. Christianity was only one element in the fostering of intermarriage and social exchange between these groups. (Springer 2004; Rembold 2014; Flierman 2017)

p. 210 The papyrus letter of Maginar

This unique survival attests to the difficulties of diplomacy when Charles's agents were operating in Italy; it also attests the skills of the agents involved. Charles, having annexed the Lombard kingdom, worked in different ways to create alliances with the Lombard principalities (aka duchies) of Spoleto and Benevento. The years 787–8 proved a turning-point in this story. Charles's decision, against papal advice, to allow the Lombard prince Grimoald, whom he was in effect holding hostage, to go back to rule Benevento made it possible to enlist Beneventan help in effectively countering Byzantine hostility. In the longer run, Spoleto remained part of the kingdom of Italy, while Benevento and other south Italian cities grew their own independent regimes. (F. Hartmann 2006.)

p. 242 The Tassilo Chalice

Still in the treasury of the abbey of Kremsmünster, the Tassilo Chalice represents the glory days of the dukedom of Bavaria under Tassilo and his wife Liutpirc (aka Liutperga), a daughter of the Lombard King Desiderius and Queen Ansa. Liutpirc and Tassilo had married probably in 763. She and Tassilo were co-patrons of this beautiful object, and with it they endowed the abbey. The upper ring of images shows Christ with the Greek characters *alpha* and *omega* and 'I' and 'S' for *ihesus soter* (Christ the Saviour) and the evangelists. Around the bottom are the words '+*Tassilo Dux fortis* +*Liutpirc virga regalis*', 'Tassilo the brave leader, Liutpirc the royal rod [or branch]'. Irish scholars, notably Bishop Virgil of Salzburg, helped make the ducal court a centre of learning. (Nelson 2007, X; Airlie 2012, III : 98–100)

p. 268 The Rhine–Mosel confluence at Koblenz, near St-Goar

For Charles and his contemporaries the confluence of these rivers was an important routeway but also a navigational hazard. In 790, Charles and his two elder sons embarked on a river journey to visit the monastery of St-Goar, Charles in one boat, his sons in others. The weather turned threatening, visibility shrank to nil, and at the confluence the water roiled. Charles and his sons lost contact. Charles feared he might drown amidst the whirlpools – as boatmen still did until modern times. Charles's sons, following on behind, fared better: they took the chance to make peace with each other. (*The Miracles of St-Goar*)

p. 300 The new coinage, 793

Charles issued a new coinage in 793, which effectively continued throughout Charles's reign. Unlike the pre-reform issue of pennies (*denarii*) weighing 1.3 grammes, and unlike an ensuing issue which bore Charles's portrait image but was very short-lived, the 793 issue consisted of pennies each of 1.7 grammes and of remarkably high fineness (about 93 per cent). The great majority of coins were characterized on the obverse by the inscription CAROLUS REX FR surrounding a cross, but a relatively small number carried on the reverse Charles's monogram, surrounding the name of the mint – as in the example shown here (PAPIA, for Pavia), found in a small hoard from Trier. The output of monogram-coins from Melle in Poitou (the major silver mine of the period) rose impressively; Italian mint outputs also increased. Foreign coins were excluded from circulation, but finds of single Arabic dirhems and increasing numbers of Charles's coins in hoards and as strays show the increasing volume of coinage travelling with traders and pilgrims along the trade routes through Italy and along the Rhine. Charles left his successor 'a monetary economy in robust health and on an upward trajectory'. (Coupland 2018: 450. Cf. Coupland 2005)

p. 320 The church at Aachen

The building of a capital at Aachen had started as a twinkle in Charles's eye c.786, and the project began in the late 780s. The church was the priority, but it was a decade or so before the octagon in its heart, surrounded by a sixteen-sided ambulatory, and the upper-storey with its beautiful marble columns, were in place. The plan was based on mathematical principles of number symbolism extracted from Scripture, especially the Book of Revelation. The inscription around the octagon, with its references to 'living stones' and to 'the lord who created this great hall', bonded people and ruler, and surrounding all was God's protection. The building of the palace came second, and in the latter years of Charles's reign it too was taking shape. (Fried 2016: 358–70; Kraus, Müller et al. 2013.)

p. 346 Lateran Mosaic with St Peter, Pope Leo and King Charles

In the late 790s, Pope Leo III transformed the built landscape on the Lateran Hill. Two imposing triclinia (banqueting halls) were constructed. The larger's mosaics as seen nowadays are reconstructions made in 1743 from sixteenth-century drawings. In the central apse Christ delivers his mission to the apostles ranged to either side him, as in Matthew 28: 19–20: 'Therefore go forth and teach all peoples, baptising them in the name of father, son and holy spirit . . . ' ('Euntes ergo docete omnes gentes, baptizantes eos in nomine Patris et Filii et Spiritus sancti . . . '). To the viewer's left, Christ enthroned hands keys to St Peter on his right, while Christ hands a banner to R. Costantinus (King Constantine) on his left. To the viewer's right, St Peter enthroned hands a *pallium* (a scarf, symbol of episcopal office) to the most holy lord Leo on his (Peter's) right and hands over to the lord king Charles to his (Peter's) left, while beneath St Peter's feet a cartouche contains the words: 'Beate Petre donas vitam Leoni PP [papae] et bictoriam Carulo regi donas' ('Blessed Peter, you give life to Pope Leo and you give victory to King Charles.'). (Luchterhandt 1999: 55–67; Williams 2010: 184–9; Fried 2014: 409–11)

p. 388 The noble warrior with his sword

The chapel of St Benedikt at Mals in the val Venosta is one of a small number of churches in the South Tyrol built in the seventh and especially the later eighth century. Far from being marginal, this region was a mesh of routeways linking Francia and south Germany with Italy. Though the lords of Mals can't be identified, they evidently constituted a rich and powerful elite whose members bought into the Frankish takeover of Rhaetia and Lombardy and displayed their wealth and power by commissioning painters of vivid frescoes (often strongly Lombard-influenced) in their churches and offering patronage to local religious communities (like the convent of St Johann at Müstair, see Chapter 5). The two donors of the little church at Mals had themselves depicted, the clerical one (to the viewer's right), carrying the church's model, the lay one (left) bearded and with well-combed hair, carrying a mighty sword symbolizing protection: a unique surviving image of a lordly layman in the age of Charles. (Philipot and Mora 1977; Nothdurfter et al. 2003; Mitchell 2013)

p. 416 A small section of the *Breve commematorium* (*The Short Report*), 808

Charles, now emperor, assumed the role of protector of the ecumenical church. According to Einhard (Vita Karoli, c. 27), 'he would send money to poverty-stricken Christians in Syria and Egypt, as well as Africa, and to Jerusalem, Alexandria and Carthage'. *The Short Report* was the result of investigations in the Holy Land by Frankish administrators carried out on the spot with the aid of local officials. A copy survives in the Public Library of Basel University. The little sample here reports on 'a monastery of 26 girls, of whom 17 nuns who serve at the Holy Sepulchre are from the empire of the Lord Charles'. Travel went in more than one religiously inspired direction. (McCormick 2011)

p. 456 A small section of the cut-marble inlays (*opus sectile*) in Charles's church at Aachen

A thread runs through Charles's interest in antique marbles and mosaics, starting from his first brief, yet (it transpired) unforgettable, visit to Ravenna (787), continuing through his request to Pope Hadrian (later in 787) to approve the sending of such items across the Alps, and eventually culminating in the extensive use of these materials at Aachen. Recent research in the interior of the church has revealed the extent of the sumptuous original *opus sectile* work on the north side of the upper storey just metres from the throne. Charles and his architects were inspired not only by key passages in the Old and New Testaments and the ideological models of Christian Roman emperors but also by the buildings and methods they saw displayed in Rome and Ravenna. (Mitchell 2012)

Notes

I. INTRODUCTION

1. Hannig 1982: 199; Nelson 2018b.
2. Bourdieu 1986; Truc 2011.
3. Leyser 1979: 1.
4. Collins 1998b; Favier 2000; Becher 1999a, Eng. trans. 2003; Barbero 2000, Eng. trans. 2004; Ehlers 2002; Kintzinger 2005; McKitterick 2008; Williams 2010; W. Hartmann 2010; Fried 2013, Eng. trans. 2016; see also Ubl 2015.
5. Hägermann 2000; Fried 2016.
6. See further P. Brown 1967; St Augustine, *Confessions*; Stafford 2006; Nelson 2006; Caine 2010: 66–84.
7. Ganz 1983; Hellmann 2000, 2018; Garipzanov 2008a, 2018.
8. Tischler 2001, I: 1–240.
9. Patzold 2013; 193, 195–7.
10. Ganz 2008: 5.
11. *Vita Karoli* c. 22, trans. Ganz. The *Lives* from which phrases are lifted are (in order of citation) those of Tiberius, Caligula, Claudius, Titus, Nero, Tiberius, Augustus, Tiberius again, and Titus.
12. Coupland 2005: 213, 2018: 432–3.
13. *Gesta Karoli* I, 24, II, 4, with acknowledgements to two earlier translators, Thorpe 1969, and Ganz 2008; cf. Nelson 2006: 26.
14. 'The Making of Charlemagne's Europe', online database, dir. Rio. For the form-documents on which charters were very often based, see Rio 2008a, 2009, and briefly, section (iv) below.
15. Davis 2015, esp. ch. 6.
16. Bullough 1962; Davis 2015: 369–72.
17. McKitterick 1989, 1990, 2004, 2008; G. Brown 1994.
18. Poetry: Godman 1985 with selected Eng. trans., 1987.
19. Letters: Garrison 1994, 1998a, 1999; papal letters: Hack 2006–7; partial Eng. trans., King 1987; Alcuin's letters, partial Eng. trans. Allott 1974.

20. Annals and Chronicles: Collins 1998a, 2005; McKitterick 2004, 2008: 33–8; Davis 2015: 179–205; Garipzanov 2010; Eng. trans. of the Royal Frankish Annals, King 1987, partial Eng. trans. of so-called minor annals.
21. Hincmar of Reims, Quierzy Letter (858), Eng. trans. Nelson 2018, online Stone blog.
22. Horse-pestilence, Ch. 10 (iv); famines. Ch. 6 (x), Ch. 10 (xii), Ch. 15 (ii); loss of trusted men, Ch. 6 (ix) and (x), Ch. 12 (viii).
23. Theophanes, *Chronicle*, eds. Mango and Scott 1997.
24. King 1987: 41.
25. Eng. trans. R. Davis 1992.
26. Heather 1991, 1996, 2009; Ewig 2001: 26–7, 38–9; Wood 2018: 21–30.
27. Wood 1994, 2018: 86–7, 93–4.
28. Rio 2008a, 2008b, 2009.
29. A phrase part-borrowed from Anderson 1974: 153. See also Fouracre 1995.
30. Goody 1966b: 1–56 illuminated this subject. For the Huosi, see Hammer 2018.
31. Fouracre 2000: 70–71.
32. Wood 2018: 61.
33. Braudel 1972–3: 354–94; Parker 1998: 47–50.
34. Reynolds 1997: 254, 'that which pertains to a kingdom or kingdoms'.
35. Lohrmann 1976: 121–99; Barbier 1990: 245–99, esp. 284–90.
36. Bernhardt 1993; McKitterick 2008: 171–8; Duindam 2011.
37. Pestell and Ulmschneider 2003.
38. Naismith 2014: 3–39.
39. Wickham 2009: 232–54.
40. McCormick 2008: 83–97.
41. Wickham 2005: 541.
42. McCormick, Dutton and Mayewski 2007: 865–95.
43. Ariès 1960, ET 1962.
44. Kempf 2013: 82–3.
45. *Life of Pope Gregory II*, Eng. trans. R. Davis 1992: 8.
46. *Empires of Faith*, Sarris 2011.
47. *Chronicle of 754*, cc. 69–81, Eng. trans. Wolf 1990: 138–45.

2. FAMILY STORIES CHARLES MIGHT HAVE KNOWN

1. Reimitz 2015: 204–9, 256–7, 264–91.
2. Fouracre 2000: 38.
3. Fouracre and Gerberding 1996: 330–49, Eng. trans. 350–70.
4. Nelson 1996: 194, n. 75, 2002: 279.
5. For the story of Swanahild and Grifo, see pp. 54–5, 58–9.
6. Wood 2004; Fouracre and Gerberding 1996: 301–19 (with discussion of the miracles at 305–7), Eng. trans. 319–26, 327–9.

7. Fouracre and Gerberding 1996: 302–4.
8. Wood 2004: 235–9, 255.
9. Fouracre and Gerberding 1996: 301–18.
10. Gerberding 1987: 92–115, 150–59.
11. Nelson 1991: 149–63; McKitterick 2004: 6–13.
12. *LHF* c. 46–51, pp. 370–74, Eng. trans. 177–80; Gerberding 1987: 146–72; Fouracre 2000: 6–7; Reimitz 2015: 240–81. See below for the two wives of Pippin 'II'.
13. Bede *HE* V, 10, 11.
14. *HE* V, 10.
15. *HE* V, 11; Scharer 2014: III, 60–61.
16. *HE* V, 11.v.
17. Wampach 1930, no. 3.
18. *HE* V, 11.
19. Wood 2001: 43.
20. Collins 1994: 235–47, 1996: 112–17; Fouracre 2000: 6–8, 78; McKitterick 2004: 124, 138–40.
21. Collins 1996: 116.
22. Gerberding 1987: 115, registers the impression made on contemporaries by Grimoald's death: *LHF* c. 30; Cont. Fred. c. 7; compare *AMP*, pp. 19–20: '*Plectrudis . . . muliebri consilio tanti regni habenas tractare presumebat. Quod cum crudelius quam oporteret astu femineo disponere decreverat, iram Niwistrium Francorum in nepotis sui interitum . . . celeriter convertit*' ('Because [Plectrud] had decided to rule with feminine cunning more cruelly than was necessary, she quickly turned the wrath of the Neustrian Franks to the destruction of her grandson and the leaders who were with him', Eng. trans. Fouracre and Gerberding 1996: 365).
23. Fouracre 2000: 45–8; Wood 2006: 30, 186, 201; cf. Innes 2000: 13–50.
24. Heidrich 2001, no. 4. See further Fouracre 2000: 45–6.
25. Heidrich 2001, no. 5.
26. Wood 2006: 116, 223–4.
27. Bede *HE* V, 10; Alcuin, *Vita Willibrordi*.
28. Smith 2016.
29. I. Wood 2001: 81–2; S. Wood 2006.
30. Drews 2009: 45–6, 174–91, 223–8.
31. *LHF* c. 48.
32. *LHF* cc. 52, 53.
33. Heidrich 2001, no. 8, 24/25 June 715; *LHF* cc. 49–51, Cont. Fred. c. 8; for Drogo's marriage to the Neustrian heiress Anstrud, *AMP* p. 16, Eng. trans. p. 362.
34. On these names, Stoclet 2013: 34, 43–5, 52–4, 63–4.
35. *LHF* c. 48; Cont. Fred. c. 6.
36. Karras 2006; Kaschke 2006: 81.
37. Goody 1966: 2.
38. *LHF* c. 49.

39. Heidrich 2001, no. 6, pp. 66–9.
40. There is no evidence that Grimoald had any son other than Theodoald, '*ex quadam concubina*', 'by some concubine': Cont. Fred. c. 6.
41. Schieffer 1994: 306–7.
42. Gerberding 1987: 133–4; Fouracre 2000: 61–2 stressed that in May 716, Lambert's remains were translated to Liège, where he was culted by Martel's branch of the family.
43. *LHF* c. 50, '*iubente avo*', 'on his grandfather's command'.
44. Fouracre 1984.
45. Cont. Fred. c. 8. See below.
46. Gerberding 1987: 129.
47. See Map 2. The otherwise good maps of both Gerberding and Fouracre lack a scale.
48. Fouracre 2000: 197 offers a genealogy of 'Plectrude, her sisters and their descendants'.
49. See above, n. 40. Cf. I. Wood 1994: 271.
50. *LHF* c. 51; Cont. Fred. c. 8.
51. Offergeld 2001: 301–3. Perhaps the story of Theodoald in *LHF* c. 51 faintly echoes that of Chlothar II in *LHF* c. 36. Cf., differently, but for partly similar reasons, Sigebert of the East Angles, Bede *HE* III, 18.
52. Gerberding 1987: 135.
53. *Ann. Mos.* s.a. 725. On Carloman, Cont. Fred. c. 23, and on the charter-evidence for his birthdate, Heidrich 1965/66: 241.
54. The choice of a child's name is usually assumed to have been the father's, but sometimes the mother seems to have chosen: see Alcuin, *Vita Willibrordi* c. 3, and Wood 2001: 80 with n. 9.
55. *AMP* s.a. 715; Haselbach 1970: 34. For a clutch of Pippinid names in western Bavaria, see Hammer 2008: 244–9.
56. Fouracre 2000: 61. Cf. Gerberding 1994: 203–14.
57. Gerberding 1994: 214.
58. Jussen 2000.
59. Pippin, D. 30.
60. Gerberding 1994: 210–13.
61. I. Wood 1994: 271, and Fouracre 2000: 62.
62. *LHF* c. 53.
63. Wampach 1930, nos. 8, 26; S. Wood 2006: 123; Mordek 1994: 346.
64. Fouracre 2000: 70–71.
65. But cf. Cont. Fred. c. 19: Martel with an army of Franks 'laid waste with terrible bloodshed the area where the Lippe flows into the Rhine and commanded that a part of that most fierce people become payers of tributes to him and he received a great many hostages from them'. Cf. Carloman's campaigns in 743 and, with Pippin, 745, and Pippin in 749.

66. Mordek 1994; Jarnut 2002: 67– 88.
67. Fouracre 2000: 71, commenting on Martel's 'energy and military skill' as among the reasons for his 'growing ascendancy'.
68. Fouracre 2000: 122, 127, n. 10.
69. Heidrich 2001, no. 9.
70. Fouracre 2000: 64–78, traces these processes with consummate skill.
71. Heidrich 2001, nos. 12, 13.
72. '. . . ad praedicandum plebibus Germaniae gentis ac diversis in orientali Reni fluminis parte consistentibus', Heidrich 2001, no. 11, c. 723.
73. Ep. 46, p. 295; cf. Ep. 21, pp. 269–70.
74. Reuter 1980: 81.
75. Tangl 1916: no. 19.
76. Karlburg, named for Martel. On Carloman: Reuter 1980: 78 with n. 73. Martel's plan to divide realm before 741: Kaschke 2006: 85–6.
77. Lifshitz 2014: 16–28, for optimistic readings of some later texts, and passim for new and often persuasive readings of mid-eighth-century manuscripts produced by nuns at Würzburg.
78. Gibbon, Decline and Fall of the Roman Empire ch. 52; Pipes' blog: www.danielpipes.org/blog/2005/03/gibbon-oxford-and-islam.
79. Wickham 2005: 340.
80. Chronicle of 754, Wolf 1990: 143–4.
81. Collins 1989: 90–91; Collins 1994: 238–9; Fouracre 2000: 87–8, 148–9.
82. Wood 2001: 10, 60; Palmer 2014: 147–50.
83. Reuter 1994.
84. Wolfram 1994; I. Wood 1995a; Fouracre 2000: 137–43.
85. Wolfram 1994; Rio 2008a: Angers no. 6, Marculf II nos. 5, 9, 39, 40, 41 and pp. 285–6.
86. S. Wood 2006: 222 and n. 16.
87. S. Wood 2006: 114; charter evidence fails, except for Heidrich 2001, no.14, see below. For the gap in the charter-record, Fouracre 2000: 100–101.
88. Ann. Petav. s.a. 723.
89. Heidrich 2001, no. 12, contra Collins 1994. On this, the AMP is too late to trust.
90. Ann. Lauresham s.a., p. 24; see interesting reflections of Collins 1994: 229–35.
91. Goody 1966: 30, 46; cf. Kasten 1997: 110.
92. Heidrich 2001, no. 12 (1 Jan 723), rejects the suggestion of Collins 1994: 229–35, that the 'Thiedold', who is the eighth attester, was Theodoald, son of Grimoald.
93. Heidrich 1965/66: 241.
94. Dierkens 1994: 292, n. 112; Schieffer 1994: 310, with n. 32.
95. See D. 8 (755).
96. Cf. Wyss 2001; Stoclet 2013: 99–178.

97. D. 12 (759).
98. D. 14.
99. *Miracula Sancti Dionysii*, ed. Mabillon, pp. 343–64, at 347–8.
100. *LHF* c. 53; Stoclet 2013: 72–85, with a vivid scenario of St-Denis as an *abbaye des dames*.
101. Kasten 1997: 244–5, 257–8, bringing clarity to modern debates about what remains a fuzzy scene.
102. Schieffer 1994: 309, is sceptical about psychological defence against stepmothers in successive generations. Cf. Kasten 1999: 61, 65–6.
103. Fouracre 2000: 157–68.
104. Hildegar of Meaux, *Vita Faronis*, c. 78, p. 193, '*carmen publicum iuxta rusticitatem*'; *LHF* c. 41.
105. Fouracre 2000: 155–74.
106. Rotrud may have died in or soon after giving birth to a third child, her daughter Hiltrud; if so the girl was aged fifteen when she had an affair with Odilo of Bavaria, see p. 57.
107. Grifo was of age by 741 when he attested a charter (Heidrich 2001, no. 14) along with his mother.
108. Becher 1993: 99, on a similar claim s.a. 744, and cf. 143 on mayors receiving oaths on behalf of kings. Childebrand, a.k.a. the Continuator of Fredegar, does not mention this.
109. Paul the Deacon, *HL*, VI, 43: see Jarnut 2002: 78, 101–5, 149–50, for the importance of these marriage-alliances.
110. See Schieffer 1992: 43; M. Hartmann 2009: 94.
111. For Childebrand's '*Hauschronik*', Kaschke 2006: 99–130; for 748, cf. above Ch. 1.
112. Geary 1985; Fouracre 2000: 96–9.
113. Cont. Fred. cc. 14, 18, 20, 21.
114. *Cod. Car.* 1 (739) and 2 (740), pp. 476–9; Cont. Fred. c. 22.
115. Cont. Fred. cc. 23, 24. I discount two much later sources at this point: the *AMP*, and the *Breviarium Erchanberti*, though Kaschke 2006: 85–6 argues for more than a grain of truth in the story of an earlier division plan in 737, stymied by the resistance of King Theuderic IV.
116. Kaschke 2006: 84. If Childebrand's silence was deliberate, it reinforced the impression that he favoured Pippin. For Drogo, Cont. Fred. c. 30; Becher 1989; Heidrich 2001, nos. 15 and 16.
117. Jarnut 1994; Jaschke 2006: 82–3; Stoclet 2013: 179–209.
118. Balzaretti 2005: 361–82, at 377.
119. Wickham 1994: 275–94.
120. Kasten 1986: 13–15, and 1997: 118–19, suggesting the eldest, Adalhard, was born *c.*751.
121. Cont. Fred. c. 21.
122. Clay 2010: 228–9, and 349–56.

123. Becher 1989 on Tassilo; Becher 2003; Kaschke 2006: 81–9 keeps a cool head, for instance playing down the influence of Swanahild and also of Odilo and Hiltrud.

124. Cont. Fred. c. 24.

125. Cf. Einhard, *VK* c. 32, on portents preceding the death of Charles; see Scharer 2014.

126. Cont. Fred. gives Martel the title *princeps* seven times in the early 720s, then again repeatedly from the mid-730s, meaning 'the leader' or 'the chief'.

127. For stays in the Oise-valley palaces, Schieffer 1992: 48. Cont. Fred. c. 24; Heidrich 2001, no. 14, 17 Sept. 741, is attested by Swanahild and Grifo. Childebrand names neither but mentions in c. 25 that Hiltrud acted 'on the malign counsel of her stepmother [i.e. Swanahild]', when she joined Odilo in Bavaria after Martel's death. (Swanahild's only previous mention is in c. 12, on events on 725; Grifo's only mention is his death-notice at c. 35.)

128. Nelson 2000: 140–41.

129. Schüssler 1985: 59–87.

130. *Ann. Lauriss.* s.a. 741; Collins 1994.

131. Ep. 48, Tangl 1916: 76–8; Clay 2010: 356–7, and cf. 212. Tangl suggested that Boniface sent alternative versions of the letter to Grifo, and to Carloman and Pippin. The awkwardness of the shift from singular to plural tenses in the letter as it survives indicates awkwardness and uncertainty on Boniface's part at the moment he dictated it.

132. *AMP*, p. 32; *ArF* s.a. 741, p. 3.

133. Cont. Fred. c. 25: '*contra voluntatem vel consilium fratrum suorum*'.

134. Fouracre 2000: 167, points out that Pippin's marriage to Count Charibert's daughter in 744 may have been connected with the count's handing over of Grifo in 741. See also Nelson 2007: IX, 98. In the St-Gall *Liber Confraternitatis*, Swanahild was commemorated as *regina*, M. Hartmann 2009: 94.

135. Fouracre 2000: 167 notes the coincidence and infers a double-deal. Pippin secured Grifo's release from Carloman's custody in 747, according to the *AMP*, pp. 39–40.

136. Cont. Fred. c. 35.

137. *ArF* 742. For a shrewd and measured account, Kaschke 2006: 86–9.

138. Kaschke 2006: 86, 'an improvised assembly', citing Airlie 2004: 115, for the armies' role as a 'political community'.

139. Cont. Fred. cc. 25, 26.

140. Ep. 50, p. 82; Concilium in Austrasia habitum quod dicitur Germanicum, ed. A. Werminghoff, MGH Conc. 2. 1, Conc. Aevi Karolini I, no. 1, pp. 1–4.

141. Fouracre 2000: 139–41; cf. Renard 2009.

142. Hartmann 1989: 48–50.

143. Nelson 2004: 96, citing Werner 1982.

144. Hlawitschka 1979: 45, n. 176, cited in Nelson 2004: 97, n. 13.

145. Reuter 1991: 58, 60, evidently referring to *Ann. Petav.* s.a. 746.

146. Cont. Fred. c. 29 (746): '[*Carlomannus] cum magno furore ... plurimos eorum ... gladio trucidavit*'; c. 30 (747): '*Carlomannus devotionis causa inextinctu succensus, regnum una cum filio suo Drohone manibus germano suo Pippino committens, ad ... Romam ob monachyrio ordine perseveraturus advenit. Qua successione Pippinus roboratur in regno.*' Cf. *ArF.* s.a. 745, p. 4, written some forty years later, stressing the genuineness of Carloman's vocation, taking care to mention that Pippin was in the know, sending his brother 'honourably, with gifts', but without any mention of Drogo.

147. *Ann. Petav.* s.a., MGH SS I, ed. Pertz, p. 11: '*Karolomannus intravit Alamanniam [ubi fertur quod multa hominum milia ceciderit. Unde compunctus regnum reliquit et monasterium in castro Casino situm adiit].*' Of the two manuscripts, that from the abbey of Massay in Berry contains the bit indicated in square brackets: Werner 1979: 132–4. Cf. Goosmann 2015: 56, 'a somewhat obscure set of annals', but cf. Stancliffe 1983: 159–60, 171, and the *Annales Petaviani*.

148. *ArF* s.a. 745, p. 4.

149. Stancliffe 1983; Heidrich 1994; Becher 1989, 1992. See Fouracre 2000: 170–74.

150. Boniface Ep. 79, pp. 171–2.

151. Foot 2005: 90–99.

152. Collins 1998a: 2–6; Collins 1998b.

153. Becher 1993.

154. McKitterick 2004: 19–20.

155. McKitterick 2008: 39–43, 159, 379, and ch. 5 passim.

156. Compare the scenario presented by Collins 1998b: 31, with that now established by the accumulated efforts of Boschen 1972, Becher 1992, and Heidrich 1994, and Becher again 1999a: 37–42 (Eng. trans. 2003: 35–7); Nelson 2004: 93–108 (repr. Nelson 2007: ch. IX); M. Hartmann 2009: 95; W. Hartmann 2010: 33–4, 39–40; Fried 2013: 61.

157. By contrast, the late tenth-century manuscript from St-Omer got the names right but the date wrong: '749'.

158. Cathwulf, Ep. *ad Carolum* (*c.* 775), ed. Dümmler, MGH Epp. 4, p. 502.

159. Story 1991: 11, 18–21; Stoclet 2013: 72–5.

160. *De divortio, Responsio* 12, p. 182: '*Haec ideo episcopi dicimus, non quo puellarum virginalia vel feminarum secreta quae experimento nescimus scientibus revelare aut nescientibus insinuare velimus, sed quoniam scriptum est: "Causam quam nesciebam diligentissime investigabam"* (Job 29: 16)'. See the searching analysis of Airlie 1998, esp. 23.

161. *Ann. Petav.* s.a. 747 – the annalist's year ran from Easter to Easter, and Easter that year fell on 24 April, 748, meaning that for the annalist, Charles had been born on 2 April 747: '*Karolomannus migravit Romam et ipso anno fuit natus Karolus rex.*' The day and month are given in a Lorsch Calendar dated by Bischoff to the first half of the ninth century: Werner 1972 (1975), 116; Becher: 1992, p. 37, n. 5.

3. THE CHILD IN THE PICTURE

1. Fried 2013: 21, for the exception; see below pp. 291–2.
2. Fried 2013: 19.
3. Dep. Seine-et-Marne, Heidrich 2001, no. 18, and cf. no. 60; cf. also Stoclet 1989. In locating Pippin's Council of Ver, 11 June 755, Boretius, MGH Capit. I, no. 11, p. 33, and Werminghoff, Conc. II, no. 8, p. 5, suggested Ver-sur-Launette, dep. Oise. There are other possibilities. See Stoclet 1989: 148.
4. Einhard, *VK*, c. 25.
5. Brühl 1968: 18–19. Martel convalesced at Verberie in 738: Cont. Fred. 21. Compare the places mentioned in narrative sources with those mentioned in charters and Quierzy emerges as a major residence.
6. McKitterick 1989, 1990 are full of thought-provoking suggestions.
7. *VK* c. 25.
8. Williams 2010: 305. Fried 2013: 36 regrets that no (contemporary) historian thought to mention Charles's wet-nurse, or any of his early teachers.
9. Berschin 1991: 139–46; Banniard 1995: the age of Martel was pre-diglossic but evolving that way; cf. Lupus, Ep. 91 (844), hoping to send noble youths from Ferrières to Prüm to learn German.
10. Heidrich 2001, no. 23, pp. 113–17. The charter is an original, but undated: circumstantial evidence means before 22 October.
11. Kasten 1997: 124–5.
12. Weidemann 1998: 211, n. (g), dates within November but further precision impossible.
13. Schieffer 2004; cf. Buc 2001.
14. Cont. Fred. c. 33: '*praecelsus Pippinus electione totius Francorum in sedem regni cum consecratione episcoporum et subiectione principum una cum regina Bertradane, ut antiquitus ordo deposcit, sublimatur in regno*'. Collins 1996: 113–17.
15. *Cod. Car.* 3, pp. 479–80.
16. Cont. Fred. c. 33 cf. *ArF* s.a. 749, names the envoys as Bishop Burchard of Würzburg, a follower of Boniface, and Abbot Fulrad of St-Denis, both with experience of transalpine diplomacy; see Stoclet 1993: 454–62.
17. Hen 2004.
18. Nelson 1986a, ch. 12. Cf. Hack 1999.
19. See Ch. 2 for councils of Estinnes and Soissons; on Pippin's way with monasteries, Semmler 1975.
20. de Jong 2001.
21. *Chron. Lauriss. brev.* s.a. 750; *Ann. Lob.* s.a. '*Hildricus rex depositus in monasterio s. Medardi est attonsus*'. *ArF* s.a. 752: '*Pippinus . . . elevatus est a Francis in regno in Suessionis civitate*'. Zacharias's successor Stephen II in 753 wrote to the leaders of the Franks in a letter carried by

Abbot Droctegang of Jumièges, urging them to put pressure on Pippin to support the interests of St Peter: *Cod. Car.* no. 5, p. 488. See below, n. 24.

22. Nelson 1977, 1987, repr. 1996; Angenendt 2004.

23. Angenendt 2004; cf. Nelson 1977, repr. 1996.

24. Claussen 2004: 27–8, and cf. 219–20, for interest in ritual in another context.

25. Pössel 2009: 116–17, 122, 124.

26. Nelson 1987, repr. 1996; Angenendt 2004.

27. Cam 1924: 568, where a man called Harvey, soon after 1148, in the shire-moot of the two counties of Norfolk and Suffolk, says, 'I declare, testify and affirm that 50 years have passed since I first began to come regularly to hundred courts and shire courts with my father, before having a household of my own, and after that on up to now.' My thanks to Susan Reynolds for this reference. Cf. Bloch 1961: 114. For baptism, Nelson 2014c.

28. Nelson 2014c.

29. *Ann. S. Amandi* s.a. 751: '*Pippinus in regem unctus est apud Suessiones*'; Schneider 2004: 250–51; cf. Schüssler 1985: 77; Gerberding 1987: 151.

30. Nelson 2007; Airlie 2012: ch. 3.

31. Foucault 1978, 2007.

32. Davis 2015.

33. Esders 2012.

34. For details on Chrodegang, see Claussen 2004: 20–28, 253–6.

35. *Vita Stephani II* cc. 16–24: an unusually detailed account to highlight the significance of Stephen's journey.

36. Cont. Fred. c. 37, pp. 302–5.

37. *Vita Stephani II* cc. 26–7, trans. Davis, pp. 63–4.

38. Pippin, D. 16, p. 22; *Cod. Car.* no. 11.

39. *Vita Constantini I*, trans. Davis, p. 91; Buc 2005: 32.

40. See Ch. 2, pp. 46–7.

41. Angenendt 1980; *Cod. Car.* 8 (756), 11 (757).

42. See also Goodson 2015.

43. *ArF* s.a. 755, p. 12.

44. The information about Pippin's grant is included in an original charter of Charles in 778, DD Kar. I, D. 122, pp. 170–71.

45. Fried 2000, and 2013: 34–5 and 636, n. 2.

46. Becher 1992: 50–54; Hartmann 2010: 42–3; Nelson 2003: 24–8.

47. *Translatio S. Germani*, ed. G. Waitz, MGH SS XV (i), pp. 5–9. The interpolation may actually have been part of the early ninth-century story.

48. Einhard, *VK* c. 33; Verhulst 2002: 16–17, 20, 69.

49. Tomas Kalmar (pers. comm.) kindly sent me the following comments: 'If a man says, "I remember losing my first milk tooth", he is telling you something about his relationship with his body – past and present. If a man says, "I remember participating in a *translatio* when I was a child", he is telling

you something about his relationship to a ritual exercise of power that seems exotic to us but was paradigmatic in Carolingian life. If he links these two – *translatio*/tooth – he is telling you something rather intimate about his personal private hermeneutic praxis.'

50. LP *Vita Stephani II* c. 52.

51. LP *Vita Pauli* c. 3.

52. LP *Vita Pauli* c. 3; on the cult of Petronilla, Goodson 2015.

53. *Ann. Petav.* s.a. 757.

54. *Cod. Car.* no. 14, p. 511.

55. Buc 2005: 34–7.

56. Angenendt 1980: 57–63.

57. *Cod. Car.* 21, 29, 32, 42, 43. Hack 2006–7: i, 278–81.

58. Hack 2006–7: i, 128–9, 442–6.

59. Helvétius 2015: 161–8.

60. Fried 2013: 38.

61. Paul the Deacon, *Liber*, trans. Kempf 2013: 76–7; Oexle 1967.

62. F. Hartmann 2009.

63. Kempf 2013: 78–81; cf. Wood 2004.

64. Sestan 1970: 367.

65. F. Hartmann 2009; Kempf 2013: 1–6, 78–81, 82–6.

66. Cont. Fred. cc. 37–8.

67. *Ann. Petav.*; *Ann. Naz.* s.a.; Hack 2006–7: ii, 697–704.

68. MGH Capit. I, no. 14, prol. p. 33, c. 6, p. 34.

69. Capit. I, no. 14 (755), c. 20, p. 36, c. 25, p. 37.

70. Capit. I, no. 16 (756), c. 9, p. 41 (dating, Mordek 1995: 1081).

71. Capit. I, no. 15 (757), c. 9, p. 38: '*Homo Francus accepit beneficium de seniore suo, et duxit secum vassallum, et postea fuit ibi mortuus ipse senior et dimisit ibi ipsum vassallum; et post hoc accepit alius homo ipsum beneficium, et pro hoc ut melius potuisset habere illum vassallum, dedit ei mulierem de ipso beneficio, et habuit illam aliquo tempore; et, dimissa ipsa, reversus est ad parentes senioris sui mortui, et accepit ibi uxorem, et modo habet eam. Definitum est, quod illam quam postea accepit, ipsam habeat.*'

72. Cf. Cam 1924.

73. For the palace as consisting of people (*homines* – including women), Hincmar, Quierzy letter, 858, MGH Capit. II, ii, no. 297, pp. 427–41, at 431; Airlie 2009.

74. See Ch. 2 for Bertrada's connections with St-Denis.

75. DD. Pippini nos. 2 (25 April 752, at Herstal), and 14 (10 June, 760, at Verberie).

76. Depreux 2002: 175.

77. D. 3, requesting perennial prayers at Prüm for our '*memoria* and that of our wife Bertrada' (p. 5).

78. D. Pippin no. 16 (14 August, 762, at Trisgodros, probably Trigorium, near Koblenz). Nelson 2004 (repr. 2007): 96–7.

79. Only two other charters, D. 1 (752) and D. 12 (759), both of which are judgments, include lists of judges within the formal record in the traditional way. Only one man seems to appear in DD. 1 and 12 and also in D. 16: Crothard/Rothard/Chrodard, and there is disappointingly little overlap between the witnesses in Pippin's two charters issued when he was still mayor of the palace (Heidrich 2001, nos. 18 (748) and 22 (751) and D. 16), and Gerhard is the only one of D. 16's counts to have appeared in earlier charters (Garehard in Heidrich no. 18 and Gerihard in D. 1). Priceless evidence for continuity of service across a reign, available for a very few Carolingians, is barely visible in Pippin's case.

80. Smith 2016: 442.

81. Ibid.: 453.

82. Cont. Fred. c. 41: 'going through Berry as far as the Auvergne, ravaging that region, and burning most of Aquitaine' (*per pago Bitorivo usque Arvernico accessit; regionem illam pervagans, et maximam partem Aquitanie igne concremavit* (760)), and forcing Waifar to give oaths and hostages; *Ann. S. Amandi Cont.* s.a. 761, p. 10: '*Pippinus fuit in Vasconia cum Karolo et Claremonte igne cremavit*'; *Ann. Petav.* s.a. 761, p. 11: '*iterum Pipinus fuit in Wasconia una cum Karolo: captoque omni pago Alvernico, Burboni castro et Claromonte igne cremavit*'. Contemporary writers did not distinguish Gascony from Aquitaine.

83. *Ann. S. Amandi Cont.* s.a. 762, p. 10: '*iterum Pippinus pergens in Wasconia cum Karolo et Carlomanno superavit Wascones*', 'again Pippin campaigned in Gascony, with Charles and Carloman, and overcame the Gascons'; *Ann. Petav.* s.a. 762, p. 11: '*Iterum domnus Pipinus cum dilectis filiis suos Karolo et Karolomanno perrexit in Wasconiam, et adquisivit civitatem Bituricas*', 'again the lord Pippin with his beloved sons Charles and Carloman campaigned in Gascony and captured the *civitas* of Bourges'. For doubts on ArF's account of Charles's and Carloman's receiving of oaths from Tassilo in 757, Becher 1993: 35–45; Kasten 1997: 128, n. 274. Cf. Cont. Fred. c. 51, for Gascons' oaths to Charles and Carloman in 768, and comments of Becher 1993: 119 and n. 525.

84. *Ann. Petav.* s.a. 762, p. 11.

85. Kasten 1997: 129, n. 280.

86. *Ann. Petav.* s.a. 763, p. 11; *Ann. Laureshamenses* s.a. 763, p. 28.

87. Kasten 1997: 130.

88. *Cod. Car.* no. 26, pp. 530–31; see also nos. 29, 33, and for Paul's gifts of rings set with hyacinths to both Charles and Carloman (as well as one to their father), probably in 758, *Cod. Car.* no. 17, p. 517; Hack 2006–7: ii, 823.

89. See below Chs. 4 and 5.

90. Hack 2006–7: i, 261–2, 454–5.

91. Cont. Fred. cc. 41–51, ed. Haupt 1982.

92. Cont. Fred. cc. 47, 50.

93. Bachrach 2001b: 241, stresses the 'complexity and sophistication' of Pippin's 'campaign strategy'. His index contains no entries for 'burning', 'ravaging', 'laying waste', or 'vineyards, destruction of'.

94. Fouracre 2000: 144–5, for the dynamics of competition within 'accepted rules and obligations'.

95. *ArF* rev. s.a. 767, p. 24.

96. McCormick 1994: 113–31, and for the quotation, McCormick 1995: 365; see also Close 2011: 73, 77–9; Helvétius 2015: 165. Cf. above Ch. 1. In his last extant letter, *Cod. Car.* no. 43, p. 558, Paul once more addressed Gisela fondly.

97. Astron. c. 21; above Ch. 2, p. 57.

98. McCormick 2004: 222–3.

99. Cont. Fred. c. 50.

100. A journey of nearly 400km, assuming he and his forces took a Roman road south to its junction with the Via Agrippa, the *via magna* roughly east–west from Lyons to Saintes.

101. Cont. Fred. c. 51. Cf. Becher 1993: 119, n. 525.

102. Cont. Fred. cc. 51, 52.

103. It was at this point, Nibelung reported, that Pippin got news that the envoys from the caliph had arrived in Francia. McCormick 2004; 231–40, deftly identifies ingredients in 'a strange brew of insightful but flawed information' (I would add, with an unappetizing dash of inconsequential chronology . . .).

104. *De ordine palatii* c. 22, l. 360, p. 72.

105. Borgolte 1976; Kennedy 1981; McCormick 2004.

106. McCormick 2004, cf. above n. 89.

107. *ArF* s.a. 777. See below Ch. 6.

108. Cont. Fred. cc. 52, 53.

109. Capit. I, no. 18, pp. 42–3. McCormick 2004: 230. By July, when Pippin issued a charter at Poitiers for St-Hilary (D. 24, datable only to the month in this ninth–tenth-century copy), he was struggling north to reach Francia and St-Denis.

110. DD. 8 (755), 12 (759), see above Ch. 2, p. 53.

111. DD. 25, 26, 27 (all dated to 23 September 768, D. 27 surviving as an original). Kings and monasteries often used immunities in alliances that were mutually strengthening; see Davies and Fouracre, eds. 1986: 272; Rio 2008a: 131–7.

112. D. 28 (September 768).

113. Cont. Fred. cc. 53, 54; Kaschke 2006: 123–5, 130.

114. Haupt 1982: 8; Collins 1998b: 116–17, and 1998b: 38 with n. 74. Cf. Ch. 2 (vi) for the Continuators as patrons/commissioners of the work rather than authors in the modern sense.

115. *Cod. Car.* 45, p. 561.

116. For Charles's height, see Ch. 1, p. 7. For Himiltrud's, see the photograph of her skeletal remains in Nelson 2014c: 435, illustration 3.

117. M. Hartmann 2009: 97–8.
118. MGH Epp. III, no. 19, p. 326; Nelson 2000, p. 142 with n. 40, was too credulous where Suger's twelfth-century claim was concerned. Cf. preferably Angenendt 1994: 68–80.

4. FAMILY FORTUNES

1. I owe this observation to Stuart Airlie.
2. Kaschke 2006: 130.
3. Samoussy: an inference from Carloman's charters DD. 43 and 44; Aachen: Müller in Krause, ed., 2013: 32–6; Rollason 2012: 431–2, 435–7, 439; Rollason 2016. Geopolitics explain why Charles did not winter again, or indeed stay at all, at Aachen until 788–9. Schüssler 1985: 60 offers a plausible reconstruction of the boundary between the kingdoms of Charles and Carloman.
4. Paris, Archives nationales K 5, no. 121, CLA XV, no. 608, Introduction to sections 3–6 and p. 63.
5. Garipzanov 2008: 175, on the monogram. For Byzantine visitors, see McCormick 1994: 131.
6. Bullough 1991b: 127. Schaller 2011: 135, 169–73, disagrees, on the grounds that Hitherius didn't visit Italy until after 769.
7. The terms 'chancellor' and 'chancery' appealed to nineteenth-century charter-scholars.
8. Stoclet 1993: 97–8, 108, 158–66; Semmler 2003; Nelson discusses D. 55 on the MCE website, xx.
9. Contra Stoclet 1993, p. 95, n. 3.
10. Rosenwein 2000, 2001.
11. Stoclet 1993: 95, n. 3.
12. Cf. Schaller 2011: 135, 169–73.
13. Hitherius received the abbacy of St-Martin, Tours, in 775 or possibly 777, Bullough 1984: p. 77 and n. 12.
14. *ArF* rev. 769, p. 29.
15. *Cod. Car.* 44, pp. 558–9; cf. Dep. 27, Hack 2006–7: ii, p. 964.
16. Mornac, D. 58, Angeac, D. 59.
17. Cap. 18, pp. 42–3. The place of issue might have been Angoulême or Angeac, but Saintes seems likeliest.
18. McKitterick 2008: 80, 237.
19. Pippin, Capits. nos. 13–16.
20. *Admonitio generalis*, eds. Mordek et al., MGH 2013, p. 180; Schmitz 2002: 279.
21. I am grateful to Julia Smith for seeing these alternatives.
22. *ArF* s.a. 769, pp. 28, 30.
23. Davis 2015: 43–5; 104–6 with n. 98; cf. Krah 1987: 7–9.

24. Capit. no. 18.
25. Capit. 24, esp. cc. 1 and 2.
26. D. 60. Historians generally assume, other things being equal, that the formulaic assertion to the effect that a charter-beneficiary turned up to receive the document in person expressed a reality. Angers, on the north bank of the Loire, was some 130km north of Chasseneuil.
27. *Vita Stephani III*, c. 16.
28. *Vita Stephani III*, esp. cc. 17–33. Davis 1992: 85, suggests that this *Life*, and the first 44 chapters of Hadrian's, were written up shortly after the Frankish conquest in 774, whereas 'much' of the *Vita* of Stephen II was 'a first-rate piece of contemporary chronicling', Davis 1992: 51.
29. McKitterick 2008: 78.
30. Jarnut 1993; repr. Jarnut 2002.
31. *Vita Stephani III*, c. 17, p. 96, and n. 42.
32. Kasten 1997: 139. There is no strictly contemporary evidence for the birth-year of Charles and Himiltrud's son; 'before 770' is inferred from his later career, see M. Hartmann 2009: 97. There is no reference in *Cod. Car.* 44 (770) to children of either Charles or Carloman.
33. *Ann. Petav.* s.a.770: '*nativitas Pipini filii Karlomanni*'. The name of Carloman's wife, Gerberga, is uniquely given by *AMP* s.a. 771, p. 58. Her anonymity, even in Einhard's *VK*, reeks of a *damnatio memoriae*.
34. There is a touching coincidence between the apogée of the League of Nations' influence and the appearance in 1932 of an article portraying Bertrada's agenda, '*elle rêvait d'inaugurer un équilibre général en occident . . . [et] d'une réconciliation européenne*': Delaruelle 1932: 215.
35. Jarnut 2002: 235.
36. *Cod. Car.* 48.
37. For Theoderic: Nelson 1998: 174–5; Heather 2016: 29–34.
38. Kamp 2001: 289, n. 74.
39. *Cod. Car.* 46, 48, are addressed to 'Bertrada and Charles', in that order.
40. Story 1991: 3, with n. 12, suggests that Cathwulf had served – and perhaps was still serving – at the Frankish court, 'in personal proximity to the king', possibly after an earlier stint as young Charles's tutor.
41. Cathwulf, MGH Epp. KA II, Epp. variorum no. 7, p. 502. The first five of a total of eight blessings, translated here, relate to the period up to 771. The remaining three blessings belong to 774, and will be discussed in their chronological place.
42. The story in Genesis of Esau and Jacob is confusing, and while Cathwulf's brief mention of it does not help, his preference for Jacob is clear. I have benefited from Jo Story's account of the list of blessings: Story 1991: 4.
43. Nelson 2004: 100–101 (repr. 2007, ch. 9).
44. Story 1991: 4.
45. Story 1991: 5–6.

46. The *castrum* of Seltz was an old Roman fortress, *Chron. Fred.* IV, 37, see Hummer 2005: 166–7. The Roman road south from Seltz led down via Brumath to Basel, then east to Constanz.

47. Seltz was within Charles's kingdom, but near the border with Carloman's, see Schüssler 1985: 60.

48. *ArF* rev. s.a. 770, p. 31 and *ArF* p. 30, record the visit to Carloman at Seltz.

49. If Bertrada went from Seltz to Tassilo's capital at Regensburg mainly by river, up the Rhine to Breisach, then 90km cross-country to Donauschingen, thence via the Danube from its source to Regensburg, this would have been a very much longer distance at 650km, but perhaps, downriver, a speedier one.

50. Conc. aevi Karolini I, no. 15; see W. Hartmann 1989: 93–4.

51. Pohl 2006. The letter was probably written by the *primicerius* Christopher, whose views on the Lombards came close to the unprintable.

52. A parallel hostility to *nefandissimi Greci* surfaces in papal letters of the 750s and 760s, and again in the 770s: F. Hartmann 2006: 172 (see below Ch. 6); Gantner 2013: 324–5; Stephen III's biographer wrote early in the pontificate of Hadrian: Davis 1992: 85.

53. Register XI, Ep. 13.

54. Gantner 2015: 329.

55. *Cod. Car.* 45, pp. 560–61 (trans. Nelson; the remainder of the letter is cited in the translation of King 1987, who gives only a summary of the first section).

56. *Cod. Car.* 47. The dating is that of Lintzel 1929, followed by Noble, 1984: 251 and n., and King 1987: 273, and it convinces, even though it would necessitate placing 47 and 46 out of chronological sequence in the *Codex Carolinus*. Cf. also Hack 2006–7: ii, 1076.

57. Hack 2006–7: ii, 992, 993.

58. *Ann. Lauriss.* s.a. 770; *Ann. Mos.* s.a. 770; *Ann. Petav.* s.a. 770.

59. *ArF, ArF* rev. s.a. 770, pp. 30, 31.

60. *Cod. Car.* 46, cf. above n. 33.

61. *Cod. Car.* 48, to Bertrada and Charles, dated by King 1987, p. 275, to 'about Easter 771', reporting the plot.

62. *VK* c. 18, p. 22: '*post annum eam repudiavit*'. This assertion is corroborated by Paschasius's *Vita Adalhardi* c. 7, ed. Pertz, p. 525: '[Adalhard, Charles's cousin and contemporary], who was then doing youthful service at the palace and being educated in the ways of the world, chose rather to be a friend of justice and truth than to consent to things unlawful. And so it came about that when the Emperor Charles repudiated the Italian king's daughter whom he had previously sought in marriage with the oaths of certain Franks, and the blessed old man [Adalhard] would not be persuaded to agree by any contrivance to the king's [i.e. Charles's] marrying again as long as [the Italian king's daughter] was alive, but instead condemned that in every way he could, and groaned that some of the Franks would thereby become perjurers and the king himself use an unlawful bed. He [Adalhard]

therefore chose rather to renounce the secular life while still a youth than to get mixed up in such business, and since he could not go against his kinsman [Charles] he showed by his flight his refusal to consent.'

63. Einhard, *VK* c. 20, p. 25. Contrast Stephen III's assertion that Charles's first partner was his 'wife': *Cod. Car.* 45.

64. *The Importance of Being Earnest*, Act 1 part 2.

65. Nelson 2009a: 11–12; Nelson 2014c: 423.

66. Stone 2012: 116–27, 247–310.

67. Fichtenau 1949: 35–6; Jarnut 1999: 67; Bredekamp 2014 oddly neglects this topic.

68. Stratmann 1997; Nelson 2000: 143–5, noting, n. 45, that Charles confirmed his brother's grant of Neuilly – his largest – to St-Remi, Réims.

69. In Picardy.

70. D. 63. The document is abbreviated. Cf. D. 73, dated 20 January 773, '*actum Longolare palatio*' (in southern Belgium).

71. Picardy, 18km south-east of Laon.

72. *ArF* s.a. 771, p. 32. Abbot Fulrad of St-Denis, a trusted adviser of Pippin, had served Carloman loyally, reaped predictable rewards for his abbey, and hesitated before joining Charles: Felten 1980: 218; Stoclet 1993: 242 with n. 2, 465–6 with n. 1. Warin and Adalard were counts in Alamannia, with ties to Hildegard's family: Borgolte 1986: 36 (Adalard), 286 (Warin).

73. *ArF* rev. 771, p. 33.

74. *AMP* 771, pp. 57–8.

75. W. Hartmann 2010: 49.

76. Cf. *LHF* cc. 40, 42, where *monarchia* identifies the position of Chlothar II in 613 and then Dagobert in 629, when each united the *tria regna* (of Burgundians, Austrasians and Neustrians).

77. This is the unerringly targeted phrase of M. Hartmann 2009: 99.

78. Einhard, *VK* c. 18, p. 23, '*filiam quam [Carolus] illa [Bertrada] suadente acceperat*'; cf. p. 22, '*cum matris hortatu* ('with his mother's encouragement') . . . *cum iam tres nepotes et totidem neptes in filii domo vidisset*'. Balance the judgement of Heidrich 1988: 10, that 'there is the impression that Charles had had enough, once and for all, of women's political influence and meddling', against the point that 'perhaps Fastrada was an exception', M. Hartmann 2009: 98, and the significant presence later in the reign of 'women at the court', especially Charles's daughters, Nelson 1996, 2002, and 2007. And see below Chs. 8, 9 and 12.

79. Walahfrid Strabo, prologue to Thegan, *Vita Hludowici Imperatoris*, and c. 2, pp. 176, 178.

80. *Divisio regni*, 806, c. 12. See below Ch. 15 (v).

81. Ch. 2, p. 61.

82. Borgolte 1986: 119–20. See D. 72 (772, or possibly 773 – the charter's date is missing).

83. Becher 1999a, Eng. trans. 2003: 122–3.
84. D. 65 (?late March, 772), Innes 2000: 50–56, 180–82.
85. I. Wood 1998; Reimitz 2015: 366–421.
86. Fried 2013: 154, citing Springer 2004, (rather inappropriately) '*passim*'. See also Rembold 2017, Flierman 2018.
87. Nelson 1988: 213–16; 1996: 108–12; Garrison 2000: 120–40; Reimitz 2015: Ch. 4.
88. Boniface Ep. 43; *Vita Lebuini antiqua*, c. 4, p. 386; Becher 1999b: 2; Springer 2004: 135–52.
89. Becher, in Stiegemann and Wemhoff, eds. 1999: 188–94, with Exponattexte IV, pp. 195–262, and Lampen ibid.: 264–72, with Exponattexte V, 273–312.
90. *ArF* rev. s.a. 775, p. 43.
91. Cont. Fred. c. 19, p. 288. Such superlatives were also part of biblically inspired papal rhetoric in the eighth century. See above, and esp. *Cod. Car.* 45.
92. Springer 2004: 182.
93. Pagan Abodrites as 'our Slavs', *Ann. Lauriss*, s.a. 798, p. 37, '*Sclavi nostri qui dicuntur Abotridi . . . et quamvis illi fanatici [i.e. pagans] erant, tamen fides christianorum et domni regis adiuvit eos et habuerunt victoriam super Saxones*'.
94. For ancient, classical and late antique historians, geographers, encyclopaedists, Anglo-Saxon chroniclers, Church historians and authors of saints' Lives, and Frankish sources on Saxons up to 772. Cf. Einhard, *VK* c. 29, p. 33 on *barbara et antiquissima carmina*, and the mid-ninth-century *Vita Faronis* c. 78, p. 193, for women dancing as they sang to celebrate the seventh-century triumphs of Chlothar II over the Saxons. More generally, see Springer 2004, chs. 1–8, pp. 162–5, 181, and also the exceptionally interesting Wood 2001.
95. For references in Gregory of Tours, Springer 2004: 97–111. For Fredegar, see above, Ch. 2. I'll continue to call this author 'Fredegar', as early medievalists conventionally do, though I'm aware that the attribution of that name dates from the sixteenth century.
96. *Chron. Fred.* IV, c. 75, pp. 244, 246; cf. Gregory of Tours *LH* 4, 14.
97. Springer 2004: 113.
98. Cont. Fred. c. 27.
99. Cont. Fred. c. 35: 'when he was heading for Lombardy and plotting against the king [Pippin]'. See Ch. 3 above. *Vita altera Bonifatii* c. 8, p. 44 hints at a delay between Pippin's taking the kingdom and his elevation to kingship because of a need 'to settle down the perturbation of peoples'.
100. *ArF* s.a. 753 and revised, pp. 10–11. Rehme some 8km south of Minden, on the river Weser, at its confluence with the Hase, and just west of the Süntel hills. These hills, seldom higher than 440m, form a 12km-long plateau indented with steep valleys. See also Clay 2010.

101. Paul the Deacon's Epitaph on Hildegard, written at Charles's behest and presumably on information supplied by Charles, indicates a marriage lasting almost exactly eleven years; *ArF* s.a. 783, p. 64 give her precise death-date as 30 April: Kempf 2013: 80–81.

102. *VK* c. 7, p. 9.

103. Goetz 1990: 125–9; Bernhardt 1993: 177, 322–3, Map 7.

104. *ArF* s.a. 772, pp. 32, 34; cf. *Ann. Petav.* s.a. 772, p. 16; *Ann. Lauriss* s.a. 772, p. 30.

105. Reuter 1991.

106. Cf. Exod. 17; 2 Kings 23.

107. Most historians have taken the Ermensul to be a singular object. Even if there were many Ermensuls, as Springer 2004: 162–5, suggests, there seems to have been one exceptionally important place of offerings. For Hildegard's brothers, quite young, though each perhaps old enough to be a *tiro* in the palace, see Borgolte 1986: 122–6, 248–52; Jarnut 2002: 125–6.

108. *Vita Sturmi* c. 23: 'since the young king wished to gain the favour of all those who had been honoured by his father, he bestowed large presents upon them . . . He summoned Sturm, renewed ties of friendship with him, and loaded him with honours and princely gifts'; see Jarnut 2002: 156–7; also D. 63 (3 November 771), a judgment between Sturm and a lay claimant to some of Fulda's property. Fulda's right was upheld.

109. The annalists box and cox with their information: *Annales Iuvavenses maximi* (Greatest Salzburg Annals), MGH SS XXX, part 2, p. 732: '*Adrianus papa factus est. Karolus in Saxoniam conquesivit Erespurc et Irminsul eorum destruxit. Tassilo Carintanos vicit*'; *Annales Sancti Emmerammi Ratisponensis maiores* (Greater Annals of St Emmeram Regensburg): '*Carolus in Saxonia conquesivit Eresburc et Irminsul, et Tassilo Carentanus* [sic]. *Adrianus papa factus est.*'

110. On Hadrian, see the discerning studies of F. Hartmann 2006.

111. *Vita Hadriani* c. 7.

112. *Vita Hadriani*, c. 9.

113. *ArF* s.a. 773.

114. *ArF* s.a. 773; *Lib. Pontif. VH* c. 22.

5. CHARLES IN ITALY

1. See Ch. 1 (iii) and many references in Ch. 3.

2. Einhard, *VK* c. 3, p. 6: '*nullis existentibus causis, spreto mariti fratris, sub Desiderii regis Langobardorum patrocinium se cum liberis suis contulit.*'

3. The graph at Nelson 2001a: 241 has been revised for this book (from 0 to 9 in 772).

4. For the *ArF*, see Ch. 1 (ii).

5. Taking the charter-count down to 775 brings the total up to 56, of which 30 had Neustrian elements.

6. In the year 772 the fall in the Neustrian element reflects Charles's military preoccupations in Saxony. In 775 the figures reflect Charles's stays at Quierzy and 7 donations to St-Denis, all surviving as originals.

7. Precious evidence on the ducal reign of Tassilo of Bavaria can be gleaned from the account of the antiquary Aventius (1477–1534), whose sixteenth-century German Chronicle version of the eighth-century Latin Annals by Tassilo's chancellor Creontius is now helpfully translated by King (1987) from the edition of S. Riezler (1881). Riezler 1881: 256–81; King 1987: 340–43.

8. The mentions of Düren as a residence in *ArF* for 769, 775 and 779 could suggest that Aachen, only 40km or so west of Düren, is meant.

9. *Lib. Pontif. VH* cc. 9, 23. F. Hartmann 2006: 113, deals briefly with Hadrian's negotiations with Desiderius in 772–3.

10. Cf. Ch. 4, p. 109 above, to *Life* of Stephen cc. 18, 20.

11. Pointedly, Helvétius 2015: 127–8.

12. Julia Smith, pers. comm., stresses the significance of this frontier-march.

13. *AMP* p. 57, and cf. Ch. 4, p. 108 above.

14. R. Davis 1992: 108.

15. *Vita Hadriani*, c. 9.

16. *Vita Hadriani*, c. 23.

17. *Vita Hadriani*, c. 25.

18. Davis 1992: 132, n. 35. See also Noble 1984: 131.

19. F. Hartmann 2006: 113, neatly adapting his ch. 4's epigraph from Greenblatt 1980: 141: 'One of the highest achievements of power is to impose fictions upon the world and one of its supreme pleasures is to enforce the acceptance of fictions that are known to be fictions' – this apropos Charles's first visit to Rome.

20. Ibid. pp. 15–28.

21. Ibid. p. 3. Cf. McKitterick 2006b: 46–51; 2010: 10–11. I have chosen not to call the author a biographer, because a *Vita* is not a piece of life-writing in the modern sense: see Ch. 1.

22. The document, known to historians as the Donation of Quierzy, is retailed in *Vita Hadriani*, cc. 42, 43.

23. R. Davis 1992: 119, and Commentary pp. 113–55. Cf. Hägermann 2000: 121, on archives and archive-keeping; and the excellent analyses of Costambeys 2007: ch. 8; Costambeys 2013.

24. Above, Ch. 1 (iii).

25. Noble 1984: 51; for an example, F. Hartmann 2006: 150.

26. R. Davis 1992: 107, calls this the 'historical' section. Cf. Hartmann's incisive chapter titles *Fakten und Fassaden* ('Facts and Façades', ch. 1) and *Schenkungen und andere Fiktionen* ('Donations and Fictions', ch. 4).

27. D. 74, an eighth-century copy.
28. D. 78. Wolfram 2013b: 251–60, puts all this in the historical context of a post-Roman hereditary prince-bishopric.
29. Wolfram 2013b: 253, 259.
30. Wolfram 2013b: 255.
31. For evidence that D. 78 was issued at Auxerre, see the note on this charter in Mühlbacher 1906: 111.
32. Heitmeier 2013: 143–75; Nelson 2015b: 234.
33. Mitchell 2013; Nothdurfter et al., 2003.
34. For Bernard, see *ArF* s.a. 773, p. 36; *AMP*, p. 60; Weinrich 1963: 11–12, 90–91.
35. D. 110 (Dec. 775); Bernard also appears in another judgment, D. 102, of 775.
36. *ArF* s.a. 773.
37. See sec. (ii) of the present chapter for the new ecclesiastical province of Tarentaise. Ross Balzaretti, pers. comm., notes that Aosta had been in Lombard control in Aistulf's reign, according to the eleventh-century Novalesa Chronicle, ed. Alessio 1982: 37.
38. *Vita Hadriani*, c. 26. On George: Hack 2006–7: ii, 1001–4, and Story 2003: 55–78, 87–91; on Vulfard: Hack 2006–7: ii, 1024–5; on Albuin: Hack 2006–7: ii, 1002, n. 53, but *pace* Hack, Bullough 1984: 73–94, convincingly argued that this was not Alcuin.
39. *Vita Hadriani*, c. 28 (Davis's translation with some phrases from King's).
40. *Vita Hadriani*, cc. 29–32 (Davis's translation, with borrowings from King's.)
41. The details of military movements in cc. 29, 30 are so circumstantial that, in the absence of other evidence, I have ventured to accept them. Unlike the *ArF*, the author of the *Life* of Hadrian makes no mention of Bernard and his forces at Mont Joux.
42. Einhard, *VK*, c. 6: 'Pippin [had fought in Lombardy] under great difficulties, for certain nobles with whom he usually consulted had opposed his wishes so strongly that they frankly (*libera voce*) declared they would desert the king and go home.'
43. *Vita Hadriani*, c. 31.
44. For hostages in threes, Kosto 2002: 134.
45. Nelson 1998: 183–4, repr. Nelson 2007: ch. X.
46. Rio 2009: 203 (Marc. II, 18; cf. I, 18, p. 151–2).
47. The motif of God scattering his enemies recurs often in the Old Testament: Ps. 68: 1; Exod.. 17: 8–16; Exod. 23: 27–8; Num. 10: 35; Joel 3.
48. *AMP*, s.a. 773, p. 60.
49. *Vita Hadriani*, c. 31.
50. *Vita Hadriani*, cc. 32–3 report the Lombards' dispersing, and defections from Desiderius in the area of Spoleto and in the former exarchate south of Ravenna. Other biblical echoes: Jos. 6: 20, Jos. 6: 1, in Cont. Fred. cc. 20, 44.

51. *Vita Hadriani*, c. 34.
52. M. Hartmann: 2009: 99–100.
53. Kempf 2013: 82–3.
54. Kempf 2013: 14, 16; and Ch. 1, p. 24.
55. D. 79, 'Idherius recognovi'; *Vita Hadriani* cc. 42, 43.
56. D. 79.
57. D. 62.
58. This probably explains why Charles chose him as an envoy to Italy in 775: *Cod. Car.* 52, 56, 57; see Ch. 6 below.
59. *Vita Hadriani*, c. 34.
60. It's unlikely that Charles ever did read the *Life* of Hadrian; the manuscript diffusion in Francia belongs to the period after Charles's death: McKitterick 2004: 121–2.
61. Goody 1966: 28.
62. *Vita Hadriani*, c. 35, ed. Duchesne I, p. 406.
63. *Vita Hadriani*, c. 35. The translation above follows closely that of King 1987: 193, who rightly renders *in extasi* as 'in consternation' (rather than Davis 1992: 138, 'with rejoicing' – a significant difference). Noble 1984: 139, sidesteps the translation issue by saying 'after Hadrian had recovered from the shock of learning that Charles was coming . . .' See now F. Hartmann 2006: 113–14, with nn. 5–7, and ch. 6, *passim*. The standard presented to Charles could have been the one depicted in the Lateran mosaic put up by Leo III in ?799, Goodson and Nelson 2010: 457–8, 465.
64. Above, Chs. 1, 3. Nelson 2002: 25–8; Smith 2016: 438–41.
65. McCormick 1986: 233, 254–5 with n. 111, 365, 372–3, noting Alcuin's Ep. 145 (798), Epp. IV, p. 235 (on his wish to be with the 'singing boys and palm-branches' when Charles returns to Aachen), and esp. 374.
66. For the *bandora*'s significance, see n. 63 above. See below, Ch. 13 (viii).
67. *Vita Hadriani*, c. 36. The Late Roman/Byzantine heritage is evident here: McCormick 1986: 255, n. 111, 372–5, 384–5.
68. *Cod. Car.* 14, p. 511.
69. Goodson 2015: esp. 183–4.
70. *Vita Hadriani*, c. 38, Davis 1992 p. 139; for the *confessio*, see Davis's Glossary, p. 238: 'originally the burial-place of one who had "confessed" Christ by martyrdom; hence the name for an area in front of an altar above a martyr's tomb, excavated to give closer access to, or sight of, the grave; some or all of the area might then be decorated with silver . . .'
71. Usually taken as referring to the agreement between Pippin and Stephen II at Quierzy in 754, Davis: cc. 26, 29; above, Ch. 3.
72. Schieffer 2002: 284.
73. *Vita Hadriani*, c. 43. The narrative of cc. 37–43 is dense: it is possible to infer that two separate oaths were taken on separate days, or even that two different accounts were spliced. I owe these suggestions to Julia Smith.

74. F. Hartmann 2006: 115–18.

75. *Cod. Car.* no. 45, p. 563, Eng. trans. King, p. 273.

76. Davis 1992: 142, with n. 69; *Vita Hadriani*, c. 43, ed. Duchesne I, p. 406: '*intus super corpus beati Petri subtus evangelia quae ibi osculantur pro firmissima cautela et aeterna nominis sui ad regni Francorum memoria propriis suis manibus posuit*'.

77. Nelson 2005c: 31.

78. MGH *Poet.* Lat. I, pp. 90–91.

79. For instances in the Carolingian period of besiegers from the north suffering terrible losses in Italy, see below, Ch. 13 (vii).

80. *Vita Hadriani*, c. 31, quoted above p. 131, 'when the Franks were willing to return home next day'; and cf. Einhard, *VK*, c. 6: Pippin's men in Lombardy 'had opposed his wishes so strongly that they frankly declared they would desert the king and go home' (n. 42 above).

81. Epp. Kar. Aevi. II, Epp. variorum no. 7, p. 502.

82. *ArF* s.a.; see also *ArF* rev.

83. *Ann. Mos.* s.a.

84. *Ann. Petav.* s.a.

85. *ArF* 774, p. 38: '*coepit et Desiderium regem cum uxore*' and '*venientes omnes Langobardi de cunctis civitatibus Italiae subdiderunt se in dominio domni gloriosi Caroli regis et Francorum*'; *ArF* rev., p. 39: '*civitatem ad deditionem compulit*'; Einhard, *VK*, c. 6: '*non prius [Carolus] destitit, quam et Desiderium quem longa obsidione fatigaverat, in deditionem susciperet*'. Cf. the surrender of Duke Tassilo, below, Ch. 8. For comparing the symbolism of power in early medieval states more generally: Drews 2009 (reviewed Van Berkel 2012), and Marsham 2009.

86. D. 80. This was the only charter Bobbio ever received from Charles. No grant from Pippin to Bobbio is documented.

87. Doubts about D. 80's reliability are voiced by Collins 1998b: 61–2; but cf. Balzaretti 2013: 100, 115–19.

88. D. 81. See Nelson 2010b: 118–26, and map.

89. Cf. Julia Smith's comments on Wilchar, quoted above, pp. 124.

90. Following the suggestion of Bullough 1984: 76–7 with n. 12.

91. For Adelchis's return in 788, see *Cod. Car.* 81, 83, 84; and below, Ch. 9.

92. *AMP*, s.a. 774. Above, Ch. 4, and for Wilchar in 773, above, pp. 124.

93. The next surviving charter, dated 2 September, was given at Worms.

94. *ArF* s.a. 774.

95. *Ann. Mos.* s.a. 774.

96. Hlawitschka 1960: 25–30; cf. Esders 2012: 425–7, 433–8.

97. A new abbess, the Lombard Richgard, was in post in 781: D. 135.

98. *Ann. Sangall. maiores* s.a. 774, p. 75. Though there is no charter-evidence of Charles having contact with Corbie after 769 (D. 57), its choice as Desiderius's monastic prison would have made sense: from Charles's standpoint, the

1,000km-distance between Corbie and Pavia posed a minimal security-risk. Adalhard, who had become a monk at Corbie in 771, soon moved to Monte Cassino, where he spent the rest of the 770s; Kasten 1986: 40.

6. PEACE AND WAR

1. Werner 1973: VII, 135; an exemplary piece of detective work.
2. Lampen 1999: 268–71; Springer 2004: 184–5. Whimsy has its place in academic discourse.
3. Nelson 2016b: 243–4. For context, see P. Brown 1967, 1971, 1996: 328–35; T. Brown 2016.
4. *Cod. Car.* no. 49, p. 568.
5. *Cod. Car.* no. 53, p. 575.
6. *Cod. Car.* no. 51, pp. 571–3.
7. *Cod. Car.* no. 54, pp. 576–7. Hack 2006–7: i, 463–5, 468–9. An internally dated letter is exceptional, Hack 2006–7: i, 141–3.
8. *Cod. Car.* no. 55, pp. 578–80.
9. F. Hartmann 2006: 216–21 convincingly explains Charles's position.
10. The Spoletans had 'elected' Hildeprand (first mentioned in the *Life* of Hadrian cc. 32, 33, Eng. trans. Davis 1992: 137 and nn. 45, 47) as their duke after his defection from Desiderius in 773. After briefly accepting St Peter's authority in 774, Hildeprand had recognized that of Charles in late 775/ early 776: see Gasparri 1978: 84–5.
11. *Cod. Car.* no. 56, pp. 580–81.
12. *Cod. Car.* no. 57, pp. 582–3. Adelchis had fled to Constantinople and would not return to Italy until 788 (and then only very briefly).
13. F. Hartmann 2006: 164–9.
14. *ArF* s.a. 773.
15. Springer 2004: 181 suggests this was in retaliation for the destruction of the Erminsul the previous year.
16. *ArF* s.a. 773: the attack occurred late in that year or possibly early in 774.
17. For Guntland, brother of Chrodegang, see Ch. 3 above; also Innes 1998b: 312–13, and 2000: 180–81 (with an emphasis different from mine).
18. J. Davis 2015: 325–9 points to possibilities for Charles's development of Ingelheim; cf. Rollason 2016: 25–7.
19. *ArF* s.a. 774. Bachrach 2001b: 80–82, citing this passage. Halsall 2003: 54, 76, pins down the distinctive traits of *scarae*: 'bands of chosen warriors', 'socially selective', and 'select bodies of troops, dispatched quickly to trouble-spots', implying that these were cavalrymen, and, p. 150, shows important evidence for pack-horses: Astron. c. 15. Astron. c. 2, implies cavalry in the 778 campaign. See below, this ch. sec (ix).
20. See Ch. 5, p. 121.

21. *ArF* s.a. 775. See Springer 2004: 182–3, 251.
22. For the suggestion about Bertrada at St-Denis, cf. Ch. 3. The eleven charters issued from Quierzy are DD. 89–91, 93–95, 98–102.
23. DD. 89, 90.
24. The abbot also got exemption from tolls for the monastery's agents trading '*in Francia et Italia*': D. 93.
25. The chief notary, who doubled as an envoy to Italy, had been promoted to this plum post in 775, in which his first appearance is D. 97. Cf. *Cod. Car.* no. 46, and Ch. 4, p. 107.
26. Palmer 2005: 266.
27. McKitterick 2008: 188–97, esp. 192.
28. In 773, by way of comparison, it is not clear when the host was summoned to Geneva and when the two armies crossed the Alps. Davis 1992: 138, n. 49, implies late September; Fried 2013: 131 makes a plausible guess late in the year 773.
29. Schieffer 2009: 43–9.
30. Nelson 1996, ch. 6; Koziol 1992, 2002, 2012; Buc 2005; Garipzanov 2008, 2018.
31. *ArF* s.a. 775.
32. *ArF* rev. s.a. 776.
33. *ArF* s.a. 776.
34. MGH Capit. I, no. 88, pp. 187–8. Dating to 776: Mordek 1995: 1089 (I do not follow Mordek 2005, arguing for 781). J. Davis 2015: 288, n. 261, and 410–11, follows McKitterick. Charles did not go to Rome in April 774 because, *pace* McKitterick, he was 'comfortable enough with his position to leave Pavia for Rome to celebrate Easter'. Charles was not, I think, 'in firm control' of Italy in February 774, but had become so by February 776. It's rather misleading to say there was 'no evidence for serious dissension in the ranks once the attack was underway', when there certainly *is* evidence for serious Frankish protest a little before God intervened to put Desiderius's troops to flight. See Ch. 5 (vi).
35. Ch. 5 above, p. 134.
36. McKitterick 2008: 111–13.
37. The *Notitia italica* is extant in six manuscripts; one of them has two incomplete copies of the *notitia*, and another two copies (one complete, another incomplete), and all scribes apparently treated the *notitia* as a capitulary.
38. Capit. I, no. 88, prol., cc. 2 and 4, pp. 187–8.
39. Einhard, *VK*, cc. 19, 21, 28; Ganz 2005: 45.
40. Rio 2017: 62.
41. Capit. I, no. 94, c. 10, p. 199.
42. F. Hartmann 2009.
43. D. 102.

44. Charles is thirteen times documented as staying at Herstal, Bruhl 1968: 19, n. 59. See DD. 60, 65, 71, 114, 116, 119, 121, 122, 123, 124, 126, 136 and 146.

45. DD. 114, 116 (dated 7 January 777). Martel's grant to Utrecht (723) had been made 'at the *villa* of Herstal'; Pippin as king is only documented once at Herstal, now upgraded to a *palatium*, D. 2 (752).

46. Marculf, I, 22, Eng. trans. Rio 2008a: 155–6, with n. 476.

47. Rio 2017: 104–5, with n. 99.

48. Esmyol 2002: 92, a 'chronic adulterer', cf. 148–52; Stone 2012, ch. 9. In Charles's later years as a widower, concubines may have, as it were, worked shifts in the equivalent of a seraglio (though on a very much smaller scale).

49. Cf. Laws of Ine c. 00, where a wet-nurse is prized as highly as a smith.

50. The only previous mention of *pagani* in the *ArF* was the killing of St Boniface by pagan Frisians, s.a. 754.

51. *ArF* s.a. 776. For the meaning of *scarae*, see above, this chapter, p. 155, and n. 19.

52. *Ann. Petav.* s.a. 776, *maiores natu*, 'men of leading families'.

53. *Ann. Mos.* s.a., p. 496; and '*aedificavit civitatem super fluvio Lippiae, que appellatur Karlesburg*' ('he built a city on the river Lippe, which is called Karlesburg'; *Ann. Maxim.* s.a. 776, p. 21, '*Franci civitatem fecerunt in Saxonia quae dicitur urbs Caroli et Francorum.*' ('The Franks made a city in Saxony which is called the town of Charles and the Franks.')

54. *Ann. Petav.* s.a. 778; Springer 2004: 184.

55. Becher 1993: 120–21, 127–8.

56. McKitterick 2008: 27–31. See Ch. 1 (ii).

57. *Ann. Mos.* s.a.; *Ann. Petav.* s.a.

58. King 1987: 48; Kennedy 1995: 261–2.

59. Bautier 1991: ch. III, p. 4, with n. 4.

60. Collins 1998b: 66, contextualizes expertly.

61. *Cod. Car.* no. 61.

62. *Ann. Petav.* s.a. 777

63. Latowsky 2005: 25–57, and 2014.

64. My excerpts largely follow the translation of Rabe 1995: 62–6, with further help from Rembold 2017. For Paulinus's later career and influence, see Davis 2015: 207–15.

65. Schaller 1997: 197. Cf. Nelson 2007 (2003), ch. XI: 52–3.

66. See below, chs. 14, 16.

67. Collins 1998b: 67.

68. Bautier 1979 (repr. 1991) remains the best study of the campaign.

69. *ArF* rev. s.a. 778, pp. 51, 53. The pass is nowadays known as Roncesvalles in Spanish, Roncevaux in French and Roncesvaux in English, from the monastery of that name several kilometres down from the pass.

70. Einhard, *VK*, c. 9, pp. 12–13. My translation draws on several others, especially that of Firchow and Zeydel 1985: 55, which can be compared with the facing-page Latin. In the 840s, Walahfrid supplied the *VK* with

chapter-headings. Ch. 9's was: '*Quid in Hispania fecerit, et de plaga, quam in exercitu eius Vascones fecerunt*', 'What happened in Spain and concerning the heavy blow the Basques inflicted on the army'. The epitaph of Eggihard which survives independently, MGH *Poet. Lat.* KA I, pp. 109–10, Eng. trans. Dutton 1993: 48, gives the battle's date – 15 August.

71. Manzano Moreno 1991: 110–16; Collins 1995a: 285 ('fruitless intervention'); and Collins 1998b: 66–8 (more cautiously), 'a tawdry campaign that could have become a complete disaster'; Hägermann 2000: 157 ('a misconceived adventure ending in defeat'); McKitterick 2008: 134 ('the disastrous ambush', 'the severity of the defeat'), 226 ('the rout in the Pyrenees'); Davis 2015: 414–15 ('a disastrous military defeat', 'one of his worst defeats').

72. Bautier 1979 (1991): 45, and 27, on the probable location of the ambush not far below the Col de Lepoeder, noting that the gradient of the path at that point is relatively gentle – 12 per cent.

73. Collins 1995b: 285.

74. King 1987: 45.

75. Liebeschütz 1950. For similar comments on Charles's canal-project, see Ch. 10 (xii).

76. Halsall 2003: 145.

77. Hägermann 2000: 155–61, esp. 159.

78. Jarnut 2002: 247–53; cf. Fouracre 2005: 19.

79. *ArF* rev. 778.

80. *ArF* s.a. 778.

81. *ArF* 779; cf. *ArF* rev.

82. *ArF* 780; cf. *ArF* rev.

83. Ganshof 1971: 18.

84. Astron. cc. 2, 3 pp. 289–91.

85. Astron. c. 2, p. 288: '*Quorum, quia vulgata sunt, nomina dicere supersedi.*'

86. Ganz 2010: 18–32.

87. Costambeys et al. 2011: 113–15, 306.

88. Airlie 2012; also Nelson 2007. Adalhard/Hincmar in the *De ordine palatii* details traditional functionaries without mentioning *aulici*, who multitasked.

89. Eggihard, see above, n. 70; Anselm present and correct in D. 102 (an original dated 775) and D.110 (dated 776).

90. Coupland 2005: 213.

91. On the three appearances of 'Roland', and the likelihood that they signify the same man, see above, Ch. 1, p. 8.

92. This was how Einhard expressed his relationship with Charles in the prologue to the *VK*.

93. Hägermann 2000: 156–71, esp. 158.

94. For advice on the vividness of traumatic memories of youthful wartime experiences in elderly people, I am grateful to Robin Jacoby.

95. The sociologist Niklas Luhmann observed, 'A complete absence of trust would prevent [one] ever getting up in the morning' (Luhmann 1979: 4). My guess would be that Charles seldom, if ever, had difficulties getting up in the morning. See further Hosking 2014.
96. Only one charter of Pippin's: D. 2 (752) *in palatio publico*.
97. Brühl 1968: 22, n. 66. *Liebling* means 'favourite', 'most loved'.
98. Brühl 1968: 19, n. 59. Two more stays in 781 and 782, and stays at Christmas and Easter in 783. Thereafter Charles established a different pattern. See Ch. 7.
99. *Anglo-Saxon Chronicle* 'E' s.a. 1085.
100. de Clercq 1936: 159, cited in Ganshof 1971: 19; on the Capitulary of Herstal, Capit. I, n. 20, pp. 47–51, see now McKitterick 2008: 186, 231; on capitularies in practice, see Pössel 2006: 255–70, and Innes 2011: 262–75; Davis 2015: 111–12, 288–9, 352.
101. MGH Capit. I, no. 20, c. 12, p. 50. I have drawn on the translations of Loyn and Percival 1975: 47–9, and King 1987: 203–5.
102. For immunities, see above, chs. 3 and 5.
103. Capit. I, no. 20, c. 9, p. 49.
104. Ibid. c. 11, p. 49.
105. Ibid. c. 21, p. 51.
106. Fouracre 1995 (2013) – fundamental.
107. MGH Capit. I, no. 82, *Capitulare de Latronibus* (804–13), c. 2, p. 180; Capit. I, nos. 71, 72, pp. 161–4; Nelson 2001c; McKitterick 2008: 186, 231.
108. The Bishops' Capitulary, translated by King, is dated there to Spring 793, but the re-dating is convincingly established by Mordek 2005: 23–31.
109. Mordek 2005: 12.
110. Verhulst 2002: 123–4.
111. Hindle 2001.
112. DD. 8, 12; Brühl 1968: 18; McKitterick 2008: 161.
113. Stollberg-Rilinger 2008 (Eng. trans. 2015) on 'presence culture' and on 'being present'.
114. D. 131; Wickham 1981: 47–8; Davis 2015: 216, 220–21, 226.
115. *ArF* 780: *'tunc sumpto consilio'* ('then having taken counsel'); cf. *ArF* rev. 780: *'initoque consilio'*.
116. M. Hartmann 2009: 100. The children were Rotrud, Carloman, Louis and Berta. Pippin and Charles remained at Worms: *Ann. Mos.* s.a. Baby Lothar had died not long after he was born: Astron. c. 3.

7. THE FAMILY DEPLOYED

1. *Ann. Mos.* 780.
2. Ch. 4. From here on, I shall sometimes identify Pippin as 'the first-born', partly for convenience, partly to make a point, and sometimes as 'son of Himiltrud'.

3. *Ann. S. Amandi*, s.a. 780: 'King Charles divided his realms (*regna*) between his sons, and journeyed to Rome.' Collins 1998b: 69–70 says that 'such a division would have needed approval however formal at a Frankish assembly', but the qualified tone of 'however formal' in effect concedes that there were no fixed rules: cf. Kaschke 2006: 149–50.

4. M. Hartmann 2009: 100.

5. Astron. c. 4 mentions a push-chair in Louis' case not just once, in Rome, but again a few months later, at Orléans (where an alternative translation might be a 'portable chair' or 'baby-seat').

6. *Cod. Car.* no. 60 (May 778).

7. For the death of baby Adelheid in 774, see above, Ch. 5.

8. The adjective was liberally applied by Hadrian and/or his notaries: see Gantner 2013, on Roman rhetoric.

9. Coronations are mentioned only by the reviser. See Brühl 1962; Nelson 1996: 102–3.

10. *Cod. Car.* no. 68 (after 15 April (Easter) and before May); *Cod. Car.* nos. 69, 70, 72, 73, 74 (the exception, 71, was a business letter about envoys). *Cod. Car.* no. 75 is dated after Hildegard's death and before Charles's remarriage on the basis of the absence of reference to the queen's spiritual co-motherhood. For the cult of Petronilla in the 750s, and the reception at Rome of the baptismal towel of King Pippin's baby daughter Gisela, see *Cod. Car.* no. 14, and above Ch. 3, and Goodson 2015: 172–82.

11. Angenendt 1980, 1990: 285, 293, 298 – path-breaking but with a tendency to flatten out unevennesses.

12. See below, Ch. 14 (vii).

13. Louis in 778 had been baptized as an infant as soon as it was possible to determine 'which one [of the twins] gave promise of a vigorous constitution'. The name had been chosen and agreed by Charles and (I am assuming) Hildegard, after Charles's return from Spain.

14. *ArF*, and reviser.

15. Geuenich 2013; and see above Ch. 6.

16. Kaschke 2008: 137–8.

17. *Ann. Mos.*, s.a. 781; *Ann. Lauriss.* s.a. 781. Neither the *ArF* nor the *ArF* reviser mentioned the name-change at all.

18. Nees 2007. See Wikipedia, 'Godescale Evangelistary', with commentary, illustrations and references.

19. Kantorowicz 1946; McCormick 1984: 1–23, 1986: 356–60.

20. For the title '*patricius* of the Romans', see Ganshof 1950.

21. Ed. from MS Montpellier, acad. medic. no. 409, fol. 344, as an Appendix to *VK*, ed. Holder-Egger, Hanover 1911: 47. The fourth is for Louis, whose helper is St Martin. The language is a mixture of Latin and a romance vernacular: '*Chlodorio rege Aequitaniorum vita! / Sanctae Martinae, tu lo iuva!*' (To Louis king of the Aquitanians, life! / You St Martin, help him!)

22. Thoma 1985.
23. Bullough 1962.
24. Above, Ch. 4; Becher 1993: 35–45, 51–8. For a second alleged oath-taking, see below, pp. 189–90. I will leave discussion of a third oath-taking, in 787, to Ch. 8.
25. Becher 1993: 44–5; Reynolds 1994: 86; Kaschke 2006: 155–72.
26. See Ch. 1.
27. Roper Pearson 1999: 66.
28. Jahn 1991: 390–95; Nelson 2007: Ch. X, p. 178.
29. Conc. Aevi Karolini I, no. 15, p. 93.
30. Jarnut 2002: 158–9; for Adalhard's reaction see *Vita Adalhardi* c. 7, p. 525. See Kasten 1986: 18–22, 24–5; Airlie 2012 (1999): 102; Nelson 2007: 182–3.
31. Crantz s.a. 772, p. 341; Nelson 2007: Ch. X, p. 178.
32. King 1987: 150; *Ann. S. Emmeram.*, s.a., p. 733.
33. *Vita Hadriani.* c. 23. See above, Ch. 6.
34. Crantz, s.a. 772, King 1987: 341.
35. Garrison: 1998a.
36. Airlie 2012 (1999): 96.
37. *ArF* s.a. 781, p. 53. Kosto 2002: 133–4 notes the valence of the number 12.
38. *ArF* 781, and reviser (with minor changes).
39. Crantz, s.a. 781, Eng. trans. King 1987, F. (b), p. 341. For details of this Bavarian source, see above Ch. 1. It was contemporary and independent, though it survives only in a sixteenth-century German translation from the original eighth-century Latin.
40. Hannig 1988: 18–20; Hack 2006–7: ii, 854; Nelson 2011a: 225–53, esp. 233–9, 244–8.
41. Nelson 1999: chs. XII, XIX; 2007: chs. X, XI, XV
42. Theophanes, Eng. trans. Mango and Scott 1997: 628.
43. See Ch. 1. Brought up at the imperial court in Constantinople, Theophanes probably knew about the betrothal at the time, though he wrote up his history much later, in 810–17.
44. *Ann. Mos.* 781; *Ann. Lauriss.* 781.
45. *ArF* rev. s.a. 788, King 1987: 122; and for the relevant events of 787, see below, Ch. 8.
46. Collins 2005: 58–9.
47. *Ann. Mos.* s.a. 782; *Ann. Lauriss.* 782.
48. *Ann. S. Max.* s.a. 782, p. 21: '*Constituit super eos [Saxones] comites ex nobilibus Francis et Saxonibus.*' See Schubert 1993: 9, 'This is plausible because it would have been unlikely that Charles wanted only Saxon nobles.'
49. Exiguous evidence on the Danes appears in *ArF* 777, 782 and 798; for Avars, see Ch. 8 below.
50. D 143 (25 July)
51. D 144* (28 July), for Lull and Leoba; D 145 (also 28 July), for Abbot Baugulf of Fulda.

52. D 146 (18 August, for Farfa); see Costambeys 2007: 229.
53. D 147* (26 September, for Modena)
54. *ArF* s.a. 782, p. 60. For the *Capitulatio* see p. 196 below.
55. *ArF* s.a. 782, pp. 60, 62. Springer 2004: 189–90, offers a convincingly subtle interpretation of the author's dilemma.
56. *ArF* rev. s.a. 782, pp. 61, 63.
57. Hägermann 2000: 212; Springer 2004: 188.
58. Goldberg 1995: 467–501 offers a good account of this strand of the historiography.
59. Körntgen 2009: 283–7. Corrections and revisions to my earlier views (in Nelson 2013a: 24–5) are offered in this present chapter.
60. My thanks go to John Gillingham for this suggestion.
61. *Ann. Petav.* s.a. 782, MGH SS I, p. 17.
62. Mordek 1995: 770, dates '782 or 785'. The rare term *capitulatio* is equivalent to capitulary.
63. Schubert 1993: 7–10, developing the case made by Lintzel 1937 (1961): 384–9. See also Lintzel 1934 (1961): 109–14, 121–2, who put the *Capitulatio* in the context of Saxon class-war between aristocrats and freemen.
64. Collins 1998b: 52–4.
65. Schubert 1993: 17.
66. Lintzel 1937 (1961): 384; Springer 2004: 222–9. See the translation of King 1987: 205–8, with very helpful comments at 25, 50–51.
67. Old Testament influence, Flierman 2016: 194–200; *Indiculus*, Wood 2001: 255; Palmer 2005: 407–8, 412–13. The recent works of Rembold 2017 and Flierman 2018 are path-breaking in many respects but I remain unconvinced by Hen 2006 on whom they rely for crucial questions of dating and Islamic influence: a convincing rebuttal is offered by König 2016: 1–40.
68. The figure of 4,500 looks like a later interpolation into the *ArF*, which was then followed by the *ArF* reviser; Springer 2004: 190.
69. Palmer 2005: 414 throws much light. See also Effros 1997.
70. *ArF* rev. s.a. 782, p. 63; Einhard, *VK* c. 9; on names and memory, compare Astron. c. 2, and Ch. 6 (x).
71. Lambert 2017: 181–200.
72. Effros 1997: 268–9, 277–88.
73. Fouracre 1986.
74. Innes 2000: 180–97; Innes 2005; Wood 2006: 217, 340–41; Davis 2011: 162–3.
75. D 148, pp. 200–202. *Scabinus/scabini* first appear in the mid-eighth century. See Fouracre 1995: 106–7; Davis 2015: 52–3.
76. D. 65 (late March 772), D. 72 (between May 772 and January 773), D. 73 (20 January 773); Innes 1998b: 309–12, and 2000: 183–4, with Fig. 10 at 265. One of the root-meanings of *mundeburdium* (with variant spellings) was guardianship: Niermeyer 1997 (revd by Burgers 2002) s.v. *mundeburdis*, meaning 3.

77. Innes 2000: 184.
78. S. Wood 2006: 217.
79. S. Wood 2006: 211, 219.
80. Capit. I, no. 75, p. 168 (the same Fulrad as the *missus* of Capit. no. 85, p. 183?).
81. Felten 1980: 141–2.
82. Davis 2015; Hosking 2014; Stollberg-Rilinger 2008 (2015).
83. Life of Augustus c. 51, Life of Tiberius c. 51.
84. *ArF* rev. 783.
85. Einhard, *VK*, c. 8.
86. Fastrada and 'his sons and daughters', see below pp. 205, 207.
87. *Ann. Petav.* s.a. 785, p. 17.
88. *ArF* s.a. 785, p. 83.
89. *ArF* rev. s.a. 785, pp. 118–19.
90. *ArF* s.a. 785, p. 83.
91. Augustine, *The City of God* XIX, 13.
92. Above, Ch. 4. Other stays at Thionville can be tracked in the charter record for 775: in May (DD. 96, 97), and in November (DD. 108, 109).
93. D. 149 (1 May, 783).
94. D. 155 (probably Christmas 786).
95. Above Ch. 1, for baby Hildegard's epitaph. See Kempf 2013: 80–83. For the burial-place, Kempf 2013: 2–13, 76–7: 'Hildegard rests in the oratory of St Arnulf in the city of Metz, because it was there that the kings descended from St Arnulf placed the bodies of those dear to them.' For Hildegard's piety, and for her commemoration, see Gaedeke in Riché et al., eds., 1987: 27–39.
96. Innes 1998a: 3–36, at 24–5, 29–33, is the key article. See also Ganz 2008: 51–2, for generous appreciation both of Notker and of his earlier translator, Lewis Thorpe.
97. Notker, *Gesta Karoli* I, 17, pp. 21–2.
98. Cf. MacLean 2003: 204–13, at 212.
99. Above Ch. 2, for the *Miracles of St Denis*, and stories that described Bertrada's staying at the monastery.
100. Stafford 2006: ch. X, p. 6.
101. Fried 1994: 26; 2013: 377–82, 601.
102. Staab 1997: 188. M. Hartmann 2009: 101.
103. Stone 2012.
104. The vision of Wetti, a monk of Reichenau, trans. Godman 1985: 215; Dutton 1993: 65–78; Ganz 2000: 181–2; Fried 2013: 17–18.
105. Fichtenau 1949; Jarnut 1999: 6–7; M. Hartmann 2009; Nelson 2015a. See Ch. 6, above, for Hildegard; for Fastrada, see Chs. 8 and 9, below.
106. D. 156, issued at Capua on 22 March; D. 157, issued at Capua on 24 March 787: '[prayers] *pro nobis uxoribusque nostris*'. In D. 158, issued at Rome on 28 March, the scribe Jacob had corrected the plural wives to a singular, '*pro uxore nostra*'.

107. Ch. 2; this chapter, above p. 192; cf. Crawford 1933: 49, 57–8, 60–65.

108. Körntgen 2009, neatly identifies, and sidelines, Christianization as means, military and political subordination as end; he also (at p. 298, n. 26) chides Schubert 1993 for anachronism in overstating the split between means and end.

109. M. Hartmann 2009: 103; Fried 2013: 185 (for the situation in 787), 380–81.

110. *ArF* rev. s.a. 785, p. 71.

111. *ArF* s.a. 785, p. 70. Attigny, on the river Aisne, in the Ardennes is always called a palace in charters. Charles had never stayed there before (though Pippin and Carloman had).

112. *Ann. Mos.* s.a.; *Ann. Lauriss.* s.a. adds details: 'Charles honoured him [the newly baptized Widukind] (no mention of Abbio) with magnificent gifts. From the death of Pope Gregory up to now 180 years have passed.' The dating from Gregory's death is intended to show the importance of this event. Widukind may or may not have become a count in Saxony: Angenendt 1990: 298; Springer 2004: 193–4; 195–200. For comparable godparental relationships, see Hadley 2009: 205, Stafford 2009: 464; Nelson 1992: 76–8, 80–81, 170 (and s.v. 'spiritual kinship'); 1999, ch. 2, p. 38; and 2014c.

113. Rembold 2017. The rest of Widukind's career comes from later sources and much of it is mythical. Lambert 2017.

114. *Cod. Car.* no. 76 (early 786).

8. BOUNDARY-CROSSINGS

1. Wickham 1981, 1986, 1988, 2005; Hodges 1997; Mitchell and Hansen 2001; Moran 2003.

2. See Ch. 6.

3. *Cod. Car.* no. 66.

4. *ArF* rev. s.a.

5. Houben 1985; West 1999: 350–54; F. Hartmann 2006: 227–43.

6. King 1987: 153, Greatest Salzburg Annals 784, p. 734: '*Ad Posanum pugna fuit*', p. 154, Greater St Emmeram Annals 785: '*Pugna Baiowariorum cum Hrodperto ad Pozana*'.

7. For Creontius/Crantz, see King 1987: 342, and for the significance of his Chronicle, Ch. 1, above.

8. King 1987: 342.

9. Jarnut 2002: 159, points out that the Franks' attack on Bolzano prefigured the all-out onslaught on Tassilo in 788.

10. See *Divisio regnorum* (806), cc. 2 and 3; below Ch. 15.

11. Becher 1993: 58.

12. Einhard, *VK* c. 20, pp. 25–6.

13. *ArF* rev. s.a. 785, p. 71. (I have ventured to alter King's translation occasionally, to clarify Einhard's borrowings.)

14. *ArF* rev. s.a. 792, p. 91.
15. Einhard, *VK* c. 20, p. 26.
16. Einhard, *VK* c. 18, p. 22.
17. Staab 1997: 186–7; Nelson 1997a: 158–9.
18. *Ann. Lauriss.* s.a. 786, p. 32; cf. *Ann. Fuld.* s.a. 785, p. 11: 'a conspiracy of East Franks, called Hardrad's, arose against the king, and was soon suppressed.'
19. Abbot Baugulf was perhaps the Count Baugulf who attested the grant of Pippin and Bertrada to Prüm in 762 (D. 16). Above Ch. 3. Abbots multitasked and did not always behave like cynical brutes. For a vignette of Baugulf in jovial, welcoming mode, at Fulda in 791, see Innes 2000: 66. For Charles's circular *De litteris colendis* ('On the cultivation of learning'), of which the copy sent to Baugulf survives, see below Ch. 11.
20. Geary 1994: 81, 84–5, 88–90; Raajmakers 2012: 203–13; Innes 2013. 'The Making of Charlemagne's Europe' database, constructed 2012–15, directed by Alice Rio and available online, is an excellent starting-point from which to explore charters from Charles's reign.
21. D. 65; see above Ch. 4.
22. D. 89.
23. D. 129.
24. D. 148, see Ch. 7 (v).
25. D. 165.
26. Hummer 2005: 106–7.
27. S. Wood 2006: 226, 228.
28. Innes 2000: 185.
29. D. 140*, issued in December 781 at the palace of Quierzy, where Charles wintered in 781–2 (*ArF* s.a. 781).
30. Nelson 2009a: 18–19. What follows in this and the next two paragraphs is mostly filched from my 2009 paper.
31. See the complaints of Pope Leo III in letters to Charles in 808–13 about the damage caused by his *missi* and their men in northern Italy: Leo III, Epp. 2, 9, 10.
32. *Chronicle of Fredegar* IV, c. 54, pp. 216–18. Cf. Becher 1993: 196.
33. See Ch. 10.
34. Rio 2008a: 175–6.
35. *Ann. Iuvavenses maximi* s.a. 785, 786, MGH SS XXX, pt. 2, p. 734.
36. *Ann. S. Emmerammi Ratisponensis maiores* s.a. 786, MGH SS I, p. 92.
37. King 1987: 342; Riezler 1881: 276.
38. King 1987: 155. *Ann. Petav.* s.a. 786: p. 17.
39. King 1987: 155, Min. (c). The Chesne Fragment is a brief independent account of the years 786–90 stemming from a continuation of *Ann. Lauriss.* from 786: Collins 2005: 57, 59. Diesenberger 2006: 111–15, shows the importance of the entries for 787–8, and suggests that they could reflect a crucial shift of some Bavarians' loyalties from Tassilo to Charles.

40. *Ann. Lauriss.* s.a. 786; King 1987: 138.
41. Cf. Exodus 4 (on signs), and 8–12 (God's plagues imposed on Egypt).
42. Palmer 2014: 146, and cf. Palmer 2011: 213–41.
43. Matt. 24: 35–6; Mk. 13: 31–2.
44. Collins 2005: 58–9; cf. McKitterick 2008: 31–43.
45. McKitterick 2008: 48
46. For the allegations, see *ArF* rev. s.a. 792, and Einhard, *VK* c. 20.
47. Staab 1997; Nelson 1997a and 2018a; see also above Ch. 7, p. 207; and below Ch. 10.
48. See above Ch. 7, p. 209 with n. 114.
49. George's letter-report, MGH Epp. IV, Ep. 3, p. 28; see Story 2003: 62, and 64–92, for the date, form and function of the Report, showing multiple connections between Anglo-Saxon and Carolingian learning.
50. Hack 2006–7: ii, 1001–4.
51. Wigbod's *Commentary on Genesis* was commissioned by Charles: de Jong 2003: 114; see Gorman 1982 and 1997; the *Epitome* of the Commentaries was published in Gorman 2008 (see Primary Sources).
52. Story 2003: 62–3. See Story 2003: 61–92 for an excellent conspectus. For more on Alcuin, see Bullough 2004: 379–80; Glatthaar et al. 2013: 47–8, 50–63. Whether or not the Decrees of 786 influenced the *Admonitio generalis* or vice versa, were moot points until Glatthaar settled the matter in 2013.
53. Definition from *Postscripts* magazine, accessed 6 April 2017.
54. Freeman 2003: ch. I, p. 1.
55. Above, Ch. 7, p. 209, citing *Cod. Car.* no. 76.
56. See below Ch. 11.
57. D. 155. Cf. above Ch. 7, p. 206, for two grants of 787, D. 156 and D. 157. See also this chapter, below, p. 229.
58. *ArF* s.a. 787, p. 72.
59. *ArF* p. 74.
60. *Ann. Lauriss.* s.a. 786; West 1999: 354–5.
61. Poet. I, pp. 68–9. Glatthaar 2010: 469–70, 472, takes seriously 'Prince Charles/ . . . arbiter of the toga-wearing world/and the glory of the Dardanian people' as representing an actual visit to Rome when Charles donned a toga.
62. D. 158.
63. *Epistola Generalis*, Capit. I, no. 30, p. 81, King 1987, p. 208; Glatthaar 2010: 469–70, 472–4; Mostert 2016: 114. Back in Francia, Charles commended the work of 'our friend and little client' (*familiaris clientulus noster*) to 'religious readers' (*religiosi lectores*) to be read in churches.
64. Wickham 1981: 147–8. Map XX.
65. *ArF* s.a. 787.
66. Compare the *ArF* reviser's rather different account, s.a. 787, p. 75: 'Charles, though he had his whole army with him gave up his planned attack and, in

response to Arichis's entreaties, and out of God-fearing respect, abstained from war.'

67. D. 156, D. 157.

68. D. 158, D. 159.

69. *ArF* s.a. 787, p. 74.

70. *ArF* s.a. 787 (the *ArF* reviser's account is much briefer).

71. McKitterick 2008: 124.

72. Airlie 2012 (1999): III, pp. 103–4.

73. *ArF* rev. s.a. 786, p. 75: '*misitque legatos, qui et ipsum ducem et omnem Beneventanum populum per sacramenta firmarent*'; King 1987: 120.

74. *ArF* rev. s.a. 788, King 1987: 122. Compare *Cod. Car.* no. 83 (after Jan. 788), in which Hadrian reports information from Capuans about active Byzantine diplomacy in Benevento in 787.

75. Chesne Fragment, p. 35.

76. Hack 2006–7: ii, 840–43, 970.

77. *Cod. Car.* no. 81, p. 614. Hadrian quoted from a lost letter (Deperdita no. 43); see Hack 2006–7: ii, 840–43; see also Nelson 2011a: 244–8, and 2016b: 248–9.

78. On *spolia*, see Wikipedia, accessed 8 April 2017, 'The repurposing of building stone for new construction, or the reuse of decorative sculpture on new monuments, is an ancient and widespread practice whereby stone that has been quarried, cut, and used in a built structure, is carried away to be used elsewhere.' See Goodson 2010: 48–9, and Marano 2016: 120–21, for legal prescription and practice.

79. Nelson 2010b: 134–40, and 2016b: 251–2, with nn. 38, 39. For relations between pope and king in the late 780s, see F. Hartmann 2006: 244–50.

80. Schieffer 1997b: 13–14.

81. *ArF* s.a. 787.

82. Fried 2013: 185 (Eng. trans. 2017: 149) shrewdly surmised this possibility.

83. Nelson 1997a: 158–9.

84. *ArF* s.a. 787.

85. *Ann. Lauriss.* s.a. SS I, p. 33; King 1987: 138. Schove 1984: 162–5, 270.

86. Glatthaar et al. 2013: 8.

87. Niermeyer 1997 s.v. *marca*, differentiates boundary, frontier and border-land (meanings 2, 3, 4 – the last esp. in Italian contexts).

88. Smith 1995: 169, 175–6; for Italy, Delogu 1995: 303–10; for Avars, Pohl 1988: 17.

89. Smith 1995: 176. For Friuli and Istria, and for the border-zone of Bavaria's eastern periphery (Capit. I, no. 44), see below Ch. 9.

90. *ArF* rev. s.a. 790, p. 87; cf. s.a. 791: 'the river Enns running midway between the lands of the Bavarians and the Huns, was regarded as a clear frontier between the two realms (*certus duorum regnorum limes*)'.

91. Capit. no. 44, c. 7; Reuter 2006: 231–50; Nelson 2009b: 34–6.

92. Smith 1995: esp. 186–9; cf. also Davis 2015: 219–22.

93. *Cod. Car.* nos. 71, 72.

94. *Cod. Car.* nos. 71, 72; Alcuin, *Carm.* XCII, p. 319; Stoclet 1993: 466, and for Maginar and Fulrad's Testament, 5–33; Bullough 1991b: 128, 130, 151–2.

95. *Epitaphium Arichis Ducis*, Carmen 33, MGH *Poet.* I, pp. 66–8.

96. *Cod. Car.* no. 80 (end 787/early 788), King 1987: 302.

97. *Cod. Car.* no. 82; Maginar's letter is edited by Gundlach in *Cod. Car.* Appendix 2. Facsimile in Atsma and Vezin eds., Ch.L.A. no. 629, pp. 59–65.

98. *Cod. Car.* no. 65; Louis of Aquitaine's charter issued at the request of Atto, Ch.L.A. no. 681; Depreux 1997: s.v. 'Aton', no. 38, pp. 114–15; Hack 2006–7: ii, 987–8, 'Prosopographie', no. 1.

99. Hack 2006–7: ii, 'Prosopographie', 1005 ('Goteramnus').

100. *Cod. Car.* no. 82, and Deperditum 43a in Hack 2006–7: ii, 970, and 'Prosopographie', no. 45, 1009–10.

101. Hack 2006–7: ii, 'Prosopographie', 1010 ('Liuderich/Leuderich').

102. Allegedly said by Sir Henry Wotton (1568–1639).

103. For an equally rare survivor of the genre of memoranda to be given *missi*, Nelson 2010b: 129–31.

104. *Cod. Car.* nos. 79, 80, 82, 83 and 84 – especially 82, 83 and 84.

105. *Cod. Car.* Appendix 2, ed. Gundlach, who dated it 'after 22 Jan. 788'. According to *Cod. Car.* no. 82, Byzantine envoys arrived at Salerno on 20 January 788. That Maginar's letter must have been written and sent on 22 January or a little after has been generally accepted. See the facsimile in Atsma and Vezin eds., Ch. L.A. 629, Paris, Archives Nationales, K7, no. 9i, pp. 59–65, from the archive of St-Denis. It was 'transcribed by a scribe from Gaul', Atsma and Vezin, p. 59; text, pp. 62–5. The translation is my own, but with a big debt to that of King 1987: 295–7.

106. Coins, Blackburn 1995: 554; charters, Poupardin 1901: 134; Erchempert, *Historia Langobardorum Beneventanorum*, c. 4, p. 236.

107. *ArF* s.a. 788, p. 82.

108. Cf. Adelperga's concern for deploying treasure in Grimoald's cause, above p. 235, and Pope Hadrian's deployment of money in north-eastern Italy, Nelson 2016b: 246.

109. Alcuin, Ep. 7, p. 32.

110. Alcuin, Ep. 8, pp. 33–4 (Alcuin ends: 'O why are you so far away? I wish you were near to make me happy as you have so often done.').

9. FRANKS, BAVARIANS AND NEW THINKING

1. Garrison 1998a: 308–10, 315–16; Airlie 1999 (repr. 2012): 110–11.

2. Garrison 1998a: 322.

3. Two texts, neither strictly contemporary, say Tassilo was given back his dukedom, but only for a short time, both in King 1987, p. 156: Lorsch Chron. c. 19, p. 118, *AMP* s.a. 787, p. 176.

4. See Ch. 8 (ii) above.

5. Cont. Fred. III, c. 26, p. 294–6, and *AMP* s.a. 743 (for these sources, see Ch. 1).

6. *ArF* s.a. 787, p. 78, see below sec. (iv); cf. Lorsch Ann. s.a. 787: 33, 'Tassilo came to the Lechfeld peacefully, and gave his son Theudo to Charles as a hostage, after which Charles returned in peace and joy to Worms', King 1987; cf. Duke Arichis's giving Charles his son Grimoald and twelve other Lombards as hostages six months before.

7. Chesne Fragment, s.a. 787, SS I, p. 33.

8. *Ann. Naz.*, s.a. 787, SS. I, p. 43. See Airlie 1999 (repr. 2012): 109, 111; for the meanings of *vassus* and the relevance of analogy, see Reynolds 2001 (repr. 2012: ch. I): 5–6, 11–12, and Airlie 1999 (repr. 2012): 106–8.

9. Godman 1985: ll. 174–9 (Latin with English translation); Godman 1987: 61, for comment.

10. From this point, the translations of passages from the Irishman's poem are my own. MGH *Poetae* I, p. 397, ll. 42–5, and abbreviating ll. 46–60.

11. Genesis 3, 4.

12. Is Charles giving Tassilo a second chance to prove himself faithful?

13. For the myth of the Franks' descent from the Trojans, see Gregory of Tours, *DLH* II, 9; Fredegar, *Chron.* III, 2; *LHF* 1.

14. For Providence's assignment to the Trojans of lands in the west, see Vergil, *Aeneid*, Book VIII.

15. Airlie 1999 (repr. 2012): ch. III, 112, acutely points out that 'Tassilo survived 787 . . . Charlemagne had to be content with re-defining him.'

16. Garrison 1994: 119: 'the newly advertised prestige of poetry'.

17. Schaller 1997: 210, and 213–17, adding, 215, n. 74, that 'the "Tassilo-poem" plays virtually no part in the works of historians'.

18. Garrison 1994: 138, and *passim*.

19. Garrison 1994: 135.

20. Airlie 1999 (repr. 2012): ch. III, 112–13. I share Airlie's view that the poem dates from 787 or 788. Cf. for African praise-poems as cross-cultural analogues, Opland 1993, 1998.

21. *Karoli Epistola generalis*, Capit. I, no. 30, pp. 80–81, part trans. King 1987: 208.

22. Glatthaar 2010.

23. Above, Ch. 8 (vii).

24. Glatthaar 2010: 457, 469.

25. *Cod. Car.* no. 41, pp. 553–4, (761–7).

26. Bernard 1998: 40–42, 55–6.

27. Diesenberger 2016: 5–8; also Buck 1997: 397–401, and, still fundamental, McKitterick 1977: 80–114.

28. For Glatthaar 2010: 474 the manifesto was for 'a commitment to a driving-mechanism for the renewal of a writing-culture'.

29. Nelson 2001c.

30. *ArF* s.a. 788.

31. See *Lex Baiwariorum* II, 8a, p. 302: 'If a duke ordained by the king in that province was so bold and insolent and goaded on by inconstancy and impudent and puffed up and proud and rebellious as to despise the decree of the king, he must lose the gift of the dignity of his duchy and in addition he must know that he was condemned to lose all hope of seeing heaven and any chance of salvation.' Cf. Siems 2017: 339 with n.181, 355–8. In Bavarian eyes, was denial of salvation a sufficient sanction?

32. Chesne Fragment s.a. 788, p. 33, says 6 July was the date of Tassilo's tonsuring at St-Goar; Diesenberger 2006: 112 plausibly surmises the same date for Theodo's.

33. Becher 1993: 74–7, with summary at 213. Cf. the reviser's invocation of the Roman Law *crimen maiestatis* (lèse-majesté or treason) against Tassilo, and hostility to Liutperga, 'always extremely opposed to the Franks' (*Francis inimicissima semper*).

34. Airlie 1999 (repr. 2012): ch. III, 105.

35. *ArF* s.a. 788, p. 80; Becher 1993: 45, 47, 64–5.

36. Becher 1993: 66–9; Pohl 1988: 14–16.

37. *ArF* rev. s.a. 782, p. 61. The khagan was the senior ruler among the Avars, while the jugur's rank seems to have been lower and his power more regional; Pohl 1988: 15, 22–31.

38. See Ch. 10, below, and King 1987: Map 4; also Pohl 1988: Anhang IV, p. 47.

39. *ArF* rev. 788, p. 81.

40. Becher 1993: 69; for the connection of the ruler's wife or widow with treasure, Nelson 1986a: 6, 8, 10, 18; Stafford 2006: ch. IX, 20–25.

41. Above, Ch. 8, and *Cod. Car.* no. 80.

42. Collins 2005: 57–9, indicates the connections between the Lorsch Annals and other sets of annals and provides a very helpful 'family-tree' of them. See also Lendi 1971.

43. Garrison 1999; Hack 2006–7: i, pt IV, II: 488–624.

44. Bischoff 1973: 55, with German translation, 22. My thanks go to Carlotta Dionisotti and Charlotte Roueché for help with the translation.

45. Above, Ch. 8.

46. Tassilo and his offspring irrevocably renounced their rights and properties at the Synod of Frankfurt in June 794: Capit. I, no. 28, c. 4. See Ch. 10.

47. McKitterick 1989: 252–4; M. Hartmann 2009: 56. The name Cotani evoked that of the Alaman duke Cotafrid/Gottfried: Jarnut 2002: 91, 103.

48. *ArF* s.a. 788.

49. Airlie 1999 (repr. 2012): ch. III, 109, spots the analogy.

50. Diesenberger 2006, is richly informative.
51. Airlie 1999 (repr. 2012): ch. III, 116–18; Nelson 2018a.
52. Einhard, *VK* c. 11: '*Tassilo tamen postmodum ad regem evocatus neque redire permissus, neque provincia, quam tenebat, ulterius duci sed comitibus ad regendum commissa est.*' Reindel 1965: 226–9, wrote of 'constitutional change'.
53. D. 162.
54. *ArF* s.a.
55. Glatthaar 2010: 25.
56. de Jong 2005: 104–5, 115–16, 118, 122; McKitterick 2008: 240; Fried 2016: 197–8, 256–7, 259–68.
57. Glatthaar et al. 2013: 28–9, n. 148, rightly drawing on Pössel 2006: 258–9. See also Collins 1998b: 112 ('a blueprint for a new society'); McKitterick 2008: 239–41, at 240 ('full of moral zeal and idealism'); Fried 2016: 268: 'The king's agenda was to renew the whole of society according to the principles of the Church Fathers and the directives of the pope . . . Yet the overriding priority was to reform learning.'
58. *Admonitio*, prologue: 180–85, Glatthaar et al. 2013: 5–7, nn. 23, 29, 30.
59. Glatthaar et al. 2013: 180–84, esp. ll. 30–34, 36–40.
60. Cf. Rothari's *ego*-declaration in his edict of 643, MGH *Leges* IV, c. 1, and those of mayors of the palace Carloman, *Conc. German.* (742), MGH *Conc.*, 2, 1, p. 2; and Pippin, *Conc. Soissons* (744), no. 4, p. 33. See also Fried 2016: 260.
61. Glatthaar et al. 2013: pp. 25–6.
62. MGH *Poet.* I, p. 495, ll. 77–82.
63. See Nelson 2013b: 288–306, at 290–94 (where my reference to 'an assembly of bishops' is misguided, cf. above n. 46).
64. de Jong 2005: 104–5, 115–18, 122.
65. See above Ch. 5 (vi).
66. Patzold 2008: esp. 177–84; Pangerl 2011: 34, 100–109, 109–21.
67. The second of only two appearances of this phrase: l. 19, preface, p. 182; l. 288, p. 220 with n. 157.
68. Cubitt 1995: 166–8; Story 2003: 63; Glatthaar et al. 2013: 47–63; for Theodulf, Nelson 2013b: 290–95; Glatthaar et al. 2013: 48–9, 55. For more on Alcuin, see Ch. 11.
69. de Jong 2005: 116.
70. E.g. the quite specific 25, 29, 40, 46; contrast e.g. 53, 60–65, 79, which could be categorized as 'general'.
71. On tithes, Story 2003: 86; Glatthaar et al. 2013: 19.
72. *Epistola*, Mordek 1995; no. 20, pp. 185–6, 1083. The figure for the *Admonitio* is that of Glatthaar et al. 2013: 86; Mordek 1995, no. 22, p. 1082, made it 41. For details, Glatthaar et al. 2013: 63–86.
73. Fried 2016: 54.

74. E.g. Noble 1992: 60, where the question, 'How do you sanctify a state?', gets an inimitable answer: 'You communicate to it the one true faith ... You call into being, or you reform, the institutional structures necessary to implement that sanctification. That is, you publish the *Admonitio generalis*'; cf. Collins 1999b: 112, 'a blueprint for a new society' (though with qualifications); Hägermann 2000: 287, 'the "Charter" of Charles's realm'; W. Hartmann 2010: 160–61, 'Christian standardisation of everyday life'; McKitterick 2008: 240 ('specific injunctions as to how the Christian society ... was to be achieved'); Glatthaar et al. 2013: 20 (rightly warning against 'anachronistic notions'); most recently Fried 2016: 'an agenda to renew the whole of society'.

75. E.g. *Admonitio* c. 1 cites Nicaea c. 5, on people who, 'excommunicated by their own bishop because of their faults are received back into communion by other ecclesiastics *or by laymen*'; c. 23 (ii): 'no-one is to entice anyone else's *servus* to the clerical or monastic order without the permission of his *lord* (*dominus*)'; c. 30, '*laymen* are not to accuse bishops or clerics unless their personal reputation has first been discussed'.

76. Nelson 2001b: 38; 2014c: 491–3.

77. Davis 2015: 278–89, and passim; Van Rhijn 2007; Van Rhijn 2016: 162–80.

78. *Admonitio* c. 63, Glatthaar et al. 2013: 214–16.

79. MGH Capit. I, nos. 23 and 25, pp. 62–4, 66–7.

80. Capit. no. 25, p. 66.

81. What follows is slightly abbreviated in places.

82. Cf. Glatthaar et al. 2013: 18, ' "generally" has more to do with people than themes'.

83. Marculf I, no. 40, p. 68; Rio 2008a: 175–6; Becher 1993: 79–85, 98, 122–3, 144, 195–201; Rio 2009: 24–6; Nelson 2014c: 499–502.

84. 'Romans' here means those living under Late Roman Law and/or in religious institutions: see Rio 2008a: 140 (with reference to Marculf I, no. 8).

85. Nelson 1996: 19, 21–6; Nelson 2008a: 223–34; Esders and Haubrichs, forthcoming.

10. THE REGENSBURG YEARS

1. *Annales Nazariani* and *Annales Guelferbytani* related members of the Murbach annals-family; Collins 2005: 58–9; also *AMP* s.a., whose author offsets 'attending to the internal needs of the kingdom' vis-à-vis 'took no army anywhere'.

2. Astron. c. 5, p. 299 (Tremp does not translate *simpliciter*), King 1987: 170.

3. *AMP* s.a. 790, p. 78; King 1987: 157. Nelson 1991 suggested that Charles's sister Gisela oversaw the production of these annals at Chelles early in the ninth century: cf. Ch. 2 above; and cf. Hen 2000; Kaschke 2006: 241–2; Kasten 1997: 149.

4. *ArF* rev. s.a. 790, p. 87, cf. 791, p. 89.

5. *ArF* rev. s.a. 790, King 1987: 123.

6. *Ann. Mos.* s.a. 780.

7. *ArF* s.a. 784.

8. *Ann. Naz.* s.a., p. 42, King 1987: 155.

9. See the insights of the late Franz Staab, 1997: 190–99.

10. *Ann. S. Amandi* s.a. 789 (there is no entry for 790). On these contemporary annals, see Kaschke 2006: 145–54.

11. For Gisela at Chelles, see above, Ch. 2 (ii).

12. *AMP* s.a. 790; for the special status of the first-born, see above Ch. 4 (iii), on Cathwulf's blessing 3.

13. *ArF* s.a., p. 8; *AMP* s.a., p. 42.

14. *Gesta of the Abbots of St-Wandrille* c. xii, p. 87. The *Gesta* were written up, on the basis of the monastery's archives and oral traditions, in tranches between *c.*830 and the 850s: I. Wood 1991: 1–14.

15. *Gesta ASW* p. 87.

16. McKitterick 2008: 282.

17. Story 2003: 184–8, esp. 186.

18. *Cod. Car.* no. 92 has nothing to do with the marriage-plan: it reveals an anti-papal plot better dated to 787 than earlier or later: see Nelson 2017b.

19. Below Ch. 13, and *Gesta ASW* p. 86, and cf. Charles to Offa, in MGH *Epp.* IV, no. 100, about trade and traders.

20. Below, Ch. 13 (ii).

21. *ArF* rev. s.a. 790: '*Rex autem quasi per otium torpere as tempus terere videretur . . .*' In previous reflections (Nelson 1999: XIII, 151; Nelson 2007: XV, 276), I missed – *mea culpa* – the possibilities of irony and strategic thinking in the *ArF* author's words.

22. Wandalbert of Prüm, *Vita et miracula sancti Goaris*, cc. XI, XII: 55–9 (my translation). Wandalbert, writing *c.*840, called Charles *imperator*. The dangers of the fogs and the whirlpools at the confluence were well-known in medieval times and remain so in more recent folklore.

23. Brunner 1979: 7–13, 60–65; Hammer 2012: 5–6; Davis 2015: 128–63.

24. Kempf 2013, *Liber Ep. Mett.* 2013, p. 77: 'Charles begot four sons and five daughters from his wife Hildegard. But before his legal marriage, he had, from the noble girl Himiltrud, a son named Pippin.'

25. Synodal decree of 786, c. xii, MGH *Epp.* IV, no. 3, pp. 23–4; Wormald 1991: 38–9; Story 2003: 86–7.

26. Staab 1997: 199–200.

27. Reuter 2005: 184, 190–93.

28. Sec. (xii) below.

29. Cf. Fried 2016: 516–18.

30. McKitterick 2008: 166. See further Schieffer 1997c: 13–14; Rollason 2016: 274–7.

31. Pohl 1988: 15; Pohl 2018: 344–402.
32. *ArF* rev s.a. See Gillmor 2005: 23–45. See below Ch. 12.
33. *ArF* s.a., *ArF* rev. s.a.; *Ann. Lauriss.* s.a., and Chesne Fragment p. 34. King 1987: 87–8, 123–4, 139, 158.
34. McCormick 1984.
35. *Karl der Große* to Fastrada, MGH *Epp. Variorum Carolo magno regnante scriptae*, edn. Ep. 20, pp. 528–9; Story 1999: 1–24.
36. For Pippin in Pannonia, see Pohl 2018: 384–9.
37. Mordek 2005: 1–52, at 6 and nn. 24, 25. Chesne Fragment s.a. 791, p. 34: 'he came to Regensburg, and there he joined his army. And there, after taking counsel with Franks, Saxons and Frisians, on account of the great and intolerable malice that the Avars had imposed on the holy church and the Christian people ... they decided to make a campaign with God's help in the regions of the Avars. And they went fast and reached the Enns and there made a three-day fast.' (*Ad Reganesburg pervenit, ibi exercitum suum coniunxit. Ibique consilio peracto Francorum, Saxonum, Frisonum, disposuerunt propter nimium malitiam et intolerabilem quem fecerunt Avari contra sanctam ecclesiam vel populum christianum ... Perrexerunt ad Anisam fluvium properantes; ibi constituerunt letanias faciendi per triduo.*)
38. MGH *Epp.* IV, *Epp. Variorum Carolo Magno regnante* no. 20, p. 528. Cf. Council of Herstal March 779, above, Ch. 6 (xi). Third-class drinkers could presumably fall back on small beer.
39. They were already prescribed in the Old Testament Book of Tobit 12: 8: '*Bona est oratio cum ieiunio, et elemosyna magis quam thesauros auri recondere*', Mordek 2005: 41, n. 177, and *passim*.
40. Capit I, no. 17, p. 42; Mordek 2005:10, n. 41.
41. *Cod. Car.* no. 76; McCormick 1986: 359–60. 23 June was the Vigil of St John's Day, 26 June St John's and St Paul's day, 28 June the Vigil of St Peter's day.
42. Lorsch Ann. 786; *Ann. Naz.* 786; Chesne Fragment 786, SS I, p. 33; *ArF* rev 785; Crantz, in Rietzler 1881: 277, King 1987: 342.
43. Hindle 2001: 44–96.
44. Wickham 2009: 375–6.
45. *ArF* rev. s.a., p. 77.
46. Hammer 2008: 235–76.
47. Hack 2006–7: i, 79.
48. Trad. Regensburg, no. 6; see Hammer 2008: 257, with n. 78.
49. Borgolte 1986: 125: a document issued at Freising, and witnessed by Adalunc, 'commissioner' of Sheriff Gerold. Gerold may have been with Charles on campaign in September.
50. *ArF* rev. s.a. 792, and attributed to the rebels of that year; Einhard *VK*, c. 20. See Kasten 1999.
51. Hack 2006–7: i, 326, n. 568. Perhaps on that occasion no miracle was credited to St Goar.

52. Bullough 1985, repr. in Bullough 1991b: 123-60, at 124.
53. Bullough 1991b: 14, with 30 n. 49; Bullough 2003b; McKitterick 2008: 347-50.
54. Bullough 1991b: 143-4.
55. *Ann. Maxim.* s.a. 792, p. 22: '*Carolus rex synodum magnam habuit in Reganesburc contra Felicem hereticum de adoptione filii Dei . . .*'
56. Close 2011: 53, 'The condemnation of Adoptionism was above all proof of the Frankish and Roman theologians' incomprehension of what the terms "adoption" and "self-emptying" meant' (my translation).
57. Cavadini 1993: 125.
58. Cavadini 1993: 80: 'Their debates were not rancorous, but remained relatively polite, civilized, and substantive' (adjectives not always applied to theologians).
59. Chandler 2002; Close 2011: 86-93.
60. Close 2011: 87. For Theodulf, see Freeman 2003]: ch. VIII. Theodulf came to Francia as a refugee from Zaragoza in Spain probably in the early 780s, see Freeman 2003: ch. VIII; he came to Aachen at Charles's behest in 789, see Nelson 2013b: 288-92, and was at the Regensburg Council in 791.
61. Below, sec. (xi); Freeman 1985: 105 (repr. 2003: ch. III, 105), and 2003: ch. I, 6-7.
62. *Ann. Maximin.* s.a. 792, p. 22: 'et libri plurimi . . . combusti sunt'. See *Cod. Theodos.* 16. 5. 66, and *Cod. Justin.* 1. 1. 3. 1; Sarefield 2004: 287-96, and 2007: 59-73. My thanks to Simon Corcoran for these references. See further McKitterick 2004: 218-20; and Bonnington 2016: 1-10.
63. *Ann. Lauriss.* s.a. 791.
64. Hägermann 2000; Fouracre 2013, ch. XI; Fried 2017: chs. 4 and 5.
65. Weber 1968: 252; Mann 1987: 22-8.
66. Nelson 2009a.
67. *Ann. Mos.* s.a. 791, *recte* 792, have 'Pippin resolved treacherously to usurp his father's realm (*regnum*) for himself by killing his father and brother [singular]'. Cf. Judges: 8 and 9.
68. Nelson 2009a: 11.
69. Notker, *Gesta Karoli*, ed. Haefele, II, c. 12, pp. 71-2.
70. *ArF* rev. s.a. 792, p. 93.
71. Notker, *Gesta Karoli*, ed. Haefele, II, c. 12. My translation draws heavily on those of Thorpe 1977: 153-4, and, especially gratefully, Hammer 2008: 263.
72. Hammer 2008: 261 and n. 98. The untitled '*Karalus*' might already have been being groomed for kingship of an enlarged Francia – though my suggestion is certainly skewed by hindsight.
73. Krah 1987: 28-40. For Peter of Verdun, see Schieffer 1997a: 167-82; for Theodold, see D. 181, wherein Charles exculpated the count and restored the inherited and acquired lands which the king had confiscated, and The-

odold's own charter, CLA XVI, no. 638, pp. 96–9, in which many estates in the Chambliois were given to St-Denis; Le Jan 1989: 265; Nelson 2009a: 30, n. 22. For the Bavarian Helmoin, Brown 2001: 134–5, 147, 164.

74. *Ann. Lauresham.* s.a. 792, p. 35, 'since the king did not wish him to be put to death, the Franks judged that he must be subjected to God's service. And . . . the king sent him, now a cleric, into a monastery', King 1987: 140; Einhard *VK* c. 20, says 'Pippin was tonsured and allowed, of his own free will, to enter the monastery of Prüm'. He died at Prüm in 811, *Ann. Laurissenses minores* s.a. 811, p. 121.

75. Hammer 2008: 241.

76. Konecny 1976: 65–6, with n. 9 at 193; Nelson 2014d: 432–9.

77. See Ch. 4.

78. *Ann. Lauresh.* s.a. 792, p. 35.

79. Leyser 1979: 77.

80. Garipzanov 2016: 62–5.

81. Naismith 2014.

82. See Ch. 6 (ix) for the case of Count Roland.

83. See Ch. 11.

84. Brown 2001: 102–23; Davis 2015: 63–77, 243–59; Nelson 2018a.

85. Freeman 2003, I: 53.

86. Freeman 2003, VIII: 186–7.

87. *Opus Caroli* I, 1, pp. 105–15.

88. For western failure to understand Greek and hence Greek theology, see above, sec. (vii); for mutual linguistic ignorance, Auzépy 1997: 291–2; for knowledge of Greek, and ignorance of Greek, at Rome, Noble 2009: 160; Gantner 2013: 310–18; for the rift between Rome and Byzantium in 776, F. Hartmann 2006: 164–72; Gantner 2013: 330–35.

89. Herrin 2013: 226 and 235, n. 15.

90. Freeman 2003, VIII: 190–91.

91. Noble 2009: 158–69, esp. 164–5.

92. Gantner 2013: 336–7.

93. *Opus Caroli* II, 16, in Freeman and Meyvaert, eds., 1998: 265, l. 20 '*Augustino meo, immo vero Dei cultori*'; see Freeman 2003 I: 75 with n. 360: 'the most theatrical' of Theodulf's settings of *testimonia* in the *Opus Caroli*.

94. Further details, Freeman 2003, II: 666–7.

95. Freeman 2003, I: 71, and III: 66. See Ch. 1, p. 4.

96. A comparable response from Charles to the public reading at court of a work of Alcuin was critical: Alcuin, Ep. 172 (April/May 799), p. 284, understandably professed himself '*caritatis calamo vulneratus*' ('wounded by the pen of love').

97. Freeman 2003, V: 598–600.

98. Dahlhaus-Berg 1975: 193.

99. Dahlhaus-Berg 1975: 38, 190–206.

100. The quotation is in fact from the First Epistle of John 4:1.

101. Theodulf used the word *rationabiliter* six times: *Opus Caroli* pp. 428, l. 28, 431, ll. 22–3, 455, l. 17, 494, l. 8, 535, l. 31, 547, l. 28.

102. Liebeschütz 1950: 17–44; Nelson 2014b: 65–82, at 69, and 2015a: 113–22, at 120.

103. *Opus Caroli* I, 8, in Freeman and Meyvaert, eds. 2003: 145–6. The text was Augustine, *De diversis quaestionibus* 74 (CC 44A: 213, line 5).

104. Einhard *VK* c. 4; Fried 2016: 391. Cf. Riché 1981: ch. XI, pp. 59–70, and Ch. 3 above.

105. *Ann. Mos.* s.a. 792, *recte* 793, p. 498.

106. Hack 2014: 53–63, now the best starting-point for research on the textual accounts of the canal-project.

107. *ArF* s.a. 793, ed. F. Kurze, *MGH SRG*, Hannover, 1895, p. 92.

108. *ArF* rev. s.a., p. 95.

109. *Ann. Lauriss.* s.a. 793, p. 35: '*Et domnus rex cum apud Reganesburg iterum celebrasset pascha, et in estivo tempore voluisset cum navibus venire in Francia, et aliquem fossatum iussisset facere inter duo flumina, id est inter Alcmona et Ratanza, et ibi multum demorasset . . . Rex tamen, Christo adiuvante, de eodem loco navigio pervenit ad Franconofurt, et ibi ipsum hiemem resedit.*' See Collins 2005: 52–70.

110. *Ann. Guelf.* s.a., ed. Pertz, *MGH SS* I, p. 45: '*Karolus resedit Reganespu-ruc . . . post haec egrediens navigio pervenit in Sualafeld ad fossatum magnum; hieme inchoante cum illis navibus et per terram tractis et per flumina venit ad Franchonofurt, et ibi hiemavit.*' See Garipzanov 2010: 123–38, convincingly suggesting the author was a Regensburg cleric.

111. *Ann.Mos.* s.a. 792, 793, p. 498: '*Hoc anno isdem Karlus rex in praefata urbe [Rehanesburg] nativitatem Domini celebrate totum pene sequente anno [793] ibidem resedit, except quod circa tempus automni ad quon-dam aquaeductum quem inter Danuvium fluvium et Radantum alveum facere caeperat, secessit ibique praefato opera sedulus insistens, partem huius anni que supererat pene perstetit; praeter quod paucis diebus ante natale Domini ad Sanctum Kilianum [Würzburg] praefatum opus imperfectum derelinquens advenit ibique eandem natalem Domini cum fine huius anni et initio alterius celebravit.*' Hack 2014: 53–62 is illuminating.

112. *Ann. Guelf.* s.a. 793, p. 45.

113. Pohl 1988: 16–21; Pohl 2018: 344–402.

114. In the 790s, the name Avaria was used by Alcuin, Ep. 112 (796), p. 162; in Capit. 49, c. 2 (806), p. 136, in reference to the area beyond the Enns into which troops can be sent.

115. In 792, Charles 'made a boat-bridge across the Danube to use in the war against the Huns', *ArF* rev. s.a. p. 93 ('Avars' were consistently called 'Huns' by the reviser).

116. My thanks go to Lukas Werther for drawing my attention to a charter of Louis the German (D. 3, dated 5 January 831, pp. 3–4, available online, RI no. 1342), in which is embedded the lost charter of Charles for Herrieden.

117. Squatriti 2002a: 16–18, 20, 40–41, 2002b.

118. Scott 1998.

119. Scott 1998: 257–8; Moreland 2000: 1–34; Näsman 2000: 35–68; Wickham 2005: 345–77, esp. 347–56; Buc 2001: 249–50.

120. Reuter 1993, repr. 2006: : 388–412, esp. 411, differentiated rulership style from institutional methods.

121. See Nelson 2015b. Nelson and Werther, forthcoming, discuss the use of Vitruvius by the engineers working on Charles's canal project.

122. Devroey 2011.

123. Davies 2010: 111–33; Werther 2014: 95–8.

124. Ettel and Wunschel 2014: 79–80; Wyss 1999: 138–41.

125. Hägermann 2000: 328–31; Werther 2014: 45–52.

126. See Werther and Feiner 2014, and previous section (x).

127. Capit. I, no. 28, cc. 4 and 5, p. 74; Devroey 2011; Witthöft 1997 (i): 219–52; Verhulst 2002: 128–9; Campbell 2010: 243–64.

128. See n. 111 above.

129. Braudel 1981.

130. P. Brown 2012: 8–14.

131. P. Brown 2012: 12.

132. Sarris 2011: 17–32.

133. Claudian, *Panegyricus*, ed. Birt 1892: 160, ll. 276–7; Anton 1968: 46, n. 5.

134. Augustine, *De civitate Dei* V, 24, eds. Dombart and Kalb, CCSL XLVII (1955): 160.

135. Verhulst 1965, repr. 1992: no. VI, and 2002: 25–6, 123–4, 128–9, 133–4; Campbell 2010: 243–64.

136. P. Brown 2012: 62.

137. Mordek 2005: 1–52, at 6–7. See above Ch. 5.

11. SAXONS, SARACENS, NORTHMEN AND THE COUNCIL OF FRANKFURT

1. *Ann. Petav.* s.a. 792, p. 18; *Ann. S. Amandi* s.a. 792, p. 14; *Ann. Guelf.* s.a. 792, p. 45.

2. *Ann. Lauriss.* s.a. 792, p. 35; cf. *Ann. Mos.* s.a. 791, *recte* 792, p. 498; 'returned to being pagans' (*rursum pagani facti sunt*). St Augustine had used the term *paganismus*, and 'ego Pippinus', when still *dux et princeps Francorum*, had issued conciliar decrees at Soissons (744) including (in some MSS) c. VI, '*Christianus populus paganismum non faciat*', *Conc.*

Aevi Karolini Part I (1906), p. 35. (I've not found another instance of the word *paganismus* in Charles's reign.)

3. Fichtenau 1978; Collins 2005: 56–7 (sceptical); McKitterick 2004: 109–10, and 2010 (judicious); see also Diesenberger 2018: 40–41.

4. *ArF* rev. s.a. 793, p. 95, cf. the same phrase s.a. 783, p. 65.

5. Genealogical scholarship has proposed (often rather speculatively) various relationships between William and other members of the extended family of the Pippinids: see Le Jan 1995, Tables 19, p. 213, and 50, p. 437.

6. Buc 2000: 202–7.

7. *Chron. Moissiac.* s.a., 793, ed. Kettemann, ii: 65–6, and i: 139–255, and Map at p. 263.

8. D. 173 (27 July 792).

9. Alcuin, Ep. 20, p. 57, and cf. Isaiah 5: 25.

10. See above, Chs. 8, 9.

11. Melleno 2014 offers a fine analysis of the rich material on commerce and politics in the northern world: it could have benefitted from a discussion of the last bit of Alcuin's Ep. 20, p. 58.

12. Alcuin, Ep. 7, p. 32.

13. *ArF* s.a. 794. This writer more than once used *synodus* for assembly.

14. See Fried 1994: 38, Map.

15. Fried 1994: 26–7.

16. D. 176, an original (22 Feb. 794, '*actum super fluvium Moin in loco nuncupante Franconofurd*'); Fried 1994: 26.

17. D. 177 (31 March 794): '*actum in Franconofurd*'.

18. D. 178, 20 July 794, '*actum Franconofurd palatio*'.

19. MGH Conc. Aevi Karolini I (1906), no. 19 G, *Capitulare Frankofurtense* c. 56, p. 171.

20. Fried 1994: 25.

21. *ArF* rev. s.a. 794, p. 95; cf. *ArF* s.a. p. 94: 'At Frankfurt there was gathered a great synod (*synodus magna*) of bishops of the Gauls, the Germans and the Italians, and Pope Hadrian's legates, whose names were Theophylact and Stephen, were there.' The legate Theophylact was very probably the same man as the bishop of Todi, George's colleague in 786.

22. Capit. I, no. 28, p. 73.

23. W. Hartmann 1997: 334, 340.

24. *Formulae Imperiales* no. 49, p. 323, '*cum Fastrada regina domni genitoris nostri Karoli piissimi augusti de Baoaria hiemandi gratia ad Franconovurd veniret*'; Staab 1997: 195, n. 66, and Nelson 1997a: 160. As usual in formulae, the gap signifies 'fill in the name as required', Rio 2009: 45–7, and for the collection, 132–4.

25. Nelson 1997a: 162–3; M. Hartmann 2009: 102. See further Staab 1997: 183–218, esp. 186–208, rebutting early medieval (Einhard *VK* c. 20: 'cruelty' (twice repeated)) and modern (Fried 1994: 26, 'young, beautiful and

cruel') charges against Fastrada, and suggesting other indications of her political influence: see above Ch. 10 (v). Information on those present at the great synod is scarce; but it seems wise not to differentiate too sharply between family occasions (complete with nannies) and synods.

26. *ArF* s.a., p. 94; *A F antiq.* s.a., p. 138; *Ann. Guelf.* s.a., p. 45 give the precise date.

27. Staab 1997: 201–3; M. Hartmann 2009: 103.

28. Theodulf *Carm.* XXIV, p. 483. For pertinent comments on earlier readings see Andersson 2014: 66. Early modern editions of Theodulf's oeuvre have been superseded by better ones.

29. Staab 1997: 205–6, with n. 105, makes sense of the poem (see his suggestions, quoted above).

30. Hildegard's 36-line epitaph written by Paul the Deacon for inscribing on her tomb at St-Arnulf's, Metz, was a much more elaborate affair, and part of a larger dynastic campaign. Hildegard was a mother of sons and kings: Fastrada had only daughters.

31. Paulinus, *Libellus Sacrosyllabus*, MGH *Conc.* II, 1, pp. 130–42, at 131: '*Quadam die residentibus cunctis in aula sacri palatii, adsistentibus in modum coronae presbyteris, diaconibus cunctoque clero, sub praesentia praedicti principis allata est epistola missa ab Elipando, auctore inhormi negotii, Toletanae sedis antistite Hispaliensi finitimae ruri. Cumque iubente rege publica voce recitata fuisset, statimque surgens venerabilis princeps de sella regia stetit supra gradum suum, adlocutus est de causa fidaei prolixo sermone et adiecit: "Quid vobis videtur? Ab anno prorsus praeterito et ex quo coepit huius pestis insania tumescente perfidiae ulcu diffusius ebulisse, non parvus in his regionibus, licet in extremis finibus regni nostri, error inolevit, quam censura fidaei necesse est modis omnibus resecare."* '

32. The reference to the lower clergy's presence 'in the shape of a crown' in a circle around the seated bishops followed the liturgical order for the holding of a synod: *Konzilsordines/Ordines de celebrando concilio,* ed. Schneider 1996: 128, 138–41. This *ordo,* p. 139, adds after the clerical participants: '*Deinde ingrediantur laici, qui electione concilii interesse meruerint*', 'Then there enter the laymen deemed worthy to be chosen to participate in the council.' This could have a bearing on the differentiation between 'family-times' and synods, above, n. 25.

33. Perhaps during discussion of the heresy of Felix: see next note.

34. Felix had, of course, been condemned earlier, at Regensburg.

35. See Ch. 10 (vii); Bonnery 1997: 767–86; Cavadini 1997: 787–808; Fried 2016: 378–81.

36. See Ch. 10 (xi); Auzépy 1997: 279–300, esp. 289–90, very helpfully offers a Byzantinist's perspective on Frankfurt.

37. Innes 2008.

38. See Ch. 13 below.

39. D. 169, p. 228.
40. Wolfram 1987: 188; Pohl 1988: 18–20; W. Brown 2001: 94 puts Fater's words into Charles's mouth, but the outcome was the same.
41. Diesenberger 2006: 110, 116.
42. Becher 1993: 67–8 (following Fichtenau) saw Archbishop Ricbod of Trier as the patron or supervisor of these annals.
43. Schieffer 1997c: 167–82, esp. 169.
44. Becher 1993: 73.
45. Schieffer 1997c: 169–70.
46. Verhulst 2002: 124.
47. Rio 2017: 162–5, for *mancipia* as unfree tenants or farmhands.
48. Mordek 2005, as cited above, Ch. 6.
49. Nelson 2014c: 504.
50. Dating: Garipzanov 2016: 59–67; context Garipzanov 2016: 67–71; Verhulst 2002; Devroey and Wilkin 2012; Naismith 2014: 28–30, 35–6, 38–9.
51. Garipzanov 2016: 70, 72, 73.
52. Bruand 2002: 160–65; Wickham 2008: 27–8; Naismith 2014: 20, 25, 30–39; Garipzanov 2016: 67–8.
53. Garipzanov 2016: 61–7.
54. Davis 2015: 278–89, with at 288, Table 5: 1, showing the learning-gap.
55. See below, Chs. 12, 13.
56. C. 13 quoted the Rule of St Benedict c. 22; and cc. 6 and 25 quoted from the Capitulary of Herstal (c. 1 and c. 13).
57. Fried 2016: 392.
58. *Admonitio* c. 42, p. 202, from the African Council (*Registri ecclesiae Carthaginensis excerpta*, c. 11, via the Dionysio-Hadriana), and Frankfurt c. 42, Capit. I, no. 28, p. 77.
59. Fouracre 1999: 151.
60. *AMP*, see above, Ch. 2 (ii).
61. Smith 2012, 2015.
62. Nelson 2001a, and below, Ch. 15.
63. Mayr-Harting 2002: 119.
64. In the new MGH edition of the *Admonitio* (see Ch. 10) the numbers of all *capitula* from 59 to 68 are reduced by one, and from 69 to 82, are reduced by two. Hence c. 76 becomes c. 74.
65. *Admonitio*, c. 74, Glatthaar et al. 2013: 228.
66. Council of Frankfurt c. 47, p. 77, in MGH Capit. II, no. 28.
67. *Vita Leobae* c. 14, p. 128; see also above Ch. 7.
68. Bloch 1961: 64.
69. W. Hartmann 1997: 331–5; Mordek 1997: 205–28; Glatthaar et al. 2013: 112–15.
70. Thegan, *Gesta Hludowici* c. 7, p. 176; Bullough 2005: 142–6; Brandes 1997: 56.

71. Alcuin, Ep. 15, pp. 40–41.
72. Alcuin, *Carm.* XXIII, p. 244, l. 23, from his elegy on his loss of his little cell at Aachen, written in the late 790s, and echoes directly *Carm.* IX, p. 229, l. 11, his elegy on the destruction of Lindisfarne, written in 793. Godman 1985: 127, 125, gives the Latin with English translations.
73. Alcuin, Epp. 16, 17, 18, 19, 20, 21, 22, pp. 42–60. For Ep. 20, see also n. 9 above.
74. Frankfurt c. 56. Bullough 1997, 2003b: 351, 359, 2004, 2005: 139–40.
75. Marenbon 1981: 30.
76. The writing may have extended into 795: Bullough 2003b: 351, 359.
77. Alcuin, *De Rhetorica*, p. 66, ll. 10–11.
78. Alcuin, *De Rhetorica*, p. 66, ll. 12–17.
79. Alcuin, *De Rhetorica*, p. 68, ll. 34–48.
80. Alcuin, *De Rhetorica*, Intro. Howell 1941: 8–10.
81. Alcuin, *De Rhetorica*, pp. 124–8, ll. 883–933, pp. 130–36, ll. 977–1050.
82. Alcuin, *De Rhetorica*, pp. 136–42, ll. 1070–116.
83. Alcuin, *De Rhetorica*, p. 146, ll. 1232–5.
84. Alcuin, *De Rhetorica*, p. 154, ll. 1357–9, 1361–3.
85. Howell 1941: 8–10.
86. Kempshall 2011: 8, for rhetoric as the art of persuasion.
87. Alcuin, *De Rhetorica*, p. 68, ll. 56–8.
88. Kempshall 2011: 10.
89. Reuter 2006: 193, and passim; Nelson 2009c: 69–81.
90. Nelson 1990, 1998, 2001a; Innes 2011.
91. Fried 2016: 392–8 (German original, '*Ein versteckter Mißerfolg: Die Synode von Frankfurt*', *Karl der Grosse*, 2013: 455–61).

12. THE BEGINNING OF THE END OF THE SAXON WARS

1. *ArF* rev. s.a. 793, p. 95; compare *ArF* s.a. 793: 'A *missus* brought news that Saxons had again broken their faith' (*missus nuntavit Saxones iterum fidem suam fefelisse*).
2. *Ann. S. Amand* s.a. 792, p. 14, King 1987: 158.
3. *Ann. Guelf.* s.a. 792, p. 45, King 1987: 158.
4. Geary 1983; Pohl 1998. On the Transformation of the Roman World project (1993–8), Wood 1997: 217–27; on the Vienna School, Hakenbeck 2011: 11–26.
5. A characteristically thought-provoking suggestion of Pohl 1999: 234.
6. Fried 2013: 154, citing Springer 2004, passim.
7. *ArF* s.a. 775, p. 43, trans. King 1987: 112.
8. Paderborn in 1999; Aachen in 2015.

9. See Ch. 4 (iv).

10. Althoff 1998: 64.

11. Bührer-Thierry 1998.

12. *Ann. Mos.* s.a. 792.

13. *ArF* rev. s.a. 798.

14. Ep. 249.

15. *ArF* s.a. 795, p. 96.

16. Becher 1993: 111–20 shows the roots of this expression in bilateral oaths of fidelity. Cf. *ex parte Saxanorum* a few lines further on.

17. The Abodrites were called 'our Slavs', *Ann. Lauriss.* s.a. 798, p. 37 ('*Sclavi nostri qui dicuntur Abotridi*').

18. *Ann. Lauriss.* 795, p. 36, trans. King 1987: 141 (with some modifications).

19. *ArF* 778, p. 52, King 1987: 80, Saxons, exceptionally, 'plundered in the Rhineland and burned churches and did things to nuns too disgusting to mention'.

20. *Ann. Petav.* s.a. 795, 796, p. 18. Cf. *Ann. Naz.* 786, p. 41, '*missis ex satellitibus suis contra eos* [the Thuringians], *qui sagaciter atque fiduciater contra eos perrexerunt, praedia possessionesque eorum devastantes*' ('sending some of his fighting-men against them, who proceeded against them with shrewdness and faithfulness, they devastated their estates and properties').

21. See the debate between Innes 2000: 143–56, and Halsall 2003: 76–81.

22. For Ricbod's supervision of the production of these annals, Fichtenau 1953, 1978; Hägermann 2000: 276, 412, 418; McKitterick 2004: 109–10.

23. *Ann. Petav.* s.a. 796, p. 18, King 1987: 160.

24. *Ann. S. Amandi* (a contemporary source), s.a. 798, p. 14: '*Carlus in Saxonia hiemavit, et tota aestate ibidem fuit, et hospites* [for *obsides?*] *capitaneos 1600 inde adduxit, et per Franciam divisit.*' For these annals, Kaschke 2006: 145–54.

25. *Ann. Lauriss.* p. 37; cf. *ArF* s.a. 798, p. 104, *ArF* rev. p. 105: 4,000 killed.

26. *ArF* s.a. 799, p. 106, *ArF* rev. p. 107. Cf. Becher 1999c: 22–6, showing how brief was Leo's stay. See Ch. 13, below.

27. *ArF* s.a. 796.

28. Alcuin, Ep. 107 (to Arn, June 796), p. 153; see also Epp. 112, 113 (to Arn).

29. Alcuin, Ep. 110 (to Charles), p. 157.

30. Pohl 1988: 23–9, 48 (Map); Collins 1998b: 89–101, with Map 3; Wilson 2016: 77–82, 203–4, 234–5, 295–352.

31. Alcuin, Ep. 111 (to Meginfrid, late August/September), pp. 159–62; see Nelson 2017b.

32. D. 213* (issued 1 December 811, at Aachen), pp. 284–5.

33. He may be identified perhaps with the Count Gaero in a judgment of Charles of *c*.782, D. 148, p. 201. See above, Ch. 7 (v).

34. D.218* (issued at Aachen, 9 May, 813), pp. 290–92.

35. Innes 2008: 252–9; Gravel 2012: 51–2, 62, 64–5, ch. II and passim; Brown et al., eds. 2013; Mersiowsky 2015 pt 1. 80–95; pt 2: 565–77, 677–88.
36. MGH Epp. KA III, no. 2, pp. 300–302. For the date, Springer 2004: 206.
37. *ArF* rev. s.a. 798, p. 103.
38. Springer 2004: 207. For *deportatio* as the penalty for *calumnia* and *infamia*, see CTh 9. 39. 2, and Breviary of Alaric (BrTh. 9. 29. 2). See also *ArF* s.a. 818, p. 148, *deportatio* and exile as penalty for *fraus et coniuratio*; *Ann. Fuld.* s.a. 820, p. 22, as penalty for *infidelitas*. My thanks go to Simon Corcoran for pointing me to the legal evidence.
39. Bardowik is not shown on the maps in most of the recent books, and when it *is* shown, it is sometimes on, sometimes (correctly) near, the Elbe.
40. Springer 2004: 209, and cf. 207. Charanis 1961 is still valuable on population transfers in the Byzantine world.
41. For *vassi sui* in this context, I have picked and chosen from Niermeyer 1997, meanings 4 and 6.
42. Springer 2004: 209; for earlier scholarship, see Goldberg 1995, and see above, Ch. 7.
43. *ArF* s.a. 798, p. 104, King 1987: 91.
44. Kosto 2002: 128–38, though making little of the Lorsch Annals, remains the best critical account of variations on the hostage theme.
45. See on transmigration, collation and mass deportations of 795, *Ann. Lauriss.* s.a. 799, 804; Diesenberger 2018: 35–57.
46. Capit. no. 27, c. 11, p. 72. The word Bortrini appears here uniquely. Siclus (sicclus), from the Hebrew *shekel*, is a liquid measure. Cf. Westphalians, Ostphalians and Angrarii, in Capit. no. 115, the *Indiculus* (Mainz hostage list) of 805/806. See Ch. 14 below.
47. See above Ch. 11.
48. The re-coinage of 793, see above, Ch. 10, had little impact on the near-coinless north, still less the north-east.
49. I am very grateful to Alice Rio for her comments on the Capitulare's postscript.
50. On Bernard, Weinrich 1963: 90–91; see Ch. 5 above.
51. *Ann. Lauriss* s.a. 796, p. 37, King 1987: 142.
52. Young Charles, *ArF* 799, 805, 806, 808, *Chron. Moissiac.* 805, 806, 808, 810; Pippin, *Ann. Alem.* 797, *ArF* 800, 801, 805–7, 810, *Ann. Guelf.* 800; Louis *ArF* 808, *Chron. Moissiac.* 803, Astron. cc. 8–11 (797–800), 13–16 (803–8), 18 (812).
53. *Laudes*, see above, Ch. 7.
54. Innes 2003; Stone 2012: 67, 138, 188–213.
55. Nelson 2007: ch. VI.
56. See Ch. 7 (iii), Ch. 10 (iv).
57. *ArF* rev. 793, p. 93.
58. Hägermann 2000: 328.

59. Collins 1998b: 94 with n. 32.

60. See above, Chs. 7 and 8, and p. 335, on losses of men.

61. *ArF* 791, *Meginfrid camerarius*, mentioned three times in this one annal. Nelson 2017a.

62. *Chron. Moissiac.* s.a. 793, *Ann. Alem.* 793, Astron. cc. 5, 13. See above Ch. 10.

63. *ArF* s.a. 798, p. 104, *ArF* rev. p. 105; '4,000 enemy slain' is the kind of high and round figure that arouses suspicions: cf. the 4,500 figure of 782.

64. *ArF* s.a. 799, p. 108, *ArF* rev. s.a. 799, p. 109; cf. Reuter 2006, and Ch. 14 below.

65. Cf. *De ordine palatii* c. 5, ll. 440, 455–6. The core of this text was written by Adalhard *c.*812, reflecting his experiences at Charles's court. See Ch. 16 below.

66. *ArF* rev. s.a. 778; see Ch. 6, above.

67. *ArF* rev. s.a. 798, see above.

68. Eric's memorial verses by Paulinus of Aquileia, *Poet.* I, *Carm.* II, pp. 131–3; Anon., Epitaphia no. X, Gerold's epitaph, p. 114.

69. Durham, *Book of Life*, Story 2005a: 102–3 ('Magenfrith' and 'Karlus'); Alcuin, Ep. 211, pp. 351–2; Anonymous, epitaph of Eggihard, *Poet.* I, pp. 109–10, trans. Dutton 1993: 48.

70. Dhuoda, *Handbook* VIII, 16, quoting Maccabees 12:46.

71. Schieffer 1990: 157–8 and *passim*; Staab 1997: 191–7.

72. *ArF* rev. s.a., p. 77, King 1987: 121.

73. Eichler 2011.

74. *ArF* Glossary, p. 201.

75. *ArF* rev. s.a. p. 93. Cf. *ArF* s.a. pp. 92, 94: '*missi apostolici cum magnis muneribus praesentati sunt*', trans. King 1987: 88: 'Papal envoys bearing great gifts were presented.'

76. *ArF* rev. s.a. 797, p. 103.

77. *ArF* rev. s.a. 797, p. 103, King 1987: 128. Note the calibration of gift-quality. Cf. Nelson 2010b: 129–40; 2011a.

78. *ArF* rev. s.a., p. 103, King 1987: 128, translating *comitatus* as 'court'.

79. Capit. II, no. 297, c. 5, p. 431. See Depreux 1997: 29–39.

80. Astron. c. 19, p. 340, King 1987, p. 179. It is hard to date this episode, given Ercanbald's longevity (he is first attested as a notary in 778) and the Astronomer's shaky chronology in his record of the latter years of Charles's reign. Tremp's suggestion of 812 for c. 19, ed. Astron, p. 340, is a guess.

81. For the Aquitanian palaces, see Gravel 2012: 317–23, with map at 318.

82. Theodulf, *Carm.* XXV (dated 795), *Poet.* I, p. 487. See also Hack 2011: 22–32.

83. Garrison 1997.

84. Alcuin, *Carm.* XXVI (dated 796), *Poet.* I, p. 246: 'Little Zaccheus has climbed up a tall tree/to watch the crowd of scribes running about;/with small letters and parchment he provides help to the needy', trans. Godman

1985: 121. The biblical reference is to the tax-gatherer short of stature in Luke 19:2–3.

85. Airlie 2012, chs. V, VI (though the evidence cited here is from the reign of Louis the Pious) and VII. For nicknames, see Garrison 1994, 1998b, 2000, 2002, 2010a, 2010b; also Nelson 2007, chs. XI, XIII–XV.

86. Charles probably assigned Alcuin income from some religious houses during those years, but none of those mentioned in his letters belonged to this first stay.

87. Bullough 2005: 146, 148.

88. Daly and Suchier, eds. 1939: 137–43, at 143, trans. Dutton 1993: 123–8, at 128.

89. For Pippin and his later career, see Ch. 14.

90. Ep. 119, p. 174. For this genre, cf. Cathwulf, above. Ch. 2.

91. Ep. 217, to Young Charles, post-4 April, 801, see Ch. 13, below, and also for Ep. 304.

92. Ep. 188: 315–16.

93. See Chs. 14 and 15, below.

94. Patzold 2014b: 52.

95. On Baugulf, who also embodied political qualities highly approved by Charles, see above Ch. 8.

96. York Annals s.a. 795. That this report reached York so quickly and in such detail indicates Alcuin's personal witness; cf. *Ann. Guelf.* s.a. 796; *Ann. S. Amandi* s.a. 796; Story 2003: 101, 103.

97. Einhard, *VK* prologue, p. 1, c. 13, pp. 15–16, trans. Ganz 2008: 17, 27–8.

98. Einhard, *VK* c. 7, p. 10, trans. Ganz 2008: 23: qualities displayed especially in the Saxon Wars; Ganz 2005.

99. For Liutgard: Alcuin, Epp. 96, 102; and M. Hartmann 2007.

100. Einhard, *VK* c. 13, p. 16, trans. Ganz 2008: 27.

101. Bullough 1991b: 146, evoking the centripetal pull of Calcutta in the Indian Raj before 1911.

102. Alcuin, Epp. 69 (c.789–96?), 224, (801), 98 (796), 111 (796), 33 (793–95), and 305 (801–4). See Bullough 2002.

103. Alcuin, Ep. 149, pp. 243–4. The modern editor has supplied the nicknames in notes to the text. That these scholars *had* nicknames is significant in itself.

104. For the Aachen park, baths and fountain, Rollason 2016: 104–5, 120–22, 134–5, 277.

105. Alcuin, Ep. 121, p. 177.

106. Paravicini.

107. McKitterick 2008: 137–8.

108. Niermeyer 1997 s.v. *ministerium*, meaning 7.

109. Ep. 107 (796), pp. 154–5.

110. Epp. 98 and 99 (795).

111. Ep. 99, p. 143, l. 27; Bullough 2004: 447, with n. 47.

112. Ep. 110 (796), p. 158.
113. Nelson 2017a.
114. Ep. 111 (796), p. 160.
115. Ep. 111, pp. 159–62.
116. Godman 1987: 11.
117. For the occasion itself, see Ch. 13, below.
118. Paderborn Epic, *Poet.* I, ll. 220–23, p. 371, Nelson 2007: ch. XV, p. 270.

13. INTERESTING TIMES, DANGEROUS TIMES

1. F. Hartmann 2006: 291.
2. Cf. Noble 1984: 61.
3. F. Hartmann 2006: 292–300. An English translation is keenly awaited.
4. This was hypothesized by Schaller 1976 and has been generally accepted by experts on poetry in the reign of Charles. Three manuscripts (from the ninth, tenth and twelfth centuries) preserve the epitaph, see *Poetae* ed. Dümmler 1881: I, p. 101.
5. Ganz 2000: 297–315, esp. 302–3. In the printed edition, *Poetae* I, pp. 113–14, the editor normalizes the punctuation.
6. The punctuation of this line is the modern editor's. On the visual effect, see below.
7. Edited by Dümmler in *Poetae* I, no. IX, pp. 113–14. The epitaph for Hadrian is still to be seen in St Peter's, Rome; for a photo, Story 2005b: 158. The translated extracts are mine; for a full English trans. Dutton 1993: 46–7.
8. Einhard, *VK* c. 19, p. 24.
9. Higgitt 2001.
10. *Ann. Lauriss.* s.a. 795, p. 36, trans. King 1987: 142. For other details about the epitaph, see Godman 1982: lxxvi–viii; Schaller 1970.
11. For more on how the marble slab might have been transported to Rome, Story forthcoming.
12. Story 2005b: 162.
13. Poetae I, *Theodulfi Carm.* XXVI, pp. 489–90. For translation and brief, thought-provoking commentary, Andersson 2014: 74–5.
14. Theodulf was a refugee from Spain, Freeman 2003: ch. VIII.
15. See e.g. Charles in Aquitaine in 769, or campaigning against Saxons in 772, or following Pippin's reforming aspirations in the *Epistola generalis* of 787.
16. Einhard, *VK* c. 18.
17. The suggestion of Andersson 2014: 74.
18. Bernard 1998: 55–61.
19. For difficulties c. 790, see above Ch. 10 (ii).

20. Story 2003: 196.
21. Capit. I, no. 13 (764/5), c. 4, p. 32. See Nelson 2014b: 72–82.
22. Capit. I, no. 22 (789), c. 75, p. 60. For *hospites*, see Niermayer 1997 s.v. meanings 7 and 8.
23. Reuter 2006: 39.
24. Story 2003: 196.
25. *Novellae Valentiniani III*, in Nelson 1996: 94–7.
26. Story 2003: 139–40, 195–6.
27. Notker, *Gesta Karoli* I, 34, pp. 47–8. I prefer Thorpe's translation here because, as a former officer in World War II, he felt a real sympathy with his subject, and his choice of tone strikes me as entirely apt. Charles's complaints about the cloaks, as recorded in his letter, connect very plausibly with the story as received by Notker: serendipity!
28. Fuhrmann 1966, 1973; Huyghebaert 1979; Goodson and Nelson 2010. For the broader context of such late antique writings, see Cooper 1999, 2009.
29. Basic orientation, Noble 1984: 134–7; the translation easiest to come by is that of Henderson 1892, now reprinted by Dutton 1993: 13–220.
30. Note the references in cc. 14, 15, and 16 to cavalrymen, horses and saddle-cloths, and groom-service, Hack 2006–7: i, 414, ii, 854–5; Nelson 2016a: 359–61.
31. *Cod. Car.* no. 60, p. 587, trans. King 1987: 287.
32. Goodson and Nelson 2010: 452–3.
33. Goodson and Nelson 2010: 448–9.
34. Goodson and Nelson 2010: 449, 454–5, 457–9. Their view challenges that of Fried 2007 on this and other grounds. See also next section.
35. Story 1999: Rio 2009: 143–4.
36. Hack 2006–7: i, 414–15, 416–20; 2006–7: ii, IV, 697–722, 822–928 (esp. 855, 910, with prosopography of envoys at 987–1028).
37. Müller, in Krause, ed. 2013: 54–72.
38. *Chron. Moissiac.* 796, ed. Kettemann, pp. 84–5: '*Ibi firmaverat sedem suam atque ibi fabricavit ecclesiam mirae magnitudinis . . . Fecit autem ibi et palatium, quod nominavit Lateranis, et collectis thesauris suis de regnis suis in Aquis adduci praecepit. Fecit autem et opera multa et magna in eodem loco.*' The palace at Aachen was named the Lateran (as Lateranis) after the pope's palace in Rome.
39. Ristow in Krause, ed. 2013: 119–22; Schaub in Krause, ed. 2013: 145–52; Heckner 2012; Story, pers. comm.
40. Ley in Krause, ed. 2013: 209–73; Heckner 2012: 25–62.
41. Pohle in Krause, ed. 2013: 98–115; Müller in Krause, ed. 2013: 143–5, 157–68, 193–209.
42. Rollason 2016: 273–89, with Figure 9-6.
43. Nelson 2000: 145–53.

44. Falkenstein 1991; Nelson 2000, 2001a; Rollason 2016: 288–9, with Figure 9-13.
45. Capit. I, no. 122, p. 241.
46. Schramm 1968: 209 (quoting an authoritative oral source, a senior canon of the *Domkirche* in the post-war years).
47. Bayer 1999: 445–52; from a St-Gall manuscript of *c*.800 giving an anthology of inscriptions, of which this is the last, entitled *Versus in Aula Ecclesiae in Aquis Palatio*. My thanks go to Jo Story for the translation (only slightly modified here).
48. Rollason 2016: 273–89, at 289, and see Figure 9-13, showing the sightline from the throne.
49. Davis 1992: 179, n. 3.
50. Davis 1992: 173.
51. Luchterhandt 1999; Goodson 2010: 81–159, and specifically on Leo: 25–6, 27–8, 144–5.
52. *Vita Stephani II*, c. 47.
53. Things didn't work out as planned: Nelson 2016b.
54. Gregory I, Reg. VII, 8, VIII, 35, IX, 52 etc. *Vita Gregorii III*, c. 14; Cont. Fred. c. 22, p. 293. Schramm 1968, I: 240.
55. Theophanes, eds. Mango and Scott 1997: 463; King 1987: 339.
56. Compare *ArF* rev. 788 with Theophanes, ed. cit., pp. 640–42; see also above, Ch. 8.
57. Whittow 1996: 144, 149–50; Herrin 2001: 64–129.
58. The date was significant: the Assumption of the Virgin Mary, patroness of Constantinople.
59. Herrin 2000; cf. Bührer-Thierry 1998; Schieffer 2018.
60. *ArF* s.a. 798, trans. King 1987: 91.
61. *ArF* rev. 798, 799; Brown 1995: 345–6; McCormick 2001: 523–31; 2008: 13–18.
62. Brandes 1997: 52–3, drawing on Löwe 1949, and three earlier discoverers (in 1859, 1874 and 1880); Schieffer 2004: 10.
63. Classen 1968: 42, 537–608; Schieffer 2004: 11–13; Nelson 2007: 17–18; cf. Hägermann 2000: 405.
64. Ep. 7, p. 32.
65. See Alcuin, Ep. 149, pp. 241–5. Wallace-Hadrill 1983: 217–25 still illuminates.
66. Nelson 2010c esp. 394–400.
67. Geary 2008. Cf. Theodulf, *Comparatio legis antiquae et modernae*, Poetae I, *Carm.* XXIX, p. 47, l. 47; Dahlhaus-Berg 1975: 36–8, citing *Opus Caroli* II, 27 (in the margin of which is: '*acute*'); Godman 1987: 83–4; Nees 1991: 127–8.
68. Nees 1991: 110–43.
69. Ep. 219 (to Arn), p. 362; Ep. 225 (to Theodulf), p. 368.

70. Ep. 225, p. 368, with citations from Isaiah 58:1 and Hosea 8:1.

71. Nelson 2013b: 293 with n. 32 at 304.

72. Still indispensable is Dahlhaus-Berg 1975.

73. Nees 2013: 177.

74. Weber 1968: 514; Mann 1987: 28.

75. Power 1937 (first published 1924): 16

76. See Campbell 2010: 264; Verhulst 2002: 127.

77. Goodson 2015; Davies 2018.

78. Gibbon, *Decline and Fall*, ch. 49.

79. Campbell 2010.

80. Rollason 2016: 140–41, 149, 156–7.

81. *ArF* s.a. 799, p. 106, Lorsch Annals s.a., p. 37; *ArF* rev. s.a. 799, p. 107, is slightly more expansive at 12 lines.

82. Schieffer 2002 offers a fine analysis; see further F. Hartmann 2011: 378–87, adding further subtleties.

83. Ep. 159, p. 257.

84. Ep. 184, p. 309, Eng. trans. King 1987: 320, no. 17, Allott 1974, no. 102. Candidus had been a student of Alcuin's.

85. Ep. 174, p. 288.

86. Matt. 24:11; 1 Tim. 4:1.

87. Compare Fried 2016: 412–15, 468–9, with W. Hartmann 2010: 217 and Palmer 2014: ch. 5. For Spanish religiosity, Fichtenau 1949: 191, 196–203. See sec. (ix) below, and Ch. 14.

88. Nelson 2007, 2014c.

89. Ep. 179, p. 297, trans. King 1987: 324, no. 21, Allott 1974, no. 102.

90. Theodulf, *Carm.* XXXII, *Poet.* I, pp. 523–4, trans. Andersson 2014 (with one or two slight changes of my own), p. 115.

91. T. Brown 1998: 81–2.

92. Goetz 2007: 207–16.

93. Alcuin, Ep. 179, p. 297.

94. *Ann. Guelf.* s.a. 799, p. 45, trans. King 1987.

95. Becher 2002: 108–9 – estimating mid-September until the beginning of October.

96. Both rated epitaphs: Gerold's brief and austere, by an anonymous author perhaps from the monastery of Reichenau, Eric's an elaborate lament by Paulinus of Aquileia.

97. See Ch. 16.

98. *ArF* s.a. 800.

99. *Vita Leonis III*, c. 10, ed. Duchesne II, pp. 3–4. For the dating, Luchterhandt 1999: 109–22. Becher 2002: 87–112, focuses on the written sources and the Paderborn meeting.

100. Luchterhandt, *Katalog* of the Paderborn Exhibition of 1999, in Stiegemann and Wemhoff, eds. 1999, I: 48–50; Luchterhandt, '*Famulus Petri*', and

'*Päpstliche Palastbau*', Stiegemann and Wemhoff, eds. 1999, I, p. 49, Abb. II, 10, fol. 186r and fol. 104r; 1999, III: 55–70, 109–22, at Abb. 2, p. 110, Abb. 8, p. 118.

101. Goodson and Nelson 2010: 460–67.

102. Wickham 2009: 232, 251.

103. D. 190 (13 June 799), a St-Denis cartulary, now in the Archives Nationales, Paris.

104. D. 319* (13 June 799), now in the Archives Nationales, Paris.

105. Kasten 1997: 138–54.

106. Alcuin, *Poet.* I, *Carm.* XII, l. 6, to Lucia (i.e. Gisla), '*femina verbipotens*', p. 237; Ep. 15, pp. 40–41 (to *dilectissima in Christo virgo Gisla*, admonishing her with *caritas*; Ep. 84, p. 127 (to *carissima soror Gisla*); Ep. 154, p. 249 (to *carissima soror, dulcis amica*); Ep. 196, p. 323, '*humillima Christi famula Gisla*' to Alcuin, '*venerandus pater*'; etc.

107. *AMP* s.a. 804, 805, for further mentions of the Young Charles. See Ch. 14.

108. *ArF* s.a. 800, p.110.

109. *Ann. Lauriss.* s.a. 800, p. 38.

110. Alcuin, Ep. 93 (Charles to Leo, 796), p. 137: 'We have sent to you Angilbert, *manualis nostrae familiaritatis auricolarius* (close to us and our most intimate counsellor).'

111. *Ann. Lauriss.* s.a. 800, p. 38, trans. King 1987: 143.

112. Anon., *Vita Alcuini*, c. 15, p. 193.

113. The second version of the story, Ermold, *In honorem Hludowici*, ll. 599–633.

114. Astron. c. 10, pp. 308–9.

115. Einhard, *VK* c. 18, pp. 22–3.

116. Richter 2001: 23–4; M. Hartmann 2007: 559–61; see further Karras 2006; Stone 2012: chs. 8 and 9; also Ch. 14.

117. For the case in point of the Empress Angilberga, see M. Hartmann 2007: 563–4.

118. M. Hartmann 2007: 567.

119. Alcuin, Epp. 50, 96, 102, 150, 190.

120. Theodulf, *Carm.* XXV, XXXI, trans. Andersson 2014: 69, ll. 83–90, 114, ll. 1–22.

121. Astron. c. 10.

122. *ArF* s.a. 800, p. 110, King 1987: 92–3.

123. Wilson 2016: 137.

124. *ArF* s.a. 800, p. 110.

125. Schramm 1968: 256; Schieffer 2000: 283–4. Charles as *patricius Romanorum* had been met a mile out from the city.

126. *ArF* s.a., p. 110.

127. *Vita Leonis* c. 20, p. 6, trans. Davis 1992: 189. For *obsequium*, see Niermeyer 1997 s.v. meanings 11 and 12. For estimates of size of retinues, Nelson 1986a: 120–26, with n. 33.

128. *Vita Leonis* c. 24, p. 7, trans. Davis 1992: 191–2.
129. Einhard, *VK* c. 28, p. 32.
130. Collins 1998b: 144.
131. Nelson 2007: ch. XII, 1–3, 3–5, 5–6.
132. *ArF* s.a. 801, p. 114, trans. King 1987: 93–4.
133. Nelson 2007: ch. XII; Palmer 2014: 132–46.
134. Compare the list of Leo's gifts listed in *Vita Leonis* c. 9, p. 3, trans. Davis 1992: 183.
135. On the author's identification as Ricbod, see above Ch. 12, and Reimitz 2015: 352–3, 360–63.
136. The earliest example was D. 197* (29 May 801), p. 265.
137. Nelson 2007: ch. XII, pp. 21–2.
138. Ep. 214, p. 358.
139. Epp. 216, p. 360, 215, p. 359.
140. Alcuin, Ep. 217, pp. 360–61. In elite circles and among poets, 'David' was Charles's nickname. See Ch. 12 (viii).
141. Hammer 2012.
142. Nelson 2005a: 11–12. See above, Ch. 12 (viii). Ch. 15 (vii) for mores at the Aachen court.
143. Astron. c. 13, p. 318 with n. 159, trans. King 1987: 173–4, and *Chron. Moissiac.* s.a. 803, ed. Kettemann, pp. 104–5. See Kasten 1997: 264–70, 276–90, 297–302, 318–19, 360–69; Kaschke 2006: 193–202, 297–323.

14. *Fin de siècle – début de siècle*

1. D. 196, pp. 263–4.
2. Davis 2015: 222–3, with nn. 217–19.
3. The earliest example was D. 197* (29 May 801), p. 265. See, definitively, Classen 1951, and Ch. 13 (xiv) above.
4. *ArF* s.a. 801, p. 114, trans. King 1987: 94. See Becher 2012.
5. Freeman and Meyvaert 2001. See Ch. 13 on Germigny.
6. Capit. I, no. 98, pp. 204–6.
7. Hack 2011.
8. Noizet 2004; Meens 2007
9. For glimpses, see Rio 2008a; 2009: 112–17.
10. Ep. 245, p. 393, trans. Allott 1974, p.121; Meens 2007: 284–5.
11. Noizet 2004: 118–19.
12. Ep. 246, pp. 398–9.
13. Ep. 247, pp. 399–401.
14. Cf. St-Denis, Ch. 3 above.
15. Epp. KA II, Ep. 249, p. 403.
16. Suetonius, *Life of Titus*, c. 8; Eutropius, *Breviarium* VII, c. 21, trans. Bird.

17. Capit. I, no. 39; see Noizet 2004: 123–9; also Rosenwein 1999: 227–8, distinguishing immunity from asylum; for the shift from particular case to norm, Becher 2006: 10–14.
18. Capit. I, no. 39, c. 2.
19. Capit. I, no. 39, c. 3.
20. Mordek 1995: 551–2, 1083–4.
21. Nelson 1996: 21–2.
22. Patzold 2007: 331–50.
23. Ep. 254, p. 411.
24. Alcuin, MGH *Poet.* I, *Carm.* XXIII, pp. 243–4, trans. Godman 1985: 124–5.
25. Innes 2011: 157.
26. Patzold 2007.
27. See Ch. 9, above; and Nelson 2018b.
28. Capit. I, no. 33, pp. 91–9.
29. Capit. no. 33, c. 33, p. 97, referring to the case of Fricco, 'who perpetrated an act of incest on a nun', but who is otherwise unknown.
30. Patzold 2007: 345.
31. *Admonitio generalis* c. 75, eds. Mordek et al., p. 228, trans. King 1987: old numbering c. 77, p. 218.
32. Epp. KA II, no. 247, pp. 400–401. Cf. the Legatine Synod of 786, Epp. KA II, c. 4, p. 22: '*ut discretio sit inter canonicum et monachum vel secularem*', 'there should be a distinction [of dress] between a canon and a monk and a secular man'. For authoritative texts, and familiarity of judges with written law, Innes 2011: 168, 170–79; cf. Innes 2009: 299–313 and also Pössel 2006: 259–70; Kikuchi 2012.
33. Capit. no. 33, p. 92.
34. Capit. no. 25, pp. 66–7.
35. Capit. I, no. 122, p. 241; Nelson 2014c; Phelan 2014: 147–207.
36. McCune 2009: 283; Diesenberger 2016: 272–3.
37. *Ann. Lauriss.* s.a. 802, pp. 38–9. See McKitterick 2004: 109, for the idea that the Lorsch Annals 'were actually conceived in reaction to the Royal Frankish Annals'; Collins 2005: 64–9 offers a different angle.
38. *Ann. Lauriss.* s.a. 802, pp. 38–9, trans. King 1987: 144–5. See Hannig 1983.
39. See Ch. 13 (vii).
40. Innes's metaphor gets closer to social realities in Charles's empire than does Hannig's rather mechanistic account of administrative overhaul. See Nelson 2010c: 389–90, on pre-modern ideas about gifts, referencing anthropological approaches.
41. *Poet.* I, *Carmen* XXVIII, p. 501, ll. 283–90.
42. *Form. Marc.* I, 11, ed. and trans. Rio 2008a: 142–4; Ganshof 1969, iii: 585–603.
43. Nees: 1991; Patzold: 2007; Innes 2011; Nelson 2018b.

44. Asser, *Life of Alfred*, cc. 14, 15, trans. Keynes and Lapidge, p. 236, nn. 30–32,

45. Stafford 1981: 3–7.

46. Story 2003: pp. 214–17.

47. de Jong 2008: pp. 280–81. The Eadburh story would buttress de Jong's view on the meaning of the *solarium*: an entrance-way at which a richly endowed visitor bearing gifts would have to wait.

48. Asserius, *De rebus gestis Ælfredi*, c. 15, '*cum ante solarium multa régi afferens dona staret . . . filium meum qui mecum in solario isto stat*', ed. Stevenson, cc. 14–15, pp. 12–14.

49. Esders 1999: 64–93.

50. *ArF* s.a. 802, 803, pp. 117–18; D. 199.

51. *ArF* s.a. 803, p. 118.

52. D. 200 (803); later termed a *villa regia*, DD *regum Germaniae, Ludowici Iunioris* no. 8 (878), p. 345. The *Capitula ecclesiastica*, cc. 2 and 3, decreed at Salz, Capit. I, no. 42 (803 or 804), p. 119, firming up regulations about tithes could have formed part of the meeting of Fortunatus and Charles.

53. *AMP*, s.a. 803, pp. 89–90.

54. D. 201 (803).

55. Krahwinkler 2005: 63–78; Štih 2010: 14–17.

56. *AMP* s.a. 803, p. 90. Hammer 2018 highlights the influential presence of the late Hildegard's kin in Alemannia.

57. Now comprehensively debunked by Springer 2004: 213–15, though not bringing into the picture the Ecclesiastical Capitulary of Salz, Capit. no. 42, (803/4).

58. D. 209 (7 July 809), pp. 279–80.

59. *ArF* s.a. 817, p. 145; Borgolte 1986: 88–90; Wolfram 2013a: 185, 262, 270, 317–18.

60. D. 199, pp. 267–8.

61. Esders 1999: 53–64, at 58.

62. Esders 1999: 60–61.

63. Capit. I, no. 67 (?805), c. 5, p. 144; see Mordek 1995: pp 689–90. Name-tags are among the most useful of the uses of literacy.

64. *Karolus Magnus et Leo Papa*, Poet. I, pp. 370–71, ll. 184–94: '*Liutgardis Karoli pulcherrima nomine coniux . . . Magnanimes inter proceres regina superbo/Gaudet equo . . .*'; ll. 213–14: '*Rhodrud ante alias rapidoque invecta puella/Fulget equo et placidum prior occupat ordine gressum . . .*'; ll. 219–23: '*Virgines interque choros turbamque sequentem/Proxima Berta nitet, multis sociata puellis./Voce, virile animo, habitu vultuque corusco,/ Os, mores, oculos imitantia pectora patris/Fert . . .*'; l. 229: '*Gisala post istas sequitur candore coruscans*'; ll. 237–40: '*Laeta super rapidum conscendit virgo caballum;/Frena superbus equus spumantia dente volutat./Hinc comitata viris, illinc stipata puellis/Innumeris circum, circumstrepit agmen equorum . . .*' 'Hence after delaying long in her gorgeous marriage-chamber the

queen comes forth, the most beautiful wife of Charles, Liutgard by name ... The queen amongst the great-hearted magnates/rejoices in her splendid horse ... The maiden Rotrud shines before the other maidens born on her swift steed and takes her calm step as she takes first place in the procession ... /Berta comes next, between the choirs of maidens and the crowd that follows her, she gleams, in the company of many girls, while in her voice, virile spirit, resplendent in dress and face,/she has a mouth, behaviour, eyes, chest, just like her father's; Gisela follows all these glittering with brightness ... The maid mounts her swift horse; the proud animal chews its reins with foaming tooth./On one side men accompany her, on the other, surrounded by countless girls, a great procession of horses make a terrific noise.'

65. MGH DK II, no. 82, p. 202.

66. Fouracre, forthcoming, provides a thorough account of the regional context and also a comparative analysis of the role of *placita* elsewhere.

67. See Ch. 16.

68. *ArF* s.a. 804, p. 118, King 1987: 95. (Einhard shows virtually no interest in the Abodrites.) In 802, Charles had 'devoted himself to hunting in the Ardennes, sending an army of Saxons and devastated the Saxons beyond the Elbe', *ArF* s.a., p. 117, King 1987: 95. Saxon-on-Saxon violence turned out to have signalled the end of Saxon resistance.

69. *Chron. Moissiac.* s.a. 804, ed. Kettemann, p. 106.

70. Einhard, *VK*, c. 7, p. 10, trans. Ganz 2008: 23–4 (with some minor alterations).

71. Capit. I, no. 32, c. 12, p. 84, shows hostages kept on royal estates. Campbell 2010. See Ch. 13.

72. Capit. I, no. 45 (806), c. 13, p. 129.

73. Kosto 2002: 142–4, citing, n. 98, the testimony of Flodoard, *Historia Remensis ecclesiae* II, 18, pp. 172–3 for Archbishop Wulfar of Reims as a minder of 15 hostages in Francia early in the ninth century.

74. Capit. I. no. 115, pp. 233–4. Kosto 2002: 123–47, esp. 142–4; Nelson 2008a: 223–34, at 224–8.

75. Pers. comm. David Ganz, to whom my thanks.

76. *Chron. Moissiac.* s.a. 804, 805, ed. Kettemann, pp. 106–7; *AMP* s.a. 805, pp. 93–4.

77. Capit. I, no. 32, c. 12, p. 84, trans. Loyn and Percival: 1975: 66.

78. Capit. I, no. 45, c. 13, p. 129, trans. King 1987: 254.

79. That Wala's mother was a Saxon is a widely held view for which I see no evidence. My thanks go to Mayke de Jong for discussing the problem with me.

80. Flodoard, *Historia Remensis ecclesiae* II, c. 18, pp. 174–5.

81. Nelson 2008a: 224–8. On population transfers, see also Charanis 1961.

82. Hrabanus Maurus, '*De procinctu romanae militiae*', c. 3, p. 444.

83. See above, Ch. 1.

84. Einhard, *VK* prol., p. 1.
85. *Ann. Petav.* s.a. 777, p. 16, trans. King 1987: 151. See Rembold 2017.
86. Einhard, *VK* c. 7, p. 10. See further Kosto 2002: 127, 137–8, 146–7; Nelson 2008a: 227–8.
87. See Munding 1920 (Primary Sources).
88. The best guide is now Davis 2015: 278–89, and see also Davis, 'Western Europe', forthcoming; see also Bougard 1997, 2009: 201–5. For complementary evidence of charters: Costambeys 2013.
89. Ch. 6 (vi) above, on Capit. 88, c. 4, p. 188.
90. Capit. 94 (787), c. 10, p. 199.
91. Capit. 95 (?787), c. 14, p. 201.
92. Capit. 99 (802–810), cc. 3, 4, 5, p. 206.
93. Capit. no. 103, pp. 211–12, Eng. trans. mine.
94. But see Depreux 1997 – an invaluable guide to Louis' regime in Aquitaine.
95. Astron. cc. 12, 13. In D. 217, Ademar was named as Count of Narbonne.
96. Astron. c. 4, p. 294, trans. King 1987: 169. Arnold was probably abbot of Noirmoutier. Bullough 1962; Kasten 1986: 106.
97. Astron. c. 4, p. 296, trans. King 1987: 169.
98. Astron. c. 6, p. 302, trans. King 1987: 171.
99. Astron. c. 7, p. 304, trans. King 1987: 171.
100. Astron. c. 7, pp. 304, 306, trans. King 1987: 171.
101. Compare Astron. c. 5 (and the holding of an assembly in Mourgoudou, pp. 296–7, in 787), with the measures described in c. 7, pp. 304–5, datable to 796, and c. 8, 797, pp. 306–7. See further Brühl 1968: 76 with n. 292.
102. Gravel 2012; 339–412.
103. Chandler 2002.
104. Astron. c. 10, pp. 308–10, trans. King 1987: 172.
105. Astron. c. 13, pp. 318–21, trans. King 1987: 174; *Chron. Moissiac.* s.a. 803, ed. Kettemann, pp. 104–5.
106. Astron. c. 15, pp. 324–5, trans. King 1987: 175–6.
107. Astron. c. 15, pp. 328–9, trans. King 1987: 176.
108. Astron. c. 17, pp. 330–33, trans. King 1987: 177.
109. Astron. c. 18, pp. 334–5, trans. King 1987: 178.
110. See n. 94 above.
111. Astron. c. 19, pp. 340–41, trans. King 1987: 178.
112. Formulary of Bourges no. 14, p. 174, with French translation, Gravel 2012: 363, and commentary 364–6. See also Rio 2009: 111–12.

15. THE AACHEN YEARS

1. *ArF* s.a. 804, p. 119
2. Helvétius 2015: 111–33, esp. 128–30.

3. I. Wood 1994: 48; Isaïa 2010: 353–68, 398–400 (not mentioning the 804 meeting).
4. Nelson 2000: 143–5; and see Ch.4, p. 108 above.
5. W. Hartmann 1989: 55 and 2010: 166 notes that Charles must have agreed this, in light of the Capitulary of Herstal, Capit. no. 20 (779), c. 1, no. 47.
6. *AMP* s.a. 804, p. 92. Little attention was paid to Rémi's cult in Charles's reign. The Council of Mainz (813), c. 33, in a local initiative, made the saint's day one to be celebrated.
7. Nelson 2005c: 30–31.
8. F. Hartmann 2006: 113–29, 153–5, especially 113, quoting the American literary scholar Stephen Greenblatt, 1980: 141: 'One of the highest achievements of power is to impose fictions upon the world and one of its supreme pleasures is to enforce the acceptance of fictions that are known to be fictions.'
9. See above, Ch. 13; and below, sec. (vii).
10. Althoff 1997: 157–84.
11. *ArF* s.a. 805, p. 120.
12. *AMP* s.a. 805, p. 94.
13. *Chron. Moissiac* s.a. 805, ed. Kettemann, pp. 107–9.
14. Capit. no. 122, pp. 241–2, dated by Mordek 1995: 41, 1093, to 802/805.
15. Capit. no. 124, pp. 244–6, dated by Mordek 1995: 41, 1093, to 805.
16. Capit. no. 124, pp. 244–6.
17. Patzold 2006: 141–62, esp. 153–7.
18. Mayr-Harting 2009: 213.
19. Nelson 2001a.
20. Davis 2015: 353, with Graph 7.1, and details of the chronological distribution of royal charters for Italian and non-Italian beneficiaries at pp. 215–16, nn. 198, 199, 200 and at p. 217, Graph 4.1, showing a huge preponderance of grants to Frankish, as compared with Italian, monastic and episcopal beneficiaries. See Mersiowsky 2015, i: 80–95, ii: 565–77.
21. Nelson 2010b: 118–29. Houses, with number of gifts in brackets: St-Denis (5), Fulda (3), Prüm (3), St-Martin, Tours (2), Lorsch (2), Hersfeld (2), Nonantula (2) and Bobbio, Echternach and Metz (1 each).
22. See the grant of the island-fort of Sirmione in Lake Garda and the Valcamonica to St-Martin, Tours (D. 81), and the confirmation to St-Denis of additional properties in the Valtellina as an immunity under royal protection (D. 94). See also Nelson 2010b: 122, Map 6.1.
23. Falkenstein 1991, 2002: 131–81; Müller, in Krause, ed. 2013: 83–92, with maps 14 and 15, from Flach 1979.
24. Mordek 2005: 5 and nn. 20, 21.
25. D. 203 (dated 20 January at Thionville); see Rio 2017: 158–9, with n. 104.
26. D. 210 (dated 12 August 810).
27. *Chron. Moissiac.* s.a. 810, ed. Kettemann, pp. 113–14.

28. *Ann. S. Amandi* s.a. 810, p. 14; Eng trans. King 1987: 166.
29. For this wider context, see Davis 2015: 259–78.
30. It is a guess that Charles chose to travel by boat in late 805, as the *ArF* author says he did in February 806, when he moved north from Thionville to Nijmegen, via the Mosel and the Rhine and arriving for Easter (12 April), *ArF* s.a., p. 121.
31. Capit. nos. 43 and 44, pp. 120–22, 122–6. Comparing the translations of King 1987 and Loyn and Percival 1975 is instructive.
32. See King 1987: 30, cf. Loyn and Percival 1975: 86, 'the last of the great general capitularies to be published'. For Ansegis, Airlie 2000: 7, 2006: 12, repr. Airlie 2012, chs. V and VII.
33. Davis 2015: 90 (here, covering secular agents), 99 (with reference to Capit. no. 94, c. 12, pp. 199–200), 117–18 (allowing for unevenness in the treatment of derelict counts). The historiography gives curiously little attention to Capit. nos. 43 and 44, though see Hägermann 2000: 487–91; Fried 2016: 472–3, and below. A recently discovered *Capitulare ecclesiasticum* (805–13), eds., Mordek and Schmidt, in Mordek 2000: 113–34 has one or two references to Capit. no. 43 (ecclesiastical).
34. King 1987: 31, noting a variant phrase in one manuscript ordering singers to return from Metz, asked, tongue-in-cheek, 'Were the bright lights of Metz – the chief musical centre of Francia – proving so attractive that those sent there to learn the art were loth to return to their own churches and pass on the skills they had acquired?' See further Hen 2001.
35. Capit. no. 43, c. 9, p. 121, c. 10, p. 122.
36. See above Ch. 14 (ii), and cf. in Capit. no. 43, c. 13, on undergoing a probationary period before committing to a Rule.
36. Capit. no. 43, c. 16, p. 122. Charles's concern over this topic, and his attention to the detail of monitoring it, was shown by the cases of Fricco, mentioned in the Programmatic Capitulary no. 33, c. 33 (of 802), and of Godbert, the subject of D. 205 (28 April 807). See Ubl 2008.
38. Mordek 2005: 5–6.
39. Capit. I, no. 44, c. 4, pp. 122–3.
40. Capit. I, no. 44, cc. 5, and 7, p. 142.
41. 60 *solidi*, see Niermeyer 1997 s.v., meaning 3, p. 82.
42. Capit. I, no. 44, c. 7, p. 123. See Nelson 2009a: 35–6, for three of these *missi*, Madalgaud, Audulf (see also Hammer 2007: 137–200) and Warner (Mitterauer 1963: 65; Le Jan 1989: i: 258).
43. Capit. I, no. 55, c. 2, p. 142.
44. Reuter 1985: 85, repr. Reuter 2006: 240. For further discussion, see By Way of Conclusion.
45. Capit. no. 44, c. 9, p. 124.
46. Capit. no. 20, c. 16, p. 51.

47. Capit. no. 28, c. 31, p. 77.

48. Capit. no. 44, c. 10, p. 124.

49. Capit. no. 44, c. 12, p. 125; for *vicedomini* see Niermeyer 1997, meaning 5, p. 1094, and *vicarii*, Niermeyer 1997, meaning 23, p. 1090.

50. *De villis* c. 16, p. 84.

51. Davis 2015: 97; cf. Nelson 2001b, 2011b.

52. *De villis*, c. 63, p. 89. See Ch. 13 (viii).

53. Ganshof 1958: 44.

54. *ArF* s.a. p. 121.

55. Schlesinger 1963: 227, 229, also noting *consors* in two of Suetonius' *Vitae Caesarum* (Titus, c. 9, Otto, c. 8) and *consors regni* in Eusebius-Jerome, *Chronicle*, on Constantine's three-way division of the empire.

56. *De bello civili* (also known as *Pharsalia*) VII, ll. 387–8. There are at least five ninth-century Frankish manuscripts of Lucan's work: Gotoff 1971: 11–19.

57. Capit. no. 45, pp. 126–7 (my translation owes much to both King 1987: 251 and Loyn and Percival 1975: 91–2).

58. Above, Ch. 13 (xii). See Classen 1971: 109–34; Hägermann 1976: 12–27; Collins 1998b: 157–8 (admirably succinct); Kaschke 2006: 298–323, esp. 305–11, 320–23.

59. Fried 2016: 477.

60. Alcuin, Ep. 132 (date uncertain), pp. 198–9. See Fried 2016: 476–7. The relevant passage is c. 5 (of five *capitula* on inheritance), 'The best born and he who lawfully followed the inheritance, and did not despise the old or the new law ... ought to have great confidence to manage the inheriting, by God's mercy.' See also Kasten 1997: 155–60, 213.

61. Theodulf, *Carm.* XXXIII, *Carm.* XXXV, pp. 526–7; see Barbero 2000 (2004): 340–42; Andersson 2014: 191–21, nos. 34, 35.

62. *Divisio* cc. 1–4, pp. 127–8.

63. *Divisio* cc. 5–6, p. 128.

64. See Ch. 8, *passim*.

65. *Divisio* cc. 7–9, p. 128.

66. *Divisio* cc. 12–14, p. 129. Trial by the ordeal of the cross seems to have been introduced by Charles: in 779. Capit. no. 20 (Herstal), c. 11, p. 49: '*stent ad crucem*', 'they must stand to the cross'. In *Divisio* c. 14, p. 129, Charles banned 'single combat or judicial duel of any sort'.

67. *Divisio* cc. 15, 16, p. 129.

68. Capit. no. 45, cc. 17, 18, pp. 129–30. The last two *capitula*, 19 and 20, p. 130, are formal commands that the sons keep to what has been set down, and that as long as Charles himself lives, 'all these decrees shall be kept, and the emperor shall enjoy the obedience of his sons and of his people lovely to God (*Deo amabilis populus noster*), with all the deference (*subiectio*) to be shown by sons to their father and by his peoples (*populi*) to their emperor and king.'

69. Werner 1967, iv: 444, 445, 448. For the daughters' liaisons, see below sec. (vii).

70. Fried 2016: 479.

71. The phrase (Peter Lewis's arresting translation of '*Aufschrecken mußten erst recht die Schutzverfügungen*') is that of Fried 2016: 479.

72. See above, Ch. 5 (v).

73. Schlesinger 1963: 196.

74. Nelson 2007: XV, 269–70.

75. *ArF* s.a. 806, p. 122.

76. Capit. no. 46, pp. 130–32, trans. King 1987: 256–8, with valuable comment, pp. 30–32, on Bishop Ghaerbald's involvement. See Eckhardt 1956: 49–59; Patzold 2008: 156, and esp. Davis 2015: 215–16, on 'how the court prompted local texts'.

77. Capit. no. 49, cc. 1, 4, pp. 135–6.

78. Innes 2011.

79. Capit. I, no. 85, pp. 183–4. See for context and *missi*, Davis 2015: 278–322, and *passim*.

80. *Unrocus comes*, *ArF* s.a. 811, p. 134; Einhard, *VK*, c. 33, p. 41 (among the counts who witnessed Charles's will, and was father of Count Eberhard of Friuli); Werner 1965, i: 136; Fulrad, lay-abbot of St-Quentin, Capit. no. 75, p. 168, Capit. no. 85, p. 183, Felten 1982: 105, 126–7, n. 68.

81. Adalhard, Kasten 1986; Hrocculf (aka Roculf, Rocolf), witness to Charles's will, Einhard, *VK*, c. 33, p. 41, Werner 1965, i: 136, McCormick 2011: 167–8, 170–75 ('a man to be reckoned with in Charlemagne's entourage'). See below, Ch. 16 (ii).

82. Gravel 2012, and especially Davis 2015.

83. Theodulf, *Carmen* XXXV, MGH *Poetae* I, pp. 526–7; see Godman 1987: 96; Andersson 2014: 120. The reference to the Young Charles's presence in western regions, Theodulf, *Carm.* XXXV, l. 11, seems to refer back to 800.

84. For the Mercian marriage project, see above Ch. 10.

85. *Carm.* XXV, MGH *Poetae* I, pp. 483–9, at ll. 177–8, trans. Godman 1985: 158–9.

86. *Carm.* XXVII, MGH *Poetae* I, ll. 87–92, trans. Andersson 2014: 75–6, commentary, poem 76–9, at 78.

87. Theodulf, *Carmen* XXXV, MGH *Poetae* I, pp. 526–36, trans. with commentary Andersson 2014: 120–21.

88. My thanks go to Franz Fuchs who discovered the original version of *Carmen* XXXV and to David Ganz who put me in touch with the discoverer.

89. See Nelson 2005a: 12, on which I draw in what follows.

90. *Carmen* XXXV, MGH *Poetae* I, ll. 25–32, p. 527.

91. Munz 1969: 46.

92. Theodulf, *Carmen* XXV, ll. 97–100, trans. Godman 1985: 154–5. Cf. Andersson 2014: 70.

93. Einhard, *VK*, c. 18, p. 22.

94. Rabe 1995: 74–6. For Nithard and Hartnid, see Treffort 1994; for the boys as twins, see M. Hartmann 2007: 562, 2009: 191. For lay-abbots, see S. Wood 2006: 247–71, and Felten 1980.

95. *Annales Bertiniani*, s.a. 867, ed. F. Grat et al., p. 77, Eng. trans. Nelson p. 138, and cf. 858, n. 5. I should now like to revise this in light of Nelson 1998: 185–7.

96. See Fried 2016: 327, partly relying on their leading-names Rich-, partly on Richwin's eminence (he attested Charles's will in 811. See further Nelson 1986a: 224–5, 236–7, and for Richwin's countship, see below Ch.16 (ii). But Richwin's identity remains uncertain.

97. At St-Riquier, Richbod became the regular abbot, Nithard a lay-abbot: both were killed, along with Hugh (son of Charles and Regina) in the ambush near Angoulême on 14 June 844. For Richbod, *Ann. Bert.* 844, pp. 46–7, trans. p. 58, 'through his mother a grandson of the emperor Charles'; for Nithard, Nelson 1986a: 235–7.

98. See Nelson 1999, XIV, p. 186.

99. It's also worth speculating about the name Theoderic, given to the baby boy born 807 to the last (as far as is known) of Charles's concubines, Adelind: see Nelson 2016b: 252, n. 29. Both Louis (Clovis) and Theoderic were dynastic founders and heroes: names to conjure with.

100. It is just possible that Rotrud died in childbirth, but that may be a speculation too far.

101. Einhard, *VK*, c. 19.

102. Nelson 2006.

103. Fried 2016: 318, 326–7.

104. Kosso and Scott 2009.

105. Capit. I, no. 51, c. 13, p. 139; for bottlenecks.

106. Schieffer 1990: 148–64.

107. For male and female godparents at the Aachen church, Capit. I, no. 122, pp. 241–2. Anecdotal evidence for gender division in church: *Ann. Bert.* s.a. 858, p. 76, Eng. trans. p. 86.

108. Fried 2016: 319.

109. Nelson 1996: 240, and 2006: 21. See further Stone 2012: 136–46.

110. Contreni 1995: 118–27.

111. Einhard, *VK*, c. 19, p. 23.

112. *Vita Adalhardi*, c. 16, MGH SS II, pp. 525–6: '*ut regnum et eius regem Pippinum iuniorem ad statum reipublicae et ad religionis cultum utiliter, iuste atque discrete honestius informaret*'. Kasten 1986: 42–7.

113. *Vita Adalhardi*, c. 32, Weinrich 1963: 19.

114. *Vita Adalhardi*, c. 33, MGH SS II, p. 527; Alcuin, Ep. 241, pp. 386–7; Kasten 1986: 50.

115. Nelson 2004b: 191.

116. D. 218, p. 292. For further comment, Nelson 2007: XI, 46, with thanks for David Ganz's expertise.

117. *Vita Adalhardi*, c. 33, trans. 47. For Bernhar and Theodrada, de Jong 2009: 21.

118. *Vita Adalhardi*, c. 34, where Paschasius shows off his musical knowledge.

119. For the hypothesis, Fried 1998: 95–6, 2008: 145–92, esp. 177–9; against, Ubl 2008: 379; M. Hartmann 2009: 105.

120. Airlie 2012: VII, 23.

121. Airlie 2012: VII, 3; Davis 2015: 206–38, 259–92. There is a striking difference between the use of capitularies in Italy and their apparent non-use in Aquitaine.

122. The contents and dates of Alcuin's Epp. 175 (799), p. 290, 237 (dated 801), p. 381, and 306 (801–4), pp. 465–6, suggest that Angilbert, hitherto still a layman, underwent an experience of *conversio* (cf. Thionville *Capitulare . . . mere ecclesiasticum* (805), no. 43, cc. 9, 10, pp. 121–2) that followed not so long after his withdrawal from the court after the consecration of St-Riquier on Easter Day, 19 April 800. See also Rabe 1995: 53, and Ch. 14, above.

123. Above, sec. (vii).

124. Moduin, *Egloga*, trans. Godman 1985: 190–97, no. 24, and *Versus de Verona*, 'In Praise of Verona', ed. and trans. Godman 1985: 180–87, no. 22, and Intro. pp. 28–33, for the genre in Italy.

125. For evidence of Lucan's *De bello civili* in the *Divisio*, see above sec. (iv), and for Theodulf's acquaintance with Lucan, see Andersson 2014: 199 (admittedly only an allusion to *Pharsalia*), and *Carmen* xxxiv, 'Quod potestas impatiens consortis est', cited from *De bello civili* I, ll. 92–3, Godman 1987: 98. For Lucan in Moduin's *Egloga*, ll. 76–7, see Godman 1987: 196.

126. Here and in the rest of this paragraph, I have followed the line of thinking of Wickham 2009: chs. 16 and 17, whose words I quote, alongside a couple of phrases of my own.

127. Communities overlap and are malleable: see Stock 1983; Rosenwein 2015.

128. Marenbon 1981: 62–6, at 63. The MGH editor, Dümmler, could date Fridugis's letter no more closely than to 804–14.

129. Contreni 1995: 737–8.

130. Eastwood 1994: 117–34.

131. Eastwood 1994: 131–2.

132. To be fair, Eastwood got the point about Charles and 'the well-educated of the time', but he didn't dwell on the sense of intellectual community between them.

133. Bullough 2003b: 358, linked it with the court of Charles. See also Mordek 1995: 502–7.

134. Ganz 2008a: 90–100.

135. Jerome, *Against Jovinian* I, 49.

136. Ecclesiasticus 25:24.

137. Bullough 2003b: 358.

138. Becher 1999a: 109, and see also 110, 111, Eng. trans. (with a few minor changes of my own) Bachrach 2003: 123, 124, see also 125. M. Hartmann 2009: 104, endorses Becher here.

139. Esmyol 2002: 92; see especially Stone 2012: 267-8, 282-3, 290-91, and ch. 9, *passim*, for a level-headed approach.

140. For what follows, see McCormick 2011; see also Borgolte 1976, 1980.

141. So, McCormick 2011: 170. Cf. McCormick 2001: 894 with n. 90 (Appendix 4, no. 279).

142. *Vita Leonis III*, cc. 84, 85, trans. Davis 1992: 219, 220.

143. McCormick 2001: 178.

144. Airlie 2005: 90-101; Innes 2005: 82-5.

145. McCormick 2001: 177.

146. Devroey 2011.

147. *Ann. Iuvavenses maximi* s.a. 803, SS XXX, pt. 2, p. 732, Eng. trans. King 1987: 21, 164.

148. *ArF* s.a. 807, p. 123.

149. McCormick 2001: 893-4, Appendix 4, no. 277.

150. McCormick 2001: 66-72, drawing on and generously acknowledging Oexle 1978: 143-57.

151. What actually survives is a very early copy of the 808 *Breve* known as the Basel Roll (from the university library where it was discovered in the mid-nineteenth century and the public library where it's now kept): McCormick 2011: 121, and Part Two, *passim*, for the documents themselves.

152. Einhard, *VK* c. 27, pp. 31-2, Eng. trans. Ganz 2008: 37 (with a few tiny changes). Walahfrid's heading for this chapter was '*In elemosinis fuerit quam profusus*'.

153. McCormick 2011, text and trans. with commentary, Document 1 [*Breve*], ll. 13-24, pp. 202-7.

154. This is the insightful comment of Borgolte 1980: 426.

155. Alcuin, Ep. 196, pp. 323-5.

156. Capit. I, no. 64, c. 18, p. 154.

157. McCormick 2011: 163-4, and 176-7. Cf. also Borgolte 1980.

158. McCormick 2011: 181-3.

159. *ArF* s.a. 809, p. 129, trans. King 1987: 101.

160. See Willjung 1998.

161. *ArF* s.a. 810, p. 130.

162. Einhard says, *VK* c. 18, that Gisela died 'a few years before her brother'; M. Hartmann 2009: 99.

163. Einhard, *VK*, c. 19, p. 24.

164. *ArF* s.a. 810, p. 132.

165. Gillmor 2005.

166. *Ann. Lauriss. Min.*, SS I, p. 121.

167. Hack 2011: 38–41.
168. Newfield 2015: 37, and *passim*.

16. 'CHARLES, BY THE BOUNTY OF DIVINE GRACE EMPEROR AND AUGUSTUS . . .'

1. *ArF* s.a. 798, p. 104; *AMP* s.a. p. 798, and cf. the meeting with Greek envoys at Salz, *ArF* s.a. 803, p. 118, *AMP* s.a. 803, p. 102. Cf. Ch. 14 (v).
2. Einhard, *VK* c. 4, p. 7, '*res gestae et domi et foris*'.
3. For the elephant's arrival in Italy, *ArF* s.a. 801, p. 116, see Hack 2011: 22–32, for the arrival of the rest of the gifts at Aachen, *ArF* s.a. 802, p. 117.
4. For the 807 embassy, *ArF* s.a., p. 123–4.
5. Einhard, *VK* c. 16
6. Above, Ch. 14 (v).
7. *ArF* s.a. 810, p. 133, trans. p. 102; Hack 2017, pp. 27–49.
8. Einhard, *VK* c. 16, cf. Theophanes, *Chronicle*, eds. Mango and Scott, s.a. 811: 678. Willeri *dux Veneticorum* was in attendance. For Heito, see Appendix, 'Prosopography'; Depreux 1997: 234–5. The much younger Hugh reappears, not in the evidence for Charles's reign, but in that of Louis: Depreux 1997: 262.
9. *ArF* s.a. 812, p. 136.
10. Coupland 2005: 223–9; Coupland 2018: 442–51.
11. MGH Epp. IV, no. 37, pp. 555–6: '*Karolus divina largiente gratia imperator et augustus . . . dilecto et honorabili fratri Michaeli glorioso imperatori et augusto*', datable to the beginning of Spring 813, *ArF* s.a. p. 137. For Frankish-Greek relations, Wickham 1998; Hack 2017. Charles's envoys, Bishop Heito and Count Hugh, were still at Constantinople when Michael was proclaimed emperor on 2 October 811; he immediately gave them leave to depart, sending with them his own envoys (*ArF* 812). According to Theophanes, *Chronicle* (eds. Mango and Scott, p. 678): '[Michael] sent an embassy to Charles king of the Franks to discuss peace and a marriage-contract for his son Theophylaktos.' This is the sole evidence for the marriage proposal, which, if true, surely involved a Carolingian bride, most probably one of Charles's grand-daughters, the daughters of King Pippin and his wife (and I think she *was* a wife, not a concubine), whom Charles had had brought to his court on their father's death. See M. Hartmann 2009: 88–9, 105, 179, 191, 198.
12. *ArF* s.a. 806, pp. 120–21, trans. King 1987: 97.
13. Haywood 1991: 109–15, 118–22 (this fine book has long been underrated).
14. *ArF* s.a. 810, pp. 130–33, trans. King 1987: 102.
15. *ArF* s.a. 801, 807, pp. 116, 124, trans. King 1987: 94, 98–9.
16. *ArF* s.a.807, p. 124, trans. King 1987: 99.

17. *ArF* s.a. 807, p. 124, carefully differentiating peace (*pax*) from truce (*indutiae*), trans. King 1987: 99.

18. *ArF* s.a. 808, p. 125, trans. King 1987: 99.

19. See Story 2003: 147–8, n. 51.

20. Epp. Leonis III Papae no. 2, p. 90. See Story 2003: 145–56, esp. 147–8.

21. *ArF* s.a. 808, 809, pp. 126–8, trans. King 1987: 99–100. For lay-abbots, see Felten 1974, 1980: 105, 145, 280–92.

22. For *embola* see Hack 2006–7: i, 156–8; and cf. Nelson 2016b: 245–6.

23. Epp. 4, Leonis III Papae Epistolae X, no. 2, pp. 89-91 Was the *mensa* intended to have a double meaning (dining-table? altar?)?

24. Reuter 1985, repr. 2006: 231–50; Reuter 1990, repr. 2006: 251–67.

25. Nelson 1996: xxviii–xxix; Nelson 2006; Innes 2008, 2009; Wickham 2009: 380–82; Costambeys et al. 2011: 329–47; Davis 2015: 423–7; Fried 2016: 164–89; de Jong 2015: 9–13.

26. Ch.13 (viii), above. See Naismith 2014 and Garipzanov 2016.

27. Haywood 1991: 112, 113–15; Hack 2017: 30–38.

28. Astron. cc. 15–18, pp. 325–35.

29. *ArF* s.a. 812, p. 137, trans. King 1987: 105; *Chron. Moissiac* s.a. 812, ed. Kettemann, p. 115.

30. *ArF* s.a. 812, p. 137, trans. King 1987: 105.

31. *ArF* s.a. 811, p. 134, trans. King 1987: 104. Heather 2009: 17–50; Garipzanov 2008b: 113–44; and for an excellent account of frontier relations, see Melleno 2014: 25, 33–52, 59–64, 71–2.

32. Smith 1995: 176.

33. Capit. I, no. 18, cc. 6, 7, p. 43, trans. King 1987: 202.

34. Capit. no. 77 (802/802) was particularly significant: Mordek 1995: 1088–9.

35. Capit. no. 77, cc. 9 and 10.

36. Capit. no. 77, c. 12, p. 171, trans. King 1987: 245. I infer that these were younger men, whose conduct unbecoming dishonoured their families and whom Charles alone could overawe.

37. Capit. I, no. 74, c. 6, p. 167 echoes Pippin's no. 18, c. 6: '*Quicumque in itinere pergit aut hostiliter vel ad placitum, nulla super suum pare praendat . . . nisi herba, aqua et ligna*', trans. King 1987: 202, 'A man travelling on military service or to the assembly is to take from his comrade nothing except grass, firewood and water . . .' Charles addressed Fulrad in the second person singular – familiarly.

38. Prinz 1971: 74–6. For horses as gifts, Capit. I, no. 57, c. 5, p. 144; Hibernicus Exul, *Carm.* II, ll. 1–11, *Poetae* I, 396, trans. Godman 1985: 174–7.

39. Felten 1980: 105, 1974: 397–431.

40. Capit. no. 18, c. 6 (above n. 33); Capit. no. 77 (802/803), cc. 9 and 10, p. 171.

41. Capit. no. 50 (early 808), cc. 2, and 8, p. 137, trans. Loyn and Percival 1975: 96–7; King 1987: 261–3.

42. Capit. no. 74, c. 7, p. 167. For *vassi, vassalli* and counts as office-holders of different ranks, see Kasten 1997: 255–62, with searching analysis by Esders 2009a: 327–45; see also Renard 2009. Both scholars, starting from rather different premises, agree that it was not defective strategy but shortage of recruits that created military problems at local and regional levels.

43. France 2002; Halsall 2003: 93–5, 149–51.

44. Capit. no. 74, cc. 5 and 6, p. 167, trans. King 1987: 265–6.

45. Capit. no. 48, c. 2; Capit. no. 49, c. 2; Capit. no. 50, c. 1.

46. Renard 2006, 2009: 8–27, rightly seeing, pp. 15, 22, the significance of Charles's immunity for Metz, D. 91, p. 132.

47. Renard 2009: 27; McKitterick 2008: 135–6, 288–91.

48. Cf. the *plebei* in Astron. c. 7, above, Ch. 14 (vii).

49. Brooks 1971, 1989, 1995; cf. Nelson 1996: 90–91.

50. Renard 2009: 4, n. 16; 13, nn. 61, 66, 67; and 27; and see above, p. 463.

51. Nelson 2007: ch. VI, 40–41.

52. Gregory, *Moralia in Job* xx. 14 (27), CC 143A, 1024; Alcuin, *De virtutibus et vitiis*, PL 101, col. 638; Theodulf, *Paraenesis ad iudices*, Poetae I, p. 516, ll. 895–6. For early medieval preaching in theory and practice, see the fine discussion of Diesenberger 2016, esp. ch. 4.

53. Capit. no. 73, pp. 164–5.

54. Capit. no. 71, cc. 1 and 2, p. 161.

55. Capit. no. 80 (autumn 811), c. 8, p. 177.

56. Rio 2008a.

57. *ArF* s.a. 811, p. 135, trans. King 1987: 104.

58. Einhard included the Will within c. 33, but his editor Walahfrid provided new chapter-headings for what he saw as different sections, and explained why at the end of his preface to the *VK*, ed. Holder-Egger, p. xxix, Eng. trans. Ganz 2008: 16: 'I Strabo ["the squinter", Walahfrid's nickname] introduced chapter-titles and divisions into this little book, where it seemed fitting, so that someone searching for particular topics should have an easier access to them.'

59. Scharer 2015: an excellent account. Innes 1997 ranges widely.

60. W. Hartmann 2010: 163–7.

61. Deliyannis 2003.

62. See sec. (iii), below.

63. Nelson 2016b: 251–2, drawing on Hammer 2005.

64. McCormick 2011: 173, 175 (Geroldings); Innes 2000: 150–51.

65. Hammer 1997: 33–43.

66. Nelson 2008a: 226 and nn. 33 and 34, 233.

67. McCormick 2011: 165–80, esp. 173–5.

68. Nelson 2017a.

69. Werner 1967: 448, no. 19 suggested Padua as his countship, followed by Fried 2016: 497 (cf. 327), but a more plausible Richoin could be the

hostage-minder of ?805 and the count of Thurgau (?808–?822), Borgolte 1986: 206–7, Art. RIHWIN.

70. The starting-point is Ganshof 1967. Cf. Nelson 2007: 78–9: '[the capitularies of the imperial years] reflect an imperial regime certainly newly ambitious and arguably newly effective'.

71. Capit. no.71, c. 1, p. 161.

72. Capit. no. 71, c. 5, p. 161, trans. Nelson 2007: ch. XIII, 81, 85.

73. Capit. no. 71, c. 9, p. 161, trans. Nelson 2007: ch. XIII, 86.

74. Capit. no. 72, pp. 162–4, trans. Nelson 2007: ch. XIII, 86–8.

75. Capit. no. 72, cc. 9, 11, pp. 163–4, trans. Nelson 2007: ch. XIII, 87, 88.

76. Capit. no. 58 (802–13), c. 3, p. 145.

77. Capit. no. 121 (801–12), p. 240.

78. Capit. no. 64 (810), c. 17, p. 153; cf. Capit. no. 65 (810), c. 5, p. 154 ('Concerning the general tribulation from which we are all suffering, that is, the mortality of animals and other plagues').

79. Capit. no. 33 (802), c. 3, p. 92.

80. Capit. no. 77 (802/803), pp. 170–72; see now Patzold 2015: 459–73, esp. 469–73, allowing for the possibility that Charles was the legislator.

81. Capit. no. 77 (802/803), c. 16, p. 172, trans. King 1987: 245; see Campbell 1989: 36, repr. in Campbell 2000: 227–46, at 244–5.

82. The inscription on Pippin of Italy's tomb in Sant'Ambrogio has been re-dated by some scholars to the Renaissance. Others continue to think it, on balance, ninth-century work. My thanks to Ross Balzaretti for expert advice.

83. There was no campaign in 807, *Chron. Moissiac.* s.a. 807, ed. Kettemann, p. 111. But did the Young Charles not campaign in 809 because of the outbreak of cattle-plague that year, according to *Chron. Moissiac* s.a. 809, ed. Kettemann, p. 112?

84. Suetonius, *Life of Augustus* c. 65: 'When members of his family died, Augustus bore his loss with far more resignation than when they disgraced themselves' (he had his daughter Julia's adulteries particularly in mind). I have used the translation of Robert Graves, *The Twelve Caesars* 1957: 86.

85. *Poet.* IV, 1, ll. 187–8, p. 50, for an allegation about the death in 811 of Pippin son of Himiltrud.

86. Thegan, *Gesta Hludovici Imperatoris* c. 22, ed. Tremp p. 210; W. Hartmann 2010: 237, 239.

87. Einhard, *VK*, c. 19.

88. Paschasius, *Vita Adalhardi* c. 16, see above Ch. 7 (i).

89. See above Ch. 13 (ix); Alcuin, Epp. 175, 176.

90. Kasten 1986: 55–6.

91. *ArF* s.a. 812.

92. Kasten 1986: 71–2; M. Hartmann 2009: 112 dates their marriage *c.* 815.

93. Kasten 1986: 71–2.

94. Astron. c. 20, pp. 340–43, trans. King 1987: 179.
95. For Gerric's status, see Adalhard (Hincmar), *De ordine palatii*, c. 16, p. 64, cf. c. 24, p. 76, and n. 179. Airlie 2006 (repr. 2012, ch. V), 1990 (repr. 2012, ch. VI).
96. Astron. c. 20, pp. 342–3, trans. King 1987: 179.
97. *ArF* 813, p. 138, trans. King 1987. 105.
98. Ermold, Poem on Louis, l. 658, trans. Dutton 1993: 134–5.
99. Hincmar, *De ordine palatii*, c. 12, p. 54, ll. 218–23, with n. 101.
100. Kasten 1986: 72–84; Nelson 2001a: 226–31.
101. Kasten 1986: 121–37; cf. Devroey 2011.
102. 'The Carolingian moment', a phrase coined in another context by Toubert 1996, has since been applied to the Carolingian political sphere at large.
103. Nelson 2001a: 228–9.
104. Quotations are from *De ordine palatii* cc. 29–36, pp. 82–97. The English translation by Herlihy 1970: 208–27, esp. 222–7, was pioneering; cf. also Nelson 1986a: 103–9.
105. Nelson 1986a: 107. Cf. Reuter 2006: 193–216; Nelson 2009d.
106. Capits. 71 and 72: see Nelson 2007, ch. XIV.
107. Keefe 2002; Phelan 2014: 94–206.
108. Nelson 2007, ch. XIII: 82 (I have found the comparison with William Gladstone apt).
109. Dahlhaus-Berg 1975: 221–35.
110. W. Hartmann 2010: 173–6; cf. Nelson 2014b: 77–82.
111. Conc. II, I, no. 38, Council of Tours, c. 51, p. 293.
112. Astron. c. 20, follows *ArF* s.a. 813 in saying Charles crowned Louis. Thegan, *Gesta Hludowici*, c. 6, pp. 182–4, said Charles delivered a long *Admonitio*, in effect a coronation oath, before telling Louis to pick up the crown from the altar and put it on his own head. The *ArF* author said Bernard was given the rule of Italy and the title of king.
113. Thegan, *Gesta Hludowici* c. 6, p. 184.
114. Einhard, *VK* c. 30, p. 34.
115. Einhard devoted *VK* c. 32 to *prodigia*. Walahfrid's title is: 'Prodigies which closely presaged his death'.
116. Einhard, *VK* c. 30, p. 35 for Charles's dieting and fasting.
117. Thegan, *Gesta Hludowici* c. 7, p. 196.
118. *Letter of Cuthbert*, eds. McClure and Collins 1994: 300–303.
119. Einhard, *VK* cc. 15, 16, 27, pp. 18, 19, 31; McCormick 2011: 143.
120. Einhard, *VK* c. 31, p. 35. For further details, Nelson 2000: 145–53.
121. Astron. c. 21, pp. 346–7.
122. Geary 1994: 48–80; Santinelli 2003.
123. Alcuin, Ep. 66.
124. Astron. c. 21, pp. 346–7.
125. Alcuin, Ep. 149, p. 244, addressed to Charles in July 798.

126. Astron. c. 21, p. 346, see Paxton 1990, pp. 136, 195.

127. Astron. c. 22, pp. 350–51.

128. Dierkens 1991.

129. Einhard, *VK* c. 31, pp. 35–6, trans. Ganz 2008: 40.

130. Nelson 2000: 143–5.

131. Augustine, *The City of God*, IV, chs. 8, 10, 11, ed. Dyson, pp. 153–4, 157; VI, ch. 7, p. 254; VII, chs. 20, pp. 291–2, 23, p. 295, 24, p. 297 and 28, p. 304.

132. Astron. c. 23, pp. 352–3.

133. D. 80, see above Ch. 5 (vii). The poem is edited by Godman 1985: 206–11. The translation is mine, but I have learned much from Godman's.

BY WAY OF CONCLUSION

1. Ganshof, 1971: chs. V–IX. For excellent accounts of Ganshof's vision of Charles's governance and the periodization of Charles's reign, see Davis 2015: 10–13, 347–65.

2. Ganshof 1971: ch. XIII, p. 259.

3. Ganshof 1971: ch. XII, pp. 247–8.

4. Ganshof 1971: ch. XII, p. 250.

5. Kantorowicz discovered and explored the theme of 'The King's Two Bodies' in the eponymous book (1957), spotting, pp. 204, n. 34, 320, n. 15 and 490, n. 113, the interest of Charles's contemporaries in baptism from this angle.

6. Hack 2009: 222, n. 269; 2015: 27–8, on the basis of Einhard, *VK*, cc. 19, and esp. 22; Kortüm 2014: 130–43.

7. *Chron. Moissiac.* s.a., ed. in Buc 2000: 205, '*Lodowicum filium suum constituit imperatorem secum ac per coronam auream tradidit illi imperium*', trans. King 1987: 148–9, '[Charles] conferred emperorship on [Louis] by means of a golden crown'; Greater St Emmeram Annals s.a.; *Ann. Lauriss.* s.a., trans. King 1987: 166. For Einhard's presence at Aachen in summer 813, see Ermold, quoted above, Ch. 16 (v).

8. Einhard, *VK* c. 30, p. 34, and the *ArF* author s.a. 813 between them showed Charles active in hunting; the authors of the *ArF* and the *Chron. Moissiac.* s.a. showed how Charles oversaw the putting-together of the outputs of the Five Councils late in the year.

9. The subtitle of Fichtenau's book was '*Soziale und geistige Problematik eines Großreiches*', 'The social and spiritual problem of a large empire'. This subtitle had disappeared from the 3rd reprint of 1968.

10. Capit. I, no. 124, Letter to Bishop Gerbald of Liège (dated by Boretius Nov. 807, re-dated Mordek to 805), in the context of the 805 famine, and confirmed in Capit. I, no. 46, Nijmegen (March 806), pp. 130–32; Verhulst

2002: 123–5. 'Spiritual weapons' were already important features of Charles's reign in 779, however.

11. Fichtenau 1968: trans. Munz, p. 103.

12. Nelson 2015a; cf. Mayr-Harting 2002: 117, n. 23.

13. Nelson 2014a. Though the UK joined the EEC in 1974, even Prime Minister Edward Heath 'could not make the British "feel" European', Judt 2005: 526.

14. Schneidmüller 2000.

15. On military matters, Capits. nos. 48, 50, 73, 74, 75. More generally, Davis 2015: 364–77.

16. *ArF* 806–11.

17. Capit. no. 64, c. 18.

18. Conc. I, 1, nos. 34–8, esp. 38, c. 51.

19. *ArF* 813.

20. Most recently, Gabriele 2011; Latowsky 2014; Purkis and Gabriele 2016.

21. Fried 2016: 1–2; see *Poet*. II, 318–19; for comment Traill 1974: 144–5; Godman 1985: 214–15; Ganz 2000: 181–2.

22. Mayr-Harting 2002.

23. Epp. IV, no. 37, pp. 555–6.

Bibliography

ABBREVIATIONS

AF	*Annales Fuldenses*
Ann. Lauriss.	*Annales Laurisshamenses*
AMP	*Annales Mettenses Priores*
ArF	*Annales regni Francorum*
BEC	Bibliothèque de l'École des Chartes
Chron. Fred./Fred. Cont.	*Chronicarum quae dicuntur Fredegarii Libri Quattuor/ Chronicarum quae dicuntut Fredegarii Continuationes*
CCSL	Corpus Christianorum, Series Latina
CCCM	Corpus Christianorum, Continuatio Medievalis
Fredegar/Fredegar Cont.	Fredegar Continuationes
LHF	Liber Historiae Francorum
MIÖG	Mitteleilungen des Instituts für Österreichische Geschichtsforschung
Monumenta Germaniae Historica	
AA	*Auctores Antiquissimi*
AG	*Die Admonitio Generalis Karls des Grossen*, ed. H. Mordek, K. Zechiel-Eckes and M. Glatthaar, *MGH, Fontes iuris germanici antiqui in usum scholarum scholarum separatim editi* XVI (Wiesbaden, Harrassowitz Verlag), 2013
DD	Diplomata: *Die Urkunden Pippins, Karlmanns und Karls des Grossen*, ed. Engelbert Muhlbacher, with A. Dopsch, J. Lechner and M. Tangl *MGH, Diplomata Karolinorum* (Hanover, Hahn, 1906)
Epp.	Epistolae: *Epistolae 4, Epistolae Karolini Aevi 4, 2*, ed. Ernst Dümmler (Berlin, Weidmann, 1895)
Form.	*Formulae merowingici et karolini aevi*, ed. Karl Zeumer (Hanover, Hahn, 1886)

LL   *Leges*

Capit. I: *Capitularia regum Francorum*, vol. 1, ed. Alfred Boretius (Hanover, Hahn, 1883)

Capit. II: *Capitularia regum Francorum*, vol. 2, ed. Alfred Boretius and Viktor Krause (Hanover, Hahn, 1897)

CEP with volume number: *Capitularia Episcoporum*, vol. 1, ed. Peter Brommer (Hanover, Hahn, 1984); vol. 2, ed. Rudolf Pokorny (Hanover, Hahn, 1995); vol. 3, ed. Rudolf Pokorny and M. Stratmann, with W.-D. Runge (Hanover, Hahn, 1995); vol. 4, ed. Rudolf Pokorny with V. Lukas (Hanover, Hahn, 2005)

Conc. II: Concilia: LL III, vol. II, part I, *Concilia Aevi Karolini*, vol. 1, part 1, ed. Albert. Werminghoff (Hanover and Leipzig, Hahn, 1906)

Poet.   Poetae Latini I, *Poetae Latini Aevi Carolini*, ed. Ernst Dümmler (Weidmann, Berlin, 1881)

SS   *Scriptores* in folio, ed. Georg Waitz et al. (Hanover, 1826–1924)

SRG   *Scriptores rerum Germanicarum*

SRL   *Scriptores rerum langobardicarum et italicarum saec. VI–IX*, ed. Georg Waitz (Hanover, Hahn, 1878)

PL   *Patrologia Latina*, ed. J.-P. Migne, 221 vols (Paris: 1844–64)

SM   *Studi Medievali*

Diplomata, i.e. charters, are cited by number preceded by D.; so, D. 55

PRIMARY SOURCES

Adalhard of Corbie, *Consuetudines Corbeienses*, ed. J. Semmler, CCM, ed. K. Hallinger, vol. I (Siegburg, Francis Schmidt, 1963), pp. 365–422; partial Eng. trans. P. E. Dutton, ed., *Carolingian Civilization: A Reader* (Peterborough, Ont., Broadview Press, 1993), pp. 192–7.

Die Admonitio generalis Karls des Grossen, eds. H. Mordek, K. Zechiel-Eckes and M. Glatthaar, MGH *Fontes iuris germanici antiqui* XVI (Hanover, Hahn, 2013); Eng. trans. P. D. King, *Charlemagne: Translated Sources* (Lambrigg, P. D. King, 1987), pp. 209–20.

Agobard, *De grandine et tonitruis*, in *Agobardi Ludgunensis Opera omnia*, ed. L. van Aacker, CCCM 52 (Turnhout, Brepols, 1981), pp. 3–15; partial Eng.

trans. P. E. Dutton, ed., *Carolingian Civilization: A Reader* (Peterborough, Ont., Broadview Press, 1993), pp. 189–92.

Alcuin, *Carmina*, ed. E. Dümmler, MGH *Poet.* II (Berlin, Weidmann, 1895).

Alcuin, *Epistolae*, ed. E. Dümmler, MGH Epp KA II (Berlin, Weidmann, 1895); partial Eng. trans. S. Allott, *Alcuin of York: His Life and Letters* (York, William Sessions, 1974).

Alcuin, *Liber de virtutibus et vitiis*, *PL* ed. J.-P. Migne, CI (Paris, Garnier, 1844–64), cols. 613–38.

Alcuin, *Vita Willibrordi*, ed. W. Levison, MGH SSrM VII, pp. 81–141, Eng. trans. C. H. Talbot (London, Sheed and Ward, 1954), pp. 3–22.

Andreas Agnellus of Ravenna, *Liber Pontificalis Ecclesiae Ravennatis*, ed. D. M. Deliyannis, CCCM 199 (Turnhout, Brepols, 2006).

Annales Alamannici, ed. G. H. Pertz, MGH SS I (Hanover, Hahn, 1826), pp. 22–30, 40–44, 47–60; and ed. W. Lendi, *Untersuchungen zur frühalamannischen Annalistik: Die Murbacher Annalen*, Scrinium Friburgense 1 (Freiburg in der Schweiz, Universitätsverlag, 1971), pp. 146–92.

Annales Bertiniani, ed. F. Grat, J. Vieillard and S. Clémencet, with an introduction and notes by L. Levillain (Paris, Société de l'histoire de France, 1964), Eng. trans. J. L. Nelson, *Ninth-Century Histories: The Annals of St-Bertin* (Manchester, Manchester University Press, 1991).

Annales Fuldenses, ed. F. Kurze, MGH SRG VII (Hanover, Hahn, 1891); Eng. trans. T. Reuter, *The Annals of Fulda* (Manchester, Manchester University Press, 1992).

Annales Guelferbytani, ed. G. H. Pertz, MGH SS I (Hanover, Hahn, 1826), pp. 23, 40–46; and ed. W. Lendi, *Untersuchungen zur frühalamannischen Annalistik: Die Murbacher Annalen*, Scrinium Friburgense 1 (Freiburg in der Schweiz, Universitätsverlag, 1971), pp. 147–81; Eng. trans. I. Garipzanov, '*Annales Guelferbytani*: changing perspectives of a local narrative', in R. Corradini et al., eds., *Zwischen Niederschrift und Wiederschrift* (Vienna, Verlag der ÖAW, 2010), pp. 123–37.

Annales Iuvavenses maiores, ed. G. H. Pertz, MGH SS I (Hanover, Hahn, 1826), pp. 87–8; re-ed. H. Bresslau, MGH SS XXX, part II (Leipzig, Hiersemann, 1934), pp. 732–40.

Annales Iuvavenses maximi, ed. H. Bresslau, MGH SS XXX, part II (Leipzig, Hiersemann, 1934), pp. 732–44.

Annales Iuvavenses minores, ed. H. Bresslau, MGH SS XXX, part II (Leipzig, Hiersemann, 1934), pp. 733–9.

Annales Laubacenses, ed. G. H. Pertz, MGH SS I (Hanover, Hahn, 1826), pp. 7–15, 52–5.

Annales Laureshamenses, ed. G. H. Pertz, MGH SS I (Hanover, Hahn, 1826), pp. 22–39; partial Eng. trans. P. D. King, *Charlemagne: Translated Sources* (Lambrigg, P. D. King, 1987), pp. 137–45.

Annales Laurissenses minores/Chronicon Laurissense breve, ed. G. H. Pertz, MGH SS I (Hanover, Hahn, 1826), pp. 114–23.

Annales Maximiniani, ed. G. Waitz, MGH SS XIII (Hanover, Hahn, 1881), pp. 19–25.

Annales Mettenses Priores, ed. B. von Simson, MGH SRG X (Hanover and Leipzig, Hahn, 1905).

Annales Mosellani, ed. I. M. Lappenberg, MGH SS XVI; ed. G. H. Pertz (Hanover, Hahn, 1859), pp. 494–9; partial Eng. trans. P. D. King, *Charlemagne: Translated Sources* (Lambrigg, P. D. King, 1987), pp. 132–7.

Annales Nazariani, ed. G. H. Pertz, MGH SS I (Hanover, Hahn, 1826), pp. 23–31, 40–44; Eng. trans. R. McKitterick, *Perceptions of the Past in the Early Middle Ages* (Notre Dame, Ind., University of Notre Dame Press, 2004), pp. 81–9.

Annales Petaviani, ed. G. H. Pertz, MGH SS I (Hanover, Hahn, 1826), pp. 7–13, 16–18, plus additions in G. H. Pertz, ed., MGH SS III (Hanover, Hahn, 1839), p. 170.

Annales regni Francorum, eds. G. H. Pertz and F. Kurze, MGH SRG VI (Hanover, Hahn, 1895); Eng. trans. B. Scholz, *Carolingian Chronicles* (Ann Arbor, University of Michigan Press, 1972), and in P. D. King, *Charlemagne: Translated Sources* (Lambrigg, P. D. King, 1987), pp. 74–131.

Annales Sancti Amandi, ed. G. H. Pertz, MGH SS I (Hanover, Hahn, 1829), pp. 102–9.

Annales Sancti Emmerammi Ratisbonensis maiores, ed. G. Waitz, MGH SS I (Hanover, Hahn, 1826), pp. 92–3; re-ed. H. Bresslau, MGH SS XXX, Part II (Leipzig, Hiersemann, 1934), pp. 733–41.

Annales Sancti Maximini Treverensis, ed. G. H. Pertz, MGH SS II (Hanover, Hahn, 1829), pp. 212–13.

Annales Tiliani, ed. G. H. Pertz, MGH SS I (Hanover, Hahn, 1826), pp. 65–7.

Annalium Lobiensium fragmentum, ed. G. H. Pertz, MGH SS II (Hanover, Hahn, 1829), pp. 194–5.

Asser, *Life of Alfred*, ed. W. Stevenson (1904); ed. with Eng. trans. and intro. S. Keynes and M. Lapidge, *Alfred the Great: Asser's Life of King Alfred and other contemporary sources* (London, Penguin Classics, 1983).

Astronomer, *Vita Hludowici imperatoris*, ed. with German trans. E. Tremp, MGH SRG LXIV (Hanover, Hahn, 1995).

Attenborough, F. L. (1922), *The Laws of the Earliest English Kings* (Cambridge, Cambridge University Press).

Augustine of Hippo, *De civitate Dei contra paganos*, ed. E. Hoffmann, *Corpus Scriptorum Ecclesiasticorum Latinorum*, 2 vols. (Vienna, 1899–1900); ed. with Eng. trans. R. W. Dyson, *The City of God against the Pagans* (Cambridge, Cambridge University Press, 1998).

Augustine of Hippo, *The Confessions*, trans. and intro. H. Chadwick (Oxford, Oxford University Press, 1991).

Bede, *Historia Ecclesiastica Gentis Anglorum*, ed. C. Plummer (Oxford, Clarendon Press, 1896); Eng. trans. J. McClure and R. Collins (Oxford, Oxford University Press, 1994).

Bibliotheca capitularium regum Francorum manuscripta: Überlieferung und Traditionszusammenhang der fränkischen Herrschererlasse, ed. H. Mordek, MGH Hilfsmittel XV (Munich, MGH, 1995).

Boniface, *Epistolae*, ed. M. Tangl, *Die Briefe des heiligen Bonifatius et Lullus*, MGH Epp. Sel. I (Berlin, Hahn, 1916); Eng. trans. C. H. Talbot, *The Anglo-Saxon Missionaries in Germany* (London, Sheed and Ward, 1954), and in E. Emerton, *The Letters of Saint Boniface* (New York, Norton, 1940, repr. 1976).

Capitulare de Villis, Eng. trans. H. R. Loyn and J. Percival, eds., *The Reign of Charlemagne* (London, Edward Arnold, 1975), pp. 64–73.

Capitularia Episcoporum, ed. P. Brommer, MGH *Conc. aevi karolini* II, i (Hanover and Leipzig, Hahn, 1906).

Capitularia regum Francorum, MGH LL I and II, ed. A. Boretius (Hanover, Hahn, 1883, 1897); partial Eng. trans. P. D. King, *Charlemagne: Translated Sources* (Lambrigg, P. D. King, 1987), also P. E. Dutton, *Carolingian Civilization: A Reader* (Peterborough Ont., Broadview Press, 1993).

Carolus to Fastrada, MGH Epp. IV, *Epistolae variorum Carolo Magno regnante scriptae* (Berlin, Weidmann, 1985), no. 20, pp. 528–9.

Carolus to Alcuin and the brethren of Tours, MGH Epp. KA II, Epp. IV, nos. 144, 247.

Carolus to Archbishop Hildebald of Cologne, MGH Epp. IV, Epp. *variorum*, no. 21.

Carolus to Offa, MGH Epp. KA II, nos. 87, 100.

Carolus to Angilbert, MGH Epp. KA II, no. 92.

Carolus to Pope Hadrian, ed. E. Munding, *Königsbrief Karls des Grossen an Papst Hadrian über Abt-Bischof Waldo von Reichenau-Pavie* (Beuron, 1920).

Carolus to Pope Leo III, MGH Epp. KA II, no. 93.

Carolus to Emperor Nikephoros, MGH Epp. *variorum*, no. 32.

Carolus to Dungal, MGH Epp. *variorum*, no. 35.

Carolus to Emperor Michael, MGH Epp. *variorum*, no. 37.

Carolus to Archbishop Æthelheard of Canterbury and Bishop Ceolwulf of Lindsey, MGH Epp. KA II, no. 85.

Cathwulf (Cathulfus) Carolo I Francorum regi, ed. E. Dümmler, MGH Epp. IV, *Epp. kar. aevi* II, *Epistolae variorum Carolo Magno regnante scriptae* (Berlin, Weidmann, 1985), pp. 502–5.

Chartae Latinae Antiquiores: Facsimile Edition of the Latin Charters, ed. A. Bruckner et al. (Zurich, Urs Graf Verlag, 1954–).

Chartularium Sangallense, Bd. I (700–840), eds. P. Erhart with K. Heidecker and B. Zeller (St Gallen, Historischer Verein des Kanton St Gallen, 2013).

Chronicon Moissiacense, ed. G. H. Pertz, MGH SS I (Hanover, Hahn, 1826), pp. 282–313 and MGH SS II (Hanover, Hahn, 1829), pp. 257–9.

Chronicon Moissiacense, ed. and with extensive commentary, W. Kettemann, 'Subsidia Anianensia, Überlieferungs- und textseschichtliche Untersuchungen zur Geschichte Witiza-Benedikts, seinen Klosters Aniane und zur sogenannten "anianischen Reform"', available online http://duepublico.uni-duisbburg-essen.de/servlets/DocumentServlet?id=18245; partial Eng. trans. P. D. King, *Charlemagne: Translated Sources* (Lambrigg, P. D. King, 1987).

de Clercq, Charles (1936), *La Législation religieuse franque de Clovis à Charlemagne* (Paris, Bureau du Recueil, Bibliothèque de l'Université).

Codex Carolinus, ed. W. Gundlach, MGH Epp. III, *Epp. merowingici. et carolingici aevi* I, ed. E. Dümmler (Berlin, Weidmann, 1892), pp. 476–657; partial Eng. trans. H. R. Loyn and J. Percival, *The Reign of Charlemagne* (London, Edward Arnold, 1975), nos. 59, 83, 92, also P. D. King, *Charlemagne: Translated Sources* (Lambrigg, P. D. King, 1987), pp. 269–307.

Conversio Bagoariorum et Carantanorum, 3rd rev edn, ed. with German trans. H. Wolfram (Graz, Böhlau-Verlag, 2013).

Dhuoda, *Liber Manualis Dhuodane quem ad filium suum transmisit Wilhelmum*, ed. and intro. Pierre Riché; French trans. B. de Vregille and C. Mondésert (Paris, Éditions du Cerf, 1975); Eng. trans. and ed. Marcelle Thiébaux, *Dhuoda. Handbook for her Warrior Son* (Cambridge, Cambridge University Press, 1998); also Carol Neel, *Handbook for William. A Carolingian Woman's Counsel for her Son*, Eng. trans., with intro. and afterword (Lincoln, Nebr., University of Nebraska Press, 1991).

Einhard, *Epistolae*, ed. E. Dümmler, MGH Epp. V, *Epp.* KA III (Berlin, Weidmann, 1899), pp. 109–45; Eng. trans. in P. E. Dutton, *Charlemagne's Courtier* (Peterborough, Ont., Broadview Press, 1998), pp. 131–84.

Einhard, *Vita Karoli*, ed. O. Holder-Egger (Hanover, Hahn, 1911); Eng. trans. Evelyn S. Firchow and Edwin H. Zeydel, *Einhard*, Vita Karoli Magni, *The Life of Charlemagne, The Latin Text with a New English Translation, Introduction, and Notes* (Dudweiler, AQ-Verlag, 1985), also in P. E. Dutton, *Charlemagne's Courtier* (Peterborough Ont., Broadview Press, 1998), pp. 15–39.

Einhard, *Vita Karoli* – and Notker, *Gesta Karoli Magni* – are now available in single volumes in English translation: L. Thorpe, *Einhard and Notker the Stammerer. Two Lives of Charlemagne* (Harmondsworth, Penguin, 1969); the more recent D. Ganz, *Einhard and Notker the Stammerer: Two Lives of Charlemagne* (London, Penguin, 2008); also T. F. X. Noble, *Charlemagne and Louis the Pious: The Lives by Einhard, Notker, Ermold, Thegan and the Astronomer* (University Park, Pa., Penn. State University Press, 2009).

Epistolae X Leonis Papae, ed. Karolus Hampe, MGH, Berlin, 1897.

Ermold le Noir (Ermoldus Nigellus), *Carmen in Honorem Hludowici Pii*, ed. and French trans. Faral, *Poème sur Louis le Pieux*, Les Classiques de l'histoire de France au moyen âge (Paris, Société d'édition "Les Belles Lettres", 1964); Eng. trans. T. F. X. Noble, *Charlemagne and Louis the Pious: The Lives by*

Einhard, Notker, Ermold, Thegan and the Astronomer (University Park, Pa., Penn. State University Press, 2009).

Formulae, ed. K. Zeumer, MGH LL V (Hanover, Hahn, 1886); partial Eng. trans, A. Rio, *The Formularies of Angers and Marculf: Two Merovingian Legal Handbooks*, Translated Texts for Historians (Liverpool, Liverpool University Press, 2008).

Fredegar, *Chronicarum quae dicuntur Fredegarii libri quattuor*, German trans. A. Kusternik, and *Chronicarum quae dicuntur Fredegarii continuations*, German trans. H. Haupt, general editor H. Wolfram (Darmstadt, Wissenschaftliche Buchgesellschaft, 1982).

Fredegar, *The Fourth Book of the Chronicle of Fredegar with its Continuations*, ed. with Eng. trans. J. M. Wallace-Hadrill (London, Nelson, 1960).

Gesta sanctorum partum Fontanellensis coenobii, eds. F. Lohier and R. F. J. Laporte (Rouen, 1936).

Hariulf, *Chronique de l'abbaye de Saint-Riquier*, ed. F. Lot (Paris, Picard, 1894).

Hincmar of Reims, *De ordine palatii*, ed. with German trans. T. Gross and R. Schieffer, *Fontes iuris germanici antiqui in usum scholarum separatim editi* (Hanover, Hahn, 1980); Eng. trans. D. Herlihy (Atlantic Highlands, NJ, Humanities Press, 1970).

Indiculus eorum qui sacramentum fidelitatis iuraverunt, ed. A. Boretius, MGH Capit. I, no. 181 (Hanover, Hahn, 1883), pp. 377–8); new edn, ed. S. Esders and W. Haubrichs, MGH Studien und Texte (forthcoming).

Karolus Magnus et Leo Papa, ed. E. Dümmler, MGH *Poet.* I [here attributed to Angilbert], Angilberti *Carmina* no. VI (Berlin, Weidmann, 1881), pp. 366–79; partial Eng. trans. P. Godman, *The Poetry of the Carolingian Renaissance* [here attributed to Einhard] (London, Duckworth, 1985), pp. 197–207.

Das Konzil von Aachen 809, ed. H. Willjung, MGH *Leges* III, vol. II, *supplementum* II (Hanover, Hahn, 1998).

Konzilsordines/Ordines de celebrando concilio, ed. H. Schneider (Hanover, Hahn, 1996).

Lex Baiuvariorum, ed. F. E. von Schwind, MGH LL nat. germ. 5, 2 (Hanover, Hahn, 1926).

Lex Ribuaria, eds. F. Beyerle and R. Buchner, MGH LL nat. germ. 3, 2 (Hanover, Hahn, 1954).

Lex Salica, ed. K. A. Eckhardt, MGH LL nat. germ. 4, 2 (Hanover, Hahn, 1969); Eng. trans. K. F. Drew, *The Laws of the Salian Franks* (Philadelphia, University of Pennsylvania Press, 1991); and *The Laws of the Ripuarian and Salian Franks*, ed. T. J. Rivers (New York, AMS Press, 1986).

Liber Historiae Francorum, ed. B. Krusch, MGH SSRM II (Hanover, Hahn, 1888); partial Eng. trans. in P. Fouracre and R. Gerberding, *Late Merovingian France. History and Hagiography 640–720* (Manchester, Manchester University Press, 1996).

Le Liber Pontificalis, Texte, introduction et commentaire, ed. L. Duchesne, 2 vols. (Paris, Thorin, 1886–92), reissued C. Vogel (1955–7), with a third volume updating commentary, bibliography and indices; Eng. trans. R. Davis, *The Lives of the Eighth-Century Popes*, Translated Texts for Historians XIII (Liverpool, Liverpool University Press, 1992).

Lucan, *De bello civili*, ed. with commentary P. Asso (Berlin and New York, de Gruyter, 2010).

Miracula Sancti Dionysii, ed. Luc d'Achery, Acta Sanctorum Ordinis S. Benedicti, Saec. III, Pars 2 (Paris, L. Bilaine, 1681), pp. 343–64.

Miracula Sancti Dionysii, ed. Achille Luchaire, 'Les *Miracula sancti Dionysii*', *Études sur quelques manuscrits de Rome et de Paris* 8 (Bibliothèque de la Faculté des Lettres de Paris, 1899) pp. 20–29, 93–8.

Munding, Emmanuel, ed., *Königsbrief Karls des Grossen an Papst Hadrian über Abt-Bischof Waldo von Reichenau-Pavie* (Beuron, 1920).

Notker Balbulus (Notker the Stammerer), *Gesta Karoli Magni Imperatoris*, ed. H. F. Haefele, MGH SRG n.s. XII (Berlin, Weidmann, 1962); Eng. trans. D. Ganz, *Einhard and Notker the Stammerer: Two Lives of Charlemagne* (London, Penguin, 2008).

Ordines de celebrando concilio, ed. H. Schneider, MGH *Die Konzilsordines des Früh- und Hochmittelalters* (Hanover, Hahn, 1996).

Pactus legis Salicae, ed. K. A. Eckhardt, MGH LL nat. germ 4, 1 (Hanover, Hahn, 1962).

Paschasius Radbertus, *Vita sancti Adalhardi*, ed. J.-P. Migne, in *PL* CXX (Paris, Garnier, 1844–64); Eng. trans. *Charlemagne's Cousins: Contemporary Lives of Adalard and Wala*, ed. A. Cabaniss (Syracuse, NY, Syracuse University Press,1967).

PL, *Patrologiae cursus completus . . . series Latina*, ed. J.-P. Migne, 221 vols. (Paris, Garnier, 1844–64).

Paul the Deacon, *Carmina*, ed. E. Dümmler, MGH *Poet*. I (Berlin, Weidmann, 1871).

Paul the Deacon, *Gesta Episcoporum Mettensium*, ed. G. Pertz, MGH SS II (Hanover, Hahn, 1829).

Paul the Deacon, *Historia Langobardorum*, ed. G. Waitz, MGH SSRL (Hanover, Hahn, 1878).

Paulinus of Aquileia, ed. D. Norberg, *Paulini Aquileiensis opera omnia, pars I: Contra Felicem libri tres*, CCCM 95 (Turnout, Brepols, 1990).

Placiti, ed. C. Manaresi, *I placiti del regnum Italiae*, I, Fonti per la historia d'Italia 92 (Rome, Istituto storico italiano, 1955).

Placitum of Rižano, 'Il placito del Risano', eds. A. Patranovič and A. Margetič, *Atti del centro di recerche storiche Rovigno* 14 (1983–4), pp. 55–75.

Poetae, ed. E. Dümmler, MGH *Poet*. I, *Poetae Latini Aevi Carolini* I (Berlin, Weidmann, 1881); partial Eng. trans. P. Godman, *Poetry of the Carolingian Renaissance* (London, Duckworth, 1985).

Suetonius, *De vita caesarum*, ed. M. Ihm, vol. 1 (Leipzig, Teubner, 1907); Eng. trans. R. Graves, *The Twelve Caesars* (London, Penguin, 1957).

Thegan, *Gesta Hludowici Imperatoris*, ed. and German trans. E. Tremp, *Die Taten Kaiser Ludwigs und Astronomus, Das Leben Kaiser Ludwigs*, MGH SRG LXIV (Hanover, Hahn, 1995); Eng. trans. T. F. X. Noble, *Charlemagne and Louis the Pious: The Lives by Einhard, Notker, Ermoldus, Thegan and the Astronomer* (University Park, Pa, Pennsylvania State University Press, 2009).

Theodulf of Orléans, *Opus Karoli contra synodum*, eds. A. Freeman with P. Meyvaert, MGH Conc. II, *Supplementum* I (Hanover, Hahn, 1998).

Theodulf of Orléans, *The Verses*, Eng. trans. T. M. Andersson, with A. Ommundsen and L. S. B. MacColl (Tempe, Ariz., ACMRS, 2014); partial Eng. trans. P. Godman, *Poetry of the Carolingian Renaissance* (London, Duckworth, 1985).

Theodulf, *Versus Teudulfi episcopi contra iudices*, Eng. trans. pp. 162–6; and Andersson, *The Verses*, 'Bishop Theodulf's Verses against the Judges', pp. 79–107.

Theodulf, *Epitaphium Fastradae reginae*, Eng. trans. Andersson, *The Verses*, p. 65.

Theodulf, *Ad Carolum regem*, Eng. trans. Andersson, *The Verses*, pp. 65–73.

Theodulf, *Super sepulcrum Hadriani papae*, Eng. trans. Andersson, *The Verses*, pp. 73–5.

Theodulf, *Ad Corvinianum*, Eng. trans. Andersson, *The Verses*, pp. 75–9.

Theodulf, *Comparatio legis antiquae et modernae*, Eng. trans. Andersson, *The Verses*, pp. 107–10.

Theodulf, *Ad reginam [Liutgardam]*, Eng. trans. Andersson, *The Verses*, pp. 113–14.

Theodulf, *Ad regem [Carolum magnum]* Eng. trans. Andersson, *The Verses*, pp. 114–16.

Theodulf, *Ad regem Carolum [iuniorem]*, Eng. trans. Andersson, *The Verses*, p. 120.

Theophanes, *The Chronicle of Theophanes Confessor: Byzantine and Near Eastern History AD 284–813*, trans. C. Mango and R. Scott with G. Greatrex (Oxford, Clarendon Press, 1997).

Die Traditionen des Hochstift Freising, vol. I (744–926), ed. T. Bitterauf, Quellen und Erörterungen zur bayerischen Geschichte, neue Folge VI (Munich, Verlag der Kommission für bayerische Landesgeschichte, 1905).

Traditiones Wizenburgenses. Die Urkunden des Klosters Weissenburg 661–864, eds. K. Glöckner and A. Doll (Darmstadt, Hessische Historische Kommission, 1979).

Die Urkunden der Arnulfinger, ed. I. Heidrich (Bielefeld, Verlag H-C-I, 2001); also ed. I. Heidrich, MGH DD. *Maiorum domus regiae e stirpe Arnulforum* (Hanover, Hahn, 2011).

Die Urkunden Pippins, Karlmanns und Karls des Grossen, ed. E. Mühlbacher et al. (Hanover, Hahn, 1906); partial Eng. trans. H. R. Loyn and J. Percival, *The Reign of Charlemagne* (London, Edward Arnold, 1975).

Urkundenbuch des Klosters Fulda, ed. E. E. Stengel, vol. 1 (Marburg, Elwert, 1958).

Visio Wettini, ed. E. Dümmler, MGH *Poet.* II (Berlin, Weidmann, 1884); partial Eng. trans. P. Godman, *Poetry of the Carolingian Renaissance* (London, Duckworth, 1985), pp. 214–15.

Vita Hadriani, Liber Pontificalis, ed. L. Duchesne (Paris, Thorin, 1886), vol. 1, pp. 486–514; Eng. trans. with notes and commentary, R. Davis, *The Lives of the Eighth-Century Popes* (Liverpool, Liverpool University Press, 1992), pp. 115–72.

Vita Leonis III, Liber Pontificalis, ed. L. Duchesne (Paris, Thorin, 1886), vol. 2, pp. 1–34; Eng. trans. with notes and commentary, R. Davis, *The Lives of the Eighth-Century Popes* (Liverpool, Liverpool University Press, 1992), pp. 173–230.

Vita et miracula sancti Goaris, ed. with commentary Heinz E. Stiene (Bern and Oxford, P. D. Lang, 1981).

Walahfrid Strabo, *Walahfrid Strabo's* Visio Wettini: *text, translation and commentary*, ed. David A. Traill (Bern, P. D. Lang, 1974).

Wampach, Camillus (1930), *Geschichte der Grundherrschaft Echternach im Frühmittelalter*, I-2, Quellenband (Luxemburg, Luxemburger Kunstdruckerei).

Wigbod, *Epitome of the Commentaries on Genesis and the Gospels*, ed. Michael M. Gorman, *Revue Bénédictine* 118 (1), 2008, pp. 5–45.

SECONDARY WORKS

Airlie, Stuart (1990), 'Bonds of power and bonds of association in the court circle of Louis the Pious', in P. Godman and R. Collins, eds., *Charlemagne's Heir: New Perspective on the Reign of Louis the Pious (814–840)* (Oxford, Clarendon Press), pp. 191–204, repr. in Airlie (2012).

Airlie, Stuart (1995), 'The aristocracy', in R. McKitterick, ed., *New Cambridge Medieval History* II (Cambridge, Cambridge University Press), pp. 431–50.

Airlie, Stuart (1998), '"*Semper fideles?*" Loyauté envers les Carolingiens comme constituant de l'identité aristocratique', in R. Le Jan, ed., *La royauté et les élites dans l'Europe carolingienne*, Centre d'histoire de l'Europe du Nord-Ouest XVII (Lille, Centre Charles-de-Gaulle), pp. 129–43, repr. in Airlie (2012).

Airlie, Stuart (1999), 'Narratives of triumph and rituals of submission: Charlemagne's mastering of Bavaria', *Transactions of the Royal Historical Society* 6th series, pp. 93–119, repr. in Airlie (2012).

Airlie, Stuart (2000), 'The palace of memory: the Carolingian court as political centre', in S. Rees Jones et al., eds., *Courts and Regions in Medieval Europe* (Woodbridge, York Medieval Press), pp. 1–20, repr. in Airlie (2012).

Airlie, Stuart (2003), 'Talking heads: assemblies in early medieval Germany', in P. A. S. Barnwell and M. Mostert, eds., *Political Assemblies in the Earlier Middle Ages*, Studies in the Early Middle Ages VII (Turnhout, Brepols), pp. 29–46.

Airlie, Stuart (2004), 'Towards a Carolingian aristocracy', in M. Becher and J. Jarnut, eds., *Der Dynastiewechsel von 751* (Münster, Scriptorium), repr. Airlie (2012).

Airlie, Stuart (2005), 'Charlemagne and the aristocracy: captains and kings', in J. Story, ed., *Charlemagne: Empire and Society* (Manchester, Manchester University Press), pp. 90–102, repr. Airlie (2012).

Airlie, Stuart (2006), 'The aristocracy in the service of the state in the Carolingian period', in S. Airlie, W. Pohl and H. Reimitz, eds., *Staat im frühen Mittelalter* (Vienna, Verlag der ÖAW), pp. 93–111, repr. in Airlie (2012).

Airlie, Stuart (2008), 'The cunning of institutions', in J. R. Davis and M. McCormick, eds., *The Long Morning of Medieval Europe: New Directions in Early Medieval Studies* (Aldershot, Ashgate), pp. 267–71.

Airlie, Stuart (2009), '"Not rendering unto Caesar": challenges to early medieval rulers', in W. Pohl and V. Wieser, eds., *Der frühmittelalterliche Staat – europäischen Perspektiven* (Vienna, Verlag der ÖAW), pp. 489–501.

Airlie, Stuart (2012), *Power and its Problems in Carolingian Europe* (Farnham, Ashgate) [Collected papers].

Alberi, Mary (1998), 'The evolution of Alcuin's concept of the *imperium christianum*', in J. Hill and M. Swan, eds., *The Community, the Family and the Saint: Patterns of Power in Early Medieval Europe* (Turnhout, Brepols), pp. 3–17.

Allott, Stephen (1974), *Alcuin of York c.732–804: His Life and Letters* (York, William Sessions).

Althoff, Gerd (1997), 'Colloquium familiare – colloquium secretum – colloquium publicum. Beratung im politischen Leben des früheren Mittelalters', in *Spielregeln der Politik im Mittelalter. Kommunikation in Frieden und Fehde* (Darmstadt, Primus Verlag), pp. 157–84.

Althoff, Gerd (1998), '*Ira regis*: prolegomena to a history of royal anger', in B. Rosenwein, ed., *Anger's Past. The Social Uses of an Emotion in the Middle Ages* (Ithaca, NY, Cornell University Press), pp. 59–74.

Althoff, Gerd (2003), *Die Macht der Rituale. Symbolik und Herrschaft im Mittelalter* (Darmstadt, Primus Verlag).

Althoff, G., Fried, J. and Geary, P., eds. (2002), *Medieval Concepts of the Past: Ritual, Memory, Historiography*, Publications of the German Historical Institute (Cambridge, Cambridge University Press).

Anderson, Perry (1974), *Passages from Antiquity to Feudalism* (London, New Left Books).

Angenendt, Arnold (1980), 'Das geistliche Bündnis der Päpste mit der Karolingern', *Historical Journal* 100, pp. 1–94.

Angenendt, Arnold (1990), *Das Frühmittelalter. Die Abendländische Christenheit von 400 bis 900* (Stuttgart, Kohlhammer).

Angenendt, Arnold (1994), '*In porticu ecclesiae sepultus*. Ein Beispiel von himmlisch-irdischer Spiegelung', in N. Staubach and H. Keller, eds.,

Iconologia sacra. Mythos, Bildkunst und Dichtung in der Religions- und Sozialgeschichte Alt-europa. Festschrift für K. Hauck (Berlin, de Gruyter), pp. 68–80.

Angenendt, Arnold (2004), 'Pro vivis et defunctis. Histoire et influence d'une oraison de messe', in S. Gouguenheim et al., eds., *Retour aux sources. Textes, études et documents d'histoire médiévale offerts à Michel Parisse* (Paris, Picard), pp. 563–71.

Anton, Hans Hubert (1968), *Fürstenspiegel und Herrscherethos in der Karolingierzeit* (Bonn, Ludwig Röhrscheid Verlag).

Auzépy, Marie-France (1997), 'Francfort et Nicée II', in R. Berndt, ed., *Das Frankfurter Konzil von 794*, 2 vols. (Mainz, Verlag der Gesellschaft für mittelrheinische Kirchengeschichte), vol. 1, pp. 279–300.

Bachrach, Bernard (2001a), 'Adalhard of Corbie's *De ordine palatii*: some methodological observations regarding chapters 29–36', *Cithara* 41, pp. 3–34.

Bachrach, Bernard (2001b), *Early Carolingian Warfare: Prelude to Empire* (Philadelphia, University of Pennsylvania Press).

Bachrach, Bernard (2002), 'Charlemagne's military responsibilities "Am Vorabend der Kaiserkrönung": das Epos "Karolus Magnus et Leo papa" und der Papst', in P. Godman, J. Jarnut and P. Johanek, eds., *Am Vorabend der Kaiserkrönung* (Berlin, Akademie Verlag), pp. 231–55.

Bachrach, Bernard (2013), *Charlemagne's Early Campaigns (768–777)* (Leiden, Brill).

Balzaretti, Ross (2005), 'Masculine authority and state identity in Liutprandic Italy', in W. Pohl and P. Erhart, eds., *Die Langobarden: Herrschaft und Identität* (Vienna, Verlag der ÖAW), pp. 361–82.

Balzaretti, Ross (2013), *Dark Age Liguria. Regional Identity and Local Power, c. 400–1020* (London, Bloomsbury).

Banniard, Michel (1995), 'Language and communication in Carolingian Europe', in R. McKitterick, ed., *New Cambridge Medieval History* II (Cambridge, Cambridge University Press), pp. 695–708.

Barbero, Alessandro (2000), *Carlo Magno. Un padre dell'Europa* (Rome–Bari, Laterza & Fili Spa). Eng. trans. *Charlemagne. Father of a Continent*, by A. Cameron (Berkeley, Calif., University of California Press, 2004).

Barbier, Josiane (1990), 'Le système palatial franc: genèse et fonctionnement dans le Nord-Ouest du Regnum', *BEC* 148, pp. 245–99.

Barbier, Josiane (1994), 'Quierzy. Résidence pippinide et palais carolingien', in A. Renoux, ed., *Palais médiévaux (France-Belgique): 25 ans d'archéologie* (Centre d'édition et de publication de l'Université du Maine, Le Mans), pp. 85–6.

Bates, David et al., eds. (2006), *Writing Medieval Biography 750–1250. Essays in Honour of Frank Barlow* (Woodbridge, Boydell).

Bautier, Robert-Henri (1979), 'La campagne de Charlemagne en Espagne (778): la réalité historique', in *Roncevaux dans l'histoire, la légende et le mythe*,

Bulletin de la Société des sciences, lettres, et arts de Bayonne, nouv. Sér. 135, Bayonne, pp. 1–47.

Bautier, Robert-Henri (1991), *Recherches sur l'histoire de la France médiévale* (Ashgate, Variorum).

Bayer, Clemens M. M. (1999), 'Die karolingische Bauinschrift des Aachener Domes', in M. Kerner ed., *Der verschieierte Karl. Karl der Große zwischen Mythos und Worklichkeit* (Aachen, Verlag Mainz), pp. 445–52.

Becher, Matthias (1989), 'Zum Geburtsjahr Tassilo III', *ZBLG* 52, pp. 3–12.

Becher, Matthias (1992), 'Neue Überlegungen zum Geburtsdatum Karls des Großen', *Francia* 19, pp. 37–60.

Becher, Matthias (1993), *Eid und Herrschaft. Untersuchungen zum Herrscherethos Karls des Großen*, Vorträge und Forschungen, Sonderband XXXIX (Sigmaringen, Thorbecke).

Becher, Matthias (1999a), *Karl der Große* (Munich, Beck). Eng. trans. *Charlemagne*, by B. S. Bachrach (New Haven and London, Yale University Press, 2003).

Becher, Matthias (1999b), '"*Non enim habent regem idem Antiqui Saxones*" Verfassung und Ethnogenese in Sachsen während des 8. Jahrhunderts', in H.-J. Häsler with J. Jarnut and M. Wemhoff, eds., *Sachsen und Franken in Westfalen. Zum Komplexität der ethnischen Deutung und Abgrenzung zweier frühmittelalterlicher Stämme*, Studien zur Sachsenforschung 12 (Oldenburg, Isensee), pp. 1–31.

Becher, Matthias (1999c), 'Karl der Große und Papst Leo III', in C. Stiegemann and M. Wemhoff, eds., *799. – Kunst und Kultur der Karolingerzeit. Karl der Große und Papst III in Paderborn*, vol. 1 (Mainz, von Zabern), pp. 22–36.

Becher, Matthias (2002), 'Die Reise Papst Leos III zu Karl dem Großen. Überlegungen zu Chronologie, Verlauf und Inhalt der Paderborner Verhandlungen des Jahres 799', in P. Godman, J. Jarnut and P. Johanek, eds., *Am Vorabend der Kaiserkrönung* (Berlin, Akademie Verlag), pp. 87–112.

Becher, Matthias (2003), 'Eine verschleierrte Krise. Die Nachfolge Karl Martells 741 und die Anfänge der karolingischen Hofgeschichtsschreibung', in J. Laudage, ed., *Von Fakten und Fiktionen. Mittelalrerliche Geschichtsdarstellungen und ihre kritische Aufarbeitung* (Cologne, Böhlau), pp. 95–133.

Becher, Matthias (2006), 'Karl der Große zwischen Rom und Aachen. Die Kaiserkrönung und das Problem der Loyalität im Frankenreich', in Lotte Kéry et al., eds., *Eloquentia copiosus. Festschrift für Max Kerner zum 65. Geburtstag* (Aachen, Thouet Verlag), pp. 1–15.

Becher, Matthias (2007), 'Karl der Große und sein Hof. Reiseherrschaft und Residenz', in M. Meier, ed., *Sie schufen Europa. Historische Portraits von Konstantin bis Karl der Großen* (Munich, C. H. Beck), pp. 308–26.

Becher, Matthias (2009), 'Dynastie, Thronfolge und Staatsverständnis', in W. Pohl and V. Wieser, eds., *Der frühmittelalterliche Staat – europäische Perspektiven* (Vienna, Verlag der ÖAW), pp. 183–200.

Becher, Matthias (2012), 'Das Kaisertum Karls des Großen zwischen Rückbes-innung und Neuerung', in H. Leppin et al., eds., *Kaisertum im ersten Jahrtausend* (Regensburg, Schnell und Steiner), pp. 251–70.

Becher, Matthias (2013), 'Der Prediger mit eiserner Zunge. Die Unterwerfung und Christianisierung der Sachsen durch Karl der Großen', in H. Kamp and M. Kroker, eds., *Schwertmission. Gewalt und Christianisierung im Mittelalter* (Paderborn, Verlag Ferdinand Schöningh), pp. 23–54.

Becher, Matthias (2015), 'Karl der Grosse im Licht aktueller Forschung. Zu den Erkenntnismöglichkeiten von angeblich Altbekenntem', *Rheinische Vierteljahrsblätter* 79, pp. 188–96.

Becher, Matthias (2018), '*Omnes iurent*! Karl der Große und der allgemeine Treueid', in R. Grosse and M. Sot, eds., *Charlemagne: Les Temps, les espaces, les hommes* (Turnhout, Brepols), pp. 183–92.

Becher, Matthias and Hen, Yitzhak, eds. (2010), *Wilhelm Levison (1876–1947). Ein jüdisches Forscherleben zwischen wissenschaftlicher Anerkennung und politischem Exil* (Siegburg, Verlag Franz Schmitt).

Becher, Matthias and Jarnut, J., eds. (2004), *Der Dynastiewechsel von 751* (Münster, Scriptorium).

Becher, Matthias and Plassmann, Alheydis, eds. (2011), *Streit am Hof im frühen Mittelalter* (Bonn, Bonn University Press).

Bernard, Philippe (1998), 'Benoît d'Aniane est-il l'auteur de l'avertissement "Hucusque" et du supplément au sacramentaire "Hadrianum"?', *Studi Medievali*, 3rd ser. 39, pp. 1–120.

Berndt, Rainer, ed. (1997), *Das Frankfurter Konzil von 794. Kristallisarionspunkt karolingischer Kultur*, Quellen und Abhandlungen zur mittelrheinischen Kirchengeschichte LXXX, 2 vols., (Mainz, Gesellschaft für Mittelrheinische Kirchengeschichte).

Bernhardt, John (1993), *Itinerant Kingship and Royal Monasteries in Early Medieval Germany*, c. *936–1075* (Cambridge, Cambridge University Press).

Berschin, Walter (1991), *Biographie und Epochenstil im lateinischen Mittelalter* (Stuttgart, Hiersemann).

Bertolini, Ottorino (1965), 'Carlomagno e Benevento', in W. Braunfels, ed., *Karl der Grosse: Lebenswerk und Nachleben*, 5 vols. (Düsseldorf, Schwann, 1965–8), vol. 1, pp. 609–71.

Beumann, Helmut (1958), '"*Nomen imperatoris*": Studien zur Kaiseridee Karls des Grossen', *Historische Zeitschrift* 185, pp. 515–49.

Bischoff, Bernhard (1973), *Salzbürger Formelbücher und Briefe aus Tassilonischer und karolingischer Zeit*, SB der Bayerischen Akademie für Wissenschaften, phil.-hist. Klasse, Heft 4 (Munich 1973).

Bischoff, Bernhard (1986), *Latin Palaeography. Antiquity and the Middle Ages*, trans. D. Ó Cróinín and D. Ganz (Cambridge, Cambridge University Press).

Blackburn, Mark (1995), 'Money and Coinage', in R. McKitterick, ed., *New Cambridge Medieval History* II (Cambridge, Cambridge University Press), pp. 548–54.

Bloch, Marc (1961), *Feudal Society*, trans. L. A. Manyon (London, Routledge and Kegan Paul).

Bockius, Ronald (2014), 'Binnenfaharzeuge im Karolingerzeit', in P. Ettel et al., eds., *Großbaustelle 793. Das Kanalprojekt Karls des Großen zwischen Rhein und Donau* (Mainz, Verlag dos Römisch-Germanischen Zentralmuseumsthmar), pp. 81–6.

Bonnery, André (1997), 'A propos du Concile de Francfort (794). L'action des moines de Septimanie dans la lutte contre l'adoptionisme', in R. Berndt, ed., *Das Frankfurter Konzil von 794* (Mainz, Selbstverlag der Geselleschaft für Mittelrheinische Kirchengeschichte), pp. 767–86.

Bonnington, Tom (2016), 'Why were book burnings so often an accompaniment to extremist and fundamentalist ideologies in the twentieth century?' *The Journal of Publishing Culture* 5, pp. 1–10.

Borgolte, Michael (1976), *Der Gesandtenaustausch der Karolinger mit der Abbasiden und mit der Patriarchen von Jerusalem*, Münchner Beiträge zur Medivistik und Renaissance-Forschung 25, Munich.

Borgolte, Michael (1980), 'Papst Leo III., Karl der Große und der *Filioque*streit von Jerusalem', *Byzantina* 10, pp. 403–27.

Borgolte, Michael (1986), *Die Grafen Alemanniens in merowingische und karolingische Zeit: eine Prosopographie*, Archäologie und Geschichte, Freiburger Forschungen zum ersten Jahrtausend in Südwestdeutschland II (Sigmaringen, Thorbecke).

Borgolte, Michael (2009), 'Ein einziger Gott für Europa. Was die Ankunft von Judentum, Christentum und Islam für Europas Geschichte bedeutete', in W. Eberhard and C. Lübke, eds., *Die Vielfalt Europas. Identitäten und Räume* (Leipzig, Leipziger Universitätsverlag), pp. 581–90.

Borgolte, Michael (2014), 'Karl der Große – ein Global Player?', in *Kaiser und Kalifen: Karl der Grosse und die Mächte am Mittelmeer um 800*, Stiftung Deutschen Historischen Museum (Darmstadt, Verlag Philipp von Zabern), pp. 16–23.

Borri, Francesco (2008), '"Neighbours and relatives": the plea of Rižana as a source for northern Adriatic elites', *Mediterranean Studies* 17, pp. 1–26.

Borst, Arno (1972), 'Kaisertum und Namentheorie im Jahr 800', in G. Wolf, ed., *Zum Kaisertum Karls des Grossen. Beiträge und Aufsatze*, Wege der Forschung XXXVIII (Darmstadt, Wissenschaftliche Buchgesellschaft), pp. 216–39.

Boschen, Lothar (1972), *Die Annales Prumienses. Ihre nähere und ihre weitere Verwandtschaft* (Düsseldorf, Schwann).

Bougard, François (1997), 'La justice dans le royaume d'Italie aux IXe–Xe siècles', in *La giustizia nell'alto medioevo (secoli IX–XI)*, Settimane XLIV, pp. 133–76.

Bougard, François (2008), 'Adalhard de Corbie entre Nonantola et Brescia (813): commutation, gestion des biens monastiques et marché de la terre', in E. Cuozzo et al., eds., *Puer Apuliae. Mélanges offerts à J.-M. Martin* (Paris, CNRS).

Bougard, François (2009), 'Laien als Amtsträger: Über die Grafen des *regnum Italiae*', in W. Pohl and V. Vieser, eds., *Der frühmittelalterliche Staat – europäische Perspectiven*, OAWD (Vienna, Verlag der ÖAW), pp. 201–15.

Bougard, François (2010), 'Le crédit dans l'occident du haut moyen âge', in J.-P. Devroey et al., eds., *Les élites et la richesse au haut moyen âge* (Turnhout, Brepols), pp. 439–78.

Bourdieu, Pierre (1986), 'L'Illusion biographique', *Actes de la Recherche en Sciences Sociales Année* 62–63, pp. 69–72.

Bourdieu, Pierre (1998), *Practical Reason* (Oxford, Blackwell).

Brandes, Wolfram (1997), '"*Tempora periculosa sunt.*" Eschatologisches im Vorfeld der Kaiserkrönung Karls des Großen', in R. Berndt, ed., *Das Frankfurter Konzil von 794*, 2 vols. (Mainz, Verlag der Gesellschaft für mittelrheinische Kirchengeschichte), vol. 1, pp. 49–79.

Braudel, Fernand (1972–3), *The Mediterranean and the Mediterranean World in the Age of Philip II*, trans. Sîan Reynolds (London, Collins).

Braudel, Fernand (1981), *Civilization and Capitalism, 15th–17th centuries*, vol. 1, *The Structures of Everyday Life*, trans. Sian Reynolds (London, Collins).

Bredekamp, Horst (2014), *Karl der Große und die Bildpolitik des Körpers. Eine Studie zum schematischen Bildakt* (Berlin, Wagenbach Verlag).

Brooks, Nicholas P. (1971), 'The development of military obligations in eighth- and ninth-century England', in P. Clemoes and K. Hughes, eds., *England before the Conquest. Studies in Primary Sources presented to Dorothy Whitelock* (Cambridge, Cambridge University Press), pp. 69–84.

Brooks, Nicholas P. (1989), 'The formation of the Mercian kingdom', in S. Bassett, ed., *The Origins of Anglo-Saxon Kingdoms* (London, Leicester University Press), pp. 159–70.

Brooks, Nicholas P. et al., eds. (1995), *St. Oswald of Worcester, Life and Influence* (London, Leicester University Press).

Brown, Giles (1994), 'Introduction: the Carolingian Renaissance', in R. McKitterick, ed., *Carolingian Culture: Emulation and Innovation* (Cambridge, Cambridge University Press), pp. 1–51.

Brown, Peter (1967), *Augustine of Hippo: A Biography* (London, Faber & Faber).

Brown, Peter (1971), *The World of Late Antiquity* (London, Thames and Hudson, repr. 1989 with rev. bibliog. 1989).

Brown, Peter (1996), *The Rise of Western Christendom: Triumph and Diversity, AD 200–1000* (Oxford, Blackwell, repr. 1997 with footnotes).

Brown, Peter (2012), *Through the Eye of a Needle: Wealth, the Fall of Rome, and the Making of Christianity in the West, 350–550* (Princeton, NJ, Princeton University Press).

Brown, Thomas S. (1984), *Gentlemen and Officers: Imperial Administration and Aristocratic Power in Byzantine Italy, AD 554–800* (London, British School at Rome).

Brown, Thomas S. (1988), 'The interplay between Roman and Byzantine traditions and local sentiment in the Exarchate of Ravenna', *Settimane* 34, pp. 127–60.

Brown, Thomas S. (1995), 'Byzantine Italy, c.680–c.876', in R. McKitterick, ed., *New Cambridge Medieval History* II (Cambridge, Cambridge University Press), pp. 320–48.

Brown, Thomas S. (1998), 'Urban violence in early medieval Italy: the cases of Rome and Ravenna', in G. Halsall, ed., *Violence and Society in the Early Medieval West* (Woodbridge, Boydell), pp. 76–89.

Brown, Thomas S. (2016), 'Culture and society in Ottonian Ravenna', in J. Herrin and J. Nelson, eds., *Ravenna: Its Role in Earlier Medieval Change and Exchange* (London, University of London, School of Advanced Study, Institute of Historical Research), pp. 335–44.

Brown, Warren C. (2001), *Unjust Seizure: Conflict, Interest and Authority in an Early Medieval Society* (Ithaca, NY, Cornell University Press, 2001).

Brown, Warren C. (2006), 'The idea of empire in Carolingian Bavaria', in B. Weiler and S. MacLean, eds., *Representations of Power in Medieval Germany, 800–1500* (Turnhout, Brepols), pp. 37–55.

Brown, Warren C. (2013), 'Laypeople and documents in the Frankish formula collections', in W. C. Brown, M. Costembeys, M. Innes and A. J. Kosto, eds., *Documentary Culture and the Laity in the Early Middle Ages* (Cambridge, Cambridge University Press), pp. 125–51.

Brown, W. C., Costembeys, M., Innes, M. and Kosto, A. J., eds. (2013), *Documentary Culture and the Laity in the Early Middle Ages* (Cambridge, Cambridge University Press).

Bruand, Olivier (2002), *Voyageurs et marchantsises aux temps carolingiens* (Brussels, De Boeck Université).

Brühl, Carlrichard (1962), 'Fränkischer Krönungsbrauch und das Problem der "Festkrönungen"', *Historische Zeitschrift* 265, pp. 265–326.

Brühl, Carlrichard (1967), 'Remarques sur les notions de "capital" et de "résidence" pendant le haut moyen âge', *Journal des Savants*, pp. 193–215.

Brühl, Carlrichard (1968), *Fodrum, gistum und servitium regis: Studien zu den wirtschaftlichen Grundlagen des Königtums im Frankenreich*, 2 vols. (Cologne, Böhlau).

Brunner, K. (1979), *Oppositionelle Gruppen im Karolingerreich*, VIOG XXV (Vienna, Böhlau).

Brunner, K. (1983), 'Auf der Spuren verlorener Traditionen', *Peritia* 2, pp. 1–22.

Buc, Philippe (2000), 'Ritual and interpretation: the early medieval case (with an addition of the Chronicle of Moissac', *Early Medieval Europe* 9, pp. 183–210.

Buc, Philippe (2001), *The Dangers of Ritual* (Princeton, NJ, Princeton University Press).

Buc, Philippe (2005), 'Warum weniger die Handelnden selbst als eher die Chronisten das politische Ritual erzeugten – und warum es niemandem auf die wahre Geschichte ankam', in B. Jussen, ed., *Die Macht des Königs* (Munich, C. H. Beck), pp. 27–37.

Buck, Thomas (1997), *Admonitio und Praedicatio. Zur religiös-pastoralen Dimension von Kapitularien und kapitulariennahen Texten (507–814)*, Freiburger Beiträge zur mittelalterlichen Geschichte Studien und Texte IX (Frankfurt, Lang).

Bührer-Thierry, Geneviève (1998), '"Just anger" or "vengeful anger"? The punishment of blinding in the early medieval west', in B. H. Rosenwein, ed., *Anger's Past. The Social Uses of an Emotion in the Middle Ages* (Ithaca, NY, Cornell University Press), pp. 75–91.

Bullough, Donald A. (1962), '"*Baiuli*" in the Carolingian "*regnum Langobardorum*"', *English Historical Review* 77, pp. 625–37.

Bullough, Donald A. (1965), *The Age of Charlemagne* (London, Paul Elek).

Bullough, Donald A. (1966), 'Urban change in early medieval Italy: the example of Pavia', *Papers of the British School at Rome*, new series 21, pp. 82–130.

Bullough, Donald A. (1969), 'Early medieval social groupings', *Past & Present* 45, pp. 3–18.

Bullough, Donald A. (1970), '*Europae Pater*: Charlemagne and his achievement in the light of recent scholarship', *English Historical Review* 85, pp. 59–105.

Bullough, Donald A. (1984), '*Albuinus deliciosus Karoli regis*. Alcuin of York and the Shaping of the Early Carolingian Court', in L. Fenske et al. eds., *Institutionen, Kultur und Gesellschaft im Mittelalter. Festschrift für Josef Fleckenstein* (Sigmaringen, Thorbecke), pp. 73-92.

Bullough, Donald A. (1985), '*Aula renovata*: the Carolingian court before the Aachen palace', *Proceedings of the British Academy* 71, pp. 267–301, repr. Bullough (1991b).

Bullough, Donald A. (1991a), '*Imagines regum* and their significance in the early medieval west', in *Carolingian Renewal: Sources and Heritage* (Manchester, Manchester University Press), pp. 39–96.

Bullough, Donald A. (1991b), *Carolingian Renewal: Sources and Heritage* (Manchester, Manchester University Press).

Bullough, Donald A. (2002), 'Alcuin and lay virtue', in L. Gaffuri and R. Quinto, eds., *Predicazione e società nel Medioevo: rifelssione etica, valore e modelli di comportimento* (Padua, Centro Studi), pp. 71–91.

Bullough, Donald A. (2003a), 'Was there a Carolingian anti-war movement?' *Early Medieval Europe* 12, pp. 365–76.

Bullough, Donald A. (2003b), 'Charlemagne's court library revisited', *Early Medieval Europe* 12, pp. 339–63.

Bullough, Donald A. (2004), *Alcuin: Achievement and Reputation*, Education and Society in the Middle Ages and Renaissance XVI (Leiden, Brill).

Bullough, Donald A. (2005), 'Charlemagne's "Men of God": Alcuin, Hildebald and Arn', in J. Story ed., *Charlemagne: Empire and Society* (Manchester, Manchester University Press), pp. 136–50.

Caine, Barbara (2010), *Biography and History* (Basingstoke, Palgrave Macmillan).

Cam, Helen M. (1924), 'An East Anglian shire-moot of Stephen's reign, 1148–53', *English Historical Review* 39, pp. 568–71.

Campbell, James (1989), 'The sale of land and the economics of power in early England: problems and possibilities', *Haskins Society Journal* 1, pp. 23–37.

Campbell, James (2000), *The Anglo-Saxon State* (London, Hambledon).

Campbell, Darryl (2010), 'The *Capitulare de Villis*, the *Brevium Exempla*, and the Carolingian Court at Aachen', *Early Medieval Europe* 18, pp. 243–64.

Carroll, Christopher (1999), 'The bishoprics in Saxony in the first century after Christianization', *Early Medieval Europe* 8, pp. 219–46.

Cavadini, John C. (1993), *The Last Christology of the West: Adoptionism in Spain and Gaul 785–830* (Philadelphia, University of Pennsylvania Press).

Cavadini, John C. (1997), 'Elipandus and his critics at the Council of Frankfurt', in R. Berndt, ed., *Das Farnkfurter Konzil von 794*, vol. 2 (Mainz, Selbstverlag der Gesellschaft für Mittelrheinisiche Kirchengeschichte), pp. 787–807.

Chandler, Cullen J. (2002), 'Between court and counts: Carolingian Catalonia and the *aprisio* grant, 778–897', *Early Medieval Europe* 11, pp. 19–44.

Charanis, Peter (1961), 'The transfer of population as a policy in the Byzantine Empire', in *Comparative Studies in Society and History* 3 (2), pp. 140–54.

Classen, Peter (1951), '*Romanum gubernans imperium*: zur Vorgeschichte des Kaisertitulatur Karls des Große', *Deutsches Archiv für Erforschung des Mittelalters* 9, pp. 103–21. Repr. in *Ausgewählte Aufsätze von Peter Classen*, eds. J. Fleckenstein with C. J. Classen and J. Fried (Sigmaringen, Thorbecke, 1983).

Classen, Peter (1968), 'Karl der Große, das Papsttum und Byzanz', in *Karl der Große. Lebenswerk und Nachleben*, 5 vols., vol. 1, *Persönlichkeit und Geschichte*, ed. H. Beumann (Düsseldorf, Schwann), pp. 537–608. Repr. in H. Fuhrmann and C. Märtl, eds., *P. Classen, Karl der Grosse, das Papsttum und Byzanz* (Sigmaringen, Thorbecke, 1985), pp. 205–29.

Classen, Peter (1971), 'Karl der Grosse und der Thronfolge im Frankenreich', in *Festschrift für H. Heimpel*, ed. Max-Planck-Instituts für Geschichte, 3 vols. (Göttingen, Vandenhoeck und Ruprecht), vol. 3, pp. 109–34.

Classen, Peter (1978), 'Bayern und die politischen Mächte im Zeitalter Karls des Großen und Tassilo III', in S. Haider, ed., *Die Anfänge des Klosters Kremsmünster*, Erganzungsband zu den Mitteilungen des Öberösterreichischen Landesarchiv II, pp. 169–87. Repr. in *Ausgewählte Aufsätze von Peter Classen*, eds. J. Fleckenstein with C. J. Classen and J. Fried (Sigmaringen, Thorbecke, 1983), pp. 231–48.

Classen, Peter (1983), '*Romanum gubernans imperium*. Zur Vorgeschichte der Kaisertitelatur Karls des Grossen', in *Ausgewählte Aufsätze von Peter Classen*, eds. J. Fleckenstein with C. J. Classen and J. Fried (Sigmaringen, Thorbecke), pp. 187–204.

Classen, Peter (1985), *Karl der Grosse, das Papsttum und Byzanz: Die Begründung des Karolingischen Kaisertums*, eds., H. Fuhrmann and C. Märtl (Sigmaringen, Thorbecke, 1985).

Claussen, Martin A. (2004), *The Reform of the Frankish Church. Chrodegang of Metz and the* Regula canonicorum *in the Eighth Century* (Cambridge, Cambridge University Press).

Clay, John-Henry (2010), *In the Shadow of Death. Saint Boniface and the Conversion of Hessia, 721–54* (Turnhout, Brepols).

de Clercq, Charles (1936), *La législation religieuse franque de Clovis à Charlemagne* (Paris, Bureau du Recueil, Bibliothèque de l'Université).

Close, Florence (2011), *Uniformiser la foi pour unifier l'Empire* (Brussels, Académie royale de Belgique).

Collins, Roger (1989), *The Arab Conquest of Spain* (Oxford, Oxford University Press).

Collins, Roger (1994), 'Deception and misrepresentation in early eighth-century Frankish historiography: two case studies', in J. Jarnut, U. Nonn and M. Richter, eds., *Karl Martell in seiner Zeit* (Sigmaringen, Thorbecke), pp. 227–48.

Collins, Roger (1995a), *Early Medieval Spain. Unity in Diversity, 400–1000*, 2nd edn (London, Macmillan).

Collins, Roger (1995b), 'Spain: the northern kingdoms and the Basques, 711–910', in R. McKitterick ed., *New Cambridge Medieval History* II (Cambridge, Cambridge University Press), pp. 272–98.

Collins, Roger (1996), *Fredegar*, Authors of the Middle Ages, vol. 4, no. 13 (Aldershot, Ashgate).

Collins, Roger (1998a), 'The reviser revisited: another look at the alternative version of the *Annales regni Francorum*', in A. C. Murray, ed., *After Rome's Fall: Narrators and Sources of Early Medieval History. Essays Presented to Walter Goffart* (Toronto, University of Toronto Press), pp. 191–213.

Collins, Roger (1998b), *Charlemagne* (London, Macmillan).

Collins, Roger (2005), 'Charlemagne's imperial coronation and the Annals of Lorsch', in J. Story ed., *Charlemagne. Empire and Society* (Manchester, Manchester University Press), pp. 52–70.

Conant, Jonathan (2014), 'Louis the Pious and the contours of Empire', *Early Medieval Europe* 22, pp. 336–60.

Contreni, John J. (1995), 'The Carolingian Renaissance: education and literary culture', in R. McKitterick, ed., *New Cambridge Medieval History* II (Cambridge, Cambridge University Press), pp. 709–57.

Cooper, Kate (1999), 'The martyr, the matrona and the bishop: gender and the rhetoric of allegiance in the Roman *gesta martyrum*', *Early Medieval Europe* 8 (3), pp. 297–317.

Cooper, Kate (2009), 'Closely watched households: visitibility, exposure and private power in the Roman *domus*', *Past & Present* 197 (i), pp. 3–33.

Corradini, R., Diesenberger, M. and Reimitz, H., eds. (2003), *The Construction of Communities in the Early Middle Ages: Texts, Resources and Artefacts* (Leiden, Brill).

Costambeys, Marios (2007), *Power and Patronage in Early Medieval Italy. Local Society, Italian Politics and the Abbey of Farfa, c.700–900* (Cambridge, Cambridge University Press).

Costambeys, Marios (2013), 'The laity, the clergy, the scribes and their archives: the documentary record of eighth- and ninth-century Italy', in W. C. Brown, M. Costambeys, M. Innes and A. J. Kosto, eds., *Documentary Culture and the Laity in the Early Middle Ages* (Cambridge, Cambridge University Press), pp. 231–58.

Costambeys, Marios (2014), 'Alcuin, Rome and Charlemagne's imperial coronation', in F. Tinti, ed., *England and Rome in the Early Middle Ages: Pilgrimage, Art and Politics* (Turnhout, Brepols), pp. 255–90.

Costambeys, M., Innes, M. and MacLean, S. (2011), *The Carolingian World* (Cambridge, Cambridge University Press).

Coupland, Simon (2005), 'Charlemagne's coinage: ideology and economy', in J. Story, ed., *Charlemagne: Empire and Society* (Manchester, Manchester University Press), pp. 211–29.

Coupland, Simon (2018), 'Charlemagne and his coinage', in R. Grosse and M. Sot, eds., *Charlemagne: Les temps, les espaces, les hommes. Construction et déconstruction d'un règne* (Turnholt, Brepols), pp. 427–51.

Crawford, S. J. (1933), *Anglo-Saxon Influence on Western Christendom 600–800* (Cambridge, Speculum Historiale).

Cubitt, Catherine (1995), *Anglo-Saxon Church Councils c. 650–c.850* (London, Leicester University Press).

Dahlhaus-Berg, Elisabeth (1975), *Nova Antiquitas et Antiqua Novitas. Typologische Exegese und isidorianisches Geschichtsbild bei Theodulf von Orléans* (Cologne and Vienna, Böhlau).

Daim, Falko (1998), 'Archaeology, ethnicity and the structures of identification. The example of the Avars, Carantanians and Moravians in the eighth century', in W. Pohl and H. Reimitz, eds., *Stragegies of Distinction* (Leiden, Brill), pp. 71–93.

Davies, Wendy (1988), *Small Worlds: The Village Community in Early Medieval Brittany* (London, Duckworth).

Davies, Wendy (1993), 'Celtic kingships in the early Middle Ages', in A. Duggan, ed., *Kings and Kingship in Medieval Europe* (London, King's College London, Centre for Late Antique and Medieval Studies), pp. 101–24.

Davies, Wendy (2010), 'Economic change in early medieval Ireland: the case for growth?' *Settimane* 57, pp. 111–33.

Davies, Wendy (2018), 'Gardens and Gardening in Early Medieval Spain and Portugal', Annual Early Medieval Europe Lecture, 2018.

Davis, Jennifer R. (2008), 'A pattern for power: Charlemagne's delegation of judicial responsibilities', in J. R. Davis and M. McCormick, eds., *The Long Morning of Medieval Europe: New Directions in Early Medieval Studies* (Aldershot, Ashgate), pp. 235–46.

Davis, Jennifer R. (2011), 'Charlemagne's settlement of disputes', in M. Becher and A. Plassmann, eds., *Streit am Hof im frühen Mittelalter*, Studien zur Wirkung des Klassischen Antike XI (Bonn, Bonn University Press), pp. 149–73.

Davis, Jennifer R. (2015), *Charlemagne's Practice of Empire* (Cambridge, Cambridge University Press).

Davis, Jennifer R. (2018), 'Inventing the *missi*: delegating power in late eighth-century Francia', in D. G. Tor, ed., *The Abbasid and Carolingian Empires: Comparative Studies in Civilisational Formation* (Leiden, Brill), pp. 13–51.

Davis, Jennifer R. (forthcoming), 'Western Europe', in E. Hermans, ed., *A Companion to the Global Early Middle Ages* (Kalamazoo, Mich. and Leeds, Arc Humanities Press).

Davis, J. R. and McCormick, M., eds., (2008), *The Long Morning of Medieval Europe: New Directions in Early Medieval Studies* (Aldershot, Ashgate).

Delaruelle, Étienne (1932), 'Charlemagne, Carloman, Didier et la politique du marriage franco-lomard (770–771)', *Revue historique* 170, pp. 213–24.

Deliyannis, Deborah M. (2003), 'Charlemagne's silver tables: the ideology of an imperial capital', *Early Medieval Europe* 12 (ii), pp. 159–77.

Delogu, Paolo (1995), 'Lombard and Carolingian Italy', in R. McKitterick, ed., *New Cambridge Medieval History* II (Cambridge, Cambridge University Press), pp. 290–319.

Depreux, Philippe (1995), 'Tassilon III et le roi des Francs: examen d'une vassalité controversée', *Revue Historique* 593, pp. 23–73.

Depreux, Philippe (1997), *Prosopographie de l'entourage de Louis le Pieux (781–840)* (Sigmaringen, Thorbecke).

Depreux, Philippe (2002), 'Ambitions et limites des réformes culturelles à l'époque carolingienne', *Revue Historique* 623, pp. 721–53.

Depreux, Philippe (2009), 'Investitures et destitutions aux temps carolingiens', in W. Fałkowski and Y. Sassier, eds., *Le monde carolingien: Bilan, perspectives, champs de recherches* (Turnhout, Brepols), pp. 157–81.

Depreux, Philippe (2013), 'Le souverain, maître de l'échange', in Irmgard Fees and P. Depreux, eds., *Tauschgeschäft und Tauschurkunde* (Cologne, Böhlau), pp. 45–64.

Devroey, Jean-Pierre (2011), Ordering, Measuring and Counting: Carolingian Capital, and the Economic Performance in Western Europe (750–900), www.Academia (Accessible online from the University of Brussels).

Dierkens, Alain (1991), 'Le tombeau de Charlemagne', *Byzantion* 61, pp. 156–80.

Dierkens, Alain (1994), '*Carolus monasteriorum multorum eversor et ecclesiasticarum pecuniarum in usus proprios commutator?* Notes sur la politique monastique du maire du palais Charles Martel', in J. Jarnut, U. Nonn and M. Richter, eds., *Karl Martell in seiner Zeit* (Sigmaringen, Thorbecke), pp. 277–94.

Dierkens, Alain (2009), 'Quelques réflexions sur la présentation des sarcophages dans les églises du haut moyen âge', in A. Alduc-Le Bagousse, ed., *Inhumations de prestige ou prestige de l'inhumation? Expressions du pouvoir dans l'au-delà IVe–XVe siècle* (Publications du CRAHM, Caen), pp. 265–302.

Diesenberger, Maximilian (2006), 'Dissidente Stimmen zum Sturz Tassilos III', in R. Meens, C. Pössel and P. Shaw, eds., *Texts and Identities in the Early Middle Ages* (Vienna, Verlag der ÖAW), pp. 105–20.

Diesenberger, Maximilian (2016), *Predigt und Politik im Frühmittelalterlichen Bayern* (Berlin and Boston, Walter de Gruyter).

Diesenberger, Maximilian (2018), 'Die Zwangsumsiedlungen der Sachsen an der Wende vom 8. Zum 9. Jahrhundert', in T. Ertl, ed., *Zwangsumsiedlungen. Erzwungene Exile: Umsiedlung und Vertreibung in der Vormoderne (500 bis 1850)* (Frankfurt am Main, Campus Verlag), pp. 35–57.

Drews, Wolfram (2009), *Die Karolinger und die Abbasiden von Bagdad. Legitimationsstrategien frühmittelalterlicher Herrscherdynastien im transkulturellen Vergleich* (Berlin, Akademie Verlag).

Dutton, Paul E. (1993), *Carolingian Civilization: A Reader* (Peterborough Ont., Broadview Press).

Dutton, Paul E. (1998), *Charlemagne's Courtier. The Complete Einhard* (Peterborough, Ont., Broadview Press).

Dutton, Paul E. (2004), *Charlemagne's Mustache and Other Cultural Clusters of a Dark Age* (New York, Palgrave).

Dutton, Paul E. (2008), 'On medieval weather in general, bloody rain in particular', in J. R. Davis and M. McCormick, eds., *The Long Morning of Medieval Europe* (Aldershot, Ashgate), pp. 167–80.

Eastwood, Bruce S. (1994), 'The astronomy of Macrobius in Carolingian Europe: Dungal's letter of 811 to Charles the Great', *Early Medieval Europe* 3, pp. 117–34.

Eckhardt, Wilhelm A. (1956), 'Die *capitularia missorum specialia* von 802', *Deutsches Archiv für Erforschung des Mittelalters* 12, pp. 498–516.

Effenberger, Arne (1999), 'Die Wiederverwendung römischer, spätantiker und byzantinischer Kunstwerke in der Karolingerzeit', in C. Stiegemann and M. Wemhoff, eds., *799. Kunst und Kultur der Karolingerzeit*, Beiträge zum Katalog der Austellung, 3 vols. (Paderborn, Philipp von Zabern), vol. 3, pp. 643–61.

Effros, Bonnie (1997), '*De partibus Saxoniae* and the regulation of mortuary custom. A Carolingian campaign of Christianization of the suppression of Saxon identity', *Revue belge de Philologie et d'Histoire* 75, pp. 267–86.

Eichler, Daniel (2011), 'Karolingische Höfe und Versammlungen – Grundvoraussetzungen', in M. Becher and A. Plassmann, eds., *Stret am Hof in frühen Mittelalter* (Bonn, Bonn University Press), pp. 121–48.

Erkens, Franz-Reiner (1996), '*Divisio legitima* und *unitas imperii*. Teilungspraxis und Einheitsstreben bei der Thronfolge im Frankenreich', *Deutsches Archiv für Erforschung des Mittelalters* 52, pp. 423–85.

Erkens, Franz-Reiner (2006), *Herrschersakralität im Mittelalter* (Stuttgart, W. Kohlhammer Verlag).

Esders, Stefan (1999), 'Regionale Selbstbehauptung zwischen Byzanz und dem Frankenreich. Die inquisition der Rechtswohnheiten Istriens durch die Sendboten Karls des Grossen und Pippins von Italy', in S. Esders and T. Scharf, eds., *Eid und Wahrheitssuche. Gesellschaft, Kultur und Schrift*, Mediävistische Beiträge VII (Frankfurt, Lang), pp. 49–112.

Esders, Stefan (2006), 'Die baierischen Eliten nach dem Sturz Tassilos III', in F. Bougard et al., eds., *Les Élites au haut moyen âge: Crises et renouvellements* (Turnhout, Brepols), pp. 282–313.

Esders, Stefan (2008), 'Die römischen Wurzeln der fiskalischen inquisition der Karolingerzeit', in C. Gauvard, ed., *L'enquête au moyen âge*, Collection de l'École française de Rome CCCLXXXXIX (Rome, École française de Rome), pp. 13–28.

Esders, Stefan (2009a), 'Rechtliche Grundlagen frühmittelalterlicher Staatlichkeit: der allgemeine Treueid', in W. Pohl and V. Weiser, eds., *Der frühmittelalterliche Staat – Europäische Perspectiven* (Vienna, Verlag der ÖAW), pp. 423–32.

Esders, Stefan (2009b), '"Öffentliche" Abgaben und Leistungen im Übergang von der Spätantike zum Frühmittelalter: Konzeptionen und Befunde', in Theo Kölzer and Rudolf Schieffer, eds., *Von der Spätantike zum frühen Mittelalter: Kontinuitäten und Brüche, Konzeptionen und Befunde*, Ostfildern, Vorträge und Forschungen 70, pp. 189–244.

Esders, Stefan (2012), 'Spätantike und frühmittelalterliche Dukate. Überlegungen zum Problem historischer Kontinuität und Diskontinuität', in H. Fehr and I. Heitmeier, eds., *Die Anfänge Bayerns. Von Raetien und Noricum zur frühmittelalterlichen Baiovaria*, Bayerische Landesgeschichte und europäische Regionalgeschichte 1 (Munich), pp. 425–62.

Esders, Stefan and Haubrichs, Wolfgang (forthcoming), 'Notitia sacramentorum', in MGH *Studien und Quellen*.

Esmyol, Andrea (2002), *Geliebte oder Ehefrau? Konkubinen im frühen Mittelalter*, Beihefte zum *Archiv für Kulturgeschichte* 52 (Cologne, Böhlau).

Ettel, Peter and Wunschel, Andreas (2014), 'Die frühmittelalterlichen Zentren Würzburg und Karlburg am Main', in P. Ettel et al., eds., *Großbaustelle 793: Das Kanalprojekt Karls des Grossen Zwischen Rhein und Donau* (Romisch Germanisches Zentralmuseum/Mosaiksteine), pp. 73–4.

Everett, Nicholas (2011), 'Paulinus of Aquileia's *Sponsio Episcoporum*: written oaths and ecclesiastical discipline in Carolingian Italy', in W. Robins, ed., *Textual Cultures of Medieval Italy* (Toronto, Ont., University of Toronto Press), pp. 167–216.

Ewig, Eugen (1956), 'Zum christlichen Königsgedanken im Frühmittelalter', in T. Mayer, ed., *Das Königtum, seine geistigen und rechtlichen Grundlagen*, Vorträge und Forschungen III (Lindau, Thorbecke), pp. 7–73.

Ewig, Eugen (1963), 'Résidence et capitale pendant le haut moyen âge', *Revue Historique* 230, pp. 25–72.

Ewig, Eugen (2001), *Die Merowinger und das Frankenreich*, 4th edn (Stuttgart, Kohlhammer).

Falkenstein, Ludwig (1991), 'Charlemagne et Aix-la-Chapelle', *Byzantion* 61, pp. 231–89.

Falkenstein, Ludwig (2002), 'Pfalz und *"vicus"* Aachen', in Caspar Ehlers, ed., *Orte der Herrschaft. Mittelalterliche Köigspfalzen* (Göttingen, Max-Planck-Institut zur Erforschung multireligiöser und multiethnischer Gesellschaften), pp. 131–81.

Favier, Jean (2000), *Charlemagne* (Paris, Fayard).

Feller, Laurent (2010), 'Introduction. Formes et fonctions de la richesse des élites au haut moyen âge', in J.-P. Devroey et al., eds., *Les Élites et la richesse* (Turnhout, Brepols), pp. 5–30.

Felten, Franz J. (1974), 'Laienäbte in der Karolingerzeit', in A. Borst, ed., *Mönchtum, Episkopat und Adel zur Grundungszeit des Klosters Reichenau* (Stuttgart, Thorbecke), pp. 397–431.

Felten, Franz J. (1980), *Äbte und Laienäbte im Frankenreich, Monographien zur Geschichte des Mittelalters* (Stuttgart, Monographien zur Geschichte des Mittelalters).

Felten, Franz J. (1982), 'Zur Geschichte der Klöster Farfa und S. Vincenzo al Volturno im achten Jahrhundert', *Quellen und Forschungen aus italienischen Archiven und Bibliotheken* 62, pp. 1–58.

Fentress, James and Wickham, Chris (1992), *Social Memory* (Oxford, Blackwell).

Fichtenau, Heinrich (1949), *Das karolingische Imperium* (Zurich, Fretz und Wasmuth), partial trans. P. Munz, *The Carolingian Empire* (Oxford, Blackwell, 1957).

Fichtenau, Heinrich (1953), 'Karl der Grosse und des Kaisertum', *MIÖG* 61, pp. 257–334.

Fichtenau, Heinrich (1978), 'Abt Richbod und die *Annales Laureshamenses*', in *Beiträge zur Geschichte des Klosters Lorsch* (Lorsch, Verlag Laurissa), pp. 277–304.

Firey, Abigail (2009), *A Contrite Heart: Prosecution and Redemption in the Carolingian Empire* (Leiden, Brill).

Flach, Dietmar (1979), *Untersuchungen zur Verfassung und Verwaltung des Aachener Reichsguter von der Karolingerzeit* (Göttingen, Veröffentlichungen von der Max-Planck-Instituts für Geschichte 46).

Fleckenstein, Josef (1959–66), *Die Hofkapelle der deutschen Könige*, 2 vols. (Stuttgart, Hiersemann, MGH Schriften XVI).

Fleckenstein, Josef (1965), 'Karl der Große und sein Hof', in W. Braunfels et al., eds., *Karl der Grosse, Lebenswerk und Nachleben*, 5 vols. (Düsseldorf, Schwann), vol. 1, pp. 24–50.

Fleckenstein, Josef (1997), 'Karl der Grosse, seins Hofgelehrten und das Frankfurter Konzil von 794', in R. Berndt, ed., *Das Frankfurter Konzil von 794. Kristallisationspunkt karolingischer Kultur*, 2 vols. (Mainz, Gesellschaft für mittelrheinische Kirchengeschichte), vol. 1, pp. 27–46.

Flierman, Robert (2016), 'Religious Saxons: paganism, infidelity and biblical punishment in the *Capitulatio de partibus Saxoniae*', in R. Meens et al., eds., *Religious Franks. Religion and Power in the Frankish Kingdoms: Studies in Honour of Mayke de Jong* (Manchester, Manchester University Press), pp. 181–201.

Flierman, Robert (2018), *Saxon Identities, 150–900 AD* (London, Bloomsbury).

Foot, Sarah (2005), 'Finding the meaning of form: narrative in annals and chronicles', in N. Partner, ed., *Writing Medieval History* (London, Hodder Education), pp. 87–108.

Foot, Sarah (2012), 'Annals and chronicles in Western Europe', in S. Foot, C. F. Robinson and I. Hesketh, eds., *The Oxford History of Historical Writing*, vol. 2: *400–1400* (Oxford, Oxford University Press), pp. 346–67.

Foucault, Michel (1978), *The History of Sexuality*, vol. 1, trans. Robert Hurley (New York, Penguin).

Foucault, Michel (2007), *Security. Territory, Population: Lectures at the Collège, 1977–1978*, trans. Graham Burchell (Basingstoke, St. Martin's Press).

Fouracre, P. (1984), 'Observations on the outgrowth of Pippinid influence in the "*Regnum Francorum*"', *Medieval Prosopography* 5, pp. 1–31.

Fouracre, P. (1986), '"*Placita*" and the settlement of diputes in later Merovingian Francia', in W. Davies and P. Fouracre, eds., *The Settlement of Dispute in Early Medieval Europe* (Cambridge, Cambridge University Press), pp. 23–43.

Fouracre, P. (1995), 'Carolingian justice: the rhetoric of improvement and contexts of abuse', in *La giustizia nell'alto medievo (secoli V-VIII)*, SSCI 42, pp. 771–803.

Fouracre, P. (1999), 'The origins of the Carolingian attempt to regulate the cult of saints', in J. Howard-Johnson and P. A. Hayward, eds., *The Cult of Saints in Late Antiquity and the Early Middle Ages* (Oxford, Oxford University Press), pp. 143–65.

Fouracre, P. (2000), *The Age of Charles Martel* (Harlow, Longman).

Fouracre, P. (2005), 'The long shadow of the Merovingians', in J. Story, ed., *Charlemagne. Empire and Society* (Manchester, Manchester University Press), pp. 5–21.

Fouracre, P. (2009a), 'Comparing the resources of the Merovingian and Carolingian states: problems and perspectives', in W. Pohl and V. Wieser, eds.,
Der frühmittelalterliche Staat – europäische Perspektiven (Vienna, Verlag
der ÖAW), pp. 1–18.

Fouracre, P. (2009b), 'England, Ireland, and Europe, c.500–c.750', in P. Stafford, ed., *A Companion to the Early Middle Ages. Britain and Ireland c.500
to c.1100* (Chichester, Wiley-Blackwell), pp. 126–42.

Fouracre, P. (2013), *Frankish History. Studies in the Construction of Power*
(Farnham, Ashgate) [Collected papers].

Fouracre, P. and Gerberding, Richard A., eds. (1996), *Late Merovingian France.
History and Hagiography 640–720* (Manchester, Manchester University Press).

France, John (2002), 'The composition and raising of the armies of Charlemagne', *Journal of Medieval Military History* 1, pp. 61–82.

Freeman, A. (1985), 'Carolingian orthodoxy and the fate of the *Libri Carolini*',
Viator 16, pp. 65–108.

Freeman, A. (2003), *Theodulf of Orléans: Charlemagne's Spokesman against
the Second Council of Nicaea* (Aldershot, Ashgate).

Freeman, A. and Meyvaert, P. (2001), 'The meaning of Theodulf's apse mosaic
at Germigny-des-Prés', *Gesta* XL (2), pp. 125–39.

Freeman, A. and Meyvaert, P. (2003), '*Opus Caroli regis contra synodum*:
an introduction', in A. Freeman, *Theodulf of Orléans* (Aldershot, Ashgate),
pp. 1–123.

Fried, Johannes (1982), 'Der karolingische Herrschaftsverband im 9. Jh. Zwischen "Kirche" und "Königshaus"', *Historische Zeitschrift* 235, pp. 1–43.

Fried, Johannes (1998), 'Elite und Ideologie; oder, Die Nachfolgeordnung Karls des
Großen vom Jahre 813', in R. Le Jan, ed., *La royauté et les élites dans l'Europe
carolingienne* (Lille, Centre d'Histoire de l'Europe du Nord-Ouest), pp. 71–109.

Fried, Johannes (2000), 'Wann verlor Karl der Große seinen ersten Zahn?'
Deutsches Archiv für Erforschung des Mittelalters 56, pp. 573–83.

Fried, Johannes (2001), 'Papst Leo III besucht Karl den Großen in Paderborn,
oder, Einhards Schweigen', *Historische Zeitschrift* 272, pp. 281–3̄6.

Fried, Johannes (2007), *Donation of Constantine and* Constitutum Constantini
(Berlin, Walter de Gruyter).

Fried, Johannes (2008), 'Ehrfahrung und Ordnung. Die Friedenskonstitution Karls
des Großen vom Jahr 806', in B. Kasten, ed., *Herrscher- und Fürstentestamente
im westeuropäischen Mittelalter* (Köln-Weimar, Böhlau), pp. 146–92.

Fried, Johannes (2013), *Karl der Grosse* (Munich, C. H. Beck).

Fried, Johannes (2016), *Charlemagne* (Cambridge, Mass., Harvard University Press).

Fried, Johannes et al., eds. (1994), *794 – Karl der Große in Frankfurt am Main.
Ein König bei der Arbeit* (Sigmaringen, Thorbecke).

Fuhrmann, Horst (1966), 'Konstantinische Schenkung und abendländisches
Kaisertum', in *Deutsches Archiv für Erforschung des Mittelalters* 22, pp.
63–178.

Fuhrmann, Horst (1973), 'Das frühmittelalterliche Papsttum und die Konstantinische Schenkung', *Settimane* 20, pp. 257–329.

Gaborit-Chopin, Danielle (1999), *La statuette équestre de Charlemagne* (Paris, Collection Solo XIII).

Gabriele, Matthew (2011), *An Empire of Memory: The Legend of Charlemagne* (Oxford, Oxford University Press).

Gaehdeke, Nora (1987), 'Die Memoria für die Königin Hildegard', in P. Riché et al., eds., *Autour d' Hildegard. Recueil d'études* (Paris, Imprimerie intégrée de l'Université Paris-X), pp. 27–39.

Ganshof, François L. (1950), 'Notes sur les origines byzantines du titre *Patricius Romanorum*', in *Mélanges Henri Grégoire* (Brussels, Institut de philologie et d'histoire orientales et slaves), pp. 261–81.

Ganshof, François L. (1959), 'À propos du tonlieu à l'époque carolingienne', *Settimane* 6.

Ganshof, François L. (1964), 'Les relations extérieurs de la monarchie franque', *Annali di Storia del Diritto* 5, 6, pp. 1–53.

Ganshof, François L. (1968a), *Frankish Institutions under Charlemagne*, trans. B. and M. Lyon (Providence, RI, Brown University Press).

Ganshof, François L. (1968b), 'Note sur les "Capitula de causis cum episcopis et abbatibus tractandis" de 811', *Collectanea Stephen Kuttner*, III, Bologna, 1967, *Studia Gratiana* XIII.

Ganshof, François L. (1969), 'Contribution à l'étude de l'application du droit romain et des capitularires dans la monarchie franque sous les Carolingiens', in *Studi in onore di Edoardo Volterra*, vol. 3 (Milan, A. Guiffrè), pp. 585–603.

Ganshof, François L. (1971), *The Carolingians and the Frankish Monarchy: Studies in Carolingian History*, trans. J. Sonderheimer (Ithaca, NY, Cornell University Press) [Collected papers].

Gantner, Clemens (2013), 'The label "Greeks" in the papal diplomatic repertoire in the eighth century', in W. Pohl and G. Heydemann, eds., *Strategies of Identification: Ethnicity and Religion in Early Medieval Europe* (Turnhout, Brepols), pp. 303–49.

Gantner, Clemens (2014), *Freunde Roms und Völker der Finsternis: Die Konstruktion von Anderen im 8. Und 9. Jahrhundert* (Vienna, Böhlau).

Gantner, Clemens (2015), 'The eighth-century papacy as a cultural broker', in C. Gantner, R. McKitterick and S. Meeder, eds., *The Resources of the Past in Early Medieval Europe* (Cambridge, Cambridge University Press), pp. 245–61.

Ganz, David (1983), 'Bureaucratic shorthand and Merovingian learning', in P. Wormald, D. Bullough and R. Collins, eds., *Ideal and Reality in Frankish and Anglo-Saxon Society: Studies Presented to J. M. Wallace-Hadrill* (Oxford, Oxford University Press), pp. 58–75.

Ganz, David (1989), 'Humour as history in Notker's *Gesta Karoli Magni*', in E. B. King et al., eds., *Monks, Nuns and Friars in Medieval Society* (Sewanee, Tenn., The Press of the University of the South), pp. 171–83.

Ganz, David (2000), 'Charlemagne in Hell', *Florilegium* 17, pp. 175–94.

Ganz, David (2004), 'The study of Caroline Minuscule 1953–2004', *Archiv für Diplomatik* 50, pp. 387–98.

Ganz, David (2005), 'Einhard's Charlemagne: the characterisation of greatness', in J. Story, ed., *Charlemagne: Empire and Society* (Manchester, Manchester University Press), pp. 38–51.

Ganz, David (2008), 'Some Carolingian questions from Charlemagne's days', in P. Fouracre and D. Ganz, eds., *Frankland. The Franks and the World of the Early Middle Ages* (Manchester, Manchester University Press), pp. 90–100.

Ganz, David (2010), 'Giving to God in the Mass: the experience of the offertory', in W. Davies and P. Fouracre, eds., *The Languages of Gift in the Early Middle Ages* (Cambridge, Cambridge University Press), pp. 18–32.

Ganz, David and Goffart, W. (1990), 'Charters earlier than 800 from French collections', *Speculum* 65, pp. 906–32.

Garipzanov, Ildar H. (2008a), *The Symbolic Language of Authority in the Carolingian World* (Leiden, Brill).

Garipzanov, Ildar H. (2008b), 'Frontier identities: Carolingian frontier and the *gens Danorum*', in I. H. Garipzanov, P. J Geary and P. Ubañcczyk, eds., *Franks, Northmen and Slavs. Identities and State Formation in Early Medieval Europe* (Turnhout, Brepols), pp. 113–44.

Garipzanov, Ildar H. (2010), '*Annales Guelferbytani*: changing perspectives of a local narrative', in R. Corradini et al., eds., *Zwischen Niederschrift und Wiederschrift* (Vienna: Verlag der ÖAW), pp. 123–37.

Garipzanov, Ildar H. (2016), 'Regensburg, Wandalgarius and the *novi denarii*: Charlemagne's monetary reform revisited', *Early Medieval Europe* 24 (1), pp. 58–73.

Garipzanov, Ildar H. (2018), *Graphic Signs of Authority in Late Antiquity and the Early Middle Ages, 300–900* (Oxford, Oxford University Press).

Garrison, Mary (1994), 'The emergence of Carolingian Latin literature and the court of Charlemagne (780–814)', in R. McKitterick, ed., *Carolingian Culture: Emulation and Innovation* (Cambridge, Cambridge University Press), pp. 111–40.

Garrison, Mary (1997), 'The English and the Irish at the court of Charlemagne', in P. Butzer et al., eds., *Karl der Grosse und sein Nachwirken. 1200 Jahre und Wissenschaft in Europa* (Turnhout, Brepols), pp. 97–123.

Garrison, Mary (1998a), 'Letters to a king and biblical exempla: the examples of Cathwulf and Clemens Peregrinus', *Early Medieval Europe* 7, pp. 305–28.

Garrison, Mary (1998b), 'The social world of Alcuin. Nicknames at York and at the Carolingian Court', in L. A. J. R. Houwen and A. A. MacDonald, eds., *Alcuin of York. Scholar at the Carolingian Court*, Germania Latina III (Groningen, Forsten), pp. 59–79.

Garrison, Mary (1999), '"Send more socks": on mentality and the presentational context of medieval letters', in M. Mostert, ed., *New Approaches to Medieval Communication* (Turnhout, Brepols), pp. 69–99.

Garrison, Mary (2000), 'The Franks as the new Israel? Education for an identity from Pippin to Charlemagne', in Y. Hen and M. Innes, eds., *The Uses of the Past in the Early Middle Ages* (Cambridge, Cambridge University Press), pp. 114–61.

Garrison, Mary (2002), 'The Bible and Alcuin's interpretation of current events', *Peritia* 16, pp. 68–84.

Garrison, Mary (2010a), 'An aspect of Alcuin: "Tuus Albinus" – peevish egotist – or parrhesiast?', in R. Corradini et al., eds., *Ego Trouble: Authors and their Identitites in the Early Middle Ages* (Vienna, Verlag der ÖAW), pp. 137–51.

Garrison, Mary (2010b), 'The emergence of Carolingian Latin literature and the court of Charlemagne', in *Classical and Medieval Literature Criticism* 127, pp. 29–48.

Gasparri, Stefano (1978), *I Duchi Longobardi*, Studi Storici 109 (Rome, Istituto Italiano per il Medioevo).

Gasparri, Stefano (2009), 'Italien in der Karolingerzeit', in W. Pohl and V. Wieser, eds., *Der frühmittelalterliche Staat – europäische Perspektiven* (Vienna, Verlag der ÖAW), pp. 63–71.

Geary, Patrick (1983), 'Ethnic identity as a situational construct in the early middle ages', *Mitteilungen Anthropologischen Gesellschaft in Wien* 113, pp. 15–26.

Geary, Patrick (1985), *Aristocracy in Provence: The Rhône Basin at the Dawn of the Carolingian Age* (Stuttgart, Hiersemann).

Geary, Patrick (1986), 'Sacred commodities: the circulation of medieval relics', in A. Appadurai, ed., *The Social Life of Things. Commodotieis in Cultural Perspective* (Cambridge, Cambridge University Press), pp. 169–91.

Geary, Patrick (1994), *Phantoms of Remembrance. Memory and Oblivion at the End of the First Millennium* (Princeton, NJ, Princeton University Press).

Geary, Patrick (1995), 'Extra-judicial means of conflict-resolution', in *La Giustizia nell'alto medioevo (secoli V–VIII)*, Settimane XLII, pp. 569–601.

Geary, Patrick (1999), 'Land, language and memory in Europe 700–1000', in *Transactions of the Royal Historical Society* 6th series, 9, pp. 169–84.

Geary, Patrick, (2002), *The Myth of Nations* (Princeton, NJ, Princeton University Press).

Geary, Patrick (2012), 'Death and funeral of the Carolingians', in Karl-Heinz Spieß and Immo Warntjes, eds., *Death at Court* (Wiesbaden: Harrassowitz Verlag), pp. 8–19.

Geary, Patrick, Garipzanov, Ildar H. and Urbanczyk, Przemyslaw, eds. (2008), *Franks, Northmen, and Slavs: Identities and State Formation in Early Medieval Europe* (Turnhout, Brepols).

Gerberding, Richard A. (1987), *The Rise of the Carolingians and the* Liber Historiae Francorum (Oxford, Oxford University Press).

Gerberding, Richard A. (1994), '716: a crucial year for Charles Martel', in Jörg Jarnut, Ulrich Nonn and Michael Richter, eds., *Karl Martell in seiner Zeit*, Beihefte der *Francia* 37 (Sigmaringen, Thorbecke), pp. 203–16.

Geuenich, Dieter (2013), 'Pippin, König von Italien (781–810)', in H. R. Sennhauser, ed., *Wandel und Konstanz zwischen Bodensee und Lombardei zur Zeit Karls des Grossen*, Acta Müstair, Kloster St. Johann, vol. 3 (Zürich, vdf Hochschulverlag), pp. 111–23.

Giese, M. (2011), 'Kompetitive Aspekte höfischer Jagdaktivitäten im Frühmittelalter', in M. Becher and A. Plassmann, eds., *Streit am Hof im frühen Mittelalter* (Bonn, Bonn University Press), pp. 263–84.

Gillmor, Carroll (2005), 'The 791 equine epidemic and its impact on Charlemagne's army', *Journal of Medieval Military History* 3, pp. 23–45.

Glatthaar, Michael (2010), 'Die Datierung der *Epistola generalis* Karls des Großen', *Deutsches Archiv für Erforschung des Mittelalters* 66, pp. 455–77.

Glatthaar, Michael, Mordek, Hubert and Zechiel-Eckes, Klaus, eds. (2013), *Die Admonitio Generalis Karls des Grossen*, German trans. and intro. MGH Fontes Iuris Germanici Antiqui XVI (Wiesbaden, Harrassowitz Verlag).

Godman, Peter, ed. (1982), *Alcuin. The Bishops, Kings and Saints of York* (Oxford, Oxford University Press).

Godman, Peter (1985), *Poetry of the Carolingian Renaissance* (London, Duckworth).

Godman, Peter (1987), *Poets and Emperors. Frankish Politics and Carolingian Poetry* (Oxford, Clarendon Press).

Goetz, Hans-Werner (1990), 'Das Ruhrgebiet im frühen Mittelalter. Zur Erschliessung einer Randlandschaft', *Blätter für deutsches Landesgeschichte* 126, pp. 123–60.

Goetz, Hans-Werner (2006), 'The perception of "power" and "state" in the early Middle Ages: the case of the Astronomer's Life of Louis the Pious', in B. Weiler and S. MacLean, eds., *Representations of Power in Medieval Germany 800–1500* (Turnhout, Brepols), pp. 15–36.

Goetz, Hans-Werner (2007), *Vorstellungsgeschichte. Gesammelte Schriften zu Wahrnehmungen, Deutungen und Vorstellungen im Mittelalter*, eds. A. Aurast et al. (Bochum, Winkler) [Collected papers].

Goetz, Hans-Werner (2009), 'Versuch einer resümierenden Bilanz?', in W. Pohl and V. Wieser, eds., *Der frühmittelalterliche Staat – europäische Perspektiven* (Vienna, Verlag der ÖAW), pp. 523–31.

Goffart, Walter (1986), 'Paul the Deacon's "*Gesta Episcoporum Mettensium*" and the early design of Charlemagne's succession', *Traditio* 42, pp. 59–93.

Goldberg, Eric J. (1995), 'Popular revolt, dynastic politics, and aristocratic factionalism in the early Middle Ages: the Saxon *Stellinga* reconsidered', *Speculum* 70, pp. 467–501.

Goldberg, Eric J. (2006), *Struggle for Empire. Kingship and Conflict under Louis the German, 817–876* (Ithaca, NY, Cornell University Press).

Goodson, Caroline (2010), *The Rome of Pope Paschal I* (Cambridge, Cambridge University Press).

Goodson, Caroline (2015), 'To be the daughter of Saint Peter: S. Petronilla and forging the Franco-Papal alliance', in V. West-Harling, ed., *Three Empires, Three Cities: Identities, Material Culture and Legitimacy in Venice, Ravenna and Rome, 750–1000* (Turnhout, Brepols), pp. 159–88.

Goodson, Caroline and Nelson, Janet L. (2010), 'The Roman contexts of the "Donation of Constantine"', *Early Medieval Europe* 18, pp. 446–67.

Goody, Jack (1966), *Succession to High Office* (Cambridge, Cambridge University Press).

Goosmann, Erik (2015), 'Politics and penance: transformations in the Carolingian perception of the conversion of Carloman', in C. Gantner et al., eds., *The Resources of the Past in Early Medieval Europe* (Cambridge, Cambridge University Press), pp. 51–67.

Gorman, Michael M. (1982), 'The encyclopedic Commentary on Genesis prepared for Charlemagne by Wigbod', *Recherches Augustiniennes* 17, pp. 173–201.

Gorman, Michael M. (1997), 'Wigbod and biblical studies under Charlemagne', *Revue Bénédictine* 107, pp. 40–76.

Gotoff, H. C. (1971), *The Transmission of the Text of Lucan in the Ninth Century* (Cambridge, Mass., Harvard University Press).

Gravel, Martin (2012), *Distances, rencontres, communications. Réaliser l'Empire sous Charlemagne et Louis le Pieux* (Turnhout, Brepols).

Greenblatt, Stephen (1980), *Renaissance Self-Fashioning* (Chicago, University of Chicago Press).

Grewe, Holger (1999), 'Die Königspfalz zu Ingelheim am Rhein', in C. Stiegemann and M. Wemhoff, eds., *799. Kunst und Kultur der Karolingerzeit*, 3 vols. (Mainz, von Zabern), vol. 3, pp. 142–51.

Grewe, Holger (2014), 'Die Pfalz zu Ingelheim am Rhein. Ausgewählte Baubefunde und ihr Interpretation', in F. Pohle, ed., *Karl der Grosse/Charlemagne*, 3 vols. (Dresden, Sandstein), vol. 1, *Orte der Macht: Essays*, pp. 188–97.

Grierson, Philip and Blackburn, Mark (1986), *Medieval European Coinage*, vol. 1, *The Early Middle Ages (5th–10th centuries)* (Cambridge, Cambridge University Press).

Hack, Achim T. (1999), 'Zur Herkunft der karolingischen Königssalbung', *Zeitschrift für Kirchengeschichte* 110, pp. 170–90.

Hack, Achim T. (2006–7), *Codex Carolinus: Päpstliche Epistolographie im 8. Jahrhundert*, Papst und Papsttum XXXV, 2 vols. (Stuttgart, Hiersemann).

Hack. Achim T. (2009), *Alter, Krankheit, Tod und Herrschaft im frühen Mittelalter. Das Beispiel der Karolinger* (Stuttgart, Hiersemann).

Hack, Achim T. (2011), *Abul Abaz. Zu Biographie eines Elephanten*, Jenaer mediävistische Vorträge 1 (Badenweiler, Bachmann).

Hack, Achim T. (2014), 'Der Bau des Karlsgrabens nach den Schriftquellen' and 'Schiffreisende im früen Mittelalter', in P. Ettel et al., eds., *Großbaustelle 793. Das Kanalprojekt Karls des Großen zwischen Rhein und Donau* (Mainz, Verlag dos Römisch-Germanischen Zentralmuseumsthmar), pp. 53–62, 105–6.

Hack, Achim T. (2015), *Karolingische Kaiser als Sportler. Ein Beitrag zur frühmittelalterlichen Körpergeschichte*, Jenaer mediävistische Vorträge 4 (Stuttgart, Franz Steiner Verlag).

Hack, Achim T. (2017), 'Vom Seekrieg zum ersten Herrscher besuch. Die Karolinger und Venedig', in R. Schmitz-Esser et al. eds., *Venedig als Bühne. Organisation, Inszenierung und Wahrnehmung euopäischer Herrsch-besuche* (Regensburg, Verlag Schnell & Steiner), pp. 27–49.

Hadley, Dawn (2009), 'Viking raids and conquest', and 'Scandinavian settle-ment', in P. Stafford, ed., *A Companion to the Early Middle Ages. Britain and Ireland c.500 to c.1100* (Oxford, Wiley-Blackwell), pp. 195–211, 212–30.

Hageneder, Othmar (1983) 'Das *crimen maiestatis*, der Prozess gegen die Attentäter Papst Leos III und di Kaiserkrönung Karls des Großen', in H. Mordek, ed., *Aus Kirche und Reich. . .Festschrift für F. Kempf* (Sigmarin-gen, Thorbecke), pp. 55–79.

Hägermann, Dieter (1976), 'Zur Entstehung der Kapitularien', in W. Schloge and P. Herde, eds., *Grundwissenschafter und Geschichte. Festschrift für Peter Acht* (Kallmünz, Lassleben), pp. 12–27.

Hägermann, Dieter (2000), *Karl der Große. Herrscher des Abendlandes: Biog-raphie* (Berlin, Propyläen).

Hakenbeck, Susanne (2011), *Local, Regional and Ethnic Identities in Early Medieval Cemeteries in Bavaria* (Florence, All'insegni del Giglio).

Halphen, Louis (1921), *Études critiques sur l'histoire de Charlemagne* (Paris, Alcan).

Halsall, Guy (2003), *Warfare and Society in the Barbarian West, 450–900* (London, Routledge).

Halsall, Guy (2018), 'Classical gender in deconstruction', in S. Joye and R. Le Jan eds., *Genre et compétition dans les sociétés occidentales du haut moyen âge* (Turnhout, Brepols), pp. 27–42.

Hamilton, Sarah (2001), *The Practice of Penance 900–1050* (Woodbridge, The Royal Historical Society, Boydell).

Hammer, Carl (1997), *Charlemagne's Months and their Bavaraian Labours. The Politics of the Seasons in the Carolingian Empire* (Oxford, British Archaeological Reports, International Series, 676).

Hammer, Carl I. (1999), 'The social landscape of the Prague Sacramentary: the prosopography of an eighth-century mass-book', *Traditio* 54, pp. 41–80.

Hammer, Carl I. (2005), 'Recycling Rome and Ravenna', *Saeculum* 56, pp. 295–325.

Hammer, Carl (2007), 'Virtual rule and *Damnatio Memoriae* in eighth-century Bavaria: the strange case of the Montpellier Psalter', in his *From Ducatus to Regnum: Ruling Bavaria under the Merovingians and early Carolingians* (Turnhout, Brepols), pp. 131–200.

Hammer, Carl I. (2008), '"Pipinus rex": Pippin's plot of 792 and Bavaria', *Tra-ditio* 63, pp. 235–76.

Hammer, Carl I. (2012), 'Christmas Day 800: Charles the Younger, Alcuin, and the Frankish Royal Succession', *English Historical Review* 127, pp. 1–23.

Hammer, Carl I. (2018), 'In the field with Charlemagne, 792', *Journal of Medieval Military History* 13, pp. 1–10.

Hannig, Jürgen (1982), *Consensus fidelium. Frühfeodale Interpretationen des Verhältnisses von Königtum und Adel am Beispiel des Frankenreiches* (Stuttgart, Hiersemann).

Hannig, Jürgen (1983), '*Pauperiores vassi de infra palatio?* Zur Entstehung der karolingischen Königsbotenorganisation', *MIÖG* 91, pp. 309–74.

Hannig, Jürgen (1988), 'Ars donandi. *Zur Ökenomie des Schenkens im früheren Mittelalter*', in R. Van Dülmen, ed., *Armen, Liebe, Ehre. Studien zur historischen Kulturforschung* (Frankfurt, Fischer Taschenbuch), pp. 11–37, 275–8.

Hartmann, Florian (2006), *Hadrian I (772–795). Frühmittelalterliches Adelspapsttum und die Lösung Roms vom byzantinischen Kaiser*, Päpste und Papsttum XXXIV (Stuttgart, Hiersemann).

Hartmann, Florian (2009), '"*Vitam litteris ni emam, nihil est, quod tribuam*". Paulus Diaconus zwischen Langobarden und Franken', *Frühmittelalterliche Studien* 43, pp. 71–93.

Hartmann, Florian (2011), 'Streit an der *cathedra Petri* oder Streit um die *cathedra Petri*? Konflikte um den Papsthron in der Deutung päpstlicher Quellen', in M. Becher and A. Plassmann, eds., *Streit am Hof im frühen Mittelalter* (Bonn, Bonn University Press), pp. 365–88.

Hartmann, Florian (2015), 'Karolingische Gelehrte als Dichter und der Wissenstransfer am Beispiel der Epigraphik', in J. Becher, T. Licht and S. Weinfurter, eds., *Karolingische Klöster. Wissenstransfer und kulturelle Innovation* (Berlin, de Gruyter), pp. 255–74.

Hartmann, Martina (2007), 'Concubina vel regina? – Zu einigen Ehefrauen und Konkubinen der karolingischen Könige', *Deutsches Archiv für Erforschung des Mittelalters* 63, pp. 545–67.

Hartmann, Martina (2009), *Die Königin im frühen Mittelalter* (Stuttgart, W. Kohlhammer).

Hartmann, Wilfried (1986), 'Der Bischof als Richter. Zum geistlichen Gericht über kriminelle Vergehen von Laien im frühmittelalter (6–11 Jht)', *Römische Historische Mitteilungen* 28, pp. 103–24.

Hartmann, Wilfried (1989), *Die Synoden der Karolingerzeit im Frankenreich und Italien* (Paderborn, Munich, Vienna and Zurich, Schöningh).

Hartmann, Wilfried (1997), 'Das Konzil von Frankfurt 794. Nachwirkung und Nachleben', in R. Berndt, ed., *Das Frankfurter Konzil von 794. Kristallisationspunkt karolingischer Kultur*, 2 vols. (Mainz, Gesellschaft der Mittelrheinische Kirchengeschichte), vol. 1, pp. 331–55.

Hartmann, Wilfried (2010), *Karl der Große* (Stuttgart, W. Kohlhammer).

Haselbach, Irene (1970), *Aufstieg und Herrschaft der Karlinger in der Darstellung der sogenannten Annales Mettenses Priores*. Ein Beitrag zur Geschichte der politischen Ideen im Reiche Karls des Großen (Lübeck-Hamburg, Matthiesen).

Haubrichs, Wolfgang (1988), *Die Anfänge. Versuche volkssprachiger Schriftlichkeit im frühen Mittelalter*, vol. 1 (Frankfurt, Hiersemann).

Hauck, K. (1986), 'Karl als neuer Konstantin 777. Die archäologischen Entdeckungen in Paderborn in historische Sicht', *Frühmittelalterliche Studien* 20, pp. 513–40.

Haywood, John (1991), *Dark Age Naval Power: A Reassessment of Frankish and Anglo-Saxon Seafaring* (New York, Routledge).

Heather, Peter (1991), *Goths and Romans, 332–489* (Oxford, Oxford University Press).

Heather, Peter (1996), *The Goths* (Oxford, Blackwell).

Heather, Peter (2009), *Empires and Barbarians: Migration, Development and the Birth of Europe* (London, Macmillan).

Heather, Peter (2016), 'A tale of two cities: Rome and Ravenna under Gothic rule', in J. Herrin and J. Nelson, eds., *Ravenna. Its Role in Earlier Medieval Change and Exchange* (London, Institute of Historical Research), pp. 15–37.

Heckner, Ulrike (2012), 'Der Tempel Salomos in Aachen – Datierung und geometrischer Entwurf der karolingiaschen Pfalzkapelle', in A. Pufke, ed., *Der karolingische Pfalzkapelle in Aachen* (Worms, Werner), pp. 25–62.

Heidrich, Ingrid (1965–6), 'Titulatur und Urkunden der arnulfingischen Hausmeier', *Archiv für Diplomatik* 11–12, pp. 71–279.

Heidrich, Ingrid (1988), 'Von Plectrud zu Hildegard. Beobachtungen zum Besitzrecht adliger Frauen im Frankenreich des 7. und 8. Jahrhunderts und zur politischen Rolle der Frauen der frühen Karolinger', *Rheinische Vierteljahrsblätter* 52, pp. 1–15.

Heidrich, Ingrid (1994a), 'Synode und Hoftag in Düren im August 747', *Deutsches Archiv für Erforschung des Mittelalters* 50, pp. 415–40.

Heidrich, Ingrid (1994b), 'Die Urkunden Pippins d. M. und Karl Martells: Beobachtungen zu ihrer zeitliche und räumlichen Streuung', in J. Jarnut et al., eds., *Karl Martell in seiner Zeit* (Sigmaringen, Thorbecke), pp. 23–34.

Heidrich, Ingrid (2001), *Die Urkunden der Arnulfinger* (Bad Münstereifel, H-C-I).

Heitmeier, Irmtraut (2013), 'Per Alpes Curiam – der rätische Straßenraum in der frühen Karolibgerzeit – Annäherung an die Gründungsumstände des Klosters Müstair', in H. R. Sennhauser, ed., *Wandel und Konstanz zwischen Bodensee und Lombardei zur Zeit Karls des Grossen*, Acta Müstair, Kloster St. Johann, vol. 3, pp. 143–75.

Hellmann, Martin (2000), *Tironische Noten in der Karolingerzeit* (Hanover, Hahn).

Hellmann, Martin (2018), http://www.martinellus.de/index/indexti.htm.

Helvétius, Anne-Marie (2012), 'L'abbaye de Saint-Maurice d'Agaune dans le haut moyen âge', *Autour de Saint Maurice. Actes*, pp. 113–31.

Helvétius, Anne-Marie (2015), 'Pour une biographie de Gisèle, soeur de Charlemagne, abbesse de Chelles', in L. Jégou et al., eds., *Splendor Reginae. Passions, Genre et Famille. Mélanges en l'Honneur de Régine Le Jan* (Turnhout, Brepols), pp. 161–8.

Hen, Yitzhak (1995), *Culture and Religion in Merovingian Gaul, A.D. 481–751* (Leiden, New York and Cologne, Brill).

Hen, Yitzhak (2000), 'The *Annals of Metz* and the Merovingian past', in Y. Hen and M. Innes, eds., *The Uses of the Past in the Early Middle Ages* (Cambridge, Cambridge University Press), pp. 175–90.

Hen, Yitzhak (2001), *The Royal Patronage of Liturgy in Frankish Gaul* (Woodbridge, The Boydell Press, for The Henry Bradshaw Society).

Hen, Yitzhak (2004), 'The Christianisation of kingship', in M. Becher and J. Jarnut, eds., *Der Dynastiewechsel von 751* (Münster, Scriptorium), pp. 163–77.

Hen, Yitzhak (2006), 'Charlemagne's *jihad*', *Viator* 37, pp. 33–51.

Henning, Joachim (2008), 'Strong rulers – weak economy? Rome, the Carolingians and the archaeology of slavery in the first millennium AD', in J. R. Davis and M. McCormick, eds., *The Long Morning of Medieval Europe* (Aldershot, Ashgate), pp. 33–54.

Herrin, Judith (1992), 'Constantinople, Rome and the Franks in the seventh and eighth centuries', in J. Shepard and S. Franklin, eds., *Byzantine Diplomacy* (Aldershot, Ashgate), pp. 91–107.

Herrin, Judith (2000), 'Blinding in Byzantium', in *Polypleuros nous. Festschrift für Peter Schreiner* (Munich, Sauer), pp. 56–68.

Herrin, Judith (2001), *Women in Purple. Rulers of Medieval Byzantium* (London, Weidenfeld and Nicolson).

Herrin, Judith (2013), 'Political power and Christian faith in Byzantium: the case of Irene, Regent 780–90, Empress 797–802', in Herrin, *Unrivalled Influence* (Princeton, Princeton University Press), pp. 198–207.

Herrin, Judith and Nelson, J. L., eds. (2016), *Ravenna. Its Role in Earlier Medieval Change and Exchange* (London, Institute of Historical Research).

Higgitt, John (2001), 'Form and focus in the Deerhurst dedication inscription', in John Higgitt, Katherine Forsyth and David N. Parsons, eds., *Roman, Runes and Ogham. Medieval Inscriptions in the Insular World and on the Continent* (Donington, Shaun Tyas), pp. 89–93.

Hindle, Steve (2001), 'Dearth, fasting and alms: the campaign for general hospitality in late Elizabethan England', *Past & Present* 172, pp. 44–86.

Hlawitschka, Eduard (1960), *Franken, Alemannen, Bayern und Burgunder in Oberitalien (774–796)* (Freiburg, Albert).

Hlawitschka, Eduard (1979), 'Studien zur genealogie und Geschichte der Morwinger und der frühen K`rolinger', *Rheinische Vierteljahrsblätter* 43, pp. 32–55.

Hodges, Richard (1997), *Light in the Dark Ages. The Rise and Fall of San Vincenzo al Volturno* (London, Duckworth).

Hosking, Geoffrey (2014), *Trust: A History* (Oxford, Oxford University Press).

Houben, Hubert (1985), 'Karl der Grosse und die Absetzung des Abt Potho von San Vincenzo al Volturno', *Quellen und Forschungen aus italienischen Archiven und Bibliotheken* 65, pp. 405–17.

Howell, Wilbur S., ed. (1941), *The Rhetoric of Alcuin and Charlemagne*, trans. and intro. (Princeton, NJ, Princeton University Press).

Hummer, Hans J. (2005), *Politics and Power in Early Medieval Europe: Alsace and the Frankish Realm, 600–1000* (Cambridge, Cambridge University Press).

Huyghebaert, Nicolas (1979), 'Une légende de formation: le Constitutum Constantini', in *Le Moyen Âge* 85, pp. 177–209.

Innes, Matthew (1997), 'Charlemagne's Will: piety, politics and the imperial succession', *English Historical Review* 112, pp. 833–55.

Innes, Matthew (1998a), 'Memory, orality and literacy in an early medieval society', *Past & Present* 158, pp. 3–36.

Innes, Matthew (1998b), 'Kings, monks and patrons: political identities and the Abbey of Lorsch', in R. Le Jan, ed., *La royauté et les élites dans l'Europe carolingienne* (Lille, Université Charles-de-Gaulle), pp. 301–24.

Innes, Matthew (2000), *State and Society in the Early Middle Ages. The Middle Rhine Valley, 400–1000* (Cambridge, Cambridge University Press).

Innes, Matthew (2003), '"A place of discipline": Carolingian courts and aristocratic youth', in C. Cubitt, ed., *Court Culture in the Early Middle Ages* (Turnhout, Brepols), pp. 59–76.

Innes, Matthew (2005), 'Charlemagne's government', in J. Story, ed., *Charlemagne: Empire and Society* (Manchester, Manchester University Press), pp. 71–89.

Innes, Matthew (2008), 'Practices of property in the Carolingian empire', in J. R. Davis and M. McCormick, eds., *The Long Morning of Medieval Europe* (Aldershot, Ashgate), pp. 247–66.

Innes, Matthew (2009), 'Property, politics and the problem of the Carolingian state', in W. Pohl and V. Wieser, eds., *Der frühmittelalterliche Staat – europäische Perspektiven* (Vienna, Verlag der ÖAW), pp. 299–313.

Innes, Matthew (2011), 'Charlemagne, justice and written law', in A. Rio, ed., *Law, Custom and Justice in Late Antiquity and the Early Middle Ages* (London, Centre for Hellenic Studies, King's College London), pp. 155–203.

Innes, Matthew (2013), 'Rituals, rights and relationships: some gifts and their interpretation in the Fulda Cartulary, c. 827', *Studia Historica* 31, pp. 25–50.

Isaïa, Marie-Céline (2010), *Rémi de Reims. Mémoire d'un saint, Histoire d'une Église* (Paris, Éditions du Cerf).

Jahn, Joachim (1991), *Ducatus Baiuvariorum: Das bairische Herzogtum der Agilulfinger* (Stuttgart, Hiersemann).

Jarnut, Jörg (1982), *Geschichte der Langobarden* (Stuttgart, Hiersemann).

Jarnut, Jörg (1984), 'Chlodwig und Clothar. Anmerkungen zu den Namen zweier Söhne Karls des Großen', *Francia* 12, pp. 645–51.

Jarnut, Jörg (1993), 'Ein Bruderkampf und seine Folgen', in G. Jenal, ed., *Herrschaft, Kirche, Kultur: Beiträge zur Geschichte des Mittelalters. Festschrift für Friedrich Prinz* (Stuttgart, Hiersemann), pp. 165–76.

Jarnut, Jörg (1994), 'Die Adoption Pippin durch König Liutprand und die Italienpolitik Karls Martell', in J. Jarnut et al., eds., *Karl Martell in seiner Zeit* (Sigmaringen, Thorbecke), pp. 217–26.

Jarnut, Jörg (1999), 'Karl der Grosse: Mensch, Herrscher, Mythos', *Paderborner Universitätsreden*, 66.

Jarnut, Jörg (2002), *Herrschaft und Ethnogenese im Frühmittelalter. Gesammelte Aufsätze von Jörg Jarnut. Festgabe zum 60. Geburtstag*, eds. M. Becher, S. Dick and N. Karthaus (Münster, Scriptorium).

Jarnut, Jörg (2004), 'Anmerkungen zum Staat des frühen Mittelalters. Die Kontroverse zwischen Johannes Fried und Hans-Werner Goetz', in D. Hägermann, W. Haubrichs and J. Jarnut, eds., *Akkulturation. Probleme einer germanisch-romanischen Kultursynthese in Spätantike und frühen Mittelalter* (Berlin, de Gruyter), pp. 504–9.

Jarnut, Jörg, Nonn, U. and Richter, M., eds. (1994), *Karl Martell in seiner Zeit* (Sigmaringen, Thorbecke).

Joch, Waltraud (1994), 'Karl Martell – ein minderberechtiger Erbe Pippins?' in J. Jarnut et al., eds., *Karl Martell in seiner Zeit* (Sigmaringen, Thorbecke), pp. 149–70.

de Jong, Mayke (2001), 'Monastic prisoners or opting out? Political coercion and honour in the Frankish kingdoms', in M. de Jong, F. Theuws and C. van Rhijn, eds., *Topographies of Power in the Early Middle Ages* (Leiden, Brill), pp. 291–328.

de Jong, Mayke (2003), '*Sacrum palatium et ecclesia*. L'autorité religieuse royale sous les Carolingiens (790–840)', *Annales: Histoire, sciences sociales* 58, pp. 1243–69.

de Jong, Mayke (2005), 'Charlemagne's church', in J. Story, ed., *Charlemagne: Empire and Society* (Manchester, Manchester University Press), pp. 103–35.

de Jong, Mayke (2006), 'Ecclesia and the early medieval polity', in S. Airlie et al., eds., *Staat im Mittelalter* (Vienna, Verlag der ÖAW), pp. 113–32.

de Jong, Mayke (2008), 'The *solarium*', in J. R. Davis and M. McCormick, eds., *The Long Morning of Medieval Europe: New Directions in Early Medieval Studies* (Aldershot, Ashgate), pp. 280–81.

de Jong, Mayke (2009), *The Penitential State: Authority and Atonement in the Age of Louis the Pious* (Cambridge, Cambridge University Press).

de Jong, Mayke (2015), 'The empire that was always decaying', *Medieval Worlds* 2, pp. 1–20.

Judt, Tony (2005), *Postwar. A History of Europe since 1945* (London, Vintage).

Jussen, Bernhard (2000), *Spiritual Kinship as Social Practice. Godparenthood and Adoption in the Early Middle Ages* (London and Newark, University of Delaware Press) (revd. Eng. version of 1991 German publ.).

Jussen, Bernhard, ed. (2005), *Die Macht des Königs. Herrschaft in Europa vom Frühmittelalter bis in der Neuzeit* (Munich, C. H. Beck).

Jussen, Bernhard (2014), *Die Franken* (Munich, C. H. Beck).

Kahl, Hans-Dietrich (1980), 'Zwischen Aquileja und Salzburg. Beobachtungen und Thesen zur Frage romanischen Restchristentums im nachvölkwanderungszeitlichen Binnen-Noricum (7.–8. Jahrhundert)', in H. Wolfram and F. Daim, eds., *Die Völker an der mittleren und unteren Donau in fünften und sechsten Jahrhundert* (Vienna, Verlag der ÖAW), pp. 33–81.

Kaiser, Reinhold (1979), 'Aachen und Compiègne: Zwei Pfalzstädte im Mittelalter', *Rheinische Vierteljahrblätter* 43, pp. 100–115.

Kaiser, Reinhold (1998), *Churrätien im frühen Mittelalter* (Basel, Schwabe).

Kamp, Hermann (2001), *Friedensstifter und Vermittler im Mittelalter* (Darmstadt, Wissenschaftliche Buchgesellschaft).

Kantorowicz, Ernst H. (1946), *Laudes Regiae: A Study in Liturgical Acclamations and Medieval Ruler Worship* (Berkeley and Los Angeles, University of California Press).

Kantorowicz, Ernst H. (1957), *The King's Two Bodies. A Study in Medieval Political Theology* (Princeton, NJ, Princeton University Press).

Karras, Ruth M. (2006), 'The history of marriage and the myth of *Friedelehe*', *Early Medieval Europe* 14 (ii), pp. 119–51.

Kaschke, Sören (2006), *Die karolingischen Reichsteilungen bis 831: Herrschtspraxis und Normvorstellungen in zeitgenössischer Sicht* (Hamburg, Dr Kovač).

Kaschke, Sören (2008), 'Tradition and adaption. Die "*Divisio regnorum*" und die fränkische Herrschaftsnachfolge', in B. Kasten, ed., *Herrscher- und Fürstentestamente im westeuropäischen Mittelalter* (Cologne, Böhlau), pp. 259–89.

Kaschke, Sören (2010), 'Fixing dates in the early Middle Ages: the *Chronicon Laurissense breve* and its use of time', in R. Corradini et al., eds., *Zwischen Niederschrift und Wiederschrift* (Vienna, Verlag der ÖAW), pp. 115–22.

Kasten, Brigitte (1986), *Adalhard von Corbie: Die Biographie von eines karolingischer Politiker und Klostervorstehers* (Düsseldorf, Droste).

Kasten, Brigitte (1997), *Königssöhne und Königsherrschaft: Untersuchungen zur Teilhabe am Reich in ber Merowinger- und Karolingerzeit*, MGH Schriften XLIV (Hanover, Hahn).

Kasten, Brigitte (1999), 'Stepmothers in Frankish legal life', in *Law, Laity and Solidarities. Essays in Honour of Susan Reynolds*, eds. P. Stafford, J. L. Nelson and J. Martindale (Manchester, Manchester University Press), pp. 47–67.

Kasten, Brigitte (2001), 'Laikale Mittelgewalten: Beobachtungen zur Herrschaftspraxis der Karolinger', in F.-R. Erkens, ed., *Karl der Grosse und das Erbe der Kulturen* (Berlin, Akademie Verlag), pp. 54–66.

Kasten, Brigitte (2004), 'Alkuins Erbrechtlichte Expertise für Karl den Grossen', in P. Depreux and B. Judic, eds., *Alkuin de York à Tours. Écriture, pouvoir et réseaux*, special issue of *Annales de Bretagne et des Pays de l'Ouest* 111, pp. 301–15.

Keefe, Susan A. (2002), *Water and the Word: Baptism and the Education of the Clergy in the Carolingian Empire*, 2 vols. (Notre Dame, Ind., University of Notre Dame Press).

Keller, Hagen (1985), 'Herrscherbild und Herrschaftslegitimation: Zur Deutung der ottonischen Denkmaler', *Frühmittelalterliche Studien* 19, pp. 290–311.

Keller, Hagen (1998), 'Zu den Siegeln der Karolinger und der Ottonen: Urkunden als "Hoheitszeichen" in der Kommunikation des Königs mit seinen Getreuen', *Frühmittelalterliche Studien* 32, pp. 400–441.

Keller, Hagen (2010), 'Wählen im früheren Mittelalter', in C. Dartmann, G. Wassilowsky and T. Weller, eds., *Technik und Symbolik vormoderner Wahlverfahren* (Munich, Oldenbourg), pp. 35–52.

Kempf, Damian (2004), 'Paul the Deacon's *Liber de episcopis Mettensibus* and the role of Metz in the Carolingian realm', *Journal of Medieval History* 30, pp. 279–99.

Kempf, Damian (2013), Paul the Deacon. *Liber de episcopis Mettensibus*, ed., trans. and intro. (Peeters, Paris).

Kempshall, Matthew (1995), 'Some Ciceronian aspects of Einhard's Life of Charlemagne', *Viator* 26, pp. 11–38.

Kempshall, Matthew (2011), *Rhetoric and the Writing of History, 400–1500* (Manchester, Manchester University Press).

Kennedy, Hugh (1981), *The Early 'Abbasid Caliphate* (London, Croom Helm).

Kennedy, Hugh (1995), 'The Muslims in Europe', in R. McKitterick, ed., *New Cambridge Medieval History* II (Cambridge, Cambridge University Press), pp. 249–71.

Kennedy, Hugh (2005), *The Court of the Caliphs: When Baghdad Ruled the Muslim World* (London, Phoenix).

Kennedy, Hugh (2016), *The Caliphate: A Pelican Introduction* (London, Penguin).

Kerner, Max (2000), *Karl der Grosse. Entschleierung eines Mythos* (Cologne, Böhlau).

Kershaw, Paul (2011), *Peaceful Kings: Peace, Power, and the Early Medieval Political Imagination* (Oxford, Oxford University Press).

Kikuchi Shigeto (2012), 'Carolingian capitularies as texts. Significance of texts in the government of the Frankish kingdom especially under Charlemagne', in O. Kano, ed., *Configuration du texte en histoire* (Nagoya, Waseda University Press), pp. 67–80.

King, P. D. (1987), *Charlemagne: Translated Sources* (Lambrigg, P. D. King).

Kintzinger, Martin (2005), *Die Erben Karls des Grossen im Mittelalter* (Ostfildern, Thorbecke Verlag).

Kluge, Bernd (1999), 'Nomen imperatoris und Christiana religio', in C. Stiege-mann and M. Wemhoff, eds., 799. Kunst und Kultur der Karolingerzeit, 3 vols. (Mainz, von Zabern), vol. 3, pp. 82–90.

Konecny, Silvia (1976), Die Frauen des karolingischen Königshauses. Die politische Bedeutung der Ehe und die Stellung der Frau in der fränkischen Herrscherhfamilie (Vienna, Verlag WGÖ).

König, Daniel G. (2016), 'Charlemagne's Jihād revisited: debating the Islamic contribution to an epochal change in the history of Christianization', Medieval Worlds 3, pp. 3–40.

Körntgen, Ludger (2009), 'Heidenkrieg und Bischofsgründung. Glaubensverber-breitung als Herrschschaftaufgabe bei Karolinger und Ottonen', in A. Holzem, ed., Krieg und Christentum. Religiöse Gewalttheofien in der Kriegserfahrung des Westens (Paderborn, Verlag Ferdinand Schöningh), pp. 281–304.

Kortum, Hans-Hemming (2014), Menschen und Mentalitäten: Einführung in Vorstellungswelten des Mittelalters (Berlin, Akademie Verlag).

Kosso, Cynthia and Scott, Anne (2009), The Nature and Function of Water, Baths, Bathing and Hygiene from Antiquity through the Renaissance (Leiden, Brill).

Kosto, Adam (2002), 'Hostages in the Carolingian world (714–840)', Early Medieval Europe 11, pp. 123–47.

Kottje, Raymund (1970), Studien zum Einfluß des Alten Testament auf Recht und Liturgie des frühen Mittelalters (Bonn, L. Röhrsche).

Koziol, Geoffrey (1992), Begging Pardon and Favor. Ritual and Politicial Order in Early Medieval France (Ithaca, NY, Cornell University Press).

Koziol, Geoffrey (2002), 'The dangers of polemic: is ritual still an interesting topic of historical study?' Early Medieval Europe 11, pp. 367–88.

Koziol, Geoffrey (2012), The Politics of Memory in Carolingian Royal Diplomas: The West Frankish Kingdom (840–987) (Turnhout, Brepols).

Krah, Adelheid (1987), Absetzungsverfahren als Spiegelbild von Königsmacht (Aalen, Scientia Verlag).

Krahwinkler, Harald (1992), Friaul im Frühmittelalter: Geschichte von einer Region vom Ende des fünften bis zum Ende des zehnten Jahrhundert (Vienna, Böhlau).

Krahwinkler, Harald (2005), 'Patriarch Fortunatus of Grado and the Placitum of Riziano', Acta Histriae 13, pp. 63–78.

Krause, Thomas R., ed. (2013), Aachen, von den Anfängen bis zur Gegenwart, vol. 2 (Aachen, Veröffentlichungen des Stadtarchivs Aachen, Bb. 14).

Krause, Victor (1890), 'Geschichte des Instituts der missi dominici', MIÖG 11, pp. 193–300.

Lambert, Peter (2017), 'The immediacy of a Remote Past: The Saxon Wars of 772–804 in the "Cultural Struggles" of the Third Reich', in P. Lambert and B. Weiler, eds., How the Past was Used: Historical Cultures c.750-2000, (London, The British Academy), pp. 181–200.

Lampen, A. (1999), 'Die Sachsenkriege', in C. Stiegemann and M. Wemhoff, eds., *799. Kunst und Kultur der Karolingerzeit*, 3 vols. (Mainz, von Zabern), vol. 2, pp. 264–72.

La Rocca, Cristina (2018), 'Perceptions of an early medieval urban landscape', in P. Linehan, J. L. Nelson and M. Costambeys, eds., *The Medieval World*, 2nd revd edn (Abingdon, Routledge), pp. 491–510.

Latowsky, Anne (2005), 'Foreign embassies and Roman universality in Einhard's Life of Charlemagne', *Florilegium* 22, pp. 25–57.

Latowsky, Anne (2014), *Emperor of the World: Charlemagne and the Construction of Imperial Authority, 800–1229* (Ithaca, NY, Cornell University Press).

Le Jan, Régine (1989), '*Prosopographica Neustrica*: Les Agents du roi en Neustrie de 639 à 840', in Hartmut Atsma, ed., *La Neustrie. Les pays du Nord de la Loire de 650 à 850*, Beihefte der *Francia* 16/1 and 16/2 (Sigmaringen, Thorbecke), pp. 231–69.

Le Jan, Régine (1995), *Famille et pouvoir dans le monde franc (7e–10e siècles). Essai d'anthropologie sociale* (Paris, Publications de la Sorbonne).

Le Jan, Régine, ed. (1998), *La Royauté et les Élites dans l'Europe carolingienne* (Lille, Université de Charles-de-Gaulle).

Le Jan, Régine (2000), 'Frankish giving of arms and rituals of power: continuity and change in the Carolingian period', in F. Theuws and J. L. Nelson, eds., *Rituals of Power: From Late Antiquity to the Early Middle Ages* (Leiden, Brill), pp. 281–309.

Le Jan, Régine (2001), *Femmes, pouvoir et société dans le haut Moyen Age* (Paris, A. & J. Picard) [Collected papers].

Le Jan, Régine (2006), 'Élites et révoltés à l'époque carolingienne: crises des élites ou crises des modèles?' in F. Bougard et al., eds., *Les Élites au haut moyen âge* (Turnhout, Brepols), pp. 403–24.

Lendi, Walter (1971), *Untersuchungen zur frühalemannischen Annalistik* (Freiburg, Universitätsverlag).

Levison, Wilhelm (1946), *England and the Continent in the Eighth Century* (Oxford, Clarendon Press).

Ley, Judith and Wietheger, Marc (2014), 'Der karolingische Palast König Davids in Aachen. Neue bauhistorische Untersuchungen zu Königshalle und Granustur', in F. Pohle, ed., *Karl der Grosse/Charlemagne*, 3 vols. (Dresden, Sandstein), vol. 1, *Orte der Macht: Essays*, pp. 236–45.

Leyser, Karl (1979), *Rule and Conflict in an Early Medieval Society* (London, Edward Arnold).

Leyser, Karl (1994), 'Ritual, ceremony and gesture: Ottonian Germany', in Leyser, *Communications and Power in Medieval Europe* [collected papers], ed. T. Reuter (London, Hambledon Press), pp. 189–213.

Liebeschütz, Hans (1950), 'Wesen und Grenzen des karolingischen Rationalismus', *Archiv für Kulturgeschichte* 33, pp. 17–44.

Lifshitz, Felice (2014), *Religious Women in Early Carolingian Francia* (New York, Fordham University Press).

Lintzel, Martin (1929), 'Der Sachsenfrieden Karls des Großen', *Neues Archiv* 48, pp. 1–32.

Lintzel, Martin (1961), *Ausgewählte Schriften*, vol. 1 (Berlin, Akademie-Verlag) [Collected papers].

Lobbedey, Uwe (2003), 'Carolingian royal palaces', in C. Cubitt, ed., *Court Culture in the Early Middle Ages* (Turnhout, Brepols), pp. 129–54.

Lohrmann, Dietrich (1976), 'Trois palais royaux de la vallée de l'Oise d'après les travaux des érudits mauristes: Compiègne, Choisy-au-Bac, et Quierzy', *Francia* 4, pp. 121–40.

Lohrmann, Dietrich (1988), 'La croissance agricole en Allemagne au haut moyen âge', in *La croissance. Chronologie, modalités, géographie*. Flaran 10. Auch, pp. 103–15.

Lohrmann, Dietrich (1989), 'Le moulin à eau dans le cadre de l'économie rurale de la Neustrie (VIIe–IXe siècles)', in Hartmut Atsma, ed., *La Neustrie. Les pays au nord de la Loire de 650 à 850*, Beiheft der *Francia* 16 (Sigmaringen, Thorbecke), pp. 367–404.

Loveluck, Chris (2005), 'Rural settlement hierarchy in the age of Charlemagne', in J. Story, ed., *Charlemagne: Empire and Society* (Manchester, Manchester University Press), pp. 230–58.

Löwe, Heinz (1949), 'Eine Kölner Notiz zum Kaisertum Karls des Großen', *Rheinische Vierteljahrsblätter* 14, pp. 7–34.

Luchterhandt, Manfred (1999), '*Famulus Petri*. Karl der Große in den römischen Mosaikbildern Leos III', in C. Stiegemann and M. Wemhoff, eds., *799. Kunst und Kultur der Karolingerzeit*, 3 vols. (Mainz, von Zabern), vol. 3, pp. 55–70.

Luhmann, Niklas (1979), *Ein Mechanismus der Reduktion sozialer Komplexität* (Stuttgart, Enke). Publ. in English as *Trust and Power* (Chichester, Wiley).

McCormick, Michael (1975), *Les annales du haut moyen âge* (Turnhout, Brepols).

McCormick, Michael (1984), 'The liturgy of war in the early Middle Ages: crisis, litanies and the crisis of the Carolinian monarchy', *Viator* 15, pp. 1–23.

McCormick, Michael (1986), *Eternal Victory: Triumphal Rulership in Late Antiquity, Byzantium and the Early Medieval West* (Cambridge, Cambridge University Press).

McCormick, Michael (1994), 'Textes, images et iconoclasme dans le cadre des relations entre Byzance et l'Occident carolingien', *Settimane* 41, pp. 95–162.

McCormick, Michael (1995), 'Byzantium and the West, 700–900', in R. McKitterick, ed., *New Cambridge Medieval History* II (Cambridge, Cambridge University Press), pp. 349–80.

McCormick, Michael (2001), *Origins of the European Economy: Communications and Commerce, AD 300–900* (Cambridge, Cambridge University Press).

McCormick, Michael (2002), 'New light on the "Dark Ages": how the slave trade fuelled the Carolingian economy', *Past & Present* 177, pp. 17–54.

McCormick, Michael (2004), 'Pippin III, the embassy of Caliph Al-Mansur, and the Mediterranean World', in M. Becher and J. Jarnut, eds., *Der Dynastiewechsel von 751* (Münster, Scriptorium), pp. 221–41.

McCormick, Michael (2008), 'Molecular Middle Ages: early medieval economic history in the twenty-first century', in J. Davis and M. McCormick, eds., *The Long Morning of Medieval Europe* (Aldershot, Ashgate), pp. 83–97.

McCormick, Michael (2011), *Charlemagne's Survey of the Holy Land: Wealth, Personnel, and Buildings of a Mediterranean Church between Antiquity and the Middle Ages* (Washington, DC, Dumbarton Oaks).

McCormick, Michael, Dutton, Paul E. and Mayewski, Paul A. (2011), 'Volcanoes and the climate forcing of Carolingian Europe, AD 750–950', *Speculum* 82, pp. 865–95.

McCune, James C. (2009), 'The sermons on the Virtues and Vices for *lay potentes* in the Carolingian Sermonary of Salzburg', *Journal of Medieval Latin* 19, pp. 250–90.

McKitterick, Rosamond (1977), *The Frankish Church and the Carolingian Reforms, 789–895* (London, Royal Historical Society).

McKitterick, Rosamond (1983), *The Frankish Kingdoms under the Carolingians, 751–987* (London, Longman).

McKitterick, Rosamond (1989), *The Carolingians and the Written Word* (Cambridge, Cambridge University Press).

McKitterick, Rosamond, ed. (1990), *The Uses of Literacy in Early Medieval Europe* (Cambridge, Cambridge University Press).

McKitterick, Rosamond (1993), 'Zur Herstellung von Kapitularien: ie Arbeit des Leges-Skriptoriums', *MIÖG* 101, pp. 3–16.

McKitterick, Rosamond (1994), *Books, Scribes and Learning in the Frankish Kingdoms, 6th–9th Centuries* (Aldershot, Ashgate) [Collected papers].

McKitterick, Rosamond (1995), *The Frankish Kings and Culture in the Early Middle Ages* (Aldershot, Ashgate) [Collected papers].

McKitterick, Rosamond (1997a), 'Constructing the past in the early Middle Ages: the case of the Royal Frankish Annals', *Transactions of the Royal Historical Society* 6th series, 7, pp. 101–29.

McKitterick, Rosamond (1997b), 'Perceptions of justice in Western Europe in the ninth and tenth centuries', in *La giustizia nell'alto medioevo (secoli IX–XI)*, Settimane XLIV, pp. 1075–102.

McKitterick, Rosamond (2004), *History and Memory in the Carolingian World* (Cambridge, Cambridge University Press).

McKitterick, Rosamond (2005a), 'History, law and communication with the past in the Carolingian period', in *Comunicare e significare nell'alto medioevo*, Settimane LXII, pp. 941–79.

McKitterick, Rosamond (2005b), 'The Carolingian renaissance of culture and learning', in J. Story, ed., *Charlemagne: Empire and Society* (Manchester, Manchester University Press), pp. 151–66.

McKitterick, Rosamond (2006a), 'Histoire et mémoire de la crise d'une élite carolingienne: l'année 785 et les *Annales regni Francorum*', in F. Bougard et al., eds., *Les Élites au haut moyen âge* (Turnhout, Brepols), pp. 267–82.

McKitterick, Rosamond (2006b), *Perceptions of the Past in the Early Middle Ages*, The Conway Lectures in Medieval Studies, 2004. (Notre Dame, Ind., University of Notre Dame Press).

McKitterick, Rosamond (2008), *Charlemagne and the Formation of a European Identity* (Cambridge, Cambridge University Press).

McKitterick, Rosamond (2009a), 'Court and communication in the early Middle Ages: the Frankish kingdom under Charlemagne', in W. Pohl and V. Wieser, eds., *Der frühmittelalterliche Staat – europäische Perspektiven* (Vienna, Verlag der ÖAW), pp. 357–68.

McKitterick, Rosamond (2009b), 'Charlemagne's *missi* and their books', in S. Baxter et al., eds., *Early Medieval Studies in Memory of Patrick Wormald* (Farnham, Ashgate), pp. 253–67.

McKitterick, Rosamond (2010), 'Entstehung und Gestaltung fränkischer Annales im Spiegel der Lorscher Annalen', in R. Corradini et al., eds., *Zwischen Niederschrift und Wiederschrift* (Vienna, Verlag der ÖAW), pp. 107–13.

McKitterick, Rosamond (2011), 'A king on the move: the place of an itinerant court in Charlemagne's government', in J. Duindam et al., eds., *Royal Courts in Dynastic States and Empires: A Global Perspective* (Leiden, Brill), pp. 145–69.

MacLean, Simon (2003), *Kingship and Politics in the Late Ninth Century. Charles the Fat and the End of the Carolingian Empire* (Cambridge, Cambridge University Press).

Mann, Michael (1987), *The Sources of Social Power*, vol. 1 (Cambridge, Cambridge University Press).

Manzano Moreno, Eduardo (1991), *La Frontera de Al-Andalus en Epoca de los Omeyas* (Madrid, Centro Superior de Investigaciones Científicas).

Marano, Yuri A. (2016), 'The circulation of marble in the Adriatic Sea at the time of Justinian', in J. Herrin and J. L. Nelson, eds., *Ravenna: Its Role in Earlier Medieval Change and Exchange* (London, Institute of Historical Research), pp. 111–32.

Marenbon, John (1981), *From the Circle of Alcuin to the School of Auxerre* (Cambridge, Cambridge University Press).

Marsham, Andrew (2000), *Rituals of Islamic Monarchy. Accession and Succession in the First Islamic Empire* (Edinburgh, Edinburgh University Press).

Martin, Thomas (1985), 'Bemerkungen zur "Epistola de litteris colendis"', *Archiv für Diplomatik* 31, pp. 227–72.

Mayr-Harting, Henry (1992), 'Charlemagne as a patron of art', *Studies in Church History* 28, pp. 43–77.

Mayr-Harting, Henry (1996), 'Charlemagne, the Saxons and the Imperial coronation of 800', *English Historical Review* 111, pp. 1113–33.

Mayr-Harting, Henry (2002), 'Charlemagne's religion', in P. Godman et al., eds., *Am Vorabend der Kaiserkrönung* (Berlin, Akademie Verlag), pp. 113–24.

Mayr-Harting, Henry (2009), 'Alcuin, Charlemagne and the problem of sanctions', in S. Baxter et al., eds., *Early Medieval Studies in Memory of Patrick Wormald* (Farnham, Ashgate), pp. 207–18.

Meckseper, Christiane (2001a), 'The Imperial Hall at Frankfurt am Main: a reinterpretation', in L. Fenske et al., eds., *Deutsche Königspfalzen: Beiträge zu ihrer historischen und archäologischen Erforschung*, vol. 5: *Splendor palatii* (Göttingen, Vandenhoeck und Ruprecht) pp. 51–70.

Meckseper, Christiane (2001b), 'Methodische Probleme der Rekonstruktion karolingischer Pfalzen-und Kirchenbauten', in L. Fenske et al., eds., *Deutsche Königspfalzen*, vol. 5: *Splendor palatii* (Göttingen, Vandenhoeck und Ruprecht), pp. 211–28.

Meens, Robert (2007), 'Sanctuary, penance and dispute settlement under Charlemagne: the conflict between Alcuin and Theodulf of Orléans over a sinful cleric', *Speculum* 82, pp. 277–300.

Melleno, Daniel (2014), *Before They Were Vikings: Scandinavia and the Franks up to the Death of Louis the Pious*. Doctoral thesis, University of California, Berkeley.

Mersiowsky, Mark (1996), 'Regierungspraxis und Schriftlichkeit im Karolingerreich das Fall Beispiel der Mandate und Briefe', in R. Schieffer, ed., *Schriftkultur und Reichsverwaltung unter den Karolingern*, Abhandlungen der Nordrhein-Westfälischen Akademie der Wissenschaften 97 (Opladen, Westdeutscher Verlag), pp. 109–66.

Mersiowsky, Mark (2015), *Die Urkunde in der Karolingerzeit. Originale, Urkundenpraxis und politische Kommunikation*, 2 vols, MGH Schriften 60 (Wiesbaden, Harrassowitz Verlag).

Metz, Wolfgang (1960), *Das Karolingische Reichsgut* (Berlin, de Gruyter).

Mitchell, John (1999), 'Karl der Grosse, Rom und das Vermächtnis der Langobarden', in C. Stiegemann and M. Wemhoff, eds., *799. Kunst und Kultur* (Mainz, Philipp von Zabern), vol. 1, pp. 95–108.

Mitchell, John (2013), 'St Johann at Müstair – the painted decoration in context', in H. R. Sennhauser, ed., *Wandel und Konstanz zwischen Bodensee und Lombardei zur Zeit Karls des Grossen*, Acta Müstair, Kloster St. Johann, pp. 373–96.

Mitchell, John and Hansen, Inge, eds. (2001), *San Vincenzo al Volturno 3. The Finds from the 1980–86 Excavations*, 2 vols. (Spoleto, Centro Italiano di Studi sull'Alto Medioevo).

Mitterauer, Michael (1963), *Karolingische Markgrafen im Südosten. Fränkische Reichsaristokatie un d bayerische Stammesadel im österreichische Raum* (Vienna, Archiv für österreichische Geschichte 123).

Moran, Matthew (2003), 'San Vincenzo in the making: the discovery of an early medieval production site on the east bank of the Volturno', in T. Pestell and K. Ulmschneider, eds., *Markets in Early Medieval Europe. Trading and 'Productive' Sites, 650–850* (Bollington, Windgather Press), pp. 249–63.

Mordek, Hubert (1992), 'Karl der Große – barbarischer Eroberer oder Baumeister Europas?' in B. Martin, ed., *Deutschland in Europe. Ein historischer Rückblick* (Munich, Deutscher Taschenbuch Verlag), pp. 23–45.

Mordek, Hubert (1994), 'Die Hedenen als politische Kraft im austrasischen Frankenreich', in J. Jarnut et al., eds., *Karl Martell in seiner Zeit* (Sigmaringen, Thorbecke), pp. 345–66.

Mordek, Hubert (1995), *Bibliotheca capitularium regum Francorum manuscripta: Überlieferung und Traditionszusammenhang der fränkischen Herrschererlasse*, MGH Hilfsmittel (Munich, MGH).

Mordek, Hubert (1997), 'Aachen, Frankfurt, Reims. Beobachtungen zu Genese und Tradition des Capitulare Frankofurtense (794)', in R. Berndt, ed., *Das Frankfurter Konzil von 794*, 2 vols. (Mainz, Gesellschaft für Mittelrheinische Kirchengeschichte), vol. 1, pp. 125–48.

Mordek, Hubert (2000), *Studien zur fränkischen Herrschergesetzgebung. Aufsätze über Kapitularien und Kapitulariensammlungen ausgewählt zum 60. Geburtstag* (Frankfurt, Lang).

Mordek, Hubert (2005), 'Karls des Großen zweites Kapitular von Herstal und die Hungersnot des Jahre 778/779', *Deutsches Archiv für Erforschung des Mittelalters* 61, pp. 1–52.

Mordek, Hubert and Glatthaar, Michael (1993), 'Von Wahrsagerinnen und Zauberern. Ein Beitrag zur Religionspolitik Karl des Großen', *Archiv für Kulturgeschichte* 75, pp. 33–64.

Mordek, Hubert and Schmitz, Gerhard (1987), 'Neue Kapitularien und Kapitulariensammlungen', *Deutsches Archiv für Erforschung des Mittelalters* 43, pp. 361–439.

Moreland, John (2000), 'Concepts of the early medieval economy', in I. Hansen and C. Wickham, eds., *The Long Eighth Century* (Leiden, Brill), pp. 1–34.

Morrissey, Robert (1997), *L'empéreur à la barbe fleurie. Charlemagne dans la mythologie et l'histoire de France* (Paris, Gallimard). Eng. trans. *Charlemagne and France. A Thousand Years of Mythology* by C. Tihanyi (Notre Dame, Ind., University of Notre Dame Press, 2003).

Mostert, Marco, ed. (1999), *New Approaches to Medieval Communication* (Turnhout, Brepols).

Mostert, Marco (2016), '. . . but they pray badly using corrected books': errors in early Carolingian copies of the *Admonitio generalis*', in Rob Meens et al., eds., *Religious Franks: Religion and Power in the Frankish Kingdoms. Studies in Honour of Mayke de Jong* (Manchester, Manchester University Press), pp. 112–17.

Müller, Harald, Bayer, C. M. M. and Kerner, Max, eds. (2013), *Die Aachener Marienkirche. Aspekte ihrer Archäologie und frühen Geschichte* (Regensburg, Schnell & Steiner).

Munz, Peter (1969), *Life in the Age of Charlemagne* (New York, G. P. Putman & Sons).

Naismith, Rory (2012), *Money and Power in Anglo-Saxon England* (Cambridge, Cambridge University Press).

Naismith, Rory (2014), 'The social significance of monetization in the early Middle Ages', in *Past & Present* 223, pp. 3–39.

Näsman, Ulf (2000), 'Exchange and politics: the eighth–early ninth century', in I. Hansen and C. Wickham, eds., *The Long Eighth Century* (Leiden, Brill), pp. 35–68.

Nees, Lawrence (1991), *A Tainted Mantle. Hercules and the Classical Tradition at the Carolingian Court* (Philadelphia, University of Pennsylvania Press).

Nees, Lawrence (1995), 'Art and architecture', in R. McKitterick, ed., *New Cambridge Medieval History* II (Cambridge, Cambridge University Press), pp. 809–44.

Nees, Lawrence (2007), 'Godescalc's career and the problems of "influence"', in J. Lowden and A. Bovey, eds., *Under the Influence. The Concept of Influence and the Study of Illuminated Manuscripts* (Turnhout, Brepols), pp. 21–43.

Nees, Lawrence (2013), 'Theodulf's mosaic at Germigny, the Sancta Sanctorum in Rome, and Jerusalem', in Cullen J. Chandler and Steven Stofferahn, eds., *Discovery and Distinction in the Early Middle Ages: Studies in Honor of John J. Contreni* (Kalamazoo, Mich., Medieval Institute Publications), pp. 187–211.

Nees, Lawrence (2017), 'The "foundation reliquary" of Hildesheim and ornamental art at the court of Charlemagne', in G. Davies and E. Townsend, eds., *A Reservoir of Ideas. Essays in Honour of Paul Williamson* (London, Paul Holberton), pp. 56–66.

Nelson, Janet L. (1986a), *Politics and Ritual in Early Medieval Europe* (London, Hambledon Press) [Collected papers].

Nelson, Janet L. (1986b), 'Dispute settlement in Carolingian West Francia', in W. Davies and P. Fouracre, eds., *The Settlement of Disputes in Early Medieval Europe* (Cambridge, Cambridge University Press), pp. 45–64.

Nelson, Janet L. (1988), 'Kingship and empire', in J. H. Burns, ed., *The Cambridge History of Political Thought* (Cambridge, Cambridge University Press), pp. 211–51.

Nelson, Janet L. (1990), 'Literacy in Carolingian government', in R. McKitterick, ed., *The Uses of Literacy in Early Medieval Europe* (Cambridge, Cambridge University Press), pp. 258–96, repr. in Nelson (1996), pp. 1–36.

Nelson, Janet L. (1991), 'Gender and genre in Women Historians of the early Middle Ages', in J.-P. Genet, ed., *L'Historiographie médiévale en Europe* (Paris, Éditions CNRS), pp. 149–63, repr. in Nelson (1996), pp. 199–222.

Nelson, Janet L. (1992), *Charles the Bald* (London, Longman).

Nelson, Janet L. (1994), 'Kingship and empire in the Carolingian world', in R. McKitterick, ed., *Carolingian Culture: Emulation and Innovation* (Cambridge, Cambridge University Press), pp. 52–87.

Nelson, Janet L. (1995), 'Kingship and royal government', in R. McKitterick, ed., *New Cambridge Medieval History* II (Cambridge, Cambridge University Press), pp. 383–430.

Nelson, Janet L. (1996), *The Frankish World* (London, Hambledon Press) [Collected Papers].

Nelson, Janet L. (1997a), 'The siting of the Council at Frankfurt: some reflections on family and politics', in R. Berndt, ed., *Das Frankfurter Konzil von 794*, 2 vols. (Mainz, Gesellschaft für mittelrheinische Kirchengeschichte), vol. 1, pp. 149–65.

Nelson, Janet L. (1997b), 'Kings with justice, kings without justice: an early medieval paradox', in *La giustizia nell'alto medioevo*, Settimane XLIV, pp. 797–823.

Nelson, Janet L. (1998), 'Making a difference in eighth-century politics: the daughters of Desiderius', in A. C. Murray, ed., *After Rome's Fall. Narrators and Sources of Early Medieval History. Essays presented to Walter Goffart* (Toronto: Toronto University Press), pp. 171–90.

Nelson, Janet L. (1999), *Rulers and Ruling Families in Early Medieval Europe* (Aldershot, Ashgate) [Collected papers].

Nelson, Janet L. (2000), 'Carolingian royal funerals', in F. Theuws and J. L. Nelson, eds., *Rituals of Power: From Late Antiquity to the Early Middle Ages* (Leiden, Brill), pp. 131–84.

Nelson, Janet L. (2001a), 'Aachen as a place of power', in M. de Jong, F. Theuws and C. Van Rhijn, eds., *Topographies of Power* (Leiden, Brill), pp. 217–41.

Nelson, Janet L. (2001b), 'Peers in the early Middle Ages', in P. Stafford, J. L. Nelson and J. Martindale, eds., *Law, Laity and Solidarities. Essays in Honour of Susan Reynolds* (Manchester, Manchester University Press), pp. 27–46.

Nelson, Janet L. (2001c), 'The voice of Charlemagne', in R. Gameson and H. Leyser, eds., *Belief and Culture in the Middle Ages. Studies Presented to Henry Mayr-Harting* (Oxford, Oxford University Press), pp. 76–88.

Nelson, Janet L. (2002), 'England and the Continent in the ninth century: I, ends and beginnings', *Transactions of the Royal Historical Society* 6th series, 12, pp. 1–21.

Nelson, Janet L. (2003), 'England and the Continent in the ninth century: II, the Vikings and others', *Transactions of the Royal Historical Society* 6th series, 13, pp. 1–28.

Nelson, Janet L. (2004a), 'England and the Continent in the ninth century: III, rights and rituals', *Transactions of the Royal Historical Society* 6th series, 14, pp. 1–24.

Nelson, Janet L. (2004b), 'Gendering courts in the early medieval West', in L. Brubaker and J. M. H. Smith, eds., *Gender in the Early Medieval World. East and West, 300–900* (Cambridge, Cambridge University Press), pp. 185–97.

Nelson, Janet L. (2005a), 'England and the Continent in the ninth century: IV, bodies and minds', *Transactions of the Royal Historical Society* 6th series, 15, pp. 1–27.

Nelson, Janet L. (2005b), 'Carolingian contacts', in M. Brown and C. Farr, eds., *Mercia. An Anglo-Saxon Kingdom in Europe* (London, Continuum), pp. 126–43.

Nelson, Janet L. (2005c), 'Charlemagne the man', in J. Story, ed., *Charlemagne: Empire and Society* (Manchester, Manchester University Press), pp. 22–37, repr. in Nelson (2007).

Nelson, Janet L. (2006), 'Did Charlemagne have a private life?', in D. Bates, J. Crick and S. Hamilton, eds., *Writing Medieval Biography, 750–1250. Essays in Honour of Professor Frank Barlow* (Woodbridge, Boydell), pp 15–28.

Nelson, Janet L. (2007), *Courts, Elites and Gendered Power* (Aldershot, Ashgate) [Collected papers].

Nelson, Janet L. (2008a), 'Charlemagne and empire', in J. R. Davis and M. McCormick, eds., *The Long Morning of Medieval Europe* (Aldershot, Ashgate), pp. 223–34.

Nelson, Janet L. (2008b), 'Frankish identity in Charlemagne's empire', in I. H. Garipzanov et al., eds., *Franks, Northmen, and Slavs: Identities and State Formation in Early Medieval Europe* (Turnhout, Brepols), pp. 71–83.

Nelson, Janet L. (2009a), 'Opposition to Charlemagne', German Historical Institute Annual Lecture 2008 (London, German Historical Institute).

Nelson, Janet L. (2009b), 'Charlemagne and the paradoxes of power', The Reuter Lecture 2005, in P. Skinner, ed., *Challenging the Boundaries of Medieval History: The Legacy of Timothy Reuter* (Turnhout, Brepols), pp. 29–50.

Nelson, Janet L. (2009c), 'England, Ireland and the Continent', in P. Stafford, ed., *A Companion to the Early Middle Ages. Britain and Ireland c.500–c.1100* (Oxford, Wiley-Blackwell), pp. 231–47.

Nelson, Janet L. (2009d), 'How Carolingians created consensus', in W. Fałkowski and Y. Sassier, eds., *Le Monde carolingien* (Turnhout, Brepols), pp. 69–83.

Nelson, Janet L. (2010a), 'Power and its limits in the reign of Charlemagne', in S. J. Ridyard, ed., *Power in the Middle Ages*, Sewanee Medieval Studies 14 (Sewanee, Tenn., The University of the South), pp. 1–23.

Nelson, Janet L. (2010b), 'The setting of the gift', in W. Davies and P. Fouracre, eds., *The Languages of Gift in the Early Middle Ages* (Cambridge, Cambridge University Press), pp. 116–48.

Nelson, Janet L (2010c), 'Munera', in J.-P. Devroey et al., eds., *Les élites et la richesse dans le haut moyen âge* (Turnhout, Brepols), pp. 383–401.

Nelson, Janet L. (2011a), 'The role of the gift in early medieval diplomatic relations', *Le Relazioni Internazionali nell'alto medioevo*, Settimane 37, pp. 225–48.

Nelson, Janet L. (2011b), 'Elites in the Carolingian empire', in F. Bougard et al., eds., *Théorie et pratique des élites au haut moyen âge* (Turnhout, Brepols), pp. 309–23.

Nelson, Janet L. (2013a), 'Religion and politics in the reign of Charlemagne', in L. Körntgen and D. Waßenhoven, eds., *Religion and Politics in the Middle Ages* (Berlin, Walter de Gruyter), pp. 1–29.

Nelson, Janet L. (2013b), 'The *libera vox* of Theodulf of Orléans', in C. J. Chandler and S. A. Stofferahn, eds., *Discovery and Distinction in the Early Middle Ages: Studies in Honor of John J. Contreni* (Kalamazoo, Mich., Medieval Institute Publications), pp. 288–306.

Nelson, Janet L. (2014a), 'Charlemagne and Europe', Raleigh Lecture on History, *Journal of the British Academy* 2, pp. 125–52.

Nelson, Janet L. (2014b), 'Opposition to pilgrimage in the reign of Charlemagne', in V. I. Garver and O. M. Phelan, eds., *Rome and Religion in the Medieval World. Studies in Honor of T. F. X. Noble* (Farnham, Ashgate), pp. 65–82.

Nelson, Janet L. (2014c), 'Religion in the reign of Charlemagne', in J. Arnold, ed., *The Oxford Handbook of Medieval History* (Oxford, Oxford University Press), pp. 490–514.

Nelson, Janet L. (2014d), 'Pater Europae? Karl der Große und Europa', in *Karl der Grosse. Orte der Macht* (Stadt Aschen, Sandstein Verlag), pp. 432–9.

Nelson, Janet L. (2015a), 'Why *Das Karolingische Imperium* still needs to be read', in A. Schwarz and K. Kaska, eds., *Urkunden – Schriften – Lebensordnungen. Neue Beiträge zur Mediävistik* (Vienna, Verlag der ÖAW), pp. 111–23.

Nelson, Janet L. (2015b), 'Evidence in question: dendrochronology and medieval history', in O. Kano and J.-L. Lemaître, eds., *Entre texte et histoire: études d'histoire médiévale offertes au professeur Shoichi Sato* (Paris, Éditions de Boccard), pp. 227–49.

Nelson, Janet L. (2016a), 'Charlemagne and the bishops', in R. Meens et al., eds., *Religious Franks. Religion and Power in the Frankish Kingdoms: Studies in Honour of Mayke de Jong* (Manchester, Manchester University Press), pp. 350–69.

Nelson, Janet L. (2016b), 'Charlemagne and Ravenna', in J. Herrin and J. Nelson, eds., *Ravenna: Its Role in Early Medieval Change and Exchange* (London, Institute of Historical Research Press), pp. 239–52.

Nelson, Janet L. (2016c), 'Revisiting the Carolingian Renaissance', in J. Kreiner and H. Reimitz, eds., *Motions of Late Antiquity. Essays on Religion, Politics, and Society in Honour of Peter Brown* (Turnhout, Brepols), pp. 331–46.

Nelson, Janet L. (2017a), 'Alcuin's letter to Meginfrid', in A. Dierkens et al., eds., *Penser la paysannerie médiévale, un défi impossible? Recueil d'études offert à J.-P. Devroey* (Paris, Éditions de la Sorbonne), pp. 111–25.

Nelson, Janet L. (2017b), 'Losing the plot? "Filthy assertions" and "Unheard of deceit" in Codex Carolinus 92', in D. Woodman and R. Naismith, eds., *Writing, Kingship and Power in Anglo-Saxon England* (Cambridge, Cambridge University Press), pp. 122–35.

Nelson, Janet L. (2018a), 'Staging integration in Bavaria', in M. Diesenberger and B. Zeller, eds., *Neue Wege der Frühmittelalterforschung. Tagensakten der Tagung zu Ehren von Herwig Wolfram* (Vienna, Verlag der ÖAW), pp. 225–37.

Nelson, Janet L. (2018b), 'Trust and mistrust in the reign of Charlemagne', in Y. Sassier and W. Fałkowski, eds., *Confiance, bonne foi, fidelité* (Paris, Classiques Garnier), pp. 87–96.

Nelson, Janet L. and Rio, Alice (2013), 'Women and laws in early medieval Europe', in J. A. Bennett and R. M. Karras, eds., *The Oxford Handbook of Women and Gender in Medieval Europe* (Oxford, Oxford University Press), pp. 103–17.

Newfield, Timothy (2015), 'Human–bovine plagues in the Early Middle Ages', *Journal of Interdisciplinary History* 46, pp. 1–38.

Niermeyer, Jan Frederik (1997), *Mediae Latinitatis Lexicon Minus*, 3rd edn (Leiden, Brill).

Noble, Thomas F. X. (1984), *The Republic of St. Peter: The Birth of the Papal State, 680–825* (Philadelphia, University of Pennsylvania Press).

Noble, Thomas F. X. (1992) 'From brigandage to justice: Charlemagne 785–794', in C. M. Chazelle, ed., *Literacy, Politics and Artistic Innovation in the Early Medieval West* (Lanham, Md., University Press of America), pp. 49–75.

Noble, Thomas F. X. (2009), *Images, Iconoclasm and the Carolingians* (Philadelphia, University of Pennsylvania Press).

Noizet, Hélène (2004), 'Alcuin contre Théodulphe: un conflit producteur de normes', in P. Depreux and B. Judic, eds., *Alcuin, de York à Tours. Écriture, pouvoir et réseaux dans l'Europe du haut Moyen Âge* (Rennes, Presses Universitaires de Rennes), pp. 113–29.

Nolte, Cordula (1995), *Conversio und christianitas. Frauen in der Christianisierung vom. 5. Zum 8. Jahrhundert* (Stuttgart, Hiersemann).

Nonn, Ulrich (2004), 'Die Nachfolge Karl Martells und die Teilung von Vieux-Poitiers', in M. Becher and J. Jarnut, eds., *Der Dynastiewechsel von 751* (Münster, Scriptorium), pp. 61–73.

Nothdurfter, Hans et al. (2003), *St Prokulus in Naturns* (Lara, Tappeiner Verlag).

Oexle, Otto G. (1967), 'Die Karolinger und die Stadt des Heiligen Arnulf', *Frühmittelalterliche Studien* 1, pp. 249–364.

Oexle, Otto G. (1978), *Forschungen zu monastischen und geistlichen Gemeinschaften im westfränkischen Bereich* (Munich, Fink).

Oexle, Otto G. (1985), 'Conjuratio und Gilde im frühen Mittelalter. Ein Beitrag zum Problem der sozialgeschichtlichen Konitinuität', in B. Schwineköper, ed., *Gilden und Zünfte* (Sigmaringen, Thorbecke), pp. 151–214.

Oexle, Otto G. (1988), 'Haus und Ökonomie im früheren Mittelalter', in G. Althoff et al., eds., *Person und Gemeinschaft im Mittelalter. Festschrift für Karl Schmidt* (Sigmaringen, Thorbecke), pp. 101–22.

Oexle, Otto G. (1995), 'Die Kultur der Rebellion. Schwureinung und Verschwörung im früh- und hochmittelaltrlichen Okzident', in M. T. Fögen, ed., *Ordnung und Aufruhr im Mittelalter* (Frankfurt am Main, Klostermann), pp. 119–37.

Offergeld, Thilo (2001), *Reges pueri. Das Königtum Minderjähriger im frühen Mittelalter* (Hanover, Hahn).

Opland, Jeff (1993), '*Scop* and *Imbongi* IV: Reading prose poems', *Comparative Literature* 45 (2), pp. 97–120.

Opland, Jeff (1998), *Xhosa Poets and Poetry* (Cape Town, David Philip).

Palmer, James T. (2005), 'The vigorous rule of Bishop Lull: between Bonifatian mission and Carolingian church control', *Early Medieval Europe* 13, pp. 249–76.

Palmer, James T. (2009), *Anglo-Saxons in a Frankish World (690–900)* (Turnhout, Brepols).

Palmer, James T. (2011), 'Computus after the Paschal controversy', in I. Warnjes and D. Ó Cróinín, eds., *Proceedings of the First International Conference on the Science of Computus in Ireland and Europe, 2008* (Turnhout, Brepols), pp. 213–41.

Palmer, James T. (2014), *The Apocalypse in the Early Middle Ages* (Cambridge, Cambridge University Press)

Pangerl, Daniel Carlo (2011), *Die Metropolitenverfassung des karolingischen Frankenreichs*, MGH Schriften 63 (Hannover, MGH).

Parker, Geoffrey (1998), *The Grand Strategy of Philip II* (New Haven, Conn., Yale University Press).

Patzold, Steffen (2006), 'Die Bischöfe im karolingischen Staat', in S. Airlie et al., eds., *Staat im frühen Mittelalter* (Vienna, Verlag der ÖAW), pp. 133–62.

Patzold, Steffen (2007), 'Normen im Buch', *Frühmittelalterliche Studien* 41, pp. 331–50.

Patzold, Steffen (2008), *Episcopus. Wissen über Bischöfe im Frankenreich des späten 8. Bis frühen 10. Jahrhunderts* (Ostfildern, Thorbecke).

Patzold, Steffen (2009), 'Bischöfe als Träger der politischen Ordung des Frankenreiches im 8./9. Jahrhundert', in W. Pohl and V. Wieser, eds., *Der frühmittelalterliche Staat – europäischen Perspektiven* (Vienna, Verlag der ÖAW), pp. 255–68.

Patzold, Steffen (2013), *Ich und Karl der Große. Das Leben des Höflings Einhard* (Stuttgart, Klett-Cotta).

Patzold, Steffen (2014), 'Die Kaiseridee Karls des Großen', in F. Pohle, ed., *Karl der Grosse/Charlemagne*, 3 vols. (Dresden, Sandstein), vol. 1, *Orte der Macht: Essays*, pp. 152–9.

Patzold, Steffen (2015), 'Das sogenannte "Capitulare Aquisgranense". Karls des Großen und die letzte Reforminitiative Ludwigs des Frommen im Jahr 829', in *Deutsches Archiv für Erforschung des Mittelalters* 71, pp. 459–73.

Paxton, Frederick S. (1990), *Christianizing Death. The Creation of a Ritual Process in Early Medieval Europe* (Ithaca, NY, Cornell University Press).

Phelan, Owen M. (2014), *The Formation of Christian Europe: The Carolingians, Baptism and the Imperium Christianum* (Oxford, Oxford University Press).

Pirenne, Henri (1939), *Mohammed and Charlemagne*, ed. F. Vercauteren, trans. B. Miall (New York, Barnes and Noble).

Pohl, Walter (1988), *Die Awarenkrieg Karls des Großen 788–803* (Vienna, Bundesverlag).

Pohl, Walter (1998), 'Telling the difference: signs of ethnic identity', in W. Pohl and H. Reimitz, eds., *Strategies of Distinction: The Construction of Ethnic Communities, 300–800* (Leiden, Brill), pp. 17–69.

Pohl, Walter (1999), 'Franken und Sachsen: die Bedeutung ethnische Prozessei m 7. und 8. Jahrhundert', in C. Stiegemann and M. Wemhoff, eds., *799. Kunst und Kultur der Karolingerzeit: Karl der Große und Papst Leo III in Paderborn* (Mainz: von Zabern), pp. 233–6.

Pohl, Walter (2006), 'Staat und Herrschaft im Frühmittelalter: Überlegungen zum Forschungsstand', in S. Airlie et al., eds., *Staat im frühen Mittelalter* (Vienna, Verlag der ÖAW), pp. 9–38.

Pohl, Walter (2007), '*Alienigena coniugia*: Bestrebungen zu einem Verbot auswärtiger Heiraten in der Karolingerzeit', in A. Pečar and K. Trampedach, eds., *Die Bibel als politisches Argument* (Munich, Oldenbourg), pp. 159–88.

Pohl, Walter (2014), 'Why not to marry a foreign woman: Stephen III's letter to Charlemagne', in V. L. Garver and O. W. Phelan, eds., *Rome and Religion in the Medieval World. Studies in Honor of Thomas F. X. Noble* (Farnham, Ashgate), pp. 47–63.

Pohl, Walter (2018), *The Avars. A Steppe Empire in Central Europe, 567–822*, trans. William Sayers (Ithaca, NY, Cornell University Press).

Pohl, Walter and Reimitz, Helmut, eds. (1998), *Strategies of Distinction: The Construction of Ethnic Communities, 300–800* (Leiden, Brill).

Pohle, Frank, ed. (2014), *Karl der Grosse/Charlemagne*, 3 vols. (Dresden, Sandstein).

Pokorny, Rudolf (1996), 'Ein Brief-Instruktion aus dem Hofkreis Karls des Großen an einen geistlichen Missus', *Deutsches Archiv für Erforschung des Mittelalters* 52, pp. 57–83.

Pössel, Christina (2006), 'Authors and recipients of Carolingian capitularies, 779–829', in R. Corradini et al., eds., *Texts and Identities in the Early Middle Ages* (Vienna, Verlag der ÖAW), pp. 253–74.

Pössel, Christina (2009), 'The magic of early medieval ritual', *Early Medieval Europe* 17, pp. 111–25.

Poupardin, René (1901), 'Étude sur la diplomatique des princes lombards de Bénévent, de Capoue et de Salerne', *Mélanges de l'école française de Rome*, 1901, pp. 117–80.

Power, Eileen (1937), *Medieval People* (Harmondsworth, Penguin).

Prinz, Friedrich (1971), *Klerus und Krieg im früheren Mittelalter* (Stuttgart, Hiersemann).

Purkis, William J. and Gabriele, Matthew, eds. (2016), *The Charlemagne Legend in Medieval Latin Texts* (Woodbridge, D. S. Brewer).

Raaijmakers, Janneke (2012), *The Making of the Monastic Community of Fulda c. 744–c. 900* (Cambridge, Cambridge University Press).

Rabe, Susan (1995), *Faith, Art, and Politics at Saint-Riquier: The Symbolic Vision of Angilbert* (Philadelphia, University of Pennsylvania Press).

Reimitz, Helmut (2000), 'Grenzen und Grenzüberschreitungen im karolingischen Mitteleuropa', in W. Pohl and H. Reimitz, eds., *Grenzen und Differenz im frühen Mittelalter* (Vienna, Verlag der ÖAW), pp. 105–66.

Reimitz, Helmut (2015), *History, Frankish Identity and the Framing of Western Ethnicity 550–850* (Cambridge, Cambridge University Press).

Reindel, Kurt (1965), 'Bayern im Karolingerreich', in H. Beumann et al., eds., *Karl der Große: Leben und Nachleben*, 4 vols. (Düsseldorf, Schwann), vol. 1, pp. 220–46.

Rembold, Ingrid (2017), *Conquest and Christianization: Saxony and the Carolingian World, 772–888* (Cambridge, Cambridge University Press).

Renard, Étienne (2006), 'Une élite paysanne en crise? Le poids des charges militaires pour les petits alleutiers entre Loire et Rhin au IXe siècle', in F. Bougard et al., eds., *Les Élites au haut moyen âge: Crises et renouvellements* (Turnhout, Brepols), pp. 315–36.

Renard, Étienne (2009), 'La politique militaire de Charlemagne et la paysannerie franque', *Francia* 36, pp. 1–33.

Reuter, Timothy, ed. (1978), *The Medieval Nobility* (Amsterdam, New York and Oxford, North Holland Publishing Company).

Reuter, Timothy (1980), 'Saint Boniface and Europe', in T. Reuter, ed., *The Greatest Englishman: Essays on St. Boniface and the Church at Crediton* (Exeter, Paternoster Press), pp. 71–94.

Reuter, Timothy (1985), 'Plunder and tribute in the Carolingian empire', *Transactions of the Royal Historical Society* 5th series, 35, pp. 75–94.

Reuter, Timothy (1990), 'The end of Carolingian military expansion', in P. Godman and R. Collins, eds., *Charlemagne's Heir: New Perspectives on the Reign of Louis the Pious* (Oxford, Oxford University Press), pp. 391–404.

Reuter, Timothy (1991), *Germany in the Early Middle Ages 800–1056* (Harlow, Longman).

Reuter, Timothy (1993), 'The medieval German *Sonderweg*? The empire and its rulers in the high Middle Ages', in A. Duggan, ed., *Kings and Kingship* (London, King's College London), repr. in Reuter (2006), pp. 388–412.

Reuter, Timothy (1994), '"Kirchenreform" und "Kirchenpolitik" im Zeitalter Karl Martells: Begriffe und Wirklichkeit', in J. Jarnut et al., eds., *Karl Martell in seiner Zeit* (Sigmaringen, Thorbecke), pp. 35–60.

Reuter, Timothy (1997), 'Response to T. N. Bisson, "The Feudal Revolution", *Past & Present* 155, pp. 177–95.

Reuter, Timothy (2001), 'Assembly politics in Western Europe from the eighth to the twelfth century', in P. Linehan and J. L. Nelson, eds., *The Medieval World* (London, Routledge), pp. 434–50.

Reuter, Timothy (2006), *Medieval Polities and Modern Mentalities*, ed. J. L. Nelson (Cambridge, Cambridge University Press) [Collected papers].

Reynolds, Susan (1994), *Fiefs and Vassals. The Medieval Evidence Reinterpreted* (Oxford, Oxford University Press).

Reynolds, Susan (1997), *Kingdoms and Communities in Western Europe, 900–1300*, 2nd edn (Oxford, Clarendon Press).

Reynolds, Susan (2001), 'Afterthoughts on *Fiefs and Vassals*', *Haskins Society Journal* 9, pp. 1–15, repr. 2012 in S. Reynolds, *The Middle Ages without Feudalism* (Farnham, Ashgate/Variorum).

Reynolds, Susan (2006), 'Empires: a problem of comparative history', *Historical Research* 79, pp. 151–65.

Riché, Pierre (1974), 'Le renouveau culturel à la cour de Pépin III', *Francia* 2, pp. 59–70.

Riché, Pierre (1981), *Instruction et vie religieuse dans le Haut Moyen Age* (London, Variorum Reprints).

Riché, Pierre (1983), *Une famille qui fit l'Europe* (Paris, Hachette littérature).

Riché, Pierre et al., eds. (1987), *Autour d'Hildegarde. Recueil d'Études* (Paris, Centre de recherches sur l'Antiquité tardive et le Haut Moyen-âge, et Centre de recherches d'histoire et civilisation de l'Université de Metz).

Richter, Michael (1998), 'Die "lange Machtergreifung" der Karolinger. Der Staatstreich gegen die Merowinger in den Jahren 747–771', in U. Schultz, ed., *Große Verschwörungen* (Munich, Beck), pp. 48–59.

Richter, Michael (2001), 'Karl der Große und seine Ehefrauen', in F.-R. Erkens, ed., *Karl der Große und der Erbe der Kulturen* (Berlin, de Gruyter), pp. 17–24.

Riezler, Sigmund von (1881), 'Ein verlorenes bairisches Geschichtswerk des achten Jahrhunderts', in *Sitzungsberichte der königlichen Akademie der Wissenschaften, philosophisch-philogisch-historische* Klasse 1, pp. 247–51, trans. P. D. King (1987), *Charlemagne: Translated Sources* (Lambrigg, P. D. King), pp. 340–43.

Rio, Alice (2006), 'Freedom and unfreedom in early medieval Francia: the evidence of the legal formulae', *Past & Present* 193, pp. 7–40.

Rio, Alice (2008a), *The Formularies of Angers and Marculf, with English Translation and Commentary* (Liverpool, Liverpool University Press).

Rio, Alice (2008b), 'High and low: ties of dependence in the Frankish kingdoms', in *Transactions of the Royal Historical Society* 6th series, 18, pp. 43–68.

Rio, Alice (2009), *Legal Practice and the Written Word in the Early Middle Ages* (Cambridge, Cambridge University Press).

Rio, Alice, ed. (2011), *Law, Custom and Justice in Late Antiquity and the Early Middle Ages* (London, Centre for Hellenic Studies).

Rio, Alice (2017), *Slavery after Rome 500–1100* (Oxford, Oxford University Press).

Rio, Alice and Nelson, Janet L. (2013), 'Women and laws in early medieval Europe', in J. M. Bennett and R. M. Karras, eds., *The Oxford Handbook of Women and Gender in Medieval Europe* (Oxford, Oxford University Press), pp. 103–17.

Rollason, David (2012), 'Palaces, forests, parks and the power of place in the early Middle Ages', *Early Medieval Europe* 20, pp. 428–49.

Rollason, David (2015), 'Charlemagne's palace', *The Archaeological Journal* 172 (2), pp. 443–8.

Rollason, David (2016), *The Power of Place. Rulers and their Palaces, Landscapes, Cities and Holy Places* (Princeton, NJ, Princeton Uninversity Press).

Roper Pearson, Kathy L. (1999), *Conflicting Loyalties in Early Medieval Bavaria. A View of Socio-Political Interaction, 680–900* (Aldershot, Ashgate).

Rosenwein, Barbara H., ed. (1998), *Anger's Past. The Social Uses of an Emotion in the Middle Ages* (Ithaca, NY and London, Cornell University Press).

Rosenwein, Barbara H. (1999), *Negotiating Space. Power, Restraint and Privileges of Immunity* (Ithaca, NY, Cornell University Press).

Rosenwein, Barbara H. (2000), 'Perennial prayer at Agaune', in B. H. Rosenwien and S. Farmer, eds., *Monks and Nuns, Saints and Outcasts* (Ithaca, NY, Cornell University Press), pp. 37–56.

Rosenwein, Barbara H. (2001), 'Writing without fear about early medieval emotions', *Early Medieval Europe* 10, pp. 229–34.

Rosenwein, Barbara H. (2003), 'Francia and Polynesia: rethinking anthropological approaches', in G. Algazi, V. Groebner and B. Jussen, eds., *Negotiating the Gift: Pre-modern Figurations of Exchange* (Göttingen, Veröffentlichungen des Max-Planck-Instituts für Geschichte), pp. 361–79.

Rosenwein, Barbara H. (2006), *Emotional Communities in the Early Middle Ages* (Ithaca, NY, Cornell University Press).

Rosenwein, Barbara H. (2015), 'Rereading "Askese und Laster": the case of Alcuin', in A. Schwarcz and K. Kaska, eds., *Urkunden – Schriften – Lebensordnungen* (Vienna, Böhlau), pp. 77–89.

Rouche, Michel (1979), *L'Aquitaine des Wisigoths aux Arabes, 418–781: Naissance d'une région* (Paris, Touzot).

Santinelli, Emmanuelle (2003), *Des Femmes Éplorées? Les veuves dans la société aristocratique du haut moyen âge* (Septentrion, Presses Universitaires).

Sarefield, Daniel C. (2004), *Burning Knowledge. Studies of Bookburning in Ancient Rome* (Columbus, OH, Ohio State University Press).

Sarefield, Daniel C. (2006), 'Book burning in the Christian Roman Empire: transforming a pagan rite of purification', in H. A. Drake, ed., *Violence in Late Antiquity: Perceptions and Practices* (Aldershot, Ashgate), pp. 287–96.

Sarefield, Daniel C. (2007), 'The symbolics of book burning: the establishment of a Christian ritual of persecution', in W. E. Klingshirn and L. Safran, eds., *The Early Christian Book* (Washington, DC, The Catholic University of America Press), pp. 59–73.

Sarris, Peter (2011), *Empires of Faith: The Fall of Rome to the Rise of Islam, 500–700* (Oxford, Oxford University Press).

Sassier, Yves (1988), 'L'utilisation d'un concept romain auz temps carolingiens: La *res publica*', *Médiévales* 15, pp. 17–29.

Schaller, Dieter (1976), 'Das Aachener Epos für Karl den Kaiser', in *Frühmittelalterliche Studien* 10, pp. 134–68.

Schaller, Dieter (1997), 'Karl der Große im Licht zeitgenössischer politischer Dichtung', in P. L. Butzer et al., eds., *Karl der Große und sein Nachwirken*, vol. 1, *Wissen und Weltbild* (Turnhout, Brepols), pp. 193–219.

Schaller, Martin (2011), 'Alte und neue Überlegungen zur Herkunft des Monogramms Karls des Großen', in *Epeironde. Proceedings of the 10th International Symposium of Byzantine Sigillography* (Wiesdan, Harrassowitz Verlag), pp. 111–77.

Scharer, Anton (2009), 'Charlemagne's daughters', in S. Baxter et al., eds., *Early Medieval Studies in Memory of Patrick Wormald* (Farnham, Ashgate).

Scharer, Anton (2013), 'Insular mission to the continent in the early Middle Ages', in C. Leyser and H. Williams, eds., *Mission and Monasticism* (Rome, Editions of Sankt Ottilien), pp. 55–62.

Scharer, Anton (2014), *Changing Perspectives on England and the Continent in the Early Middle Ages* (Farnham, Ashgate).

Scharer, Anton (2015), 'Das Testament Karls des Großen', in A. Schwarcz and K. Kaska, eds., *Urkunden – Schriften – Lebensordnungen. Neue Beiträge zur Mediävistik* (Vienna, Böhlau), pp. 151–60.

Scheibe, Friedrich-Carl (1958), 'Alcuin und der *Admonitio generalis*', *Deutsches Archiv für Erforschung des Mittelalters* 14, pp. 221–9.

Schieffer, Rudolf (1989), '"*Redeamus ad fontem*". Rom als Hort authentischer Überlieferung im frühen Mittelalter', in A. Angenendt and R. Schieff, eds., *Roma – caput et fons. Zwei Vorträge über das päpstliche Rom zwischen Altertum und Mittelalter* (Opladen, Westdeustche Verlag), pp. 45–70.

Schieffer, Rudolf (1990), 'Väter und Söhne im Karolingerhause', in R. Schieffer, ed., *Beiträge zur Geschichte des Regnum Francorum. Referate beim wissenschaftlichen Colloquium zum 75. Geburtstag von Eugen Ewig am 28 Mai 1988* (Sigmaringen, Thorbecke), pp. 149–64.

Schieffer, Rudolf (1992), *Die Karolinger* (Stuttgart, Kohlhammer).

Schieffer, Rudolf (1993), 'Karolingerische Töchter', in G. Jenal and S. Haarländer, eds., *Herrschaft, Kirche, Kultur: Beiträge zur Geschichte des Mittelalters. Festschrift für F. Prinz zum 65. Geburtstag* (Stuttgart, Hiersemann), pp. 125–39.

Schieffer, Rudolf (1994), 'Karl Martell und seine Familie', in Jörg Jarnut, Ulrich Nonn and Michael Richter, eds., *Karl Martell und seiner Zeit* (Sigmaringen, Thorbecke), pp. 305–15.

Schieffer, Rudolf (1997a), *Die Karolinger*, 2nd edn (Stuttgart, Kohlhammer).

Schieffer, Rudolf (1997b), 'Vor 1200 Jahren: Karl der Große last sich in Aachen nieder', in P. L. Butzer, et al., *Karl der Große und sein Nachwirken*, 2 vols. (Turnhout, Brepols), vol. 1, pp. 3–21.

Schieffer, Rudolf (1997c), 'Ein politischer Prozess des 8. Jahrhunderts im Vexierspiegel der Quellen', in R. Berndt, ed., *Das Frankfurter Konzil von 794*, vol. 1, pp. 167–82.

Schieffer, Rudolf (2000), 'Charlemagne and Rome', in J. M. H. Smith, ed., *Early Medieval Rome and the Christian West: Essays in Honour of Donald A. Bullough* (Leiden, Brill), pp. 279–95.

Schieffer, Rudolf (2001), 'Karl der Große – Intentionen und Wirkungen', in F.-R. Erkens, ed., *Karl der Große und das Erbe der Kulturen* (Berlin, Akademie Verlag), pp. 3–14.

Schieffer, Rudolf (2002), 'Das Attentat auf Papst Leo III', in P. Godman et al., eds., *Am Vorabend der Kaiserkrönung* (Berlin, Akademie Verlag), pp. 75–85.

Schieffer, Rudolf (2004a), '"Die Folgenschwerste Tat des ganzen Mittelalters?" Aspekte des wissenschaftlichen Urteils über den Dynastiewecjsel von 751', in M. Becher and J. Jarnut, eds., *Der Dynastiewechsel von 751* (Munster, Scriptorium), pp. 1–14.

Schieffer, Rudolf (2004b), 'Neues von der Kaiserkrönung Karls des Großen', *Bayerische Academie der Wissenschaften, Sitzungsberichte* 2, pp. 3–25.

Schieffer, Rudolf (2005), 'Die Einheit des Karolingerreiches als praktisches Problem und als theoretische Forderung', in W. Maleszek, ed., *Fragen der politischen Integration im mittelalterlichen Europa* (Ostfildern, Thorbecke), pp. 33–47.

Schieffer, Rudolf (2007), 'Karl der Große und die Einsetzung der Bischöfe im Frankenreich', *Deutsches Archiv für Erforschung des Mittelalters* 63, pp. 451–67.

Schieffer, Rudolf (2009), 'Die internationale Forschung zur Staatlichkeit in der Karolingerzeit', in W. Pohl and V. Wieser, eds., *Der frühmittelalterliche Staat – europäischen Perspektiven* (Vienna, Verlag der ÖAW), pp. 43–9.

Schieffer, Rudolf (2014), 'Karl der Große und Europa', in *Kaiser und Kalifen. Karl der Große und die Mächte am Mittelmeer um 800*, ed. Stiftung Deutsches Historischen Museum (Darmstadt, Stiftung Deutsches Historisches Museum and von Zabern), pp. 322–9.

Schieffer, Rudolf (2018), 'Karl der Grosse und das Kaiserreich der Greichen', in R. Gross and M. Sot, eds., *Charlemagne. Les temps, les espaces, les hommes. Construction et déconstruction d'un régime* (Turnhout, Brepols), pp. 285–90.

Schlesinger, Walter (1963), 'Kaisertum und Reichsteilung. Zur *Divisio regnorum* von 806', *Beiträge zur deutschen Verfassungsgeschichte des Mittelalters* (Göttingen, Vandenhoeck & Ruprecht), pp. 193–232.

Schmid, Karl (1972), 'Zur Ablösung der Langobardenherrschaft durch die Franken', *Quellen und Forschungen aus italienischen Archiven und Bibliotheken* 52, pp. 1–36.

Schmieder, Felicitas (2005), 'Fastrada – Karl der Große, die Bayern und Frankfurt am Main', in *Millennium 2/2005, Jahrbuch zu Kultur und Geschichte des ersten Jahrtausends n. Chr.* (Berlin and New York, Walter de Gruyter), pp. 329–35.

Schmitz, Gerhard (2002), 'Echte Quellen – Falsche Quellen: Müssen zentrale Quellen aus der Zeit Ludwigs des Frommen neu bewertet werden?' in F.-R. Erkens and Hartmut Wolff, eds., *Vom Sacerdotium und Regnum. Geistluche und weltliche Gewalt im frühen und hohen Mittelalter. Festschrift für Egon Boshof zum 65. Geburtstag* (Cologne, Weimar and Vienna, Böhlau), pp. 275–300.

Schmitz, Gerhard (2004), 'Echtes und Falsches, Karl der Große, Ludwig der Fromme und Benedictus Levita', in O. Münsch and T. Zotz, eds., *Scientia Veritatis. Festschrift für Hubert Mordek zum 65. Geburtstag* (Ostfildern, Thorbecke Verlag), pp. 153–72.

Schneider, Olaf (2004), 'Die Königserhebung Pippins 751 in der Erinnerung der karolingischen Quellen', in M. Becher and J. Jarnut, eds., *Die Dynastiewechsel von 751* (Münster, Scriptorium), pp. 243–75.

Schneidmüller, Berndt (2000), 'Sehnsucht nach Karl dem Großen. Vom Nutzen eines toten Kaisers füdie Nachgeborenen', *Geschichte in Wissenschaft und Unterricht* 51, pp. 284–301.

Schove, Derek J. (1984), *Chronology of Eclipses and Comets*, AD 1–1000 (Woodbridge, Boydell Press).

Schramm, Percy E. (1968), 'Karl der Große als Kaiser (800–814) im Lichte der Staatssymbolik', in Schramm, *Kaiser, Könige und Päpste: Gesammelte Aufsätze*, 4 vols. (Stuttgart, Hiersemann), vol. 1, pp. 264–302.

Schubert, Ernst (1993), 'Die *Capitulatio de partibus Saxoniae*', in D. Brosius et al., eds., *Geschichte in der Region. Zum 65. Geburtstag von Heinrich Schmidt* (Hanover, Hahn), pp. 3–28.

Schulze, Hans K. (1973), *Die Grafschaftsverfassung der Karolingerzeit in der Gebieten östlich des Rheins* (Berlin, Duncker und Humblot).

Schulze-Dörrlamm, Mechthild (2014), 'Die Stadt Mainz um 800', in P. Ettel et al., eds., *Großbaustelle 793. Das Kanalprojekt Karls des Großen zwischen Rhein und Donau* (Mainz, Verlag dos Römisch-Germanischen Zentralmuseumsthmar), pp. 75–8.

Schüssler, Heinz (1985), 'Die fränkische Reichsteilung von Vieux-Poitiers (742) und die Reform der Kirche', *Deutsches Archiv für Erforschung des Mittelalters* 13, pp. 47–112.

Scior, Volker (2009), 'Bemerkungen zum frühmittelalterlichen Boten- und Gesandtschaftswesen', in W. Pohl and V. Wieser, eds., *Der frühmittelalterliche Staat – europäische Perspektiven* (Vienna, Verlag der ÖAW), pp. 315–29.

Scott, James C. (1998), *Seeing Like a State: How Certain Schemes to Improve the Human Condition Have Failed* (New Haven, Conn., and London, Yale University Press).

Semmler, Josef (1965), 'Karl der Grosse und das fränkische Monchtum', in W. Braunfels, ed., *Karl der Grosse: Lebenswerk und Nachleben*, 5 vols. (Düsseldorf, Schwann, 1965–8), vol. 2, pp. 255–89.

Semmler, Josef (1975), 'Pippin III und die fränkischen Klöster', *Francia* 3, pp. 88–146.

Semmler, Josef (1977), 'Zur pippinidisch-karolingischen Sukzessionskrise 714–23', *Deutsches Archiv für Erforschung des Mittelalters* 33, pp. 1–36.

Semmler, Josef (2003), *Der Dynastiewechsel von 751 und die fränkische Königssalbung* (Düsseldorf, Droste Verlag).

Sestan, Ernesto (1970), 'La Storiografia dell'Italia longobarda: Paolo Diacono', *Settimane* 17, pp. 357–86.

Siems, Harald (2017), 'Herrschaft und Konsens in der "Lex Baiuvariorum"', in V. Epp and C. H. F. Meyer, eds., *Recht und Konfession im Mittelalter* (Ostfildern, Thorbecke), pp. 299–359.

Smith, Julia M. H. (1995), '*Fines imperii*: The Marches', in R. McKitterick, ed., *New Cambridge Medieval History* II (Cambridge, Cambridge University Press), pp. 169–89.

Smith, Julia M. H. (2002), 'Confronting identities: the rhetoric and reality of a Carolingian frontier', in W. Pohl and M. Diesenberger, eds., *Integration und Herrschaft: Ethnische Identitäten und soziale Organisation im Frühmittelalter* (Vienna, Verlag der ÖAW), pp. 169–82.

Smith, Julia M. H. (2012), 'Portable Christianity: relics in the medieval West', in *Proceedings of the British Academy* 181, pp. 143–67.

Smith, Julia M. H. (2014), 'Care of relics in early medieval Rome', in V. Garver and O. Phelan, eds., *Rome and Religion in the Early Medieval World. Studies in Honour of Thomas F. X. Noble* (Farnham, Ashgate), pp. 179–205.

Smith, Julia M. H. (2015), 'Les relques et leurs étiquettes', in B. Anennatten et al., eds., *L'abbaye de Saint-Maurice d'Agaune, 515–2015*, 2 vols. (Agaunum, Abbey of St Maurice), vol. 1, pp. 221–57.

Smith, Julia M. H. (2016), 'Pippin III and the sandals of Christ: the making and unmaking of an early medieval relic', in R. Meens et al., eds., *Religious Franks. Religion and Power in the Frankish Kingdoms: Studies in Honour of Mayke de Jong* (Manchester, Manchester University Press), pp. 437–54.

Sot, Michel (2009), 'Le palais d'Aix: Lieu de pouvoir et de culture', in W. Fałkowski and Y. Sassier, eds., *Le Monde carolingien* (Turnhout, Brepols), pp. 243–51.

Springer, Matthias (2004), *Die Sachsen* (Stuttgart, Kohlhammer).

Squatriti, Paolo (2002a), 'Digging ditches in early medieval Europe', *Past & Present* 176, pp. 11–65.

Squatriti, Paolo (2002b), 'Mohammed, the early medieval Mediterranean, and Charlemagne', *Early Medieval Europe* 11 (3), pp. 263–79.

Staab, Franz (1997), 'Die Königin Fastrada', in R. Berndt, ed., *Das Frankfurter Konzil von 794*, 2 vols. (Mainz, Selbstverlag der Gesellschaft für mittelrheinische Kirchengeschichte), vol. 1, pp. 183–217.

Stafford, Pauline (1981), 'The king's wife in Wessex', *Past & Present* 91, pp. 3–26.

Stafford, Pauline (2006), *Gender, Family and the Legitimation of Power* (Aldershot, Ashgate).

Stafford, Pauline, ed. (2009), *A Companion to the Early Middle Ages. Britain and Ireland c. 500 to c. 1100* (Oxford, Wiley-Blackwell).

Stancliffe, Clare (1983), 'Kings who opted out', in P. Wormald et al., eds., *Ideal and Reality in Frankish and Anglo-Saxon Society. Studies presented to J. M. Wallace-Hadrill* (Oxford, Blackwell), pp. 154–76.

Stiegemann, Christoph and Wemhoff, Matthias, eds. (1999), *799 Kunst und Kultur der Karolingerzeit: Karl der Große und Papst Leo III in Paderborn*, 3 vols. (Mainz, von Zabern).

Štih, Peter (2010), 'Istria at the onset of Frankish rule, or the impact of global politics on regional and local conditions', in Štih, *The Middle Ages Between the Eastern Alps and the Northern Adriatic: Select Papers on Slovene Historiography and Medieval History*, trans. F. Smrke (Leiden, Brill), pp. 212–29.

Stock, Brian (1983) *The Implications of Literacy* (Princeton, NJ, Princeton University Press).

Stoclet, Alain J. (1989), '*Evindicatio et petitio*. Le recouvrement des biens monastiques en Neustrie sous les premiers Carolingiens', in Hartmut Atsma, ed., *La Neustrie* (Sigmaringen, Thorbecke), vol. 2 pp. 125–49.

Stoclet, Alain J. (1993), *Autour de Fulrad de Saint-Denis* (Geneva, Droz).

Stoclet, Alain J. (1999), Immunes ab omni teloneo. *Études de diplomatique, de philologie et de l'histoire sur l'exemption du tonlieu au haut moyen âge et spécialement sur la praeceptio de navibus* (Turnhout, Breols).

Stoclet, Alain J. (2000), 'La *Clausula de unctione Pippini regis*, vingt ans après', *Revue Belge de Philologie et d'Histoire* 78, pp. 719–71.

Stoclet, Alain J. (2013), *Fils du Martel: La naissance, l'éducation et la jeunesse de Pépin, dit 'le bref' (v.714–v.741)* (Turnhout, Brepols).

Stollberg-Rilinger, Barbara (2008), *Des Kaisers alte Kleider. Verfassungsgeschichte und Symbolsprache des Alten Reiches. Vol. 2, durchgesehene und aktualisierte Auflage* (Munich, C. H. Beck). Eng. trans. *The Emperor's Old Clothes: Constitutional History and the Symbolic Language of the Holy Roman Emperor* by Thomas Dunlap (New York and Oxford, Berghahn Books, 2015).

Stone, Rachel (2012), *Morality and Masculinity in the Carolingian Empire* (Cambridge, Cambridge University Press).

Stone, Rachel (2018), 'Sisters prepare death for sisters, aunts for nieces? The missing competition between Carolingian women', in S. Joye and R. Le Jan, eds., *Genre et compétition dans les sociétés occidentales du haut moyen âge* (Turnhout, Brepols), pp. 135–50.

Story, Joanna (1999), 'Cathwulf, kingship, and the royal abbey of Saint-Denis', *Speculum* 74, pp. 1–21.

Story, Joanna (2003), *Carolingian Connections: Anglo-Saxon England and Carolingian Francia, c.750–870* (Aldersot, Ashgate).

Story, Joanna (2005a), *Charlemagne: Empire and Society* (Manchester, Manchester University Press).

Story, Joanna (2005b), 'Charlemagne's black marble: the origin of the epitaph of Pope Hadrian I', *Papers of the British School at Rome* 73, pp. 157–90.

Story, Joanna (2007), 'Frankish annals in Anglo-Norman Durham', in M. Becher and Y. Hen, eds., *Wilhelm Levison (1876–1947). Ein Jüdisches Forscherleben zwischen wissenschaftlicher Anerkennung und politischer Exil*, Bonner Historische Forschungen 61 (Marburg, Verlag Franz Schmitt), pp. 145–80.

Story, Joanna (2010), 'Aldhelm and Old St Peter's Rome', *Anglo-Saxon England* 39, pp. 7–20.

Stratmann, Martina (1997), 'Schriftlichkeit in der Verwaltung von Bistümern und Klostern zur Zeit Karls der Großen', in P. Butzer et al., eds., *Karl der Grosse und sein Nachwirken. 1200 Jahre Kultur und Wissenschaft in Europa* (Turnhout, Brepols), pp. 251–76.

Tellenbach, Gerd (1979), 'Die geistigen und politischen Grundlagen der karolingischen Thronfolge: Zugleich eine Studie über kollectiven Willensbildung und kollektives Handeln in neunten Jahrhundert', *Frühmittelalterliche Studien* 13, pp. 184–302.

Theuws, Frans and Nelson, J. L., eds. (2000), *Rituals of Power: From Late Antiquity to the Early Middle Ages* (Leiden, Brill).

Thoma, Gertrud (1985), *Namensänderungen in Herrscherfamilien des mittelalterlichen Europa* (Munich, Kallmünz-Oberpfalz).

Tischler, Matthias M. (2001), *Einhards* Vita Karoli. *Studien zur Entstehung, Überlieferung und Rezeption*, 2 vols. (Hannover, Hahnsche Buchhandlung).

Tischler, Matthias M. (2008), 'Die "*Divisio regnorum*" von 806 zwischen handschriftlicher Überlieferung und historiographischer Rezeption', in B. Kasten, ed., *Herrscher- und Fürstentestamente im westeuropäischen Mittelalter* (Cologne, Böhlau), pp. 193–258.

Toubert, Pierre (1996), 'The Carolingian moment (eighth–tenth century)', in A. Burguière et al., eds., *A History of the Family*, trans. S. Hanbury-Tenison et al., 2 vols. (Cambridge, Mass., Belknap Press), vol. 1, pp. 379–406.

Traill, David A. (1974), *Walahfrid Strabo's* Visio Wettini: *Text, Translation and Commentary* (Bern, P. D. Lang).

Treffort, Cécile (1994), 'Nithard, petit-fils de Charlemagne. Note sur une biographie controversée', *Société des Antiquaires de Picardie, Bulletin du 1re trimester*, pp. 415–33.

Treffort, Cécile (2004), 'La place d'Alcuin dans la redaction épigrahique carolingienne', in P. Depreux and B. Judic, eds., *Alcuin de York à Tours. Écriture, pouvoir et réseaux dans l'Europe du haut moyen âge* (Rennes, Presses Universitaires de Rennes), pp. 353–69.

Truc, Gérôme (2011), 'Narrative identity against biographical illusion', *Études Ricœuriennes* 2 (1), pp. 150–67.

Ubl, Karl (2008), *Inzestverbot und Gesetzsgebung: die Konstruktion eines Verbrechens (300–1100)* (Berlin, de Gruyter).

Ubl, Karl (2015), 'Karl der Große und die Rückkehr des Gottesstaates, Narrative der Heroisierung für das Jahr 2014', *Historische Zeitschrift* 300, pp. 374–90.

Ullmann, Walter (1969), *The Carolingian Renaissance and the Idea of Kingship* (London, Methuen).

Untermann, Matthias (1999), '"*Opere mirabilia constructa*". Die Aachener "Residenz Karls des Großen", in C. Stiegemann and M. Wemhoff, eds., *799. Kunst und Kultur der Karolingerzeit*, 3 vols. (Mainz, von Zabern), vol. 3, pp. 152–64.

Van Berkel, Maaike (2012), 'Review of W. Drews, *Die Karolinger und die Abbasiden von Bagdad, Legitimationsstrategien frühmittelalterliche Herrscherdynastien im transkulturellen Vergleich*', *Early Medieval Europe* 20 (1), pp. 96–7.

Van Rhijn, Carine (2007), *Shepherds of the Lord: Priests and Episcopal Statutes in the Carolingian Period* (Turnhout, Brepols).

Van Rhijn, Carine (2016), '"Et hoc considerat episcopus, ut ipsi presbyteri non sint idiotae". Carolingian local *correctio* and an unknown priests' exam from the early ninth century', in R. Meens et al., eds., *Religious Franks. Religion and Power in the Frankish Kingdoms: Studies in Honour of Mayke de Jong* (Manchester, Manchester University Press), pp. 162–80.

Verbruggen, Jan Frans (1965), 'L'armée et la stratégie de Charlemagne', in W. Braunfels, ed., *Karl der Grosse: Lebenswerk und Nachleben*, 5 vols. (Düsseldorf, Schwann), vol. 1, pp. 420–36.

Verhulst, Adriaan (1965), 'Karolingische Agrarpolitik: Das Capitulare de Villis und die Hungersnöte von 792/93 und 805/806', *Zeitschrift für Agrargeschichte und Agrarsoziologie* 13, pp. 175–89, repr. in Verhulst (1992).

Verhulst, Adriaan (1992), *Rural and Urban Aspects of Early Medieval Northwest Europe* (Aldershot, Ashgate).

Verhulst, Adriaan (2002), *The Carolingian Economy* (Cambridge, Cambridge University Press).

Waldhoff, Stefan (2003), *Alcuins Gebetbuch für Karl den Großen: seine Rekonstruktion und seine Stellung in der frühmittelalterlichen Geschichte der libelli precum* (Münster, Aschendorff Verlag).

Wallace-Hadrill, J. M. (1971), *Early Germanic Kingship in England and on the Continent* (Oxford, Clarendon Press).

Wallace-Hadrill, J. M. (1983), *The Frankish Church* (Oxford, Clarendon Press).

Weber, Max (1968), *Economy and Society*, eds. G. Roth and C. Wittich, Eng. trans. University of California Press (New York, Bedminster Press).

Weidemann, Margarete (1998), 'Zur Chronologie der Merowinger im 7. Und 8. Jahrhundert', *Francia* 25, pp. 177–230.

Weinrich, Lorenz (1963), *Wala: Graf, Mönch und Rebell: Die Biographie eines Karolinger* (Lübeck and Hamburg, Matthiesen Verlag).

Weise, Georg (1923), *Zwei fränkische Königspfalzen: Berichte über die an den Pfalzen zu Quierzy und Samoussy vorgenommenen Grabungen* (Tübingen, Universität).

Wemhoff, Matthias (2014), 'Zentralität, Sakralität, Repräsentativität. Auswirkungen der karolingischen Herrschaft in Sachsen', in *Kaiser unf Kalifen. Karl der Große und die Mächte am Mittelmeer um 800* (Darmstadt, Stiftung Deutsches Historisches Museum and von Zabe), pp. 116–29.

Werner, Karl Ferdinand (1965), 'Bedeutende Adelsfamilien im Reich Karls des Großen', in W. Braunfels et al., eds., *Karl der Große. Lebenswerk und Nachleben*, 5 vols., vol. 1, *Persönlichkeit und Geschichte*, ed. H. Beumann (Düsseldorf, Schwann), pp. 83–142.

Werner, Karl Ferdinand (1967), 'Die Nachkommen Karls des Großen bis um das Jahr 1000 (1.-8. Generation), in W. Braunfels et al., eds., *Karl der Große. Lebenswerk und Nachleben*, 5 vols. (Düsseldorf, Schwann), vol. 4, pp. 403–83.

Werner, Karl Ferdinand (1973), 'Das Geburtsdatum Karls des Großen', *Francia* 1, pp. 115–57, repr. in Werner (1979).

Werner, Karl Ferdinand (1979), *Structures politiques du monde franc* (London, Variorum).

Werner, Karl Ferdinand (1980), '*Missus-marchio-comes*: entre l'administration centrale et l'administration locale de l'Empire carolingien', in W. Paravicini, ed., *Histoire comparée de l'administration* (Munich, Artemis Verlag), pp. 191–239.

Werner, Karl Ferdinand (1985), 'Qu'est-ce que la Neustrie?', 'Les rouages de l'administration' and 'Armées et guerres en Neustrie', in P. Périn and L.-C. Feffer, eds., *La Neustrie. Les pays au nord de la Loire de Dagobert à Charles le Chauve* (Créteil, Les Musées et Monuments départementaux de Seine-Maritime), pp. 29–38, 41–6, 49–52.

Werner, Matthias (1982), *Adelsfamilien im Umkreis der frühen Karolinger* (Sigmaringen, Thorbecke).

Werther, Lukas (2014), 'Kanalbau und künstliche Wassführung in Frühmittelalter – eine Ausnahme?', in P. Ettel et al., eds., *Großbaustelle 793 Das Kanalprojekt Karls des Großen zwischen Rhein und Donau* (Mainz, Verlag dos Römisch-Germanischen Zentralmuseumsthmar), pp. 95–8.

Werther, Lukas and Ferner, Dorothea (2014), 'Der Karlsgraben im Fokus der Archäologie', in P. Ettel et al., eds., *Großbaustelle 793. Das Kanalprojekt Karls des Großen zwischen Rhein und Donau* (Mainz, Verlag dos Römisch-Germanischen Zentralmuseumsthmar), pp. 33–40.

West, Charles (2013), *Reframing the Feudal Revolution: Political and Social Transformation between the Marne and Moselle, c.800–c.1100* (Cambridge, Cambridge University Press).

West, Geoffrey V. B. (1999), 'Charlemagne's involvement in central and southern Italy: power and the limits of authority', *Early Medieval Europe* 8, pp. 341–67.

Whittow, Mark (1996), *The Making of Orthodox Byzantium* (London, Macmillan).

Wickham, Chris (1981), *Early Medieval Italy. Central Power and Local Society 400–1000* (London, Macmillan).

Wickham, Chris (1986), 'Land disputes and their social framework in Lombard-Carolingian Italy 700–900', in W. Davies and P. Fouracre, eds., *The Settlement of Disputes in Early Medieval Europe* (Cambridge, Cambridge University Press), pp. 105–24, repr. in Wickham (1994).

Wickham, Chris (1988), *The Mountains and the City* (Oxford, Oxford University Press).

Wickham, Chris (1994), *Land and Power: Studies in Italian and European Social History, 400–1200* (London, British School at Rome).

Wickham, Chris (1998), 'Ninth-century Byzantium through western eyes', in L. Brubaker, ed., *Byzantium in the Ninth Century: Dead or Alive?* (Aldershot, Ashgate, Variorum), pp. 245–56.

Wickham, Chris (2005), *Framing the Early Middle Ages. Europe and the Mediterranean 400–800* (Oxford, Oxford University Press).

Wickham, Chris (2008), 'Rethinking the structures of the early medieval economy', in J. R. Davis and M. McCormick, eds., *The Long Morning of Medieval Europe* (Aldershot, Ashgate), pp. 19–31.

Wickham, Chris (2009), *The Inheritance of Rome. A History of Europe from 400–1000* (London, Allen Lane).

Williams, Hywel (2010), *Emperor of the West. Charlemagne and the Carolingian Empire* (London, Quercus).

Wilson, Peter H. (2016), *The Holy Roman Empire* (London, Allen Lane).

Witthöft, Harald (1997), '*Denarius novus, modius publicus* und *libra panis* im Frankfurter Kapitulare. Elements und Struktur einer materiellen Ordnung in fränkischer Zeit', in R. Berndt, ed., *Das Frankfurter Konzil von 794* (Mainz, Selbstverlag der Gesellschaft für Mittelrheinische Kirchengeschichte), pp. 219–52.

Wolf, Kenneth Baxter (1990), *Conquerors and Chroniclers of Early Medieval Spain* (Liverpool, Liverpool University Press).

Wolfram, Herwig (1987), *Die Geburt Mitteleuropas* (Vienna, Siedler Verlag).

Wolfram, Herwig (1994), 'Karl Martell und das fränkische Lehenswesen. Aufnahme einer Nichtbestandes', in J. Jarnut et al., eds., *Karl Martell und seiner Zeit* (Sigmaringen, Thorbecke), pp. 61–78.

Wolfram, Herwig (2001), 'The creation of the Carolingian frontier system c. 800', in W. Pohl, I. Wood and H. Reimitz, eds., *The Transformation of Frontiers from Late Antiquity to the Carolingians* (Leiden, Brill), pp. 233–45.

Wolfram, Herwig (2013a), Conversio Bagoariorum et Carantanorum. *Das Weißbuch der Salzburger Kirche über die erforlgreiche Mission in*

Karantanien und Pannonien, ed., German trans. with commentary (Ljubljana, Laibach), 3rd rev. edn.

Wolfram, Herwig (2013b), 'Expansion und Integration – Râtien und andere Randgebiete des Karolingerreichs in Vergleich', in H. R. Sennhauser et al., eds., *Wandel und Konstanz zwischen Bodensee und Lombardei zur Zeit Karls des Grossen. Kloster St. Johann in Müstair und Churrätien* (Zurich, vdf Hochschulverlag), pp. 251–60.

Wood, Ian (1991), 'Saint-Wandrille and its historiography', in I. Wood and G. A. Loud, eds., *Church and Chronicle in the Middle Ages* (London, Bloomsbury), pp. 1–14.

Wood, Ian (1994), *The Merovingian Kingdoms, 450–751* (Harlow, Longman).

Wood, Ian (1995a), 'Teutsind, Witlaic and the history of Merovingian *precaria*', in W. Davies and P. Fouracre, eds., *Property and Power in the Early Middle Ages* (Cambridge, Cambridge University Press), pp. 31–52.

Wood, Ian (1995b), 'Pagan religions and superstitions east of the Rhine from the fifth to the ninth century', in G. Ausenda, ed., *After Empire: Towards an Ethnology of Europe's Barbarians* (Woodbridge, Boydell), pp. 253–79.

Wood, Ian (1997), 'Report: the European Science Foundation's programme on the transformation of the Roman world and emergence of early medieval Europe', in *Early Medieval Europe 6* (2), pp. 217–27.

Wood, Ian, ed. (1998), *Franks and Alemanni in the Merovingian Period. An Ethnographic Perspective* (Woodbridge, Boydell).

Wood, Ian (2001), *The Missionary Life: Saints and the Evangelisation of Europe* (Harlow, Longman).

Wood, Ian (2003), 'Beyond satraps and ostriches: political and social structures of the Saxons in the early Carolingian period', in D. H. Green and F. Siegmund, eds., *The Continental Saxons from the Migration Period to the Tenth Century. An Ethnographic Perspective* (Woodbridge, Boydell), pp. 271–90, with discussion 290–97.

Wood, Ian (2004), 'Genealogy defined by women: the case of the Pippinids', in L. Brubaker and J. M. H. Smith, eds., *Gender in the Early Medieval World* (Cambridge, Cambridge University Press), pp. 234–56.

Wood, Ian (2018), *The Transformation of the Roman West* (Leeds, ARC Humanities Press).

Wood, Susan (2006), *The Proprietary Church in the Medieval West* (Oxford, Oxford University Press).

Wormald, Patrick (1991), 'In search of King Offa's "Law-Code"', in I. Wood and N. Lund, eds., *People and Places in Northern Europe, 500–1600. Essays in Honour of Peter Sawyer* (Woodbridge, Boydell), pp. 25–45.

Wyss, Michael (1999), 'Saint-Denis', in C. Stiegemann and M. Wemhoff, eds., *799. Kunst et Kultur der Karolingerzeit* (Mainz, von Zabern), vol. 3, pp. 138–41.

Wyss, Michael (2001), 'Un établissement carolingien mis à jour à proximité de l'abbaye de Saint-Denis: La question du palais de Charlemagne', in

A. Renoux, ed., *Aux marches du palais. Qu'est-ce qu'un palais médiéval* (Le Mans, Université de Maine), pp. 191–200.

Zielhofer, C., Leitholdt, E., Werther, L., et al. (2014), 'Charlemagne's summit canal: an early medieval hydro-engineering project', *PLoS One* 9 (9), e108194. https://doi.org/10.1371/journal.pone.0108194.

Ziolkowski, Jan M. (2008), 'Of arms and the (Ger)man: literary and material culture in the *Waltharius*', in J. R. Davis and M. McCormick, eds., *The Long Morning of Medieval Europe* (Aldershot, Ashgate), pp. 193–208.

Zotz, Thomas (1993), 'Carolingian tradition and Ottonian-Salian innovation: comparative perspectives on palatine policy in the empire', in A. Duggan, ed., *Kings and Kingship in Medieval Europe* (London, King's College London Centre for Late Antique and Medieval Studies), pp. 69–100.

Zotz, Thomas (1998), 'Le palais et les élites dans le royaume de Germanie', in R. Le Jan, ed., *La royauté et les élites dans l'Europe carolingienne (début du IXe siècle aux environs de 920)* (Lille, Université Charles-de-Gaulle), pp. 233–47.

Zotz, Thomas (2001), 'Pfalzen der Karolingerzeit: Neue Aspekte aus historischer Sicht', in L. Fenske, J. Jarnut and M. Wemhoff, eds., *Deutsche Königspfalzen: Beiträge zu ihrer historischen und archäologischen Erforschung*, vol. 5. *Splendor palatii* (Göttingen, Veröffentlichungen des Max-Planck-Instituts für Geschichte 11), pp. 13–23.

Zotz, Thomas (2009), 'Grundlagen, Grenzen and Probleme der Staatlichkeit im frühen Mittelalter. Zur Bedeutung und Funktion der Königspfalzen', in W. Pohl and V. Wieser, eds., *Der frühmittelalterliche Staat – europäische Perspektiven* (Vienna, Verlag der ÖAW), pp. 515–20.

Acknowledgements

To all included below, with heartfelt thanks

For reading chapters and/or the whole thing, and much else: Stuart Airlie, Wendy Davies, Paul Fouracre, Christine Groothues, Fritz Groothues, Billy Nelson, Alice Rio and Julia Smith, and for much help during the years of writing, Jenny Davis, Caroline Goodson, Jo Story and Francesca Tinti.

For various kinds of help: Ross Balzaretti, Simon Corcoran, Simon Coupland, Carlotta Dionisotti, Serena Ferente, David Ganz, Martina Hartmann, Ulrike Heckner, Irmtraut Heitmeyer, Judith Herrin, Robin Jacoby, Mayke de Jong, Thomas R. Kraus, Angelika Lampen, Régine Le Jan, Manfred Luchterhandt, Michael McCormick, Harald Müller, Marie-Adélaïde Nielen, Frank Pohle, Susan Reynolds, Charlotte Roueché, Christoph Stiegemann, Joanna Story, Lacey Wallace, Matthias Wemhoff and Lukas Werther; and for the constructively critical anonymous persons who read my manuscript for the publisher.

For their professionalism, patience and kindness, librarians at the following libraries: British Library, Institute of Classical Studies, Institute of Historical Research, King's College London, Öffentliche Bibliothek der Universität Basel, Queen's College, Oxford, Senate House, Victoria & Albert Museum and Warburg Institute.

For those who kept me going: my Newnham friends (1961 vintage, and still friends) – Katya Benjamin, Jane and Howard Brenton, Celia and Christy Hawkesworth, Jan and Harry Marsh, Margaret Dickinson and Johnny Parry and Sarah Meron.

Pauline and Bill Stafford, Susan Kruse and Gordon Gallacher; Mary and Andrew Porter, Paul and Joanna Fouracre, Henrietta Leyser. Marguerite Dupree and Rick Trainor, Michael Wood and Rebecca Dobbs,

Ted White and Mary Restieaux, Georgina Reuter, Margot Finn, Judith Bennett and Cynthia Herrup.

Fellow music-lovers who made music and heard music with me, and gave me the CDs I live with; friends and colleagues, past and present, in/on/at: the Bucknell Group, IHR seminars, the OHME team, *History Workshop Journal*, *Past and Present*, at KCL in the University of London, at the *RHS*, at the British Academy, on the TRW project, and many former students and colleagues teaching at universities in Britain, in Continental Europe and in the USA; those who taught me much and have influenced all I have written.

My neighbours in south-east London, especially Maggi Cook and Ernesto Spinelli, Pauline Buchanan-Black and Jon Fitzmaurice, Paul and Carrie Winstanley.

Those no longer living but ever remembered: in particular Tim Reuter, Patrick Wormald, Jenny Wormald, and David King (whose *Charlemagne: Translated Sources* (1987) made a revival of Charlemagne studies in the UK thinkable).

For their parts in getting this book published: Ellen Davies, Matthew Hutchinson, Charlotte Ridings, Richard Duguid and Simon Winder.

For my family: my children Lizzie and Billy and their spouses Hugh and Ellen respectively; Ros Lovett, Andrew and Mary Nelson; my nieces and nephews and their partners, my great-nieces and great-nephews, my grandchildren Eli, Ruth, Martha, Dorie and John Paul – and last but absolutely not least, my sister and brother-in-law, to whom I dedicate this book.

Index

Paderborn, Saxony: assembly (777),
89, 164–6, 202–3, 207; Pope Leo
III arrives in (799), 372
Paderborn Epic, 345, 492
Paris, 23
Parker, Geoffrey, 21
Patzold, Steffen, 394
Paul I, Pope, 75, 78–9, 85–6, 99
Paul the Deacon: epitaphs, 80, 133,
203, 235; on Himiltrud, 275;
Homiliary, 249–50; poetry, 161,
248; Roman influence, 147; *Deeds
of the Bishops of Auxerre*, 173;
History of the Lombards, 56
Paulinus of Aquileia: and the
Adoptionist heresy, 283, 284; on
Charlemagne's stance against
heresy, 305; correspondence with
Alcuin, 341, 343; on Louis's
humility, 377; at Pavia, 338; poetry,
166–7, 248; Roman influence,
147; and Saxon conversion,
166–7, 326
Pavia, 144, 179, 182, 186; siege of
(773–4), 119, 133, 134, 135, 141–3
pestilence, 454
Pétau, Denis, 149
Peter, Bishop of Verdun, 287, 311
Peter of Pisa, 161, 248
Petronilla, St, church of, 78
Pförring, 244
pilgrims, 351–2
Pippin (brother), 79
Pippin (son of Carloman), 91, 100
Pippin (son of Drogo), 41, 43
Pippin (son of Himiltrud): birth (791),
91, 100; hunchback, 107; at Pavia
(774), 133; at Worms (780), 181; at
Eresburg (783–4), 207; and the
miracle of St Goar, 272–5;
conspiracy of (792), 214–15, 285–8,
307; enters Prüm Abbey, 418, 438;
death, 438, 440

Pippin, King of Italy (son, *formerly*
Carloman): baptism in Rome, 181,
183–4; anointed king of Italy, 182,
186; capitulary (787), 161; at
Regensburg (792), 284; campaign
against the Avars (796), 326,
333–4; advised by Alcuin, 338–9;
government of, 409; at Thionville
(806), 425; conquest of Venice, 453;
death, 453, 475
Pippin 'I,' 16, 35, 37
Pippin 'II,' 17, 36, 38–9, 41–5
Pippin 'III' (father of Charlemagne):
historical sources for, 40–41; birth
and baptism, 43, 46–7; and the
monastery of St Denis, 52–4, 68–9;
occupies Burgundy, 56; joint
regime with his brother Carloman,
59–60; marries Bertrada, 60–61,
63; consecration as King of the
Franks, 69–72; form of governmet,
81–3; at the palace of Quierzy, 24;
refounds the monastery of Prüm,
83–4; campaigns in Aquitaine,
85–7; divides kingdom between his
sons, 85, 93; death, 90–92; burial
at St Denis, 96; charters of, 93, 95,
505n77; 'Donation of Quierzy'
(754), 419
Pippinid dynasty, 35–47, 52–5
plainchant, 249
Plectrud (wife of Pippin II), 17, 38,
39, 42, 43–4, 45, 46, 497n22
poetry, 167, 244–8, 345, 350–51,
445
Poitiers, battle of (732), 50, 55
population transfers, 329–31
Potho, Abbot of San Vincenzo,
212–13
Power, Eileen, 364
Probatus, Abbot of Farfa, 158
'Programmatic Capitulary'. *See
Capitulare missorum generale* (802)